98

FOLKLORE

AN ENCYCLOPEDIA
OF BELIEFS, CUSTOMS, TALES,
MUSIC, AND ART

FOLKLORE

AN ENCYCLOPEDIA
OF BELIEFS, CUSTOMS, TALES,
MUSIC, AND ART
VOLUME I
A-H

Edited by
Thomas A. Green

ABC-CLIO
Santa Barbara, California
Denver, Colorado
Oxford, England

Library of Congress Cataloging-in-Publication Data

Folklore: an encyclopedia of beliefs, customs, tales, music, and art / edited by
    Thomas A. Green.
        p.   cm.
    Includes bibliographical references and index.
    1. Folklore—Encyclopedias.   I. Green, Thomas A., 1944– .
GR35.F63   1997
398'.03—dc21   97-25924

ISBN 0-87436-986-X (alk. paper)

02 01 00 99 98 97 10 9 8 7 6 5 4 3 2 1

ABC-CLIO, Inc.
130 Cremona Drive, P.O.Box 1911
Santa Barbara, California 93116-1911

This book is printed on acid-free paper ∞.
Manufactured in the United States of America

ADVISORY BOARD

CONTRIBUTORS LIST

Robert Ackerman
University of the Arts
Philadelphia, PA

Linda Kinsey Adams
Indiana University
Bloomington, IN

Randal S. Allison
Texas A & M University
College Station, TX

Pertti Anttonen
University of Helsinki
Helsinki, Finland

Satu Apo
University of Helsinki
Helsinki, Finland

Ronald L. Baker
Indiana State University
Terre Haute, IN

Paul Barber
Fowler Museum of Cultural History
University of California, Los Angeles
Los Angeles, CA

Dan Ben-Amos
University of Pennsylvania
Philadelphia, PA

Regina Bendix
University of Pennsylvania
Philadelphia, PA

Ann Richman Beresin
University of Pennsylvania
Philadelphia, PA

Robert D. Bethke
University of Delaware
Newark, DE

Margaret K. Brady
University of Utah
Salt Lake City, UT

Simon J. Bronner
Pennsylvania State University,
Harrisburg
Harrisburg, PA

Margaret Bruchez
Blinn College
College Station, TX

Charles Camp
Maryland State Arts Council
Baltimore, MD

William M. Clements
Arkansas State University
State University, AR

Keith Cunningham
Northern Arizona University
Flagstaff, AZ

Frank de Caro
Louisiana State University
Baton Rouge, LA

Linda Dégh
Indiana University
Bloomington, IN

D. Bruce Dickson
Texas A & M University
College Station, TX

John Dorst
University of Wyoming
Laramie, WY

Thomas A. DuBois
University of Washington
Seattle, WA

Bill Ellis
Pennsylvania State University,
Hazleton
Hazleton, PA

Alessandro Falassi
University for Foreigners of Siena
Siena, Italy

Claire R. Farrer
California State University, Chico
Chico, CA

Gary Alan Fine
University of Georgia
Athens, GA

John Miles Foley
University of Missouri
Columbia, MO

Georgia Fox
Texas A & M University
College Station, TX

Leslie C. Gay Jr.
University of Tennessee
Knoxville, TN

Mark Glazer
Pan-American University
Edinburg, TX

Christine Goldberg
Independent Scholar
Los Angeles, CA

Joseph P. Goodwin
Ball State University
Muncie, IN

Sylvia Grider
Texas A & M University
College Station, TX

Stephanie A. Hall
American Folklife Center
Washington, DC

Lauri Harvilahti
University of Helsinki
Helsinki, Finland

Gustav Henningsen
Danish Folklore Archives
Copenhagen, Denmark

David J. Hufford
Milton S. Hershey Medical Center
Pennsylvania State University
Hershey, PA

Bruce Jackson
State University of New York, Buffalo
Buffalo, NY

Nan Johnson
Ohio State University
Columbus, OH

Michael Owen Jones
University of California, Los Angeles
Los Angeles, CA

Rosan Augusta Jordan
Louisiana State University
Baton Rouge, LA

Barbro Klein
Stockholm University
Stockholm, Sweden

William E. Lightfoot
Appalachian State University
Boone, NC

Timothy C. Lloyd
Cityfolk
Dayton, OH

Marsha MacDowell
Michigan State University Museum
East Lansing, MI

Howard Wight Marshall
University of Missouri
Columbia, MO

Robert McCarl
Boise State University
Boise, ID

Charlie McCormick
University of Pennsylvania
Philadelphia, PA

Wolfgang Mieder
University of Vermont
Burlington, VT

James Moreira
Memorial University of Newfoundland
St. John's, Newfoundland, Canada

Joanne Mulcahy
Lewis and Clark College
Portland, OR

Patrick B. Mullen
Ohio State University
Columbus, OH

W.F.H. Nicolaisen
King's College, Aberdeen
Aberdeen, Scotland

Dorothy Noyes
University of Pennsylvania
Philadelphia, PA

Kathleen Malone O'Connor
University of Pennsylvania
Philadelphia, PA

Felix J. Oinas
Indiana University
Bloomington, IN

Juha Pentikäinen
University of Helsinki
Helsinki, Finland

Thomas Pettit
Odense University
Odense, Denmark

Leah Carson Powell
Independent Scholar
Albuquerque, NM

Cathy Lynn Preston
University of Colorado
Boulder, CO

Michael J. Preston
University of Colorado
Boulder, CO

Leonard Norman Primiano
Cabrini College
King of Prussia, PA

Frank Proschan
Indiana University
Bloomington, IN

Roger deV. Renwick
University of Texas, Austin
Austin, TX

Danielle M. Roemer
Northern Kentucky University
Highland Heights, KY

Owe Ronström
Independent Scholar
Stockholm, Sweden

Neil V. Rosenberg
Memorial University of Newfoundland
St. John's, Newfoundland, Canada

Rachelle H. Saltzman
Iowa Arts Council
Des Moines, IA

Jack Santino
Bowling Green State University
Bowling Green, OH

Patricia E. Sawin
University of Southwestern Louisiana
Lafayette, LA

Gregory Schrempp
Indiana University
Bloomington, IN

Hasan El-Shamy
Indiana University
Bloomington, IN

Sharon R. Sherman
University of Oregon
Eugene, OR

Amy Shuman
Ohio State University
Columbus, OH

Contributors List

Guntis Šmidchens
University of Washington
Seattle, WA

Paul Smith
Memorial University of Newfoundland
St. John's, Newfoundland, Canada

Emily Socolov
Independent Scholar
Austin, TX

Richard Sweterlitsch
University of Vermont
Burlington, VT

Timothy R. Tangherlini
University of California, Los Angeles
Los Angeles, CA

Gerald Thomas
Memorial University of Newfoundland
St. John's, Newfoundland, Canada

Jeff Todd Titon
Brown University
Providence, RI

Peter Tokofsky
University of California, Los Angeles
Los Angeles, CA

Tad Tuleja
Independent Scholar
Austin, TX

Edith Turner
University of Virginia
Charlottesville, VA

Leea Virtanen
University of Helsinki
Helsinki, Finland

John Michael Vlach
George Washington University
Washington, DC

Kathryn E. Wilson
University of Pennsylvania
Philadelphia, PA

Margaret R. Yocom
George Mason University
Fairfax, VA

Katharine Young
University of California, Berkeley
Berkeley, CA

M. Jane Young
University of New Mexico
Albuquerque, NM

Contents

FOLKLORE

AN ENCYCLOPEDIA
OF BELIEFS, CUSTOMS, TALES,
MUSIC, AND ART

List of Entries

Volume I

PREFACE

This volume is a comprehensive general reference work for students, scholars, and general readers on forms (e.g., Ballad, Folktale, Legend) and methods of inquiry and analysis (e.g., Fieldwork, Historic-Geographic Method, Linguistic Approach) relevant to the study of folklore. Entries survey and evaluate the historical and current approaches incorporated in the study of these forms and the foundations and current applications of these methods. In addition, the historical dimension is addressed further by entries devoted to theories that have been abandoned within contemporary folkloristics (e.g., Evolutionary Theory, Myth-Ritual Theory). The encyclopedia as a whole and the individual entries focus on folklore forms and methods from a cross-cultural, theoretical perspective in an effort to present an internationally applicable overview of the topics. This general theoretical volume does not contain biographical entries. Rather, individuals are treated within the context of entries devoted to their theoretical concerns.

The methods and theories that underlie specific ethnic and national traditions, such as African-American folklore or Jewish folklore, are considered in the entry Ethnic Folklore. To pursue specific ethnic or national traditions (e.g., Asian folklore, Native American folklore, the folklore of British children), readers are referred to the bibliographies following relevant general entries (Ethnic Folklore, Children's Folklore, and so forth).

Despite efforts made to confine this volume to general topics and to recruit an international list of contributors, it was impossible to comprehensively cover such a far-ranging field as folklore in a single work of this type. Although every attempt has been made to include major topics from a broad spectrum of the genres that constitute the world's folk traditions and methodologies from folklore and related disciplines used to analyze these traditions—insofar as material exists to document such traditions and scholars could be found to examine them—any overview within this format cannot be exhaustive. Emphasis in this volume is on those bodies of North American and European scholarship that have influenced each other most profoundly since the discipline's inception: those of Eastern Europe and the former Soviet Union, the United Kingdom, Scandinavia, and the United States. The entries in this volume, however, provide an introduction to the scholarship in general and facilitate the pursuit of more specialized topics.

For some topics, the labels North American scholars employ differ from those utilized by their European counterparts (e.g., folklorists in the United States favor the label "historic-geographic method," but Finnish scholars tend to employ "historical-geographic") or the respective groups adopt different spellings ("oikotype" versus "oicotype"). The North American term or spelling has been used in this volume, followed in certain cases by other common labels or spellings.

The topics treated in this work range from traditional subjects such as Ballad, Festival, and Joke, to cutting-edge entries such as Computer-Mediated Folklore, Cultural Studies, and Postmodernism. In most cases, a longer, more comprehensive essay format for entries (e.g., Folktale, Legend) has been favored over shorter entries. Exceptions have been made, of course, for those genres that have attracted more scholarly interest than others and, consequently, have generated scholarly literatures of their own (e.g., Magic Tale, Urban Legend). Similarly, categories of traditional phenomena that have international distribution and are of interest to both scholarly and general audiences (e.g., Evil Eye, Vampire) have their own entries as well. Also, there are topics that have been treated in the literature as "umbrella categories" (e.g., Material Culture). These entries are coordinated with their customary subsets (in the case of Material Culture: Architecture, Folk; Art, Folk; and Costume, Folk). Finally, less conventional categories—such as Assault, Supernatural and Enigma, Traditional—are employed as a means of developing consensus on overlapping phenomena that customarily have been distributed among a dozen or more entries.

The richness and diversity of the world's folk traditions and the literature devoted to them make it inevitable that much must be summarized or omitted entirely in an encyclopedia of this type. Readers, therefore, are urged to explore their relevant interests not only by means of the references included at the end of each entry but also through the general works in the list that follows this preface.

Thomas A. Green

❊❊❊❊❊❊❊❊❊❊❊❊❊❊❊❊

General Reference Works in English

Brunvand, Jan Harold. 1986. *The Study of American Folklore: An Introduction*. 3d. ed. New York: W. W. Norton.

Cocchiara, Giuseppe. 1981. *The History of Folklore in Europe*. Trans. John N. McDaniel. Philadelphia: ISHI Press.

Dorson, Richard M. 1972. *Folklore and Folklife: An Introduction*. Chicago: University of Chicago Press.

Dundes, Alan, ed. 1965. *The Study of Folklore*. Englewood Cliffs, NJ: Prentice-Hall.

Leach, Maria, and Jerome Fried, eds. 1950. *Standard Dictionary of Folklore, Mythology, and Legend*. New York: Funk and Wagnalls. (Rev. ed. 1972).

Oring, Elliott, ed. 1986. *Folk Groups and Folklore Genres: An Introduction*. Logan: Utah State University Press.

Toelken, Barre. 1979. *The Dynamics of Folklore*. Boston: Houghton Mifflin.

Acknowledgments

I am indebted to Texas A&M University for a Mini-Grant awarded to me in 1992 in order to support the preliminary stages of work on this volume. A Faculty Development Leave from the College of Liberal Arts at Texas A&M in 1994 allowed me to devote extra time to the project at a crucial stage in its development. Brad Markowitz provided extraordinary help during the final stages of compiling the present work, above and beyond the usual duties of a research assistant. Gary Kuris provided advice, structure, and encouragement throughout. Most of all, Valerie Green—as proofreader, editor, computer consultant, sounding board, and friend—far exceeded any reasonable spousal expectations in good spirits. My thanks to you all.

T.A.G.

Standard Folklore Indices and Classifications

The following works are cited within entries in the short forms shown in brackets.

Aarne, Antti, and Stith Thompson. 1964. *The Types of the Folktale: A Classification and Bibliography*. 2d. rev. ed. Folklore Fellows Communications, no. 184. Helsinki: Academia Scientiarum Fennica. [Cited as AT, Type, or Tale Type, followed by the appropriate number.]

Baughman, Ernest W. 1966. *Type and Motif-Index of the Folktakes of England and North America*. Indiana University Folklore Series, no. 20. The Hague: Mouton. [Cited as Baughman Type or Baughman Motif, followed by the appropriate letter or number.]

Child, Francis James. [1882–1898] 1965. *The English and Scottish Popular Ballads*. 5 vols. New York: Dover. [Cited as Child, followed by the appropriate number from 1 through 305.]

Laws, G. Malcolm Jr. 1957. *American Balladry from British Broadsides: A Guide for Students and Collectors of Traditional Song*. American Folklore Society, Bibliographical and Special Series. Vol. 8. Philadelphia. [Cited as Laws, followed by the letter J through Q followed by the appropriate number.]

———. 1964 *Native American Balladry: A Descriptive Guide and a Bibliographical Syllabus*. Rev. ed. American Folklore Society, Biographical and Special Series. Vol. 1. Philadelphia. [Cited as Laws, followed by the letter A through I, followed by the appropriate number.]

Thompson, Stith. 1955–1958. *The Motif-Index of Folk-Literature*. Rev. ed. 6 vols. Bloomington: Indiana University Press. [Cited as Motif, followed by the appropriate letter and numbers.]

ACADEMIC PROGRAMS IN FOLKLORE, INTERNATIONAL

Research, teaching, and study of folklore as a formal academic discipline outside North America. Any investigation into the current status of folklore and of its discernible progress in the academic world internationally is, from the very outset, apt to run into terminological problems as well as organizational variations. The term *folklore* for the discipline and/or for the materials the discipline studies, though originating in English in William Thoms' famous letter to *Antheneam* of 1846, has not found general acceptance in university circles in the British Isles. Currently, it is used only in the official title of the Department of Irish Folklore in University College Dublin, the department being a direct descendant of the former Irish Folklore Commission. The preferred term elsewhere, in the few academic institutions in which folklore is a recent newcomer to the curriculum (Edinburgh, Cardiff), is *ethnology*. Sometimes, this term also is used in Scandinavia, as in the title of the journal *Ethnologia Europaea*, but *folkliv, folkminne/folkeminde, folkekultur, folkedigtning*, and the like also occur in institutional titles. In some instances, these terms imply a strict separation of the study of material and nonmaterial culture, and the relationship of this group of terms to the use of *ethnology* is not always clear. Sometimes, the latter is understood to be the umbrella term; at other times, it is thought of as coequal with folklore. Relevant chairs or institutes in universities in German- or Dutch/Flemish-speaking countries usually are designated by the term *Volkskunde*, generally in deliberate juxtaposition to *Ethnologie;* in the former socialist countries, *ethnography* predominates. In Greece, we find *lagrophia*, and in Italy, *storia delle tradizioni popolari* as well as *etnografia*. The term *ethnology* is frequently qualified by the epithet *regional*, and other designations restrict the scope of inquiries to areas and groups within national borders. The Finno-Ugric countries have their own terminologies.

These and other variations on the surface appear to point to a fragmented discipline, but in reality, they hide a remarkable singleness of purpose. The activities generated and the subject matter studied all have some bearing on and are frequently roughly identical with what in North America is termed *folklore*. They can, therefore, legitimately be included in any attempt to measure the status of and programmatic development in this field of study. Apparently, there has never been a global survey of the teaching of folklore in academic institutions, and no systematic inquiry has been conducted in Europe since the late 1960s. Two surveys were undertaken, however, in

1953–1954 and in 1965, the former on behalf of the Commission Internationale des Arts et Traditions Populaires (CIAP) and the latter in conjunction with its successor, the Societé Internationale d'Ethnologie et de Folklore (SIEF). These surveys yield a certain amount of information with regard to the presence of folklore studies in European institutions of higher learning. The 1965 survey, for example, ascertained that, at that time, there were about 150 chairs-cum-institutes in "folklore" in European academic establishments. In some countries, practically every university offered courses and conducted research in the subject; in others, formal offerings were more sporadic or nonexistent. It also was quite common for the pursuit of folklore studies to be linked to or incorporated within departments devoted to adjacent areas of academic endeavor (e.g., geography, cultural history, German), rather than conducted within independent departments. It would be misleading, however, to gauge the presence and development of folklore studies in Europe solely in terms of the universities, for much research in the field in the last two centuries has been carried out by individuals or clusters of individuals attached to academies, archives, and museums; many of the incumbents of related research posts also have had part-time or honorary lecturing positions in universities. A rich crop of publications testifies to the range and intensity of the research carried out by individual scholars or as cooperative ventures.

One reason why development and evolution are so difficult to measure for the field of folklore studies involves the change in direction that the discipline has undergone in certain parts of Europe, especially in reaction to the politicization of the topic in the 1930s and early 1940s. A sociological orientation is now not unusual, often coupled with expressions of a social conscience. The investigation of modern phenomena often takes precedence over more traditionally oriented approaches. In a sense, such directional shifts may be interpreted as progressive, as may the increase in the number of students entering this field. Occupational opportunities in the public sector are practically nonexistent in Europe, unlike the United States.

The most obvious advance in academic folklore on the international scene has been through joint projects such as the *European Folklore Atlas*, the *International Folklore Bibliography*, and the *International Dictionary of Regional European Ethnology and Folklore*; through conferences and symposia organized, in most instances, by national and international scholarly societies such as CIAP and SIEF, the International Society for Folk-Narrative Research, or the fledgling International Society for Contemporary Legend Research; or through the summer schools organized by the revitalized Folklore Fellows of Helsinki. Within SIEF, the Ballad Commission has been particularly successful in arranging annual symposia that have resulted in fruitful personal contact among scholars not only within Europe but also across the Atlantic. Therefore, in terms of a wide definition of what folklore is and of what folklorists do, it can be said that the research, teaching, and study of the subject undoubtedly are prospering in much of Europe, and the current situation can with justification be described as encouraging.

W.F.H. Nicolaisen

See also Academic Programs in Folklore, North American.

✳✳✳✳✳✳✳✳✳✳✳✳✳✳✳✳✳

References
Anttonen, Pertti J. 1993. Profiles of Folklore 2: Department of European Ethnology, Lund University, Sweden. *NIF Newsletter* no. 2 (21):1–11.
Erixon, Sigurd. 1951. Ethnologie regionale ou folklore. *Laos* 1:9–19.
———. 1955. The Position of Regional Ethnology and Folklore at the European Universities: An International Inquiry. *Laos* 3:108–144.
Nicolaisen, W. 1965. Regional Ethnology in European Universities (French summary). *Volkskunde* 66:103–105.

ACADEMIC PROGRAMS IN FOLKLORE, NORTH AMERICAN

History and development of folklore programs in North American colleges and universities. The academic study of folklore and folklife has made considerable progress since 1940 when Ralph Steele Boggs reported only twenty-three U.S. colleges and universities with folklore courses; however, departments or even minidepartments of folklore projected in the late 1960s and early 1970s and degree-granting programs in folklore have not developed. Most academic folklorists teach folklore courses in departments other than folklore, typically in English and anthropology departments or in American studies programs.

In North American colleges and universities, folklore was first taught by literary scholars as part of literature and philology courses. This literary study of folklore began at Harvard University around 1856 when Francis James Child began collecting English and Scottish folk ballads from books, broadsides, and manuscripts. Although Child did not develop separate folklore courses or a folklore program, he incorporated folklore in his English courses, created the Folklore Collection in the Harvard College Library, and trained several notable U.S. folklorists, including George Lyman Kittredge, successor to Child's English professorship in 1894. Through the efforts of Child and Kittredge, Harvard became the center for the literary study of folklore in North America in the late nineteenth and early twentieth centuries, and it remains a center for the comparative study of oral literature today. Bartlett Jere Whiting and others carried on Child's and Kittredge's tradition of library research in folk literature, and in the 1930s, Milman Parry and Albert B. Lord initiated field research in European oral epics, leading to the development of the Milman Parry Collection of Oral Literature now in the Harvard College Library. The university's Center for the Study of Oral Literature supports graduate study in allied areas and complements Harvard's undergraduate degree program in folklore and mythology, awarded through its Committee on Degrees in Folklore and Mythology.

In 1883, Franz Boas was beginning fieldwork among the Eskimos of Baffinland, and by 1888, he was serving on the faculty of Clark University and collecting folklore from Native Americans in British Columbia. In 1899, Boas began a long career as an anthropology professor at Columbia University, which, through his reputation, became the center for the anthropological study of folklore in North America. Inspired by Boas, several of his students—including Robert H. Lowie, Ruth Benedict, Melville Herskovits, and Melville Jacobs—and other anthropologists began to incorporate folklore, especially Native American folklore, into their courses. Boas also encouraged scholars such as Marius Barbeau, who collected French-Canadian folklore, to study North American ethnic traditions. After Boas retired, Ruth Benedict and George Herzog combined efforts to keep Columbia a center of folklore activity well into the middle of the twentieth century.

The academic study of folklore also is indebted to a group of Americanists—Perry Miller, F. O. Matthiessen, Bernard DeVoto, Ralph Barton Perry, and Howard Mumford Jones—who established the first degree-granting program in American studies at Harvard in 1937. These Harvard Americanists expanded the study of American literature and culture from an emphasis on formal culture to include folk and popular cultures. They also established a place for folklore within interdisciplinary American studies programs, which today rank third after English and anthropology among departments and programs offering folklore courses at U.S. institutions. Although the early literary folklorists stressed the library study of older European folklore and the anthropological folklorists emphasized the field study of tribal traditions, the Americanists promoted the interdisciplinary study of American folk cultures against a background of American cultural history.

The first department of folklore in the United States was established at Franklin and Marshall College in 1948 when Alfred L. Shoemaker was appointed assistant professor of American folklore. Although the department was called the Department of American Folklore, the program was based on European folklife and *Volkskunde* models, and four of the six courses offered dealt with Pennsylvania folklore and folklife. Franklin and Marshall's short-lived folklore department first appeared in the catalog for 1949–1950 but remained in the catalog only through 1951–1952.

Although separate courses in folklore were introduced at several universities in the 1920s and 1930s, a degree-granting program in folklore did not exist until 1940 when Ralph Steele Boggs founded an interdisciplinary curriculum in folklore, offering an M.A. degree and a doctoral minor, at the University of North Carolina, Chapel Hill. Professor Boggs, a specialist in Latin American folklore, also spread the study of folklore to Mexico, where he introduced folklore studies and taught a folklore techniques course at the National University in 1945. Through its curriculum in folklore, the University of North Carolina remains one of the leading centers for the study of folklore in North America. Supported by major research collections—including the papers of D. K. Wilgus, the labor song collection of Archie Green, the Southern Folklife Collection, the John Edwards Memorial Collection, and the American Religious Tunebook Collection—and a large library collection in southern literature and culture, the North Carolina program is especially strong in the study of folksong and southern folklife. The program also emphasizes African-American folklore, ethnographic filmmaking, occupational folklore, public sector folklore, and immigrant folklore. The curriculum in folklore at North Carolina is designed mainly for graduate students, though undergraduates may put together an interdisciplinary degree with an area in folklore.

Trained by Kittredge and inspired by the historic-geographic studies of the Finnish folklorists of the late nineteenth and early twentieth centuries, Stith Thompson, who joined the English faculty at Indiana University in 1921, introduced the first folklore course there in 1923 and directed a number of folklore theses and dissertations of graduate students in the English department. Thompson founded the first U.S. doctoral program in folklore, emphasizing the comparative study of folk narratives, at Indiana University in 1949. After Thompson's retirement in 1955, his successor, Richard M. Dorson, expanded the concept of folklore studies at Indiana and elevated an expanded folklore program to departmental status in 1963. A graduate of the Harvard program in the history of American civilization, Dorson provided an Americanist orientation for a generation of folklorists trained at Indiana University between 1957 and 1981. Warren E. Roberts, Thompson's protégé in comparative folktale studies and recipient of the first U.S. doctorate in folklore in 1953, introduced the first course in material culture at Indiana in 1961; he also contributed significantly to broadening the scope of the Indiana program, which now combines humanistic and social scientific approaches. The program emphasizes theoretical approaches to folklore and, true to its comparative heritage, continues to cover many of the world's folk traditions. A program in ethnomusicology within the department and the renowned Archives of Traditional Music strengthen the teaching and research programs. Nearly 60 percent of all university teachers of folklore who hold doctorates in the subject have been trained at Indiana University.

Under the direction of MacEdward Leach, the University of Pennsylvania introduced the second U.S. doctoral program in folklore in

1959. After receiving a Ph.D. in Middle English literature at the University of Pennsylvania in 1930, Leach remained on the university's English faculty and changed an epic and short story course into an introductory folklore course and a literary ballad course into a folk ballad course. Eventually, Leach developed an interdisciplinary graduate program in folklore at the University of Pennsylvania and trained a number of folklorists, including Kenneth S. Goldstein, who eventually became chair of the program. At first, studies in ballads and folksongs and in folklore and literary relations were emphasized in the university's program; however, by the time Leach retired in 1966, the Department of Folklore and Folklife had developed into a broad program covering the entire range of folklore studies. Influenced by sociolinguistic approaches and the ethnography of communication, the program stresses social scientific approaches to folklore. Presently, around a third of all university teachers of folklore who hold doctorates in the subject received their training at the University of Pennsylvania.

Today, only two universities in the United States—Indiana and Pennsylvania—have folklore departments, but the University of California, Los Angeles (UCLA) is another major center for the study of folklore in North America. UCLA first offered a folklore course in 1933 when Sigurd B. Hustvedt, another student of Kittredge, introduced a graduate course in the traditional ballad. In 1937, Wayland D. Hand, a specialist in folk belief and custom, joined the German faculty, and two years later, he introduced a general folklore course. Under Hand's direction, an interdepartmental folklore program was established in 1954, offering around two dozen courses in folklore and related areas. Currently, the Folklore and Mythology Program at UCLA awards interdisciplinary master's and doctoral degrees in folklore and mythology. The interdisciplinary nature of the UCLA program gives it identity and strength, for students may choose from over seventy-five folklore and allied courses in departments throughout the university. A research institute, the Center for the Study of Comparative Folklore and Mythology, and other university research centers strengthen UCLA's teaching program.

In Canada, Memorial University of Newfoundland and Université Laval have folklore programs, one anglophone and the other francophone, and both programs award doctoral degrees in folklore. In 1962, Herbert Halpert, a student of Benedict and Herzog at Columbia and of Thompson at Indiana, joined the Memorial faculty, and through the encouragement and support of place-names scholar E. R. Seary, head of the Department of English, he developed a folklore program within the Department of English. In 1968, Halpert founded the Department of Folklore, which now offers a full range of folklore courses and emphasizes a balanced approach to folklore studies. Three archives support the teaching mission: the Centre d'Études Franco-Terreneuviennes, the Centre for Material Culture Studies, and the Folklore and Language Archive. Université Laval, with folklore studies dating from 1944 when Luc Lacourcière was appointed to a chair in folklore, offers courses and undergraduate and graduate degrees in folklore through its *programmes d'arts et traditions populaires* in the Département d'Histoire. Laval's program emphasizes French folklore in North America.

Although only Indiana, Memorial, Laval, Pennsylvania, and UCLA award the Ph.D. degree in folklore and only Harvard, Indiana, Laval, Memorial, Pennsylvania, and Pitzer College offer the B.A. degree in folklore, the M.A. degree in folklore is more common in North America. In addition to master's programs in folklore at UCLA, Indiana, Laval, Memorial, North Carolina, and Pennsylvania, an M.A. in folklore also is offered in the Department of Anthropology at the University of California, Berkeley, and an M.A. in folk arts is offered through the Tamburitzans Institute of Folk Arts in the School of Music at Duquesne University. Western Kentucky's program in folk studies is housed in the Department of Modern Languages and Intercultural Studies and offers an undergraduate minor as well as an M.A. degree in folk studies.

At least 80 North American institutions offer majors in other disciplines (notably, English, anthropology, and American studies) that permit either a folklore minor or a folklore concentration. These programs range from formal curricula to informal concentrations at all degree levels. For example, an M.A. and a Ph.D. in anthropology or English with a folklore concentration is offered at the University of Texas, Austin, and undergraduates there may design a special concentration in folklore. Undergraduate majors as well as graduate majors in anthropology at Texas A & M University also may elect a concentration in folklore. Degrees in folklore at the University of Oregon are coordinated through its Folklore and Ethnic Studies Program, which is supported by the Randall V. Mills Archive of Northwest Folklore. At Oregon, master's students create their own plans of study through individualized programs, and doctoral students may elect folklore as an area in English or anthropology. Through its Program in Folklore, Mythology, and Film Studies, the State University of New York, Buffalo awards an M.A. in English or humanities and a Ph.D. in English with a folklore and mythology concentration.

George Washington University's Folklife Program grants an M.A. in American studies or anthropology and a Ph.D. in American studies with a concentration in traditional material culture. Well situated in Washington, D.C., the Folklife Program utilizes the resources of the Smithsonian Institution, the American Folklife Center, and other museums, libraries, archives, and historical societies in the area. The Folklore Program at Utah State University is administered through the American Studies Program, and undergraduate and master's degrees in American studies with a folklore emphasis are offered. Folklore concentrations also are available in history or English at Utah State.

Master's candidates may elect areas in general folklore, public folklore, or applied history/museology. Ohio State University has offered folklore courses since the 1930s and now has a Center for Folklore and Cultural Studies, allowing undergraduate and graduate students a folklore concentration in an interdisciplinary program. A folklore archives and the Francis Lee Utley Collection in the university library support the academic program, which emphasizes folklore and literary relations and narrative theory.

Although more folklore courses are offered in English and, to a lesser degree, anthropology departments than in any other departments or programs, folklore courses are found in a wide variety of academic departments and programs, from architecture to women's studies. At a number of institutions, folklore courses, often cross-listed, are housed in more than one department. Though degrees in folklore and departments of folklore have not developed to the extent anticipated in the late 1960s and early 1970s, folklore courses and concentrations in allied departments and programs, after a slow beginning, have increased significantly in North America since that time. Public institutions, doctoral-granting institutions, and large institutions are more likely to offer folklore courses than private institutions, two-year institutions, and small institutions.

Ronald L. Baker

See also Academic Programs in Folklore, International.

✳✳✳✳✳✳✳✳✳✳✳✳✳✳✳✳✳

References

Baker, Ronald L. 1971. Folklore Courses and Programs in American Colleges and Universities. *Journal of American Folklore* 84:221–229.

———. 1978. The Study of Folklore in American Colleges and Universities. *Journal of American Folklore* 91:792–807.

———. 1986. Folklore and Folklife Studies in American and Canadian Colleges and Universities. *Journal of American Folklore* 99:50–74.

———. 1988. The Folklorist in the Academy. In *One Hundred Years of American Folklore Studies*, ed. William M. Clements. Washington, DC: American Folklore Society.

Boggs, Ralph Steele. 1940. Folklore in University Curricula in the United States. *Southern Folklore Quarterly* 4:93–109.

Bronner, Simon. 1991. A Prophetic Vision of Public and Academic Folklife: Alfred Shoemaker and America's First Department of Folklore. *The Folklore Historian* 8:38–55.

Bynum, David E. 1974. Child's Legacy Enlarged: Oral Literary Studies at Harvard since 1856. *Harvard Library Bulletin* 22:237–267.

Dorson, Richard M. 1950. The Growth of Folklore Courses. *Journal of American Folklore* 63:345–359.

———. 1972. The Academic Future of Folklore. In Richard M. Dorson, *Folklore: Selected Essays*. Bloomington: Indiana University Press.

Leach, MacEdward. 1958. Folklore in American Colleges and Universities. *Journal of American Folklore Supplement*, pp. 10–11.

ACCULTURATION

Cultural modification of groups' and individuals' material culture, behaviors, beliefs, and values caused by borrowing from or adapting to other cultures. Whenever cultures regularly contact one another, change takes place in a limited number of ways: One group may destroy the other, one may completely adopt the other's culture and become a part of it, the two may merge to create a fusion culture, or both may adapt and borrow from one another. The group that is politically or economically subordinate to the other usually does the most immediate and extensive borrowing. Major references to the subject of acculturation include the "Exploratory Formulation" published by H. G. Barnett and colleagues in 1954 as the result of a Social Science Research Council Summer Seminar and the report of a 1979 symposium sponsored by the American Association for the Advancement of Science.

The process of acculturation, without a doubt, has been going on as long as cultures have been coming in contact with one another, and the concept of acculturation was first employed in a manner close to its present sense as early as the 1880s. But acculturation has been the subject of a good deal of intensive analysis in the fields of cultural study only since the 1930s. The emphasis that led to closer scholarly examination of acculturation, particularly in the United States, grew out of the earlier concern for salvaging so-called memory-cultures and the assumption that "pure" cultures that had not been "contaminated" by acculturation were somehow superior and more important. In 1936, a committee appointed by the Social Science Research Council and consisting of Robert Redfield, chair, Ralph Linton, and Melville J. Herskovits published a three-page "Memorandum for the Study of Acculturation" that urged special attention to the matter and the exchange of information gathered on the subject by researchers working with different cultures. There is little evidence that the sort of exchange among researchers that Redfield, Linton, and Herskovits anticipated took place, but the call greatly affected the course of cultural study. Redfield, Linton, and Herskovits themselves heeded the call, and each of them wrote classic books on acculturation.

From the research of the committee members and that inspired by their report emerged many important studies and widely accepted conclusions concerning acculturation. It is, first of all, important to note that the term *acculturation* as used within the fields of cultural analysis refers only to change that comes about by borrowing, although popular usage also applies the term to the process of socialization by which individuals (usually children) learn to function within their own culture. As it is used within anthropology and folklore, the term *acculturation* usually is limited to changes caused by intercultural influencing that affects and modifies a broad range of the deep structures of culture; the term *diffusion* is used to describe changes that take place in individual elements or parts of cultures adopted without change. The Navajo and Zuni tribes of the U.S. Southwest, for example, have been in close contact for several hundred years and have experienced a good deal of diffusion, but their total sociocultural systems seem to have been little acculturated by one another because the two cultures share a long-standing tradition of mutual hospitality and reciprocity—"guest-friend" relationship roles that encourage mutual acceptance.

Classic research studies, furthermore, demonstrate that the degree and extent of acculturation within a culture depends on and ultimately occurs at the behest of the culture that is doing the borrowing (the receptor culture), rather than the culture from which the other is borrowing (the donor culture). An individual culture's emphasis upon and mechanisms for maintaining its cultural boundaries, the relative degree of flexibility of its varied internal structures, and the degree and functioning of its mechanisms for self-correction are all major cultural traits that directly and indirectly affect acculturation. The existing values and patterns of the receiving culture serve as a filter that controls the process of acculturation and allows the enthusiastic and whole-hearted acceptance of some traits while providing for the firm rejection of others. Thus, acculturation does not proceed at an even rate in terms of all elements of culture within the same group. Research also has indicated that technology tends to be altered more readily than nontangible elements such as beliefs or values.

Perhaps the single most important fact to emerge from the classic studies of acculturation is that acculturation is not only inevitable and extremely dynamic but also highly creative. Researchers made much of the melancholy process of change as cultures adapted to new situations, and they based their observations upon the unspoken romantic assumption that the precontact cultures represented a "golden age" and that acculturation in response to contact was somehow unavoidably corrupting and evil. In marked contrast with this tacit assumption, the description of the borrowing of the Navajo tribe—and other cultures—as incorporative acculturation presented a very different model, explaining that cultures borrowing traits often reinterpret them in form and/or meaning so that a culture may be always changing and yet always retain its integrity. The Navajo, for example, borrowed sheep, horses, silversmithing, weaving, and ceremony and mythology from other cultures, but they reinterpreted all that they borrowed so that the new traits became and remain their own.

Research on acculturation published in the 1980s and 1990s supports earlier research and agrees with previous discoveries—though in different language—that acculturation must be recorded and studied as a multivariate and multidimensional process. This research develops and employs highly sophisticated statistical models and tools that enable quantitative analysis as a supplement to the earlier classic qualitative studies. The researchers who are developing this approach to understanding acculturation emphasize the psychological consequences of acculturation upon individuals.

Keith Cunningham

See also Anthropological Approach.

✱✱✱✱✱✱✱✱✱✱✱✱✱✱✱✱✱

References

Barnett, H. G., Leonard Broom, Bernard J. Siegel, Evon Z. Vogt, and James B. Watson. 1954. Acculturation: An Exploratory Formulation. *American Anthropologist* 61:973–1000.

Herskovits, Melville J. 1938. *Acculturation: The Study of Cultural Contact*. New York: Augustin.

Linton, Ralph, ed. 1940. *Acculturation in Seven American Indian Tribes*. New York: Appleton-Century.

Padilla, Amado M. 1980. *Acculturation: Theory, Models, and Some New Findings*. Boulder, CO: Westview Press.

Redfield, Robert. 1953. *The Primitive World and Its Transformations*. Ithaca, NY: Cornell University Press.

Redfield, R., R. Linton, and M.J. Herskovits. 1936. Memorandum for the Study of Acculturation. *American Anthropologist* 38:149–152.

AESTHETICS

The study of the creation and appreciation of beauty. Philosophical approaches to the subject of aesthetics center on the *perception* of beauty in the experience of art. Folkloristic approaches to the subject define those formal features within folklore that constitute its artfulness in communal and/or personal terms. Folklorists speak of aesthetic issues most often in terms of style, artistry, and the relation of tradition and innovation. An aesthetic analysis may pertain to a single genre or to the folklore of an entire community. In either case, aesthetic standards may be examined from a contrastive perspective (i.e., in relation to some other genre or community) or from an in-group perspective. Folkloristic research in aesthetics contributes vitally to theoretical understandings of cultural relativism and the importance of communal tastes in the creation of art. The topic of aesthetics also holds importance for public sector researchers, as it raises issues related to the evaluation and presentation of folklore.

TRADITION AND INNOVATION

The study of material culture in particular has furnished significant insights into aesthetics. One of the early classics in the area is Franz Boas' *Primitive Art*

(1927). Through examination of traditional arts from around the world, Boas identifies several fundamental criteria of artistry: symmetry (a balance of component elements), rhythm (the regular, pattern-forming repetition of features), and the emphasis or delimitation of form (the tendency toward representative or abstract depiction). The complex interplay of these features makes artwork from one culture distinguishable from that of another.

Since these features underlie all art, however, Boas stresses further the importance of communal tastes in the execution of "primitive" art. Boas writes of a communal "emotional attachment to customary forms," limiting acceptance of innovation. The fact that the form and details of a given implement may vary little from one artist to the next does not derive from a lack of creativity on the part of the folk artist; rather, the artist responds to the community's greater interest in preserving the traditional. Under these circumstances, the aesthetic merit of a given product resides not in its uniqueness but in the artist's ability to realize and execute communal norms, confining individual variation to small details of ornamentation or style.

As Boas and later scholars demonstrate, this stress on the customary is further bolstered by the communal creation of objects. In a traditional barn raising or quilting bee, for instance, individual tastes or experimentation are limited by the communal execution of the work. Communal production, characteristic of many varieties of traditional material culture, thus exerts a leveling influence on artistic variation and helps ensure the maintenance of a communal aesthetic over time. When traditional performers become separated from this ambient collective tradition of evaluation and production, their work may change greatly, incorporating new ideas and departing to some degree from old standards. Richard Bauman addresses changes of this sort in his study of a folk raconteur turned professional. Similarly, Michael Owen Jones examines the conscious interplay of tradition and innovation in the products of a professional Kentucky mountain chairmaker. Jones stresses that aesthetic choices do not occur mechanistically but as the result of personal decisions and values over time.

Given this analytical framework, a prime issue for the folk art collector lies in the question of whether to value typicality in a piece of folklore (an act presumably valued in the traditional community) or to privilege instead those works that transgress typical norms or tastes (an act valued in elite art circles). Judgments of this sort have direct bearing on folk artists, as the monetary value attached to a given work may influence artistic trends within the community itself. Collector interest in a particular physical form or color scheme, for instance, may alter a community's evaluation of that form and lead to its triumph over other types. An obscure performer or style may thus become central, while a community's own evaluative standards lose cogency. By contrast, changes that appear significant to an outside audience may be regarded as minor creative alterations within the ambient community itself, of little consequence to the tradition or its maintenance. Alterations in technique, materials, or use only become significant if they transgress important rules within the community's aesthetic system. Questions of aesthetics thus present intriguing issues for both public sector and academic folklorists alike.

AESTHETICS IN COMMUNICATION

Aesthetics becomes an explicit concern of linguistic folklorists through the writings of Roman Jakobson. Jakobson's attention to poetics provides a new basis for the analysis of the aesthetic form and uses of language. In Jakobson's analysis, poetic language draws ordinary words into new frameworks of meaning through attention to criteria (e.g., rhyme) normally ignored in speech. This new axis of *equivalence* distinguishes the poetic utterance from the ordinary. Studies such as William Pepicello and Thomas Green's examination of riddling demonstrate the ways in which folklore can capitalize artfully on such normally unnoticed similarities between words or utterances. The study of ethnopoetics further examines the ways in which equivalence operates in the narrative traditions of many cultures, converting seemingly utilitarian components of speech (e.g., grammatical case, conjunctions, tense) into markers of artistic structure. In this way, minute aesthetic features become markers of larger aesthetic patternings, themselves constitutive of the narrative's symbolic import.

From the outset, the performance perspective of folklore studies stressed the importance of aesthetic inquiry. Dan Ben-Amos' classic definition of folklore as "*artistic* communication in small groups" (emphasis added) has led others to pay particular attention to the ways in which aesthetic merit is achieved in a given performance. For Richard Bauman, the performance itself becomes framed through communally recognized aesthetic features that distinguish it from ordinary discourse: for example, special language, altered use of voice or body, or special opening and closing formulas. Aesthetic features become instrumental, helping the performer designate the performance as a special moment during which the rules of ordinary communication are temporarily suspended.

CONTRASTIVE ANALYSIS

Folklorists have often addressed aesthetic features within a given genre or community from a contrastive perspective. The aesthetic values of a certain kind of folklore, for instance, may be contrasted with the values of elite art or with those of some other community. Typical of a genre-based approach is Max Lüthi's study of European *Märchen* (see Folktale entry). Concentrating on the formal aspects of the genre (e.g., characters, setting, plot), Lüthi demonstrates the *Märchen's* distinctiveness from elite narrative literature. Similarly, Breandán Breathnach's study of Irish folk music contrasts the means of ornamentation and style in folk music with that of European art music. The features favored by the elite tradition (e.g., variation in intensity of sound—"dynamics") remain unexploited by the folk performer, and other features (e.g., grace notes, rhythm) become prime means of varying and evaluating performances.

John Michael Vlach offers a community-based approach to contrastive aesthetics in his examination of African-American arts. In his discussion of quilting, for instance, Vlach not only stresses the survival of West African techniques and styles but also examines how the particular aesthetic embodied in such works contrasts with the Euroamerican aesthetic of quilt form. Whereas Anglo quiltmakers of the nineteenth century valued geometric regularity and naturalistic representational depiction, African-American quilters valued works that employed both "improvisational" patternings and stylized figures.

Such contrastive analysis is particularly enlightening when the groups or genres compared have existed side by side for an extended period, leading to the more or less conscious creation and maintenance of contrastive evaluative standards. Differential aesthetics can become a means of creating and defending cultural boundaries, of resisting a threatened loss of communal identity.

IN-GROUP VALUES: ETHNOAESTHETICS

Often, however, the folklorist seeks to explicate a communal aesthetic on its own terms, without reference to some contrasting system. An examination of this type turns to native concepts and categories. Gary Gossen's study of Chamula verbal categories, for instance, discusses the importance of "heat" in Chamula evaluations of oral performance. Genres differ from each other in Chamula culture through differences in attendant heat, and one performance differs from another in its ability to create the proper degree of heatedness. Heat becomes the conceptual basis of Chamula verbal aesthetics, relating it in turn to aspects of Chamula mythology.

Gary Witherspoon and Barre Toelken point to the similar centrality of the concepts of process and cosmic interrelation in the aesthetics of Navajo people. Navajo aesthetics locates beauty in the act of creation rather than in the product and stresses the relation of that act to many others occurring in tandem throughout the universe. Beauty is a central and profoundly meaningful concept rather than a marginal or superfluous one. Aesthetics can thus provide insight into deep philosophical questions of native metaphysics and worldview.

Although folkloristic approaches to aesthetics may appear diffuse and unsystematized, they indicate the fundamental importance of aesthetics for the study of folklore. Aesthetics helps link the performer and the community, the personal and the communal. It provides a crucial focus for researchers interested in the artistry of human communication.

Thomas A. DuBois

See also Art, Folk; Artifact; Ethnoaesthetics; Ethnopoetics; Linguistic Approach; Performance; Repertoire; Texture; Tradition.

✳✳✳✳✳✳✳✳✳✳✳✳✳✳✳

References

Bauman, Richard. 1975. Verbal Art as Performance. *American Anthropologist* 77:290–311.

———. 1986. *Story, Performance and Event: Contextual Studies in Oral Narrative.* Cambridge: Cambridge University Press.

Ben-Amos, Dan. 1971. Toward a Definition of Folklore in Context. *Journal of American Folklore* 84:3–15.

Boas, Franz. 1927. *Primitive Art.* New York: Dover.

Breathnach, Breandán. 1971. *Folk Music and Dances of Ireland.* Dublin: Mercier.

Gossen, Gary. 1974. *Chamulas in the World of the Sun.* Cambridge, MA: Harvard University Press.

Jakobson, Roman. 1960. Closing Statement: Linguistics and Poetics. In *Style in Language*, ed. Thomas A. Sebeok. New York: John Wiley.

Jones, Michael Owen. 1989. *Craftsman of the Cumberlands: Tradition and Creativity.* Lexington: University Press of Kentucky.

Pepicello, W. J., and Thomas A. Green. 1984. *The Language of Riddles*: New Perspectives. Columbus: Ohio State University Press.

Toelken, Barre. 1979. Worldview and the Traditional Material Artifacts of the Navajo. In *The Dynamics of Folklore*, ed. Barre Toelken. Boston: Houghton Mifflin.

Vlach, John Michael. 1978. *The Afro-American Tradition in Decorative Arts.* Cleveland, OH: Cleveland Museum of Art.

Witherspoon, Gary. 1977. *Language and Art in the Navajo Universe.* Ann Arbor: University of Michigan Press.

ANECDOTE

Narratives that concentrate on representative incidents regarding named individuals or groups. As the etymology of this term indicates (Latin *anecdota*, "unpublished items," from the Greek *anekdotos*, "unpublished"), anecdotes have always been closely associated with oral tradition. They share their particular folk-narrative niche with closely related genres such as *joke*, *legend*, *exemplum*, *rumor*, *tall tale*, (see related entries) and the kind of humorous story that in German is called *schwank*. Several traits, therefore, tend to overlap among these genres, and it is not always easy to separate one from the other.

What is peculiar to the anecdote, though not exclusively so, is its concentration on named individuals or groups, especially the former. Consequently, anonymity is not one of its chief properties. Anecdotes focus particularly on well-known historical or contemporary personalities, both those in the public eye in general (royalty, famous military figures, politicians, scientists, film stars, athletes, writers) and those locally regarded as "worthies." Whether anecdotes told about these individuals are intended to enhance or to denigrate them, the anecdotes relate incidents seen as typical of the individuals' actions or other qualities. In performance, an anecdote is often used to underpin or confirm in its pointedness a characteristic previously ascribed to an individual ("To show you what I mean, let me tell you a story I heard about so-and-so"). Whether they are believed to be true or known to be apocryphal, anecdotes can be powerful rhetorical tools thinly disguised as narrative entertainment. Mutatis mutandis, these hallmarks also apply to anecdotes told about distinguishable, named groups, whether in praise (soldiers of a particular regiment, a famous clan, Londoners during World War II) or in mocking contempt (the East Frisians, the Irish, the people of Aarhus, the men of Gotham, city officials).

Although allegedly relating the actions or sayings of named individuals, anecdotes essentially express general human traits or universal human concerns, such as stupidity, cleverness, boastfulness, curiosity, cowardice, miserliness, laziness, drunkenness, gaucheness, ignorance, credulity, absent-mindedness, shrewdness, courage, quick-wittedness, slow-wittedness, and so on. The diplomatic gaffe of an ambassador representing a powerful country or the simple mistake made in a foreign language by a prominent politician not only creates a certain amount of schadenfreude and exposes the imperfections of those in high places but also, in some representative fashion, compensates for our own occasional lack of tact or behavioral competence and our own linguistic struggles when abroad. Thus, anecdotes are convenient vehicles for overt or covert social criticism. Drunkenness may itself be deplored or lead to hilarious narrative accounts: The story of a drunken priest highlights the incongruity of the condition and the status of the person afflicted. Courage may be admired in the strong, but it gains much poignancy when displayed by the timid in adversity. Group rivalry between sports teams, neighboring cities, universities, fraternities, the different armed services, ethnic communities, religious persuasions, and so on may find otherwise elusive expression in the short, sharply focused narrative of the anecdote.

Structurally, anecdotes, like jokes and contemporary legends, rely heavily on and therefore work toward a final revelation or punch line. But unlike the other two genres, they do not lose their effectiveness in repetition; quite the contrary, those who tell anecdotes are often asked to repeat them to reinforce a particular view or opinion of an individual or group in an entertaining manner. Antti Aarne and Stith Thompson's *Types of the Folktale* lists many of the traditional anecdotes in section 1200–1999 ("Jokes and Anecdotes"), together with other monoepisodic stories. The majority of motifs are likely to be found under J ("The Wise and the Foolish"), K ("Deceptions"), W ("Traits of Character"), and X ("Humor") in Stith Thompson's *Motif-Index of Folk-Literature*. Despite the popularity of the anecdote in oral tradition, folklorists have paid comparatively little attention to the anecdote as a genre per se. Not surprisingly, the anecdote, with its strong affinity to the short story, also has become a well-honed literary genre.

W.F.H. Nicolaisen

See also Blason Populaire; Esoteric/Exoteric Factor; Ethnic Folklore; Folktale.

✳✳✳✳✳✳✳✳✳✳✳✳✳✳✳✳✳✳

References

Aarne, Antti, and Stith Thompson. 1964. *The Types of the Folktale*. 2d ed., rev. Folklore Fellows Communications, no. 184. Helsinki: Academia Scientiarum Fennica.

Brunvand, Jan Harold. 1986. *The Study of American Folklore: An Introduction*. New York: Norton.

Dégh, Linda. 1972. Folk Narrative. In *Folklore and Folklife: An Introduction*, ed. Richard M. Dorson. Chicago: University of Chicago Press.

Grothe, Heinz. 1984. *Anekdote*. Sammlung Metzler Band 101. Stuttgart: Metzler.

Ranke, Kurt. 1972. *European Anecdotes and Jests*. European Folklore Series, no. 4. Copenhagen: Rosenkilde and Bagger.

Thompson, Stith. 1946. The *Folktale*. New York: Holt, Rinehart and Winston.

———. 1966. *Motif-Index of Folk-Literature*. 2d ed. 6 vols. Bloomington: Indiana University Press.

Animism

Term derived from the Greek *anima*, meaning spirit or soul, and used to signify either: (1) the belief in indwelling spirits (souls, ghosts, and other invisible beings) inherent in people, animals, plants, or even lifeless things and often presented in personalized or anthropomorphized images, or (2) the theory that accounts for the origin of religion on the basis of this kind of anima. The anima is believed to be like a soul, a self, or an ego, able to leave the body either temporarily (e.g., in sleep, ecstasy, or fright) or permanently (e.g., on the occasion of death).

The theory of animism as the basis of the earliest form of religion was set forth by the pioneer English anthropologist E. B. Tylor (1832–1917) in his book *Primitive Culture*. Tylor bridged the evolutionary and diffusionist theories of culture of his times in his own psychologically inspired reasoning. The general evolutionary perception of that age proposed a gradual development of the natural, social, and spiritual worlds toward more complex and higher modes of existence. In the evolution of man's religious ideas, monotheistic Christianity was placed at the pinnacle of the developmental scale as the highest form of spirituality.

Tylor stated that primitive religion was rational in its own way, supporting his premises with an image of the "ancient savage philosophers." The theory of animism was thought to reveal the psychological mechanisms of primitive man and the original form of religion in human history. However, Tylor's hypotheses were not based on reliable scientific data, and the premise of unilinear cultural evolution ultimately could not prevail in the face of accumulating evidence regarding early man. Scientific accumulation of knowledge on the so-called primitive religions and on continuous contacts between these tribes and peoples of different modes of production and belief systems forced scholars to abandon the theory that claimed that the nineteenth-century aboriginal tribes represented the pristine state of human cultural evolution.

Despite the fact that the theoretical value of animism has been disproved, it played an influential role in the study of man for decades before the rise of functionalism in the field of anthropology. It also made an important contribution to the search for the origins of human civilization.

Juha Pentikäinen

See also Evolutionary Theory; Religion, Comparative.

✻✻✻✻✻✻✻✻✻✻✻✻✻✻✻✻✻

References

de Vries, Jan. 1977. *Perspectives in the History of Religions*. Trans. Kees W. Bolle. Berkeley: University of California Press.

Eliade, Mircea. 1969. *The Quest: History and Meaning in Religion*. Chicago: University of Chicago Press.

Evans-Pritchard, E. E. 1965. *Theories of Primitive Religion*. Oxford: Oxford University Press.

Hodgen, Margaret T. 1936. *The Doctrine of Survivals: A Chapter in the History of Scientific Method in the Study of Man*. London: Alleson.

Tylor, Edward B. 1958. *Primitive Culture: Researches into the Development of Mythology, Philosophy, Religion, Art and Custom*. 2 vols. (Vol. 1, *The Origins of Culture*; Vol. 2, *Religion in Primitive Culture*.) Gloucester, MA: Smith.

ANTHROPOLOGICAL APPROACH

Subject selection, definitions of folklore, data selection, research methods, and theories of folklore research closely related to and associated with those employed in cultural anthropology. Folklore and anthropology arose together as disciplines in response to the interests and concerns of an England that had accepted Charles Darwin's theory of evolution and social Darwinism. An important and long-standing difference between the disciplines from the time of their common English origins—a difference that grew out of and in turn shaped the disciplines' definitions of themselves—was their subject selection. From the beginning in England, there was a division of labor and laborers so that anthropology traveled through space and folklore traveled through time to explore the evolutionary stages of man. From the beginnings of their histories, anthropologists researched contemporary people and cultures other than their own around the world, and folklorists researched the lore of their own people as it existed in the past through an examination of peasant culture as a stage of their own cultures' histories.

The disciplines of folklore and cultural anthropology have varied greatly through the times and spaces they have shared but perhaps no more so than in their definitions of folklore. The Russian structural folklorist Vladimir Propp strongly denied that material culture and custom—he called the complex of custom and belief "spiritual culture"—were folklore and argued that these genres of tradition should be left to ethnologists. The American folklife movement insisted just as strongly that material culture and custom—from the 1950s on, Don Yoder also insisted that folklore included something very akin to Propp's "spiritual folklore"—were an essential part of folklore and demanded that greater attention be paid to them. At various times in various places, members of both professions have claimed as their province various combinations of verbal lore, customary and material culture, and the folk.

Another issue of concern between members of each discipline is whether the data of the field are to be garnered through written records or firsthand experience (library or field research). Some early folklorists—Andrew Lang, for example—and anthropologists were content to draw their data from the recorded observations of others. Later folklorists and anthropologists often insisted upon conducting field research themselves and gathering their own materials for analysis supplemented by their observations. Both field- and nonfield-based research has been conducted by scholars in folklore and in anthropology at various times throughout the disciplines' histories.

There have been many anthropological approaches to folklore based upon cross-cultural theories. Some of these theories quickly fell out of fashion. Max Müller's *solar mythology* claimed that folklore was devolutionary. He defended the idea that it was possible to work backward, transcend the "disease of language," experience anew the wonder of an age in which primitive man worshiped the sun, and discover that the folklore of the present was but a dim reflection or a broken-down myth of the time when the sun was king. Müller's theory—and his reputation—were destroyed by the power of the pen when Andrew Lang published a brilliant parody using Müller's methods to prove that both "Max" and "Müller" were reflections of solar myth.

Max Müller and Andrew Lang were united, however, in their reliance upon published materials for research. Lang's own *survivals theory* was in keeping with the widespread acceptance of evolutionary patterns of thought in the England of his time, and his wit and tenacity won the day. His vigorous defense of the idea that all peoples and cultures evolved in a fixed, orderly progression of stages so that ontogeny recapitulates phylogeny was a folkloristic attempt to understand the present by studying the past, just as anthropologists have sought to understand their cultures by studying others— different responses to the same theory. Lang's theory, however, had its day and slowly lost its influence in both folklore and anthropology over a period of decades.

Other anthropological approaches to folklore also foundered when field-tested and gradually were disproved and discarded by folklorists. The *myth-ritual theory*, an essentially literary approach espoused by Sir James Frazer and others who sought to discover the patterns and forms of the ritual of early man underlying literature, was, like Max Müller's solar mythology, essentially devolutionary and therefore in conflict with the evolutionary theory that dominated Western thought. Consequently, myth-ritualism was destined to be discarded. Although the process was more gradual, the myth-ritual theory, like solar mythology, also lost its influence and adherents over the years.

The *pattern theory of culture, ethnography, functionalism, structuralism*, and *symbolic anthropology* are all anthropological theories that underlie or are elements of widely accepted and employed anthropological approaches to folklore in the 1990s. Because of its generative relationship to other anthropological approaches to folklore, Ruth Benedict's pattern theory of culture, it can be argued, is the anthropological theory most basic to folklore scholarship in the last days of the twentieth century. Benedict asserted the idea that all parts of culture are related and reflect—albeit sometimes in different ways—the same values and beliefs, so that unconscious canons of choice produce a unified whole of behaviors, values, and beliefs. Benedict's theory implies that culture is one, each part evincing the whole, so that oral and material and customary folklore are all windows into culture. The widespread acceptance of Benedict's theory revolutionized the definition of culture and the study of folklore. A good deal of controversy was generated within the discipline of folklore by this anthropological approach (in two books published in 1972, Richard M. Dorson both condemned and commended the idea that lore including ordinary conversation could be used to understand values). Thus, it is somewhat surprising to see that Benedict's ideas have been so widely accepted that they have become a truism and the basis of a great deal of research and general knowledge in the 1990s, even among people who may not know that she was the scholar who first popularized the pattern theory of culture. Folklore was the principal cultural item she studied. Her concept of the great significance of folklore follows from the definition of culture she popularized and has led to a number of anthropological approaches to folklore.

The importance of Ruth Benedict's pattern theory of culture is matched by the influence of the method she used to report her research—the *ethnography*. Ethnography is a method of studying cultures in which researchers immerse themselves in ways of life to perceive them as they are lived and then write articles and books recounting and interpreting their fieldwork. Such studies are designed to enable others to experience what it is like to be members of the cultures studied. The method existed long before Benedict, but it was popularized because it was the method she and her colleagues employed. Clifford Geertz, along with many other contemporary anthropologists in the 1970s, 1980s, and 1990s, further emphasized ethnography as an important and successful way of exploring culture, and ethnography has become a major literary genre and anthropological approach to folklore in the late 1990s.

Structuralism is another anthropological approach to folklore. Syntagmatic structuralism is concerned with discovering the basic, surface structures of folklore—the method is most often applied to oral lore—and has become one of the most frequently employed methods of folklore research today. Vladimir Propp's morphological analysis, the oral-formulaic method, and William Labov's system of narrative analysis are widely employed structural analysis methods applied to the study of narrative and other oral forms, and there have been a number of widely accepted structural analyses of conversational genres such as riddles and proverbs. Claude Lévi-Strauss' paradigmatic structuralism—the quest for underlying deep structures (usually sets of binary oppositions)—was extremely popular for a period of time in the middle of the twentieth century. Lévi-Strauss claimed that his sets of binary opposites were universal and reflected the basic nature of human thought. The theory had become less influential and widely accepted in folklore by the 1990s.

Benedict's insistence that all spheres of culture are meaningfully related provided a rationale for approaches attempting to discover how folklore functions. The idea that all forms of folklore satisfy some important psychological, social, or cultural function is a basic axiom of most folklore research in the 1990s.

Symbolic anthropology, interpreting symbols in the context of the processes of social and cultural life, is another anthropological approach to folklore. Victor Turner disagreed with the rigidity and conformity that he felt had become a part of structural and functional anthropology and argued instead for an analysis of symbols. Turner and other symbolic anthropologists saw symbols as conscious and unconscious representations and objects of power. His method and his insistence upon interpreting symbols from the broadest possible perspective as complex data reflecting multivalence and condensation have been widely accepted as an anthropological approach to folklore; moreover, his approach is yet another way of saying, as did Benedict, that all cultural traits have meaning. Anthropology in general, throughout its long history, has studied man; folklore has studied the products of the human imagination; and symbolic anthropology studies the products of the human imagination in order to understand man.

Anthropology and folklore both developed and changed over their histories from Tylor to Turner. Folklore continued to broaden its field of study, method, and theoretical orientations as it developed as a discipline. In the 1990s, functional, structural, and symbolic anthropology are all part of anthropological approaches to folklore. The major feature of the discipline of folklore in the last decades of the twentieth century is the fact that it is eclectic. In the 1990s, most folklorists pursue research in terms of a limited number of topics, but most recognize as an ideal a truly complete anthropological approach. This approach would examine people of all cultures as revealed by research methods emphasizing the firsthand experiencing of material culture, custom, and oral lore.

Many American folklorists and American graduate programs have defined their field of study not in terms of lore—item or genres—but in terms of anthropological approaches to folklore. In the 1990s, folk cultural field research concentrating upon people and their lore is one of the most commonly used methods for dissertation research in major American folklore graduate schools, and for that reason, such research is apt to be one of the most important approaches to folklore for at least the next generation of graduate students.

Keith Cunningham

See also Acculturation; Anthropology, Symbolic; Cultural Relativism; Ethnography; Evolutionary Theory; Fieldwork; Functionalism; Myth-Ritual Theory; Structuralism.

✳✳✳✳✳✳✳✳✳✳✳✳✳✳✳✳✳

References

Ackerman, Robert. 1991. *The Myth and Ritual School: J. G. Frazer and the Cambridge Ritualists*. New York: Garland.

Benedict, Ruth. 1934. *Patterns of Culture*. Boston: Houghton Mifflin.

Dorson, Richard M. 1972. Concepts of Folklore and Folklife Studies. In *Folklore and Folklife: An Introduction*, ed. Richard M. Dorson. Chicago: University of Chicago Press.

Geertz, Clifford. 1973. *The Interpretation of Culture*. New York: Basic Books.

Kroeber, A. L., and C. Kluckhohn. 1963. *Culture: A Critical Review of Concepts and Definitions*. New York: Vintage Books.

Lévi-Strauss, Claude. 1963. *Structural Anthropology*. New York: Basic Books.

Müller, Friedrich Max. 1856. Comparative Mythology. In *Oxford Essays*. London: John W. Parker.

Propp, Vladimir. 1984. *Theory and History of Folklore*. Minneapolis, MN: University of Minneapolis Press.

Turner, Victor. 1967. *The Forest of Symbols: Aspects of Ndembu Ritual*. Ithaca, NY: Cornell University Press.

Tylor, E. B. 1873. *Primitive Culture*. Vol. 1. London: John Murray.

ANTHROPOLOGY, SYMBOLIC

The study of the nature of the symbols used in different cultures, in ritual, in performances, and in daily life where full meaning requires more than literal expression. A symbol has two components—a solid, visible, or otherwise sensory sign and the idea to which it points. Symbolic anthropology interprets symbols in the context of the processes of social and cultural life.

In the history of the symbolizing process, investigators are able to trace symbolization to *Homo erectus*, who lived a million to a hundred thousand years ago, before *Homo sapiens*. Symbolization was evidenced in the signs of ocher pigment on the bones of these earliest hominids. Later (circa 35,000 to 19,000 years ago), the caves of Lascaux and Altamira were filled with pictures of shamanic scenes, pictures that themselves are thought to have been objects of power. Human beings appear to possess a predisposition for symbolization (indeed, this trait is shared by some animals). The practice of producing an alternative object to the ordinary one—a picture of a bull, for example—is deep in the techniques of ritual and usually goes beyond representation. There exists the ordinary object, the bull, and the picture of it— two things thrown together. Within the depiction lies not only meaning and ideological message, a teaching device, but also actual sacredness and efficacy. The nature of the sacredness is very hard to determine.

The use of the word *symbol* was first known to have appeared in ancient Greece, though undoubtedly a reflexive process about what we call *symbols* was afoot much earlier. Certainly, the history of the concept is considerably older than the discipline of anthropology. The word *symbol* itself derives from the Greek *sym*, meaning together, and *ballein*, meaning to throw—that is, two things thrown together. A pair of friends would mark their alliance by breaking a precious token in half, whereupon each treasured one of the halves as a mark of identification. The church took up the Greek idea of a mark or symbol and termed the creed itself a symbol. Later, the church developed a field of symbolic theology in which *symbol* began to take on its present meaning based on the mysteries inherent in a religious object—its double nature, outward and inward.

Symbolism came under the close attention of thinkers during the romantic movement in the nineteenth century, mainly in the theorizing of Johann Bachofen (1815–1887)—specifically, his notion of an original "mother right" among early humanity and his theory that the symbolism of funerary rituals was related to fertility. However, as we have seen, symbolism in the activities of the world's peoples was flourishing for ages without scholarly analysis. It is how we look back on symbolism now that appears to determine our definitions. We already see two ways of looking at symbols—as a mark or really a sign and as having power—which Jung as a scholar began to recognize in the early twentieth century in his work on the living symbol and dream archetypes. In modern religious studies, Mircea Eliade held that symbols are true parts of religion itself; he pointed out that an ordinary object could become genuinely sacred while remaining just the same as it is.

Clearly, to obtain an unbiased view of symbolism, only genuine participant study can pinpoint what is actually going on, even at such simple occasions as a folk wedding or when a hunter takes an animal.

Within the discipline of anthropology, the basic thinking on symbolism was founded on the concepts of Émile Durkheim and his school centered in France in the first decade of the twentieth century. Durkheim taught the primacy of the *social* in symbolic analysis and held that symbols were always social representations. Durkheim even attempted to bring theology down to earth by claiming that symbols were the building blocks society constructed for itself for the task of deifying itself. After Durkheim, the study of symbolism became ramified and divided, notably in the work of the folklorist Arnold van Gennep, who broke free of Durkheim's strictures by drawing attention to the liminal, in-between phase in rites of passage, that no-man's-land beyond the provenance of normal social structures and their self-deifying tendencies.

Others, notably the linguist Edward Sapir, began to reveal the complexity of a symbol as multivalent, that is, possessing many meanings and condensing them. David Schneider, a down-to-earth functionalist and authority on kinship and marriage, showed how the major (though hidden) symbol driving our conceptions of kinship and marriage was semen itself, at the core. In the 1930s and 1940s, the study of kinship became central in anthropology. (Interestingly, kinship studies have been vindicated by contemporary theorists working on the symbolism of the body.)

Then Victor Turner appeared on the scene, breaking from the sole focus on kinship and social structure and resuscitating van Gennep's work from the oblivion it had suffered while most anthropologists were following the course of structural functionalism, which taught, as Durkheim had, that symbols serve the main structures of society and follow them in style. Turner claimed a distinctly creative and different character for the symbols of rites of passage—*liminal symbols*, as he termed them; these symbols might even carry a revolutionary message, subverting social structures while sheltered in that temporarily antistructural phase of the rite of passage. Turner became the principal analyst of symbolism in anthropology, emphasizing—and here he followed Durkheim—that symbols were factors in social processes. However, he argued that these processes were not necessarily structure-bound.

In his analysis of the symbol itself, Turner exposited the important likeness between the symbolic object (the signifier) and its meaning (what is signified). Symbols were semantically "open": The meaning was not absolutely fixed. Turner saw how a symbol might become an independent force that was a product of many forces, even opposing ones. He was much influenced by the symbolic anthropologists, psychologists, and other theorists who went before him—Freud, with his polarization of the symbol into the ideological pole and the sensory pole of meaning (Turner cited the example of the Ndembu initiation symbol, the "milk tree," whose sensory pole was the bodily and emotional experience of milk and whose ideological pole, dynamized by the sensory pole, connoted the tribal virtues and the principle of matriliny), and also Jung, with his insight that a live symbol works and possesses power when pregnant with meaning but dies when it is dissected and analyzed. On the basis of this insight, Turner realized that there is no need for participants to render into words what symbols say, for symbols transmit their messages in a number of sensory codes simultaneously. Yet Turner himself analyzed. He followed Sapir in his discovery of the multivalence and condensation of meaning in dominant symbols. He noted conscious and unconscious levels in the symbols' meanings. He perforce had to alternate between regarding symbols as representations and as objects of power. He described the shrine pole of the Ndembu hunters of Zambia as not so much an object of cognition, a mere set of referents to known phenomena, but rather as "a unitary power," the slaughterous power of the hunter spirit itself. His analysis of symbolism stood, whether he took the representationist view or the power view.

Other symbologists abounded. Raymond Firth pointed out that the relation between the two elements of a symbol, the signifier and the signified, was that of concrete to abstract, particular to general. Claude Lévi-Strauss saw symbols as key items in the universal cognitive structures of the mind. Clifford Geertz's definition of a symbol, similar to Firth's, was "any object, act, event, quality, or relation which serves as a vehicle for a conception." He explained how symbols are layered in multiple networks of meanings and warned that the symbols of each culture should be studied in situ, without attempting a universalist theory. Mary Douglas was a universalist, regarding symbols as corresponding to the attitudes held by a culture toward the human body—which is very much a basic universal.

Further hints of the independent character of symbols have appeared. Roy Wagner showed how symbols become independent entities, ever obviating themselves in new forms. He became interested in the way a percept in the brain may be formed at some central location in the visual system by using stimuli that could not possibly produce that percept at an earlier, more primary location. The precept requires its own special, internal "retina" for the formation of the image. In other words, a percept with its rich meaning—a symbol, for instance—arrives in human minds as a manufactured item produced in its own peculiar way. Wagner said that this "abstracting" process is not the kind of abstraction that produces items useful in logic and the like but is part of the generative and ongoing process of complex symbol production itself. This appears to be parallel to the processes that produce poetry.

Barbara Babcock pointed out an important characteristic of symbols in festivals and celebrations that is of particular interest to folklorists: a well-marked surplus of signifiers—multitudes of symbols produced to bespeak the meaning of the celebration in an exuberantly fantastic multiplication of color, cloth, masks, costumes, and fireworks, even to the point of indeterminate nonsense. This surplus creates a self-transparent discourse that mocks and subverts the monological arrogance of "official" systems of signification. Here are hints of Victor Turner's "antistructure," which, he said, is the mark of the rite of passage; there are also reminders of Mikhail Bakhtin's praise of the vitality of the people's second life, as expressed in *Rabelais and His World*.

Another extension of symbol theory comes from Don Handelman's work on the symbolic type, again of significance in the study of folk festivals. The symbolic type may be a Hopi clown, the *wau* (a disreputably disguised uncle in Iatmul initiation in New Guinea), a lascivious old man figure in Pakistani weddings, or the hobbyhorse intruder muddling the neat figures of Morris dancing. There are many examples in folklife literature of this clumsy, contradictory figure, often suggestive of overfertility; it is a figure that will not stabilize like the respectable gods of the Hopi, for instance, or the royals in *Midsummer Night's Dream*. The fool figure classically appears within the boundaries of rites of passage or yearly rites, demonstrating uncertainty and also process itself, and thereby it is able to shift ritual occasions through their sequential phases.

Another school, that of critical anthropology and postmodernism, looks at modern symbolism under the rubric of commodity fetishism, including the symbolism of store goods, advertising, and land development, as displayed in the contemporary popular scene.

Meanwhile, in the most contemporary discussion, the Africanist Michael Jackson has held that the controversial question of whether the effect of a symbol is objective or subjective should be subsumed under the performance and experiencing of the ritual process—thus downplaying the word *symbol* as a nonissue: If one actually experiences ritual, mere representation is left behind. Is symbology really the way to study human ritual or action sequences of deepest fundamental importance? Robert Desjarlais has looked back on a generation of anthropologists who worked under the guiding assumption that culture consists of networks of symbols and webs of significance, so much so that later ethnographers even considered human bodies as texts, emotions as discourses, and healings as symbolic. He has argued that here we have drifted away from experience of the body. We must go back and consider ritual direct, from the plane of the body and not as interpreted through the mind.

In short, an anthropology of the senses is emerging that is returning to the study of bodily experience. And paradoxically, we are gaining an even richer understanding of what we have called symbolic objects. Our understanding is richer because the object (such as a sacred tree, a ritual food, or perhaps a song) may be given a deeper respect—a respect that ethnographers (and certainly the people themselves) often have actually felt, with something like Rudolf Otto's awe. We may now be able to accept that, for example, the whale meat from the self-sacrificing spirit being, the whale, is both bodily delicious and charged with the whale's spirituality—a direct process in which representation has no part. This brings symbolism out in its full dimensions; we see no cutoff point where logic steps in and says, this is only blubber.

From this summary, incomplete as it is, the depth and diversity of thought on symbols in anthropology can be inferred. Symbols are all around us. To paraphrase Vasilii Kandinsky, there is no form, there is nothing in the world, that says nothing.

Edith Turner

See also Anthropological Approach; Freudian Psychology; Jungian Psychology; Phenomenology; Semiotics.

✳✳✳✳✳✳✳✳✳✳✳✳✳✳✳✳✳✳

References

Babcock, Barbara. 1978. Too Many, Too Few: Ritual Modes of Signification. *Semiotica* 23:291–302.

Desjarlais, Robert. 1992. *Body and Emotion: The Aesthetics of Illness and Healing in the Nepal Himalayas*. Philadelphia: University of Pennsylvania Press.

Douglas, Mary. 1966. *Purity and Danger*. London: Routledge and Kegan Paul.

Durkheim, Émile. [1911] 1954. *The Elementary Forms of the Religious Life*. London: Allen and Unwin.

Firth, Raymond. 1973. *Symbols: Public and Private*. Ithaca, NY: Cornell University Press.

Geertz, Clifford. 1973. *The Interpretation of Culture*. New York: Basic Books.

Handelman, Don. 1990. *Models and Mirrors: Towards an Anthropology of Public Events*. Cambridge: Cambridge University Press.

Lévi-Strauss, Claude. 1963. *Structural Anthropology*. New York: Basic Books.

Turner, Victor. 1967. *The Forest of Symbols: Aspects of Ndembu Ritual*. Ithaca, NY: Cornell University Press.

Turner, Victor, ed. 1982. *Celebration: Studies in Festivity and Ritual*. Washington, DC: Smithsonian Institution Press.

Wagner, Roy. 1986. *Symbols That Stand for Themselves*. Chicago: University of Chicago Press.

APPLIED FOLKLORE/FOLKLORISTICS

Using folklore or folklorists' methods, investigative techniques, and skills as a personal resource or to affect policy, develop technology, or alter social, cultural, and economic conditions. Applied folklore is often contrasted with academic research and teaching folklore courses per se (although these might include a degree of advocacy and intervention). Typical venues are museums, the entertainment industry, arts agencies and parks and recreation departments that document and present folk traditions, the health and social welfare professions, cultural resources management programs, community redevelopment agencies, human resources development departments and management consulting firms, and education programs.

Early folklorists did not hold full-time appointments teaching and researching folklore owing, in part, to the absence of chairs of folklore studies and degree-granting programs. They documented, interpreted, and presented folklore avocationally or as a resource in their professions. Wilhelm and Jacob Grimm, the compilers of celebrated collections of household tales, practiced law; the latter also published a study of ancient Teutonic legal customs. Employed by his government as a circuit physician, Elias Lönnrot (whose dissertation concerned magical medicine of the Finns) traveled to remote areas where he met "seers" ("wise men" and "wise women") as well as masters of narrative poetry from whom he collected beliefs and songs that he recast into the *Kalevala*, which became the Finnish national epic. Poets Sir Walter Scott and John Greenleaf Whittier and writers Joel Chandler Harris and Zora Neale Hurston, among others, collected and interpreted folklore and drew upon it for their literary creations. Hungarian composer Béla Bartók based many scores on folk music. The American regionalist Thomas Hart Benton included folksong themes, fiddling, and other Ozark folklife in his murals and lithographs.

Folklore has long been manipulated for political purposes. In 1630, the king of Sweden decreed that ancient traditions be documented; as records of the way of life in ancient times, they would demonstrate to older European countries that Sweden, too, had a long history. The Antiquities Council, founded in Stockholm in 1666, implored the local clergy to gather old narrative songs because they contained "much truth about the heroic deeds of the forefathers." Nineteenth-century nationalism motivated some of the folklore collecting in Germany, Finland, Ireland, and other countries suffering from outside cultural or political domination. In the twentieth century, Nazi Germany exploited the Aryan myth, Soviet Russia promoted folklore for its propaganda value, and Communist China attempted to indoctrinate children through folksongs, dance, and puppetry. On the other side of the coin, labor and civil rights activists and social reformers have used folklore to educate, agitate, and rally people to a cause.

Folklore was also used to help immigrants adjust to their new social environments. Jane Addams established Hull House in Chicago in 1889 as a place where people could gather to celebrate familiar holidays, dress in traditional costume, sing the old songs, and reminisce. In 1900, she created a labor museum with tools and products, photographs, and demonstrations. By showing similarities in crafts and work, the museum linked various nationalities, revealed a continuity in experiences from the native country to the new, and bridged the gap between immigrants and their children. Phyllis H. Williams, who interviewed and observed more than 500 Italian immigrants over 11 years' time, published a volume in 1938 on southern Italian folkways in Europe and the United States. A handbook for social workers, medical personnel, and teachers, the work surveyed both Old World and New World traditions and advised the reader on how to ease the adjustment of families and individuals. In the 1940s, Rachel Davis DuBois, a social worker, utilized folklore in schools to increase understanding among people of different ethnic backgrounds. Dorothy Mills Howard created child development programs through which children became aware of the folklore process and how it operated in their lives and communities.

Public agencies in the United States have played a role in applied folklore, from the Bureau of American Ethnology (founded in 1879) to the Archive of Folksong (established in 1928 and renamed the Archive of Folk Culture in 1981) and the Works Progress Administration's Federal Project Number One, which operated between August 2, 1935, and August 31, 1939. The latter included folklore documentation, festivals, or publications by the art, music, theater, and writers' projects in addition to the Historical Records Survey. During World War II, the National Research Council created the Committee on Food Habits, dedicated to the belief that studies of ethnic and regional customs revolving around food were crucial to solving nutritional problems.

More recently, three federal organizations have been active in folklore applications in the United States. The Office of Folklife Programs at the Smithsonian Institution sponsors research, exhibits, films, and publications as well as a Festival of American Folklife (established in 1967), defending this annual event for its advocacy on behalf of cultural equity. The National Endowment for the Arts' Folk Arts Program (founded in 1974) funds local traditional festivals, workshops, demonstration programs in schools, and other activities that present folk art and artists, in part to help perpetuate traditional art forms, skills, and knowledge. This organization also provides the first years of funding for folk arts coordinator positions in arts councils; by the late 1980s, 50 of the 56 states and territories and several cities had hired people to document and present traditional arts, performers, and craftspeople. In 1976, the American Folklife Preservation Act established the American Folklife Center as the country's first national agency devoted to the study, preservation, and presentation of folk culture. Located in the Library of Congress, the center provides technical assistance, carries out model documentary projects, and organizes public forums in the name of cultural conservation.

The folksong and folk dance revivals of the 1950s and 1960s brought many to the halls of academe seeking information, resources, and training. Some became scholars; others continued to pursue careers in the arts as singers, musicians, puppeteers, dancers, choreographers, directors of folk dance troupes, radio programmers, creative writers, journalists, editors, filmmakers, and consultants to the entertainment industry (advising on costume, dialect, sets, and scripts). Folklore studies complement and supplement arts training by providing (1) knowledge about varied forms and examples of folklore through time and space, (2) familiarity with bibliographical tools and archive resources, and (3) an understanding of the historical, social, cultural, and biographical contexts in which folklore is generated and perpetuated. Arts practitioners enrich their repertoires, tend to be more concerned with authenticity, and usually add an interpretive, educational dimension to entertainment.

Many folklorists find employment in public agencies such as state arts councils, city cultural affairs divisions, and parks and recreation departments (sometimes referring to their specific field as "public folklore" or "public sector folklife programming"). They locate and document the behaviors of individuals who are the active tradition-bearers. Through films, tape recordings, festivals, exhibits, publications, and interpretive programs, they honor local artists and performers, educate the public about the community's history and culture(s), and foster intergroup communication and cooperation. Apprenticeship programs and venues for showcasing artists help perpetuate the traditions. Attention to folklore in these agencies democratizes support of the arts and enlarges the public served.

The same is true for museums of art, history, and science and industry in which folklorists have found employment as curators and directors. Those trained in folklore studies know their way around archives and historical collections, can establish the traditionality and cultural representativeness of objects, and are able to discern and communicate the meanings, symbolic significance, and functions of the things that people make. With their interviewing and observation skills, folklorists can elicit information from resource persons while locating and presenting craft demonstrators for educational programs. Oriented to the documentation and study of traditional, expressive behavior in everyday life, folklorists are well suited to working in living-history museums and community cultural centers, and they can help prevent or overcome elitist tendencies in other museums. Their efforts and emphases assist established residents in valuing their heritage, newcomers in understanding what daily life was like for early settlers, and tourists in comprehending the social and cultural forces shaping the region.

Increasingly, teachers, curriculum planners, and educational consultants are seeking training in folkloristics and utilizing folklore materials and folkloristic methods. Effectiveness in the multicultural classroom requires that a teacher communicate with those whose heritages differ from one another's and from the teacher's own; the teacher must also discover what the various traditions are and uncover fundamental similarities. Learning to do folklore fieldwork develops these skills. Student fieldwork projects promote experiential learning, nurture the enjoyment of discovery, and can help reduce intergroup stereotyping and dissonance as individuals learn about each other. The sharing of folklore in the classroom establishes common ground between the student and teacher, among the students, and between generations when class assignments involve the student in conversations with younger siblings or with parents and grandparents.

Incorporating comparative folklore into the curriculum internationalizes students' studies. Folklore provides a sense of immediacy, capturing students' attention and interest as it confers a sense of identification with the subject. In language arts, exposure to folk poetry and narratives (or analysis of the students' own verbal art) can help students learn about meter, rhyme, structure, motivation and character, and symbolism; the classics then become less formidable. Having students in composition classes write about their own folklore, community traditions, or the lore of colleagues provides interesting subject matter and turns the writing exercise into a meaningful and rewarding experience. In history and social studies, students who document family traditions or record narratives, songs, and descriptions of customs from community members gain insights into historical events and processes that impersonal textbooks cannot convey. Investigating modern legends, beliefs, and rituals can help the student understand more fully the impact of social and technological change.

Folklorists in the helping professions, such as medicine and social work, supplement and complement the knowledge and skills of coworkers because their training prepares them to document and interpret relevant traditions historically, culturally, and behaviorally. Folklorists seek to understand the overlooked knowledge, especially by learning the traditional idioms and modes of thought from which it arises, posing questions aimed at understanding the patient's point of view and describing it sympathetically. They advise medical personnel about health beliefs and healing practices that are traditional either cross-culturally or within a given group, suggesting ways to integrate folk medicine with scientific medicine and to translate concepts from one system of care to another. Practitioners in health and social work who study folklore increase their ability to understand patient or client behavior and enhance their delivery of services.

Folklorists in human resources management and organization development provide understanding and assistance in meeting the needs of the multicultural workplace. They also document and analyze the meanings and significance of stories, rituals, metaphoric language, and customs in an organization, including such functions as enculturating members, expressing values and assumptions, serving as coping mechanisms, or fostering community and cooperation. Through the use of fieldwork techniques, knowledge of folklore forms, and an understanding of what traditional symbolic behavior expresses and does, those trained in folkloristics are better able to uncover the sources of interpersonal tensions, to help improve communication and leadership, and to contribute to strategic planning by ascertaining and assessing the organization's culture.

Environmental planning, rural and economic development, and tourism benefit from folklorists' involvement by utilizing their knowledge of ethnic and regional subcultures, their abilities to document and interpret traditions, and their inclination to work with local communities to help them define and achieve their own goals. The cultural resources management aspect of environmental planning involves inventorying cultural resources, determining their significance, mitigating the effects of intervention, and presenting and interpreting community traditions to others. Social impact assessments entail investigating how a proposed development (such as an industrial park, a shopping center, or a recreational facility) will affect communities, including the impact on the communities' traditions, quality of life, and collective ethos. Folklorists understand the basis of community identity in common traditions; they also are among the most adept at discovering attitudes, values, and tastes, using folklore as a diagnostic tool and information source. Their knowledge of craft traditions, vernacular architecture, and local customs is crucial to rural development and tourism; they can clarify what aspects of culture need to be preserved or developed, and they are able to assess how alternative economic interventions will strengthen or weaken and enhance or disrupt the local culture and community.

Folklorists also use their knowledge and skills to develop programs for and with senior citizens, in art therapy and urban planning, and as archivists, librarians, photographers, marketers, public relations specialists, and program officers on humanities councils, to name a few fields. Some are involved in technological developments. By the late 1960s, specialists in artificial intelligence were experimenting with computer programs that mimic human storytellers, using folklorists' research on narrating, dialect use, and the structure of folktales and myths. Concerned about the demise of the apprenticeship system in modern industry and seeking to develop computerized expert systems for use in training, some firms have employed folklorists to interview older designers and craftspeople to document their procedures and understand their processes of conceptualization.

Various conceptual, logistic, ethical, and political issues surround applied folkloristics. Issues of authenticity and context confront museum curators, festival organizers, and teachers who present folk artists or experts. Interpreters or re-creators of folklore are practiced performers but not necessarily representative of the cultural heritage. Demonstrating to the public may discomfort local artists and craftspersons, and it removes the art or craft from its natural context in family and community. Spotlighting esoteric traditions and highlighting differences may reinforce stereotypes. For some, "cultural conservation" suggests artificially sealing off some elements of culture from further development—in effect, embalming them. There is also concern about the deliberate staging of cultural pluralism by organizers of festivals serving as cultural brokers who select, manipulate, or sometimes alter the cultural symbols and strategies of a group through their decisions about which segments or members of the community to invite as participants and what traditions to include or exclude. Because public sector folklife programs have such broad or vague goals as furthering public awareness, appreciation, and support of traditional culture, it has proved difficult to develop adequate measures of their success. The fact that so much programming in the folk arts depends on a few governmental agencies (and the decisions of their directors) raises concerns over the exercise of power and control. Folklorists in the private sector must guard against misapplication or abuse of their findings. Efforts at cultural resources management or economic development may disrupt some segments of a community while benefiting others. Folklorists have resolved some of these issues through the use of a partnership approach or participatory action research in which the impetus for programs or inquiry originates with the community or organization, representatives of all interests are included, and collaboration occurs to understand the problems and to plan and take action.

To conclude, applied folklore has evolved from a simple and sometimes simplistic use of folklore forms and examples per se to the discipline of applied folkloristics with a body of theory, methods, and techniques that establishes research problems and hypotheses along with a code of ethics. From the inception of their field two centuries ago, folklorists have focused on populations often ignored by others (children, the elderly, various ethnic groups), providing a forum through publications, exhibits, festivals, and films for underrepresented groups or individuals and their traditions. Some folklorists have become activists on behalf of particular groups (such as Alice Fletcher, the first woman president of the American Folklore Society [1905], who studied the lore of the Winnebago and Omaha and lobbied for the passage of federal legislation giving Native Americans greater control over their lands). Whether they work in academe or applied fields, folklorists are trained to identify, document, analyze, and present forms and examples of traditional symbolic expression in which ordinary people engage in their everyday interactions. They appreciate these traditions and respect the bearers of them. They understand and can interpret the historical, social, cultural, and biographical circumstances of traditional behavior. With such skills, knowledge, and abilities informed by values and philosophy, folklorists are particularly suited to both pursuing theoretical research that increases understanding of the species and participating in applications that improve the quality of life and benefit the welfare of individual members.

Michael Owen Jones

See also Occupational Folklife/Folklore; Organizational Folklore; Public Sector Folklore.

✳✳✳✳✳✳✳✳✳✳✳✳✳✳✳✳✳✳

References

Baron, Robert, and Nicholas R. Spitzer, eds. 1992. *Public Folklore.* Washington, DC: Smithsonian Institution Press.

Bauman, Richard, Patricia Sawin, and Inta Gale Carpenter. 1992. *Reflections on the Folklife Festival: An Ethnography of Participant Experience.* Indiana University Special Publications of the Folklore Institute, no. 2. Bloomington.

Camp, Charles, ed. 1989. *Time and Temperature: A Centennial Publication of the American Folklore Society.* Washington, DC: American Folklore Society.

Dorson, Richard M., ed. 1961. *Folklore Research around the World: A North American Point of View.* Indiana University Folklore Series, no. 16. Bloomington, IN (also published as a special issue of *Journal of American Culture,* vol. 74, no. 294).

Feintuch, Burt, ed. 1988. *The Conservation of Culture: Folklorists & the Public Sector.* Lexington: University Press of Kentucky.

Jackson, Bruce, ed. 1989. *Teaching Folklore.* Rev. ed. Buffalo, NY: Documentary Research.

Jones, Michael Owen, ed. 1993. *Putting Folklore to Use: Essays on Applied Folkloristics.* Lexington: University Press of Kentucky.

Loomis, Osmond, coordinator. 1983. *Cultural Conservation: The Protection of Cultural Heritage in the United States.* Washington, DC: Library of Congress.

Sweterlitsch, Dick, ed. 1971. *Papers on Applied Folklore.* Folklore Forum Bibliographic and Special Series, no. 8. Bloomington, IN.

Wilson, William A. 1976. *Folklore and Nationalism in Modern Finland.* Bloomington: Indiana University Press.

ARCHETYPE

Word derived from the Greek *archētypon,* signifying the first stamp, pattern, or model. As a term, *archetype* is instrumental in two major theoretical approaches to the study of culture: (1) the Finnish School employing the historic-geographic method toward reconstructing the original form of an international tale type (or other relatively intricate items of lore that exist in a variety of forms), and (2) Jungian analytical psychology. In the works of the Finnish

A woodcut by Albrecht Duerer depicting the battle between St.George and the Dragon. This battle is a Christian account of the archetypal struggle of the hero slaying the monster, which signifies the conflict between life and death, right and wrong.

School, *archetype* denotes the reconstructed first form argued hypothetically to be the original form of the item under scrutiny. The term *archetype* is also closely linked to the psychological postulates advanced by C. G. Jung. Jung proposed that a number of primordial images common to all individuals of a given nation or historical epoch and—to some extent—to any human being exist in the collective unconscious of the social group (race). These images are externalized (expressed) in the form of streams of intuitive notions, bits of common knowledge, or apprehensions recurrent to mankind. In this respect, the archetype is analogous to Adolf Bastian's concept of the elementary idea (*Elementargedanke*), which holds that certain thoughts may be generated independently by different peoples at various time periods due to the psychic unity of mankind. Jung labeled this phenomenon *transcendental imagination*.

By their nature, according to this reasoning, archetypes are preexisting determinants of mental/psychological experiences that render an individual disposed to behave in a manner similar to that manifested by his or her racial ancestors. Typically, archetypes are primordial potentials for generating thoughts, images, and emotions (to be differentiated from learned feeling, or sentiments). Archetypes exist only in the collective unconscious of the individual; they impose themselves on a person when the conscious mind is inactive and is generating no images, as during sleep, or when the consciousness is caught off guard, as in telling impersonal tales. They tend to personify natural processes and to present them in concrete terms—god and devil, life and death, male and female, for example—a characteristic of mythological imagery. Less pivotal belief-characters (such as spirits, fairies, ogres, and dragons), as well as abstractions (such as good and evil) and individuals in the social group (or mother and father), also serve as prominent archetypes. In daily living, archetypes are experienced as emotions and mental images associated with such significant events in the life of a human as birth or death or with a stage in life (adolescence or becoming a man or woman, for example).

Of the many archetypes Jung designated, four seemed to him to be more recurrent, laden with emotional significance, and traceable directly to ancient myths of origins. Consequently, Jung considered them separate personality systems. These four are: the *persona*, the *anima*, the *animus*, and the *shadow*. The persona (or outermost aspect of personality) conceals the true self; it is the mask that an individual wears publicly and is comparable to the concept of role-playing. The anima is the feminine characteristics in the male. The animus is the masculine characteristics in the female. The shadow (or darker self) is the inferior, animal-like part of the personality; it is something primitive in our human nature. Yet, the most important archetype in Jung's system is the *self*; it comprises all aspects of the unconscious and is an integrative force that provides stability and unity to the structure of personality.

Thus, a cultural account of a hero slaying a monster (dragon) that had impounded water (Motif A1111, "Impounded water"; AT 300, "The Dragon Slayer") would signify conflict between life and death, right and wrong, and so forth; meanwhile, a wager between truth and falsehood (Motif N61, "Wager that falsehood is better than truth"; AT 613, "The Two Travelers [Truth and Falsehood]") would be symbolic of conflict between god and devil, good and evil. Similarly, an elaborate folktale in which a youth sets out to learn fear (Motif H1376.2, "Quest: learning what fear is"; AT 326, "The Youth Who Wanted To Learn What Fear Is") and encounters many socially significant individuals and groups, of whom only one succeeds finally in teaching him fear, would be indicative of the struggle between individual and society; it is the struggle of a youngster with no independent social identity seeking to wrest his place in society (represented by parental authority) by going through the process (archetype) of individuation.

Hasan El-Shamy

See also Historic-Geographic Method; Jungian Psychology; Monogenesis/Polygenesis; Psychological Approach.

✳✳✳✳✳✳✳✳✳✳✳✳✳✳✳✳✳✳

References

Campbell, Joseph. 1949. *The Hero with a Thousand Faces*. New York: Pantheon.

Jung, C. G. 1916. *Psychology of the Unconscious*. Leipzig, Germany: Franz Deuticke.

Jung, C. G., and C. Kerényi. 1969. *Essays on a Science of Mythology*. Princeton, NJ: Princeton University Press.

Koepping, Klaus-Peter. 1983. *Adolph Bastian and the Psychic Unity of Mankind*. New York: University of Queensland Press.

Stephens, Anthony. 1983. *Archetypes: A Natural History of the Self*. New York: Quill.

Van Eenwyk, J. R. 1991. Archetypes: The Strange Attractors of the Psyche. *Journal of Analytical Psychology*. 36:1–25.

von Franz, Marie-Louise. 1975. C. G. *Jung: His Myth in Our Time*. Trans. William H. Kennedy. New York: Putnam's.

ARCHITECTURE, FOLK

Regional traditions in building. In the study of cultural traditions past and present, folk architecture has found its niche among academic fields that document, conserve, and interpret cultural heritage. Folk architecture, also known as traditional or vernacular architecture, values concepts based on enduring patterns that often express regional or ethnic personality. Tradition is the chosen utilization of older, agreed-upon, and sometimes transplanted ideas in a new thing. Though tradition is manifest in every sort of experience, it is the conservative, community-based tradition accrued over time and trial that provides the rootstock for the ordinary structures and landscapes that constitute folk architecture. Researchers interested in traditional building study all kinds of domestic, agricultural, industrial, and sacred structures. Like other expressions of cultural heritage, folk architecture has patterns and decorations that have evolved over generations of execution and variation.

When people build, they intend to build structures that look good, whether they are constructing a new house, a church, or a garden shed. "Style" makes the surfaces of buildings look good in the context of the expectations of the community.

Vernacular architecture operates in a system related to high-style design but separate from many of its pressures and goals. Traditional architecture continually changes, even if subtly and slowly, and one can chart the nuances of social and cultural history in the varieties of buildings and their revealing individualized details.

However, though change for the high-style designer means trying to forge beyond boundaries of popular taste, change in folk design occurs within the flexible boundaries of custom. An 1880s traditional farmhouse in Maine, Iowa, or California may sport a stylish Gothic dormer window above the front door to express the owner's participation in the popular culture of the day.

Folk buildings are not anonymous; their builders simply have not been identified. All buildings reflect the individual designer, builder, or owner's personality. To be conservative is not necessarily to be old-fashioned or resistant to fashions moving through the community. There are countless examples of conservative traditional builders who adapt to new technology and ideas if they fit with the customary view of what architecture should be like.

For example, the owners of a late-nineteenth-century farm on the moors of central Scotland built a stone house, byre (stable), and barn in a

A

Figure 1. The basic building block in British-American house types was a one-room, "single-cell" or "single-pen" house. Most single-cell log cabins were well made and represented temporary economics, not temporary architecture; almost all log cabins were covered with horizontal weatherboarding (as in this example) to protect the log walls, provide added insulation, and present the look of a fashionable white frame building. (A) The John Wells house, a single-pen horizontal log house in Callaway Country, Missouri, circa 1840. (B) The Wells house plan; additions to the rear of a log house were typically frame construction, as indicated here.

B

0   5   10

FEET

40

A

Figure 2. The Georgian cottage house type, with its broad central hall, meant high status in early-nineteenth-century Missouri, but it proved less popular than the I house type and faded by the time of the Civil War. (A) Kentucky emigrant and tobacco planter Thomas Hickman's 1818 brick house, Howard County, Missouri. (B) Hickman house plan.

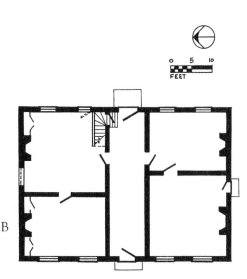

B

traditional manner but asked the masons to install a carved finial or knob upon the front peak of the barn's gable roof. Such finials, like the finials on chairs and presses, reflect to the eighteenth century's deep shift to bring Georgian style and order to the small steading. The owners thereby acknowledged fashion while doing business as usual as thrifty farmers.

In the context of traditional architecture, style pertains to visual elements of decoration and ornament. Styles change in the context of popular design and taste, influenced by a small number of designers whose ideas are disseminated in the mass media. Houses may be based on folk ideas of suitability and at the same time be designs selected from catalogs, magazines, displays of prefabricated houses, or model houses in new suburbs. The range of domestic shelters the student of vernacular architecture studies runs from the archaeological remains of one-room, half-timbered houses in colonial America to the connected adobe rooms of a Native American pueblo in Arizona to a grand Gothic mansion of white wood along a big city boulevard to the small shotgun house of the sharecropper to the mobile home and tract house.

Makers of traditional buildings are craftsperson-builders or artisans who—like the carpenter who made roof trusses in Ste. Genevieve, Missouri, resembling those of medieval France—are bearers of the knowledge of how to build a new thing on the footings of folk tradition. Folk builders reuse parts of old structures or entire structures as they expand and tinker with their landscapes and take advantage of local climate and terrain. Construction may depend upon locally available materials, but even builders in remote areas import construction materials when desired or needed.

Traditional builders acquire most of their skills through apprenticeship,

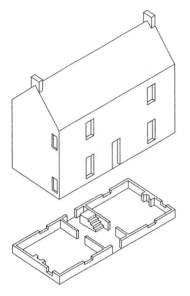

Figure 3. One of the quintessential folk house types in the United States has parallels and antecedents in the British Isles: the so-called I house (generalized sketch and plan, Missouri).

practice, and emulation of respected models and artisans, rather than through classes at schools of design. Instead of being called an architect, the maker of a commonplace traditional building was and continues to be called a builder or contractor, craftsperson, bricklayer, carpenter, and so on. Special cases result in special names; the group of skilled stonemasons from northern Italy who settled and built in Paradise Valley, Nevada, were called "cement men" and "pic-à-pierre."

One feature of folk design that differentiates it from high-style design is the degree to which the client and members of the community participate in the design process. Forms are often familiar. Neighbors understand what is being built and why. The contractor knows similar buildings; work is attuned to the needs of the client. People apply decorative details and variations to give the building special character.

For studies of diffusion and cultural connections, typologies continue to be useful. Typology—classification—is important because, on many levels, form and surface structure are important. Form is reasonably stable through time and different regions and gives the researcher discernible patterns with which to trace routes of diffusion and variation. Floor plan (horizontal layout) is important because form is relatively stable over time and scholars can use form to study cultural diffusion.

Looking for background patterns and comparative examples is only one of numerous approaches to the study of buildings as culture. We can learn about comparable buildings in other regions, communities, or countries; folk buildings vary regionally and culturally more than they vary chronologically through time.

In looking at building types, several elements can be documented and analyzed. In 1968, Henry Glassie implemented a three-part approach to typology, in which the elements form, construction, and use were employed to classify and identify different types of houses and agricultural structures with European parentage. In 1981, Howard Marshall, a student of Glassie's, added a fourth element, decoration (stylistic detailing), when analyzing folk buildings in the Little Dixie region of British Missouri. Other scholars concentrate on different elements, such as function or the decoration that overlays a structure. Although Glassie, a theoretical and methodological innovator, has also written about new and different areas of material culture research, his early books continue to be the basis for many studies.

The hunt for origins and paths of diffusion, the classic approach in examining folk architecture, usually leads to more questions. Some building types can be seen as successfully established; other types of structures simply do not take root in a new environment. We have yet to understand completely why certain features of folk culture do not get carried to new places. For example, one of the oldest settings for people and their possessions, produce, and animals is a building type that comes in two basic forms in the British Isles and Europe—the longhouse and the housebarn. The longhouse has been built for hundreds of years in the British Isles, alongside separate house and byre farm steadings that developed in late medieval times. In this long, one-story building that is one room deep, the spaces for the family, the dairy, the storehouse, and the beasts are lined up to form a row of rooms with special purposes. The longhouse or housebarn tradition is deeply ingrained in the shared cultural heritage of western Europe, Scandinavia, and the British Isles. However, though a number of distinctive European and British folk-building elements were carried to the Americas—seen most clearly and immediately in the prevalence of the "I house" type across British America—the longhouse or its continental cousin, the housebarn, was rarely situated in North America. Finding vast tracts of new land and forest, immigrants were quick to assert control, order, and ownership. One way of asserting control was to break apart and scatter the old European longhouse and housebarn over space into a series of buildings. Perhaps the saga of the longhouse—its interruption or rejection—helps illustrate the point that ethnic groups, even in substantial numbers, do not necessarily reestablish old and familiar patterns. People may adopt and adapt other forms of architecture when the new forms have a good fit with the character of the group's sense of place and architectural preferences. One of the challenges of the folk architecture researcher is to try to disentangle the various vines of architecture and view architecture's parts both as reflections of old folk ideas and as continually evolving new ideas as well.

One may investigate roles played by the Industrial Revolution and the factory system as factors in the processes of folk architecture. Shifts in

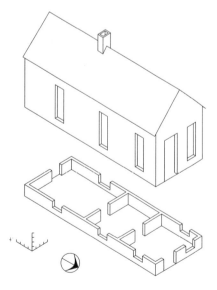

Figure 4. Shotgun house (generalized sketch and plan, Missouri).

Figure 5. The T-shaped house became popular in the late nineteenth century; it retained the interior spaces of traditional houses but presented to the public a facade decorated with the "carpenter Gothic" ornament of the day (birthplace of World War I Allied forces Gen. John J. Pershing, Laclede, Linn County, Missouri).

technology brought changes in traditional building. The influence of pattern books and carpenter's manuals in the nineteenth century is interesting in terms of the accommodations builders made and make still to new tools and techniques that become widespread nationally. Mail-order house plans for a "vernacular cottage" from a Sunday newspaper today provide a self-selected style that means much in terms of private values. Mobile homes (manufactured housing) sell fast in growing communities not only because they are relatively inexpensive and efficient but also because their interior spaces and their layer of "style" makes them livable to people. Prefabricated housing is a very old tradition in the United States; the dynamics of a production model speak to folk ideas, or the company loses business.

American folklorists who study folk buildings tend to study those of the colonial period through the mid-twentieth century. Most leave precontact Native American architecture to experts in archaeology and today's built environment to scholars in American studies or anthropology. Yet the entire range of traditional buildings needs attention, and the increasingly complicated matter of ethnicity in folk architecture is gaining importance in this as in every area of cultural study. Part of the success of folk architecture studies is due to the tendency of researchers to study built environments of ethnic groups, socially marginal communities, and remote places where little or no field documentation has been accomplished.

Sorting out the ethnic elements in a building or neighborhood can be a complex undertaking. All may not be what it seems. Some patterns in folk houses are embedded in time and are difficult to interpret. John Vlach has shown that the shotgun house, the narrow dwelling of African-Americans in certain regions, likely resulted from the wedding of West African social space to Caribbean dwelling forms, transmitted to the American South in the processes of evolution in the colonial and early national periods. The shotgun house type was carried in people's minds and employed in many places when African-Americans built their own houses, spreading outward and upward from the New Orleans, Louisiana, area, along riverways in the nineteenth century. In regard to rural Chinese communities in northern California, architectural historian Christopher Yip has shown us the complexity and rich symbolism in the construction and ornamentation of the interiors of frame buildings that were relatively simple in outward appearance. Sacred places (joss houses) in these communities carried minimal exterior ornamentation. A people suppressed by society and economy, whatever form the subjugation or manipulation may take, tend to express identity or ethnicity in private spaces—the inside of the dwelling, the garden plot behind, the altar, or the fireplace mantle.

Studying architecture gives entry into broader areas of behavior, so the land itself becomes our artifact. People live in environments and not merely in buildings. Landscape study is part of the folklorist's work as constellations of buildings in a community, valley, or region are seen in the frame of habitat and climate. Environment influences how folk buildings are thought of and built. In 1900, a Lowland Scottish coal-mining family arriving by train at a prairie village in north Missouri would have found no suitable stone for the "cottage" they know and want, so the Midwest's great hardwood forests would serve for the Scots, as for all, in the construction of a dwelling that in form and use might well have been identical to those in the home village.

One of the tools brought to the study of old buildings by scholars such as Warren Roberts, Henry Glassie, and John Vlach is intensive field research. Discovering and measuring ordinary, scruffy, and often derelict buildings up close is at the heart of our work. Photographing a barn from the road provides visual and structural information; spending the afternoon crawling through the dusty, smelly barn balancing tape measure, cameras, flashlight, and clipboard adds a level of intimacy that is helpful in a holistic reading of the structure in its distinctive place and time. So field research and its products—the measured architectural drawing, fieldnotes, and detailed photographic coverage—are integral components in the study of vernacular architecture.

Field study is fundamental because folk buildings have not been accorded the historical documentation that high-style buildings have received. Combined with the recording of the physical scene, including elements of the material culture of a farmstead or household and the landscape itself, we include oral interviews and discussions with knowledgeable citizens. To these field techniques can be added research in public records to establish property histories as well as research in historical photograph collections, ordnance survey maps, manuscript archives, museums, and a variety of libraries and repositories.

There always will be debates over terms when describing culture. Many folklorists divide culture into categories reflecting the degree of tradition found among cultural items in the categories. For example, some use a three-fold division of folk, popular, and elite, as positioned in the literature by Henry Glassie in his pathbreaking *Pattern in the Material Folk Culture of the Eastern United States* (1968). R. W. Brunskill posed two categories, vernacular and "polite." We try to avoid culturally biased terms such as *primitive, naive, untrained*, and *country*. Actually, buildings, each exhibiting different shares of traditionality or progressivist design (style), can be located somewhere along a horizontal scale from conservative through commonplace to futuristic. Viewed this way, folk buildings are at the more conservative, community-oriented, and indeed restrictive end of the scale.

Folk architecture specialists frequently are involved with historical preservation groups and agencies in their local districts. More and more, preservation agencies will deal with traditional buildings and cultural landscapes, and the folklorist's theories and practical approaches to the study of artifacts in context will be helpful in the coming years.

Traditional buildings comprise the bulk of the built environment globally and thus are significant within a broad context. Traditional buildings provide clues to understanding historical patterns and intersections between methods of design, form, construction, and function as people alter buildings to meet trends and changing economies while still finding ways to accommodate them to personal and aesthetic ideals. Folk architecture's ideas and preferences are versatile. They endure and change, and they can be studied through field research and observation. From Thomas Jefferson's Monticello to Abraham Lincoln's log cabin to Elvis Presley's Graceland, architecture is a crucial element in our lives. All of us shape our personal spaces to one degree or another according to deeply held traditions in our family or community or both. When we have choices, we select forms and styles in a dwelling that reflect a number of forces in us as people, whether these forces are obvious and objective—to impress our neighbors, mark success, or meet a limited budget—or obscure and subjective—for psychological comfort and safety, order, balance, predictability, or tradition.

Howard Wight Marshall

See also Material Culture.

✳✳✳✳✳✳✳✳✳✳✳✳✳✳✳✳✳

References

Brunskill, Ronald W. 1970. *Illustrated Handbook of Vernacular Architecture*. New York: Universe Books.

Bunting, Bainbridge. 1976. *The Early Architecture of New Mexico*. Albuquerque: University of New Mexico Press.

Carter, Thomas R., and Bernard L. Herman, eds. 1989. *Perspectives in Vernacular Architecture*, vol. 3. Columbia: University of Missouri Press.

———. 1991. *Perspectives in Vernacular Architecture*, vol. 4. Columbia: University of Missouri Press.

Cummings, Abbott Lowell. 1979. *The Framed Houses of Massachusetts Bay, 1625–1725*. Cambridge, MA: Belknap.

Fenton, Alexander, and Bruce Walker. 1981. *The Rural Architecture of Scotland*. Edinburgh: John Donald.

Gailey, Alan. 1984. *Rural Houses of the North of Ireland*. Edinburgh: John Donald.

Glassie, Henry. 1975. *Folk Housing in Middle Virginia: A Structural Analysis of Historic Artifacts*. Knoxville: University of Tennessee Press.

———. 1977. *Pattern in the Material Culture of the Eastern United States*. Philadelphia: University of Pennsylvania Press.

Hubka, Thomas. 1984. *Big House, Little House, Back House, Barn: The Connected Farm Buildings of New England*. Hanover, NH: University Press of New England.

Marshall, Howard Wight. 1981. *American Folk Architecture: A Selected Bibliography*. Washington, DC: Library of Congress, Publications of the American Folklife Center, no. 8.

———. 1981. *Folk Architecture in Little Dixie: A Regional Culture in Missouri*. Columbia: University of Missouri Press.

———. 1995. *Paradise Valley, Nevada: The People and Buildings of an American Place*. Tucson: University of Arizona Press.

Mercer, Eric. 1975. *English Vernacular Houses: A Study of Traditional Farmhouses and Cottages*. London: Her Majesty's Stationery Office.

Pocius, Gerald L. 1991. A Place to Belong: *Community Order and Everyday Space in Calvert, Newfoundland*. Athens: University of Georgia Press.

Roberts, Warren E. 1988. *Viewpoints on Folklife: Looking at the Overlooked*. Ann Arbor, MI: UMI Research Press.

Smith, Peter. 1975. *Houses of the Welsh Countryside*. London: Her Majesty's Stationery Office.

Upton, Dell, and John Michael Vlach, eds. 1986. *Common Places: Readings in American Vernacular Architecture*. Athens: University of Georgia Press.

Vlach, John Michael. 1993. *Back of the Back House: The Architecture of Plantation Slavery*. Chapel Hill: University of North Carolina Press.

Wells, Camille, ed. 1986. *Perspectives in Vernacular Architecture*, vol. 2. Columbia: University of Missouri Press.

Wiliam, Eurwyn. 1986. *The Historical Farm Buildings of Wales*. Edinburgh: John Donald.

ARCHIVES AND ARCHIVING

Repositories of material in formats ranging from transcribed fieldnotes through photographs and films documenting folklore, folklife, and related areas and the techniques used for the collection, preservation, and cataloging of such materials.

Unpublished material relating to folklore and folklife studies may be found in ethnomusicology, anthropology, oral history, local history, sociolinguistic, and cultural archives as well as in archives dedicated to the preservation of folklore and folklife documentation. There are over 200 such ethnographic archives in the United States and Canada alone. Some archives are specific to particular topics or genres, such as folksong or cowboy lore. Others may specialize in the conservation of particular formats, such as sound recordings or photographs. Still others provide for the care of all formats of cultural documentation in all genres. Researchers working in this field must learn to make use of all such archives, as they contain the primary resources for the study of folk culture.

The creation of the first folklore/folklife repositories coincided with the emergence of folklore as a formal discipline and was a manifestation of both the genesis of the field and the field's early concepts. By establishing archives, scholars declared the importance and vitality of their new field of study, ensured that the results of their research would be passed on to the next generation of scholars, and hoped to preserve examples of traditions they feared would disappear through industrialization and urbanization. As research in the field developed, the pragmatic necessity of creating safe storage for the growing collection of a particular researcher or institution often gave rise to the foundation of public archives.

All these motives probably contributed to the establishment of the world's first archive for collections of folklore. The Folklore Archive of the Finnish Literature Society was created at the same time as the society (in 1831) and opened its public quarters in 1888. Its first collections were those of Elias Lönnrot, the compiler of the *Kalevala*. This body of Finnish lore provided an inspiration to other collectors, who then added their materials to the collections.

The folklore movement in Europe was paralleled by similar efforts to preserve traditions in many parts of the world, resulting in the creation of archives devoted to the preservation of folklore. The establishment of archives became imperative with the development of new documentary technologies. As folklorists began to use fragile formats such as recordings, film, and still photography regularly in their fieldwork, they found that those formats required expert preservation, and they therefore established a number of special format archives for that purpose.

The first public archive dedicated to collecting and preserving folklore and folklife in the United States was established in 1928 at the Library of Congress. The Archive of Folksong was originally concerned with the preservation of sound recordings. Today, it is part of the American Folklife Center and has been renamed the Archive of Folk Culture. It is a repository for all formats of ethnographic documentation.

Folklife archives often are research institutions as well as repositories, and their staffs initiate ethnographic research and compile the collected materials. Archivists also have found ways to sponsor or support fieldwork in order to add to their collections. Archivists at universities with folklore programs often encourage and preserve student collections. Some are able to provide training in fieldwork and collections management through internships. Others provide for the loan of documentary equipment, such as tape recorders, to collectors who then may place their documentation in the archive.

Folklorists often joke that in order to become an effective field-worker, one must learn everything there is to know. Folklife archivists must master the skills of a field-worker and those of archival science as well. Managing materials in fieldwork situations is practical experience for managing collections in an archive. But an archivist must be able to preserve and duplicate various media, which may entail such things as knowing the technical specifications for the preservation of audiotapes, the chemistry of different types of film, and the methods for conserving aging manuscripts. Folklife archivists usually are trained folklorists who have studied archival science or learned it through on-the-job experience. Some also have training in library science, history, or another related discipline; all should be familiar with computer networking and database construction.

Archivists first arrange a collection. When possible, mixed-media documentary collection materials are processed together in keeping with the collector's intent in compiling them. The documentary goals of the collector are a guiding principle in organizing and providing access to ethnographic documentation. This means that the better collections are documented and organized by a collector before they arrive at the archive, the more thoroughly the collector's purpose and method can be conveyed to researchers. Ideally, a collection arrives at an archive already arranged by the collector. If a collector fails to give the collection a clear order and it is no longer possible to contact the collector for further information (as is often the case with historical collections), the archivist must decide on an order. This frequently involves attempting to reconstruct the collector's purpose as much as possible in order to arrange the materials in a coherent way.

The next step is to preserve collection materials by housing them in protective enclosures or by duplicating them onto more durable media. Many ethnographic materials have finite life spans. The primary task of the archivist is to preserve the information the materials contain through duplication. Duplicates also can be used as reference copies so that the life of the originals may be lengthened. Funding is not always available for duplication, and the originals of sound and video recordings must be preserved because duplicates may lose signal with each generation. For these reasons, preservation care and storage for the original media are generally needed as well. With manuscript materials, it is often desirable to preserve the original. For example, a paper disc sleeve from an instantaneous disc recording of Zora Neale Hurston made by Herbert Halpert, containing fieldnotes by the collector, has intrinsic value as an artifact to folklorists interested in the history of the various formats of documentary media. Many ethnographic media have finite life spans.

For documentary materials to be useful, the archivist must have the original technology used to play or read the item. Early recording equipment must be collected and preserved so as to duplicate cylinder, wire, and disc recordings. Early film, video, and computer technologies need to be collected and preserved as well.

Finally, the archivist creates tools to provide access to the collection for researchers. The most basic of these are catalog records on a computer database, collection inventories, and collection descriptions that provide a guide for readers. For modern collections, searchable databases often can be constructed using the field-worker's computer files. These access tools are another important means of providing links among the various media in mixed-media ethnographic collections. Even if photographs must be housed separately from recordings and manuscripts, all the different parts of the collection may be located and their relationships to one another explained clearly for researchers by means of well-written access tools.

Archives sometimes publish books or recordings of materials from collections, thereby providing access to a selected portion of their collections. Books or recordings created by other organizations from an archive also may be available. Today, archivists and publishers are exploring the possibilities of interactive computer duplicates of collection materials made available on a network or CD-ROM (compact disc read-only memory).

Whatever public products stem from collections in archives, the rights of the individuals documented in ethnographic work must be considered. The laws regarding rights to unpublished materials change frequently, and the interpretation of these laws is sometimes difficult. Archivists must stay abreast of these changes and also determine their own archival policies concerning the use of their materials. Generally, the archivist is responsible for obtaining permissions when the institution publishes or disseminates collection materials. When researchers publish archival materials, the responsibility to obtain permission falls on them. Field-workers often ask participants in their research to sign release forms giving them permission to use performances and photographs in their publications. Such permissions do not transfer to an archive. But should the collection become part of an archive, these permission forms provide a valuable source of addresses and phone numbers so that performers may be contacted in case materials are published.

Archives provide a fine training ground for folklorists and for future archivists. Field-workers may benefit from experience in collection management training so they may better care for the materials they collect, and aspiring archivists may find their best preliminary training in an ethnographic archive. Many archives sponsor interns or provide classes for this purpose. Folklife, ethnomusicology, and cultural archives make it possible for scholars to explore the range and variation of traditions over time and to compare traditions across cultures and regions. The archive may be the first stop in a folklorist's preparation for field research or an additional, later step as questions arise during an ethnographic study. Any number of issues may be addressed in archival research: Other folklorists may have compiled collections on the same or a related subject, local historians may have collected materials that provide useful cultural background, or linguists may have documented language variations or examples of natural speech that may provide clues to the culture in question. The unique unpublished recordings, photographs, and moving-image materials found in archives can provide field-workers with indispensable cultural data to take with them into the field.

It is difficult to predict from the outset what useful information archives may yield, and archival research consequently proves most fruitful when approached with an open mind. It is advisable to prepare for a visit to an archive by doing preliminary reading and by contacting the archive ahead of time to obtain brochures and background information about collections.

Every archive will have its own system for retrieving information. Some archives have cataloged materials at the item level, so that song or narrative titles may be searched and retrieved. In larger archives, this level of detail often is not possible and collections can only be searched in more general ways. Researchers must allow more time for working with unpublished materials than with published works, as the organization, indexing, and descriptions of the collections are irregular. In addition, most of the research must be conducted in the archive, for unique materials usually cannot be removed for study. Duplication of materials is sometimes possible, depending on the restrictions of the collection or archive. Transcriptions of recordings are sometimes available for duplication, but not all archives are able to provide them. Transcriptions, furthermore, are often inaccurate or lacking in important information available in the original sound recording.

A general understanding of the history of cultural documentation and the constraints of ethnographic archiving can facilitate an archival search. Pioneers of ethnographic research were often pioneers of recorded sound as well. For example, folklorist Robert Winslow Gordon experimented with transferring cylinder recordings to disc recordings for archival preservation. Such experimentation with documentary and preservation technology continues to the present day.

The developing technologies worked changes on ethnographic techniques. Lengthy recorded interviews became a research method with the invention of the tape recorder. Earlier collections of folklore on cylinders and discs usually focused on collecting individual songs, stories, and other items of a length that fit on one side of the recording medium. Folklorists used their fieldnotes to add information about the selections recorded. A modern researcher seeking information about the cultural background of songs sung in the 1930s, for example, may be frustrated to find that the collector of a historical ethnography turned the disc recording machine off just as the singer began to explain the provenance of the song or that only a few verses of a long ballad were recorded. But the rest of the information the researcher seeks may be jotted on the protective disc sleeve or painstakingly written into notebooks. Similarly, photographic documentation of culture changed as photography became less cumbersome and society became more accustomed to the camera. Researchers using historical collections need to become aware of what they can expect to find there and how to gain the most from the materials available.

Changing technology also affected archival practice. In the 1950s, ethnographers eagerly took up the new medium of reel-to-reel tape recording, allowing them to record long interviews, cultural events, and ambient sound without concern for duration. But these long recordings posed new problems for the archivist. Formerly, songs, stories, and other short items recorded on identifiable tracks on discs or cylinders could be readily cataloged. Interviews and other long recordings collected with tape recorders could not so easily be broken down and cataloged by item. In addition, as tape recording became inexpensive and tape recorders became increasingly portable and as the number of scholars in the field increased, the quantity of recorded folklore documentation contributed to archives became overwhelming. Increased use of photography and videotape added to the large bodies of ethnographic documentation that folklife archivists now needed to preserve and make accessible.

Today, folklore archives often can only catalog collections at a general level. Archivists typically rely on the fieldnotes, photograph logs, and audio- or videotape logs of the folklorists who created the collections they house. Researchers may be startled to find that materials available through the 1950s have been carefully cataloged (complete with song titles, references to individual performers, and cross-references to other collections) but that the more modern archival holdings are far less accessible. Researchers doing work with modern collections will need to examine manuscripts of tape logs and fieldnotes of collectors to determine which recordings will be most useful to their study. Fortunately, in the 1980s, many field-workers began using computers in the field. Computer-readable fieldnotes and logs can be entered into archival databases to create searchable collection information. As technology provides field-workers with better methods of managing their collections, they will be able to donate more accessible documentation to archives, making work with the collections far easier for both archivists and researchers.

The possibilities for data retrieval created by computers are causing many ethnographic archivists to change their methods of cataloging materials. In the past, concern for the care of various documentary formats caused archivists to break up collections by format: recordings might go to one repository or storage facility, and photographs would go to another. Modern use of computers is helping archivists to create cross-references to materials stored in different environments so that the different media from the work of one ethnographer can be brought back together for researchers to use. Modern archivists are going back to old collections and reexamining how they were cataloged to provide more comprehensive access in the future.

Archivists today must keep abreast of the ever changing technologies of modern ethnography, while learning about new ways to preserve materials from older collections. For example, early recordings and photographs are deteriorating to the point that they must be duplicated, quite possibly for the last time. Modern technologies of digital recording and scanning may provide a method of preserving the most information possible in those preservation duplicates. This new technology is still developing, however, and the stability of the various formats of digital preservation are a modern area of archival discussion. Digital technology is being used in the field as well, so archivists must learn about the preservation needs of the various digital formats and to make sure that they have access to equipment to read those formats.

The future of folklife archives may extend far beyond archival walls. Collections may become available to researchers through the Internet and other on-line information services. These far-reaching developments in ethnographic archiving were described in the 1994 report on the state of the discipline by the Archiving Section of the American Folklore Society:

> Historic collections once broken up by format can now be reunited for the researcher by means of digitized versions of the sound recordings, photographs, and texts linked together on a multi-media server or CD-ROM. Online communications are making it possible for archives to share their collection finding aids and catalog records with the world. A new standard cataloging format for multi-format collections, Mixed Materials MARC, makes possible standardized cataloging of ethnographic collections as whole intellectual works, rather than as separate media. . . .

The computer and information revolutions provide marvelous new possibilities for compiling, preserving, and providing access to ethnographic collections. However, these new options come at a time when ethnographic archives are losing funding and staff and are often unable to support the technology that makes these techniques possible. Archives need computers to build the databases, staff trained in using them, and staff to develop catalogs and other access tools.

Ethnographic archivists today may look forward to providing more complete access to their collections and to reaching scholars globally in a way never before possible, if they receive the intellectual and material support needed to realize these goals.

Stephanie A. Hall

See also Academic Programs in Folklore, International; Academic Programs in Folklore, North American; Applied Folklore/Folkloristics.

✳✳✳✳✳✳✳✳✳✳✳✳✳✳✳✳✳

References

Bartis, Peter, and Hillary Glatt. 1994. *Folklife Sourcebook: A Directory of Folklife Resources in the United States.* Washington, DC: Library of Congress.

Hall, Stephanie, and Lani Herrmann. 1994. The State of the Discipline: Remarks from the Archiving Section. Report prepared by the Archiving Section of the American Folklore Society for its report on the state of the discipline.

Hatuala, Jouko, and Urpo Vento. 1965–1966. The Folklore Archives of the Finnish Literature Society. The *Folklore and Folk Music Archivist*, 8:39–53.

Kodish, Deborah. 1986. *Good Friends and Bad Enemies.* Urbana: University of Illinois Press.

List, George. 1972. Archiving. In *Folklore and Folklife: An Introduction*, ed. Richard Dorson. Chicago: University of Chicago Press.

Stielow, Frederick J. 1986. Relations with the Public and the Law. In *The Management of Oral History Sound Archives*, ed. Frederick J. Stielow. New York: Greenwood.

ARGOT

A special linguistic code whose purpose is to conceal and to exclude. Also called *cant*, this genre of folk speech differs from standard language principally in vocabulary. However, argots based upon a language (the use of *Romanes* by Gypsies in English-speaking societies, for instance) or dialect differing from that in mainstream social use may diverge from standard speech in more complex ways. Argot's nonstandard diction allows its users to communicate with one another secretively. Hence, it most usually occurs among speakers with reasons to hide what they are saying from uninitiated listeners. Argots may merge with other folk speech genres such as jargons and slang.

Groups that have developed argots include persons whose activities are regarded as either illegal or immoral in some social contexts—for example, professional criminals, drug users, and homosexuals. Other groups may develop argots because their activities, though not illegal, require secrecy. Occupations that depend, in part, on tricking clients—gambling and carnival operations, for instance—may generate argots, as may competitive activities in which one team of players wishes to conceal its intentions from another team. Some ethnic groups use their native language as an argot in occupational contexts. Others may employ their language in the same way in social situations to guarantee the privacy of their communication. Argots also may have generational significance; adolescents, for example, often adopt vocabulary usages that exclude their parents from their communications. Argots may also develop in ritual situations, thus allowing religious specialists to deal with topics of esoteric spirituality without revealing sacred secrets to the profane masses. Another possible context for argot development involves communication among members of one sex that is designed to exclude persons of the other sex.

Argots received scholarly attention as early as the fifteenth century, though the first formal dictionary of a cant was probably issued in the 1700s. Francis Grose's *Classical Dictionary of the Vulgar Tongue*, first published in 1785, remains an important source of vocabulary usage by British criminals. Folklorists had included argot in their new discipline by the late 1800s. In 1890, the *Journal of American Folklore* published materials on *Shelta*, an argot used by British tinkers. Most studies of argot by folklorists and others (many of which have appeared in the periodical *American Speech*) have focused only on the compilation of word lists and their definitions. These glossaries may provide general comments about the group that uses the argot but often do not deal with specific usages in particular contexts.

More contextually oriented research could identify (1) particular situations in which groups employ specific words and phrases from the argot vocabulary, (2) whom such groups intend to exclude through their use of argot, and (3) the sociopsychological functions, such as group integration, that argots may perform in addition to their practical role in promoting secrecy and privacy of communication. Moreover, the playful dimension of argot, though noted by several commentators, has not received the attention that it deserves. Often, what appear to be attempts at communicative concealment may be artful linguistic flourishes that demonstrate the verbal agility of the speakers more than their desire for secrecy.

William M. Clements

See also Esoteric/Exoteric Factor; Language, Secret.

✳✳✳✳✳✳✳✳✳✳✳✳✳✳✳✳✳✳

References

Bronner, Simon J. 1988. *American Children's Folklore*. Little Rock, AR: August House.

Coltharp, Lurline. 1965. *The Tongue of the Tirlones: A Linguistic Study of a Criminal Argot*. University: University of Alabama Press.

Goodwin, Joseph P. 1989. *More Man Than You'll Ever Be: Gay Folklore and Acculturation in Middle America*. Bloomington: Indiana University Press.

Grose, Francis. [1785] 1963. *A Classical Dictionary of the Vulgar Tongue*. Ed. Eric Partridge. London: Routledge and Kegan Paul.

Hardy, Richard E., and John G. Cull. 1975. *Drug Language and Drug Lore*. Springfield, IL: Thomas.

Kirshenblatt-Gimblett, Barbara, ed. 1976. *Speech Play: Research and Resources for the Study of Linguistic Creativity*. Philadelphia: University of Pennsylvania Press.

Maurer, David W. 1981. *Language of the Underworld*. Eds. Allan W. Futrell and Charles B. Wordell. Lexington: University Press of Kentucky.

Murray, Thomas E. 1993. The Folk Argot of Midwestern Gangs. *Midwestern Folklore* 19:113–148.

Art, folk

The creation of aesthetic forms that emulate or reproduce techniques and designs taught, learned, and displayed primarily in situations of informal interaction. Much of what people make in everyday life and the procedures they employ in making these things are derived from the behavior of predecessors and peers. With time and repetition, these objects and behaviors become pervasive and commonplace. When they do, they are thought of as traditional. Rooted in the past and associated with particular groups or communities, they are called "folk" because of the continuities and consistencies they exhibit in form and design, materials, or techniques of manufacture.

Art entails the creation of aesthetic forms, that is, products or performances capable of being perceived by the senses, acting upon people's feelings, and being judged according to standards of excellence as well as personal preference (taste). In principle, folk art comprises both nonutilitarian objects (such as paintings and sculpture) and useful products (crafts and architecture) as well as dancing, singing, and music making. Many researchers, however, limit folk art to material culture. Some restrict it further to ornamentation, decorative designs, and sculptural forms lacking utility. Others include useful objects that may elicit aesthetic responses in the course of making and using them, such as unadorned but well-designed chairs or clay vessels, iron or wooden implements, baskets, duck decoys, musical instruments, fishing flies and lures, and customized cars.

*Folk art comes in diverse forms. Here is a "snake" rocking chair of black walnut
by Chester Cornett of Wheeling, WV, who had a vision of a chair in 1967.*

Most folk art belongs to ordinary, day-to-day experiences: the way people decorate their homes and work spaces, dress or adorn themselves, create altars and ornaments or other objects for holidays, prepare and serve food, and craft such things as quilts, furniture, pottery, rugs, clothing, toys, gifts for friends, and paintings of special or memorable events. Some people fashion particular things as an occupation or preoccupation, becoming noted in their communities as, for example, carvers, weavers, needlelace makers, boatbuilders, chairmakers, stonemasons, or makers of headstones and grave markers.

Many nonutilitarian creations display the virtuoso's skill. One person makes highly detailed miniature chairs, sofas, and rocking horses from discarded soft drink cans. Others fashion amazingly lifelike dolls from cornhusks or dried apples and small figurines from concrete. Some build elaborate birdhouses with fancy trim, carve chains from matchsticks, and construct larger-than-life animals or small-scale windmills as yard decoration. Certain Native Americans in California and Mexico weave decorated baskets no larger than a fingernail.

Objects intended for practical use also exhibit skill and mastery of technique and even great ingenuity and virtuosity. Technical excellence in carving a paddle or wooden buoy, weaving a blanket, preparing a meal, building a haystack or boat, or setting stones in a fence without mortar suffices to evoke admiration. One or more formal principles (unity, harmony, rhythm, balance) will likely be evident, and the product will serve its purpose with distinction. For example, a rocking chair with deeply curved back, sculpted armrests to enhance comfort, and legs at just the right angle to the rockers so that a slight breeze will set the chair in motion is a joy to use.

Folk art has been studied from four perspectives. One perspective views forms and examples of folklore as artifacts because they have histories. Hypothesizing that many examples of traditional objects hark back to earlier eras, some folklorists have conceptualized folk art as survival, continuity, or revival. Survivals are objects and behaviors known to have been more common historically or more compatible with former norms rather than with present norms. Living-history farms, open-air museums, and pioneer villages typically associate folkways, crafts, and arts with the past. Colonial Williamsburg (Virginia), Upper Canada Village (Ontario), Skansen Open Air Museum (Stockholm), the Welsh Folk Museum at St. Fagan's (Cardiff, Wales), and other sites consist of restored or reconstructed buildings and period furnishings, tools, and utensils, as well as role-playing interpreters in costume who discuss life in the past, demonstrate skills, and answer questions.

Numerous exhibits and publications also point out the durability of tradition and the continuity of attitudes, behaviors, and objects. Tourist markets perpetuate the making of things for which there once was widespread local use. Ethnic display events perpetuate traditional foods, dances, and crafts from the Old Country. Activities such as decorating homes, donning costumes, coloring eggs, creating shrines or altars, and building floats during holidays all help to define events and make them special. Taking part in traditions creates a sense of continuity and connectedness with others. Sometimes, people revive or revitalize forms and designs, such as the making of storytelling dolls among Pueblos, pottery production in rural North Carolina, or lei making in Hawaii. Motivations range from self-esteem to financial benefit and community redevelopment.

A second perspective views folk art creations as describable and diffusible entities. Folklorists establish genres, such as textiles, metalwork, and ceramics, in addition to subgenres (pottery, for example, can be further categorized on the basis of purpose or use—cream pitchers, butter jars, and milk crocks—or according to glazes, such as salt, lead, and alkaline). Researchers also configure types and subtypes from the many examples of houses, barns, outdoor bake ovens, chairs, garments, rugs, wooden clogs, sickles, harrows, and foods, among other forms. Questions asked about the distribution of types and subtypes leads to mapping, illustrated by Swedish, Austrian, and other European folklife atlases. Recognition of widespread examples of what seem to be the same design, technique, or form raises questions about origins. Although folklorists attribute some designs to polygenesis or multiple origins (for example, variations of a multihooked, swastika-like motif), they hypothesize that most similarities result from monogenesis (single origin) with subsequent diffusion through space and time as people travel or migrate. Procedures for tracing origins, changes, and stability are called the historic-geographic method.

A third orientation considers folk art creations to be aspects or manifestations of culture. Researchers seek to establish what other elements of culture art correlates with and how and why. Religious carvings or paintings and the colors and designs of baskets or pots sometimes parallel patterns and values in the oral literature, music, and philosophy of a society. Art may express social status. Residents of some Newfoundland outports put handhooked rugs with asymmetrical designs in their parlors where hierarchical relationships between themselves and privileged guests dominate. They place rugs with symmetrical, repetitive designs in the kitchen, where they entertain friends on an egalitarian basis. To compete for passengers and gain a modicum of wealth and status, Filipino jeepney drivers paint their vehicles with colorful scenes, elegant names, and provocative sayings (sometimes sexual), hang crocheted curtains reminiscent of those in village homes, and decorate their vehicles with rosary beads, holy pictures, and miniature altars. Folklorists postulate that some art conveys norms of behavior, validates or reinforces culture, and also provides escape from social pressures through fantasy or wish fulfillment.

A fourth perspective treats folk art as behavior. Some researchers hypothesize panhuman symbols such as the egg as life force or seek evidence of psychic processes (projections of unconscious archetypes such as the anima, animus, and shadow figure). Others have inferred unwritten laws or rules that people intuitively learn and unconsciously follow while creating aesthetic forms. For instance, food encodes social relationships and events (apparent in the structure of a meal); designers of folk houses or other objects employ an artifactual grammar in composition and construction. Some folklorists study art in a biographical context, examining repertoire, content, and style in relation to events and experiences in the maker's life. Others explore the unique situation in which a traditional object is formed, observing the impact of personality, customer influence, feedback, and reinforcement as well as uncovering the multiple meanings attributed to the object and its creation.

Aesthetic forms have instrumental effects. Some people artfully arrange linens in a cabinet, flowers on a table, nuts and bolts in containers, kitchen utensils in a drawer, or jars of homecanned goods on a shelf (by type and color of food). Ordering delimits a form, making it separable, recognizable, and accessible. Technical excellence in tools, furniture, pottery, and baskets enhances their utility and maximizes efficiency in use.

Art also has hygienic value. Many people create aesthetic forms during critical junctures in their lives or in times of anguish or turmoil (illness, retirement, marital problems, loss of a loved one). Physical expression helps objectify complex, unconscious, or vague feelings and issues. Doing something rhythmic and repetitive when troubled tends to calm, free the mind, or unlock emotions. Once produced, forms can symbolize achievement, garner praise, and increase self-esteem. Creating memory paintings, applying craft skills learned in youth at a later point in life, or making things in traditional ways with or for others can comfort through symbolic connectedness.

Art triggers aesthetic experiences. A positive response involves physiological reactions such as muscular tension and release along with a heightened awareness of form, the subordination in importance of other stimuli, and the suspension of time. The percipient likely feels a sense of unity with the object and with others. Immersion in pleasurable activities can help resolve tensions and reenergize a person.

Since no society has been discovered without traditions or aesthetic forms and experiences in everyday life, these behavioral tendencies appear to be inherited predispositions in human beings. If so, then folk art may be crucial to the adaptation of the species and survival of individual members.

Michael Owen Jones

See also Craft, Folk; Material Culture.

✳✳✳✳✳✳✳✳✳✳✳✳✳✳✳✳✳✳

References

Bronner, Simon J. 1985. Chain Carvers: *Old Men Crafting Meaning*. Lexington: University Press of Kentucky.

Eff, Elaine. 1988. *The Screen Painters of Baltimore*. Direct Cinema Limited. Color, ½″, 28 min. videotape.

Ferrero, Pat. 1981. *Quilts in Women's Lives*. California State University, San Francisco. Color, 16mm., 28 min. film.

Fry, Gladys-Marie. 1990. *Stitched from the Soul: Slave Quilts from the Ante-Bellum South*. New York: Dutton Studio Books, in association with the Museum of American Folk Art.

Glassie, Henry. 1989. *The Spirit of Folk Art: The Girard Collection at the Museum of International Folk Art*. New York: Abrams.

Johnson, Geraldine Niva. 1985. *Weaving Rag Rugs: A Women's Craft in Western Maryland*. Knoxville: University of Tennessee Press.

Jones, Michael Owen. 1989. *Craftsman of the Cumberlands: Tradition and Creativity*. Lexington: University Press of Kentucky.

Joyce, Rosemary O. 1989. *A Bearer of Tradition: Dwight Stump, Basketmaker*. Athens: University of Georgia Press.

Sherman, Sharon. 1991. *Spirits in the Wood: The Chainsaw Art of Skip Armstrong*. University of Oregon. Color, ½″, 28 min. videotape.

Vlach, John Michael. 1978. *The Afro-American Tradition in Decorative Arts*. Cleveland, OH: Cleveland Museum of Art.

ARTIFACT

Any object made or modified by humans. The term derives from the Latin *arte factum*, meaning something made with skill. The object expresses the mental template of its maker and the culture at large, through the shaping of raw materials that result in the artifact's tangible form. The attributes seen in an artifact are based on traditional, functional, and/or technological requirements of the user and culture. For these reasons, few artifacts have only one attribute or meaning.

The varied approaches used during the last century to study artifacts began with the description and classification of objects, usually by museum curators. The artifacts were grouped according to type, based on their morphological features. Nineteenth-century evolutionary theory, combined with the diffusionist theories of early twentieth-century anthropologists, contributed to the development of stylistic analyses of artifacts, as well as interest in the techniques and technology used in making them. The early fieldwork of cultural anthropologists such as Bronislaw Malinowski, Franz Boas, and Ruth Benedict and archaeologists such as A. V. Kidder focused on the interrelationship of objects to sociocultural patterns and structures.

Since the 1960s, the study of artifacts has drawn on a number of disciplines in the physical and social sciences to extract information not readily apparent to the observer. The most recent efforts now inform an integrated approach that includes aspects of the previous approaches. Artifacts now "speak" to the observer as repositories of human communication and interaction. Reading the text of an artifact, rather than just focusing on its physical attributes, is another way of accessing the culture being studied.

Although artifacts occupy a central place in anthropology and folklore studies, each discipline differs in its approach and analyses. It is understood that through artifacts, researchers in both disciplines can attempt to comprehend the beliefs, values, attitudes, ideas, and assumptions of a society or group of people at a given point in time. So the main distinction that separates the two disciplines is the factor of time.

For the archaeologist, the *processes* (both mental and physical) by which an artifact is produced are less tangible than for the folklorist since archaeologists often study cultures that are extinct. At best, the archaeologist can only hope to accurately guess at these processes through the reconstruction of events and scientific study.

For the folklorist, however, the artifact or folk object is part of an informal learning process whereby, through tradition, the mental and physical aspects of the object's manufacture are seen in the creative process of the producer and are recorded by the folklorist. In turn, when the artifact's form is read like a text, then certain motifs can be recognized and compared to known traditions. In this context, the artifact is complete and historical, so there is no mystery as to its relative context or creator.

Regardless of disciplinary orientation, the artifact continues to play a central role in bringing the culture to the researcher. In this sense, the artifact, as reference point, mirrors for posterity the ideas and systems of the culture that produces it purposefully or accidentally.

Georgia Fox

See also Text.

✳✳✳✳✳✳✳✳✳✳✳✳✳✳✳✳

References

Babcock, Barbara A. 1992. Artifact. In *Folklore, Cultural Performances, and Popular Entertainments*, ed. Richard Bauman, pp. 204–215. New York: Oxford University Press.

Bronner, Simon J. 1985. Visible Proofs: Material Culture Study in American Folkloristics. In *Material Culture: A Research Guide*, ed. Thomas J. Schlereth, pp. 127–153. Lawrence: University of Kansas Press.

———. 1992. The Idea of the Folk Artifact. In *American Material Culture and Folklife: A Prologue and Dialogue*, ed. Simon J. Bronner. Logan: Utah State University Press.

Deetz, James. 1967. *Invitation to Archaeology*. Garden City, NY: Natural History Press.

Noel-Hume, Ivor. 1985. *A Guide to Colonial Artifacts of Colonial America*. New York: Knopf.

Prown, Jules D. 1988. Mind in Matter: An Introduction to Material Culture Theory and Method. In *Material Life in America, 1600–1860*, ed. Robert Blair St. George. Boston: Northeastern University Press.

Walls, Robert E. 1990. Folklife and Material Culture. In *The Emergence of Folklore in Everyday Life*, ed. George H. Schoemaker. Bloomington, IN: Trickster.

Assault, Supernatural

Attack by a spirit or by spiritual means. The term *supernatural* has had many meanings, some of them very complex and culturally specific. However, a cross-culturally applicable concept can be derived from the simplest common denominator of the word's various usages. Most basically, *supernatural* refers to *spirits*, sentient beings that can exist and act without a physical body. *Supernatural assault*, then, is assault by spiritual means. This definition is well suited to a great many folk beliefs, but it does leave an ambiguous category of "extraordinary" creatures who sometimes assault humans, according to certain traditions. These range from werewolves and other shape-shifters to occupants of unidentified flying objects (UFOs) who abduct people from their beds. Some believe that such creatures have spiritual significance, others think that they in fact *are* spirits of some kind, and still others believe them to be entirely physical. This uncertain category will be considered last.

The idea that human beings could be supernaturally injured appears to be both ancient and ubiquitous. The events taken to constitute such assault are quite varied, including ordinary illness or injury in which a supernatural cause is inferred, special classes of illness considered always to result from supernatural attack in which the evidence of a particular supernatural cause is still indirect, and experiences in which the perception of the supernatural attacker is a central feature. Each of these kinds of assault has been associated with practically every sort of supernatural agent, from witches to ghosts to vampires to demons. The result is a very complex set of categories, and many of the characteristics attributed to each kind of attacker differ from one locale to another. A cross-cultural description follows that sets out rough conceptual categories of supernatural assault found in many traditions around the world. Each is briefly illustrated with reference to one or two specific traditions. This process inevitably downplays local, culture-specific differences. This is a necessary result of summary description and not an indication that these local variations are of lesser importance. This discussion is presented in sufficiently general terms to apply to the traditions of most cultures, but it should be understood that although the general statements that follow refer to widely found phenomena, they are not necessarily universal in application.

The human soul is supernatural, that is, although it spends part of its career in a body, it does not require that body for its existence. In some traditions, the soul exists before the body and chooses the body in which it will be born. In practically all traditions, the soul animates the body and survives the body at death, and under some circumstances, it can leave the body and return during life. In some traditions, people are believed to have more than a single soul. Supernatural assault sometimes may produce a direct physical

Vampire attacks are among the most famous types of supernatural assault and are common to many different cultures.

effect, such as bruises or scratches, but effects on the body are more often seen as operating through effects on the soul.

During life, one's soul can be dislodged. The resulting condition of "soul loss" is often called "magical fright" or "fright illness" in the literature because the condition is often believed to be produced by sudden fear or emotional shock. The most frequently described tradition of soul loss is the Latin American *susto*, but similar traditions are found in many parts of the world. This is usually an explanation attached retrospectively to explain a condition of sickness. The characteristics of such sicknesses are often distinctive, as in the case of *susto*, and are probably not merely derived from local names for medically recognized diseases. Some of them may truly be culture-bound syndromes; others may represent the recognition of sicknesses not yet known to modern medicine. Many circumstances can cause soul loss, including such natural events as seeing a terrible accident or hearing of the unexpected death of a loved one. But this loss also can be caused by sorcery or by a ghost or other spirit, and then it is a consequence of supernatural assault. In these cases, the person who has suffered the magical fright may have no memory of the event, in which case the event took place entirely at the spiritual level.

Another widely believed supernatural cause of illness is the "evil eye." The best-known example of this concept is the Italian *mal ojo*, but the idea is found in many places. In many versions, an attack by means of the evil eye barely qualifies as assault because the damage is done unintentionally. Most commonly, sickness or misfortune is brought on one person by the envy of another. As with supernatural magical fright, the victim—and in this case, the perpetrator—is unaware that anything is happening at the time.

Some living persons, because of training or a special aptitude, can leave their physical bodies and travel as disembodied spirits. In this state, they are believed to be able to see and interact with other spirits. This technique is used by some healers to find and bring back a lost soul and cure a case of magical fright. Some wicked people can travel in soul form to do harm. They may attempt to kill persons or terrify them and disturb their sleep. In English tradition, this is called "hagging" or "witch riding." The victim is held helpless and oppressed to the point that breathing becomes difficult.

Normally, a person's soul "goes on" to the afterlife or to be reincarnated at death, but some souls remain close to where they have lived or return under special conditions. Since this is not the normal course, these ghosts are especially likely to be dangerous. Some people with special knowledge and aptitude are able to cause these ghosts to do their bidding.

Ghosts can assault people in a great variety of ways. Haunted locations are places to which ghosts are bound either because of intense attachment during life or because of the circumstances of their deaths. Whatever the reason, most haunted places are dangerous. Earth-bound spirits are themselves in a "sick" state (otherwise, they would have progressed), and their anger, envy, and other negative emotions cause them to accost people who trespass in their places. (It should be noted, though, that some haunting ghosts are said to be innocuous or even friendly, and sometimes, a haunting ghost handsomely repays good treatment.) The assaults committed by such ghosts range from intentionally causing fear by producing weird sounds and apparitions to effecting a variety of transitory physical effects and inducing terrible dreams to causing potentially fatal diseases. In animist traditions, ghosts are not the only spirits associated with particular places, and in Southeast Asia, for example, there are many risks encountered from "wild spirits."

Ghosts sometimes return to particular people rather than places. Their motives may be very positive but still result in assault. This is the case when a ghost returns to admonish a parent or spouse who is abusing someone the ghost cared for in life. Sometimes, a ghostly assault is an act of revenge, visited on a person who inflicted injury in life. The avenging ghost may strike a person and cause a cancer to grow at the site of the blow, harass the guilty party into confession, or otherwise make life miserable. Less severe is the case of a ghost whose purpose is to force a living relative into a more prudent and honorable life path, as in the case of the Hawaiian tradition of *aumakua*, which has been translated as "behavioral direction visions."

A common reason for ghostly return is the absence of proper burial and mourning. This situation has been especially difficult for some of the refugee groups who fled Southeast Asia in the 1970s. In the process of fleeing, many relatives were killed under conditions that prevented proper funerary rites, and many problems, including illness and sometimes death, have been attributed to the resulting ghostly returns.

An assaulting spirit actually may seek to displace one's soul in order to possess the body. Motives for such possession vary, and many traditions allow for benign possession, as for mediumistic communication between the living and the dead. But most traditions also acknowledge harmful possession. In Christian tradition, it has generally been believed that demons—fallen angels who were never in human form—carry out possession of this type. Such nonghost possession is found in many traditions, but ghosts also are widely believed to possess the living. The act of possession itself may be perceived as an assault in which the victim struggles and feels an alien spirit entering the body by force, attempting to push out the soul of the rightful owner. In other cases, the victim is unaware of anything but gaps of "missing time" and must have the events of the possession recounted. During possession, the victim's body may do antisocial acts or physically harm itself. Somewhat less intrusive is the attachment of spirits to the living in a way that influences their behavior, sometimes called "obsession." In spiritist traditions, such influences may be either good or bad; for other believers, the influences are more consistently detrimental. Most traditions have techniques for identifying harmful spirit possession or influence and treating it by expelling the offending spirits.

In many cultures, there exists the concept of supernatural sexual assault. In European tradition, such attacks were carried out by both male (incubi) and female (succubi) demons. Some held that the demon actually had no gender but merely took the form opposite to its victim. Reports of sexual assault by spirits continue to the present.

Magical assault is sometimes carried out at a distance through the principles of magic described by Sir James George Frazer in *The Golden Bough*: that like produces like (the principle of similarity) and that once in contact, things continue to act on each other even after contact has been severed (the principle of contagion). Both principles are illustrated by the use of an effigy that includes, for example, some of the victim's hair or nail parings (contagion) to cause that person pain and sickness by injuring the effigy (similarity). This and a variety of other techniques of magical assault, such as "bone pointing," are found all over the world. A more directly supernatural kind of sorcery is spirit magic, in which a spirit is bound by the sorcerer to do his or her bidding. Spirit magic is often used for healing and other benign purposes (many healers have one or more spirit helpers or "guides," what the Laotian Hmong call "tame spirits" in translation), but the same spirits can do all kinds of mischief.

Magical assault, like the attack of a ghost, sometimes may be directed against an evil one. In Japan, for example, the experience known as hagging or witch riding in English is called *kanashibari,* which is sometimes translated as "metal bound." The term derives from the magic of Fudomyoo, a Buddha who fights against evil. His statue is placed at the entrance to temples, where it is said to bind evil ones so that they cannot move, preventing them from entering. In medieval Japan, Ninjas and Buddhist monks were said to be trained to bind their opponents as if by metal strings. Similar "spellbinding" traditions, used against enemies and evildoers, are very widely found.

It was noted earlier that some categories of assault (and attackers) are ambiguous with regard to the previously outlined definition of supernatural. These types of assaults and attackers do not constitute an entirely new category so much as a boundary where opinion, often within a single tradition, differs on the physical/spiritual nature of events. Fairies sometimes appear to be a physical race with magical powers, but others consider them to be spirits. Some Newfoundlanders, for example, said that the fairies were fallen angels who were not bad enough to be consigned to hell. Fairies often mislead wanderers and sometimes strike them or wound them with fairy weapons. Bell's palsy, a neurological condition causing temporary paralysis on one side of the face, was attributed to fairies by some Newfoundlanders. Fairies also can cause blindness and all sorts of other injury. Similar races of "little people" are found all over the world.

The activities of witches are sometimes similarly ambiguous. During the witchcraft persecutions in Europe, there was a great debate over whether witches flew in their physical bodies or after leaving their physical bodies behind. The European witchcraft tradition clearly included the possibility that witches might not only leave their human bodies but also either change them or enter alternative bodies such as those of animals. In such a case, injury to the animal would then be found on the body of the witch at a later time, confirming the identity. The belief in shape shifting is found universally, and shape-shifters usually are very dangerous. Shape shifting is often associated with witchcraft, as in the Navajo "skinwalker" who transforms itself by putting on the skin of a coyote or wolf. This image is similar to the European werewolf; here too the transformation process appears supernatural, but the result seems to be a physical agent who can do direct bodily harm. Another related belief is that witches can "slip out of their skins" and travel about invisibly, a belief reported from the U.S. South. Although this sounds like a metaphorical description of witches traveling in spirit form, some informants say that, though invisible, the witches can be touched when they are out of their skins and that they feel rubbery, like raw meat.

Vampires also share some of this physical/supernatural ambiguity. Traditional vampires, unlike the movie variety, do not live above ground in closed caskets that they can conveniently open and exit at night. Rather, their bodies remain in the buried casket, and their travel and attacks seem to involve either spectral appearance or shape shifting. Some accounts suggest that a burrow connects the casket with the surface and that the vampire can leave in the form of a small animal. But the blood of the victim, in European belief, somehow gets to the corpse of the vampire, which is found filled with it when the vampire is finally identified and destroyed. In other traditions, creatures like the vampire (such as the "viscera sucker" of the Philippines) seem to take vital essence rather than physical nourishment from their victims. The result, of course, can be the same: sickness and death.

One final ambiguous category indicates the continued vigor of traditions of supernatural assault. This is "UFO abduction." Until the mid-1980s, even people fascinated by UFOs considered those who claimed to have been taken aboard the flying objects to be part of a lunatic fringe. But by the late 1980s, the topic of UFO abduction was being taken much more seriously. Stories in the media documented the increasing number of people claiming to have been taken against their will to strange craft, where they were subjected to painful physical and sexual examinations and had semen or ova taken from them. At present, there are at least dozens of investigators and abductee support groups in the United States, and a substantial number of mental health professionals are taking the abductees' claims seriously. Although many investigators are convinced that recent abduction events have been carried out by a technolog-ically advanced alien civilization, others, including many abductees, believe that what is happening is metaphysical rather than physical. Abductees are often accosted in their bedrooms and paralyzed in events much like those involved in hagging. Subsequently, they may be taken right through the ceil-ings of their rooms. The differing opinions on how this occurs recall the earlier debate about whether the flight of witches was physical or spiritual. The alien hybridization program has many elements reminiscent of fairy abduction, which sometimes included sexual union between fairies and humans.

There have been many theories about why the belief in supernatural assault recurs in so many cultural settings, and most of them probably supply pieces of the explanation. Such a belief can serve social control functions, suggesting, for example, consequences for antisocial behavior—consequences against which wealth and power cannot necessarily protect. Also, as an explanation of disease, the belief offers a course of action. Psychoanalytic authors have suggested explanations in terms of repressed sexuality.

In addition to such theories, there is now evidence that a substantial number of supernatural belief traditions (both negative and positive) are partially supported by experiences that occur cross-culturally. Such experiences seem to play a central role in the formation and persistence of these traditions. The category that has been most completely described is what Newfoundlanders call "the Old Hag" or hagging, although the perpetrator may be either male or female. In this experience, people awaken to find themselves paralyzed, although fully awake. They may hear shuffling footsteps approach; they may see a grotesque creature clamber up on the bed and squat on their chests, making it difficult to breathe; or they may be overwhelmed by a "sense of presence." The great majority of victims are convinced that something evil is in their immediate vicinity. Most surprising is the fact that this type of experience, complete with its complex set of grotesque features, is found in different cultural settings all over the world, including modern North America where most victims have no cultural frame in which to place the event. This experience is what sleep researchers and physicians call "sleep paralysis." There are known physiological mechanisms that explain the paralysis, but the peculiar, cross-culturally stable patterning of the subjective experience is still puzzling.

The sleep paralysis experience is a universally available empirical basis for supernatural assault traditions, and it has been attributed to each of the spiritual attackers described earlier. Although this event is the most thoroughly described, it appears that there may be other ubiquitous experiential foundations for these assault traditions, just as there are for more positive belief traditions (such as the near-death experience). For example, in multiple personality disorder, the alter personality sometimes claims to be a demon or other spirit alien to the host. This does not happen only to those with a strong prior belief in possession. There may well be many other underlying experiential categories. In order to find such patterns and make theoretical sense of them, it is first necessary to take traditions of the supernatural seriously—that is to inquire into them as though they may refer to actual experiences. To do this, one must not only seek the cultural repertoire of beliefs but also interview those who claim to be direct observers. Many will reveal a retrospective interpretation of mundane events. But others may give us new knowledge about phenomena that are genuinely puzzling, as is sleep paralysis. In turn, such empirical elements put the traditions in a new light, making their logical structures more understandable. Sleep paralysis by itself, occurring among about 20 percent of the population, provides an empirical basis for the belief that evil spirits exist. If that belief is established, the reference to such powerful agents in theories of disease etiology is not so difficult to understand.

David J. Hufford

See also Evil Eye; Exorcism; Night Hag; Magic; Possession; Vampire; Werewolf; Witchcraft.

✼✼✼✼✼✼✼✼✼✼✼✼✼✼✼✼✼✼✼

References

Barber, Paul. 1988. *Vampires, Burial, and Death: Folklore and Reality*. New Haven, CT: Yale University Press.

Davis, Winston. 1980. *Dojo: Magic and Exorcism in Modern Japan*. Stanford, CA: Stanford University Press.

Dundes, Alan. 1981. *The Evil Eye: A Folklore Casebook*. New York: Garland.

Goodman, Felicitas D. 1988. *How about Demons? Possession and Exorcism in the Modern World*. Bloomington: Indiana University Press.

Hufford, David. 1982. *The Terror That Comes in the Night: An Experience-Centered Study of Supernatural Assault Traditions*. Philadelphia: University of Pennsylvania Press.

Noll, Richard. 1992. *Vampires, Werewolves and Demons: Twentieth Century Reports in the Psychiatric Literature*. New York: Brunner/Mazel.

Otten, Charlotte F., ed. 1986. *A Lycanthropy Reader: Werewolves in Western Culture*. Syracuse, NY: Syracuse University Press.

Perkowski, Jan L. 1989. *The Darkling: A Treatise on Slavic Vampirism*. Columbus, OH: Slavica.

Rubel, Arthur J., Carl W. O'Nell, and Rolando Collado-Ardon. 1984. *Susto: A Folk Illness*. Berkeley: University of California Press.

Simons, Ronald C., and Charles C. Hughes. 1985. *The Culture-Bound Syndromes: Folk Illnesses of Psychiatric and Anthropological Interest*. Dordrecht, Netherlands: D. Reidel.

Summers, Montague. 1960. *The Vampire, His Kith and Kin*. New Hyde Park, NY: University Books.

———. 1966. *The Werewolf*. New York: Bell.

AUDIENCE

A word derived from the Latin *audientia*, meaning a hearing or listening. In folklore scholarship, the term *audience* may refer to a variety of social groups (or individuals) who constitute the actual (or intended) receiving party in a transmission process. Depending on the dynamics of the activity involved, the term may signify a listener to verbal or musical communication or a spectator of visual presentation or activity. In a broader sense, closely related labels (e.g., *the public, fans, clients*) also are used to refer to a customary audience or to consumers of a material culture product (artifact). Typically, an audience is physically present with the source of the communication; the audience may also be intended (as in the case of producing a commodity for a certain category of a population) or imaginary (symbolic interactional—e.g., in AT 894, "The Ghoulish Schoolmaster and the Stone of Pity," a persecuted heroine tells her sorrows to a stone, which bursts out of compassion for her).

During the early stages of folklore scholarship, only casual references were made to the audience, especially with reference to narrative materials (e.g., *Märchen*, ballads). The most pronounced emphasis placed by a folklorist on the audience came in the 1920s as part of Walter Anderson's "Law of Self-Correction." Anderson credited the audience of orally communicated tales with censoring narrators into conforming to established characteristics of a tale text, thus exerting a stabilizing influence on traditions. Other folklorists defined some genres in terms of the presence or absence of an audience and its expectations. For example, Iouri Sokolov argued that one can chant a song for one's self but that there is no solitary tale telling since narrating a tale presupposes the presence of an audience; similarly, C. W. von Sydow distinguished between the long *chimerates* and *novellates*, on the one hand, and the short animal fables and jocular fables, on the other, according to a raconteur's purpose vis-à-vis a listening audience.

Subsequent theoretical developments led to the inclusion of the audience as a basic factor in studying lore. One such development was the anthropological functional approach, which was heavily influenced by behavioristic theories of learning wherein labels such as *cues* and *intervening variables* designated the context for a learning process. Under the terms of functional studies, the audience becomes a component of the context within which cultural institutions operate, and recurrent practices are learned or unlearned.

As did Anderson earlier, many folklorists came to view social reward by an audience as a major factor in motivating narrators, singers, minstrels, dancers, and other performers to publicly perform their art or exercise their craft. Stith Thompson pointed out the impact of such rewards on raconteurs; Albert Lord reported the influence of a "critical audience" on minstrels' performances; Bengt Holbeck concluded that if meaning in tales were to be understood, the traditional audience had to be seen in conjunction with the narrators. Likewise, in the field of material culture, the role of the consumer is emphasized. Warren E. Roberts noted a craftsperson's eagerness to produce "satisfactory items" due to a close personal contact with the customer and expectations to serve the customer again, and Henry Glassie pointed out the folk artist's sensitiveness to the "audience's needs and pleasures."

This form of interaction (as compared with feedback) between a source and a recipient in terms of effect (reward and punishment or absence thereof) received further indirect elaboration in the "ethnography of speaking" espoused by Dell Hymes and in "performance-centered" approaches advocated by Roger Abrahams, Richard Bauman, and others. The new nomenclature for this formula is the *responsibility/accountability* assumed by a speaker/performer to an audience (and vice versa). Imbedded in this view of "cultural behavior"—to use Hymes' words—is the audience's response, which will reward or punish the performer. According to behavioristic learning theories, effect is the basic force responsible for the continuity and discontinuity of behavior, especially that category of traditional cultural behavior that may be designated as "folkloric behavior."

Hasan El-Shamy

See also Performance; Psychological Approach; Superorganic Theories; Tradition.

✱✱✱✱✱✱✱✱✱✱✱✱✱✱✱✱✱

References

Anderson, Walter. 1923. *Kaiser und Abt* (Emperor and abbot). Folklore Fellows Communications, no. 42. Helsinki: Academia Scientiarum Fennica.

Bauman, Richard. 1975. Verbal Art as Performance. *American Anthropologist* 77:290–311.

Glassie, Henry. 1972. Folk Art. In *Folklore and Folklife: An Introduction*, ed. R. M. Dorson. Chicago: University of Chicago Press.

Holbeck, Bengt. 1987. *Interpretation of Folktales: Danish Folklore in European Perspective*. Folklore Fellows Communications, no. 239, Helsinki: Academia Scientiarum Fennica.

Hymes, Del. 1975. Breakthrough into Performance. In *Folklore: Communication and Performance*, eds. Dan Ben-Amos and Kenneth Goldstein. The Hague: Mouton.

Lord, Albert B. 1960. *The Singer of Tales*. New York: Atheneum.

Roberts, Warren E. 1972. Folk Crafts. In *Folklore and Folklife: An Introduction*, ed. R. M. Dorson. Chicago: University of Chicago Press.

El-Shamy, H. 1967. Folkloric Behavior. Ph.D. dissertation, Indiana University, Bloomington.

Sokolov, Iouri. 1950. *Russian Folklore*. New York: Macmillan.

Thompson, Stith. 1946. *The Folktale*. New York: Holt.

von Sydow, C. W. 1948. *Selected Papers on Folklore*. Copenhagen: Rosenkilde and Bagger.

AUTHENTICITY

Clearly identifiable authorship or the uniqueness of a folklore item, such as an authentic piece of folk art as opposed to mass-produced copies of it; also, the ability of cultural objects or performances to evoke a sense of genuineness among those who partake of them, such as the strong emotional or even physical response of audiences witnessing a ritual. The term derives from the Greek *authentes*, meaning made by one's own hand, original, or genuine. In classic and medieval usage, *authenticity* was primarily applied to objects and scriptures, particularly in the religious and legal realms.

The intellectual, social, and political transformations that began with the Enlightenment brought forth individual experience as a second realm of authenticity, which remains central to modern philosophy. In the breakup of feudal life worlds that would eventually lead to the formation of bourgeoisies and democracies, upper-class literati in Western societies began to question the sincerity of social interaction, as civilized manners and behaviors increasingly removed people from expressing themselves in plain, truthful, and unpremeditated ways. Intellectuals thus sought to discover places and states of being where authenticity flourished undisturbed by what Jean-Jacques Rousseau termed the "wound of reflection." Excessive civilization had, from this perspective, covered over authentic ways of being and expression, and thus the search began for peoples or social classes that remained in primeval states in order to then recover authenticity from such examples and employ it for the recovery and renewal of the self.

Aside from the exotic savages encountered in the colonial expansion, one such locus of authenticity was thought to be the European peasantry. Labeled *the folk,* this group and its material and spiritual artifacts became the focus of folklore studies, which emerged around 1800. The search for authenticity was thus a core concern in the formation of the discipline, and the material and the experiential component of authenticity became intertwined. The concept served as a powerful means to legitimate the subject matter but itself remained curiously unexamined. Only in the 1980s did authenticity undergo increasing analytic scrutiny, particularly with regard to questions of cultural commodification (as in the mass marketing of indigenous artifacts) and the politics of culture (as in the use of folklore materials for diverse sociopolitical goals). Eventually, the absolute nature of the concept was questioned, and the notion of authenticity as a socially negotiated quality emerged instead.

Despite its ancient Greek roots, the meaning of the term *authenticity* is thoroughly modern. It emerged in the mid-eighteenth century, concurrently with both the political transformations brought about by the French Revolution and the socioeconomic changes initiated by the Industrial Revolution. Both the political and the economic changes furthered the growth of increasingly individualistic worldviews in place of the communal ethos dominant in feudal societies. The excitement of dramatic change and technological progress therefore also entailed a sense of loss of community, and the romantically inspired search for authenticity around the turn of the nineteenth century attempted to counteract this loss. Emphasizing the need for getting in touch with their own innermost feelings and emotions, romantic writers and thinkers sought to uncover the lost origins of poetry. This was closely entwined with the perception of natural purity, on the one hand, and civilization as a spoiling agent, on the other. Works such as Ossian (later discovered to be a fraud) inspired the collection of folksong and folk narrative on a grand scale, as upper-class individuals hoped to regain their own lost authenticity by reading and imitating folk poetry. A vocabulary relying on tropes such as cleanliness and genuineness of natural manifestations, threatened loss of paradise, and alienation from society was employed by the romantics, who were initially driven by a largely emotional desire to recoup the authentic. Although this vocabulary lingers to the present, the desire to restore authentic origins moved from the emotional realm and became an increasingly scholarly, scientific preoccupation. Scholars began to devise techniques of collecting and representing the essence of folkness in the form of texts and artifacts. In the work of Jacob and Wilhelm Grimm, for instance, one recognizes the effort to turn the sociopolitical quest for authenticity into a scientifically valid enterprise. Folklore materials, the standards used in collecting them, and the groups and individuals from whom scholars collected were subjected to explicit or implicit authenticity criteria. This perception of more and less genuine groups and cultural productions grew into a rarely questioned scientific canon. The ideology that relative isolation from modern forces such as mass communication and technological advances preserves cultures in a purer (hence, superior) state continued to inform choices in fieldwork sites until the romantic mystique of fieldwork itself began to be examined.

In contrast to authenticity standards in the domain of high culture, where individual, known authorship of artistic production served as a means to determine originality, the authenticity of an item of folklore was established by proving anonymous authorship and continuity through traditional channels of communication. Individual performers living within presumably untainted communities were considered only as vessels through whom folklore materials were passed on. In a variety of theoretical folkloristic projects, such as those of the historic-geographic school, the scholar's task consisted of cleansing from folklore materials the impurities that had crept into them through human error and establishing the original or Ur-form. In the public sphere, the appeal of authenticity was considerable as well. Folkloristic notions of originality and cultural purity fueled applications in anything from (romantic) nationalist rhetoric to small-scale preservational or restorational associations.

In the second half of the twentieth century, folklorists began to move from an item- or text-oriented focus that had disregarded intentionality and creativity on the part of the folk to a processual approach in which actors and audiences were recognized as active shapers of folklore. Simultaneously, scholars faced a variety of cultural manifestations that forced them to examine the latent dichotomies informing much of their thinking. By adhering to the folk-versus-nonfolk dichotomy and the corresponding differentiation between the genuine or authentic versus the spurious, folklorists artificially isolated the materials they studied from the cultural processes in which they were embedded. Issues such as the mechanical reproduction of folk art or the touristic exploitation of costume, festival, and foodways brought forth the *folklorismus* discourse in Europe and the concept of fakelore in the United States. Both notions were initially conceived to separate out authentic folk culture from the machinations of mass markets. Closer examination of issues such as the commodification of cultural goods in the larger framework of the politics of culture forced scholars to recognize the artificial boundaries that they themselves had constructed around folklore and folk communities. Cases where the purported authenticity of folkloric materials was foregrounded began to be studied, for instance, in the intersection of folk art and the art market, the display of ethnicity, or the encounter of tourists and natives. Agents in these settings clearly constructed authenticities according to arbitrary criteria suiting their particular needs. Such insights helped the discipline to recognize its own complicity in endowing some cultural goods with greater significance than others. The hegemonic implications of disciplinary theory and practice in the discourse on authenticity thus finally became an object of analysis itself.

Regina Bendix

See also Fakelore; Folklorismus/Folklorism; Tradition; Invented Tradition.

✹✹✹✹✹✹✹✹✹✹✹✹✹✹✹✹✹

References

Appadurai, Arjun. 1986. Introduction: Commodities and the Politics of Value. In *The Social Life of Things*, ed. A. Appadurai. Cambridge: Cambridge University Press.

Bendix, Regina. 1992. Diverging Paths in the Scientific Search for Authenticity. *Journal of Folklore Research* 29:103–132.

Benjamin, Walter. [1936] 1968. The Work of Art in the Age of Mechanical Reproduction. In *Illuminations*, ed. H. Arendt (trans. Harry Zohn). New York: Harcourt, Brace.

Berman, Marshall. 1972. *The Politics of Authenticity*. New York: Atheneum.

Cohen, Erik. 1988. Authenticity and Commoditization in Tourism. *Annals of Tourism Research* 15:371–386.

Evans-Pritchard, Deirdre. 1987. The Portal Case: Authenticity, Tourism, Tradition, and the Law. *Journal of American Folklore* 100:287–296.

Handler, Richard. 1986. Authenticity. *Anthropology Today* 2(1):2–4.

Handler, Richard, and William Saxton. 1988. Dyssimulation: Reflexivity, Narrative, and the Quest for Authenticity in "Living History." *Cultural Anthropology* 3:242–260.

Kirshenblatt-Gimblett, Barbara. 1988. Authenticity and Authority in the Representation of Culture. In *Kulturkontakt-Kulturkonflikt*, eds. I. M. Greverus et al. Notizen, vol. 28, pp. 59–70. Frankfurt: Institut für Kulturanthropologie und Europäische Ethnologie.

Staub, Shalom. 1988. Folklore and Authenticity: A Myopic Marriage in the Public Sector. In *The Conservation of Culture*, ed. Burt Feintuch. Lexington: University of Kentucky Press.

Trilling, Lionel. [1971] 1974. *Sincerity and Authenticity*. London: Oxford University Press.

AUTOGRAPH BOOK

A volume for collecting handwritten verse and prose. This written material can be traditional or original, comically irreverent or high-mindedly serious. It can represent very personal feelings or repeat customary formulas. Messages are usually quite brief, perhaps consisting only of a traditional greeting phrase with the writer's signature ("Best wishes, Spike").

Also called *friendship books* and *memory books*, autograph books existed as early as the fifteenth century. A vogue for keeping them emerged early in the 1800s and continued as a mark of gentility until the beginning of the twentieth century. Writers of autographs at least until the mid-nineteenth century treated the custom as an opportunity for offering homiletics on such subjects as friendship ("Remember well and bear in mind, / A constant friend is hard to find"). Although some might compose their own messages, most writers probably drew upon traditional materials that originated or were preserved in almanacs, school readers, and collections of sentimental verse. Later in the century, messages became more comic, a trend that has continued until the present.

During the 1900s, the custom of keeping autograph books has flourished most among children, who employ a variety of folk rhyme formulas ("Roses are red, / Violets are blue, / There has never been a friend / That's better than you") as well as visual manipulations ("U R 2 Good 2 B 4 Gotten") to memorialize relationships. Sometimes, symbols take the place of a word or concept (a heart substituted for the verb "love" or a "smiley face" representing happiness). Autograph book inscriptions also may comment humorously and sometimes sardonically about such concerns as schoolwork and boy-girl relationships. Though writers still stress the importance of friendships, twentieth-century autograph verse is often comically insulting. Inscriptions may be preserved in albums designed especially for the purpose. Today, school yearbooks, produced even for elementary schools, are designed to accommodate autographed sentiments from one's classmates. In fact, administrators may set aside part of a day at the end of the school year for an "annual" party, during which students write in each other's yearbooks.

Most studies of autograph books published by folklorists have focused entirely on the verses and prose written therein. Changes through time in the nature of the sentiments expressed have received considerable attention. Some attempts also have been made to typologize autograph verse on the basis of form and to view the content of the verse as reflecting the worldview of the writers and collectors. Little attention, though, has been paid to the dynamics of autograph exchange. A study by folklorist Stephen Stern provides some rare insights into why particular children write particular sentiments.

A related autograph book custom involves the collection of signatures from celebrities. Some participants in this custom specialize in particular kinds of celebrities (for instance, country-and-western musicians); others are more general in their approach. Some sites where a number of celebrities may be available for autographs market special books to collect their signatures. The Disney theme parks, for instance, sell books in which children can collect signatures from people dressed in the costumes of Disney characters.

William M. Clements

See also Children's Folklore; Inscription.

✳✳✳✳✳✳✳✳✳✳✳✳✳✳✳✳✳

References

Bronner, Simon J. 1988. *American Children's Folklore*. Little Rock, AR: August House.

Green, Thomas A., and Lisa Devany. 1989. Linguistic Play in Autograph Book Inscriptions. *Western Folklore* 48:51–58.

Knapp, Mary, and Herbert Knapp. 1976. *One Potato, Two Potato: The Folklore of American Children*. New York: Norton.

McNeil, W. K. 1968. The Autograph Album Custom: A Tradition and Its Scholarly Treatment. *Keystone Folklore Quarterly* 13:29–40.

———. 1969. From Advice to Lament: New York Autograph Album Verse, 1820–1850. *New York Folklore Quarterly* 25:175–194.

———. 1970. From Advice to Lament Again: New York Autograph Album Verse, 1850–1900. *New York Folklore Quarterly* 26:163–203.

Stern, Stephen. 1973. Autograph Memorabilia as an Output of Social Interaction and Communication. *New York Folklore Quarterly* 29:219–239.

Zeitlin, Steven J. 1974. As Sweet as You Are: The Structural Elements in the Signed High School Yearbook. *New York Folklore Quarterly* 30:83–100.

B

Ballad

Narrative song that is characterized chiefly by concentration on a single episode, dramatic development through dialogue and action, and objective tone and that is structurally rooted in repetitive verbal patterns and tight, balancing scenes. This definition—which applies mainly to the classical ballad, as distinct from the broadside, native American, and blues ballads—augments only slightly a definition formulated over half a century ago by Gordon Gerould. There is, however, a shift in emphasis in current approaches to the definition. Whereas Gerould attempted to define a substantive body of poetry, as epitomized by the anthologies of Francis James Child and Svend Grundtvig, a contemporary reader focuses on Gerould's attention to stylistic features and argues that balladry should be understood not as a canon of folksongs but as a way of telling a story in song using a particular narrative technique. As a result, contemporary ballad studies show a marked concern for the poetic processes of composition and interpretation, with particular emphasis on the role of formulas and other verbal and structural patterns.

Ballads are found throughout Europe and, as a result of outward European migration, in northern Africa, the Americas, and Australia, with analogues reported in India, the Orient, and Oceania. But the desire to deal with an apparently global tradition is frustrated by the need to grapple with regional forms whose differences are as apparent as their common characteristics. The most obvious distinctions are metrical. In northern Europe, ballads are stanzaic, commonly written in rhymed quatrains of alternating tetrameter and trimeter lines or, less frequently, four tetrameter lines. Couplet stanzas, often thought to be an older form, normally have interspersed refrains, whereby they are equivalent to quatrains. By contrast, many southern and eastern European ballads are stichic and exhibit varying metrical and acoustic structures: The Spanish *romanceros* are based on octosyllabic verses linked by assonance rather than rhyme; verses in Romanian ballads, normally trochaic trimeter or tetrameter, are subject to considerable variation in metrical length. It should be noted, however, that ballad scansion is variable within the confines of the melody, and rhythm is dictated primarily by four-beat melodic phrases grouped in four-line strophes. Hypermetrical or abbreviated constructions are common enough that it seems quite inappropriate to describe them as "irregular," and when ballads are sung, inconsistencies that might otherwise be apparent on the printed page are smoothed out.

One might argue here, in light of defining the ballad from the perspective of narration, that prosody is a secondary consideration having little to do with the actual way a story is told. It has been shown, however, that form has a direct bearing on style. Stichic ballads permit expansion and development more easily than strophic ones, and thus they tend to be more descriptive. Since this has implications for how formulas and other repetitive patterns function in the various traditions, researchers attempting to understand the precise details of balladic style have tended to deal with regional forms as distinct entities.

Although it is difficult to generalize about ballads on a broad scale, one can perhaps identify two overarching elements that encompass the most significant stylistic features: (1) a paratactic linking of concise narrative images (noted by David Buchan), the so-called gapped quality of the ballad, and (2) a reliance on repetition. Forgoing descriptive detail and elaborated character or scene development, the ballad tells its story through flashes of imagery, a process M.J.C. Hodgart likened to the cinematic technique of "montage." Each action and scene is clearly articulated, with actors characteristically frozen in tableau, glancing back over a shoulder, taking the hand of another, shouldering a cape, or peering over a castle wall; Lajos Vargyas described balladry as a poetry of gestures. Many other metaphors applied to the genre also point to its highly concentrated narrative style. Thomas Gray recognized the ballad tendency to "begin in the fifth act," often at a moment of imma-nent conflict; from there, it is said to "leap and linger" from one scene to the next. To the overall narrative structure, Wilhelm Grimm applied the analogy of rows of mountain peaks with the valleys between hidden from view. These characterizations, along with such typical features as a propensity for over-statement and understatement, highlight the degree to which the ballad subscribes to Axel Olrik's "epic law" of tableaux scenes. Its ideas are clear, focused, and, at the same time, intrinsically dramatic.

Repetition, within individual songs and within the broader tradition, is central to ballad technique. Indeed, Francis Gummere's notion of incremen-tal repetition (that is, narrative development through sequences of verbally patterned lines, stanzas, or stanza groupings) is a crucial one in that it shows a compositional unity between repetition and the paratactic linkages inher-ent in ballad structure. Recent Danish scholarship, particularly the work of Flemming Andersen, expands on the idea by showing that repetition has both *static* and *dynamic* functions. Static repetition includes reiterations of a single idea for the sake of intensity—"You lie, you lie, you bonny may / So loud I hear you lie." With dynamic repetition, the idea behind the pattern is modified in some way, however slightly, so that each iteration moves the narrative forward. This includes both the "progressive" forms, such as incre-mental repetition, and noncontiguous "recurrent" repetitions, which often act as frames for scenes and larger narrative units. In addition to internal repetition, commonplaces (formulas) and stylized poetic diction intrinsic to each regional tradition are standard generic conventions that further demonstrate the importance of verbal patterning in balladry.

For the most part, ballad theory has struggled to understand the cultural basis of ballad style. Early in the twentieth century, communal creationists and cultural devolutionists attempted, from contrasting perspectives, to explain ballad style in terms of long-term transmission processes. The debate was finally resolved by the notion of "communal re-creation," advanced by Cecil Sharp in England and Phillips Barry in the United States. This concept assumed individual authorship but declared it irrelevant to ballad process and focused instead on the continual reshaping of texts through a total interaction between the ballad story, the singer, and his or her community. Philological studies of the same period focused on the genre's relationship to epic, metrical romance, and other ostensibly medieval forms.

Present research tends to be more synchronically oriented and attempts to locate the role of formulas and other repetitive patterns within the larger framework of ballad poetics. Two main schools of thought have emerged, one focusing on composition, the other on interpretation. Influenced by Milman Parry and Albert B. Lord's oral-formulaic theory, several scholars have proposed that ballad style emanates from an oral re-creative process. David Buchan's work, in particular, suggests that preliterate ballad-makers relied not only on formulaic repetitions but also on complex structuring mechanisms that enabled them to maintain tight control over the organization of stanzas, scenes, and the narrative as a whole. Changes in ballad style at later stages in the tradition are thus seen to result from a literate poetic sensibility, one no longer bound by the patterned conventions of oral art.

Other analyses, such as those by Barre Toelken, Otto Holzapfel, Edith Rogers, and Flemming Andersen, have discovered a tendency for formulas to appear in stable narrative environments. The ideas embodied within the formulas thus become habitually associated with certain narrative events, such that image and action cohere as a compound structural unit. At a basic level, then, the formula foreshadows a certain course of events. From a more dynamic perspective, the two parts of the compound often establish a qualitative tension: The delicateness suggested by "he's taen her by the lily-white hand" contrasts starkly with the brutality of the acts of rape or murder that normally follow this formula. The interplay of image and action drives the narrative forward, often at an accelerated pace, but at each step of the way, ancillary tensions are generated by contrastive associations built into the stereotyped motifs. It is this apparently simple yet superbly artful way of telling a story in song that is the essence of balladry.

James Moreira

See also Folk Song, Narrative.

✱✱✱✱✱✱✱✱✱✱✱✱✱✱✱✱

References

Andersen, Flemming G. 1985. *Commonplace and Creativity*. Odense University Studies from the Medieval Centre, no. 1. Odense, Denmark: Odense University Press.

Bronson, Bertrand. 1959–1972. The *Traditional Tunes of the Child Ballads*. 4 vols. Princeton, NJ: Princeton University Press.

Buchan, David. 1972. The *Ballad and the Folk*. London: Routledge & Kegan Paul.

Catalán, Diego, J. Antonio Cid, Beatriz Mariscal, Flor Salazar, Ana Valencio, and Sandra Robertson. 1984. *Catálogo general del romancero*. 3 vols. Madrid: Seminario Menéndez-Pidal.

Child, Francis James. [1882–1898] 1965. *The English and Scottish Popular Ballads*. 5 vols. New York: Dover.

Entwistle, William J. [1939] 1951. *European Balladry*. Oxford: Clarendon.

Grundtvig, Svend, et al. [1853–1876] 1966–1976. *Danmarks gamle folkeviser*. 12 vols. Copenhagen: Universitets-Jubilæets Danske Samfund (Akademisk forlag).

Holzapfel, Otto. 1980. *Det balladeske fortællemåden i den ældre episke folkeviser* [The Balladic Narrative Method in the Older Epic Folk Songs]. Odense, Denmark: Odense Universitetsforlag.

Jonsson, Bengt, Svale Solheim, and Eva Danielson. 1978. *Types of the Scandinavian Medieval Ballad*. Instituttet for sammenlignende kulturforskning, Serie B, Skrifter LIX. Oslo: Universitetsforlaget.

Richmond, W. Edson. 1989. *Ballad Scholarship: An Annotated Bibliography*. New York: Garland.

Vargyas, Lajos. 1973. *Hungarian Ballads and the European Ballad Tradition*. 2 vols. Budapest: Akadémiai Kiadó.

Bard

Originally, an ancient Celtic poet-minstrel, who composed and performed songs eulogizing heroic deeds of chiefs and warriors. In Ireland and in Gaelic-speaking Scotland, the bardic tradition was still alive until the eighteenth century. In Wales, the original tradition disappeared after the Middle Ages but continued in the form of yearly festivals called *Eisteddfod*. An important part of the program consisted of competition in composing poems in the classical poetic devices. Romanticism gave birth to literary products eulogizing the bardic art, such as *The Poems of Ossian* by James Macpherson, *The Bard* by Thomas Gray (1757), and *An Essay on the Ancient Minstrels of England* by Bishop Thomas Percy (1765), and also to organizations and festivals promoting the revitalization of the bardic traditions—for example, the society of Welsh bards *Gorsedd* (founded in 1792), the Irish festival *Oireachtas* organized by the Gaelic League (and held since 1818), and the *Mod*, the equivalent event in Gaelic-speaking Scotland that was organized by the Gaelic Language Society.

In addition, *bard* is often used as a general term for singers and/or composers of (especially) epic folk poetry. The synonyms are *minstrel* or *troubadour*.

In Western Europe, the bardic traditions have left such epic monuments as the *Beowulf* (eighth century A.D.), the *Nibelungenlied* (thirteenth century A.D.), and the *Song of Roland* (eleventh century A.D.). The *Iliad* and *Odyssey* will be treated later in this entry.

In most parts of Europe, the bardic traditions in their oral form disappeared before the nineteenth century. In certain areas along the eastern border of Europe, some of the epic poetry cultures have survived to the present—the south Slavic epics performed by bards called *guslar*, Russian *bylina* poetry, or Finnic *Kalevala* poetry, for example.

South Slavic epic poetry saw centuries of dynamic, productive output that continued well into the twentieth century. The performers of both Finnish and Russian folklore, in the golden age of collection in the nineteenth century, were largely peasants living in remote regions, people engaged in hunting or itinerant occupations. The art of singing was still common in the nineteenth century (and to some extent in the twentieth century), but active professional singing of heroic and mythical songs was on the way out. Female singers performing largely lyric-epic and lyric songs often remained productive longer than their male counterparts.

In spite of the fact that most of the bardic traditions are dying out, there are several epic poetry cultures still alive, especially in various parts of Asia and Africa. The tradition is kept up, in many cases, by the elderly, those of seventy or eighty, and it will die with them. For instance, the epic of *Džangar* is still known among the Oirats in northwest China (Xinjiang), but most of the singers are very old. Formerly, this epic was known among the Kalmyks in the Volga region, in Mongolia, and also among the Buriats, who inhabit the region around Lake Baikal. The epic of *Geser* was spread mainly within the sphere of Tibetan cultural influence in Tibet, Mongolia, and among the Buriats and also in Nepal, Bhutan, Sikkim, and Ladakh. This heroic epic can still be encountered in some rather inaccessible areas. Convincing evidence of existing epics is to be found among various Turkic peoples (e.g., the Kirghiz *Manas*) and also among other peoples living in the Middle East, Central Asia, and Siberia. There are also rich epic poetry cultures in some parts of Southeast Asia and the Indian subcontinent.

Formerly, unfamiliarity with the material and inadequate knowledge of local oral traditions, cultural history, and other relevant contextual information led some scholars to assert that there were no bardic traditions in Africa. At present, there is enough evidence to demonstrate that there are several rich and influential epics in different parts of the continent—for example, the *jeli* (often called *griots*) among the Mande-speaking populations in West

Africa, the epics called *mvet* of Cameroon, Gabon, and Equatorial Guinea, or the *Nyanga* epic from Zaire. The performing of the epics (such as *Sunjiata*) is often only one of the manifold social roles of the bards.

On the basis of new fieldwork methods and materials, it is possible to draw a more complete picture of the art of the bards from all over the world, considering topics such as the variety of epic genres, modes of performance, differences between mythic, historical, and lyric-epic songs, and roles in society. One of the most interesting areas of contemporary research focuses on the coexistence and mutual influence between oral and literary epics and the use of epics in modern culture. In many cases, dominant concepts or ideologies have helped to strengthen the vitality of the impulsive use of epic poetry. This kind of situation also inspired a large number of new epic songs. Bardic poetry has been in constant use as a productive tradition adapting to new situations.

THE PROBLEM OF BARDIC ART AND
ORAL COMPOSITION

In 1795, Friedrich Wolf argued in his *Prolegomena ad Homerum* that Homer could not have composed such long poems as the *Iliad* and *Odyssey*. According to him, the Homeric poems were composed orally in the form of short songs and edited later to obtain the unity they ultimately had. Wolf maintained that the Homeric poems were composed before the Greeks were acquainted with writing. For that reason, he contended, it was not possible to create such long epic texts as the Homeric epos.

Milman Parry and Albert B. Lord suggested that the performers of south Slavic epic songs created their texts in the performance situation by means of formulas, themes, and an overall structure, the "stable skeleton of narrative." The production of folk poetry varied thus from one performing situation to another—the singers were using a method that Parry and Lord referred to as *composition in performance*. Parry's basic aim was to prove that the *Iliad* and the *Odyssey* too were composed orally in a traditional style. South Slavic epic poetry was proved to be oral and traditional. Since the Greek heroic epics also revealed the same type of features of traditionality and orality, Parry and Lord asserted that they were composed using the same mode of composition. In his study *The Singer of Tales*, published in 1960, Lord presented a summary of Parry's theses as well as his own research. It is necessary to note, however, that only the starting point of the Parry-Lord theory was literary in the sense that the authors aimed at solving the classical Homeric question. During the years since Lord's work appeared, this approach, originally devoted to classical literature, has expanded into a universal school. In the bibliography *Oral-Formulaic Theory and Research* by John M. Foley, over 1,800 monographs on materials from more than 90 language areas are mentioned. In addition to the Homeric and south Slavic epic, the advocates of the oral-formulaic school have focused on the Anglo-Saxon *Beowulf*, as well as a number of other classic epics and living traditions.

Milman Parry and Albert Lord's argument can be supported by many bardic traditions. In fact, an oral singer can produce an epic song longer than the *Iliad* and *Odyssey* and the Finnish *Kalevala* put together. The Tajik singer of the *Gurguli* epics Hikmet Rizo has sung a version with a total length of 101,596 verses. Sayaqbay Qaralaev, one of the best-known Kirghiz epic singers (*manasci*), has produced a version of the *Manas*-cycle (Manas, Semetey, Seytek) totaling more than half a million verses. Another famous Kirghiz singer, S. Orozbaqov, has produced a version that comprises over 180,000 verses.

By using a set of narrative techniques, a singer is capable of composing long epics without having memorized them or created them beforehand. Singers are able to use this technique to vary and compose long narrative structures during performance. As singers produce their versions of epics, they make use of the line sequences commonly encountered in tradition, some of which are suitable for setting the scene for several plot structures or describing different events, others for rather few entities. In studies of epic singing among various peoples, one often finds mention of singers who are able to repeat a long narrative poem after only a single hearing or rapidly producing a new poem on a given theme.

The singer has at his or her disposal the traditional means of epic poetry: metrical patterns, parallelism, alliteration, rhyme, anaphora, or other devices of diction. During the composition process, the bard elaborates on the song according to his or her own preferences and the circumstance. In order to perform an entire epic song, the singer has to master simultaneously a number of systems. The memory of the singer works on multilevel representations containing features of surface and meaning structure. Formulas, ideas, and images join in a coherent whole; certain scenes and themes include particular details and clusters of forms. As a result of this composition process, bardic art is simultaneously innovative and traditional.

The training of the bard takes place over a long period, involving numerous stages of development. A. B. Lord's account of the south Slavic oral-formulaic learning process is famous. According to Lord, this process consists of three stages. The first is a period of passive listening, during which the singer learns the general themes and plot structures of his region. This stage is followed by a period of practice, during which the singer-to-be, who already knows how to sing, gradually learns to fit the material learned into traditional metrical and musical frameworks. The third stage is the making of the singer: the first performance of an entire song before a critical audience. Albert Lord mentioned the learning capabilities of the Bosnian master singer Avdo

Medjeović, describing a situation in which another singer—Mumin Vlahovljak—performed a song that Avdo had never heard. After Mumin had finished, Avdo praised the song but stated that he could perform it better. Although Mumin's version was already thousands of lines in length, Avdo's interpretation was even longer. Avdo's poem was more complete than that which Mumin had presented, and it made use of standard elements characteristic of Avdo's repertoire in its construction.

Although the skill of the gifted singer made it possible to improvise on the basis of traditional forms and to repeat a song after hearing it only once, as a general collective expression it was considered that the epic poems had to be repeated in a traditional, standard form. The study of epic poetry nonetheless reveals signs of considerable variation. Among the features of epic poems (and indeed of folklore in general) is a tendency to preserve the linguistic and poetic conventions that have become familiar and primary in the community and also to produce folklore tied to the history, social development, and cultural conditions of the community. One may find abundant examples of these concepts in studies of epic songs among various peoples. In some poetic cultures, the performers generally produce relatively fixed entities (small-scale epics); in others, the singers compile poems by drawing on traditional devices in relatively free combinations (large-scale epics). According to this distinction, Finnish-Karelian and Russian bards normally belong to the former category; the epic poetry of the southern Slavs, especially the Bosnian and the Herzegovinian Moslem singers as well as those in numerous Mongolian and Turkic traditions, belong largely to the latter category.

In addition, it has to be noted that there are abundant examples of epic traditions in which diverse genres play an important role. Epics in such traditions might contain chapters in verse hagiography or panegyric, prose sections (or prosimetric) forms, fragments of lyric elegy or laments, or even proverbs and riddles.

The mode of performance may be flexible and varied. The singers can perform on various occasions, for different audiences, and they are able to choose the chapter to be performed according to the context. Such "eposes in the making" clearly show how important it has been to challenge the literary-based concept of the epics and bardic traditions.

Lauri Harvilahti

See also Ethnopoetics; Folk Song, Narrative.

❋❋❋❋❋❋❋❋❋❋❋❋❋❋❋❋❋❋❋

References

Foley, John Miles. 1985. *Oral-Formulaic Theory and Research: An Introduction and Annotated Bibliography*. New York: Garland.

Honko, Lauri, ed. 1990. *Religion, Myth, and Folklore in the World's Epics*. New York: Mouton de Gruyter.

Honko, L., S. Timonen, and M. Branch. 1993. *The Great Bear: A Thematic Anthology of Oral Poetry in the Finno-Ugric Languages*. Helsinki: Finnish Literature Society.

Johnson, John, ed. 1992. *The Epic of Son-Jara: A West African Tradition*. Text by Fa-Digi Sisòkò. Bloomington: Indiana University Press.

Lord, A. B. 1960. *The Singer of Tales*. Cambridge, MA: Harvard.

Oinas, Felix, ed. 1978. *Heroic Epic and Saga: An Introduction to the World's Great Folk Epics*. Bloomington: Indiana University Press.

Reichl, Karl. 1992. *Turkic Epic Poetry: Traditions, Forms, Poetic Structure*. New York: Garland.

Belief Folk

A broad genre of folklore that includes expressions and behaviors variously called superstition, popular belief, magic, the supernatural, old wives' tales, folk medicine, folk religion, weather signs, planting signs, conjuration, hoodoo, root work, portents, omens, charms, and taboos. Alan Dundes has formulated a structural definition of folk belief (underlying patterns remain the same even if the content changes) in order to avoid the pejorative connotations of many of the terms just listed. Superstitions are traditional expressions that have conditions and results (if a black cat crosses a person's path, he or she will have bad luck; a halo around the moon means rain the next day). In some superstitions, the conditions are causal (the black cat is the cause of bad luck), and in some, they are not (the halo is a sign of rain, not the cause of it). The belief that spilling salt means bad luck has a cause condition (spilling the salt) and a result (bad luck). Since spilling the salt causes the bad luck, a conversion ritual is possible—in this case, throwing the salt over one's shoulder in order to negate the bad luck.

The underlying structure is not always apparent in the spoken belief, as in the widespread expression "knock on wood." The cause condition here is not spoken but is part of the context of behavior. Someone says, "I've been driving for thirty years and never had an accident" and follows with "knock on wood." The unspoken cause condition and result—that is, that saying an event has not happened will actually cause it to happen—shows the magic power of uttering words. The only expressed structural element is the conversion ritual—knocking on wood—which then negates the result element—an accident taking place. This example also illustrates the need to examine the behavioral context in order to understand the folk belief; the verbal expression only contains a part of the meaning of the event. Using the structural definition helps us to better see the contextual elements and to avoid making judgments about the people who practice the belief.

Folklorists and anthropologists who studied superstition in the nineteenth and early part of the twentieth century definitely were making judgments about the tradition-bearers of folk belief. One school of thought saw superstitions as survivals of primitive rituals, so that knocking on wood, for instance, would be based on an appeal to vegetation gods. The problem with this theory is that it is not based on evidence of actual belief or behavior in the past; rather, it is a hypothesis that works backward from present-day evidence. Also, the survivalist theory does not tell us much about belief in practice in present-day situations; people who knock on wood are not aware of appealing to vegetation gods. Earlier scholars associated superstitions with the peasantry in rural environments, which caused them to neglect the study of superstitious behavior in urban, industrial, or middle- and upper-class environments. There was an implicit condescension toward the bearers of folk belief as the "other," groups of people whose culture suffered arrested development.

Folklorists have long recognized the need for a neutral term to designate traditional beliefs in order to avoid ethnocentric bias in studying human behavior: In 1930, Alexander Krappe wrote, "Superstition, in common parlance, designates the sum of beliefs and practices shared by other people in so far as they differ from our own. What we believe and practise [sic] ourselves is, of course, Religion." More recently, in 1977, Lawrence W. Levine noted that "in the cultures from which the [African-American] slaves came, phenomena and activities that we might be tempted to dismiss as 'superstitious' were legitimate and important modes of comprehending and operating within a universe perceived of in sacred terms. To distinguish these activities and beliefs from religion is a meaningless exercise." Religious beliefs and folk beliefs may be similar in terms of structure and function; their differences lie in the way they are perceived by different groups. As many folklorists have pointed out, folk beliefs are found not just among isolated, uneducated, or exotic groups but among all peoples.

Given the diversity and cross-cultural spread of folk belief, one of the central problems in the scholarship in this field is classification. What scheme will be able to handle the seemingly unending variety of topics and examples from different cultures all around the world? Wayland D. Hand formulated a classification based on "the cycle of life," which has proven useful in organizing folk belief collections. The categories are: (1) birth, infancy, childhood; (2) human body, folk medicine; (3) home, domestic pursuits; (4) economic, social relationships; (5) travel, communication; (6) love, courtship, marriage; (7) death and funereal customs; (8) witchcraft, ghosts, magical practices; (9) cosmic phenomena: times, numbers, seasons; (10) weather; (11) animals, animal husbandry; (12) fishing and hunting; (13) plants, plant husbandry; and (14) miscellaneous. These categories are subdivided into more specific topics—for instance, the fourth category (economic, social relationships) is divided into (a) prosperity, wealth; (b) works, trades, professions; (c) religion;

(d) friends, enemies; (e) recreation, sports, games; and (f) lying, thievery, legal guilt, murder, etcetera. The stuff of human drama, this list gives some idea of the range of topics and concerns that make up folk belief.

The cycle of life classification system is based on the concept of the rite of passage as formulated by Arnold van Gennep. Rites of passage take place at points in the life cycle where important transitions from one stage of life to another occur. Ritual and magic tend to be concentrated at these points to aid in the transition; Hand's classification system illustrates this with major categories of folk belief located at birth, marriage, and death. In many circumstances, folk belief as part of human cultural activity can only be understood as it relates to ritual. For example, beliefs about marriage are often expressed as part of the ritual of weddings, so that the traditions of throwing rice at the newly married couple or wearing "something old, something new, something borrowed, something blue" have to be studied in terms of the overall customs and behavior associated with the wedding itself.

In the past, folklorists tended to collect superstitions as statements of belief without exploring related behavior or varying degrees of belief, concentrating on texts and ignoring contexts. Developments in the anthropological study of magic and ritual, specifically the work of Bronislaw Malinowski and other functionalists, have caused folklore research in folk belief to become more contextual. Malinowski conducted fieldwork on magic and ritual among Trobriand Islanders, and out of this research, he formulated the anxiety-ritual theory: Wherever there is uncertainty in life, anxiety will arise, and magic and ritual will be used to gain a sense of control. Numerous researchers have pointed out how the anxiety-ritual theory applies to various occupational groups involved with high-risk work. For instance, the research of Patrick B. Mullen indicates that commercial fishermen have a system of occupational folk belief that helps them to cope with the physical and financial risks of their work. When they start out on a long fishing trip in potentially dangerous waters, they perform rituals such as throwing coins overboard, they avoid saying words such as "alligator" or "rabbit," and they avoid particular actions such as turning the hatch cover upside down in order to ensure a safe and profitable trip. The pattern of anxiety and ritual can be observed among athletes involved in big games, actors on opening night, students taking exams, and lovers who are suspicious of their mates—in other words, among any group or in any individual who faces any form of uncertainty and anxiety.

Scholars have criticized this functional explanation of superstitious behavior because it concentrates on abstract cultural forces as determinants of behavior to the exclusion of varying individual causes. The idea that folklore, in this case folk belief, is only a reflection of preexisting cultural patterns such as anxiety-ritual oversimplifies the complex ways in which folklore can be an imaginative means of dealing with life. Folk belief in a specific context can serve many other individual needs as well as relieve anxiety. For instance, some commercial fishermen who work as deckhands have been known to follow the traditional occupational belief in throwing coins overboard to buy wind in order to get off work early, and coal miners who do not want women working in the mines can cite the traditional belief that women are bad luck in mines. In both cases, folk belief is used in individual creative ways as part of strategies to control specific situations, not to relieve anxiety. A person who expresses a folk belief may not actually believe it and may be using it to parody another's behavior, to challenge accepted rules rather than reinforce them. In order to comprehend the multiple meanings and functions of folk belief, we have to examine the specific circumstances in which it occurs, noting such features as verbal expression, behavior, responses of others present, and so forth.

Recently, folklorists have begun to apply performance theory to the study of folk belief in order to get at the ways in which expressions of belief do more than simply reflect worldview but actually help to reconstruct the culture itself. Folk belief as part of a dynamic, ongoing tradition is not static but continually undergoing change as individuals adapt received knowledge to specific circumstances. Performance theory provides an approach for examining the nuances of verbal expression and behavior when superstitions are discussed or acted upon. Definitions of folklore from a performance perspective seem to exclude folk belief since they emphasize *artistic* communication and the utterance of a belief or the practicing of a superstition is not ordinarily thought of as an artistic expression. An argument could be made that these behaviors contain an artistic component in that they often depend on metaphor and analogy, but even if they are not artistic communication, they are subject to certain formulas and framing devices, in performance terms, the keys that set them off from other kinds of expressions and establish clues to their rhetorical purpose. Gary R. Butler has done extensive research on folk belief in a French Newfoundland community, applying concepts of performance to identify and analyze narrative and conversation frames in the "discourse of belief."

As Butler and others have discovered, folk beliefs are often expressed in other genres of folklore, such as narratives (memorates and legends), customs, rituals, foodways, proverbs, and rhymes. Examples of the cross-genre nature of folk belief also indicate the cross-cultural pervasiveness of superstitious behavior. Memorates are stories told from a first- or secondhand point of view with a belief at their core—for instance, a story about a personal encounter with a ghost would be a memorate because the belief in ghosts is essential to the narrative. A story one tells about a friend walking under a ladder and then being hit by a car also would be classified as a memorate because it is based on a superstition. The storyteller does not necessarily have to believe in the core folk belief; for example, a person could tell about starting a trip on Friday and

*Tom Thumb is an example of the folk belief in the diminutive fairy child,
a popular character in French and English folklore.*

having good luck on the trip, a story that would counter the traditional belief in Friday as an unlucky day. Often, folk beliefs are expressed in narrative form to prove or disprove them.

Legends are usually removed from the first- or secondhand point of view of the memorate; they are told about events in the past that were not observed by the teller or someone the teller knows. In addition, certain kinds of legends also have folk belief at their core. The legend of the Flying Dutchman is about a ship doomed to sail the seas for eternity because of the actions of a blasphemous captain. The central belief here is that blasphemy (the cause condition in structural terms) can bring about a supernatural punishment (the result), indicating an area where religious and folk beliefs overlap.

Customs and rituals also contain folk beliefs that are essential to their meanings. The aforementioned wedding customs have many beliefs associated with them, mostly ones meant to guarantee good luck for the bride and groom as they begin a new stage of life. Folk beliefs are also an integral part of holiday customs, where they often intersect with foodways. In the southern United States among certain groups, there is a custom of eating black-eyed peas (always made with salt pork) on New Year's Day to ensure good luck for the rest of the year, an example that illustrates how belief, custom, and foodways interact. Beliefs exist as folk knowledge and are then put into practice as customary behavior. It is through the behavior that the belief itself is usually learned; a child may never hear that it is good luck to have black-eyed peas on New Year's but will learn the belief when the dish is served. A novice coal miner may not hear that it is bad luck to whistle in the mine until he whistles and is fired for breaking the taboo. Folk beliefs do not exist solely in the abstract but also in actual practice and behavior. Again, folklore is not merely a reflection of an abstract cultural worldview; it exists in everyday life as a means of creating culture.

Often, folk beliefs are expressed as proverbs or rhymes in situations in which such communication is appropriate. Weather signs can be more easily remembered and passed on if they are given in the form of a rhyme: "Red sun at night, sailor's delight; red sun at morning, sailor's take warning." Children's rhymes sometimes have expression of folk belief in them, such as "Step on a crack, and you'll break your mother's back." Some children may believe this to the extent that it affects their behavior: While walking down a sidewalk, they will avoid stepping on any cracks out of fear that they may hurt their mothers. An expression such as "An apple a day keeps the doctor away" is also a folk medical belief that has come to be expressed in the fixed form of a traditional proverb. "Rats leave a sinking ship" can be used as a metaphorical proverb to express contempt for someone who abandons a failing project, but it is also a folk belief, an omen of impending disaster.

Omens, portents, and signs indicate human concern with the uncertainty of the future; science cannot predict what the future holds, but folk belief provides ways for people to believe they can foretell future events. We have everything from astrology, numerology, tarot cards, and palm reading to Ouija boards, children's games, and jump rope rhymes for predicting the future. Many of these devices could be thought of as divination rituals, ways of divining the future. For example, children make folk toys out of folded paper, which they then inscribe with predictions and color codes. By moving the folded paper with their fingers a certain number of times and identifying colors within, they can predict whom they will marry, what kind of cars they will drive, what kind of houses they will live in, and so forth. Children's traditional play activities often have underlying belief elements that help to explain the child's concerns and developing worldview.

Folk beliefs are often part of complex cultural processes that involve not only belief but also values and other behaviors and that find expression in different genres of folklore. The widespread cross-cultural belief in the evil eye is expressed verbally as a direct statement, through gestures and sayings as a conversion ritual, and through elaborate cures to take away the effects of the evil eye; underlying this complex of behaviors are certain values that help to explain its meanings. Known in Spanish as *mal de ojo* and in Italian as *mal'occhio* and found throughout the Mediterranean and other parts of the world settled by ethnic groups from the Mediterranean region, the concept of the evil eye varies from culture to culture, but certain patterns persist. Often, the evil eye is given unintentionally by someone who is praising a person or an object. "What a beautiful vase on your mantel," someone remarks; two days later, the vase falls and breaks. "What a darling little girl," comments another; the next day, the child becomes ill, and the doctors cannot diagnose what is wrong with her. The evil eye may be the cause, according to folk belief.

The underlying value that seems to inform the belief and the behavior lies in the importance of envy. The assumption is that to praise a person or an object is an indirect expression of envy. The belief in the power of the evil eye is actually, then, a warning against envy because even the unconscious feeling of envy can cause destruction and illness. The cultures that have a belief in the evil eye also have folkloric means of dealing with it; there are conversion rituals that, when used with expressions of praise, can prevent the evil eye from having an effect. For example, in Puerto Rico, if one praises a young girl, one also touches her lightly on the head to ward off the evil eye. Among Italian-Americans, the praise is accompanied by a blessing: "What a darling little girl; God bless her." There are also traditional cures for the evil eye in Italian and Italian-American culture. A bowl of water is placed near the person suspected of having an illness caused by the evil eye, oil is dropped into the water, and words from Scripture are recited. The movement of the oil indicates the efficacy of the cure. In a large city in the northern United States, an Italian-American woman has even performed the cure over the telephone, indicating the way folk belief adapts to technological change. Since the ritual involves both healing and religion, the evil eye can be studied as both a medical and a religious phenomenon.

Folk medicine and folk religion are major areas of study in themselves, but both are fundamentally concerned with the study of belief and associated behavior. Folk medical beliefs or folk cures are traditional ways of dealing with health problems. They are often used in conjunction with scientific medicine, and, in fact, there is no clear distinction between folk and scientific medicine in terms of efficacy. Herbal cures, for instance, have been tested by traditional usage over long periods of time and are often found to have an empirical basis when examined scientifically. Studies of folk medicine have concentrated on rural and isolated areas that do not offer easy access to medical facilities; these communities have a correspondingly greater dependency on folk medical practices. Here, as with many other kinds of folk belief, the belief itself may be carried forward in narrative form. Mary Lozier, who lived for years in an isolated hollow in the mountains of Kentucky, told the story of her young son being bitten by a deadly copperhead snake. The boy's grandmother knew of a traditional poultice made from chopped onions, which she placed on the snakebite to draw out the poison. By the time the boy's father, John, came home with the car, the boy was able to run out to meet him to tell him he was bitten by a snake. The narrative indicates a strong degree of belief, describes the actual practice of the belief in a specific situation, and serves to pass on the tradition to listeners.

Other studies of folk medicine show that when rural people migrate to cities, they take their folk practices with them and adapt them to the new environment. An Appalachian migrant in Detroit will not be able to gather wild yellowroot, which is used for coughs and colds, but she can often find packaged ground yellowroot at the drugstore. Because of a traditional distrust of doctors and hospitals, some ethnic groups turn to folk medicine even when other forms of medicine are available. Mexican-Americans in south Texas continue to consult traditional healers, *curanderos*, for such problems as *susto*, a sickness caused by a magic spell, because medical doctors might dismiss such a cause as ignorant superstition. Many Native Americans still prefer traditional medicine men to non–Native American doctors for religious reasons and cultural identity.

Faith healing is an area in which folk medicine and folk religion overlap since religious belief is the foundation for the curing process. Various forms of faith healing exist in different religions and cultures: The healing may be done by an individual within the church who has healing powers, or self-healing may be accomplished through prayer. Jesse Hatcher, an elderly African-American man from the Blue Ridge Mountains of Virginia, told visitors to his farm of the time he prayed to God to heal a goiter on his neck and found the goiter gone the next day. The memorate is once again the means of expressing belief by giving evidence in support of it.

Weather and planting signs are used to determine future courses of action. Weather beliefs usually have the sign condition structure since the conditions on which they are based are not seen as causal. Cloud formations, sunspots, wind direction, and halos around the moon do not cause the weather to change but rather are indications that help to predict the weather. Weather beliefs are not usually designed to attempt to control the weather but are used in outdoor occupations such as farming and fishing to plan activities ahead of time. Planting signs are used by farmers and gardeners to determine the best time to plant particular crops. Farmers' almanacs are important in this tradition because they print the signs of the zodiac in relation to the calendar. By consulting the almanac, the farmer will know what crops to plant under which signs in order to grow the biggest and best crops. As with folk medicine, planting by the signs is often used in conjunction with current scientific agricultural techniques.

These examples from rural and ethnic groups should not be taken as an indication that folk belief is confined to cultures outside the mainstream; there is copious evidence to suggest that folk beliefs and associated behaviors are widespread throughout the population—at all income and education levels, in urban and suburban environments, and in technological fields of endeavor. Alan Dundes pointed out the influence of the magic number three on scientific and medical patterns and in academic textbooks. So-called New Age activities are another area in which folk beliefs currently are being widely practiced. Many New Age beliefs are borrowed from other cultures, such as the Native American culture, or are revived based on historical records of pre-Christian religions. We find educated, middle-class people in urban areas carrying crystals in pockets or purses in order to ensure good luck in their daily lives or people practicing ancient forms of belief such as Wicca, calling themselves witches. These new forms of traditional behavior have not been widely studied by folklorists, but they should be seriously examined by scholars interested in folk belief as part of human behavior.

The study of folk belief has come a long way from the nineteenth-century concern with primitive survivals to the late-twentieth-century concern with everyday behavior, from a model based on the progress of civilization to a model based on the social construction of reality. The early scholars thought of themselves as standing at the most developed point of civilization, examining inferior modes of thought of primitives and peasants. Contemporary scholars see *themselves* as practicing certain forms of folk belief, constructing their scholarly schemes for ordering the world in some of the same ways others use religion or folk belief to construct their own patterns. The anxiety-ritual theory, after all, fits the structural pattern of superstition with a cause condition (uncertainty) and a result (magic). This scholarly paradigm shift has taken place over a century of time, and many of the insights into folk belief, culture, and human behavior are still ahead of us if the model of progress has any validity at all.

Patrick B. Mullen

See also Belief Tale; Charm; Divination; Medicine, Folk; Religion, Folk.

✳✳✳✳✳✳✳✳✳✳✳✳✳✳✳✳✳

References

Butler, Gary R. 1990. *Saying Isn't Believing: Conversation, Narrative and the Discourse of Belief in a French Newfoundland Community.* St. John's, Newfoundland: Institute of Social and Economic Research.

Dundes, Alan. 1975. *Analytic Essays in Folklore.* The Hague: Mouton.

Hand, Wayland D., ed. 1964 [1961]. *Popular Beliefs and Superstitions from North Carolina,* vols. 6 and 7 of The Frank C. Brown Collection of North Carolina Folklore, ed. Newman Ivey White. Durham, NC: Duke University Press.

Jahoda, Gustav. 1969. *The Psychology of Superstition*. London: Penguin.

Krappe, Alexander H. 1930. *The Science of Folklore*. New York: Barnes and Noble.

Lessa, William A., and Evon Z. Vogt, eds. 1979. 4th edition. *Reader in Comparative Religion: An Anthropological Approach*. New York: Harper and Row. See these chapters: George C. Homans, "Anxiety and Ritual: The Theories of Malinowki and Radcliffe-Brown," Bronislaw Malinowski, "The Role of Magic and Religion," and A. R. Radcliffe-Brown, "Taboo."

Levine, Lawrence W. 1977. *Black Culture and Black Consciousness: Afro-American Folk Thought from Slavery to Freedom*. New York: Oxford University Press.

Malinowski, Bronislaw. 1948. *Magic, Science and Religion and Other Essays*. Boston: Free Press.

Mullen, Patrick B. 1978. *I Heard the Old Fishermen Say: Folklore of the Texas Gulf Coast*. Austin: University of Texas Press.

van Gennep, Arnold. 1960. *The Rites of Passage*. Chicago: University of Chicago Press.

Belief Tale

Folk narratives that, in the context of their telling, have degrees of belief as a factor. Folklorists classify folk narratives into a multitude of categories (genres) that overlap and cause confusion because these genres are based on different principles, such as content (themes, motifs, concepts, and ideas), context (degree of belief, social function, and distance between storyteller and audience), and texture (point of view, imagery, tone, and other stylistic variables). *Belief tale* is sometimes used as a term synonymous with *legend* because *legend*, in its broadest sense, is thought of as a story in which belief is a contextual factor that is either wholly or partially believed or rejected. Some folklorists define *belief tales* more narrowly as stories about the supernatural and distinguish them from historical legends about individuals and events. The classification problem in this case arises from using content and context in inconsistent ways; the broad category is based on context (belief), and the narrow is based on content (supernatural events).

Another problem is that the classification systems often combine etic categories, imposed from the outside by scholars, and emic ones, based on native distinctions. A particular story may be told as a joke in certain circumstances (emic), but based on the scholars' examination of content, it may be classified as a belief tale (etic). For instance, old sailors tell a story about a man who was becalmed while out on his sailboat; he followed an ancient folk belief and threw a half-dollar overboard to buy wind. The wind came, blew his sails and mast down, and overturned the boat, and his wife and children were drowned. The same basic story is often told without the tragic ending and with a punch line: "If you get that much wind for a half-dollar, fifteen cents' worth would have been plenty." Both stories contain the core folk belief about buying the wind, but the first story would be classified as a legend or belief tale by a folklorist, and the second story, with the same content except for the ending, would be called a joke by storyteller and audience alike.

The classification of belief tales is further complicated by shifting points of view. The story on buying the wind is told about an event that happened in the past and was not observed by the storyteller or by someone he or she knew. Because the event was removed from the experience of the storyteller, folklorists classify it as a legend, as opposed to a memorate—that is, a belief tale based on first- or secondhand personal experience. If someone tells a story about his or her own experience of throwing coins overboard to buy wind, then that narrative is a memorate. But, we might ask, who cares about this distinction? Certainly, the persons telling the stories do not care what folklorists label their narratives; again, we have the problem of scholarly categories not having much to do with actual behavior in specific situations.

Folklorists are now more interested in the processes of tradition, the ways in which belief, behavior, and storytelling about belief interact in everyday life. Telling ghost stories may serve to reinforce a belief in ghosts, or it may make fun of the belief in ghosts. Stories about supernatural events can help to relieve anxiety over fears of the unknown and provide ways of expressing emotions that may be difficult to articulate directly. For example, some people tell of visitations by the recently deceased. Often, the spiritual visitor reassures the person about the afterlife and advises the loved one not to mourn excessively. The belief tales based on these experiences help the person to cope with the loss and get through the mourning period.

The belief tale concentrates on inexplicable experiences in human life and helps to explain the mysterious and unknown. Whether the stories are ancient ones passed down as legends or new ones based on personal experience in the recent past, they are concerned with the supernatural and become part of the ongoing debate about the existence of a spiritual realm beyond the empirically observable world.

Patrick B. Mullen

See also Belief, Folk; Legend.

✳✳✳✳✳✳✳✳✳✳✳✳✳✳✳✳✳

References

Bennett, Gillian. 1987. *Traditions of Belief: Women, Folklore, and the Supernatural Today*. New York: Penguin Books.

Dégh, Linda, and Andrew Vázsonyi. 1976. Legend and Belief. In *Folklore Genres*, ed. Dan Ben-Amos. Austin: University of Texas Press.

Hand, Wayland D., ed. 1971. *American Folk Legend: A Symposium*. Berkeley: University of California Press.

Honko, Lauri. 1964. Memorates and the Study of Folk Beliefs. *Journal of the Folklore Institute* 1:5–19.

Mullen, Patrick B. 1978. *I Heard the Old Fishermen Say: Folklore of the Texas Gulf Coast.* Austin: University of Texas Press.

von Sydow, C. W. 1948. *Selected Papers on Folklore.* Copenhagen: Rosenkilde and Bagger.

*B*LASON *POPULAIRE*

Brief characterization of a group of which one is not a member. Sometimes, *blason populaire* (literally, popular emblem) is used as a synonym for *ethnic joke*, but the term more accurately applies to the stereotype that informs the joke. Ethnicity has been the most usual factor in generating such outgroup (or exoteric) folklore. But other kinds of outgroups (religious, geographical, or occupational, for example) may become the targets for pithy depictions; these, in fact, appear in a variety of folklore genres.

Perhaps the simplest form of *blason populaire* is the group nickname. Although they may communicate nothing specific in their characterizations of the groups they target, terms such as *nigger* or *spick* suggest derogation through their harsh, cacophonous sounds. Slightly more complex is the use of group names to characterize objects and behaviors (*Indian giver* or *French letter*). The *blason populaire* may also appear in traditional similes: "as tight as a Scotsman" or "like a Chinese fire drill." In addition, proverbs can arise from *blasons populaires*: "A Swabian has no heart but two stomachs."

Ethnic jokes and other narratives provide the opportunity for more developed use of the *blason populaire* in folklore. Such forms may assign particular characteristics to particular groups and play upon conventional stereotypes, such as that of the "dumb blonde." But specific characterizations often rest on a foundation that seems to figure into *blasons populaires* in general: that of the Other, one whose most important traits stem from differentness from the group among whom the *blason populaire* circulates. Hence, in ethnic jokes in the United States, where such virtues as efficiency, cleanliness, and orderliness are valued, the target of exoteric folklore, no matter what the particular group, is depicted as inefficient, dirty, and disorganized. *Blasons populaires* often imply the lack of humanity of their targets. For example, when Europeans began to contact the indigenous peoples of the Western Hemisphere in the sixteenth century, they often depicted them as naked cannibals, their alleged eating habits and lack of clothing assigning them to subhuman status. During particular periods in a group's history, members of group may be the target of *blasons populaires*. During the last half of the nineteenth century, for instance, Irish immigration to the United States produced stereotypical depictions of

Irish men and women in various media. Joke cycles occasionally center for a while upon a particular group. The next time the cycle comes around, the same jokes may target another group. *Märchen, novelle,* folksongs, and material culture also make use of *blasons populaires.*

Research into *blasons populaires* by folklorists has focused mostly upon their manifestations in ethnic jokes. Some studies simply have reported and cataloged the phenomenon, but others have delved more deeply into the sociological, historical, and cultural factors that generate the stereotypical attitudes that the *blason populaire* captures. Seldom have studies of *blasons populaires* examined how these exoteric characterizations emerge in performance, an important exception being Keith Basso's investigation of depictions of the "whiteman" among Western Apaches. Sociologists and psychologists, who often rely on questionnaires rather than the ways *blasons populaires* occur in traditional culture, also have worked with these exoteric characterizations.

William M. Clements

See also Esoteric/Exoteric Factor; Ethnic Folklore; Joke.

✳✳✳✳✳✳✳✳✳✳✳✳✳✳✳✳✳

References

Basso, Keith A. 1979. *Portraits of "the Whiteman": Linguistic Play and Cultural Symbols among the Western Apache.* Cambridge: Cambridge University Press.

Birnbaum, Mariana D. 1971. On the Language of Prejudice. *Western Folklore* 30:247–268.

Davies, Christie. 1990. *Ethnic Humor around the World: A Comparative Analysis.* Bloomington: Indiana University Press.

Dundes, Alan. 1971. A Study of Ethnic Slurs: The Jew and the Polack in the United States. *Journal of American Folklore* 84:186–203.

———. 1975. Slurs International: Folk Comparisons of Ethnicity and National Character. *Southern Folklore Quarterly* 39:15–38.

Gaidoz, Henri, and Paul Sebillot. 1884. *Blason populaire de la France.* Paris: Leopard Serf.

Joanne, Wm. Hugh. 1957. A Culture's Stereotypes and Their Expression in Folk Clichés. *Southwestern Journal of Anthropology* 13:184–200.

———. 1959. The Esoteric-Exoteric Factor in Folklore. *Fabula* 2:205–211.

Roebuck, A. A. 1944. *A Dictionary of International Slurs (Ethnophaulisms).* Cambridge, MA: Sci-Art.

Boast

Formulaic praise of self or one's property and associates. The boast as a distinct verbal art genre almost always occurs in association with other forms, and boasting may occur in folklore when the boast as genre is not present. In most cases, formulaic boasts are specific to particular contexts, especially those defined by age and gender. They are often a component of competitive displays that may be ends in themselves or that may lead to further competition, even physical violence.

Verbal dueling, usually an activity of adolescent males, provides an important context in which boasts occur cross-culturally. For example, the ritual exchange of insults that characterizes what is called "dozens," "joning," or "snaps" among young African-American males focuses principally on derogating the opponent and his family. But frequently, boasts of one's prowess, especially sexual, contribute to the duel's outcome, which depends upon verbal agility and one's ability to undercut the opponent's masculinity. Reducing the opponent to an image of passivity can be achieved at least partially through boasting of one's active masculinity, a technique that also has been reported in verbal dueling among Turkish youths.

Boasts also occur in longer forms of folk literature. One characteristic of the epic hero, be he Achilles or Odysseus from Homeric Greece, Beowulf from Old English tradition, or the protagonists of the Balkan epics reported by Milman Parry and Albert Lord, is his boasting, an act that may figure into council scenes, serve as preparation for battle, or comprise a warrior's account of an action in which he has participated. The humor of the American frontier produced similar boasts, which probably served to burlesque the characters' uncivilized manners. Davy Crockett or Mike Fink would claim to be "half horse, half alligator" and able to "lick [his] weight in wildcats" before scuffling with an opponent. The toast, a long narrative poem recited by African-American males, often features a boastful protagonist who extols his own violent disregard of convention. Among Native Americans of the plains, boasts became part of the formula for coup tales, stories in which warriors recounted their military exploits, especially those that evinced particular daring. The tall tale provides another folk literary context for the boast. The focus of tall tales, though, may not be praise of self as much as of the country where one lives. For example, tall tales often include boasts about a land's fertility and richness, the size and accessibility of its game, and the beauty of its women.

Boasts also may assume a negative cast, though their ultimate purport redounds to the boaster's credit. For example, American humor includes boasts about the excessively inclement weather and general insalubrity of rural areas and the toughness of city neighborhoods. On one hand, these boasts derogate, but on the other, they stress the speaker's prowess in being able to survive unpleasant, dangerous conditions.

Formulaic boasting seems to flourish in societies that stress the so-called "masculine" virtues of aggressiveness toward other males, women, and the environment. Folklore research has tended to examine such boasting in terms of its linguistic patterning and psychological importance, the latter usually informed by Freudian assumptions.

William M. Clements

See also Verbal Duel.

✳✳✳✳✳✳✳✳✳✳✳✳✳✳✳✳✳

References

Abrahams, Roger D. 1970. *Deep Down in the Jungle: Negro Narrative Folklore from the Streets of Philadelphia*. 1st revised ed. Chicago: Aldine.

Blair, Walter, and Franklin J. Meine, eds. 1956. *Half Horse, Half Alligator: The Growth of the Mike Fink Legend*. Chicago: University of Chicago Press.

Boatright, Mody C. 1949. *Folk Laughter on the American Frontier*. New York: Macmillan.

Chadwick, H. Munro. 1912. *The Heroic Age*. Cambridge: Cambridge University Press.

Dundes, Alan, Jerry W. Leach, and Bora Ozkok. 1970. The Strategy of Turkish Boys' Verbal Dueling Rhymes. *Journal of American Folklore* 83:325–349.

Welsch, Roger. 1972. *Shingling the Fog and Other Plains Lies*. Lincoln: University of Nebraska Press.

BROADSIDE BALLAD

In its more general sense, a narrative song (ballad) printed on one side of a single sheet of paper (broadside) and sold by a mobile peddler of the market-place, fairground, and street corner sort. The broadside phenomenon emerged in Europe in the early years of the sixteenth century, flourished in major Old World and, later, American cities and towns up to the middle of the nine-teenth century, and continued in less progressive locales (Ireland, for instance) into the early years of the twentieth century; it may be found in towns and villages of some developing nations, such as Brazil and India, even today. In lay speech, the phrase *broadside ballad* (or more commonly, just *ballad* or *ballet*) was not restricted to narrative songs but applied to any street-hawked printed songs at all; for the past two hundred years or so, however, folklorists have reserved the word *ballad* for a song that recounts a plotted story.

Each year from the early sixteenth century onward, many such newly made song-stories appeared for the first time on broadsides and were peddled in public places. Some were fictional, but most chronicled imaginatively some current, newsworthy event, such as a military victory, a sensational crime, or a society scandal. Few of them, however, changed their original status as popu-lar literature to become folklore; that is to say, like their many nonliterary broadside kin—proclamations, pamphlets, tracts—they were bought, read, or sung a few times and then forgotten. They did not, as we say, "enter folk tradition," becoming imprinted in memory and re-created in divers day-to-day social encounters, sung by mothers to children by evening candlelight, by upstairs maids to each other after a lengthy day's domestic service, or by a soldier to his comrades over a campfire far from home. But over time, the public showed a distinct preference for hearing, for singing, for remembering, and for experiencing again and again ballads from broadsides that exhibited a fairly distinctive set of traits. So in British folksong tradition, to take just one European example, the public had developed a preference for a certain "style" of such ballads by the latter half of the eighteenth century, and it is this style that folklorists have in mind when they talk about the broadside ballad in a *specific* sense: They do not mean just any song printed on broadside, and they do not mean—in the general sense mentioned earlier—just any narrative song printed on broadside. (Of those, we just say that they "appeared on broadside" or some such thing, as we do, for example, of the many lengthy, virtually unsingable song-tales printed in the older, heavy, ornate Gothic or black letter typeface common in Tudor and Stuart England that never became folklore.) What folklorists do mean in a *specific* sense is a folksong exhibiting a certain set of formal conventions, the development and popularization of which was closely bound up with broadside printing and dissemination. Indeed, in folklore terminology, a broadside ballad may never actually have appeared on a broadside at all—it only needs to exhibit the relevant stylistic traits of the genre!

In the tradition we know by far the most about, that of the British Isles and its North American continuation, these characteristics are best described in terms of their differences from the other major ballad style originating in Europe, the older medieval or "Child" ballad style. Thus, a broadside ballad, first of all, usually tells its story in a more linear, expository way than does the medieval ballad, which is more allusive, dramatic (with much direct, unascribed speech that retards the forward movement of the narrative), internally repetitive, and tableauxed in style. Consider, for example, the step-by-step account in "The Flying Cloud," a nineteenth-century broadside ballad of slavery and piracy:

> And when I struck Belfrazer shore I met with Captain
>   Moore,
> The commander of the Flying Cloud belonging to
>   Baltimore.
> He cordially invited me a slavery voyage to go
> To the burning shores of Affaric, where the sugar cane
>   does grow.

The Flying Cloud was a clipper ship, four hundred tons or
    more.
She could easily sail round any ship that sailed from
    Baltimore.
Her sails were as white as the driven snow and on them
    not one speck;
She had thirty-two brass guns, my boys, she carried upon
    her deck.

    And in a short time after we had struck the African
        shore
    Eighteen hundred of those poor souls on board with us
        we bore.
    We made them walk out on our planks as we stored
        them down below;
    Scarce eighteen inches to the man was all that she
        would go.

The very next day we set to sea with our cargo of slaves.
It would have been better for them poor souls had they
    been in their graves.
For the plagued fever came on board and swept one half
    away;
We drew their bodies up on deck and hove them in the
    sea.

    And in a short time after we struck the Cubian shores.
    We sold them to the planters there to be slaves for
        ever more,
    To hoe in the rice and coffee fields beneath the burn-
        ing sun,
    To worry out a wretched life till their career was done.

As this excerpt from "The Flying Cloud" suggests, a second, related feature of the broadside ballad style is its relative concreteness and specificity: People, places, dates, professions, and motives are all detailed. The broadside ballad universe is quite distinguishable from the adumbrated, stylized, and more homogeneous medieval ballad world—and even more so, for that matter, from the extremely generalized world of another folksong type, the nonnarrative lyric song: Each story tends to be particularized, situated, and contextualized. To put this trait another way, a broadside ballad contains far more information of the quantifiable sort than does its medieval forebear, as the first two stanzas of "The Greenland Whale Fishery" illustrate:

It was in the year eighteen hundred and one,
On March the twentieth day,
Our sheets were spread, and our anchors weighed,
And for Greenland we bore away, brave boys,
And for Greenland we bore away.

"Speed" it was our Captain's name,
And our ship the "Lion" bold,
And we sailed away to that cold countrie,
For to face the storms and the cold, brave boys,
For to face the storms and the cold.

A third distinguishing feature of the broadside ballad, in contrast with the oft-noted impersonality and objectivity of the narrator point of view prominent in the medieval ballad, is that it strives for subjectivity. Songs often pass explicit moral judgment on the events at hand or express overt sentimentality. They expose clearly their characters' attitudes and values, often going so far as to instruct the listener how to react emotionally or ethically to the events recounted. More often than not, this subjectivity is emphasized with the device, rare in the older ballad format, of a first-person narrator, as in "The Sheffield Apprentice":

My friends, who stand around me my wretched fate to see,
Oh, don't mourn for my downfall, but oh! do pity me.
A long while I've proved innocent, still death had sentenced me.
Oh, farewell, pretty Polly! I'll die a-loving thee.

A fourth characteristic is that broadside ballads treat their subjects more realistically than do medieval ballads. In the newer ballad style, for example, supernatural personnel are rare: We find few revenants (ghosts who return from the dead to bid their sweethearts a final farewell), household spirits, and magical plants that, embodying the souls of dead lovers, sprout and entwine above the deceaseds' graves. Similarly, broadside ballad language itself is less exaggerated, stylized, and formulaic, paralleling more closely the everyday standard language: Few broadside ballad horses in folk tradition are shod in gold and silver, fewer heroines dressed in red while their accompanying retainers are clad in green, fewer trips away from home are described in the same way ("He hadn't been in fair England / A week but barely three"). Of course, like all folklore, broadside ballads are imaginative art and do exhibit stock epithets ("Come all you gallant Christians, I pray you lend an ear"), but the broadside style of telling a story seems far more bound by empirical constraints than the medieval style; thus, broadside representations and language are more prone to reflect the world as experienced in everyday life.

Finally, a closely related trait should be noted: the distinctive world portrayed in the broadside ballad. In the medieval ballad, social organization, material culture, and customs and habits are distinctly premodern: Many heroines have pageboys at their command, live in castles, or can escape a parentally arranged marriage only by dying. In contrast, broadside ballads depict a more familiar, more recognizable world. Perhaps the clearest example of this sort of difference can be seen in the dramatis personae themselves. Even in twentieth-century versions, protagonists of medieval ballads are usually leisure-class men and women, often nobility and sometimes even royalty. Protagonists of broadside ballads, however, are much more commonly working people—laboring men and women, artisans, merchants, and formally trained professionals such as physicians and sea captains. And in this more modern world, heroines and heroes enjoy more options in all aspects of life than do their medieval forebears, most notably in the folksong's favored topic, love relationships:

> It's of a rich merchant, I can't call his name,
> He had but one daughter and a daughter of fame,
> She courted a great many but slighted them all,
> For the sake of a sailor both handsome and tall.

This ballad tells of a father who disapproves of his daughter's choice of mate and has the sailor pressed to sea, but the daughter, disguised in male clothing, follows her lover and shares his nautical life. The two eventually return home to marry.

The five traits mentioned in the preceding passages constitute the primary textual markers of the broadside ballad as a folksong type. Other tendencies may be found in the genre that have less to do with the broadside ballad's literariness and more with its poetics—for example, an affection for 7/7/7/7 meter and for *abba* tunes, especially in the Irish-influenced strand of English-speaking tradition—but those qualities are not pervasive enough for definitional purposes. All five primary traits (most notably, the last two) are doubtless a function of the historical conditions attending the broadside ballad's more contemporary era (in Britain, the medieval ballad style had virtually ceased to be employed as a vehicle for new songs by 1700). The five traits also reflect the broadside ballad's greater dependence on print, as opposed to orality, for its origin, transmission, and reproduction.

In England by the mid-eighteenth century and in North America somewhat later, this broadside song-story style had achieved clear prominence in the folk aesthetic. Printers and the song makers they employed or contracted with turned out a much more varied set of items for sale on street corners and market stalls, but the public accepted into its personal performance repertoire of songs for everyday social use mainly ballads that manifested the characteristics described. Even amateur village rhymesters who were moved to share with family, workmates, and friends songs on topics of strictly local interest that might never see a printed page—the drowning of some neighbor's son in a nearby stream, a Maine woods logging accident—were as likely as not to follow the broadside model, as in this twentieth-century example:

> Come all you Newfoundlanders and listen to my song,
> I'll tell you 'bout the moose we killed and the man that did
>   us wrong,
> On a sunny morn, October third, I'm telling you no lies,
> When Izzie Walters hollered out saying, "Get your guns,
>   my b'ys!"
>
> "There is a moose down in the reach, he's coming up the
>   lane,
> Jim Keeping's got him rounded up, I think he must be
>   tame."
> Our guns and ammunition we got without delay,
> Lou Lemmon had the first shot I'm very sure to say.
>
> George Croucher had the second shot if you want to
>   know his name,
> Bill Munden had the third shot which brought him to his
>   end.
> There were men, women, and children all gathered round
>   the hill
> All looking for a piece of meat their appetite to fill.

Just as the populace preferred a certain way of telling a story in song when accepting popular culture into folk tradition, so too did it prefer certain topics. Ballads of armed conflict, by land and sea; of crime and outlaws; of tragedies and disasters (earthquakes, train wrecks, coal-mining cave-ins); of occupational experience (in Britain, especially of agricultural work and seafaring and in North America, of lumbering and cowboying); of sports and pastimes (horse races, foxhunting); and, of course, of the most popular topic by far (and the one most often made up rather than based on actual events), love relationships, with recurring plot-types about female warriors, returned and unrecognized lovers, murdered sweethearts, and so on. Over the years, these were the broadside songs that people preferred to learn, to pass on, and to remember. We base this assertion not on the numbers and kinds of actual broadsides preserved in museums, archives, and libraries or on printers' inventory and sales figures but on just what songs folklore collectors have found prominent in the repertoires of ordinary men and women over the last century or so.

The broadside ballad declined in popularity after the midpoint of the nineteenth century, with the greater availability and affordability of professional entertainment and the general decline of singing as a custom in everyday life. Concomitantly, the broadside style of song became overshadowed by the more sophisticated ditties that were heard in music halls and traveling shows, played on radios and phonographs, and transcribed in sheet music and songbooks. Increasingly, the public preferred songs of loftier topic and finer sentiment, of more mature humor, of greater inventiveness and skill, and of more general interest The public now favored songs that were less dependent on the apparently dated plot-types (not to mention language, meter, and even tunes favored by the broadside muse) and songs that were more closely identified with particular professional composers and performers, rather than with anonymous, itinerant versifiers or with the even more anonymous "tradition." In short, the broadside ballad style did not survive well in an era that was more technologically advanced, more market-driven, more consumer-oriented, and more supportive of bourgeois sensibilities.

Roger deV. Renwick

See also Ballad; Chapbook; Folk Song, Narrative.

✳✳✳✳✳✳✳✳✳✳✳✳✳✳✳✳✳✳

References

Dugaw, Dianne. 1989. *Warrior Women and Popular Balladry, 1650–1850.* Cambridge Studies in Eighteenth-Century English Literature and Thought, vol. 4. Cambridge: Cambridge University Press.

Laws, G. Malcolm Jr. 1957. *American Balladry from British Broadsides: A Guide for Students and Collectors of Traditional Song.* American Folklore Society, Bibliographical and Special Series, vol. 8. Philadelphia.

———. 1964. *Native American Balladry: A Descriptive Study and a Bibliographical Syllabus.* Rev. ed. American Folklore Society, Bibliographical and Special Series, vol. 1. Philadelphia.

Paredes, Américo. 1958. *"With His Pistol in His Hand": A Border Ballad and Its Hero.* Austin: University of Texas Press.

Würzbach, Natascha. [1981] 1990. *The Rise of the English Street Ballad, 1550–1650.* Cambridge: Cambridge University Press.

C

CANTOMETRICS

A method for defining societies' singing styles and correlating them with other cultural features. Coined by Alan Lomax, *cantometrics* refers to a method devised in the 1960s by Lomax, Victor Grauer, and other participants in the Columbia University Cross-Cultural Study of Expressive Style, which identifies stylistic patterns in singing from societies throughout the world. Based on 36 variables grouped under 7 headings, culture-specific approaches to singing receive ratings that have allowed the definition of 10 performance regions. Song performance features in each region correlate with and derive from social structure.

The cantometric method emerged with the availability of a body of recorded song samples from across the globe. Significant, recurrent features of performance, based on as few as ten individual examples from a society, have become the measures for creating a cantometric profile of the society's singing style. Such a profile identifies these characteristics of singing: vocal qualities, use of ornamentation (for example, glissandos and tremolos), dynamic features, melodic features, rhythmic features, level of cohesiveness, and group organization. Subcharacteristics of each of these general traits are scaled between two poles: For example, melodic form (one of nine melodic features) ranges from complex to simple, and vocal width (one of six vocal qualities) ranges from narrow to wide.

Similar profiles among several societies produce song-style regions, which correspond roughly to culture areas in George P. Murdock's *Ethnographic Atlas*. Song-style region 1, for example, represents pockets of hunter-gatherer cultures in Africa; region 6 corresponds to the tropical gardener cultures of Oceania and central Africa, and region 8 is the Old High Culture that extends from north Africa throughout most of southern and central Asia.

Moreover, the method adds an explanatory dimension to the construction of profiles and the definition of regions. Researchers using cantometric scales hypothesize correlations between singing performance and social structure. For example, harsh vocal timbres predominate in cultures that stress the development of aggressiveness in males. Narrow vocal widths and a high degree of nasality occur in cultures with tightly controlled sexuality. Rhythmic regularity reflects the inculcation in childhood of habits of obedience and adherence to structured rules, and irregular rhythms occur in cultures with indulgent child-rearing practices.

Lomax and his colleagues, who have done similar measures on dance and other expressive though nonverbal aspects of culture, have generated the bases for defining singing styles and the ways in which to scale them. They also have produced tapes for classroom use that afford students a global sample of singing styles and enable them quickly to master ways to identify specific performances according to song-style regions. Familiarity with these tapes also instructs students in constructing cantometric profiles.

To some extent, objections to cantometrics reflect folklorists' uneasiness with broad syntheses of data. Moreover, a society's song-style profile, critics aver, may reflect the scorer's subjective judgment, though informal experimentation has shown considerable consistency among individuals using the system. A general profile also can blur important variations within the society. That Lomax tended to release information about cantometrics piecemeal over a 20-year period also contributed to hasty, often negative appraisals of what was essentially work in progress.

William M. Clements

See also Choreometrics.

✳✳✳✳✳✳✳✳✳✳✳✳✳✳✳✳✳✳

References
Lomax, Alan. 1959. Folk Song Style. *American Anthropologist* 61:927–954.
———. 1967. The Good and the Beautiful in Folksong. *Journal of American Folklore* 80:213–235.
———. 1968. *Folk Song Style and Culture*. Washington, DC: American Association for the Advancement of Science.
———. 1972. The Evolutionary Taxonomy of Culture. *Science* 177:228–239.
———. 1976. *Cantometrics: A Method in Musical Anthropology*. Berkeley: University of California Extension Media Center.
Murdock, George Peter. 1967. *Ethnographic Atlas*. Pittsburgh, PA: University of Pittsburgh Press.

CARNIVAL

Traditional celebrations that climax on the days immediately preceding Ash Wednesday throughout the Catholic world. Precise origins of carnival are unknown and most likely indeterminable. The place of the festival in the Christian calendar suggests that apparent links to pre-Christian celebrations, such as Roman Saturnalia and Bacchanalia, are formal rather than directly historical. However, some scholars believe the church simply adopted pre-Christian customs into its liturgy when it found they could not be eliminated. Carnival has been documented in European cities from the fourteenth century and in towns and villages in the following centuries. Elements of carnival eventually crossed the Atlantic and Mediterranean to mix with the traditions of indigenous and former slave populations in North and South American and in certain African countries, creating new forms of celebration. Common to carnival throughout its historical and geographic ranges are masking and costuming (generally restricted to the three to five days before Lent but also occurring sporadically from as early as St. Martin's Day, November 11, or Epiphany, January 6), public dramas and private ceremonies, and the stylized expression of social and political attitudes. Local social or occupational groups, known variously as guilds, schools, or cliques, often serve as festival organizers and actively prepare carnival celebrations throughout much of the year. More generally, carnival is an occasion for individuals to behave in manners that either invert or exaggerate the behavior practiced at other times of the year.

Carnival costuming ranges from the extravagant and elaborate regalia worn by performers in those groups known as samba schools in Brazil and troupes of Mardi Gras "Indians" in New Orleans to a bit of makeup or a nose mask worn by parade spectators. Costumes may draw on mundane materials, such as agricultural waste and rags, or utilize exquisite paraphernalia in their designs. In European tradition, fool and wild man figures predominate. Animals, witches, and local demons and comical figures frequently appear in Europe and elsewhere. Some costumes are ephemeral, making their only appearance during the few days before Lent in a single year; other traditions (such as those in southwest Germany or in certain Belgian towns) require that local residents preserve their costumes for use each year. Through such repeated appearances, these durable costumes come to represent the localities where they are worn. In all of these cases, costuming and the change of identity it creates encourage alternative behavior—from growling like a bear to revealing private body parts. However, individuals do not have complete license to behave as they choose during carnival.

Carnival dramas range in complexity from an individual reading a text or singing a ballad to parades, processions, and choreographed dances and festival plays lasting a day or more. These dramas frequently reorient the distinctions made between public and private spheres. For example, readings of "scandal sheets" (poetic accounts of local escapades, such as the priest who "lost" his foulmouthed parrot) make public knowledge that previously was passed through private gossip. Likewise, the practice of wearing underwear or nightshirts on the streets during carnival brings the private out into the open. Visits to homes by troupes of performers collecting donations for community celebrations and/or their own inebriation thrust reckless outdoor behavior into the private domain. Although these diverse displays form the centerpiece of the public carnival spectacle, smaller groups of locals hold annual balls, parties, and formal ceremonies behind closed doors.

The relative freedom of behavior afforded by the joyous carnival mood seems to encourage participants to voice their opinions about current affairs. Whether in the form of scandal sheets, street theater, or politically apropos costumes (e.g., that of a Chernobyl victim), carnival antics regularly mock local, national, and international citizens, institutions, and events, giving the playful festival atmosphere an underlying tone of seriousness. The politics of carnival also encompass struggles over the privilege to enact and shape the celebration. Historically, these struggles were played out between church and secular authorities and plebeian populations. More recently, competing ethnic groups have battled over control of the festival in urban settings, and established carnival organizers and local officials have tried to stage regulated, presentable festivals in opposition to the wilder revelry advocated by some participants.

Peter Tokofsky

See also Charivari/Shivaree; Festival.

✳✳✳✳✳✳✳✳✳✳✳✳✳✳✳✳✳

References

Bakhtin, Mikhail. 1984. *Rabelais and His World*. Translated by Hélène Iswolsky. Bloomington: Indiana University Press.

Cohen, Abner. 1993. *Masquerade Politics: Explorations in the Structure of Urban Carnival Movements*. Oxford: Berg.

Damatta, Roberto. 1986. *Carnival as a Cultural Problem: Toward a Theory of Formal Events and Their Magic*. Kellogg Institute Working Paper no. 79. Notre Dame, IN: Helen Kellogg Institute for International Studies.

Kinser, Samuel. 1990. *Carnival, American Style: Mardi Gras at New Orleans and Mobile*. Chicago: University of Chicago Press.

Le Roy Ladurie, Emmanuel. 1979. *Carnival in Romans*. Trans. Mary Feeney. New York: George Braziller.

Mezger, Werner. 1991. *Narrenidee und Fastnachtsbrauch: Studien zum Fortleben des Mittelalters in der europäischen Festkultur*. Constance, Germany: Universitätsverlag.

Catch Question

A type of traditional enigma designed to "catch" the respondent by frustrating expectations. The catch question may exploit syntactic ambiguities: "I saw Esau sitting on a see-saw, how many s's in that?—None" (the word *that* has no s's). Or the catch question may use homonyms: "I know three monkeys. One's called Doh, one's called Ray. What's the third one called?—Me.—Oh, I didn't know you were a monkey." Or the question may give a personal application to an apparently general question: "What do virgins eat for breakfast?—I don't know" (thus, the respondent must not be a virgin).

Just as it shifts the frame of reference, the catch question also shifts the performance frame. Its efficacy results from a surprising emergence in another kind of discourse. In the middle of a riddling session, someone asks, "What has four legs, a tail, and barks?" The respondent, expecting a metaphorical or punning solution, ponders, gives up, and at last volunteers, "A dog?" The poser gives a condescending smile and replies, "Oh, you've heard that one." The catch question may break into ordinary conversation: "You know your great-grandfather?—Yes.—No you don't, he's dead!" Sometimes, it comes disguised as a clever question with a recondite answer: "Where did King John sign the Magna Carta?—At the bottom."

The catch question is used to embarrass, obliging the respondent to utter an obscenity, make an unintended admission, or simply appear foolish. It may serve to upset the accepted hierarchy of wit, pulling the rug from under a clever person. Or it may simply introduce variety into a riddling session.

A subtype of the catch question is the mock-obscene or double-entendre riddle, found widely around the world and often in cultures with strict norms of sexual propriety. The mock-obscene riddle presents a question with an apparently sexual solution. The respondent betrays awareness by offering this answer or by blushing; the poser then provides an innocent solution. An example is this Italian riddle: "You stick it in hard, it comes out soft. What is it?—Spaghetti." Such catches are generally exchanged among children, as a way of introducing a forbidden but endlessly interesting topic, and in cross-gender gatherings of adolescents, among whom, as Anniki Kaivola-Bregenhøj has said, the mock-obscene riddle acts as "kindler of an erotic atmosphere."

Dorothy Noyes

See also Enigma, Folk.

✳✳✳✳✳✳✳✳✳✳✳✳✳✳✳✳✳✳

References
Abrahams, Roger. 1983. *The Man-of-Words in the West Indies*. Baltimore, MD: Johns Hopkins University Press.
Kaivola-Bregenhøj, Anniki. 1978. *The Nominativus Absolutus Formula*. Folklore Fellows Communications, no. 222. Helsinki: Academia Scientiarum Fennica.
Opie, Iona, and Peter Opie. 1959. *The Lore and Language of Schoolchildren*. Oxford: Oxford University Press.

CHAPBOOK

A nineteenth-century English word coined to signify the small, ephemeral books sold, among items such as needles and thread, by itinerant peddlers called chapmen. Chapbooks also were sold in shops. By 1700, chapbooks had become an important part of the stock of such peddlers, and their subject matter included prophecies and fortune-telling, fables and fairy tales, and stories of devils and angels, love and hate, and scoundrels and heroes.

Chapbooks, with their modern typography, replaced the earlier black letter broadside ballads; usually measuring 3½″ by 6″, they also were easier to carry about than a pile of ballad sheets. By the end of the seventeenth century, they were typically printed in octavo, a sheet of paper folded three times to make 8 leaves or 16 pages, but chapbooks of 4, 8, 12, and 24 pages were also common. Printed on both sides of a sheet of paper, they were a better value than broadside ballads and became the main reading matter available for the poor, although they also were read by more well-to-do individuals. Chapbooks containing ballads were called "garlands."

In the nineteenth century, chapbooks were increasingly produced for children. No longer printed on coarse rag paper, they were better produced and often smaller in size. The quality of woodcuts and other illustrations was improved, and the illustrations were sometimes colored. Broadside ballads, no longer printed in black letter, replaced chapbooks for adult readers of the poorest class. During the eighteenth and nineteenth centuries, more than 250 firms and individuals were involved in the production of chapbooks in London alone, with many more in such cities and towns as Newcastle upon Tyne, Banbury, Northampton, Gloucester, and York. Chapbooks were printed in Belfast, Dublin, Glasgow, Edinburgh, Aberdeen, and throughout the English-reading world.

Ephemeral literature seems to exist wherever its means of production exist, and it is often late in its history before it becomes an object of study; its forms differ somewhat from country to country. *Folhetos* (pamphlets or little books)—or, colloquially, *folhetes*—are known to have been printed in Brazil since the late nineteenth century. Often 4″ by 6½″ in size and of 8, 16, 32, and occasionally 64 pages, these little books are much like English chapbooks. Printed on newspaper-weight paper, they contain stories in verse (with the exception of a small number of prayers in prose), thus differing from English chapbooks, which often were written in prose. In subject matter, *folhetos* reflect the culture in which they are produced. Most stories represent a series of trials, and their heroes and heroines are either saints or sinners. Almost all have explicit, serious messages, even though many are humorous and a few are pornographic. A recent title, *A contagiosa AIDS matando a humanidade* (Contagious AIDS killing humanity), reflects both a highly conservative view of sexual behavior and a plea for help for AIDS victims.

Because of the interest of middle-class visitors and their common use of the Portuguese phrase *literatura de cordel* (stories on a cord) for *folhetos*, such a little book is now commonly called a *cordel*, even though the items produced in Brazil differ from the Portuguese chapbooks to which they are related. The relationship between the little ephemeral books of Brazil and Portugal may be

An illustration of a mermaid from a chapbook. The subject matter of chapbooks often consisted of fairy tales and mythic creatures.

thought of as analogous to the relationship between chapbooks produced in England and the United States. Products of different people in different places, they differ accordingly.

The growing awareness of the existence and importance of ephemeral literature in many countries outside of the Western European tradition—Egypt and Pakistan, for example—and the increasingly detailed study of broadsides and chapbooks within the European tradition since the 1970s have resulted in a virtual revolution in our understandings of the place of these materials in society. The woodcuts used for chapbooks and broadsides once were called "crude" and their printing "vile," but those words are now understood to reveal more about the privileged perspectives of those who uttered them than about the materials themselves. Working with limited resources, chapbook printers produced little books, many of enduring value.

Michael J. Preston

See also Broadside Ballad.

✱✱✱✱✱✱✱✱✱✱✱✱✱✱✱✱✱

References

Ashton, John. 1882. *Chap-Books of the Eighteenth Century.* Reprint. New York: Benjamin Blom.

Neuburg, Victor E. 1968. *The Penny Histories: A Study of Chapbooks for Young Readers over Two Centuries.* London: Oxford University Press.

———. 1972. *Chapbooks: A Guide to Reference Material on English, Scottish and American Chapbook Literature of the Eighteenth and Nineteenth Centuries.* Reprint. London: Woburn.

———. 1977. *Popular Literature: A History and Guide, from the Beginning of Printing to the Year 1897.* Harmondsworth, England: Penguin.

Preston, Cathy Lynn, and Michael J. Preston. 1995. *The Other Print Tradition: Essays on Chapbooks, Broadsides, and Other Ephemera.* New York: Garland.

Preston, Michael J., M.G. Smith, and P.S. Smith. 1977. *Chapbooks and Traditional Drama: An Examination of Chapbooks Containing Traditional Play Texts, Part 1: Alexander and the King of Egypt Chapbooks.* CECTAL Bibliographical and Special Series, no. 2. Sheffield, England: University of Sheffield.

Shepard, Leslie. 1969. *John Pitts: Ballad Printer of Seven Dials, London (1765–1844) with a Short Account of His Predecessors in the Ballad & Chapbook Trade.* London: Private Libraries Association.

Slater, Candice. 1982. *Stories on a String: The Brazilian "Literatura de Cordel."* Berkeley: University of California Press.

Spufford, Margaret. 1981. *Small Books and Pleasant Histories: Popular Fiction and Its Readership in Seventeenth-Century England.* Athens: University of Georgia Press.

———. 1994. The Pedlar, the Historian and the Folklorist: Seventeenth Century Communications. *Folklore* 105:13–24.

Watt, Tessa. 1991. *Cheap Print and Popular Piety: 1550–1640.* Cambridge: Cambridge University Press.

CHARIVARI/SHIVAREE

Ritualized forms of popular justice intended to draw public attention to transgressions of the moral or social order and thus enforce community standards, appropriate behavior, and traditional rights. Also known as *Katzenmusik, Polterabend,* and *Haberfeldtreiben* in Germany; *Thierjagen* in Holland; *cencerrada* in Spain; *scampanate* in Italy; *ceffyl pren* in Wales; riding the stang, skimmington, tin panning, kettling, Devon's stag hunt, and rough music in England and Scotland; and serenade, tin panning, and belling in North America, these traditional events show great variation over their distribution. Elements of charivaris derive from forms of punishment and folly that are over a millennium old, and they coalesced into a coherent ritual form by the Middle Ages. With the increasing dominance of civil authority over social life, charivaris have largely disappeared; they continue today primarily in isolated rural communities or in substantially altered form and function.

Central to all forms of the charivari is clamorous noise, usually produced with pots and pans, tins, bells, horns, or other traditional local instruments. Typically, participants gather at a designated public place and noisily proceed to the home of the offender, where they mock the victim with skits (particularly dramatizations of the offense), continue their clamor, and engage in festive activities including costuming, drinking, and licentious sexual activity. The scene may be repeated for several nights, and on many occasions, the crowd eventually invades the home of the victim, levies payment of cash or alcohol in exchange for ceasing the spectacle, or forces the subject from his or her home and subjects him or her to a variety of traditional punishments.

These include riding a donkey while seated backward, riding a pole, satirizing, and even beating and death. Mockery also can have traditional local form, such as a particular style of poetic proclamation or versified satire sung to the tunes of popular songs. Historically, the most common reasons for initiating a charivari were perceived domestic problems: quick remarriage by a widow or widower, extreme discrepancy between the ages of spouses, wife or husband beating, adultery, licentious conduct by a married person, a child born out of wedlock, or even marriage to an outsider. Locals also directed charivaris against strikebreakers or unpopular officials and policies. A related North American form, whitecapping, victimizes dissidents and oppressed or marginalized groups, such as African-Americans and immigrants. Best known in the form of Ku Klux Klan lynching, whitecapping does not include the clamor of charivaris, but it retains aspects of the traditional processional drama and punishment.

Some historical and by far the most common contemporary charivaris may be more aptly termed *reverse charivaris*. Rather than punishing their victims, they affirm the social belonging of the subjects by playfully celebrating their foibles and social transitions. Thus, newlyweds may be subjected to derision or be the focus of a street serenade; baby showers and retirement parties also feature mockery of the person entering a new stage of life. Similarly, during festivals such as carnival, celebrants may draw on elements of the charivari to satirize the behavior of individuals (for example, a drunk driver running his car into a tree), but the only punishment is the publicity the "victim" receives, and typically he or she enjoys the attention. Although reverse charivaris affirm local standing, they simultaneously remind participants, as traditional charivaris do, that the community watches over behavior.

Peter Tokofsky

See also Custom; Rites of Passage.

✳✳✳✳✳✳✳✳✳✳✳✳✳✳✳✳✳

References

Davis, Natalie Zemon. 1975. The Reasons of Misrule. In Natalie Zemon Davis, *Society and Culture in Early Modern France*, pp. 97–123. Stanford, CA: Stanford University Press.

Le Goff, Jacques, and Jean Claude Schmitt, eds. 1981. *Le Charivari*. Paris: École des Haute Études en Science Sociales.

Palmer, Bryan D. 1978. Discordant Music: Charivaris and Whitecapping in Nineteenth-Century North America. *Labour/le travailleur* 3:5–62.

Thompson, E. P. 1993. Rough Music. In *Customs in Common: Studies in Traditional Popular Culture*, ed. Edward P. Thompson. New York: New Press.

CHARM

Folk belief and practice in which humans use magic to bring about particular outcomes in activities where there is uncertainty. Charms can be verbal or material, they can involve action, and they seem to be cross-cultural and found in all historical periods. Charms are important in several different areas of folk belief scholarship, including folk medicine, folk religion, ritual, and custom.

One of the most common forms of behavior involving charms is the practice of keeping or carrying amulets, fetishes, or talismans—material objects thought to ward off evil forces or bring good luck. People in ancient Rome used garlic to keep witches away; in medieval times, monks used the mullen plant as a charm against devils although the plant also was thought to be used in witches' brew; the Chinese sometimes carry peach wood or peach stones to ward off evil; and many people carry a rabbit's foot or hang horseshoes over doors for good luck in the contemporary United States. In religious terms, carrying a saint's medal or small statue is thought to help people avoid accidents on trips. This practice is not confined to Catholics; Protestant commercial fishermen in the Gulf of Mexico often carry saints' medals given to them by priests at annual blessings of the fleet. Scholars must examine the ritual context in order to understand why Protestants would carry Catholic medals. As with any kind of folk belief, it is important to study charms within the specific context of belief and behavior.

Verbal charms or incantations are an important part of healing traditions among many cultural groups. For example, the practice of bloodstopping in Appalachia depends on reciting a verse from the Bible several times. The verse is learned from certain family members and is usually thought of as a secret ritual that has to be learned and practiced in very specific ways. People who believe that excessive bleeding can be stopped through this verbal charm tell stories about the times they have witnessed the charm succeed, saving the lives of individuals who would have bled to death before they reached a hospital.

Often, to be effective, use of a verbal charm also must be accompanied by certain actions. For instance, Italian fishermen have a charm for dispersing a waterspout that could sink their boats. They recite words from Scripture, make the sign of the cross with a special knife, and say "tail of the rat" to keep the magic from harming anyone. As with bloodstopping, this charm must be learned from a special person under certain conditions—in this case, from an elderly woman on Christmas Eve. Again, stories are told about experiences that validate when a person has seen this charm work to break up a waterspout. Catholic Croatian fishermen in the Adriatic have a similar charm for waterspouts, but it involves an inscription, combining material and behavioral methods: They draw a Star of David on a piece of paper and throw it overboard in the direction of the waterspout. This is another instance of using the religion of others as a source for folk belief.

Folk charms are associated with particular groups or communities, but knowledge of charms can pass to a broader, mass-media context. Traditional African-American charms have been popularized through music, novels, and the public interest in conjuration. Chicago blues singer Muddy Waters sang, "Got my mojo working, but it just don't work on you." The mojo, an amulet that can be made of different materials, is a powerful love charm; hence, the singer referred to his frustration that his mojo was not working on the woman he loved. Recordings of Waters' song have been played all over the world, and other singers have done versions of it. Charms are a cross-cultural phenomena, so that even though specific amulets and incantations vary widely, the concept of using a magical means for controlling fate seems universal.

Patrick B. Mullen

See also Magic; Medicine, Folk.

✻✻✻✻✻✻✻✻✻✻✻✻✻✻✻✻✻

References

Dundes, Alan, ed. 1973. *Mother Wit from the Laughing Barrel: Readings in the Interpretation of Afro-American Folklore*. Englewood Cliffs, NJ: Prentice-Hall. See these chapters: Ruth Bass, "Mojo," and Mimi Clar Melnick, "'I Can Peep through Muddy Water and Spy Dry Land': Boasts in the Blues."

Leach, Maria, ed. 1984. *Funk and Wagnalls Standard Dictionary of Folklore, Mythology, and Legend*. San Francisco: Harper and Row. See these entries: "Amulets," "Charms," "Fetish," and "Talisman."

Lessa, William A., and Evon Z. Vogt, eds. 1979. 4th edition. *Reader in Comparative Religion: An Anthropological Approach*. New York: Harper and Row. See these chapters: James G. Frazer, "Sympathetic Magic," Claude Lévi-Strauss, "The Effectiveness of Symbols," and Bronislaw Malinowski, "The Role of Magic and Religion."

Wigginton, Eliot, ed. 1972. *The Foxfire Book*. Garden City, NY: Doubleday.

CHILDREN'S FOLKLORE

Those traditions that are learned, transmitted, and performed by children without the influence of adult supervision or formal instruction. Historically, concepts of childhood have varied widely. According to social historian Philippe Aries, in western Europe up until about the twelfth or thirteenth centuries, children were depicted in paintings and other visual media as miniature adults, complete with adult clothing and facial expressions. By the seventeenth century, there was a growing tendency to recognize and acknowledge children as separate from adults and worthy of special attention regard-

123

ing their dress, food, behavior, and so forth. Today (and certainly in the United States), children are generally regarded as a privileged class with special schools, toys, amusements, and medical care.

It was only in the late nineteenth century that the peculiar traditions of childhood—or children's folklore—were noticed, collected, and documented. The focus of scholarly interest in children's folklore has been primarily on western European culture.

The distinctive folklore that children acquire and perform on their own exists within what folklorists characterize as the "child-to-child conduit." In general, scholars agree that such childhood traditions are an integral part of the overall enculturation process because through mastering the rules of the games or the literary structure of oral genres such as riddles and rhymes, children learn some of the fundamental aspects of cooperation and strategy that are so integral to contemporary Western society. Furthermore, much of the interaction that takes place when children play games together involves negotiation of rules and the status of various players more than the actual performance of the game itself. Many researchers believe that analyzing the social interactions in which the games are embedded is at least as important as documenting the exact texts and tunes of the songs children sing or the rhymes they recite during hand-clap routines.

Children's folklore contains practically all of the principal genres of tradition, including games, narratives of many kinds, songs, customs, and material culture. The defining characteristic, of course, is that the targeted traditions circulate within an informal children's network or folk group. A growing body of recent research concerns scatological materials, which are more common among children than many more conservative educators have been willing to accept.

Comparative scholarly research makes it clear that many of these genres of children's folklore are extremely widespread, enjoying international distribution in form if not in language. Riddling, storytelling, and games, for example, are almost universal among European, Australian, Canadian, and American children.

One notable aspect of children's folklore is the rapid transmission of the ever changing materials over vast distances, such as from one coast of the United States to the other in a matter of days. The general hypothesis is that children, just as adults, rely on the media (including long-distance telephone service as well as television and other electronic media) for the spread and transmission of these shared materials. The mass media certainly play a role in the transmission of traditions that involve popular culture, such as games played with various action figures or the wearing of Halloween costumes based on media characters.

Another characteristic of children's folklore is that many of the genres involve both a kinesic component and an oral component, as in singing games, jumping rope and its distinctive rhymes, or hand-clapping routines. The physical action and the verbal texts are so integrated that children find it almost impossible to satisfactorily perform one without the other, as evidenced when researchers ask for jump-rope rhymes without letting the children jump rope as they recite them. Likewise, many children who are accustomed to the traditional versions of the game cannot maintain the intricate rhythms of jumping rope unless they recite the rhymes. Folklorists in the past who collected the verbal components without the physical components of the games were usually collecting "fossilized" memories from adult informants rather than collecting from the children, the active bearers of the traditions.

Perhaps one reason for the widespread distribution of children's traditions is inherent in the very nature of tradition itself, namely, the informal, noninstitutional nature of the acquisition, maintenance, and transmission of these various cultural items, whether they be oral, customary, or material. The informality and expansiveness of this vast communicative network is due, in large part, to its lack of dependence on literacy and fixed form. Children, although taught in school to read and write, operate among themselves in a world of informal and oral communication, unimpeded by the necessity of maintaining and transmitting information by written means. In fact, one could theoretically regard the performance, process, and content of children's folklore as a paradigm for folklore in general.

The concept of the folk group is fundamental to folkloristics. Folk groups, quite simply, are groups of people, no matter how large or how small, who are validated and bonded primarily by the traditions they share. Children, therefore, constitute one of the largest and most accessible folk groups that folklorists regularly study.

Of course, within the larger folk group of children as a whole are innumerable smaller and more intimate folk groups in which children interact and transmit their almost infinite repertoire of folklore. It is also likely that any individual child can be part of numerous such groups, including the child's family, grade cohort and playground playmates at school, neighborhood playmates of varying ages, daycare members, as well as many others such as groups at church, at camp, on vacation, and so forth. The guiding principle in recognizing children's folk groups is that they provide a context in which the children can teach, learn, and share their distinctive traditions without outside influence or interference.

Because the concept of the folk group is integral to folklore theory, researchers do not regard those materials that adults teach to children as being within the purview of children's folklore. The social matrix within which playground supervisors or day-care attendants teach songs, games, and such to groups of children under their care is quite different from the process of transmission when children learn from and teach one another. If, however, a child who has learned a particular item from a teacher at school in turn teaches a

Ole Luk Oie, a nursery spirit of Danish and Swedish children's folklore. This tiny elf is believed to protect sleeping children and ensure good dreams.

version of that item to younger brothers and sisters at home and then that item becomes part of the active repertoire of that small folk group, the item would be of interest to folklorists.

Age is also a factor that must be taken into consideration in identifying children's folklore because the traditions commonly shared by children are quite distinctive from those of adolescents. In general, childhood has been regarded as the span from kindergarten through about the sixth year of school or about ages 5 through 12. Recently, the pervasiveness of child care for the children of working parents has lowered the age bracket to about age 4 because the social context of many day-care centers is quite conducive to very young children learning traditional items from the older children with whom they are in such constant contact. The limited language acquisition and undeveloped physical coordination of very young children prevent children's folklore from circulating among those younger than about 4 years of age.

Until the 1960s, the main studies of children's folklore were in the English language, undertaken primarily in England and the United States. Since the mid-1970s, Australian folklorists have produced a sizable and well-regarded body of scholarship and collections. Scholars throughout Europe also have begun to publish collections and analytical studies based on their fieldwork.

The earliest studies of children's folklore were the massive collections undertaken by the noted British scholar Lady Bertha Gomme (1894—1898) and the American William Wells Newell, a founder of the American Folklore Society and first editor of the *Journal of American Folklore* (1888–1900). Both of these early scholars in the discipline of folklore were interested in preserving what they regarded as the dying traditions of childhood; both also focused on games, especially games with an spoken or sung component.

Since the 1940s, American and British folklorists have produced a large body of scholarship, encompassing both field-collected material and analytical studies. Dorothy Howard was a pioneer in the technique of collecting directly from children rather than focusing on adult memories of their childhood traditions; she advocated this technique in her 1938 dissertation on ball-bouncing rhymes, one of the first analytical studies of childlore. Howard continued her study of children's folklore throughout her long lifetime. The most influential phase of her career was the period she spent studying and collecting children's folklore in Australia in 1954–1955 on a Fulbright grant. Her work greatly influenced a number of younger scholars, including New Zealand native Brian Sutton-Smith and June Factor of Australia, founder of the *Australian Children's Newsletter* and the author, collector, and editor of numerous studies of Australian childlore.

Perhaps the most significant of Dorothy Howard's protégés were the British husband-and-wife team of Peter and Iona Opie, who depended on her early in their careers for advice and support. The Opies devoted their professional lives to the documentation of the world of childhood, including not only folklore but also literature and commercially produced toys and games.

A number of studies have followed the trend established in the Opies' *Lore and Language of Schoolchildren*, the most highly regarded collection in the field. The annotated collections of Simon Bronner and Mary and Herbert Knapp are widely used as textbooks in American folklore courses. In Finland, Leea Virtanen edited a similar volume, *Children's Lore*. There are, of course, numerous other studies in this field.

In 1979, the Children's Folklore Section of the American Folklore Society was established. This section has flourished over the years and produces the journal *Children's Folklore Review*. A *Handbook of Children's Folklore* was published in 1995.

A perusal of the early studies of children's folklore reveals the outdated and largely discredited theoretical styles and trends of the times. For example, Lady Gomme, an ardent survivalist, was convinced that the words and lyrics of children's songs and rhymes contained references to or were survivals of ancient rites. In the game of London Bridge, for example, she saw evidence of ancient "foundation sacrifices" made when bridges were built.

Children's folklore also was used in the service of another popular late-nineteenth-century theory, namely, devolution. According to this theory, children's traditions were really misunderstood remnants of adult traditions that had filtered down or "devolved" from adults of previous generations to the current generation of children. Another feature of this theory held that children represented the savage stage of human development and therefore had to be civilized (in part, by learning how to behave) before they could become responsible adults.

Those who study and document children's folklore today grapple with what Brian Sutton-Smith termed the "triviality barrier" or the lack of respect stemming from the refusal of scholars in other fields and disciplines to take seriously any research dealing with the world of children. Folklorists are unusual among humanists and social scientists for their acceptance of children and their traditions on the children's own terms, as a folk group worthy of study in its own right rather than an adjunct of an older or more sophisticated body of informants.

Collecting and documenting children's folklore presents both problems and delights for the serious researcher. In general, children do not perform their folklore within earshot of adults, in order to avoid the interference or derision of those adults who are on the other side of the "triviality barrier." Folklorists, therefore, must first convince the children from whom they wish to collect that they are seriously interested in the materials and that the children will not be punished for revealing any traditions of which adults generally disapprove, such as scatological jokes and rhymes.

The spontaneity of much children's folklore frequently precludes advance notice of its performance. Consequently, folklorists must be ready to note down or observe these performances as they occur, which frequently makes video taping or audio recording difficult. However, members of a play group who are very comfortable with a particular adult researcher usually are willing to perform their traditional lore "on cue" if the researcher asks them to do so. The ideal research situation would be to document the same item both as a spontaneous performance and under prearranged circumstances and then compare the two.

Another approach to collecting children's folklore is by way of what many call "adult memory culture"—adult memories of the traditions they knew as children. This was the preferred method of the early-nineteenth-century folklorists. Since many adults have a tendency to remember selectively, this method is less reliable than collecting directly from the children themselves. Adult memory culture, however, does provide a diachronic context for contemporary children's folklore.

Sylvia Grider

See also Family Folklore.

****

References

Aries, Philippe. 1962. *Centuries of Childhood: A Social History of Family Life*. New York: Vintage.

Bronner, Simon. 1988. *American Children's Folklore: A Book of Rhymes, Games, Jokes, Stories, Secret Languages, Beliefs and Camp Legends for Parents, Grand-Parents, Teachers, Counselors and All Adults Who Were Once Children*, ed. Simon Bronner. Little Rock. AR: August House.

Gomme, Lady Alice Bertha. [1894–1898] 1964. *The Traditional Games of England, Scotland, and Ireland*. 2 vols. Reprint. New York: Dover.

Howard, Dorothy. 1938. Folk Rhymes of American Children. Ed. D. dissertation, New York University.

Knapp, Mary, and Herbert Knapp. 1976. *One Potato, Two Potato: The Secret Education of American Children*. New York: W. W. Norton.

McDowell, John H. 1983. Children's Folklore. In *Handbook of American Folklore*, ed. Richard Dorson. Bloomington: Indiana University Press.

Mechling, Jay. 1986. Children's Folklore. In *Folk Groups and Folklore Genres: An Introduction*, ed. Elliott Oring. Logan: University of Utah Press.

Newell, William Wells. [1883] 1963. *Games and Songs of American Children*. Reprint. New York: Dover.

Opie, Iona, and Peter Iona. 1959. *The Lore and Language of Schoolchildren*. Oxford: Clarendon.

Sutton-Smith, Brian. 1970. Psychology of Childlore: The Triviality Barrier. *Western Folklore* 29:1–8.

CHOREOMETRICS

A method for describing and rating dance and everyday movements in general qualitative terms, with the aim, according to Alan Lomax, of "recording and noting regularities and contrasts in movement patterns which are sufficiently frequent and gross to produce units universally applicable in cross-cultural studies." The basic ideas behind this method are that movement style in dance is a crystallization of the most frequent and crucial patterns of everyday activity and that the distribution of dance styles in the world corresponds closely to the distribution of cultures. Thus, in this method, dance is considered only as a representation and reinforcement of cultural patterns.

Choreometrics is an offspring of the Cantometrics Project, which was created in the 1960s by ethnomusicologist Alan Lomax. He and dance researchers Irmgard Bartinieff and Forrestine Paulay developed a rating system, based on a revised version of Rudolf Laban's effort-shape scheme, that describes the characteristic stances and modes of using energy that underlie social interaction, work, and other types of activity in a particular culture. Film sequences collected from all over the world, showing people in dance and at work, have been, for practical reasons, the main empirical source. On a special coding sheet, a number of parameters are rated and measured, such as the most active body parts, number of parts used, shape of transition, shape of main activity, energy of transition, energy of main activity, degree of variation, and spread of flow through the body.

The key concepts underlying the Choreometrics Project are style, dance type, culture type, global units, and universal and cross-cultural attributes. Taken together, they indicate both the kind and level of goals and the theoretical and methodological problems inherent in the study of dance. Historically, the ideas behind the project are closely related to the German *Kulturkreis* school in ethnology and the diffusionist school in folklore (the historic-geographic or Finnish School), which emphasize typologies, distribution, and mapping of cultural styles and artifacts. The main problems of the method are the claims for the universal validity of the results, the modeling of culture upon languages ("people belong to movement communities just as they belong to speech communities"), the assumption that cultures are objectively existing bounded entities that can be mapped globally, the idea of a close relation between dance and everyday movements in all cultures, and the assertion that this relationship can be measured on the basis of a limited number of filmed examples.

Owe Ronström

See also Cantometrics.

✳✳✳✳✳✳✳✳✳✳✳✳✳✳✳✳✳

References
Köngäs-Maranda, Elli. 1970. Deep Significance and Surface Significance: Is Cantometrics Possible? *Semiotica* 2: 173–184.
Lomax, Alan. 1968. *Folk Song Style and Culture*. Washington, DC: American Academy for the Advancement of Science.

CLEVER QUESTION/WISDOM QUESTION

A type of traditional enigma in which the solution cannot be guessed from the question but lies in specialized cultural knowledge. The clever question is found as a pastime in cultures that emphasize the oral examination in question-and-answer form as a means of socialization.

In many Protestant U.S. communities, the tradition of catechism in religious instruction has given rise to the posing of biblical questions. In strict groups, this instructive pastime often substitutes for other amusements viewed as immoral. Biblical clever questions do not address central questions of faith and doctrine but stretch the wits in a different way, as in the question, "How many names in the Bible begin with an *h*?" Others, although their solutions are still literal, come closer to trick questions ("Who in the Bible speaks and yet goes to neither Heaven nor Hell?—Balaam's ass").

In the United States, the clever question has become a profitable means of structuring and encouraging popular participation in mass culture. The manufacturers of baseball cards expanded their market after World War II by covering the backs of the cards with questions about batting averages and World Series scores, thus giving their customers a way to use the cards in interaction and multiplying the number of cards to be collected. A radio station connects with its listeners by offering a prize to the first person who calls in and correctly names, for example, the first drummer of the Beatles. Television quiz shows increase the prestige to be gained in a display of knowledge by carrying it to a national audience, with the added inducement of financial gain. The board game Trivial Pursuit takes the burden off the players' shoulders by posing the questions for them.

Even the high-culture industry has learned from popular culture's example. A few years after the Trivial Pursuit fad of the early 1980s, the literary scholar E. D. Hirsch declared the "culturally literate" to be those who could successfully identify a series of quotations, literary figures, scientific theories, and other things "that literate Americans know." Hirsch's proposed list of 5,000 items constituting the Western cultural lexicon provoked a more anxious form of trivial pursuit among those seeking to be literate and created a miniature publishing boom in rival lists and dictionaries.

The Christian catechism and university entrance exams demand the display of knowledge encapsulated in succinct answers to specific questions as the price of admission to a group. In the same way, the clever question can be a means of gaining entry or prestige. The lasting effects of adolescent male ludic competitions provide the comic subject for Barry Levinson's film *Diner*, in which a young man subjects his fiancée to an excruciating football trivia quiz before he consents to marry her.

The popularity of the clever question in the contemporary United States also relates to a lingering utilitarian contempt for most forms of amusement as "wasted time": Practices such as Trivial Pursuit and crossword puzzles can be defended as educational. Finally, games of clever questions exemplify an important assumption in the socialization of Americans: Knowledge, construed as a collection of discrete facts, leads to advancement and financial reward. The ethos of competitive accumulation (of both facts and goods) is played out in miniature in boys' trading of baseball cards and in the nightly broadcast of *Jeopardy*.

Dorothy Noyes

See also Enigma, Folk.

****

References

Abrahams, Roger D., and Alan Dundes. 1972. Riddles. In *Folklore and Folklife*, ed. Richard M. Dorson. Chicago: University of Chicago Press.

Green, Thomas A., and W. J. Pepicello. 1979. The Folk Riddle: A Redefinition of Terms. *Western Folklore* 38:3–21.

Taylor, Archer. 1943. The Riddle. *California Folklore Quarterly* 2:129–147.

COMMUNAL ORIGINS THEORY

The assumption that an aspect of culture was invented by a social group as a whole, rather than by an outstanding individual. This hypothesis has its roots in eighteenth-century romantic mystical philosophy, which attributed benevolent qualities to "savages," and in nineteenth-century romantic nationalism and associated ideologies that glorified ethnic and national groups (often labeled *races*). The general cultural atmosphere of the romantic period promoted debates about the inevitability of historical processes and the creative powers of the folk.

Friedrich Karl Savigny—one of the founders of the historical school and mentor to Jacob and Wilhelm Grimm—argued that "each historical process does not spring from conscious individual intention but rather carries in itself its own organic life, which develops through the effect of a force inaccessible to reason." Reflecting this mystical postulate, Jacob Grimm stated that "every epos must compose itself." Taken along with the conviction that "the folk creates," the two basic building blocks of the communal origins theory were put together.

By combining these two beliefs about creativity as an inevitable historical process and the folk as an active entity, the view that certain artistic cultural expressions arose through inevitable accident at the hands of unsophisticated social groups was formulated.

The most explicit expression of this idea is associated with Francis B. Gummere's explanations of how ballads originated through a singing-dancing throng. Gummere asserted that in the "primitive" stage of the development of poetry and in certain surviving cases, groups of illiterate individuals, without the ability to conceive of the future or to relate their experiences either to the past or to the experiences of other groups, gathered in festive settings, and through singing, accurate rhythm keeping, and dancing, these individuals expressed sentiments about local events that held immediate appeal and reflected a common interest. This, according to Gummere, was the cultural foundation of poetry: "In point of poetic process here is the social as opposed to the individual element. This festal throng and its rude choral verse are just as much a fact, apart from question of value, as a young man in the library and his poem."

The exact process by which such a creative exercise actually works has never been observed. Half a century after the introduction of Gummere's theory, ballad scholars such as D. K. Wilgus argued that "no adequate summary of Gummere's theory of communal origins has ever been made, possibly because no critic seems to have understood the peculiar union of faith and method by which Gummere convinced a generation of literary scholars that the ballad must be studied as a survival of primitive poetry." Today, the communal creation theory has been largely discredited. Arguing for a process of "communal *re*-creation" of narrative poems composed by individual authors constitutes a more plausible theory of ballad origins.

Hasan El-Shamy

See also Ballad; Bard; Evolutionary Theory; Folksong, Narrative.

****

References

Cocchiara, Guiseppe. 1981. *The History of Folklore in Europe*. Trans. by John N. McDaniel. Philadelphia: ISHI.

Gummere, Francis B. 1909. *The Popular Ballad*. New York: Dover.

Streenstrup, J.C.H.R. 1914. *The Medieval Popular Ballad*, trans. E. G. Cox. Boston: Ginn.

Wilgus, D. K. 1959. *Anglo-American Folksong Scholarship since 1898*. New Brunswick, NJ: Rutgers University Press.

COMMUNITAS

A concept of symbolic anthropology, meaning an antistructural fellowship typical of ritual contexts. The term is from the Latin word meaning community. Communitas is a social relationship that differs from the normal social and ideological order of things (i.e., the ordinary structure of the community).

The term was introduced by Victor W. Turner (1920–1983), one of the most prominent figures in the anthropological study of religion and symbolic analysis of ritual. In developing his own theory and terminology of symbolic anthropology for the study of religious symbols and ritual contexts, Turner singled out models that were observable in most ritual contexts. His labels for these common sequences in the ritual process were *communitas* and *liminality*. These concepts were very closely interrelated and represented further developments of Arnold van Gennep's ideas on liminal phases. In Turner's opinion, communitas represented one of the two major models for human interrelatedness, juxtaposed and alternating between the structured and hierarchical systems and the unstructured community emerging within liminal periods.

The concept of "structure" coincides with that of "social structure." It is suggested that communitas and "antistructure" characterize the liminal stage within a ritual process, where the juridical and political character of structure is challenged; communitas, by contrast, is a description for the community liminality. The distinction between the structure and status system and the liminal and communitas as their counterparts stresses not only their difference but also their complementary nature in the understanding of social and ritual life within a society.

Thus, the existence of this polarity between structure and antistructure is not limited to ritual contexts only but is also seen to characterize the whole human community. Social life is analyzed as a kind of dialectical process: All human interactions are perceived as consisting of two opposite and alternating forms, the stratified society and the egalitarian, closely knit liminal fellowship—communitas. According to Turner, every individual and community has to face alternating exposures to either structure or communitas. Transitions within the ritual procedures or within the individual's life history govern one's life experiences in any society.

Communitas can be characterized as a social form of liminality. Communitas is a relationship between those individuals who are not segmented according to roles and status but who confront one another in an unstructured way. Although communitas is supposed to be antistructural by its nature, it is not possible to maintain the spontaneity and immediacy of communitas for very long. Communitas then produces its own structure in which free relationships between individuals become converted into norm-governed relationships between social personae. The relationships or structure that communitas produces can be distinguished into three categories: (1) *existential* or *spontaneous* communitas; (2) *normative* communitas, in which, under the influence of time, the need to mobilize and organize resources, and the necessity for social control among members of the group in pursuance of these goals, the existing communitas is reorganized into a better social system; and (3) *ideological* communitas, which is a label one can apply to a variety of utopian models of societies based on communitas.

Juha Pentikäinen

See also Rites of Passage.

✳✳✳✳✳✳✳✳✳✳✳✳✳✳✳✳✳

References

Helander, Eila. 1986. *To Change and To Preserve: A Study of the Religiosity of Evangelical University Students and Graduates in Trinidad.* Helsinki: Finnish Society for Missiology and Ecumenics. Annals of the Finnish Society for Missiology and Ecumenics, no. 50.

Pentikäinen, Juha Y. 1986. Transition Rites. In *Transition Rites*, ed. Ugo Bianchi. Rome: "L'Erma" di Bretschneider.

Turner, Victor W. 1969. *The Ritual Process: Structure and Anti-Structure*. Chicago: Aldine.

———. 1974. *Dramas, Fields and Metaphors: Symbolic Action in Human Society*. Ithaca, NY: Cornell University Press.

COMPARATIVE MYTHOLOGY

Broadly construed, any study of mythology that attempts to reach conclusions through cross-cultural investigation; in a narrower usage, a tradition of philologically based comparative investigation of mythologies within the Indo-European language family. The precise delimitation, history, and classification of this language family has been a matter of some controversy. In his recent summary, *Comparative Mythology*, Jaan Puhvel delineates the following language groups as underlain by the Indo-European protolanguage: Indic, Iranian, Tocharian, Anatolian, Armenian, Greek, Italic, Celtic, Germanic, Baltic, and Slavic. One of the prime motives behind the study of Indo-European mythology has been the assumption that Indo-European civilization formed the essential source of Western civilization; the research of certain recent scholars, notably Martin Bernal, suggests the necessity of reexamining this assumption in light of evidence supporting a greater Afro-Asiatic influence. Traditions of comparative study also have developed within other, non-Indo-European language families (e.g., the Malayo-Polynesian family); these have sometimes incorporated methods from the Indo-European model. Because it is historically and methodologically so important, the distinction between the "narrower" and "broader" conceptions of comparative mythology will be used throughout the present discussion.

Comparative mythology in the narrower sense was set in motion in the late eighteenth and early nineteenth centuries, less by considerations specific to mythology than by discoveries in the field of comparative philology. Such scholars as William Jones, Franz Bopp, and Jacob Grimm demonstrated parallels between certain languages of Europe, the Middle East, and Asia, which in turn led to the reconstruction of Proto-Indo-European as a parent language. These philological researches lent major impetus to the detailed investigation and historical reconstruction of the relationships between the mythologies of the various Indo-European societies. Attempts to reconstruct the history and content of pantheons proved a particularly compelling pursuit, one that was frequently accompanied by nationalistic concerns.

Such historical reconstructions of mythologies via philology reached a crescendo under the intellectual leadership of Friedrich Max Müller, a scholar schooled in German comparative philology but working at Oxford amid the emerging social evolutionism of middle- and late-nineteenth-century England. Müller's comparativism rested on a partially secularized variant of the biblical ethnography that had, in previous centuries, provided a means of accounting for cultural parallels noted among widely dispersed peoples. In biblical ethnography, such parallels were held to be remnants of the degenerated original revelation of Eden; in Müller's version, they were remnants of an original period of natural poetic sensibility and speech, which had achieved an archaic greatness in India. Though many of Müller's efforts were devoted to the mythicoreligious works of India and to tracing connections to other Indo-European societies, his works sometimes also suggested that one might expect to be able to follow out such historical interconnections through the entire world.

The attempt to explain the occurrence of mythological parallels as matters of historical interrelationship became, through the course of the nineteenth century, increasingly polarized against the methods of evolutionary anthropology, which sought to explain such parallels as independent invention; this in turn would confirm the thesis of unilinear evolution. E. B. Tylor, the leading evolutionist, thought that mythology offered evidence of the erroneous form of reasoning that defined the first evolutionary stage; he juxtaposed the mythologies of numerous societies in order to demonstrate the universal character of human thought at this stage. Logically, historical-diffusionist principles and evolutionary principles are incompatible; they provide competing explanations of the occurrence of ethnographic parallels. It is one of the ironies of Müller that, committed as he was to historical-philological reconstruction, he also put forward theories about the origin of mythology that could easily be read as asserting universal psychic processes—processes lying quite beyond anything specific to the Indo-European tradition.

The most famous of the more generic aspects of Müller's theories of myth was the "solar" hypothesis—essentially, the claim that mythology was produced as a spontaneous poetic reaction to observed celestial phenomena; the thesis was enthusiastically embraced by many followers. The solar hypothesis was accompanied by a postulated "disease of language," processes of inevitable change in language, including a contraction in the range of meanings of particular terms. Such changes rendered the original poetic utterances unintelligible, if not bizarre, for later generations, who designated such utterances as "mythology." The solar and the disease hypotheses were illustrated by Müller largely through Indo-European material, but many of his followers, swept up in the solar hypothesis, were much more interested in a programmatic theory of myth interpretation than in working out specifically Indo-European issues. And methodological distinctions that are clear in the abstract are often muddy in practice. From Müller onward and even in James Frazer's world-spanning myth study, *The Golden Bough*, it is often simply unclear whether, at any given moment, the comparative dimension rests on a universal human psychology or a postulated cultural-historical interrelationship.

Comparative mythology of the narrower kind underwent a change—in certain respects, a decline—toward the end of the nineteenth century. Several reasons can be cited. The methods of Müller and his followers had many shortcomings, most notably a tendency to rest great claims on small bits of evidence—in some cases, a postulated cognate relation between words or even single syllables. The vast sweep of world languages characteristic of Müller and his followers conveyed the impression of enormous linguistic erudition. But their work was frequently carried out on the level of words and syllables, and much of it required little more than patience and a set of dictionaries. The smallness of the data was mirrored, inversely, by the extravagance of the speculation. It was largely the looseness and ad hoc nature of the methods that Andrew Lang, gadfly of the solar mythology movement, attacked, once even parodying such methods by using them to prove that Müller was himself a solar myth. Increasing data and types of data rendered some of the original postulated connections untenable.

Finally, as has been suggested, much of the swirl surrounding Müller had been stimulated by those aspects of his theories that were least intimately bound up with Indo-European mythology specifically. So the seeming contraction of interest in comparative mythology in the narrower sense at the end of the nineteenth century perhaps marked not so much a decline in Indo-European mythology as a decline in certain extravagant theories, such as the solar hypothesis and the disease of language, on whose coattails Indo-European mythology had ridden into an unusually prominent place in scholarly and popular consciousness. Comparative mythology of the narrower type, following the decline of Müller's school, tended to become the specialized province of disciplines concerned directly with Indo-European languages, such as departments of classical languages and literatures, and it was supported by such fields as ancient history and archaeology.

The most influential theories of myth in the twentieth century have not been constrained by an Indo-European border but have instead been comparative in the broader sense—seeking to isolate underlying commonalities in myths of different cultures, often with little interest in historical interrelationships. Among these one may count the "myth-ritual" school, the Freudian and Jungian schools, and the structuralist school of Claude Lévi-Strauss. The myth-ritual school and the Freudian and Jungian schools retained some of the assumptions of nineteenth-century evolutionism, especially the so-called comparative method. This method, a corollary of unilinear evolution, consisted of the assumption that one could expect to find correlations between non-European "primitive" cultures and the culture of the European historical past. The Freudian and Jungian schools also frequently invoked a further parallelism—between the psychic development of the individual and the general cultural evolution of humanity, so that, for example, childhood anxieties would have counterparts in the myths and rituals of "primitive" peoples.

Lévi-Strauss utilized the methods of structural linguistics (especially as developed by Roman Jakobson and Ferdinand de Saussure) to discover and analyze underlying patterns in myths and in their transformations through time and space. Though he dealt with patterns at many levels, Lévi-Strauss' most celebrated and controversial claims had to do with postulated universal patterns, which he attributed to universal properties of the human mind. Vis-à-vis previous comparativists, Lévi-Strauss was distinguished by his insistence that the successful interpretation of a myth necessitates an understanding of its "structure": It is not any particular image or scenario but rather the way in which elements of a myth work as an ensemble that makes signification possible. The structures that Lévi-Strauss explored were, for the most part, varieties of binary oppositions arranged as proportions; for example, he claimed that the opposition of "raw" versus "cooked" in myth encoded a universal human distinction between "nature" and "culture." Lévi-Strauss' interest in developing formal methods to decode meanings did much to bring about the now assumed interrelationship between comparative mythology and semiotic theory—a development that has remained fruitful even in the aftermath of the structuralist movement.

Each of the schools of myth research mentioned here has its own particular methods and theories, but they all operate on the assumption that myth is uniform enough to allow the scholar to abstract general conclusions from a cross-cultural pool of data. But the twentieth century also has seen some movements in the study of mythology that have carried anticomparativist tendencies; most significant among these are the "functionalism" of Bronislaw Malinowski and certain interpretations of Boasian "historical particularism." Neither one of these perspectives totally precludes comparison; yet each, in its own way, affirms the value of detailed analysis of myth in context over the search for recurrent, cross-cultural patterns. Malinowski, in "Myth and Primitive Psychology," specifically developed his functionalist approach as a counter to the speculative exuberance that was characteristic of Müller.

A significant revitalization, with innovations, of comparative mythology of the narrower type occurred in the mid-twentieth century, stimulated by the prolific writings of Georges Dumézil. Dumézil's success rested largely on the fact that he was able to devise strategies of comparison that incorporated a functionalist emphasis on myth in sociopolitical context—an orientation that he developed through an acquaintance with the Durkheimian tradition of comparative sociology. What Dumézil compared, among Indo-European mythologies, was not so much lexical items as sets of interrelated sociopolitical institutions. Most persistent was his claim that widely dispersed Indo-European mythologies expressed a common, underlying, tripartite "ideology," in which society was seen as built around three main activities or "functions"—epitomized in priest (magico-religious/juridical order), warrior, and cultivator. An interesting quirk of Dumézil's "comparative mythology," then, was that the real object that was compared from society to society was not necessarily mythology but rather "ideology." Ideology might be expressed in myth, but it might also be expressed in numerous other possible forms, such as genealogies, class divisions within social structure, or narrative genres other than myth. An example of the last is found in *Archaic Roman Religion*, in which Dumézil juxtaposed the war and eventual merging of the Romans and the Sabines, as recounted in Livy's history of Rome, with Scandinavian accounts of a war and eventual merging of two tribes of gods, the Æsir and the Vanir. Taking a clue from the fact that the Vanir, like the Sabines, represented the values of fecundity and opulence, Dumézil found a commonality between the Roman and the Scandinavian narratives. In each case, claimed Dumézil, there was a depiction of the completion of the tripartite ideology through the addition of fertility, the third function. In this sense, the Roman and Scandinavian accounts, one "historical" and the other "mythical," reflected a shared Indo-European ideology.

One of the main criticisms of Dumézil is reminiscent of a criticism that had been made of Müller—that the methods of comparison allowed the scholar to incorporate too much, eventually obliterating any border around the Indo-European family. In Müller's approach, this happened because of the smallness of the pieces compared: One could always find a syllable that could be postulated as cognate with some syllable in the next language family. In Dumézil's approach, the same thing happened, but it happened because of the largeness—the abstractness and generality—of the entity compared, that is, the tripartite ideology. For it could reasonably be argued that what was depicted in Dumézil's tripartite ideology was not so much an Indo-European speciality as a set of functional prerequisites for any society. In fact, Dumézil's arguments frequently have been picked up by scholars working in societies without any demonstrable connection with the Indo-European world. Once again, theories originating within the study of Indo-European mythology have had, for some scholars, the effect of breaking down the alleged distinctiveness of Indo-European mythology vis-à-vis other mythologies. Dumézil's methods have occasioned many criticisms, but even the critics have often applauded his fresh insights into the relation of myth and society and his refocusing of interest on Indo-European mythology and/or mythology in general.

The present climate is not particularly favorable to cross-cultural methodologies; emphasis is on the local and the incommensurable, and there is acute skepticism of methodologies that suggest "totalizing" ambitions. Still, there are signs that the present-day skepticism is discovering its own limits and that a conviction is returning regarding the value and even the necessity of a discourse of human commonalities and interrelatedness to complement the discourse of differences. Fueled by developments within maturing fields such as cognitive science, we can expect a resurgence of interest in comparative mythology in both the narrower and broader forms—that is, both bounded by particular, historically related language families and oriented toward human universals. The vastly enlarged pool of ethnographic and textual data now available will permit analyses to be more empirically grounded than was possible in Müller's time, yet our findings may prove to be no less amazing than anything devised in Müller's speculative flights.

Gregory Schrempp

See also Evolutionary Theory; Myth-Ritual Theory; Philological Approach; Structuralism.

✳✳✳✳✳✳✳✳✳✳✳✳✳✳✳✳✳✳

References

Bernal, Martin. 1987. *Black Athena*. Vol. 1. New Brunswick, NJ: Rutgers University Press.

Dumézil, Georges. 1970. *Archaic Roman Religion*. Vol. 1. Chicago: University of Chicago Press.

Frazer, James. 1911. *The Golden Bough*. Vol. 1. London: Macmillan.

Lévi-Strauss, Claude. 1969. *The Raw and the Cooked*. New York: Harper & Row.

Littleton, C. Scott. 1982. *The New Comparative Mythology*. Berkeley: University of California Press.

Malinowski, Bronislaw. 1954. *Magic, Science, and Religion and Other Essays*. New York: Doubleday Anchor Books.

Müller, Friedrich Max. 1856. Comparative Mythology. In *Oxford Essays*. London: John W. Parker.

Puhvel, Jaan. 1987. Comparative Mythology. Baltimore, MD: Johns Hopkins University Press.

Schrempp, Gregory. 1983. The Re-Education of Friedrich Max Müller. Man 18:90–110.

Tylor, E. B. 1873. Primitive Culture. Vol. 1. London: John Murray.

COMPUTER-MEDIATED FOLKLORE

Folklore generated by the computer-user subculture or, more generally, any folklore communicated through computer networking (electronic messaging).

Electronic messaging began in the late 1960s as a brainstorming tool for computer programmers. Today, a giant maze of electronic pathways referred to as "the Network" (or usually, just "the Net") links computer users around the world via fiber-optic telephone cables, making it possible to send almost instantaneous messages (electronic mail, or E-mail) to a user on the other side of the globe.

An outgrowth of these networks since about 1980 has been a proliferation of topical information-sharing forums in which individual users can take part. Topics range broadly and include academic specialities and subspecialties and also hobbies and special interests. Thus, small, temporary communities defined by special interests provide the context and the occasion (and computer networking provides the medium) for communication that is both like and not like that which folklorists more commonly study. Familiar genres such as contemporary legends and topical jokes are frequently communicated via the Net, along with audience commentary, additional variants, and analysis. The extent to which the medium and its technology influence the content and performance of folklore transmitted via the Net, however, and the exact nature of that influence are topics still being explored.

Although hackers like to distinguish between themselves (experts and aficionados) and mere users (who use the computer as a work tool rather than playing more creatively with the medium), the conventions and the jargon that the hacker subculture has evolved have spread widely among all users, and obvious lack of familiarity with the forms is the mark of the uninitiated (or *newbie*). Folklore actually generated by and for computer-mediated communication has been chronicled in electronic format by the computer-networking community itself since 1975. Expanded and updated on an ongoing basis, versions of *The New Hacker's Dictionary* were published in book form in 1983 and in 1991.

Hacker folklore that already has been widely noticed includes the use of *emoticons* such as the sideways smiling faces (smileys) used to make up for the lack of visual cues to indicate emotional content in hastily constructed prose. For example, the basic smiley :-) is inserted when the writer wants to indicate that what he or she has just written should not be taken too seriously or as an insult. Variations on the basic smiley, however, have proliferated in ways that indicate a premium on humor and creativity rather than on clearer communication. The same figure, moreover, can have multiple interpretations. For instance, the figure 8-) is sometimes said to be a user wearing glasses and sometimes an excited user (i.e., a user with wide eyes). A number of glossaries of smileys are in circulation on the Net, as are a number of files on frequently asked questions (FAQ files). Compilations of folklore such as topical jokes or urban legends are often available as FAQ files posted in order to avoid tedious repetitions.

Rosan Augusta Jordan

See also Xeroxlore.

✳✳✳✳✳✳✳✳✳✳✳✳✳✳✳✳✳✳

References

Cerulo, Karen A., Janet M. Ruane, and Mary Chayko. 1992. Technological Ties That Bind: Media-Generated Primary Groups. *Communication Research* 19:109–129.

Dorst, John. 1990. Tags and Burners, Cycles and Networks: Folklore in the Telectronic Age. *Journal of Folklore Research* 27:179–190.

Fox, William S. 1983. Computerized Creation and Diffusion of Folkloric Materials. *Folklore Forum* 16:5–20.

Jennings, Karla. 1990. *The Devouring Fungus: Tales from the Computer Age*. New York: W. W. Norton.

Raymond, Eric, ed. 1991. *The New Hacker's Dictionary*. Cambridge, MA: MIT Press.

CONDUIT THEORY/MULTICONDUIT THEORY

A theory developed by Linda Dégh and Andrew Vázsonyi to explain why folklore genres persist in a limited number of remarkably stable and crystallized conventional forms while in the processes of transmission and dissemination. Reproduction in context results in limitless personal and culture-specific variants. The theory asserts folklore texts do not pass through an orderly, regulated trail from person to person but generate their own, specific chain linkages that carry messages through society. These linkages, named *conduits*, consist of individuals united by similar mind-sets— people who react similarly to similar messages and thereby qualify as senders and receivers of similar messages within given systems of communication. If a message—a folklore text—travels through its proper conduit, it goes unchanged from one person to another; however, if the message, on its course, reaches an inappropriate individual, it will either reach a dead end or survive by undergoing modifications, and thereby, the message deviates from its original trail and lands in another conduit whose members respond to the modified message. The forms of oral transmission are as diverse as people, and the eventualities of affinity between people and folklore are as multifarious. Thus, the legend conduit unites legend fanciers, the joke conduit is made up of a sequence of witty people, and tales progress through the tale conduit shaped by storytellers. Furthermore, within a single genre, type clusters, episodes, minor incidents, motifs, and formulas also constitute their own conduits to be identified as subconduits or microconduits. In transmission, further ramifications of the conduit result in a complex, multiconduit system that is the key to the folklore process.

Observation of multiconduit systems in natural contexts or reproduced in laboratory experiments can contribute to the understanding of the nature of folklore transmission, as affinities link contents and forms, variants emerge, degeneration and regeneration of texts lead to the "extraordinary stability" observed by Walter Anderson when amassing widespread and multifarious variables of the riddle tale AT 922. Conduit analysis also explains how personal preferences lead to innovation and specialization in the building of regional, ethnic, and personal repertoires of magic tales, ghost stories, saint's legends, murder ballads, or tall tales.

The conduit theory is based on the realization that participation in the communication of folklore depends on spontaneity, the participant's freedom to tell or not to tell a story. Transmission of traditional messages in natural contexts is essentially free; arbitrary limitation of this freedom encroaches upon the normal functioning of the conduit.

Studying people's ability to remember and forget, learn and re-create, psychologists, anthropologists, and folklorists experimented with serial reproduction of prose material. Experiments by Frederick Bartlett, Robert Lowie, Walter Anderson, and others were based on the artificial lining up of volunteers, not traditional bearers. This work showed that denying participants the right of choice leads to the gradual devolution of the text. In the retelling procedure, participants react with psychological defense mechanisms by forgetting or falsely remembering, forcing the message into inadequate conduits. The conduit theory argues for the analysis of the mistakes made by participants in artificial serial reproduction situations, complementing such findings with independent psychological personality testing.

Linda Dégh

See also Performance; Repertoire; Transmission.

✳✳✳✳✳✳✳✳✳✳✳✳✳✳✳✳✳✳

References

Anderson, Walter. 1923. *Kaiser und Abt: Die Geschichte eines Schwankes* (Kaiser and abbot: The history of a joke). Folklore Fellows Communications, no. 42. Helsinki: Academia Scientiarum Fennica.

———. 1951. *Ein Volkskundliches Experiment.* Folklore Fellows Communications, no. 141. Helsinki: Academia Scientiarum Fennica.

Bartlett, Frederick C. 1920. Some Experiments on the Reproduction of Folk Stories. *Folklore* 31:30–47.

Dégh, Linda. 1993. The Legend Conduit. In *Creativity and Tradition in Folklore: New Directions,* ed. Simon J. Bronner. Logan: Utah State University Press.

Dégh, Linda, and Andrew Vázsonyi. 1975. The Hypothesis of Multi-Conduit Transmission in Folklore. In *Folklore, Performance and Communication,* ed. D. Ben-Amos and K. Goldstein. The Hague: Mouton.

———. 1976. Legend and Belief. In *Folklore Genres,* ed. Dan Ben-Amos. Austin: University of Texas Press.

Fine, Gary Alan. 1992. *Manufacturing Tales.* Knoxville: University of Tennessee Press.

Hemenway, Robert. 1976. The Functions of Folklore in Charles Chesnutt's "The Conjuring Woman." *Journal of the Folklore Institute* 13:283–309.

Lewis, Mary-Ellen B. 1976. Burns' "Tale O' Truth": A Legend in Literature. Journal of the Folklore Institute 13:241–262.

Lowie, Robert H. 1942. Some Cases of Repeated Reproduction. Reprinted in The Study of Folklore, ed. Alan Dundes. Englewood Cliffs, NJ: Prentice-Hall.

Oring, Elliott. 1978. Transmission and Degeneration. *Fabula* 19:193–210.

Wehse, Rainer. 1983. Volkskundliche Erzählforschung. In *Märchenerzähler, Erzählgemeinschaft*. Kassel, Germany: Röth.

CONTEXT

The conditions or circumstances, either transitory or lasting, within which a given item of lore (or some other aspect of culture or society) is expressed. From the perspective of the individual (or group) eliciting the expression, each external element perceived at the time it is being produced has motivational value (i.e., it becomes a "stimulus situation"); thus, such perceptions affect the item itself as it is being performed. The conception of stimulus situations, as stated by social psychologists, deals with objects and situations in their contextual relationships; the individual experiences and reacts to social objects, persons, groups, cultural items (e.g., furniture, tools, words, music) in terms of meaningful relations prevailing in the characteristic patterns of these stimulus agents.

In folklore scholarship, awareness of the roles played by such intermediary, contextual forces on a given item (and vice versa) may be seen as resulting from the influence of empirical observation by folklorists. This is due also to the impact of psychological learning theories on the functional approach to culture studies, especially the terms proposed by Bronislaw Malinowski and presented to folklorists by William Bascom. In anthropology, the need for contextual data grew from attempts to comprehend correctly social and cultural phenomena, especially verbal texts, radically different from the anthropologist's own. The works of Franz Boas in North America and those of the Finnish School in Europe were both criticized for reducing the field of folklore to the study of lifeless texts severed from their normal social and cultural contexts.

Thus, anthropologists and folklorists began to see the need for additional information about the "given" norms and values of the community whose verbal lore was being studied. For example, in their research on the Dahomean tales of West Africa, Melville and Frances Herskovits recognized the need to study Dahomean culture as a whole. Their fieldwork was facilitated by a knowledge of contextual data on patterns of family life, economic structure, educational techniques, aesthetic values, religious concepts and ritual, and political development. Similarly, in studying Clackamas Indian narratives from North America, Melville Jacobs realized the importance of social and cultural forces on the process of narrating; thus, he sought to establish the role of these forces as a prerequisite to understanding the narratives themselves.

Consequently, folklorists began emphasizing the roles of these conditions in the study of the various fields of lore—especially the impact of such factors as economic conditions, religious beliefs, audience, and the time and place of an activity—on traditional expressions. Linda Dégh emphasized the importance of the narrating community in understanding a given narrative; Alan Dundes expanded folklorists' principal interests to include "text, texture, and context." Studies emphasizing context, often at the expense of the text, were labeled "contextual"; scholars applying such an approach were designated as "contextualists."

Another aspect of the contextual approach may be explained in terms of the influence of frames of reference on how individuals perceive the properties of physical, as well as social and cultural, objects within a given set of conditions (context); for example, with reference to physical perception, what determines judging an item as light or heavy, small or big, and so on. Meanwhile, regarding kinship relations, a narrator may perceive a certain character in a folklore text as a man, a king, a brother to a sister, a brother to a brother, a husband to a wife or woman, and so forth. Each of these perceptions would entail the relevant traditional roles associated with the character (e.g., kindness, rivalry). In a cognitive behavioristic analysis of these roles, Hasan El-Shamy demonstrated that the narrator's judgment with respect to each kinship relationship is a function of the total series of relationships that serve as a frame of reference in the given situation. Such psychological processes, which are responsible for the style or semantics of texts, are typically termed *part-whole* or *frame of reference* perceptual principles and are an aspect of the broader concept of context.

Hasan El-Shamy

See also Audience.

✳✳✳✳✳✳✳✳✳✳✳✳✳✳✳✳✳

References

Dégh, Linda. 1969. *Folktales and Society: Storytelling in a Hungarian Peasant Community*. Bloomington: University of Indiana Press.

Herskovits, Melville J., and Frances Herskovits. 1958. *Dahomean Narrative, A Cross Cultural Analysis*. Evanston, IL: Northwestern University Press.

Jacobs, Melville. 1959. *The Content and Style of an Oral Literature: Clackamas, Chinook Myths and Tales*. Chicago: University of Chicago Press.

———. 1964. *Pattern in Cultural Anthropology*. Homewood, IL: Dorsey.

Malinowski, Bronislaw. 1944. *A Scientific Theory of Culture*. Chapel Hill: University of North Carolina Press.

El-Shamy, H. 1967. Folkloric Behavior. Ph.D. thesis, University of Indiana, Bloomington.

————. 1979. *Brother and Sister. Type 872**: *A Cognitive Behavioristic Text Analysis of a Middle Eastern Oikotype*, Folklore Monograph Series, vol. 8. Bloomington, IN: Folklore Publications Group.

COSMOLOGY

The culturally appropriate view of and way to study or contemplate the universe in its creation and present aspect. A people's cosmology includes their cognitive and ideational accounts of how the universe came into being and its physical characteristics. Often, the accounts include a set of moral imperatives as well. The accounts may be in prose or in poetry and usually are highly metaphorical and full of allusion. In some societies, cosmology may be fully known only to a select and highly trained few. In other societies, any member of the group who expresses an interest will be taught the cosmology. In mainstream U.S. culture, young people often complain of being forced to learn cosmology through attendance at Sunday schools or similar religious training classes.

Cosmologies usually include not only philosophy and moral precepts but also theories about how and why the universe came into being. They provide a rationale for who we are, what we represent, why we are here, and what our proper behavior should be. Often, in discussing cosmology, as much attention is given to the consequences of a failure to believe or behave properly as to the details of the construction of the universe.

Cosmology is closely related to cosmogony, which is an account of the physical creation—and usually also the ordering—of the universe; cosmogony, however, does not normally include morality or offer exemplars of proper behavior. The terms *cosmology* and *cosmogony* also are used by those in other disciplines, especially by astronomers. However, folklorists put a slightly different spin on these words. For an astronomer, *cosmogony* refers to the physical construction—or coming into being—of the universe, and *cosmology* concerns ideas on the functioning of the universe.

Folklorists usually look for cosmology in the myth sequences of a people and expect the cosmology to be peopled with animals that have the ability to speak or at least communicate, with feats of will and character seldom seen in the modern world, and with beings who are larger than life and greater than human; they also expect to find in cosmology lessons on how not to live as well as how to construct a proper life.

Once having established the universe, the world of the people, and acceptable patterns of living, the cosmology portion of mythic narrative is completed. Additional episodes that follow the cosmology usually are considered to be an integral portion of mythic narrative but qualitatively different from the cosmological portion of the narrative. There may be competing cosmologies in operation in any given culture; in contemporary American culture, for example, the Judeo-Christian-Muslim account, creationism, and science all offer differing cosmologies. However, once a cosmology is accepted by a person or group and established within a culture, it remains essentially fixed; myth, by contrast, is subject to change in response to a changing world and interactions within it.

Claire R. Farrer

See also Culture Hero; Myth.

✳✳✳✳✳✳✳✳✳✳✳✳✳✳✳✳

References

Blackburn, Thomas C. 1975. *December's Child: A Book of Chumash Oral Narratives.* Berkeley: University of California Press.

Boas, Franz. 1894. Chinook Texts. *Bureau of Ethnology*, Bulletin 20. Washington, DC: Smithsonian Institution.

Farrer, Claire R. 1991. *Living Life's Circle: Mescalero Apache Cosmovision.* Albuquerque: University of New Mexico Press.

Kroeber, Alfred L. 1976. *Yurok Myths.* Berkeley: University of California Press.

Costume, Folk

Any manner of stylizing, marking, or manipulating the appearance of the human body with culturally understood symbols and forms. The term *costume* includes not only clothing but also other body adornments, such as jewelry, cosmetics, hairstyles, masks, tattoos, and scarification, and it can refer to everyday adornment as well as dramatic, ritual, or festival costuming. Costume draws on the expressive power of the individual body to produce social identities within the terms of community aesthetics. Folkloristic studies of costume generally consider how adornment style participates in the bodily performance of individual and group identity, as well as how folk manipulate and transform adornment signs and practices within the framework of their own aesthetics.

Costume often is conceived as a symbolic language, composed of clothing signs. Petr Bogatyrev, in his influential study of folk costume in modern Slovakia, pointed out that costume is both an object and a sign having multiple functions, such as the ritual, aesthetic, practical, and ideological. In contexts in which a costume's practical function is downplayed, costume functions as a sign; it becomes an ideological reality. As ideological reality, costume embodies the associations individuals have with the social structures of family, economy or polity, region, ethnicity, religion, and caste or class. The type of

A Bahamian Junkanoo dancer with horned-toad mask and brilliantly colored costume participates in Miami/Bahamas Goombay Festival, a celebration of south Florida's black Bahamian immigrants.

folk costume discussed by Bogatyrev often has emerged in colonial or touristic contexts in which self-conscious presentation to outsiders is a key way of negotiating identity. In western and eastern Europe, such folk costumes are invariably codifications of past peasant styles representing regional differences, and they often involve symbolic inscription on women's bodies as regional or ethnic symbols. In this way, folk costume is implicated in the maintenance of the cultural or political boundaries of ethnic groups, regions, or nations, particularly in touristic, festival, or colonial contexts.

Folk costume plays a key role in the negotiation of personal and community boundaries, both inside and outside folk groups. Significantly, folklorists who discuss adornment have concentrated on costume's socializing force—its relationship to the maintenance of individual and group identities and the articulation of power relations. This important work on folk costume has considered adornment as an important means of communicating an individual's relationship to a group or community and its traditional values. According to Don Yoder, folk costume expresses identity in a symbolic way, functioning as a "badge of identity" for members of ethnic, religious, and occupational groups. Costume outwardly represents the identity of the folk community and expresses the individual's manifold relationships to and within that community. In many plain religious sects discussed by Yoder, such as the Amish, Mennonites, and Shakers, the rejection of fashion in plain dress historically articulated group separation from mainstream society by embodying the principles of sectarian doctrine and establishing a "hedge" against the temptations of the world. In this way, sect members would be perceived and perceive themselves as different from others. Thus, folk costume promotes group solidarity and maintains personal and group boundaries as individuals embody a community by reshaping their bodies in keeping with group values.

In addition to outwardly embodying identities, costume also plays a key role in the definition and reconfiguration of personal identities and social boundaries within any folk group. In ritual contexts such as rites of passage, for example, adornment practices articulate an individual's relationship to the community by marking culturally significant moments in that individual's life. Young men and women passing from childhood to adulthood often adopt adult attire (such as long trousers or skirts) as a symbol of their new status in the community. Their change in status is accomplished, in part, by the reconfiguration of their physical appearance in costume—physical transformation embodies personal transformation. Marriage and mourning costumes, contrasted with everyday clothing, indicate the wearers' participation in ritual passage and transformation. In this way, clothing induces individuals to become or remain members of a community by physically representing their integration into the community and their acceptance of group values and distinctions related to age, sex, and status. Within this approach, clothing perpetuates a dominant social code by defining hierarchies and marking separations.

Costume also possesses the power to reconfigure those hierarchies and separations. In other ritual and festival contexts, costume transforms the body's everyday appearance and redefines its boundaries temporarily in fanciful costuming, masking, or clothing that represents and helps enact new, fictional, or performative roles. Masquerade and cross-dressing are major media for inversion and other renegotiations of social boundaries, commonly adopted when individuals try on new roles or identities and when the barriers between individuals are broken down during a period of license. In carnival contexts, elaborate costumes are an important way in which a sense of fun and license is engendered. A key feature of such carnival costumes is often their aesthetic of excess. Elaborate and expensive, these carnival costumes exaggerate and distort the features and proportions of the body, opening up the body and extending its boundaries. This exaggeration and excess contribute to the sense of spectacle and a carnivalesque aesthetic that celebrates the excesses of the body and its pleasures. Costume signs in carnival contexts are multivalent and often potentially subversive; that is, they involve the play and transformation of everyday attire, renegotiating its conventional meanings, if only temporarily.

Costume is likewise dynamic and subversive in cultural contexts in which dress is contested or manipulated through what Elizabeth Wilson has termed "oppositional dress." In oppositional dress, the body is transformed into a site of struggle by disenfranchised groups or disaffected subcultures as they attempt to define themselves by redefining the appearance and meaning of their bodies. Oppositional dress can take several forms, usually through processes of refusal and appropriation. For instance, retentions or revivals of traditional dress by indigenous peoples in colonial contexts in the face of pressures to adopt fashionable, Western dress constitute a form of refusal—self-definition as a strategy of resistance to colonial control or Western cultural imperialism. In some cases, traditional dress becomes a symbol of political movements for economic and political independence. Mahatma Gandhi's use of traditional Indian textiles and dress as a symbol of resistance to British imperial control in the mid-twentieth century signified both economic and cultural independence. By advocating traditional dress, he redefined the colonial social body as Indian, not British, and reasserted the power of native Indian materials, industries, and production techniques. Resistance through costume also can take the form of revivals of indigenous or traditional dress in postcolonial situations, as expressed by women in Islamic revolutionary contexts who readopt the *chador*, the full veiling prescribed by traditional Islamic law. Again, this costume signifies in complicated ways, both reinscribing women's bodies in traditional gender roles and challenging outside religious or cultural control.

In other cases, new costume forms emerge as subcultures or groups within complex societies appropriate normative clothing forms in an oppositional way. In Western societies, feminist groups historically sought equality through dress reform by appropriating men's jackets and ties for women's professional costume. In western Europe and the United States, the wearing of black clothing to articulate alternative or decadent sensibilities by nineteenth-century dandies and twentieth-century bohemians was an appropriation of both customary mourning costume and historically respectable bourgeois male dress, exaggerated for everyday wear. This alternative costume draws on the contradictory associations of the color black with death, sexuality, respectability, and monasticism to articulate a complicated stance against mainstream respectability. In these cases, the conventional meaning of any costume style changes, even as its new status as oppositional still relies on the memory of previously respectable associations.

Appropriation also plays a central role in the oppositional costuming practices of contemporary youth subcultures, such as punks who reassemble conventional working-class clothing with symbols of transgression and violence (rips and tears, crosses, and multiple body piercings). Members of these subcultures express complex and contradictory sexual and social identities through adornment practices that appropriate normative or fashionable commodities, signs, and values and reassemble them in terms of their group aesthetic, with the aim of shocking. Dick Hebdige has characterized the style of subcultural groups as a "signifying practice" that draws on the polysemic range of meanings in clothing signs by appropriating available images and symbols from dominant culture and manipulating them in ways that defy conventional assumptions about appropriate appearance. Such styles insist on shifting the terms of any discourse of dress by adding new elements, inverting old elements, and transgressing norms as a means of articulating a challenge to accepted values, foregrounding a sense of difference and asserting self-possession or personal power in the face of powerlessness. This signifying practice is fundamentally polysemic in that appropriated signs do not lose their previous associations—they merely gain new meanings that are foregrounded in uneasy tension with older, more conventional associations. This juxtaposition of seemingly conflicting meanings highlights and expresses larger conflicts in society that these groups wish to address.

In local settings, folk costume does not develop in isolation, and much of contemporary folk costume is polysemic in nature. Like language and other aspects of material folklife such as foodways and architecture, contemporary costume bears the signs of historical struggles, contacts, borrowing, and exchanges in any locality. In the context of colonization and cultural displacement, new creole forms emerge from the interaction of different cultural groups' adornment practices. An example of such creolization is the new forms of African-American hairstyling that emerged from the collision and renegotiation of different cultural notions about the body in the African diaspora. Kobena Mercer referred to these styles as "ethnic signifiers" that reflect African understandings about hair while incorporating European styles to create new styles specific to African-Americans. These styles, which may appear to be "African" or "white" but with a difference, articulate the complex cultural heritage of African-Americans and, according to Mercer, are inevitably politicized in the context of inequality or cultural hierarchy.

Even though the trend toward global, transnational flows of fashion commodities continues, folklorists can expect to see folk costumes increasingly characterized by creole forms and styles. Mainstream fashion is an influence on folk costume that often shapes style and form at a local level. Although some scholars have postulated a distinction between rapidly changing fashionable dress and relatively unchanging folk dress (or what Ted Polhemus and Lynn Proctor have called "anti-fashion"), sustained costume studies reveal a more dynamic folk design process in which fashionable and folk ideas commingle, collide, and interact in local settings. Individuals appropriate new ideas and integrate them into their wardrobes within the terms of their own cultural aesthetic (which might include cut, color, accessory, or rules of assemblage). In addition, international fashion designers increasingly appropriate ideas for styles from folk or "street" fashions, ransacking the past and present for novelty and inspiration and thereby further complicating any clear distinction between "fashionable" and "folk" costume.

More recently, folklorists have moved from looking at clothing merely in terms of an outward, identifiable form or signification to considering the relationship between costume and the body. Costume not only reflects social or group identities but also constitutes them in bodily practice as an integral part of the everyday and habitual practices through which the body is culturally managed and supervised in any culture, practices that produce relationships of power. Thus, dress practices cannot be understood in isolation from other bodily practices, such as food consumption, deportment, gesture, and speech, that stylize the "natural" physical body and render it culturally comprehensible by imbuing it with recognizable attributes linked to identities. Costume, then, is linked to the study of "bodylore" and provides a lens through which to see how identities are formed, contested, or redefined through the body and its appearance, boundaries, and sensations.

Kathryn E. Wilson

See also Carnival; Festival; Mask; Material Culture.

References

Bogatyrev, Petr. 1971. *The Function of Folk Costume in Modern Slovakia*. Trans. Richard Crum. The Hague: Mouton.

Hebdige, Dick. 1979. *Subculture: The Meaning of Style*. London: Routledge.

Hollander, Ann. 1993. *Seeing through Clothes*. Berkeley: University of California Press.

Mercer, Kobena. 1987. Black Hair/Style Politics. *New Formations* 3:33–54.

Polhemus, Ted, and Lynn Procter. 1978. *Fashion and Anti-Fashion: An Anthropology of Clothing and Adornment*. London: Thames and Hudson.

Roach, Mary Ellen, and Joanne Bubolz Eicher. 1965. *Dress, Adornment and the Social Order*. New York: John Wiley & Sons.

Wilson, Elizabeth. 1985. *Adorned in Dreams: Fashion and Modernity*. Berkeley: University of California Press.

Yoder, Don. 1972. Folk Costume. In *Folklore and Folklife: An Introduction*, ed. Richard Dorson. Chicago: University of Chicago Press.

———. [1969] 1990. Sectarian Costume. In *Discovering American Folklife: Studies in Ethnic, Religious and Regional Culture*, ed. Don Yoder. Ann Arbor, MI: UMI.

CRAFT, FOLK

Skill or process of creating goods, usually by hand. Craft first attracted folkloristic interest in the nineteenth century because the skills involved clearly showed transmission through tradition and because the products of these skills could be compared across time and space. Craft was essential to utilities in daily life and also could have decorative and spiritual functions. In addition to the skills and processes that provide the basic equipment of domestic life—tools, furnishings, houses, clothes—crafts include ritual, religious, and artistic objects, and they foster beliefs about the highly skilled workers who produce them, as in oft-collected legends of blacksmiths.

The concept of craft is closely related to perceptions of art. Craft in nineteenth-century conceptions of folk cultures characterized folklore more than art because of the assumption that art represented originality and leisure and craft symbolized work and repetition more in keeping with the stereotype of folk culture. In a modification of this view, scholars pointed to arts such as Pennsylvania-German painted furniture that grew out of traditional crafts. Up until the 1970s, the dominant perspective viewed craft as having utilitarian intent and application and art as having a principally aesthetic character. Thus, many of the objects categorized as art were decorative, and crafts were treated as tools. The limitation of this simplification emphasizing form and function is that artifacts have multiple functions, and the artistic appreciation of skill and beauty in folk design can apply to nondecorated objects. Considering craft and art as behavior rather than form, scholars recognized craft and art as parts of each other, a symbolic kind of action. Craft had an active role, referring to the process of construction and its integration with aesthetic or artistic judgments and traditions.

The shifts in the conception of craft and art reflect changes since the nineteenth century in the kinds of approaches used to study craft. Many early folkloristic studies of craft considered the products of traditional crafts in a "natural history of civilization" or cultural evolution from the primitive to the industrial. Another early approach took up questions of diffusion and transmission of tradition across cultures and used variations among crafts to interpret cultural borrowings and map regions. Because crafts reflected daily life, another approach arose to document the folklife or historical folk culture of a regional-ethnic community. Closely related to the examination of crafts as products meant for an entire community is the role of craft as the product of an individual with creative and aesthetic goals. Especially since the 1970s, other approaches have arisen that focus on craft as a form of communication. The process of creating, consuming, using, and changing crafts has received attention as an important type of nonverbal behavior humans use to express themselves.

EVOLUTION

In 1871, following Charles Darwin's theories of origin and development in nature, Edward Tylor promoted the study of cultural evolution through "survivals." Traditional crafts among tribal societies in the world, he surmised, were evidence of a low, "primitive" stage of development that led to the highest level of industrial invention in "civilization." Evolutionists following Tylor organized crafts by technological type and typically arranged them by level of advancement to form a global evolution of civilization.

DIFFUSION

One problem with early evolutionary doctrine was that it did not explain similarities in customs and crafts among widely separated groups. The comparisons that were made were typically ahistorical in that the cultural occurrence was assumed to be part of a universal level of advancement rather than a period in a group's history. If cultures move and influence custom because of historical migrations and cultural contact, however, then the progressive explanation for civilization could be challenged. In addition to questions of origin and development, questions of diffusion and transmission arose to show that cultures not only developed in place but also moved and influenced others. Crafts became important evidence of such movements because types of crafts could be visibly traced and comparisons could be made according to date of manufacture. The most prominent example is the explanation for the similarity of many Native American and Asian folk shelters and crafts. In 1904, Waldemar Bogoras, for example, wrote on the comparable material culture in Siberia and Alaska, supporting a migration from Asia across the Bering Strait into North America.

A notable movement called the *Kulturkreiselehre* (culture-cluster school) arose in German-speaking countries to examine diffusion of folk ideas as demonstrated in folk crafts. Fritz Graebner, Wilhelm Schmidt, and Wilhelm Koppers, to name some notable figures in this movement, reconstructed the diffusion of crafts by determining clusters of cultural traits that moved together. The assumption was that migrations and contacts reduced the importance of the environment. Mapping diffusion according to this assumption could lead to a failure to deal with historical accidents, local or individual developments, and social change.

COMMUNITY AND INDIVIDUAL

Rather than slavishly following an all-encompassing culture, traditional craftsworkers observed by many scholars expressed their individuality within community traditions. Reacting to the German emphasis on cultural clusters, Franz Boas leaned toward the study of the variety of cultures, rather than their inevitable unity. Fieldwork among Eskimos during the 1880s alerted him to the control that a people maintained over their traditions and over the integrity of a cultural whole as a small community. He argued that the focus of research should be not on survivals but on the processes by which culture has developed.

This accounting for craftswork taking on the character of negotiation between individual and community could be accomplished by studies of the history and ethnography of individual societies. Although diffusion emphasizes

Toys are a common type of folk craft. Here, Japanese kite craftsman Hideo Matsutani displays one of his works. Kites play a very important role in Japanese culture.

similarities over space, individual and community studies offer views of variance influenced by personality and local conditions. A movement related to this idea is in folklife or folk cultural (from the Swedish *folkliv* and the German *Volksleben* and *Volkskunde*) studies emerging during the late nineteenth century, usually emphasizing holistic study of everyday practices, artifacts, and expressions in community context. Crafts became significant as representations of living traditions pointing to the integrated life and labor of regional-ethnic communities. From its relatively minor role in English-American folklore scholarship during the late nineteenth century, folklife study gained prominence in the United States, particularly after World War II.

Rather than using models of closed peasant societies, many American studies have applied an ethnographic approach centering on the personality and process by which individuals have the need to create and the urge to express themselves. Influenced especially by Michael Owen Jones' *The Hand Made Object and Its Maker* (1975), these studies have offered a special folkloristic mission to describe the role of tradition as evidenced by the creative process of handcrafting in complex, industrial societies. A spate of "life histories" and psychologically oriented studies of craftsworkers maintaining tradition and innovation in urban and industrial settings appeared to underscore the continual relevance of handwork and tradition in modern life. In such studies, craftsworkers' motivations and social functions were examined closely. Rather than belonging to one community, craftsworkers had many communities to serve and had individual reasons for presenting the styles and forms they followed.

COMMUNICATION

The results of close examinations of individual craftsworkers suggested that the process of craft is an everyday activity that often arises in response to certain situations. Although popular belief in postindustrial societies suggested that humans would not be involved in creative activities because of the rise of electronics and a service economy, folkloristic studies, since the 1980s particularly, have proposed a close examination of the symbols and metaphors communicated when humans "make things." Crafting in such a view becomes a metaphoric model for doing, rather than a technical procedure for turning out a product. With craft, there is the suggestion of drawing on tradition and innovation for use, of taking time to convert nature into something personal and meaningful. Stories and environments can be crafted as well as chairs and baskets.

The material process of crafting grasps ideas in ways that speech cannot. In addition to the recovery of historical crafts, such as basketry or pottery, that is common in scholarship, some folklorists suggested many noncanonized traditions, such as cooking meals, renovating houses, arranging yards, and folding papers, as everyday efforts of grasping ideas through craft processes. In a study of the construction and readjustment of tract houses in Los Angeles, Michael Owen Jones argued that such modern activities revealed processes of tradition and creativity. Homeowners often announced their intentions for establishing an identity through the process of construction. The approach implied more directly behavioral interpretations rather than sociocultural ones, with attention to the reactions and responses of particular individuals to the patterns, qualities, or symbols of activities as well as objects.

Such an approach broadened the scope of the concept of folk craft from the materials of tradition to the process involved. Some kinds of materials previously neglected in folkloristic study became open to inquiry. Tourist and revival crafts came under study because they presented opportunities to examine the meanings of tradition as it is altered when sold or used in certain situations. Such examinations have also considered the role that consumption and reuse play in the perception of crafts in contemporary society. In addition, the role of ceremonial crafts in rituals and festivals received renewed attention as vehicles for symbolic communication.

Many of these studies were situational, much as ethnographic studies of speech communication are, and had as their goal the uncovering of ways that meaning is communicated and perceived. Some authorities on verbal behavior, such as W.F.H. Nicolaisen, began using craft as an essential metaphor for folklore because it stressed the process of bringing materials into an aesthetic form relying on individual creativity and communal tradition. Craftsmanship was a model of action, a "praxis," as some scholars have described it, appropriate to cultural expression generally, for it recognized individuals making use of material at hand in response to audience and environment, injecting variety into a process of repetition.

Simon J. Bronner

See also Art, Folk; Material Culture.

✳✳✳✳✳✳✳✳✳✳✳✳✳✳✳✳✳✳

References

Boas, Franz. [1927] 1955. *Primitive Art*. New York: Dover.

Bronner, Simon J. 1985. *Chain Carvers: Old Men Crafting Meaning*. Lexington: University Press of Kentucky.

———. 1986. *Grasping Things: Folk Material Culture and Mass Society in America*. Lexington: University Press of Kentucky.

Glassie, Henry. 1968. *Pattern in the Material Folk Culture of the Eastern United States*. Philadelphia: University of Pennsylvania Press.

Jones, Michael Owen. 1975. *The Hand Made Object and Its Maker*. Berkeley: University of California Press.

Roberts, Warren E. 1988. *Viewpoints on Folklife: Looking at the Overlooked*. Ann Arbor, MI: UMI Research.

Vlach, John Michael. 1981. *Charleston Blacksmith: The Work of Philip Simmons*. Athens: University of Georgia Press.

CULTURAL RELATIVISM

A key methodological concept in anthropology that is universally accepted within the discipline. This concept is based on theoretical considerations that are fundamental to the understanding of "scientific" anthropology, just as they are basic to the understanding of the anthropological frame of mind. Cultural relativism posits that all cultures are of equal value and need to be studied from a neutral point of view. The study of any culture has to be done with a cold and neutral eye so that a particular culture can be understood on its own merits and not those of another culture. Historically, cultural relativism has been combined with historical particularism—the notion that the proper way to study culture is to study one culture in depth. The implications of cultural relativism and historical particularism have been significant to anthropology and to the social sciences in general.

The roots of cultural relativism go to the rejection of the comparative school of the nineteenth century on the basis of exact and specific ethnological information. This information rejected the comparative school's methodology and, as a result, its evolutionary conclusions. Furthermore, because the basis of cultural relativism is a scientific view of culture, it also rejects value judgments on cultures. There is, in this view, no single scale of values that holds true for all cultures and by which all cultures can be judged. Beliefs, aesthetics, morals, and other cultural institutions can only be judged through their relevance to a given culture. For example, labels of good and bad are culture specific and cannot be imposed in cultural analysis. The reasoning behind this view is, of course, that what is good in one culture may be bad in another. This indicates that every culture determines its own ethical judgments to regulate the proper behavior of its members. An offshoot of this view is the assumption that most individuals would prefer to live in the culture in which they have been enculturated. It must be added that the *cultural* in cultural relativism and historical particularism refers to specific cultures and not to a more abstract, singular, and general concept of culture.

The reasoning behind all this comes from two distinct sources: the reaction to the inaccuracies of the evolutionary schemes of the comparative school and the desire to study culture from an objective value perspective. To be a scientific concept, culture has to be studied as an object without evaluative consideration. When we are not able to do that, we no longer have a science of culture. Among the many anthropologists associated with this point of view are Franz Boas and his students Alfred Kroeber, Robert Lowie, Melville Herskovits, Ruth Benedict, Paul Radin, Margaret Mead, and Ruth Bunzel. Franz Boas was the key theoretician in this group.

Boas published his views on the comparative method in 1896 in "The Limitations of the Comparative Method of Anthropology," the first exposition of cultural relativism. According to the tenets of cultural relativism, there are no inferior or superior cultures; all cultures are equal. To order cultures in an evolutionary scheme is unfeasible. All premises of good and bad and/or upper and lower are culture-bound and ethnocentric. Put that way, we can see that schemes of evolution are ethnocentric, not objective.

According to Boas, there are four major limitations to the comparative method: (1) It is impossible to account for similarity in all the types of culture by claiming that they are alike because of the unity of the human mind, (2) the existence of like traits in different cultures is not as important as the comparative school claims, (3) similar traits may have developed for very different purposes in differing cultures, and (4) the view that cultural differences are of minor importance is baseless. The differences between cultures were, Boas asserted, of major anthropological significance. Boas did not stop his critique of the comparative school there. He also delineated a methodology to replace it. His new method emphasized that culture traits have to be studied in detail and within the cultural whole and that the distribution of a culture trait within neighboring cultures also should be examined. This approach suggests that a culture needs to be analyzed within its full context.

Boas thought that this approach would help the anthropologist understand the environmental factors that shape a culture, explain the psychological factors that frame the culture, and illuminate the history of a local custom. Boas was trying to establish the inductive method in anthropology and abandon the comparative method. He emphasized that the primary goal of anthropology was to study individual societies and that generalizations could come only on the basis of accumulated data. Thus, he argued that anthropology should be an objective and inductive science. In an age when the scientific method was important, this change in the discipline resulted in the establishment of anthropology in universities. Boas' students were among the first to establish some of the most important anthropology programs on U.S. campuses.

Moreover, Boas attacked racism throughout his career; he summarized his views on racism in *The Mind of Primitive Man* (1911). According to Boas, the sweep of cultures, to be found in association with any subspecies, was so extensive that there could be no relationship between race and culture.

Following Boas and his emphasis on studying as many societies as possible, Alfred Kroeber, the best-known anthropologist of the period, produced a good deal of ethnography. In his "Eighteen Professions" (1915), which is a credo, Kroeber affirmed two of the basic tenets of cultural relativism: (1) All men are completely civilized, and (2) there are no higher and lower cultures. Much later in his career, Kroeber made three additional points in regard to cultural relativism: (1) that science should begin with questions and not with answers, (2) that science is a dispassionate endeavor that should not accept any ideology, and (3) that sweeping generalizations are not compatible with science. Another major cultural relativist of the period was Robert Lowie, whose work is most significant among his peers for its development of cultural relativism.

Lowie probably came closer to Boas' views on the proper practice of anthropology than any other anthropologist of his time. He was deeply rooted in the philosophy of science and accepted cultural anthropology as a science. His views and criticism of theoreticians such as Lewis Henry Morgan were based on this scientific worldview. His critique of Morgan's evolutionary theory was based on epistemology, namely, that Morgan's evolutionary scheme for the development of kinship systems was speculative and had no proof. Furthermore, Morgan's data were often erroneous, according to Lowie.

Additional refinements of the concept of cultural relativism were suggested by Ruth Benedict. For Benedict, cultural anthropology was the discipline that studied the differences between cultures. This approach was fully Boasian in character. In this approach, the *s* that was added to the word *culture* by Boas and others became crucial. The interest had shifted from culture to cultures. In addition, when the focus shifted to a particular culture, there was a concern with what happened to the individual in that culture. A culture was integrated, and it was more than the sum of its parts. Finally, every culture was different from every other culture. Benedict took the Boasian program a step further through the concept of cultural configurations or patterns that allowed her to engage in cross-cultural comparison. Although her use of this approach was extremely reductionistic, it represented a new direction in cultural relativism by transcending the data collection of historical particularism and attempting to organize the data in an explanatory manner.

The attempt to understand cultures on their own terms and the attempt to pursue objective ethnography are the major accomplishments of cultural relativism. These accomplishments have sometimes led to a lack of theoretical depth and an undervaluation of the ethnographer's own culture. However, the battle against ethnocentrism and the objective view of cultures remain permanent contributions of cultural relativism.

Mark Glazer

See also Anthropological Approach; Esoteric/Exoteric Factor; Ethnic Folklore.

✳✳✳✳✳✳✳✳✳✳✳✳✳✳✳

References

Benedict, Ruth. 1934. *Patterns of Culture*. New York: Houghton Mifflin.

Boas, Franz. 1911. *The Mind of Primitive Man*. New York: Macmillan.

———. 1948. *Race, Language and Culture*. New York: Macmillan.

Garbarino, Merwin S. 1977. *Sociocultural Theory in Anthropology*. New York: Holt, Rinehart, and Winston.

Goldschmidt, Walter. 1990. *The Human Career*. Cambridge: Basil Blackwell.

Harris, Marvin. 1968. *The Rise of Anthropological Theory*. New York: Thomas Y. Crowell.

Kroeber, Alfred. 1915. The Eighteen Professions. *American Anthropologist* 17:283–289.

———. 1944. *Configurations of Culture Growth*. Berkeley: University of California Press.

———. 1949. An Authoritarian Panacea. *American Anthropologist* 51:318–320.

Lowie, Robert. 1936. Lewis H. Morgan in Historical Perspective. In *Essays in Anthropology Presented to A.L. Kroeber*, ed. Robert Lowie. Berkeley: University of California Press.

———. 1937. *History of Ethnological Theory*. New York: Farrar and Rinehart.

———. 1944. Franz Boas. *Journal of American Folklore*, 57:288–296.

CULTURAL STUDIES

Interdisciplinary, transdisciplinary, and often counterdisciplinary projects to describe, analyze, and theorize the ways in which cultural practices are entangled with and within relations of power. Cultural studies (sometimes termed *cultural criticism* or *cultural critique*) is an international set of discursive practices in which culture is viewed as a site of serious contest and conflict over meaning. The questions of how meaning is made, what meaning is made, who makes meaning, and for whom meaning is made are explored through borrowings from Marxist—in particular, revisionist (sometimes known as "neo-" or "post-") Marxist—writings on class; feminist writings on women's cultures; postcolonialist writings on race, ethnicity, and nation; lesbian-and-gay-studies writings on gender and sexuality; and poststructuralist and postmodernist writings on language and other signifying systems. Positioning itself, as noted in a collection of essays edited by Lawrence Grossberg, Cary Nelson, and Paula Treichler, as being "committed to the study of the entire range of a society's arts, beliefs, institutions, and communicative practices," cultural studies rejects the traditional humanities' equation of "culture" with "high culture." Instead, these essayists concluded, cultural studies practitioners work to disclose the politics that underlie hierarchical distinctions such as high and low or elite, popular, and folk, arguing that all "forms of cultural production need to be studied in relation to other cultural practices and to social and historical structures." Cultural studies practitioners work within an intellectual and political tradition that seeks not only to record culture but also to intervene actively in it.

Initiated by Raymond Williams' attempt to define the relations between culture and society, E. P. Thompson's work on class identity, and Richard Hoggart's work on literacy, cultural studies was first institutionalized as a discipline with the creation of the Center for Contemporary Cultural Studies at Birmingham, England, in 1964, under Hoggart's directorship. In 1968, Stuart Hall became its second director. Focusing on how meanings are generated and circulated in industrial societies, participants in the Birmingham Center developed an interest in class-based power relations, in the production, marketing, and consumption of popular forms of expressive and material culture as well as vernacular uses of those forms, and in subcultural theory. Key to British cultural studies discussions during this period were continental influences, especially the work of Marxist theorists Theodor Adorno, Antonio Gramsci, and Louis Althusser.

As cultural studies grew into an international set of discursive practices, its focus became more diverse. For example, scholars in American cultural studies, though influenced by the Birmingham model, have also been drawn

161

to the work of anthropologists Clifford Geertz and Victor Turner, literary and social theorist Mikhail Bakhtin, and writers associated with the initiatives of multiculturalism—for example, Patrick Brantlinger, Chandra Mukerji, and Michael Schudson. Cultural studies now encompasses critiques of sociocultural constructions of gender, race, ethnicity, nationalism, and sexuality in addition to class and maps the interrelations of the traditional, the emergent, the local, and the global in addition to (though frequently as part of) the popular. Still heavily revisionist-Marxist, its practitioners draw insights from the writers associated with poststructuralism (Jacques Derrida, Jacques Lacan, Julia Kristeva, Michel Foucault, Michel de Certeau, and Gilles Deleuze), from the theorists of postmodernism (Walter Benjamin, Jean-François Lyotard, and Frederic Jameson) as well as postcolonialism (Edward Said) and subaltern studies (Gayatri Chakravorty Spivak).

Folkloristics intersects with cultural studies when it follows Américo Paredes' challenges of the 1970s "to place questions of the politics of culture at the heart of the discipline of folklore." As Charles L. Briggs and Amy Shuman noted in their 1993 "New Perspectives" issue of *Western Folklore*, this means, on the one hand, "understanding that folklore is already (in Derrida's terms) a politics of culture" and, on the other hand, understanding that the discipline of folkloristics is, through its representational practices, also a politics of culture. In other words, when folklorists address how folklore is shaped by and in turn shapes sociocultural power relations, they participate in the cultural studies project.

Exploring the matrix of folk, vernacular, popular, and local performances as a politics of culture, folklorists have begun to theorize cultural production from both global and local positionings. Marxist folklorist Jack Zipes, for example, has disclosed the workings of ideology in popularly reproduced fairy tales. John Dorst has described the traditionalizing practices of an elite U.S. suburb that, in a postmodern turn, inscribes and markets itself through "pamphlets, brochures, glossy travel magazines, gallery displays, postcards, tourist snapshots, amateur art, styles of interior decoration, and suburban architecture and landscaping." And Susan Davis has analyzed the way in which public parades, although frequently used to assert the dominant culture's ideological agendas, may also function for subordinated groups "as vehicles for protest as well as for historical commemoration." José Limón has historicized and localized the study of social contradictions of race, class, and gender in Mexican-American social poetry, and Barbara Babcock has explored how Cochiti women "have contrived to tell stories" through their pottery about men's storytelling, thereby subverting "masculine discursive control" and disturbing "the distribution of [local] power profoundly." Alesia García has articulated the ways in which indigenous storytelling functions as a form of cultural resistance and preservation. Deborah Kapchan has explored the emergent politics of gendered performances in the Moroccan marketplace, and Arjun Appadurae and colleagues, focusing on south Asian expressive traditions, have brought together a set of essays that cumulatively call for a "full and direct encounter between the problematics of performance and textuality, on the one hand, and of social and cultural history, on the other." Situating their work in respect to a movement "toward somewhat larger-scale ideas of context, in which broader ideological frameworks, historical currents, and social formations are brought into the conceptualization of" such key concepts among folklorists as "context," Appadurae and colleagues foregrounded a process that is furthered in "Common Ground: Keywords for the Study of Expressive Culture," a 1996 special issue of the *Journal of American Folklore* edited by Burt Feintuch that invoked Raymond Williams' seminal work.

Finally, disclosing folkloristics as a politics of culture, folklorists such as Richard Bauman and John W. Roberts have addressed the ways in which the discipline has been, from its early foundation in romantic nationalism, participatory in the dominant culture's appropriations of folk culture as a means of enhancing hegemonic ideological agendas. Like their anthropological colleagues, folklorists have begun to critique the scientific essentialism of folkloristic paradigms and methods, in particular, as Camilla Collins has argued, the fallacy of scientific objectivity and the subject-object relations constructed with the discourse of older participant-observation positionings. In short, the broad range of folkloristic representational practices, as well as the ways in which those practices are enmeshed within the socioeconomic politics of our supporting institutions, have been resituated through discursive practices that are increasingly self-conscious and politically aware.

Cathy Lynn Preston

See also Deconstruction; Feminist Perspectives on Folklore Scholarship; Gender; Marxist Approach; Postmodernism.

✵✵✵✵✵✵✵✵✵✵✵✵✵✵✵

References

Appadurai, Arjun, Frank J. Korom, and Margaret A. Mills. 1991. *Gender, Genre, and Power in South Asian Expressive Traditions.* Philadelphia: University of Pennsylvania Press.

Babcock, Barbara A. 1993. "At Home, No Women Are Storytellers": Potteries, Stories, and Politics in Cochiti Pueblo. In *Feminist Messages: Coding in Women's Folk Culture*, ed. Joan Newlon Radner. Chicago: University of Illinois Press.

Brantlinger, Patrick. 1990. *Crusoe's Footprints: Cultural Studies in Britain and America.* New York: Routledge.

Briggs, Charles, and Amy Shuman, eds. 1993. Theorizing Folklore: Toward New Perspectives on the Politics of Culture. *Western Folklore* (Special Issue) 52:2–4.

Collins, Camilla A., ed. 1990. Folklore Fieldwork: Sex, Sexuality, and Gender. *Southern Folklore* (Special Issue) 47:1.

Davis, Susan. 1986. *Parades and Power: Street Theatre in Nineteenth-Century Philadelphia.* Berkeley: University of California Press.

Dorst, John D. 1989. *The Written Suburb: An American Site, An Ethnographic Dilemma*. Philadelphia: University of Pennsylvania Press.

Feintuch, Burt. 1995. Common Ground: Keywords for the Study of Expressive Culture. *Journal of American Folklore* (Special Issue) 108:430.

Grossberg, Lawrence, Cary Nelson, and Paula Treichler, eds. 1992. *Cultural Studies*. New York: Routledge.

Hoggart, Richard. 1957. *The Uses of Literacy*. Fair Lawn, NJ: Essential Books.

Kapchan, Deborah A. 1996. *Gender on Market*. Philadelphia: University of Pennsylvania Press.

Kirshenblatt-Gimblett, Barbara. 1988. Mistaken Dichotomies. *Journal of American Folklore* 101:140–155.

Limón, José. 1992. *Mexican Ballads, Chicano Poems: History and Influence in Mexican-American Social Poetry*. Berkeley: University of California Press.

Mukerji, Chandra, and Michael Schudson, eds. 1991. *Rethinking Popular Culture: Contemporary Perspectives in Cultural Studies*. Berkeley: University of California Press.

Preston, Cathy Lynn, ed. 1995. *Folklore, Literature, and Cultural Theory: Collected Essays*. New York: Garland.

Thompson, Edward P. 1963. *The Making of the English Working Class*. New York: Pantheon.

Williams, Raymond. 1958. *Culture and Society, 1780-1950*. New York: Columbia University Press.

———. 1961. *The Long Revolution*. New York: Columbia University Press.

———. 1976. *Keywords: A Vocabulary of Culture and Society*. London: Fontana/Croom Helm.

Zipes, Jack. 1983. *The Trials and Tribulations of Little Red Riding Hood: Versions of the Tale in Sociocultural Context*. South Hadley, MA: Bergin & Garvey.

CULTURE HERO

The central figure in a myth or myth cycle whose story tells that he lived at the beginning of—or before—time, experienced extraordinary adventures and achievements, conquered or tamed environments for human use, gave life, provided the things needed to exist, and was responsible for the life designs that exist in cultures. Oedipus of Greece, Se'ehe of the Pima Native Americans, Cu Chulainn of Ireland, Manixi of New Guinea Highlands, and I'itoi of the Papago, for example, are culture heroes.

Most scholars who have analyzed culture heroes have attempted either to discover the formulaic structure of the myth cycles or to interpret them as meaningful expressions of societal values, beliefs, and behaviors. In 1864, Johann Georg von Hahnhe published the earliest documented analysis of the formulaic pattern of culture hero myth cycles in the modern sense. Many mythologists since then—including Alfred Nutt, Otto Rank, Vladimir Propp, Joseph Campbell, Jan de Vries, and Clyde Kluckhohn—have applied the method to the study of culture heroes. Most of these studies have agreed that folk culture heroes are a very common part of myth traditions of the world. They have also noted that there are distinct similarities in the biographies of heroes from many cultures and that there are clearly detectable trends toward regularities in the narrative content and structures of culture hero myths. This research has proved that duplication, triplication, and quadruplication of elements, reinterpretation of borrowed narratives to fit preexisting cultural aesthetics, and endless variation upon central themes are constant structural tendencies of hero tales.

Structural mythologists advanced many other theories and descriptions as a result of their attempt to discover and explain the formulaic pattern of culture hero myth cycles. Lord Raglan's myth-ritual theory held that the worldwide monomyth—the culture hero narrative structural pattern—reflected a birth, initiation, and death ritual for an individual, possibly a royal personage, who also was considered the incarnation of a god. He also concluded that the similarities of the cycles around the world proved culture heroes were not historical, that religious ritual was the source of all myths, and that, in turn, myths were the precursors of all other folklore.

Following the division in approaches developed in linguistics, Claude Lévi-Strauss argued for a structuralist approach to myth that sought to reveal culture hero stories' "deep" structure rather than their surface structures. He analyzed many myths from many cultures and found binary opposition underlying them all. He used his analyses to develop his theory that myth and mythic thought proceeded from an awareness of binary opposition toward their progressive mediation.

Joseph Campbell's popular books and lectures presented a simple, three-part summation of the pattern of culture hero myths: separation, initiation, and return. Campbell's pattern was a composite that drew single incidents from the lives of many heroes from multitudinous cultures in order to create a hypothetical monomyth.

Otto Rank applied the psychoanalytic approach to myth developed by Sigmund Freud and adapted by Carl Jung to the analysis of culture hero stories as a guide to understanding the unconscious mind. Clyde Kluckhohn supported psychoanalytical interpretations of culture hero stories that held that some themes and the linking of certain features of them exemplify a large number of ego defense mechanisms, and he provided supporting examples from his fieldwork with the Navajo. These mythologists, with the exception of Kluckhohn, based their varied theories upon library research rather than fieldwork and shared the methodology of structural analysis of culture hero texts.

R. R. Marett issued the first call in the modern era for research interpreting culture heroes as meaningful expressions of societal values, beliefs, and

The mythical adventures and achievements of Oedipus define his role as a culture hero in Greek folklore.

behaviors. In his 1914 presidential address to the Folk-Lore Society and in subsequent presentations, he argued that researchers had to understand and interpret oral folklore as a meaningful expression of a culture. His call was very much in keeping with the ideas and methods of the functional movement in anthropology. Two years later, Franz Boas published his seminal work *Tsimshian Mythology* in which he emphasized the importance of fieldwork in order to understand folklore in general and myth in particular. Boas, however, attempted to use myths primarily to reconstruct the past of cultures rather than to understand how they function in the present. The first forty years of the twentieth century were, in retrospect, a golden age for the collection of culture hero stories and for attempts to interpret culture hero stories in terms of their meaning to the people who were their customary audience and performers. Many of Boas' students collected culture hero tales in their natural contexts, and some—most notably Ruth Benedict—used their data for understanding how the stories functioned in cultures.

Functionalism gained even more support in the 1950s when William Bascom presented his functional approach to folklore in his presidential address before the American Folklore Society. By the 1990s, it had become a truism that culture hero stories function directly, indirectly, and inversely within cultures.

Many field research–oriented anthropologists and folklorists of the 1960s, 1970s, 1980s, and 1990s applied a functionalist approach to the study of culture heroes. Brian M. Du Toit collected a cycle of stories about a culture hero of the Gadsups of the New Guinea Highlands, recorded their performance and cultural context, and interpreted the stories as meaningful expressions in the culture of their audience and performers. Tomás ó Cathasaigh analyzed the concept of the hero in Irish myth and concluded that myths and their structures evince native ideology and explore a culture's concepts of the nature of men and the gods.

Many theories developed by the functionalist researchers who attempted to discover and understand the formulaic structure of culture hero myth cycles had few adherents in cultural studies by the 1990s, but the general conclusions they reached remained very important. Cultural studies of the 1990s, in general, accepted the later functionalist field studies that interpreted culture hero myths as meaningful expressions of societal values, beliefs, and behaviors. The most promising methodology for future folk culture hero research is a structural-functional approach uniting the study of lore with the study of the folk and the study of the past with the study of the present.

Keith Cunningham

See also Hero/Heroine, Folk; Myth-Ritual Theory.

✽✽✽✽✽✽✽✽✽✽✽✽✽✽✽✽✽

References

Campbell, Joseph. 1949. *The Hero with a Thousand Faces*. New York: Pantheon.

Du Toit. 1964. Gadsup Cultural Hero Tales. *Journal of American Folklore* 77:315–330.

Kluckhohn, Clyde. 1959. Recurring Themes in Myths and Mythmaking. *Deadulus: Journal of the American Academy of Arts and Sciences* 88:268–279.

ó Cathasaigh, Tomás. 1985. The Concept of the Hero in Irish Mythology. In *The Irish Mind*, ed. Richard Kearney. Dublin: Wolfhound.

Ragland, Lord. 1934. The Hero of Tradition. *Folklore* 45:212–231.

Rank, Otto. 1952. *The Myth of the Birth of the Hero*. New York: Robert Brunner.

CUSTOM

An activity performed with such regularity that it is considered expected behavior or a part of social protocol. Simply put, custom is the traditional and expected way of doing things. Customs that assume the authority of unwritten law are called *mores*, and some customs and mores may become part of a written legal system.

Custom includes a vast aggregate of human behavior. Ethnographers regard customary actions as part of the daily routine in people's lives. Folklorists tend to consider custom as a component of folk belief or folkways. Recent folklore studies generally do not deal with the national or broadly practiced ethnic customs but instead are restricted to collecting and analyzing customs maintained by discrete folk groups. For example, the agricultural customs practiced by the Pennsylvania Dutch or the occupational customs of Chicago firefighters are the type of customs that received attention from folklorists. Moreover, recent folklore publications also indicate that folklorists who deal with custom focus their efforts on rural customs, religious customs, occupational customs, and children's play customs. More often than not, those studies that employ the term *folkways* refer exclusively to rural practices, especially those closely associated with agriculture and animal husbandry.

People learn customs and when to use them appropriately in a variety of ways. Sometimes, a knowledgeable member of the group tells the uninitiated or by action indicates what kind of behavior is expected in a particular situation. The family unit, for example, plays a major role in continuing customs by telling children when and how certain practices are expected in particular contexts.

Folklorists consider customs to fall into four major categories: (1) calendar customs (i.e., practices associated with certain dates or times of the year), (2) rites of passage customs (i.e., practices associated with pivotal moments in the human life cycle), (3) customs associated with significant communal events (i.e., festivals and other large group celebrations), and (4) customs linked to folk belief (i.e., practices that result from holding certain beliefs). Although these categories serve the academic purpose of cataloging, rarely do they not overlap in actuality.

Calendar customs in the United Sates are less common than they are in Europe. Although most Americans celebrate calendar holidays, such as the Fourth of July or Thanksgiving, they may maintain regional and familial traditions that distinguish the way in which one group of people commemorates these holidays from the ways of other groups. Since the mid-nineteenth century, celebrating Thanksgiving has been a national custom, but rather than focus their attention on Thanksgiving as a national harvest celebration, folklorists research regional and family customs that develop as part of celebrating Thanksgiving. How special foods are prepared and served, who performs what activities associated with preparing and serving the meal, and even deciding when and where the meal is to be served are ruled by custom. The males in some extended families in Vermont, New Hampshire, Maine, and upstate New York customarily spend Thanksgiving Day morning and early afternoon deer hunting while the women remain at home to prepare the traditional turkey meal. In some families, this hunt customarily marks the opportunity for younger children, in the company of their fathers, uncles, and older brothers, to go on their first hunt. Seldom are any animals shot this day, but the hunt and male bonding accompanying it manifest an important social dimension associated with Thanksgiving Day, and for some of the participants, the custom becomes a rite of passage.

The calendar offers various groups opportunities for practicing different customs. Ringing in the New Year may be replaced by shooting in the New Year among German- and Italian-Americans. Recently arrived ethnic groups such as the Vietnamese and Cambodians have introduced the celebration of Tet with its accompanying customs into American culture. Many Catholics continue to have their throats blessed on St. Blaise's Day, February 3.

Regional customs often mark the changing seasons. Vermonters customarily start their tomato and pepper plants indoors on or shortly after Town Meeting Day, the first Tuesday of March. Many Vermonters who tap maple trees for their sap customarily celebrate the beginning of a new sugaring season by using the first maple syrup for sugar-on-snow, which is customarily accompanied by dill pickles and plain doughnuts.

Some U.S. calendar customs, such as sending Father's Day and Mother's Day cards or passing out sweets and flowers on St. Valentine's Day, are supported more by commercial interests than by folk tradition.

Rites of passage serve to mark major transitions in the lives of individuals, and customs associated with them are important ways for folk groups to recognize the changes. From conception to death, folk groups have produced an enormous number of customs that measure the growth and development of its members. Deciding on the name of a child may be left up to the whim of parents, but in many cases, family or ethnic custom dictates that the parents follow the custom of naming the child after an ancestor or other relative. Customarily, the tooth fairy trades candy or money for the child's baby tooth when it falls out. Although this tradition may have had ancient roots in superstition, the custom as now practiced in most of the United States simply marks a stage in the physical transition of a child into adulthood, and it also promotes a safe and easy way for parents to dispose of an unneeded tooth. Peers may punch the arm of the birthday child, one punch for every year of age. Customs associated with courtship and marriage persist in the United States. Among some Mexican-Americans, it is customary for a group of the young man's friends to visit the girl's family to ask permission for the courtship to begin. Decorating cars after a wedding and parading through the bride's and groom's neighborhoods while honking the car horn remain part of community and ethnic traditions. In parts of the southern and midwestern United States, the marriage celebration does not end until after the newlyweds' first night is disrupted with a surprise and customary shivaree. The bride and groom are expected to invite the nighttime revelers into their home and give them food and drink. Customs associated with dying and death are equally widespread. Some families consider it customary to stop their clocks to mark the time that someone in the house died. In parts of the South, pottery and medicine bottles decorate graves. A widespread practice that is held after the graveside ceremony is the meal to which the mourners are invited in order to celebrate life. In many places, it is customary for the survivors to maintain their relative's gravesite and to decorate it with flowers, candles, or other ornaments on the anniversary of the death and on particular calendar celebrations.

Folk festivals provide the opportunity for a large degree of community involvement. In the Scottish-American Highland games held annually in New Hampshire, descendants of Scottish families can celebrate their heritage. The women prepare the customary dishes of Scotland; the children, dressed in kilts, perform the Highland dances, and the men compete in games that test their strength. Folks in backwater communities of Louisiana celebrate Mardi Gras following old customs unlike those practiced in the massive, more commercialized Mardi Gras celebration in New Orleans. Among many Italian-Americans, December 26 is visiting day. They customarily leave their front doors open, set out drinks on nearby tables, and arrange for viewing the gifts received on Christmas. Then they visit their neighbors' homes, calling on folks who themselves may be out making other visits. The custom provides the opportunity to show generosity to friends and to display signs of prosperity.

Festivals also provide a context in which to perform various customs. Native Americans gather for national powwows, at which they share, invigorate, and revitalize traditional, tribal, and newly created pan–Native American customs. Most state and national folk festivals are hybrid products of surging popular interest in folk traditions, especially folk music, storytelling, and crafts. Many of these would not exist on the scale they do without federal and state support and without large, professionally oriented organizations behind them.

Certain customs are closely associated with folk belief, sometimes making it difficult—and perhaps unnecessary—to distinguish custom and ritual. But the custom and ritual, at least in the abstract, are different. Ritual is usually performed in order to affect the future. Custom, in the abstract, is practiced to influence the present. To break custom can bring criticism or censure from members in the folk community. The practice of dressing a male infant in blue and the female in pink, for instance, partly derives from a primitive European belief that blue protects infants from harm. Although the belief itself generally has died out in the United States, many Americans follow the practice because "that's the way things are done." Similarly, if the gender of an expected child is not known, baby gifts are bought in a neutral color—yellow or green. The origin of this custom is probably unknown to most of those who follow it, but custom demands that the practice be followed.

To avoid bad luck, some people customarily throw salt over the left shoulder after having accidentally knocked over a saltshaker. But when the original belief associated with the custom disappears, customary actions often continue to be practiced. These actions may take be associated with new beliefs, or they may simply be practiced by habit. Many Americans may still knock on wood even though they do not know or believe in the Germanic belief behind the custom.

In the broadest sense, much of folklore is itself a part of custom because folklore is appropriate and often expected behavior in certain contexts. An ill person by custom seeks advice from the herb doctor; custom tells the Native American storyteller to wait until winter to tell certain tales; the singer frames the performance of a song with customary opening and closing formulas. Though remedies, tales, and songs are not necessarily considered customs, the practice of each may be decided by folk custom.

Material culture may also be directed by custom. Historically, custom dictated whether a chimney was built inside or outside the house or where outbuildings were located in relationship to the house. Custom may also limit the functional design for the interior of a house. For many years in the East and Midwest, lilac bushes were customarily planted in the front yards of country homes. Even the most modern styles of housing may reflect customary expectations as folk tastes adopt them to a certain way of life.

As folklorists look at folk traditions in the workplace, they discover a whole range of customs. Richard Dorson's research among lumberjacks in the Upper Peninsula of Michigan discerned a code of behavior that prescribed a number of customs. For example, the jack, after spending months in the woods, was by custom expected never to walk away from a fight, to be courteous toward women, and to spend all of his wages on drinks for himself and his fellow lumberjacks. Lumberjacks also hold their own carnivals at which they customarily compete in various games that demonstrate their logging skills. In other occupations, custom dictates a hierarchy—for example, new workers on an assembly line may be expected to do the unpleasant tasks. The customary coffee break provides both white- and blue-collar workers with a time for gossip, sharing stories, and playing practical jokes. In this context, too, new workers learn more about the social and work protocols expected of them.

Determining when a traditional craft should be undertaken also may be bound with custom. In some regions of the United States, it is a custom for a young girl to complete her first quilt—usually a doll-sized version—before reaching puberty. The finished quilt is stored in her hope chest until she marries, and eventually, it is used to bundle her first child.

Families may have their own customs, such as parents sitting at the head of the table or the youngest child opening the first gift on Christmas morning. Custom may dictate that the main meal on Sunday will be eaten in the early afternoon, although dinner meals throughout the rest of the week are eaten in the evening.

Richard Sweterlitsch

See also Belief, Folk; Foodways.

✳✳✳✳✳✳✳✳✳✳✳✳✳✳✳✳✳✳

References

Brewster, Paul G., ed. 1952. Beliefs and Customs. *The Frank C. Brown Collection of North Carolina Folklore*, ed. Newman Ivey White. Vol. 1. Durham, NC: Duke University Press.

Hand, Wayland. 1970. Anglo-American Folk Belief and Customs: The Old World's Legacy to the New. *Journal of American Folklore* 7:136–155.

Newall, Venetia. 1971. *An Egg at Easter: A Folklore Study*. Bloomington: Indiana University Press.

Smith, Robert Jerome. 1972. Festivals and Celebrations. In *Folklore and Folklife: An Introduction*, ed. Richard M. Dorson. Chicago: University of Chicago Press.

Summer, William Graham. 1960. *Folkways*. New York: Mentor Books.

D

DANCE, FOLK

Concept of a specific type or repertoire of dances belonging to the folk, developed in the latter part of the eighteenth century, in close relation to the social, political, and economic development in western and central Europe. In other parts of the world, the notion of folk dance as distinct from other kinds of dance has been less common or even totally absent (as, for example, in parts of Africa and eastern Siberia). During the nineteenth and especially the twentieth centuries, the notion was exported to most parts of the world, with the result that it is now likely that one may find something called "folk dance" everywhere.

Common definitions of the concept usually rest on a combination of at least three criteria: (1) the social and/or geographical origin of the dances and/or the dancers; (2) the forms and types of dances and/or the ways of dancing; and (3) the ways, forms, and means of transmission of the dances. However, the term *folk dance* often is used in a more general and descriptive sense also as a generic label (in much the same way as, for example, the terms *ballet, jazz, rock,* and *latin* are used) for a large and varied repertoire of dances, practiced in organized forms by specially recruited and trained groups for the purpose of either recreation or stage performance.

A standard textbook definition, compiled from a list of the most commonly used criteria, might read: Folk dances are dances that belong to and represent a specific part of the lower strata of the population, usually the peasantry (or all the lower strata of the population or the entire population) of a culturally and/or geographically bounded region or nation; the dances being collectively and anonymously created and choreographed and passed on in tradition from generation to generation, orally or nonverbally, in nonwritten form, outside formal educational institutions. As a result, folk dances exist in many different variants and are performed by unself-conscious, nonprofessional dancers primarily for functional purposes (e.g., for magical or religious rites, ceremonies, and initiations or for the promotion of social cohesion or cultural identity).

To date, there is no generally accepted definition of folk dance, and it must be understood that such a definition, for logical and empirical as well as social and political reasons, is impossible to establish. Nevertheless, over the years, there have been many attempts to define the term, resulting in a growing confusion about the meaning and use of the concept. The confusion has a variety of causes. One obstacle is the many different usages of the word *folk*. Another is the idea that folk dance is an authentic representation of an

Smoki snake dancers of Prescott, AZ. The snake dance is enacted to expedite the peoples' prayers to the gods.

ancient heritage and cultural identity of a folk or a nation. This belief has led to a quest for typical and representative dances, and political rhetoric sometimes deliberately obscures the two different denotations of the word *typical* in this context (i.e., "the most commonly used" versus "the most characteristic and distinctive"). Furthermore, the idea of the folk as a homogeneous, culturally and geographically bounded entity has encouraged a static view of folk dance and a neglect or even denial of local and regional variations, class differences, transcultural influences, processes of improvisation, innovation, creation, and change. This in turn has created a need among some scholars and performers to introduce a distinction between "unchanged," "true," or "authentic" folk dances (e.g., "folklore," "folk dance in its first existence," "survivals") versus "changed," "false," or "unauthentic" folk dances (e.g., "folkish" or "folkloristic dances," "folklorism," "fakelore," "folk dance in its second existence," or "revival dances").

The often uncritical and naive application of the specifically European folk concept of folk dance to non-European societies during the nineteenth and twentieth centuries has led to further confusion and elicited severe criticism. As a result, a set of related terms have been introduced, such as a *national dances* and *primitive dances*. These labels rose to prominence in the late nineteenth and early twentieth centuries. *National dances* was not only a synonym for *European folk dances* but also applied to all forms and types of non-European dances; *primitive dances* was usually applied to dances in "primitive" societies, especially in Africa and Asia.

During the last decades of the twentieth century, a growing dissatisfaction with the term *folk dance* among scholars and performers led to the introduction of yet other terms, such as *traditional dance* (used to include also other orally transmitted forms, such as the Indian *kathak*), *popular dance* (modern ballroom recreational dances but also often including folk dance, especially in Great Britain), *ethnic dance* (a term introduced in the 1960s referring to the dances of minorities in multicultural societies, especially in the United States), and *vernacular dance* (introduced by the U.S. dance ethnologist Joann Kealiinohomoku to include jazz dance and other popular forms).

Like *folk dance*, most of these terms and concepts have been vaguely defined, usually by combining some or all of the criteria mentioned earlier. In practice, most of these terms have been used to describe more or less the same dance types or forms as were previously studied as folk dance. Often, these terms have been arranged, implicitly or explicitly, in an evolutionary hierarchy, from primitive dances through folk dances and popular (or social) dances to classical dances (the two middle categories may sometimes be reversed).

The difficulties in defining *folk dance* originate with the fact that many of the criteria ascribed to folk dance are contrastive and can only be understood in relation to other forms of dance in specific historical contexts. In the history of folk dance, it is possible to identify at least three periods when such contrastive relations have stood out as especially important.

Crucial to most definitions is the notion that folk dance only exists in societies that also maintain art or classical dance forms. This idea can be traced back to the political and social situation in western and central Europe in the late eighteenth century. Introduced by German and French bourgeoisie intellectuals, the category "folk" intentionally was constructed in a distinct contrast to the ruling classes of postfeudal Europe. Thus, the theatrical and social dances of the cultivated few were understood to be new—individually created for aesthetic purposes by well-known, artistically self-conscious choreographers and dance masters. In contrast, folk dances were held to be old, collectively and anonymously created, and performed for functional purposes by unself-conscious peasants far from the towns and castles of the nobles. Whereas the dances of the nobles were perceived to be complex in structure and technically sophisticated—dances whose creation and performance demanded special training—folk dances were understood to be simpler, possessing natural dignity.

From this period stems the ambivalent discourse about folk dance as, on the one hand, uncultivated and therefore less valuable and as, on the other, natural and therefore more valuable. This ambiguity has been a constant feature of the concept since the late eighteenth century. Also, the emphasis on the most rustic and ancient of the dances found among the rural classes, a constant feature in definitions of folk dance, can be explained as an intended contrast against the classical and aristocratic social dance forms of the time. We also can trace the ambiguity concerning who is to be considered the folk to this period. Though some argued that only the peasants could be taken into account, others maintained that other members of the population, such as workers, could also be classified as folk. Nevertheless, it remained self-evident for both sides that the noble classes had to be excluded.

The second important period in the history of folk dance was the late nineteenth century. Then, folk concepts (such as folk dance, folk music, folk costumes, and folklore) were again evoked by the European urban bourgeoisie, this time to contrast the music and dance forms of the modern industrialized society and the urban working class. In Hungary and other eastern European countries and in Germany, folk dance, folk music, and folk costumes became fashionable among young intellectuals as symbols of a national awakening and of a growing dissatisfaction with the cosmopolitan elite culture. In Sweden, students and intellectuals founded the first folk dance organizations, which propagated "authentic folk dances" on a massive scale, in order to fight what were considered to be the foreign and degenerative influences of modern, urban life on the ancient Swedish folk dance traditions. Around the turn of the twentieth century, similar organizations had been founded in most European countries.

Through this contrastive use, folk dance developed even stronger associations with the old as opposed to the modern, the peasantry as opposed to the urban working class, the native as opposed to the foreign, and the national as opposed to the international. As a result, an ideal model of the peasantry as the bearers of a distinctive and homogenous national culture was firmly established, a model that still is prominent in the field of folk dance today.

Before and immediately after World War II, folk dancing again became popular in western Europe and the United States, often as a means to promote regional or national cultural identity but also as a symbol of peace and feelings of international understanding. In San Francisco, New York, Amsterdam, Stockholm, and many other cities, so-called international folk dance clubs were established, where young urban people met to practice dances from different parts of the world, especially the British Isles, the Balkans, the Nordic countries, and Israel. Although some of the dances belonged to the traditional repertoire of these countries, others were new compositions in folk style, made specifically to meet the demands of these new organizations.

After World War II, folk dancing became very popular in the new socialist states in Eastern Europe. In Yugoslavia, a whole generation enrolled in amateur organizations to learn the folk dances of their new confederates. This movement, described as *folkloromanija* by the Serbian ethnochoreologist Olivera Mladenovic, had its counterparts in all socialist countries and was enthusiastically supported by the prevailing regimes as a means to instill new socialist national and cultural identity in the population. During this period, parts of the old romantic concept of folk merged with the socialist notion of "the people" to form a rather unique Eastern European definition of folk, which later came to influence the discourse about the folk and folk dance in many Western countries, as well as in the Third World.

The postwar interest in folk dance brought about the development of a class of highly stylized, typified, and formally representative national folk dances intended for stage use, together with certain types of events (international folklore festivals) at which such dances could be performed. To improve the standards of folk dancing, professional state folk dance and folk music ensembles were set up in all Eastern European socialist countries, (e.g. the Kolo ensemble in Belgrade, Yugoslavia, in 1948). These ensembles were modeled upon existing state ensembles in the Soviet Union (especially the Pyatnitskij and Moisejev ensembles), and sometimes they even were under the direct control of Soviet advisers. The creative mixing of old folk dance traditions with the organized forms of folk dance cultivated in the amateur associations, modern dance theater, and ballet gave rise to a new dance genre, which, under the name of folklore, was exported to Egypt, Sudan, Iraq, Mongolia, and many other countries in the Third World. Paradoxically, this very national, even nationalistic, genre today has become one of the most international dance genres in the world and probably the one that attracts the biggest number of participants and audiences. Folk dance is an obligatory part of the national state inventory, even in countries where distinctions between classical or folk dances never existed (for example, Tanzania).

Therefore, a range of different usages and levels of meaning are stored in today's folk dance concept. As the concept became more polysemic and multivalent, it became easier to utilize—but also more difficult to define.

Research on Folk Dance

There are many noteworthy documents on dance and dancing by explorers, travelers, and ethnographers dating many centuries back (i.e., the famous Indian dance book *Bharata Natya Shastra*, from the first centuries A.D.), as well as some important studies by folklorists and musicologists from the last century. However, a genuinely systematic folk dance research began only in the first part of the twentieth century. In most parts of the world, dance research never has been an independent academic discipline. The bulk of dance studies have been carried out by European (most notably, Eastern European) and U.S. scholars trained in musicology, ethnomusicology, folklore, ethnology, anthropology, and related disciplines. Therefore, the theories and methods used in folk dance research have developed in close connection to these disciplines, and they have followed the same trends.

Over the years, folk dance scholars have pursued several goals simultaneously. There has been a profound difference between those scholars emphasizing structural aspects of the dance itself (forms, types, and structures) and those emphasizing dance in culture or "dance as culture" (functions and meanings of dance and dancing). There also have been crucial differences between the historically oriented research that developed in Europe, addressed questions of origin and distribution, and emphasized recording and documentation, on one hand, and the type of anthropologically and linguistically inspired research that has dominated in the United States, on the other. Although European scholars have tended to focus mainly upon the folk dance traditions of their own countries, many of the dance scholars in the United States have devoted more attention to dance among Native Americans or the peoples of Europe and Southeast Asia. As a result, much of the European folk dance research has tended to be, implicitly or explicitly, preconditioned and circumscribed by nationalist ideologies, and much of the U.S. research has tended to lack historical depth and to describe dance as mirroring other (and by implication, more important) aspects of culture.

Since the late 1960s, dance research has grown considerably in scope and in depth, both theoretically and methodologically. As a result, many of the differences between the European and the U.S. research traditions have been reduced, and important links have been built between the "danceologists" and "culturologists." Although issues of forms, types, and structures of dances and dance as a cultural expression remain important, recent international economic, political, and cultural changes have called forth new fields and questions. For example, small and cheap but technically advanced video cameras have made it possible to document and analyze not only dances but also entire dance events, which has led to a growing number of studies on improvisation, creation, and dancing as process. Continuing massive urbanization and large-scale migration from the poor regions of the world to the rich areas has led to a growing interest in the meanings and functions of dance among migrants in urban and multicultural societies. The creation and rapid, worldwide distribution of new forms and types of dancing, as well as contexts and reasons for dancing, has led to an interest in the roles of dance in transcultural processes and culture building at large.

Folk dance researchers today often call their subject "ethnochoreology," "dance ethnology," or "dance anthropology" ("anthropology of dance"), depending on their education, professional affiliation, and fields of interest. Although there are special national organizations for folk dance researchers in some countries (for example, in the Nordic countries), most ethnochoreologists and dance anthropologists are members of national and international anthropological, ethnological, and musicological scientific associations. This can be explained by close theoretical and methodological connections and also by the continuing strong personal connections between researchers in these fields.

Two major trends in modern dance studies that may arise from this situation can be identified. First, there is a strong tendency to give up the notion of "folk dance" for "dance," to pass on from "folk dance research" to "dance studies"—which gives room for studies of all kinds of dance, in all parts of the world. Second, there is a tendency to extend the scope of interest from dance as an object to dancing as a process. Taken together, these tendencies imply a broadening of perspectives that may lead to a more general focus on dance as human expressive behavior.

EXAMPLES OF DANCE RESEARCH

For many reasons, it is impossible to survey the folk dances of the world except in the most general and abstract way. For example, an overview from the perspective of how the body is used would probably only reveal that there is a tendency to stress floor activity, legwork, and footwork in Europe, a tendency to stress hand, arm, and upper torso movements in Asia, and a tendency to use all the body, often polyrhythmically, in Africa. The meaningfulness of such an overview must be seriously questioned. An important reason for the difficulties involved in this type of study is, of course, the overwhelming variety of forms and types of folk dances, styles and ways of dancing, and occasions and reasons for dancing. Other reasons, as noted earlier, are the problems of definition regarding folk dance and the theoretically, methodologically, and empirically still rather limited scope and content of folk dance research. Though there are relatively many studies of folk dance in Europe, especially Eastern Europe, there still are few from most other parts of the world. Even in Europe, the results of the research are often fragmentary, scattered, and difficult to compare and synthesize. Nevertheless, attempts at developing an overview have been made, the most notable and initially promising perhaps being Alan Lomax's grand-scale *choreometrics* project. The results, however, raise as many questions as the study attempts to answer.

A limited overview of existing folk dances in Europe today, however, is possible. Historical studies of folk dance in Europe have revealed the existence of several different layers of dance types and forms. The most ancient layer, surviving mainly as parts of old rituals and ceremonies, consists mainly of dances with a rather simple formal structure, which are performed collectively by large groups. There are, in addition, some more complicated solo dances with turns, skips, jumps ,and movements imitating animals. The medieval layer consists mainly of collectively performed round dances and chain dances, and the Renaissance layer consists more of solo dances, dances performed with sticks and weapons. To the baroque layer belong a rich variety of group dances in squares and lines (*contredanse*, country dances), and during the eighteenth and nineteenth centuries, couple dances, such as the waltz, schottische, and polka, became popular over most parts of Europe. The twentieth-century layer is primarily composed of a large number of couple dances (e.g., foxtrot, one-step, tango, jive) and by a type that could be termed "mass solo dances" (in many countries, these are called "disco dances"), a new phenomenon in the Western world.

The folk dances in Europe also could be surveyed from a geographical perspective. In southeastern Europe, there is a predominance of chain dances and round dances (the Serbian *kolo*, Bulgarian *horo*, Greek *choros*, Rumanian *hora*), often led by a specially gifted dancer. In central Europe, couple dances of different kinds are predominant (*csardas*, polka, waltz); in northern and western Europe, both couple dances (schottische, polka, *polska*, waltz, *krakowjak*) and group dances of different kinds (chain dances, round dances and "contra dances" in squares and lines) have been popular.

From a structural point of view, it may be noted that a very common pattern in European dances can be schematically written A-B-B1 (a step, followed by a different step in the same direction, then the last step again but with reversed direction). This simple formula is known all over Europe and the Near East—from the Turkish *hasap*, the Romanian *sirba*, the *branle simple* of the medieval aristocracy, the dancing to ballad singing in the Faroe Islands, and the foxtrot of today's dance restaurants. A structural analysis of a number of dances from Bulgaria and the former Yugoslavia demonstrates that many other and more complex dances, with longer motives and more phrases, are built on the same structural pattern as well. A similar structural analysis of Hungarian men's dances, *legenyes*, by the Hungarian dance researchers György Martin and Ernö Pesovar has revealed the existence of a kind of dance vocabulary, consisting of a large number of short formulas that are repeated and combined in different ways, according to certain structural rules. A subsequent structural analysis of chain dances in Europe by the Danish ethnochoreologist Lisbet Thorp has shown that most chain dances are constructed by combining a fairly small number of formulaic motives in different ways, according to a kind of "grammar."

These and many other studies point to redundancy as a fundamental quality in folk dancing. The redundancy leads to a well-known phenomenon in the field of folk dance (as well as in other forms of folklore) that could be described by paraphrasing the English historian Peter Burke: The same dance is different, and different dances are the same. A dance may be differently performed at different occasions and by different dancers, yet it is considered as the same dance. Likewise, two dances can be made up almost entirely by the same set of motives or phrases and still be considered different.

Owe Ronström

See also Choreometrics.

✳✳✳✳✳✳✳✳✳✳✳✳✳✳✳✳

References

Buckland, Teresa. 1983. Definitions of Folk Dance: Some Explorations. *Journal of the English Folk Dance Society.* 4:315–332.

Dunin, Elsie, ed. 1989. *Dance Research Published or Publicly Presented by Members of the Study Group on Ethnochoreology.* Los Angeles: International Council for Traditional Music, Study Group on Ethnochoreology.

Giurchescu, Anca. 1983. The Process of Improvisation in Folk Dance. *Dance Studies* 7:21–56.

Hanna, Judith Lynne. 1979. *To Dance Is Human: A Theory of Nonverbal Communication.* Austin: University of Texas Press.

Kaeppler, Adrienne L. 1978. Dance in Anthropological Perspective. *Annual Review of Anthropology* 7:31–49.

Kurath, Gertrude P. 1960. Folk Dance of the USSR: Bibliography. *Ethnomusicology* 4:142–150.

Martin, György. 1982. A Survey of the Hungarian Folk Dance Research. *Dance Studies* 6:9–45.

Martin, György, and Ernö Pesovar. 1961. A Structural Analysis of the Hungarian Folk Dance. *Acta Ethnographica* 10:1–27.

Staro, Placida. 1985. Bibliografia sulla danza popolare italiana. *Culture musicali* 4:147–194.

Torp, Lisbet. 1990. *Chain and Round Dance Patterns: A Method for Structural Analysis and Its Application to European Material.* Copenhagen: Museum Tusculanum Press.

DECONSTRUCTION

The critical activity that attempts to subvert the idea that there can ever be closure in interpretation. This activity, whose formal origin is attributed to the French philosopher and literary critic Jacques Derrida, defies classification as a theoretical branch of poststructuralism due to its transitory and often playful rendering of its own construction, which continually reinterprets and redefines the function and form of the idea of deconstruction.

As an activity, deconstructionism subverts the meaning or the truth of an interpretation by revealing that which an interpretation must necessarily repress—conflicting and anomalous interpretations—in order to give the illusion of meaningfulness. In doing so, the deconstructionist grants an audience to the multiple meanings available for interpretation and thereby endlessly defers the anticipation of arriving at an ultimate conclusion. The deconstructionist, then, is generally skeptical of the traditional methods used in interpretation whereby closure is achieved. This is not to suggest that the deconstructionist views interpretation as meaningless; rather, the deconstructive activity presumes that interpretation is capable of infinite meaningfulness.

One of Derrida's most effective conceptual activities used in subverting the idea of closure is the anomalously spelled *différance*. This term plays on the French verbs for "to differ" and "to defer" by insinuating both of their meanings. In doing so, the term confronts Ferdinand de Saussure's notion that meaningful language depends on the recognition of distinctive signs by proposing that meaning must be infinitely deferred since the play of meaning goes on and on. In other words, meaning cannot be passed between minds through words since additional oppositional distinctions lie, for instance, on both sides of the original distinction that informs the transmitted sign, and these oppositional distinctions extend outward in a chain that lures the listener from the speaker's intended meaning.

In deconstructionism's desire to upset the traditional methods of interpretation, deconstructionist texts often prove difficult to read. This difficulty is not due to any inherent complexities of the activity, but it serves as another attack on the certainty upon which interpreters and their audiences traditionally have relied. Deconstructionism, continuing its attack on traditional interpretation, encourages a suspicion of all research and scholarship that has laid claim to a stable interpretive context for the research, for stability has little place in an activity that values continual rereadings.

Although there tend to be few folklorists who explicitly adopt the critical activity of deconstructionism (i.e., the rigorous inversion of the binary and a teasing out of the multiple meanings) in their scholarship and research, the idea that meaningful closure is illusory is being reflected in much of the discipline's current work. This reluctance to adopt a deconstructive activity is shared with many other academic disciplines as well, for the admission that terms such as *meaning* and *truth* are relative at best and fictions at worst undermines the perceived role of the educational institution and its efforts at interpretive analysis, critical investigations, transmission of knowledge, and, therefore, the institution's mission.

Charlie McCormick

See also Cultural Studies; Postmodernism.

✲✲✲✲✲✲✲✲✲✲✲✲✲✲✲✲

References

Barnes, Julian. 1990. *A History of the World in 10½ Chapters*. New York: Vintage International.

Derrida, Jacques. 1977. *Of Grammatology*. Trans. Gayatri Chakravorty Spivak. Baltimore, MD: Johns Hopkins University.

Hutcheon, Linda. 1988. *A Poetics of Postmodernism: History, Theory, Fiction*. New York: Routledge.

Norris, Christopher. 1982. *Deconstruction: Theory and Practice*. New York: Methuen.

Warshaver, Gerald E. 1991. On Postmodern Folklore. *Western Folklore*. 50:219–229.

DIACHRONIC/SYNCHRONIC

Distinctive approaches to the study of language that have been extended to folklore studies. Ferdinand de Saussure sharply differentiated a diachronic (or historical) approach to the study of language, which views language as constantly dynamic, from a synchronic (or nonhistorical) approach, which perceives language in unchanging stasis at a particular point in its continual development. The distinction has entered the discourse of folklore studies in two ways.

When Claude Lévi-Strauss introduced his structural study of myth, he suggested that two ways of reading myth corresponded to *langue* (Saussure's synchronic approach) and *parole* (the diachronic approach). Interpreting myth diachronically resulted in a narration that presented the elements of myth in the nonrevertible sequence demanded by the story chronology. For Lévi-Strauss, understanding myth synchronically meant that one should focus on recurrent patterns that appear at different points in the narration. Reading several instances of a recurrent pattern in relation to occurrences of other patterns allowed an understanding of how the myth reflected the tendency of the human mind to work toward mediated binary opposition. Some folklorists and other students of narrative have used the term *syntagmatic* synonymously with *diachronic* and *paradigmatic* to equate with *synchronic*.

The distinction between the terms *diachronic* and *synchronic* has had more significant impact on folklore studies through their application to general methods of research and analysis. Diachronic approaches to folklore involve looking at particular genres or specific text-types in terms that remove them from their performance context. These approaches (for example, the historic-geographic method) work toward constructing genre and text-type histories, but they do so by conceiving folklore as an artifact that can be isolated from its immediate contexts. Synchronic approaches, influenced by the ethnography of speaking introduced by Dell Hymes and John J. Gumperz, view folklore as text and/or process within a specific context that includes the immediate performance situation, the cultural background in which that situation occurs, and the psychosocial influences that have affected the participants (performers and audience) of the community.

Critics of diachronic approaches have argued that focusing on the historical or cross-cultural dynamism of texts without contexts makes folklore a lifeless entity, analogous to a collection of museum specimens. Critics of synchronic approaches have suggested that they lose what is distinctive in the study of folklore, substituting the methods and interpretive tools of ethnography and sociolinguistics for those that have developed within the history of folklore studies. The study of folklore becomes an examination of behavior rather than of the products of artistic creativity.

The gulf between diachronic and synchronic approaches to folklore study was wide in the late 1960s and throughout the 1970s. Although the first generation of academically trained folklorists in the United States had defined folklore study in diachronic terms, many of their successors, whose manifesto was a special issue of the *Journal of American Folklore* published in 1971, advocated synchronic perspectives. That gulf persisted into the 1990s, but its significance for folklore studies lessened as some folklorists found ways of bridging it and as new concerns in folklore study emerged.

William M. Clements

See also Paradigmatic/Syntagmatic.

✳✳✳✳✳✳✳✳✳✳✳✳✳✳✳✳✳

References

Abrahams, Roger D. 1993. After New Perspectives: Folklore Study in the Late Twentieth Century. *Western Folklore* 52:379–400.

de Saussure, Ferdinand. 1966. *Course in General Linguistics*. Trans. Wade Baskin. New York: McGraw-Hill.

Georges, Robert A. 1980. Toward a Resolution of the Text/Context Controversy. *Western Folklore* 39:34–40.

Hymes, Dell H. 1974. *Foundations in Sociolinguistics: An Ethnographic Approach*. Philadelphia: University of Pennsylvania Press.

Hymes, Dell H., and John J. Gumperz, eds. 1964. *The Ethnography of Speaking*. Washington, DC: American Anthropological Association.

Jones, Stephen. 1979. Slouching toward Ethnography: The Text/Context Controversy Reconsidered. *Western Folklore* 38:42–47.

Lévi-Strauss, Claude. 1955. The Structural Study of Myth. *Journal of American Folklore* 67:428–444.

Paredes, Américo, and Richard Bauman, eds. 1971. *Toward New Perspectives in Folklore*. Austin: University of Texas Press.

DIALOGISM

The term used by late-twentieth-century scholars to describe Mikhail M. Bakhtin's (1895–1975) epistemology of mutually influencing relations among entities. Bakhtin himself employed the term *dialogue* (also *dialogization*). Dialogue served as Bakhtin's master metaphor in a semiotic "architectonics" (i.e., in Michael Holquist's terms, a "science of relations") that emphasized the concepts of emergence, relativity, tension, selection, and value. To Bakhtin, no entity had meaning in isolation. There are three basic aspects of this assertion. First, in conversational dialogue (Bakhtin's simplest framing of the term), utterances respond to one another and thereby take on meaning relative to one another. Somewhat analogously in epistemological dialogue, any entity (e.g., the human self, a literary text or character or author, an interpretive strategy, an ideology) acquires meaning only in terms of its interaction with other entities (other human selves, literary texts). This interaction may occur between entities of like kind (e.g., one character in a text in light of other characters in the same text) or between entities of differing kinds (e.g., a character's identity relative to the author's identity or the tenets of an ideology relative to the *chronotope* [i.e., the circumstances of time and space and the sociocultural contexts implied thereby] in which that ideology developed). Second, dialogue is mutually influencing to the entities involved. Thus, not only does an entity A take on significance in relation to entities B and C, for example, but *simultaneously* B and C also acquire meaning relative to their interaction with A. Third, meaning also depends on the particular power relationships obtaining among the entities. In other words, meaning arises within and exists in tension. It emerges in dialogue among *different* entities, each of which has its own viewpoint to promote. In a dialogic relationship, meanings may, for example, be altered, deleted, conjoined, or substituted as each particular viewpoint or "voice" struggles for dominance.

Any dialogue involves interaction among a multiplicity of voices operating simultaneously on several different levels—that is, in the condition Bakhtin termed *heteroglossia*. In any act of meaning-making, participants must choose which voices-in-dialogue to heed. Thus, meaning is the result of the value-based action (i.e., choice or "authorship") of its participants and not simply of the participants' perception. The quality of "novelness," which in literature is demonstrated most strongly in the genre of the novel, is that condition of human perception that is most sensitive to heteroglossia.

Because meaning is always positional (i.e., emergent within a situation of relationships), no single viewpoint can ever *validly* claim or completely maintain absolute, unitary authority (i.e., the perspective Bakhtin termed *monologism*). Confrontation with the Other will always arise because response to the

Other is intrinsic to the development of meaning. Bakhtin used the term *carnival* to refer not only to a type of medieval festival but also to any popularly based situation of fluidity that challenges the stasis of authoritative, official (i.e., monologic) culture. In carnival, novelness is most potently symbolized in the *grotesque body*—the body of extensions, apertures, and effluvia that is constantly open to the Other and thus constantly in the act of becoming.

Danielle M. Roemer

See also Carnival.

✻✻✻✻✻✻✻✻✻✻✻✻✻✻✻✻

References

Bakhtin, M. M. 1981. *The Dialogic Imagination: Four Essays*. Ed. Michael Holquist, trans. Caryl Emerson and Michael Holquist. Austin: University of Texas Press.
———. 1984. *Rabelais and His World*. Trans. Hélène Iswolsky. Bloomington: Indiana University Press.
Holquist, Michael. 1990. *Dialogism: Bakhtin and His World*. New York: Routledge.

Dilemma Tales

A narrative verbal puzzle (Motifs H620, "The unsolved problem: enigmatic ending of tale," and Z16, "Tales ending with a question"). Presenting a dilemma tale to an audience constitutes a synthesis between riddling and narrating activities. These two broad attributes of the genre may be clarified further. With reference to riddling, the dilemma tale belongs to the category of the "puzzle" in which emphasis in solving the problem is placed on the riddlee's own abilities (such as intellectual or motor skills); in this respect, a puzzle differs from a "true riddle," in which emphasis is on the riddle's structure and contents that contain clues to the camouflaged answer. As for the narrative component, the dilemma tale is typically a traditional "fantasy" prose narrative, told with the intent of entertaining or instructing and training; although some dilemma tales may contain a historical or belief component, they seem not to be narrated as legends or belief narratives.

A dilemma tale differs from similar nondilemma tales that incorporate true riddles or puzzles as part of the plot; in this category, the tale's characters (dramatis personae) may debate among themselves and offer answers, but members of the audience are not required to participate, and they remain spectators (e.g., AT 851, "The Princess Who Cannot Solve the Riddle"; AT 875A, "Girl's Riddling Answer Betrays a Theft"; and AT 1579, "Carrying Wolf, Goat, and Cabbage across Stream"). By contrast, in the dilemma tale situation, the audience is required to take part by offering answers to the problem the tale poses. The various and often conflicting solutions offered by members of the audience (each acting in dual roles as listener to the tale and as riddlee) reflect the personal viewpoints of the members proposing them; also, the answers would be based on the cultural norms (mores, folkways, laws). Consequently, the community's value system becomes a subject for debates and reevaluations. For example, a tale that appears as an African dilemma (AT 653A, "The Rarest Thing in the World") poses a situation in which three brothers, each using a precious commodity or service in resuscitating a girl, asks the question, To whom does she belong? Typically, the means utilized are information, transportation, and treatment; these may be viewed as aspects of the economic or a related culture institution whose worth will be debated.

Most of the dilemmas posed constitute decision making ("Choices," Motifs J200-J499); meanwhile, the puzzles posed belong to themes addressed under other motifs (Motifs H630, "Riddles of the superlative," and H660, "Riddles of comparison").

Although the dilemma tale has been reported from various parts of the world, its strongest presence is in sub-Saharan Africa, especially the western and central regions. Since many African dilemma tales also are known throughout the world as nondilemma tales, the occurrence of these narratives in the northern and eastern regions of Africa (in Arab, Berber, and adjacent areas) poses an interesting problem. In view of the close geographic and historical contacts between the two portions of Africa, two arguments may be advanced: (1) The northern Africans borrowed dilemma tales from the south and provided stable answers for them, thus converting them into nondilemma tales, or (2) the sub-Saharan groups took nondilemma tales from the north and omitted the concluding episodes that rest on value systems different from their own, thus converting them into dilemma tales. A third argument is that both traditions developed totally independently.

Hasan El-Shamy

See also Enigma, Folk.

✳✳✳✳✳✳✳✳✳✳✳✳✳✳✳✳✳

References

Aarne, Antti, and Stith Thompson. 1964. *The Types of the Folktale: A Classification and Bibliography*. Helsinki: Academia Scientiarum Fennica.

Bascom, William. 1975. *African Dilemma Tales*. The Hague: Mouton.

El-Shamy, Hasan. 1980. *Folktales of Egypt: Collected, Translated and Annotated with Middle Eastern and African Parallels*. Chicago: University of Chicago Press.

Thompson, Stith. 1958. *Motif-Index of Folk-Literature*. 6 vols. Bloomington: Indiana University Press.

Discourse analysis

The study of language in social interaction. A branch of sociolinguistics, discourse analysis offers insights into daily processes of expressive behavior and interaction. By accounting for minute features of conversation, the field provides a means of examining folklore as part of a unified communicative system.

Discourse analysis developed as a refinement of descriptive linguistics. Like sociolinguistics, it proceeds from the observation of what language accomplishes (i.e., its functions), discovering the structures and means by which that accomplishment takes place. Discourse analysis focuses in particular on the moment of interaction, be it face-to-face or transmitted by mass media.

Folklorists have made ready use of discourse analytical methods. Annikki Kaivola-Bregenhøj draws on studies of comprehension and memory to discuss the ways in which a single narrator remembers and performs his or her repertoire. Gary Butler similarly draws on insights into conversational roles and communicative function to shed light on such familiar genres as proverb and memorate. Deborah Tannen explores conversational style as expressive behavior. Discourse analytical frameworks deepen folkloristic understandings of performance.

Discourse analysts themselves have undertaken studies of interest to folklorists. The field is characterized by an interest in socially relevant topics. Volume 4 of the *Handbook of Discourse Analysis*, for instance, offers examinations of such phenomena as gendered speech and the social use of xenophobic urban legends. Doctor-patient and politician-constituent relations form the focus of other discourse-analytical works. Such studies enrich understandings of communication and its role in social life.

A number of ethnographers have adopted discourse-analytical frameworks for addressing social issues. Conflicts between Native American modes of communication and those of Anglo schoolteachers are explored by Susan Philips. Group conflict and its resolution have been studied in ethnographies of Pacific societies.

With its descriptive apparatus and theoretical significance, discourse analysis demonstrates the tremendous expressive content of daily interaction and life.

Thomas A. DuBois

See also Linguistic Approach.

✳✳✳✳✳✳✳✳✳✳✳✳✳✳✳✳✳

References

Butler, Gary. 1991. *"Saying Isn't Believing": Conversation, Narrative and the Discourse of Tradition in a French Newfoundland Community*. St. John's, Newfoundland:

Institute of Social and Economic Research.

Ensink, T., A. van Essen, and T. van der Geest, eds. 1986. *Discourse Analysis and Public Life: Papers of the Groningen Conference on Medical and Political Discourse.* Dordrecht, Netherlands: Foris Publications.

Kaivola-Bregenhøj, Annikki. 1989. Factors Influencing the Formulation of Narration. *Studia Fennica* 33:73–89.

Philips, Susan Urmston. 1983. *The Invisible Culture: Communication in Classroom and Community on the Warm Springs Indian Reservation.* New York: Longman.

Tannen, Deborah. 1984. *Conversational Style: Analyzing Talk among Friends.* Norwood, NJ: Ablex.

Tracy, Karen, ed. 1991. *Understanding Face-to-Face Interaction: Issues Linking Goals and Discourse.* Hillsdale, NJ: Lawrence Erlbaum.

van Dijk, Teun A., ed. 1985. *Handbook of Discourse Analysis: Volume 4, Discourse Analysis in Society.* London: Academic Press.

Watson-Gegeo, Karen Ann, and Geoffrey White, eds. 1990. *Disentangling: Conflict Discourse in Pacific Societies.* Stanford, CA: Stanford University Press.

D<small>ITE</small>

A statement that implies but does not recount a narrative. C. W. von Sydow coined the term *dite* in 1937 to help classify a broad body of materials grouped as *Sagn* (a concept comprising both narrative and nonnarrative statements of folk belief). He defined it as "what people have to say about one thing or another without characterizing that which is said as true or false, believed in or fictitious."

He divided this concept into two subcategories: (1) the *affirmate*, a statement that points out a generalized fact ("In that place, a light has been seen"), and (2) the *consiliate*, a precept that asserts what should or should not be done in a given case ("One should spit three times when a cat runs across the road"). Sydow also characterized whimsical or fanciful dites as *ficts*, expressions that have no basis in truth (such as "that stone will spin round whenever it catches the smell of newly baked bread").

In Anglo-American taxonomies, many of Sydow's dites would be termed *proverbs* or *superstitions*. But Sydow intended the term *dites* to contrast with *memorates* and *fabulates*, these being fully developed narratives that tell exactly what happened in a given instance. The dite may be a summary of a given narrative, he noted, or a dite may inspire an informant to expand it into a narrative.

For this reason, many scholars have seen such brief texts as types of legend. Susan Kalcik, for instance, found "kernel narratives" told in conversational contexts in which those present were familiar with the full story. Such "metonyms" (as condensed, allusive narratives also are called) still function as complete, finished performances in context. Linda Dégh argued that "the

191

legend text" itself consists of *all* elements, fully narrated or not, as long as they form part of a contentious conversational dynamic.

But some dites express beliefs that are *never* narrated. Sylvia Grider described the common claim that Halloween sadists put razor blades in trick-or-treat goodies as a "legend" but never found it related in the form of a story. Similarly, John Widdowson studied verbal threats that control children's behavior by invoking evil (often supernatural) entities as completed linguistic performances, not summary narratives. In such cases, the term *dite* may be appropriate and useful. Likewise, the term *fict* accurately characterizes the widespread whimsical claim (rarely corroborated by experience) that certain statues on college campuses move or otherwise respond when a virgin passes.

The dite concept, however, assumes that we agree on how much plot constitutes a narrative. Robert Georges observed that many brief texts in context could equally be considered legend or belief statements. The distinction between legend and dite is often fuzzy, and so the latter is best understood as a term describing form rather than defining genre: A dite has the potential to be a narrative, but *in its present form*, the full story is left unexpressed.

Bill Ellis

See also Belief, Folk; Belief Tale; Legend.

✻✻✻✻✻✻✻✻✻✻✻✻✻✻✻✻

References
Ellis, Bill. 1989. When Is a Legend? In *The Questing Beast*, eds. Gillian Bennett and Paul Smith. Sheffield, England: Sheffield Academic Press.

Hand, Wayland D., ed. 1971. *American Folk Legend: A Symposium*. Berkeley: University of California Press.

von Sydow, Carl Wilhelm. 1978. *Selected Papers on Folklore*. Copenhagen: Rosenkilde and Bagger and New York: Arno.

Widdowson, John. 1977. *If You Don't Be Good: Verbal Social Control in Newfoundland*. St. John's, Newfoundland: Memorial University of Newfoundland.

DIVINATION

Intuitive, revealed, and inspired knowledge obtained through the use of diverse methods, techniques, tools, and devices, eliciting the nature of time and events, the path of human life and destiny, and the unfolding of a meaningful cosmos. A general term, *divination* (from the Latin *divinus*, meaning "one inspired by the gods" or "soothsayer") refers to the culturally encoded processes of extraordinary human insight arising spontaneously from intuition and reflection or through the extrahuman agency of inspiration and prophecy by indwelling spirits and the direction of deities. Divination entails perspectives on time and space spanning regression into the past and foreknowledge of the future. Another related term, the *mantic arts* (from the Greek *mantis*, meaning "prophet") is often used to refer to the range of techniques and methods that form systems of divination, from the systematic interpretation of the personal and idiosyncratic to the perception of meaningful patterns in the natural world and the cosmos. Many types of divination have been named by the suffix *mancy*, (e.g., oneiromancy, hydromancy, and geomancy), identifying their status as disciplines that engender inspired and prophetic activity. Divination is a subject of interest within the study of folklore and folklife because it is a realm of human experience that is virtually always initially expressed and practiced orally, even though it is often later recorded in writing, in art and architecture, and in the material culture of domestic space. Divination is also equally folkloristic in that it is universally a folk practice, embraced by the common people and expressing their concerns, as well as an elite, empowered, hierarchically privileged practice of rulers, aristocracies, and professional adepts.

Since its historical range is enormous, its cultural and linguistic expression complex, and its range of tools and techniques bewilderingly diverse, divination may be best categorized along phenomenological lines. Such an approach facilitates cross-cultural and diachronic comparison and analysis. The following phenomenological categories, therefore, are offered as a comprehensive listing not of particular manifestations of divination but of types of divinatory experience.

Personal visionary and auditory experiences form a wide range of divinatory media, particularly dreams (or oneiromancy) and conscious presentiments, such as second sight, visions, soothsaying, psychic awareness, and extrasensory perception (or ESP). The mediation of knowledge communicated by the world of spirits is another important arena of divination, especially when communicated by the spirits of the dead as in necromancy, shamanism, séance, and channeling. These inspired communications can be transmitted in various ways: by indwelling spirits, gods, and the powers of nature both during and after possession and mediumship, as in speaking in tongues (or glossolalia); by prophecy via direct divine inspiration as found within Judeo-Christian-Islamic scriptures, the Zoroastrian Avesta, the Hindu Vedas and Upanishads, and so forth; by the wisdom literature embodied in the Greek and Chaldean theurgic oracles; and by other mythopoeic oracles such as archives of interpretive verses in West African and Afro-Caribbean Ifa divination.

The principle of meaningful chance and the importance of randomization are central to many divining systems. Thus, the perception and interpretation of signs or omens of luck, fate, or meaningful chance are represented in divination by lots (or sortilege, also called cleromancy); divination by the flight of arrows or the casting of arrowheads; divination by the use of mirrors; or divination by games of chance such as dice (or lithomancy). The meaningful randomization of numeric and symbolic forms together is central to several interrelated families of divining systems, including alphabetic and numeric correspondence and the creative and cosmogonic power of numbers known as numerology, as in the medieval systems that continue into modernity of Jewish *gematriya* and Islamic *jafr*, inspired by the Pythagorean and neo-Pythagorean numerology of late antiquity. Related is the practice of name reading (or onomancy) and various types of name magic that calculate the numerical values of the letters in names and interpret their effect (for good or ill) on the life path or destiny of the individual so named. Other systems based upon meaningful chance (or randomization) of numbers and pictorial symbols usually combine with narrative or poetic traditions of interpretation. These ideographic and pictographic systems are exemplified by the relationship of numeric and pictorial images as in the tarot and other types of card reading and their traditional narrative interpretation; the relationship of alphabetic symbols and oral traditional lore in the casting of runes; the I Ching hexagrams formed by the fall of coins or yarrow stalks and their traditional narrative corpus of interpretation in the Book of Change; and the figures of Ifa formed by the numerological sequence of the casting of palm nuts or divining shells and their mythopoeic archive of interpretive Ifa verses.

Divination systems that concentrate on meaningful patterns in the relationship between earth and all heavenly bodies include the diverse historical and cultural expressions of astronomy and astrology worldwide (Babylonian-Chaldean, Hindu, Chinese, Mayan, Greco-Roman, Islamic, and European), much of which survives recombined in modern practice. Astronomy and astrology were considered twin disciplines in medieval thought, both Islamic and European. Astronomy was based on acute physical and mechanical observation of the heavenly bodies and the mathematical calculation of their regular movements. These measurements were accompanied by the complex systems of associative significance encoded by astrology. Astrology's aim was to discover the essence of universal harmony that lay in the relations between the spheres. This harmony of solids and motion was seen in the revolutions of the spheres (spherical bodies moving in what was then believed to be circular patterns). Thus, metaphysical speculations on the cosmic significance of number and practical calculations and observations required for advanced astronomy went hand in hand. Astrology is a symbolic system that has blended easily with other systems of belief and practice since late antiquity. The combinations produced, among others, astrological medicine; astrological divination, as in geomancy; astrologically grounded alchemy; and other astrological magical practices, such as astrological talismanry. Astrology charts and analyzes the meaningful patterns of structure in the heavens, that is, the constellations that form the signs of the zodiac, the spatial relationships of heaven and earth that form the houses of the zodiac, and the changing inter-relationship of transiting planetary and luminous bodies with each other over time that form the ongoing process of cosmic history. The particular nature and "influence" of the heavens upon the earth can be read as a portrait of the life path of each individual (natal astrology), the meaning and outcome of particular events in time and space (horary astrology), and the unfolding of the life course of rulers, governments, and nations in history (judicial astrol-ogy). Thus, astrology as a system of divination is formed of two interrelated activities: (1) the casting of a chart of any one of the relationships mentioned earlier through mathematical and astronomical calculation, and (2) the intu-itive, inspired, and revealed process of narrative interpretation of the chart's significance in relation to a particular question (whether it be the destiny of a person according to date and time of birth, the meaning of a particular event, the timing of a life passage, the beginning or ending of some enter-prise, or the guiding of the ship of state and interactions between nations and governments).

Many other divining systems rely upon the structuring and interpretation of patterns of meaning in the earth, as encoded in its topography, its weather formations, and its natural forces and objects. Various systems of earth divina-tion, known as geomancy, survive in living practice. For example, within the Islamic world, there are diverse practices within the larger science of Islamic geomancy, *ilm al-raml* (the science of the sand), and the divination of micro- and macrocosm represented by Chinese geomancy, *feng-shui* (divination by "wind and water"), continues in both the East and where it has been trans-planted in the West. Divining the earth has often been specialized into vari-ous elemental subspecialties (according to the Greeks, the basic elements out of which all existence substance is composed are earth, water, fire, and air). Divining the presence of minerals in the earth or water or other objects is known in European and North American cultures as hydromancy, or culti-vating visions in pools or surfaces of water (an activity long religiously associ-ated with spiritual questing and interior reflection), and pyromancy, or seeing visions within candle flames or firelight have, since ancient times, been means used in diverse cultures for inspiration by the higher mind, by the gods, and by the elemental spirits of nature. Other expressions of elemental divination must include crystal gazing and stone reading, that is, seeing visions within spheri-cal, ovoid, or other shapes of clear, colored, or reflective stones. Stone reading, allied with the magical and medical use of crystals, gemstones, and minerals in Greco-Roman antiquity, became widespread in the late medieval and Renaissance West and continues in modern times. Crystal gazing usually involves use of clear and translucent colored quartzes; diamonds and other translucent gemstones (such as emerald, beryl, ruby, sapphire, and topaz);

opaque and mirrorlike stones and gems (such as polished hematite, black obsidian, jet, and black onyx); or opalescent and reflective stones, frequently in
spherical or semispherical shapes or cut as cabochon jewelry (such as varieties
of agates, moonstone, rainbow and golden obsidian, tiger's eye and cat's eye,
and opals). The interior reflection and mirrorlike intensity of stone reading and
crystal gazing are direct parallels to the guided searching of mirrored surfaces of
water described earlier. Related to this type of earth divination is the reading of
meaningful patterns in natural materials such as tea leaves or coffee grounds,
which are believed by tea- and coffee-drinking cultures worldwide to bear the
print of life left by the one who held the cup and drank the brew.

Finally, patterns of meaning within the bodies and movements of animate
creatures are divined as animal signs and omens. Within the cultures of
Mediterranean antiquity and pre- and early-Christian Europe, as well as
diverse tribal cultures worldwide, these patterns of meaning have been established and communicated through augury and auspices, as in interpreting the
passage and flight of birds and their cries (or ornithomancy), as well as interpreting the behavior and movements of herd animals such as the horse and
the behavior and movements of fish, insects, or reptiles. Through the perception and interpretation of animal portents and prodigies, the diviner alerts the
community to the often malign significance of spontaneous appearances of
extraordinary, anomalous, or unnatural animal forms. The divining of portents
focuses individual and communal awareness on the advent of unavoidable
hazards, whether stemming from the gods or from the forces of nature or
human society. The reader of portents advises how to minimize and contain
their danger by propitiating the forces that sent them with rituals of purification and sacrifice. Portents also can function as signs foretelling and confirming a path of extraordinary destiny communicated to an individual or
community by the gods and personifications of fate.

As a subset of divining the body, there are divining systems, elements of
which can be found virtually worldwide, that concentrate on the observation
and analysis of the meaningful characteristics of the human body alone,
believing it to be a microcosm of the meaningful universe. The divination of
meaningful patterns in the human microcosm is generally identified as physiognomy, or anthroposcopy. The divination of the bodily and facial features
can be broken down into several subsystems, among which are phrenology, or
reading the character and mental capacity from the conformation of the skull,
and metoposcopy, interpreting the lines that appear in the soles of the feet and
the palms of the hands, the latter being identified independently as chiro-
mancy, or palmistry. As a discipline in itself, palmistry reads the character and
destiny of the individual from the convergence of lines and markings on the
palm and the shape of the fingers and nails. Meaningful patterns also have
been gleaned from human and animal remains in ancient and tribal cultures

worldwide through practices entailing sacrifice of the living creature and extraction of the organs (the viscera) or gathering of the skeletal remains of a creature already dead by natural causes. The first method is generally known as haruspicy, the sacrifice to the gods or powers to propitiate and incline them to impart hidden knowledge of present and future situations to the questioner. The reading and documentation of answer given by the gods or powers lie in the interpretation of the physical characteristics of the internal organs of the sacrificed creature. The second method relies on similar interpretive techniques but does not employ sacrifice—for example, scapulimancy and plastromancy, the induction (through the application of heat) of cracks and reading their meaningful patterns in the bones and shells of once living animals gifted to the diviner by land and sea.

It must be noted that there is considerable overlap of the characteristics of these systems, and many forms of divination share several sets of the qualities and methods listed here. Scholars often have categorized these divinatory phenomena and experiences as discrete and separate categories, whereas in individual systems of divination, the phenomena are found interlinked and interdependent. A given form of divination, for example, may involve a series of ritual acts, including the incubation of dreams, casting of symbols using physical means, numerological and astrological calculations, consultation and performance of inspired or revealed oral and/or written bodies of interpretation, sacrifices to the deities in thanks for their inspired communications and propitiating their proper action on behalf of self or client, and the preparation and administration of medicines or talismanic remedies.

The diversity of these dispersed and disparate historical and geographic practices, the complexity of their rationales and cultural and artistic forms, and the variety of their techniques and tools are consistent only in an overarching purpose that might best be described as healing. This healing purpose operates in individual terms as identification of the personal and immediate causes of spiritual, psychological, emotional, and physical ills and asks for guidance in order to effect healing through appropriate action or response. The healing purpose operates also in communal terms to pinpoint the causes of domestic, communal, tribal, or national disease and disharmony and prescribes a cure often requiring a sacrifice or some other expiation that restores the health of society. Its ultimate referent is the discovery of the root cause and nature of disorder on a planetary, celestial, and cosmic scale, which offers healing through counseling individual and/or communal action to reestablish the universal or divine order. Thus, divining systems are devoted not only to knowing what is hidden about human and extrahuman affairs but also to providing tools and techniques for healing the disturbances that underlie and motivate recourse to divination. The sacrificial, ritual, verbal, and material prescriptions that often append the act of divination encompass a range of healing processes, techniques, substances, and interactions. This dual preventative and curative function encompasses roles that modern society has separated and secularized. In the Western context, for example, these functions include, among others, psychological therapy, spiritual ministry, physical medicine, family counseling, communal arbitration, government liaison, international negotiation, environmental lobby, and science and technology advising.

The history of the scholarly literature on the subject of divination and the mantic arts is extremely diverse, with the greatest emphasis on historical and literary systems. Theoretical discussions and analytical categorizations of divination have been offered by the history of religions approach to this material, such as the useful summary by Evan M. Zeusse in the *Encyclopedia of Religion* (1987), which emphasizes the types of religious experience and categories of perception that are the dominant features of particular divinatory systems even though they may be (and usually are) found in combination. Zeusse's typology of divination offers three main rubrics of experience and perception within which to understand divination: *intuitive divination* through dreams and visionary experience; *possession divination* by spirits and deities of nonhuman agents and of human agents; and lastly, *wisdom divination*, or systems of knowledge and techniques of interpretation based on numeric, geologic, and bodily patterns. Zeusse also distinguishes the ecstatic (intuitive and possession divination) from the nonecstatic (wisdom divination), based upon Plato's criteria of categorization (*Phaedrus* 244 and *Timaeus* 72) and the criteria of many later thinkers. He correctly emphasizes the importance of concepts and practices of sacrifice in relation to all divining systems since all divining is seen as a gift of wisdom and healing that requires a propitiating response on the part of the diviner and/or the client to the gods, ancestors, spirits of nature, powers and directions, or the cosmos as a whole.

The divination systems of the ancient and late antique world based in the cultures of the Middle East and the Mediterranean (Babylonian-Mesopotamian, Canaanite—ancient Israelite, Egyptian, Greco-Roman), which left partial to extensive textual and archaeological records, have perhaps received the greatest share of academic attention from scholars of ancient Near Eastern languages, historians, and classicists, second only to the study of Indian and Chinese divination by south and east Asian specialists. Attention has been focused on the place of divination primarily as religious and philosophical institutions of the aristocracy and ruling body, administered through a priestly class or technical college or guild of practitioners. Systems of divination that flourished during the medieval period in the West, whether Islamic, Jewish, or Christian in orientation—astrology, numerology, cards, geomancy, necromancy, hydromancy, pyromancy, dreams and second sight, physiognomy, foreknowledge and insight through the holiness of saints and spiritual masters, divination by judicial ordeal, divining by means of sacred scripture, and so forth—have been treated less intensively by historians and religious studies scholars whose attention has focused more strongly upon the normalization of religious institutions and sacred texts during the medieval period. Although there are many medieval texts devoted to these forms of divination (particularly astrology and geomancy), it is also true that many of these practices are found within the interstices of textual and historical record, with little material or archaeological evidence to document their forms and methods.

The study of living systems of divination, predominantly in the contexts of close-knit pastoral and nomadic societies worldwide since the nineteenth century, has been an outgrowth of the anthropological attention paid to the religious beliefs and practices of diverse and discrete tribal and peasant communities in sub-Saharan Africa as well as North Africa; of Native American communities of North and South America; of the shamanistic communities of the Alaskan, Canadian, and Siberian tundra; of Polynesian and Melanesian islanders; of the Malay Archipelago; of Aboriginal Australia; and of the folk traditions of south and east Asia. This anthropological attention has been devoted primarily to the study of folk and traditional systems of divination outside of the context of complex or urban communities or to the survival and adaptation of such traditional systems as a result of modernization.

Divination has not been widely considered in folklore and folklife scholarship. Two works on divination, however, are often referred to by folklorists—William Bascom's *Ifa Divination* and Evon Z. Vogt and Ray Hyman's *Water Witching U.S.A.* These two works addressing two different forms of geomancy, although dated in theory and approach, are still considered classics and are used consistently in folklore and folklife classroom presentations of divination. Interestingly, these books do not share any common method or theoretical perspective. Their representative character regarding the study of divination lies in two approaches: treating divination from a folklore perspective and treating divination as a folk system without recourse to folklore methodology.

Bascom's *Ifa Divination* offers a consistent folkloristic emphasis on oral forms of religious practice. Ifa divination involves a series of steps beginning with dream inspiration, followed by repeated geomantic castings of figures using cowrie shells or palm nuts, and distributing that pattern of figures in wood dust on a divining tray or other surface. Numerological calculations of these castings result in the "figures of Ifa," the deity of divination. It is the visual representation of the numbers that is drawn in wood dust on the tray. Recourse is then made to the oracles of Ifa in order to interpret those figures, after which counsel is given on the correct sacrifices to be made to the Ifa deities. The final step in the cycle of Ifa divination is the prescription of spir-

Pythia pronouncing the oracle of Apollo at Delphi. This legendary Greek oracle is an example of theurgic divination.

itual and physical medicines by the diviner to remedy the spiritual, familial, and social problems that spark the client's original motivation to seek out divination. Contexting Ifa divination within its social and material nexus (through text and illustration), Bascom's work appropriately emphasizes the folkloristic importance of the selection and performance of oral traditional interpretive verses that are the oracles of the gods accompanying the physical process of casting the figures of Ifa, the master-disciple relationship and received traditions by which diviners are trained and the Ifa oracles are transmitted, and the status and social interactions of the diviner serving the small community. Bascom's approach as a folklorist is not limited to emphasis on oral forms or the folk community but also extends to the credibility given to his informants and the interview process, which is one of the unique hallmarks of folklore method and allows folklore fieldwork to openly engage the world of belief within the framework of nonparticipant observation.

Vogt and Hyman's *Water Witching U.S.A.* treats a folk system—dowsing—from a nonfolkloristic perspective, emphasizing historical and sociological analysis. The diverse names for this form of divining detailed in the work reflect the historical, cultural, and linguistic origins and geographic dispersion of this practice. Divining by a rod, wand, pendulum, or other device is known by many names—dowsing in England, water witching in the United States, *radiesthésie* (or radio-electric detection) in France, and *pedelforschung* (or pendulum research) in Germany. According to early textual references, dowsing began in Renaissance Europe as a mining technique to divine from the surface the presence and depth of underground minerals. It rapidly spread to searching for underground water and lost objects and even came to be applied to seeking out criminals and missing persons. Through intuitive-psychic and, according to other views, electromagnetic connection with the unseen subsurface or otherwise distant objects, the diviner locates and identifies the objects, signaled by the movement of wand or pendulum. For Vogt and Hyman, dowsing qualifies as a folk system, at least in the United States, since it originated and is predominantly practiced in rural areas by ordinary, less educated individuals within folk communities, although it has also come to exist as an urban phenomenon as well. Vogt and Hyman's only truly theoretical examination of water witching is as magical divination, a designation undergirded by a reworked version of the two-tiered model—in this case, "the magical mind" and "the scientific mind." According to this model, which Vogt and Hyman critique and yet in the end support, the beliefs and practices of the "folk," particularly the rural folk—such as dowsing—are dominated by "the magical mind" and associated with an "emotional and unreflective attitude," which make the beliefs and practices superstition. In this view, the authors mirror a trend in folklore scholarship that has long associated and devalued magic as superstition. The most significant drawback of *Water Witching U.S.A.* as a work utilized by folklorists is its lack of folklore content. This work reflects no particular emphasis on oral forms (although a brief section on "witching folklore" is included). There is little attention to the traditional received nature of transmission of practice or training of practitioners. And most telling, there is an a priori distrust and rejection of informant belief, experience, and testimony, which is counter to folklore methodology. Vogt and Hyman's consequent method of fieldwork, using the set questionnaire without reflecting any interviews that may have been conducted, represents a much more statistically oriented approach to social data gathering and analysis, coming out of an older and less sophisticated strata of folklore and sociology theory.

On the methodological approaches available as models for the study of divination, a number of critiques of divination as religious practice and as folk practice must be offered. The weakness of religious studies and history of religions typologies in the study of divination is their inability to reflect the complexity and interactive quality of these systems, which often rely, as has been noted, on several categories in their performance. Since discovering the presence and nature of folk divining practices is more difficult due to the paucity of written sources and material remains, the scholarly examination of divination from antiquity through the Middle Ages has concentrated on the relationship of institutional religious forms and sanctions to popular forms of divination existing outside of the institutional religious context and interacting with it at different levels, from conflict to complementarity. Thus, insufficient attention has been given to systems of divination considered in their own right, independent of institutional religious contexts; to the interaction between practitioners of divination and the folk; and to folk rather than elite systems of divination. The complex interactions between educated and elite cultural systems of divination arising to serve royal courts and wealthy aristocracies and the dissemination of popular variants of court systems among the diverse divining practices of the common people, as well as the reverse trend of the intellectualization of folk divining into elite narrative traditions, have yet to be adequately studied. Finally, very little attention has been given to modern systems of divination, which rely upon dissemination by mass media and have a broad popular appeal and expression within the complex urban societies of the West. Modern European and North American divinatory beliefs and practices communicated by print and other forms of mass media—such as astrology, numerology, tarot, channeling, Ouija board and other forms of mediumistic divination, speaking in tongues and prophecy, I Ching, runes, crystal gazing, ESP and precognitive dreaming, past-life regression, astral and out of body experience, urban dowsing, and psychometry—have not received the depth and seriousness of scholarly treatment as the same or similar systems have in either historical or anthropological contexts.

ESP, for example, is a topic in the context of modern divination that relies upon the conceptual categories of parapsychology and the modern study of paranormal phenomena. ESP, in traditional folk contexts, would have been termed "second sight," and according to Finnish folklorist Leea Virtanen's 1977 study of historical and contemporary memorates regarding ESP experiences, it embraces the faculties of telepathy, clairvoyance, and precognition of future events. The use of such parapsychological terminology may seem unrelated to a discussion of divination, but the phenomena identified with ESP cover a range of mental, emotional, and sensory perceptions that are central to all forms of intuitive divination, such as precognitive dreams and visions, auditory and olfactory sensations, inner voices and directives, illusions and hallucinatory experiences, heightened and changed emotional and physical states, perception of signs and omens in animals and plants, and so forth. The rubrics of extrasensory perception and psychokinesis, also known as psi awareness and psi activity, distinguish a polarity of experience from spontaneous awareness to focused action. Similarly, particular forms of divining rely on the spontaneous reception of knowledge through intuitive, unconscious, and otherwise altered mental states or acquisition of knowledge through the use of techniques and instruments of divination.

Regarding modern systems of divination practiced in the West, it also may be appropriate to consider the significance of the term *psychic* in relation to the impact of mass media on popular belief and practice. Many of the systems listed earlier that are widely practiced in the contemporary West are often allied with the term *psychic*, and thus media characterizations of such phenomena often use the term in various pairings—for example, *psychic astrology, psychic numerology, psychic tarot reading,* or merely *psychic reading.* The meaning of the term *psychic* in these contexts is difficult to identify concretely but seems to refer to a wide range of skills that are generally understood to be intuitive and precognitive and that function in conjunction with the various techniques of divination. Thus, astrology, which is based in numerological and astronomical calculation and its symbolic interpretation of potential destiny, is wedded in the term *psychic astrologer* with the notion of the reader's precognitive ability to predict and achieve certitude in interpretation of past, present, and future events. Similarly, numerology as a system of significance is combined with belief in the efficacy of psychic prediction to yield luck in numbers and money with such diverse applications as choosing the winning lottery number; selecting the correct day to go to gambling casinos in order win at slot machines and card tables or the right number of the horse or dog to bet on at the racetrack; and propitious or malign days for important life events and passages (weddings, divorces, birthdates, major trips, and so forth). Finally and perhaps most characteristic is the appellation *psychic tarot reader.* The client's belief and trust in the reader's ability to effectively apply the traditional oral narrative interpretation of numerical and pictorial symbol (whether in the 78-card tarot deck, the regular 52-card playing deck, or any number of other types of card decks available) to his or her needs is reliant upon the reader possessing the innate faculty of psychic prediction (of future events and situations), intuitive and inspired interpretation (of past and present events and situations), and empathic awareness of persons, places, and objects. Psychic ability, with its attendant faculty of empathy or sensing the emotions of persons, places, and objects, can involve direct physical contact (laying on of hands, placing an object on the face or body) or nonphysical apprehension (which can include visual or auditory experience) or emotional sensation alone. The generic label *psychic reader* includes several interrelated faculties and types of divinatory prediction that operate independent from divining tools such as psychometry, séance with the dead, discovering past lives, and others. A specific application of the empathic talent as part of the psychic reading is the practice of psychometry, or the empathic reading of objects brought by the client (photographs, jewelry, or small mementos of family, loved ones, children, close friends, or suspected enemies). The perspective that objects bear a unique and personal emotional "signature" that can be read by the psychic encompasses two interrelated beliefs: (1) the reader's innate ability to perceive empathically, whether in physical contact or not, and (2) the principle of contagious magic—that objects are believed to absorb the emotional and spiritual energies and intentions of persons and events by direct physical contact or propinquity. In the modern Western context, with its prevailing rationalism and empiricism, the intuitive, empathic, and precognitive faculties assigned to the psychic are often considered to be extraordinary and the result of a unique and personal gift, innate to the individual. This gift cannot be taught or otherwise transmitted, although there is a strong folk belief, which survives in this popular context, that these faculties are inheritable (similar to folk beliefs that the seventh son or daughter has second sight or that second sight runs in families) and arise spontaneously. It is perhaps an irony that the diverse rituals and techniques of divination that continue in living folk and popular practice around the world are all that remain and survive intact of many of the great religious and philosophical traditions of the ancient and medieval worlds. The relegation of divination as a folk practice to the fringes of religious attention and historical and contemporary inquiry is, from this perspective, all the more questionable. The cultural range of the treatments of divination as a living practice within folklore scholarship and treatments of folk systems outside of folklore as a whole has been amazingly narrow. Such treatments are limited, for the most part, to individual examples within tribal and simple societies or rural communities within complex societies that have strong oral traditional elements and folk art forms. If the subject of divination and its theoretical exploration within folklore and folklife is restricted to early definitions of the "little" community, if religious belief and practice are limited to oral and traditionally received forms, and if religious material culture is confined to a narrow characterization of folk art, then the range of contemporary belief, practice, artifact, environment, and lifeways that relate to divining worldwide is not being addressed. A vast range of contemporary systems of divination, communicated by various forms of print and electronic media (as well as oral traditional received forms), are yet to be found by folklorists—systems that exist within and outside living world religious systems, in rural and urban communities within complex societies, and in simple agrarian and nomadic communities.

Kathleen Malone O'Connor

See also Belief, Folk; Magic; Religion, Folk.

****

References

Abimbola, Wande. 1976. *Ifa: An Exposition of Ifa Literary Corpus*. Ibadan, Nigeria: Oxford University Press.

Bascom, William. 1969. *Ifa Divination: Communication between Gods and Men in West Africa*. Bloomington: Indiana University Press.

———. [1980] 1983. *Sixteen Cowries: Yoruba Divination from Africa to the New World*. Bloomington: Indiana University Press.

Campbell, Joseph, and Richard Roberts. 1987. 3rd edition. *Tarot Revelations*. San Anselmo, CA: Vernal Equinox Press.

Caquot, André, and Marcel Leibovici, eds. 1968. *La Divination: Études recueillies*. 2 vol. Paris: Presses Universitaires de France.

Cumont, Franz. 1960. *Astrology and Religion among the Greeks and Romans.* New York: Dover.

Evans-Pritchard, Edward E. 1937. *Witchcraft, Magic, and Oracles among the Azande.* Oxford: Clarendon.

Fahd, Toufic. 1966. *La Divination arabe: Études religieuses, sociologiques et folkloriques sur le milieu natif de l'Islam.* Leiden, Netherlands: E. J. Brill.

Feuchtwang, Stephan. 1974. *An Anthropological Analysis of Chinese Geomancy.* Vientiane, Laos: Vithagna.

Fontenrose, Joseph. 1978. *The Delphic Oracle: Its Responses and Operations.* Berkeley: University of California Press.

Jaulin, Robert. 1966. *La Géomancie: Analyse formelle.* Paris: Mouton.

Lessa, William A. 1968. *Chinese Body Divination: Its Forms, Affinities and Functions.* Los Angeles: United World.

Lewis, I. M. 1989. *Ecstatic Religion: A Study of Shamanism and Spirit Possession.* London: Routledge.

Lewy, Hans. 1978. *Chaldaean Oracles and Theurgy: Mysticism, Magic and Platonism in the Later Roman Empire.* Paris: Études Augustiniennes.

Loewe, Michael, and Carmen Blacker, eds. 1981. *Oracles and Divination.* Boulder, CO: Shambhala.

Roeder, Guenther. 1960. *Kulte, Orakel und Naturverehrung im alten Ägypten.* Zurich: Artemis Verlag.

Trachtenberg, Joshua. 1984. *Jewish Magic and Superstition: A Study in Folk Religion.* New York: Atheneum.

Turner, Victor. 1975. *Revelation and Divination in Ndembu Ritual.* Ithaca, NY: Cornell University Press.

Virtanen, Leea. [1977] 1990. *That Must Have Been ESP! An Examination of Psychic Experience.* Trans. John Atkinson and Thomas DuBois. Bloomington: Indiana University Press.

Vogt, Evon Z., and Ray Hyman. 1979. 2nd edition. *Water Witching U.S.A.* Chicago: University of Chicago Press.

Wilhelm, Hellmut. 1977. *Heaven, Earth and Man in the Book of Changes: Seven Eranos Lectures.* Seattle: University of Washington Press.

Drama, Folk

Performances deploying recognizably dramatic techniques in the presentation of traditional materials under the auspices of a recurrent social activity of which they are a regular but subsidiary feature. To this theoretical paradigm, lived reality will conform only to one degree or another. There is no traditional drama. There are only traditional performances that are more or less dramatic and dramatic performances that are more or less traditional; there are also traditional dramatic activities that are more or less performances. And the theoretical ideal is the optimum combination of these elements (traditional, dramatic, performance) rather than the maximum degree of any one of them. An activity can be insufficiently dramatic to qualify as drama but too dramatic to qualify as traditional or insufficiently traditional to qualify as a tradition but too traditional to qualify as drama.

An activity qualifies as performance to the degree that it is possible to distinguish between those who perform and those who observe the performance. However convincing the new identities assumed by participants in a dance-induced trance may be, for example, the activity is more akin to ritual than to drama if all participate, and the trance is observed or celebrated rather than performed. With whatever gusto children throw themselves into the roles of cowboys and Indians, mothers and fathers, doctors and patients, if no one is watching or if the children are not aware of those who are watching, their activity is more akin to game than to drama, played or enjoyed rather than performed. But, at the opposite extreme, if the distinction between active performers and passive spectators becomes too marked, too akin to the theatrical, the traditional status of the activity is threatened under other headings.

A performance qualifies as dramatic to the degree that it deploys recognizably mimetic features and to a mimetic end: the representation of reality other than that of the performance event itself. A physical performance, however spectacular the costumes or movements of performers are, is dramatic only to the extent that these aspects are designed and taken to be mimetic. Is a costume of ribbons, straw, or hair merely visual spectacle, or is it a means to the representation of a god or a beast? Are painted faces a device to conceal identity, of ritual significance, merely decorative, or representative of a different ethnic identity? Are movements, postures, and gestures purely locomotive (as in a dance), purely entertaining (through grotesque drollery), or mimetically imitative of some other being in the process of doing something else? Correspondingly with regard to verbal performance (song and speech), an utterance is dramatic only to the degree that some attempt is made to give the impression the speaker is someone other than him- or herself. Telling a folktale is not traditional drama; it may modulate into the dramatic if direct speech is rendered, through posture, gesture, or voice, in character. At the opposite extreme, again, there are performances that are so close to regular, theatrical drama in costuming, acting style, dialogue, and staging (and in the distinction between performers and spectators) that their credentials as traditional dramatic performances are compromised. Mimesis is an aspect of traditional drama, not its ultimate aim.

A dramatic performance is, in itself, traditional to the degree that there is substantial continuity in subject and/or form between individual performances. But here, too, both too little and too much are equally problematic. Some traditions (for example, the English mummers' plays) evince fairly extreme stability over time, but this may be a more recent phenomenon and, indeed, symptomatic of the tradition's loss of vitality. The late-medieval

German *Fastnachtspiele*, in every other way analogous to the mummers' plays—short dramatic interludes performed by small groups of men in the course of the community's seasonal perambulation—may be more typical of traditional drama. In a given town (Nuremberg is the best-documented example), a new play would be written each year, but it would be traditional in the recurrence of overall form (prologue, dramatic interlude, epilogue, dance), structures (speech sequence, altercation), plot items (fight, cure, trial, contest, wooing), characters (peasants, fools), and tone (unrepentant scatology). Absolute discontinuity (a totally new play each time, with different characters, plots, themes, and structures) would qualify the activity as regular theater; absolute continuity (a sequence of performances evincing exact recapitulation of cast, costume, movement, and gesture and verbatim reproduction of the text) suggests attitudes and purposes that would be more characteristic of (and might define the activity as) ritual rather than drama. Because it is the relationship to context that is definitive of traditional drama, there will be neither extremely little nor extremely much continuity between performances. The recurrent context prompts and requires a degree of continuity in the performance that is a part of it, but this context, as a living social and personal reality, will vary from one occurrence to the next, and the performance, which is subsidiary and therefore responsive, will vary likewise.

Traditional drama is traditional primarily by virtue of its context and particularly its subservient relationship to that context. The context is recurrent: a set of circumstances whose occurrence prompts a dramatic performance but that do not reoccur for the sole sake of the performance; the drama is therefore dependent upon and subsidiary to the context. A series of dramatic performances, however repetitive in content (*commedia dell'arte*, pantomime, puppet theater), does not qualify as traditional if its auspices are specifically theatrical, that is, if the social activity concerned (going to the theater, sitting on the beach in front of the Punch-and-Judy stall) is for the sake of the dramatic performance itself. Traditional drama is always part of something else that would live (if less vitally) without it. Much medieval drama and Renaissance pageantry are delicately poised on this functional axis: Were performances of the medieval mystery cycles, which qualify as traditional drama under most other headings, theatrical occasions accompanied by some pious festivity, or were they piously festive occasions accompanied by some drama (which only in the latter case qualifies as traditional)? Did Renaissance monarchs go to their banqueting houses to see masques (which would make these theatrical occasions) or were masques put on to provide diversion at royal banquets (which would qualify them as traditional)?

It is this contextual factor that militates against traditional drama being too dramatic (in terms of mimesis) or too theatrical (in terms of the distinction between performers and audience): The purpose of the performance, ultimately, is less, more, or other than an entertainment achieving absolute mimesis; other factors are operative and even dominant. And unlike the other features that define traditional drama, subservience to context is the one criterion of which there can be too little but not too much.

Traditional drama was one of the terms suggested in the 1970s and 1980s in the pursuit of an acceptable alternative to the term *folk drama,* whose connotations were considered no longer accurate or appropriate and which had become associated with a research approach that had gone out of fashion. *Indigenous theater* also was mooted, but *vernacular drama* may be a better alternative. Originally referring to homebred as opposed to imported slaves in the Roman Empire and later applied to language, handwriting, and architecture, *vernacular* has appropriate connotations of the local and the useful—not to mention the underprivileged—for those who see traditional drama as essentially different from and opposed to the theatrical traditions of the social and cultural elite. The important segment of traditional drama forming part of seasonal or occasional customs might then usefully be distinguished within the overall field as *customary drama.*

From its inception in the mid-nineteenth century and until fairly recently, research on traditional drama was almost exclusively approached from a survivalist perspective, focusing on ultimate origins, which were believed to be the fertility rituals of savage communities. Folk drama, largely in the form of the English mummers' plays and analogous European forms, was therefore seen as a direct survival of the fertility-inducing ritual (involving the death and rebirth of a king, scapegoat, god, or the fertility principle itself) posited by anthropologists of the evolutionary school, such as Wilhelm Mannhardt and James G. Frazer. The connection was manifest in the seasonal incidence (typically, the dead of winter when fertility needed invigorating), the animal or vegetal costumes, the exclusively male performers, the ambient scatology, and appropriate action such as death and revival or wooing and mating.

This approach had both positive and negative consequences for the study of the traditions concerned. On the positive side, the ancient pedigree accorded the otherwise humble and obscure customs of modern villages considerable significance for the study of primitive religion and mentality and hence for the later cultural traditions believed to spring from them. In consequence, folk drama was appealed to in "myth and ritual" approaches to ancient Greek drama, medieval theater, and the Elizabethan stage, to medieval literature as diverse as the *Elder Edda* and the grail romances, and to witchcraft, as providing evidence of the prehistoric ritual for which prehistoric evidence was inevitably scarce. This celebrity came at the price, however, of neglect and distortion in other ways. Only those forms of folk drama with credibly ritual features were accorded attention, to the neglect of those not so endowed, and the focus of study was these supposedly ritual features rather than others that might, from perspectives other than ultimate origins, be interesting or significant. Given that the period concerned is as recent as about 1850–1950, we are surprisingly ill informed about aspects of the performance itself (such as the text or the comic figures and episodes) and, above all, about aspects of the context (such as who performed the plays, for whom, why, and on which subjects). Indeed, the major legacy of the ritual origins theory, whatever its merits, is the neglect of the living traditions of folk drama that might have been observed in hundreds of villages in the period concerned in England; the picture is similar—and for similar reasons—in much of Europe.

The general shift of folkloristics in the 1970s to a more social orientation manifested itself in this field in the widening of focus to encompass other dramatic traditions, together with an increasing awareness of material outside the European sphere, and, above all, in the emphasis accorded to the recording and analysis of recent traditions and their contexts; this was accomplished by direct observation where possible, by interviewing those with memories (as performers or spectators) of now defunct local traditions, and by searching in local documentary (typically journalistic) sources. This approach, too, has its drawbacks, particularly the reluctance to contemplate historical dimensions and the consequent lack of work on the undoubted significance of traditional drama within late medieval and early modern cultural history—for example, as an influence on (as opposed to the origin of) the early theater.

Distinctions within the field of traditional drama can be made according to a number of criteria, which include (not surprisingly, given their significance in its definition) the auspices of performance, i.e., the recurrent social activity of which the performance is a part.

Of such auspices, the most significant, certainly in scholarship and probably also in tradition itself, are the customary auspices, and of these, the seasonal customs are the most familiar. In most parts of the world, the passing year is marked by the recurrence of regular calendrical festivals. Their precise incidence depends on cultural factors such as religion and agricultural practices, but there is a distinct tendency to reflect the near universal rhythms of light and darkness, warmth and cold, rain and drought. Many such observances involve spectacular displays, often with quasi-religious status, and many such spectacles (or parts of them) evince distinctly dramatic features. Their incidence can be strictly calendrical, on the same date each year (in relation to the locally relevant calendar), or merely seasonal (for example, concurrent with the onset or completion of agricultural tasks, which vary slightly from year to year). Other customs providing the milieu for dramatic performances have a biographical rhythm, marking important phases or transitions in the human life cycle (birth, maturity, couple-formation, death), as, for example, the wake-games of Ireland. A third, smaller cluster of customs are purely sporadic, prompted by events (political, social, domestic) unrelated to any other rhythm; most familiar is the demonstrative parade (charivari) provoked by domestic behavior found unacceptable by the community.

Traditional dramatic performances also can occur under purely recreational auspices, that is, when a group of people gather under circumstances and in a mood conducive to entertainment, some of which can have mimetic characteristics. Some of these occasions are afforded by seasonal festivals, but the dramatic performances are less organically embedded in the occasion and can feasibly occur under other auspices. Many of the semidramatic dance-games more recently associated with children previously were dramatic entertainments at convivial gatherings of adults or adolescents. Dramatic skits of various kinds likewise figure among gatherings of pupils and students of North American educational institutions.

Some performances, finally, are effectively utilitarian, in that they are a means to a quite practical end, such as selling goods or services. Advertising cures for sale has been accompanied by entertainment of a distinctly dramatic character, from the medieval charlatan to the Wild West medicine show. And the spiel of other vendors, in street markets, for example, also can acquire dramatic elements.

An alternative system of typology can be applied on the basis of the immediate context of performance, particularly in terms of the processes by which performers and audience are brought together. Amidst much variation, there are basically two such alternative systems.

When performers and spectators already are gathered at the venue, the context is an assembly, be it in an enclosed indoor space or an outdoor one defined by some focal point or perimeter. There will be considerable variation in the degree to which an area is physically adjusted for the performance. The more this is the case (for example, with a substantial raised stage and/or seating arrangements for spectators) and the more this is done in advance, the closer the performance is to the theatrical and the less traditional its contextual status becomes. Most performances qualifying as purely recreational under the preceding heading tend to belong, contextually, to the assembly.

Many if not most performances qualifying as customary, however, are associated with a different physical context, one in which there is a deliberately achieved encounter between performers and spectators; further divisions are possible in terms of the movement of the groups (relative to each other and to the surrounding topography) by which this is brought about. Many take the form of a parade, in which the performers progress through the landscape, performing for spectators encountered along the way as they move and/or at a number of stations where the performers halt. Instances of this type range from the medieval mystery cycles and passion plays performed on wagons in the streets of European cities to the sword-dance plays of twentieth-century Yorkshire and Durham. Much less common is the reverse form, the interception, in which passersby are encountered (and transformed into spectators) by stationary performers, on the model of the more familiar beggars and buskers of modern cities. The stationary tableaux with which medieval and Renaissance cities welcomed incoming mayors and monarchs conform to this pattern, as do the mountebank and street-vendor shows under the utilitarian heading. Most familiar of all is the customary house visit, in which performers penetrate, welcome or not, into the homes of those who thus become spectators. The reverse of this pattern, the reception of in-coming visitors by performing hosts, is virtually restricted to the welcomes accorded by noble households to visiting monarchy in the Renaissance period. Some customs combine the parade through the community with visits to a number of houses in what may be best described as a perambulation.

The matter and form of traditional drama naturally vary a great deal, but there are nonetheless several widely recurrent features. Some of these features perhaps reflect the limited theatrical resources and other than purely theatrical ambitions common to most traditions, as well as the shared tendency to be linked to particular auspices, such as seasonal festivals.

Given the wish or need to make an impression within a context that does not guarantee attention, characters (and the costumes used to achieve them) tend to the unusual or the spectacular. For example, the more or less accurate impersonation of beasts (bears, horses, bulls, goats, rams) exists alongside figures from the fauna of local myth and fantasy (dragons, giants, trolls, ethnic grotesques), with an elaboration varying from the blacking of the face to unwieldy contraptions manipulated by several performers.

Similar factors favor dramatic structures that (whatever the plot motivating them) involve fairly simple but striking patterns. There are simple confrontations between two figures of an antagonistic nature (two gods, two warriors, hero and monster, man and wife, master and servant) or a sexual nature (female and wooer/seducer); there are also multiple confrontations between two groups distinguished on ethnic, political, or religious lines. These horizontal patterns are matched vertically by downward and upward movements. The variously achieved "slaying and revival" theme common to many traditions, of which much was made by scholars employing a ritualist approach, may owe its ubiquity, if not its origins, to a simple dramaturgical circumstance: A figure falling down and getting up is the most striking visual effect that can be achieved in traditions whose theatrical resources are largely confined to the bodies of the performers and what is done with them.

Whatever the specific matters and forms involved, the dominance of context over mimesis gives traditional drama a characteristically presentational, rather than fully representational, dramaturgy. While consciously representing something other than themselves and the time and place of performance, performers remain conscious of themselves as presenting a show to an audience in a given time and place. Dramatic illusion, though aimed for or gestured at to one degree or another, is therefore breached consistently by awareness of context and relationship to the audience: in prologues and epilogues that refer to the occasion (for example, the season or the venue and purpose of the show) and facilitate the transition between the real and dramatic worlds; by the elaborate introduction of new figures; by direct address from within the fiction of the play world to the audience or even interaction (verbal and/or physical) with spectators.

Thomas Pettit

See also Charivari/Shivaree; Custom; Evolutionary Theory; Festival; Fool; Mask; Mumming; Myth-Ritual Theory.

✳✳✳✳✳✳✳✳✳✳✳✳✳✳✳✳✳✳

References

Bergeron, David M. 1971. *English Civic Pageantry 1558–1642*. London: Arnold.

Billington, Sandra. 1984. *A Social History of the Fool*. Brighton, England: Harvester.

Brody, Alan. 1969. *The English Mummers and Their Plays*. London: Routledge & Kegan Paul.

Chambers, E.K. 1969. *The English Folk-Play*. Oxford: Clarendon.

Glassie, Henry. 1975. *All Silver and No Brass: An Irish Christmas Mumming*. Bloomington: Indiana University Press.

Green, Thomas A., ed. 1981. *Folk Drama Issue. Journal of American Folklore*, 94(4). Washington, DC: American Folklore Society.

Helm, Alex. 1981. *The English Mummers' Play*. Woodbridge, England: Brewer.

Kirby, Michael, ed. 1974. *Indigenous Theatre Issue. The Drama Review*, 18(4). New York: School of the Arts, New York University.

O Suilleabhain, Sean. 1967. *Irish Wake Amusements*. Cork, Ireland: Mercier.

Schmidt, Leopold, ed. 1965. *Le Théatre populaire européen*. Paris: Maisonneuve & Larosse.

Weimann, Robert. 1978. *Shakespeare and the Popular Tradition in the Theater*. Baltimore, MD: Johns Hopkins University Press.

E

EMIC/ETIC

A conceptual framework that distinguishes between two strategies used to categorize human behavior: *emic*, often referred to as native, ethnic, internal, or insider point of view in relation to a specific cultural system, and *etic*, representing scholarly, analytical, or external constructs employed by outsiders, primarily for the purpose of cross-cultural, comparative study.

Linguist Kenneth Pike coined the terms *etic* and *emic* from the corresponding linguistic terms *phonetic* (referring to the classification of speech sounds) and *phonemic* (referring to sound features as they are related to each other in a particular language system). He intended for *etic* and *emic* to mean for human behavior what the terms *phonetic* and *phonemic* mean for language study. An etic approach, Pike argued, is nonstructural, whereas in emic approaches, the emphasis is on systemic relationships in a specific culture. For example, an etic approach as conceived by Pike might describe dance costumes worn at a festival one by one, listing colors, sizes, and numbers of sequins and feathers, whereas an emic approach might describe the function of a particular group of dancers as a whole, how their costumes complemented each other, and how one group's costumes competed or clashed with another group's costumes at the same festival, as well as how the dance festival itself functioned in general for that particular community. Emic approaches strive to present comprehensive systems of relationships present within one specific culture, but etic units are nonstructural and free-floating.

When Pike introduced the two terms in 1962, he thought of etics as a starting point from which a scholar could begin to grasp a culture's emic categories; he envisioned describing emic units as the goal of a final analysis. Ideally, he proposed, the two vantage points would be stereoscoped into one unified vision, the etic terms gradually being modified until they accommodated the emic units of description. He emphasized that these two complementary perspectives did not constitute a dichotomy but rather combined to give the analyst a three-dimensional perspective: two views of the same data collapsed into one unified understanding.

Anthropologist Marvin Harris criticized Pike's "emic bias" and turned the equation around: One had to collect emic units to develop etic units. "Etic analysis is not a steppingstone to the discovery of emic structures, but to the discovery of etic structures," Harris wrote. "The goal is neither to convert etics to emics nor emics to etics, but rather to describe both and if possible to explain one in terms of the other." Harris' interpretation of the etic/emic concepts permits the acknowledgment of hidden or unseen systems that have a direct bearing on human systems of meaning. (For example, Hindus do not kill cattle, and yet the mortality rate of bull calves is unnaturally high; as Harris implied, a strictly emic analysis would not permit the etic deduction that Hindus allow male calves to starve to death since emically, Hindus do not kill cattle.) Harris' conception also permits diachronic analysis, the comparison of the same culture at different points in time.

Alan Dundes adopted the etic/emic distinction in proposing a more logical system for the international classification of narrative units than current tale type and motif indexes. He proposed that *motifemes* (also known as *emic motifs*, both terms equivalent to Vladimir Propp's *function*) be used as the primary structural unit in narrative classification. Thus, using Dundes' example, the motifeme of "helpful animal," holding a slot on the emic plane, could be filled by any number of appropriate etic "allomotifs," such as cow, cat, bird, and so forth. The motifeme itself would be positioned according to its relationship to a higher sequential context (such as a particular episode or tale type). To date, however, few have accepted Dundes' challenge to develop a more logical classification system; the job is apparently too massive.

On a broader basis, the etic/emic distinction has burgeoned into several brands of ethnoscience, ethnosemantics, new ethnography, and ethnography of speaking that emphasize not just rigid descriptions but also analyses of cultural dynamics. The diversity of culture is acknowledged, and native categories for sorting out the world are eagerly sought. The new ethnographers emphasize developing good emic descriptions now in order to develop good etic frameworks in the future. Ideally, after enough detail is gathered, generalizations and hypotheses about human behavior can be made cross-culturally. The emic/etic movement is often criticized, however, for becoming bogged down in microscopic emic detail while failing to significantly advance etic theory.

Linda Kinsey Adams

See also Linguistic Approach; Motifeme.

✳✳✳✳✳✳✳✳✳✳✳✳✳✳✳✳✳✳

References

Dundes, Alan. 1962. From Etic to Emic in the Structural Study of Folktales. *Journal of American Folklore* 75: 95–105.

Harris, Marvin. 1964. *The Nature of Cultural Things*. New York: Random House.

———. 1976. History and Significance of the Emic/Etic Distinction. *Annual Review of Anthropology* 5:329–350.

———. 1979. *Cultural Materialism: The Struggle for a Science of Culture*. New York: Random House.

Headland, Thomas N., Kenneth L. Pike, and Marvin Harris. 1990. *Emics and Etics: The Insider/Outsider Debate*. Vol. 7 of the *Frontiers of Anthropology* series. Newbury Park, CA: Sage Publications.

Pelto, Pertti, and Gretel Pelto. 1978. *Anthropological Research: The Structure of Inquiry.* New York: Harper and Row.

Pike, Kenneth L. 1971. *Language in Relation to a Unified Theory of the Structure of Human Behavior.* Paris: Mouton.

ENIGMA, FOLK

A cluster of genres that share a structure of puzzle and solution and a norm of dialogic performance. The *riddle* and such related forms as the *clever question, catch question, riddle joke,* and *neck riddle* generally take an overtly interrogative form. The poser asks a puzzling question, and the respondent attempts to guess the answer; the proffered solution is then accepted, rejected, or, if the respondent could give no answer, provided by the poser.

Enigmas are not ordinary questions; the poser does not want the information contained in the answer. They also are not rhetorical questions, in which the answer is assumed beforehand or contained in the question. They are true questions in that they demand an answer. But the answer, like the question, is conventional, and the enigma is constituted of both elements together.

Traditional enigmas are one of the most widespread and earliest documented forms of verbal art, found in Sanskrit hymns, the Bible, and Greek tragedy (as in the famous riddle of the Sphinx from *Oedipus Rex*). There appears, however, to be a correlation between the prevalence of riddling in a society and the presence of oral interrogation as a means of carrying on such business as the education of children and the exercise of justice. Where questioning is important in the work of a culture, it is important in play as well.

Cross-culturally, enigmas are most important among children, although they are never limited to them entirely. Many scholars have observed the ways in which riddling functions to socialize and enculturate children. In African cultures in which skills in argumentation are vital to adult prestige and power, children engage in vigorous debate over the acceptability of riddle solutions. In European peasant cultures, riddles seem to be less flexible and serve principally to teach cultural rules and categories. In Madagascar, Lee Haring argues, the importance of the enigma lies primarily in its question-and-answer form, which becomes the paradigm for more complex dialogic interactions in adult speech genres.

Although children generally perpetuate riddling traditions on their own, without encouragement from adults, adults also appropriate the enigma as a technique of formal pedagogy. The Socratic method and the Christian catechism, not to mention school entrance examinations, are part of a worldwide use of enigmas in initiation ceremony, as the means of access to a restricted code and entry into a restricted group. Deliberate obscurity and special or archaic language often enhance the exclusionary power of the enigma. An outsider who successfully penetrates this obscurity displays intelligence and resource and thus worthiness to be accepted into the group.

Enigmas construct a hierarchical relationship between poser and respondent. The questioner has authority over the questioned and may refuse a solution. Certainly, a refusal may be disputed by the larger group or undercut by the questioner's failure to provide the acceptable alternative solution, and a group may set limits to the questioner's control of the floor in a riddling session. However, as a rule, the riddler retains authority as long as he or she shows competence in the role. Good riddlers often take advantage of their skill to humble rivals in other domains, and riddling sessions easily become contests for prestige and power.

Young children seem to understand riddling as a model of parental authority. Their first riddles are simply questions with arbitrary answers, as arbitrary as adult instructions and reasonings often appear to be. To be the riddler is to have a parallel authority within the riddling frame: A solution is right "because I say so." Moreover, play with enigmas prepares participants for other hierarchies of knowledge. Not everyone in a society has the right to ask questions or to acquire privileged information; low position generally means low access. However, playing at riddles also teaches a helpful lesson in coping: Someone in a low position can rise in or overturn the hierarchy by virtue of cleverness. In narratives incorporating neck riddles, the protagonist triumphs by posing or guessing an apparently insoluble riddle. In the same way in life, younger children can gain prestige among their elders by skillful riddling performance, old women rich in traditional knowledge can disconcert their university-educated grandchildren by posing questions they cannot answer, or a presuming folklorist from outside the community may be put in his or her place with an embarrassing catch.

The power relationships negotiated in the riddling process often are reflected in the content of enigmas. West Indian riddles often present the object described as the property of the father, the chief authority figure ("My father have a cock and every time it crow, it crow fire—A gun"). In Malagasy riddles, paradoxes based on size allude to inversions of power relations ("When the little one comes, the great one takes off his hat—The great water pot").

Riddling sessions form part of various larger events and forms of sociability. A riddling session may open an evening of singing and storytelling in European peasant cultures or come in the middle of an event to revitalize interaction after a long series of monologic performances. Often, the riddling brings children and outsiders into active participation, not only out of a desire to test and initiate newcomers but also for a quite practical reason: A community's stock of riddles is generally limited, and it is not easy to find a native adult who has not heard them all before. In Scotland in the 1960s, Kenneth

S. Goldstein found that the only adults to riddle were the "travelers" or "tinkers," a subculture of peddlers, who, because of their itinerant lifestyle, had constant access to new enigmas.

In some cultures, riddling is restricted to specific occasions. In traditional Philippine Tagalog society, riddles were told during wakes, at harvest time, and in courtship, and these are important occasions for riddling in many societies. The confusing language of riddles seems to be significant in the dangerous periods of wake and harvest, when spirits are believed to be uncomfortably close to living people. It has been suggested that, like the interlocked designs and mazes sometimes used as apotropaic devices on doorways and talismans, the enigma serves to block and turn away evil spirits. Aesthetically, the binary form of the riddle, both linking and separating its halves, mimics the situation of the wake, when the dead are both part of the group and distinct from it. The frequency of the "living and the dead" motif in neck riddles performed during West Indian wakes comments directly on the disruption of everyday classifications at such liminal times.

In courtship, the conjunctive potential of enigmas is played upon. Posing a riddle to a specific person is a way of creating a binary interaction within a larger group without committing the participants to more risky personal topics. Putting the respondent on the spot may be a practical test of wit and resource in a potential mate: The Queen of Sheba used this tactic with Solomon, as did Turandot with her suitors. More common is the apparently obscene catch question, used to stimulate an erotic awareness. Even the general suggestion of unspoken levels of meaning inherent in enigmatic discourse may serve to create a consciousness between riddler and respondent. Often, the content of riddles in peasant cultures plays on traditional gender distinctions, and the structure of the *true riddle*, with its postulation of a unity bringing apparent opposites together, has as its base metaphor, James Fernandez suggests, the conjunction of the sexes.

Enigmas, then, both conjoin and separate; they confuse and they clarify, depending on the emphases of the culture, the performer, and the particular riddle. In intimating a deeper level, alluding to things hidden, they allow the unspeakable to be spoken. Neck riddles tell of incest, sacrifice, and pollution at society's foundations; the riddle proper points up the problems of fit between the world and our representations of it; riddle jokes insist on the scandals and disasters that undermine our confidence in the systems we have made. The apparent triviality of the form, its small size, and its fixity allow us to contemplate flux and chaos with relative impunity.

VISUAL AND GESTURAL ENIGMAS

The enigma follows cultures into literacy. Literate peoples may develop riddles that depend for their solution upon a knowledge of orthography:

> The beginning of every end,
> The end of every place,
> The beginning of eternity,
> The end of time and space.
>
> (*the letter E*)

The rebus is a kind of enigma that exploits ambiguities in the literate code as the true riddle exploits ambiguities in the oral one. The familiar contemporary forms of the rebus play on the multiple readings of letters, numerals, and punctuation marks:

> r/e/a/d/i/n/g
>
> (*Reading between the lines*)

> YYUR
> YYUB
> ICUR
> YY4 me
>
> (*Too wise you are; too wise you be; I see you are too wise for me*)

Others use the position of words on the page:

> I have to   paid
>   because
> work   I am
>
> (*I have to overwork because I am underpaid*)

A riddle about reading, the rebus entertains children struggling to master the conventions of written language; it enables them to distinguish "text"—a linear sequence of conventional signs—from "picture," a spatial arrangement of iconic signs.

Older forms of the rebus (Latin for "by things", that is, a representation using things instead of words) exploit iconic signs instead of the alphabet. In this way, they may convey a message that is understandable but less compromising than an explicit verbal representation. When the young Julius Caesar was administrator of the Roman mint, he put the picture of an elephant on the coinage. Since he was a private citizen at that time, he could not use his own portrait, but the word for elephant in Oscan dialect sounded like "Caesar." We also may think of the early Christian use of a fish symbol to mark secret meeting places: The Greek word *ichthys* could be read as an acrostic for "Jesus Christ Son of God Savior."

Rebuses are also found in heraldic emblems, playing with the folk etymologies of proper names. Thus, the city of Solsona in Catalonia has a blazing sun on its arms, a reference to the Latin word *Sol*. And the abbot of Ramsey in thirteenth-century England made his arms legible even to the illiterate with a drawing of a ram in the sea.

The pictorial rebus leads us to such contemporary amusements as the *droodle*, a visual form of the riddle joke. The droodle is a simple, apparently abstract drawing, revealed by the poser to stand for some absurdly complex phenomenon. Thus, the narrator of Antoine de Ste.-Exupéry's *The Little Prince* draws what looks to his parents like the outline of a man's hat: He tells them it is really a boa constrictor that has swallowed an elephant. Other droodles rely on an unfamiliar perspective to confuse the viewer: A circle inside a bigger circle is revealed as a bald fat man seen from above.

The enigma also takes gestural or mimetic form. In some cases, this gestural form allows the observance of speech prohibitions, as in the Native American northern Athapaskan enigmas about bears. In the Athapaskan culture, it is considered dangerous to mention bears in the presence of women, for women are said to have the ability to warn the animals of approaching hunters through their dreams. So one man who has found a bear's den communicates his discovery to another man by walking clumsily with his toes pointed inward or by throwing a handful of hair into the fire (to recall how the bear's skin is singed after the kill).

Other gestural enigmas enhance the interactional potential of the riddle by turning it into full-scale dramatic play. In nineteenth-century England, the genteel amusement of the literary charade, a verse form describing each syllable and then the complete word of the solution, became a performance using costuming and staging.

Charlotte Brontë's novel *Jane Eyre* provides an artful but realistic rendering of an upper-class house party playing at charades. The hero, Mr. Rochester, and Blanche Ingram, a woman in search of a suitable husband, enact a charade for which the solution is "Bridewell," a prison. A mimed wedding procession stands for the first syllable, "Bride"; the biblical Rebecca giving water to Isaac's servant is "Well"; and Mr. Rochester, in rags and chains, performs the complete word. The performance provides the occasion for the opulent Miss Ingram to display herself in suggestive and flattering guises, for much flirtatious byplay between herself and Mr. Rochester, and for Mr. Rochester to convey to Jane, his true love in the audience, that marriage with Miss Ingram would be a prison to him. Like the oral riddling session or the literary charade, the performed charade allows multiple levels of communication between participants.

Both visual and performed enigmas, then, carry on the main preoccupations of oral riddles. The visual enigma further exploits the ambiguities of representation. Performed riddles enact the disjunctions and conjunctions between the sexes or between actors and their roles. The dyadic interaction of poser and respondent remains at the heart of the form.

Dorothy Noyes

See also Catch Question; Clever Question/Wisdom Question; Neck Riddle; Rebus; Riddle; Riddle Joke.

✳✳✳✳✳✳✳✳✳✳✳✳✳✳✳✳✳

References

Abrahams, Roger D., and Alan Dundes. 1972. Riddles. In *Folklore and Folklife*, ed. Richard M. Dorson. Chicago: University of Chicago Press.

Augarde, Tony. 1984. *The Oxford Guide to Word Games*. Oxford: Oxford University Press.

Fernandez, James. 1986. Edification by Puzzlement. In *Persuasions and Performances*, ed. James Fernandez. Bloomington: Indiana University Press.

Goldstein, Kenneth S. 1963. Riddling Traditions in Northeastern Scotland. *Journal of American Folklore* 76:330–336.

Haring, Lee. 1992. *Verbal Art in Madagascar*. Philadelphia: University of Pennsylvania Press.

Hart, Donn. 1964. *Riddles in Filipino Folklore: An Anthropological Analysis*. Syracuse, NY: Syracuse University Press.

Köngäs-Maranda, Elli. 1971. The Logic of Riddles. In *The Structural Analysis of Oral Tradition*, eds. Elli Köngäs-Maranda and Pierre Maranda. Philadelphia: University of Pennsylvania Press.

McDowell, John. 1979. *Children's Riddling*. Bloomington: Indiana University Press.

Mishlin, Craig. 1984. Telling about Bear: A Northern Athapaskan Men's Riddle Tradition. *Journal of American Folklore* 97:61–68.

Pepicello, W. J., and Thomas A. Green. 1984. *The Language of Riddles*. Columbus: Ohio State University Press.

Roemer, Danielle. 1982. In the Eye of the Beholder: A Semiotic Analysis of the Visual Descriptive Riddle. *Journal of American Folklore* 95:173–199.

Sutton-Smith, Brian. 1976. A Developmental Structural Account of Riddles. In *Speech Play*, ed. Barbara Kirshenblatt-Gimblett. Philadelphia: University of Pennsylvania Press.

EPIC

A collection of narrative poems of varying length that presents a specific universe of beliefs and occurrences of a people within the cultural context. Epics often have a central figure, a protagonist, whose adventurous life experiences form the substance of the epic narrative.

There are both written and oral epics. Literary epics are extended narrative poems that establish a particular universe of the imagination by means of, for example, cosmogonic mythologies and sacrificial ritual drama. Oral epics constantly change, but epics preserved in the written form have become records of particular worldviews, histories, and religious attitudes, such as *Mahābhārata*, *Shah-namah*, *Beowulf*, *Manas*, and the *Kalevala*.

In folkloristics, epic is a narrative couched in poetic language and subject to special rules of texture, structure, style, and form. Usually, epics contain hundreds or thousands of verses and present a complex narrative full of wonders and heroism, often centered around the exploits of a main personage. The generous use of stock phrases and conventional scenes explains how

Assyrian depiction of the colossal figure of Gilgamesh, hero of the Babylonian epic poem (circa 2000 B.C.).

223

a performer can innovate and still adhere to the required poetic form. Innovations introduced by performers within traditional epic frameworks lead to many different versions of the same narrative. Great variability occurs because different performers assemble different episodes within a given epic—not only because individual passages are expanded, contracted, or altered.

Epics may remain in traditional circulation longer than other oral poetry. Even when particular epics disappear, their substance is either cannibalized for later epics or transformed into, for instance, folktales.

All types of epics—classical or folk, literary or oral, long or short—are directly related to worldview. The epic characteristically involves its audience in the fundamental issues of human existence, such as evil and good, suffering and reward, guilt or innocence, human nature and its destiny, and the origin and destruction of the cosmos and the people in it. Epics often are dramas of violent conflicts between the human and divine worlds, and as such, they often pose problems of history, theology, fate, death, regeneration, and salvation. For this reason, epics are dominated by protagonists whose destinies reinforce essential religious concepts. Such concepts materialize in the roles of the hero or heroine as shaman or warrior, in certain concepts of space, order, time, and deity, as well as in fundamental interpretations of the meaning of death and salvation.

The theme of the shaman who travels to the netherworld and establishes defenses against the evil forces that impinge on the human world is less common, however, than the theme of the warrior in the world of the living who conquers not by supranormal powers but by such qualities as strength, courage, and personal honor. Certain theories developed in the comparative analysis of myth may explain this widespread tradition. Comparative studies have suggested the religious significance of a proto-Indo-European warrior tradition and have argued that the warrior occupies an important median position in a three-class human social hierarchy.

Another prevalent epic theme describes founding the world anew: reestablishing world order, time, and space by means of the holocaust of battle. Narratives turn into epics when, drawing on the poetic power of the blood shed by popular heroes or heroines, they serve as the songs of peoples who are striving to establish national or ethnic identities, to legitimize traditions of particular places and events, and to validate authority.

The Finnish epic the *Kalevala*, compiled and edited by Elias Lönnrot (1802–1884), serves to illustrate these epic features. This epic presents a more unified interpretation of the history of the world than do the Finnish folk narratives from which Lönnrot drew. Utilizing a variety of folk materials, he developed a narrative that proceeds from primal creation to destruction of the supreme god, Väinämöinen. In Lönnrot's nineteenth-century Lutheran Christian worldview, the *Kalevala* described the "good" pagan Finnish prehistory before the advent of Christianity; the latter, of course, was considered the high point of "real history" (i.e., western European academic history). The *Kalevala* ends with the victory of the Christian faith over the pre-Christian religion of the ancient Finns. As a consequence, the pagan myths of the epic are arranged according to the Christian linear concept of time and history, a concept in which time is seen as a segment of a line with beginning and end points and in which God creates the world but then withdraws to appear again during the eschatological events that end the world. Though the structure of the epic is fundamentally Western and Christian, the worldview of the rune singers is cyclic. Nevertheless, the *Kalevala*, like epics in general, provides an ethnic and historical reference point that validates identity and solidarity within the group.

Even outside their original contexts, the epics of many peoples have proved to be universally appealing. During the performance of epics, channels open to a more pliable time and space; thus, the primal "drama of transformation" itself becomes a powerful means of renewal.

Juha Pentikäinen

See also Bard; Hero/Heroine, Folk; Oral-Formulaic Theory.

✳✳✳✳✳✳✳✳✳✳✳✳✳✳✳✳✳

References

de Vries, Jan. 1963. *Heroic Song and Heroic Legend*. New York: Oxford University Press.

Lord, Albert B. 1960. *The Singer of Tales*. Cambridge, MA: Harvard University Press.

Oinas, Felix J., ed. 1978. *Heroic Epic and Saga: An Introduction to the World's Great Folk Epics*. Bloomington: Indiana University Press.

Pentikäinen, Juha Y. 1989. *Kalevala Mythology*. Trans. Ritva Poom. Bloomington: Indiana University Press.

Vansina, Jan. 1985. *Oral Tradition as History*. Madison: University of Wisconsin Press.

Epic laws

Superorganic and transcultural "laws," which give rise to the traditional structure of narratives. The concept of epic laws was introduced by Danish scholar Axel Olrik, who formulated eighteen such laws at the beginning of the twentieth century.

Although the Norwegian folklorist Moltke Moe introduced, in 1889, the concept of fundamental epic laws to denote the operative forces in the process of traditional composition, the scholar who focused particular attention on the question of regularities in narrative formation was Axel Olrik, who developed the theory of epic laws in narration in 1908. Olrik argued that, cross-culturally, narrative tradition is governed by universally applicable rules; he made a departure from the terminology of his time to employ the concept of *Sagenwelt* (world of folk narrative, folktale world) to characterize the cross-culturally applicable rules that operate within folk narratives. Although Olrik agreed that particular national traits also exist in narrative, he believed that, in comparison with general regularities, these variations were analogous to differences in dialects. Olrik stated that these principles were termed *laws* because they limited the composition of oral literature by means of a strict set of rules.

The first rule concerns the formalized opening and closing sentences that begin and end narratives (the Law of Opening and the Law of Closing). The Law of Repetition concerns the reiteration that occurs at many levels: For example, events, dialogues, phrases, and single words are often repeated three times, thus forming a kind of rhythmic emphasis at different structural levels. The Law of Three alludes to the fact that, for instance, there are three tasks or that a task is performed in the course of three days. According to Olrik's theory, there are usually only two people occupying the narrative's "stage" at one time (the Law of Two to a Scene). Opposed character types come into confrontation: protagonist and villain, good and bad, rich and poor (the Law of Contrast). The weakest and youngest proves in the end to be the strongest and cleverest (the Importance of Initial and Final Position). The Law of Action means that characteristics are not described by means of a series of adjectives but in terms of deeds and events whose content should indicate concretely the characteristics of the personage described. According to Olrik, the *Sage* (local legend, plural *Sagen*) follows its own textural norms, which differ from those that govern written literature; these rules of oral narrative are called the Law of the Single Strand, the Logic of the Sage, and so on.

The way in which Olrik set forth his laws indicates that he considered them to be universally true, irrespective of time, nationality, or culture. Epic laws were, he believed, superior to and in control of the individual narrator. Olrik's epic laws, therefore, were superorganic. The essence of this notion is that, in addition to the organic level that is controlled by man, there is also a superorganic level that is beyond human influence but that largely governs human behavior. Olrik felt that the narrators obey epic laws blindly and unconsciously. Carried to the extreme, this view of the significance of epic laws might lead one to underestimate the individual and social component in the narrative cycle. A competent tradition-bearer, however, not only reproduces previously learned material but also, according to mastered rules, transforms familiar elements into new performances.

Many of Olrik's observations are undoubtedly of considerable value for studying folk prose, and his hypotheses may be applicable to other genres as well. It should be emphasized that Olrik's arguments were based on studying texts and not on the analysis of the communication process itself. Scholars should try to discover the unwritten rules of communication for each particular genre; Olrik's laws should be studied as hypotheses, taking into account the differences between genres and the nature of the holistic communication process as both an individual and a social phenomenon.

Axel Olrik maintained that epic laws are superorganic and transcultural. This is highly improbable. It would be more correct to say that they are conventional patterns of composition, varying among different genres and within different cultural areas. Moreover, Olrik's epic laws focus on a range of different qualities. They may be stylistic commonplaces or statements of details of style, form, content, or structure, to which certain analogs may be added by continuing to analyze techniques of narrative performance.

Juha Pentikäinen

See also Aesthetics; Superorganic Theories.

✳✳✳✳✳✳✳✳✳✳✳✳✳✳✳✳✳

References

Dundes, Alan. 1975. *Analytic Essays in Folklore*. The Hague: Mouton.

Dundes, Alan, ed. 1965. *The Study of Folklore*. Englewood Cliffs, NJ: Prentice-Hall.

Oinas, Felix J., ed. 1978. *Heroic Epic and Saga: An Introduction to the World's Great Folk Epics*. Bloomington: Indiana University Press.

Olrik, Axel. 1915. *Personal Impressions of Moltke Moe*. Helsinki: Academia Scientiarum Fennica.

———. [1921] 1992. *Principles for Oral Narrative Research*. Trans. Kirsten Wolf and Jody Jensen. Bloomington: Indiana University Press.

Pentikäinen, Juha Y. 1978. *Oral Repertoire and World View: An Anthropological Study of Marina Takalo's Life History*. Helsinki: Academia Scientiarum Fennica.

———. 1989. *Kalevala Mythology*. Trans. Ritva Poom. Bloomington: Indiana University Press.

Erotic Folklore

Traditional and emergent sexual practices and representational practices that are expressive of love, desire, and sociosexual relations. Erotic folklore and folklife encompass the sexual acts we engage in, our beliefs about those acts and the bodies we perform them with, the language (both literal and figurative) we use to articulate our desires and fears, the material erotic objects we make, and the stories, jokes, rhymes, songs, gestures, and games we perform. Erotic folklore constitutes the entire domain of that which is variously identified as "romantic," "bawdy," "vulgar," "obscene," "pornographic," or simply "the dirty bits," each expression being indicative of a differently situated politicized aesthetic concerning the body and its sexualities, as well as a response to degrees of sexual explicitness in representational practices. As a physical, emotional, psychic, and intellectual creative power and as a form of discourse, the erotic is the product of both the essentialist needs of our bodies and the cultural representations that construct those needs and those bodies.

Cultural theorists of the 1980s and 1990s, such as Michel Foucault, Sherry B. Ortner, Harriet Whitehead, and Thomas Laqueur, argue that the body and its sexualities, like gender, are sociocultural constructions, that the terms and dynamics of sexual desire are a political language, and that representations of desire are forms of political power. Thus, one way to view erotic folklore is as a rhetoric that seeks to construct sociocultural relations by traditionalizing and thereby naturalizing extant or emergent power relations. As a political language and a political power, erotic representational practices may be used to construct and reinforce hegemonic interests (those of dominant sociocultural groups) or to construct and reinforce the variant interests of differing folk groups, localized communities, imagined communities, and subcultures.

At once participatory in and contestive of public rhetorics, erotic folklore is, as Horace Beck says, "part of every society. Its form, its degree of prevalence set one group off from another." And as Gershon Legman argues, erotic folklore stands in relation to the larger corpus of various peoples' folklore "in about the same proportion as the physical sexual parts stand [in relation] to the body," if not more. He suggests the figure of about 22 percent. Yet until recently, as Legman repeatedly notes, "the record of erotic folklore . . . has only seldom—and then usually only privately—been committed to print" due to private and public censorship. To censor is to erase, and the erasure of erotic folklore from public discourse is a form of political control of bodies (both one's own and those that may differ from one's own in respect to gender, class, race, ethnicity, sexuality, and nationality). Furthermore, censorship distorts one's view of what it means to be human. As Vance Randolf cogently notes, "If a collection of folksongs [and by extension, folklore in general] contains no obscenity, it cannot fully reflect the taste and preference of the people."

One way in which people encode their "taste and preference," while seeking to construct their own and others' lives, is through language usage. Diction level and choice of metaphors, even in a very small sample of the English erotic lexicon of a particular sexuality, are quite suggestive. Heterosexuals, for example, may "copulate," "fornicate," "sleep together," "have conjugal relations," "make love," and engage in "coitus." In other words, they "do it"—"it" being "the act" or the "Big F"—which has also been known as "niggling" (1565–1820); "bulling," "tiffing," and "quiffing" (eighteenth century); "nubbing" (eighteenth and early nineteenth century); "hogging" and "tomming" (nineteenth century); "grinding," "getting a valve job," or "getting an oil change" (nineteenth and twentieth century); and "putting your floppy in someone's disk drive" (twentieth century). Similarly, the male genitalia—

the "penis", "privy part," "prick," "whang," or "whacker"—which is frequently envisioned as the active agent, may be provided with a "Christian" name ("Peter," "Dick," or "John") or euphemized as a man's "third leg" or as one of various "tools" and "instruments." The female body and female genitalia are envisioned, most frequently in the passive mode, as, for example, a landscape to be cultivated, an instrument to be played, or a fruit to be harvested. The extent to which such language usage constructs a system of gender dominance has been noted by many, but just as language may be used to construct domi-nant ideologies, it also can be used to deconstruct and contest assertions of dominance. This idea is hinted at (either intentionally or unintentionally) in the recuperative language of the title of Barbara Babcock's essay "Taking Liberties, Writing from the Margins, and *Doing It* with a Difference" (empha-sis added)—a feminist disclosure of male uses of the female body as a semiotic object.

Similarly, plastic and visual art objects, both those for everyday use and otherwise, encode a variety of human erotic acts as well as cultural attitudes toward those acts. For example, a pre-Columbian Andean culture, the Moche (or Mochica), crafted pots that were decorated with three-dimensional body parts (penis and vulva) and with three-dimensional subjects caught in various erotic positions: conventional heterosexual intercourse, heterosexual anal intercourse, male homosexual anal intercourse, lesbian digital stimulation of the vagina, fellatio, cunnilingus, male masturbation, and zoophilia. Although the erotic has been associated with the spiritual in many cultures (for exam-ple, in ancient Greece and Persia), artifacts like the Moche stirrup-spout pots suggest the ways that the erotic can simultaneously be a source of a more worldly humor: In this case, the drinking spout configured as a penis or a vulva requires that the drinker perform a type of displaced fellatio or cunnilingus in order to quench his or her thirst. Analogously, the margins of medieval European manuscript pages were sometimes decorated with figures engaged in a variety of erotic acts, and forms of twentieth-century photocopy and fax lore provide graphic visual representations of erotic fears and pleasures.

And what our linguistic lexicons and our art objects encode, our sex manuals (ancient and modern), conduct books, collections of literary and vernacular tales and songs, and inscriptions of folklife elaborate on. Sex manuals, for example, circulated in China as early as the second century B.C., Rome had Ovid's *Ars Armatoria* by the end of the first century B.C., and India produced the *Kamasutra* sometime between the third and fifth centuries A.D. Each is a complex mixture of public and folk practice and fantasy that, to varying degrees, is inflected by theological and ideological prescription. During the Middle Ages, bawdy folktales were appropriated for literary use (*The Arabian Nights*, Boccaccio's *Decameron*, Chaucer's *Canterbury Tales*). Also, early modern Europe transmitted sexual practices and fantasies through (among other genres) song, both in oral performance and print; examples may be found in Thomas D'Urfey's *Wit and Mirth, Or Pills to Purge Melancholy* (1719–1720) and Vivian de Sola Pinto and Allan Rodway's *The Common Muse: An Anthology of Popular British Ballad Poetry, XVth-XXth Century* (1957). Additionally, books such as *Aristotle's Masterpiece*, an anonymous compendium of information drawn from earlier printed sources and period folklore and first printed in the late seventeenth century, documented early modern beliefs concerning the body, its genders, and its sexualities.

Western modernity has had its Freudian case studies, its Kinsey reports, and the work of Havelock Ellis and of William H. Masters and Virginia E. Johnson. A myriad of popular articles frequently linking sex, etiquette, and domestic and public economy have appeared in women's and men's magazines. Oral historians, such as Steve Humphries, have recorded vernacular personal narratives about the heteroglossic erotic life of a nation during a specific historical period. Similarly, cultural anthropologists Elizabeth Lapousky Kennedy and Madeline D. Davis have used women's oral histories to document the life of a particular sexual community in Buffalo, New York, from 1930 to 1960. Other anthropologists have inscribed the erotic life of diverse cultures and subcultures: Owen M. Lynch's *Divine Passions: The Social Construction of Emotions in India* (1990); Richard Parker's *Bodies, Pleasures, and Passions: Sexual Culture in Contemporary Brazil* (1991); *Ritualized Homosexuality in Melanesia*, edited by Gilbert Herdt (1984); Will Roscoe's *The Zuni Man-Woman* (1991); and Esther Newton's, *Mother Camp: Female Impersonators in America* (1979).

In turn, folklorists have focused on various representational practices. For example, collected folktales as well as folksongs and ballads (although sometimes elliptical, particularly when "adapted" for public consumption) encode various peoples' attitudes toward the body, sexuality, and hierarchical social systems based on class and gender. Different textual traditions and situated performances of "Cinderella," "Little Red Riding Hood," "Beauty and the Beast," and "Bluebeard," for example, at once assume and construct heterosexuality as a cultural norm while exploring, according to differently situated scholarly interpretations, the erotic in children's developing sexualities, the relationship between sex and violence, incest, and the erotic attraction of the gender-ambivalent cross-dresser. Similarly, romantic songs and ballads construct heterosexual and homoerotic relations while sometimes documenting various cultural-specific erotic taboos. For example, in Anglo-American ballads of domestic tragedy, sibling incest is invoked in versions of "Lizzie Wan," "The King's Dochter Lady Jean," "Bonny Hind," "The Cruel Brother," "Babylon," and "Sheath and Knife."

Folktales and their popular redactions in particular have been critiqued by Western feminist scholars Marcia Leiberman, Kay Stone, and Jane Yolen as misogynistic constructions of female gender, female sexuality, and cross-gender relations, as well as for their production of an erotic economy based on the mystique of romance and female domesticity. However, scholars also have suggested that such tales, when contextualized by specific performance frames, may be negotiated by women for their own purposes. Finally, such tales also have been analyzed as sites for the disclosure of male fears of both female and male sexuality.

Other textual and performance traditions revel in graphic sexual representation and witty euphemism. Although publicly censored (for example, the blank space that potentially categorized sexual themes in the Stith Thompson *Motif-Index* was not redressed until Frank Hoffmann began the task in 1973), sexually explicit folklore not only survives but also thrives, providing, as do the trickster figures of bawdy tales, important forms of psychological and cultural renewal. As social theorist Mikhail Bakhtin has argued, bawdry—with its emphasis on the "grotesque" material body—is at the heart of cultural deconstruction and renewal: "The essence of the grotesque is precisely to present a contradictory and double-faced fullness of life. Negation and destruction (death of the old) are included as an essential phase, inseparable from affirmation, from the birth of something new." In this way, bawdy stories (folktales, as well as personal narratives, anecdotes, and contemporary legends), poems, jokes, songs, ballads, blues, graffiti, gestures, and toasts encode attitudes toward the body and the erotic while using representations of the body and the erotic for purposes of psychological release, group and dyadic bonding, and sociopolitical commentary.

As editor of *Kriptadia: The Journal of Erotic Folklore* and author of *The Horn Book: Studies in Erotic Folklore* (1964), *The Rationale of the Dirty Joke* (1968), *No Laughing Matter: Rational of the Dirty Joke, Second Series* (1975), *The Limerick* (1964), and *The New Limerick* (1977), as well as innumerable articles, prefaces, and introductions, Gershon Legman has been, in the twentieth century, the leading bibliographer and editor of sexually explicit folklore. But of particular importance for folklorists are the field collections of scholars such as Vance Randolph, whose *Pissing in the Snow & Other Ozark Folktales* (1976), *Roll Me in Your Arms: "Unprintable" Ozark Folksongs and Folklore*, Volume 1 (1992), and *Blow the Candle Out: "Unprintable" Ozark Folksongs and Folklore*, Vol. 2 (1992), when contextualized within Randolph's entire collected corpus, bawdy and nonbawdy, offer what Rayna Green has described as "a picture of expressive behavior unparalleled by any other American region's or group's study."

Although Randolph's field collections record the erotic representational practices of a particular region during a particular time, other scholars have focused on different communities and various genres. Ewan MacColl and Peggy Seeger's *Travellers' Songs* (1976) records, in the context of a broad singing tradition, the bawdy songs collected primarily in Scotland from a specific social and ethnic group, and Guy Logsdon's *The Whorehouse Bells Were Ringing* (1989) documents the bawdy song tradition of a specific occupational group (American cowboys). Roger Abrahams' *Deep Down in the Jungle: Negro Narrative Folklore from the Streets of Philadelphia* (1964) situates a localized racial community's representational practices within their immediate sociocultural context, and Bruce Jackson's *Get Your Ass in the Water and Swim Like Me* (1974) records and analyzes African-American toasts (recitations and brags). Rayna Green's "'Magnolias Grow in Dirt': The Bawdy Lore of Southern Women" (1977) decenters any notion that "trashy talk" is limited to male performers, and Joseph P. Goodwin's *More Man Than You'll Ever Be* (1989) not only contextualizes erotic representational practices within a particular sexual community (Midwestern American male homosexuals) but also explains how members outside of that community may misunderstand its representational practices. And Wendy Woenstein, Mary and Herbert Knapp, and Sandra McCosh have recorded children's erotic jokes, rhymes, riddles, games, catches, and pranks.

Psychoanalytic approaches to bawdry, particularly those stemming from the works of Sigmund Freud (1856–1939), explore the ways in which sexual humor functions variously as seduction, aggression, and exposure. Such approaches have been foregrounded in Legman's work as well as that of Martha Wolfenstein's and Alan Dundes' analyses of a wide-ranging collection of cultural phenomena: photocopy lore, oral jokes, folktales, sacred stories, children's toys and rhymes, and even the Easter Bunny. Among Dundes' classic articles are his study of heterosexual homoeroticism in the game of American football and his study of male pregnancy envy, anal eroticism, and ritual homosexuality in aboriginal Australia, native North and South America, Africa, Europe, and the United States in respect to a sacred ritual object and secular toy—the bullroarer.

An alternative to the psychoanalytic approach to erotic materials has focused on localized folk performances whose meanings are contextualized within specific sociocultural relations of a specific time and place. An important study in this respect has been Margaret Mills' *Rhetorics and Politics in Afghan Traditional Storytelling*. Inscribing an evening of storytelling by two Moslem elders who were brought together by a Marxist subgovernor so that an American woman might record their performances, Mills' book offers a record of a situated and contextualized performance in which bawdry is used as a means of establishing a homosocial bond between the storytellers and their all-male audience. The men in this audience are distinctly contestive of sociocultural and hence ideological influences that emanate from outside their worldview (that of both the Marxist subgovernor and the American female folklorist). Similarly, Cathy Preston's "'Cinderella' as a Dirty Joke: Gender, Multivocality, and the Polysemic Text" addresses the function of gender and class in negotiating the way meaning is made of differently situated American performances of a bawdy joke.

Finally, folklorists—for example, Debora Kodish and the contributors to a 1990 special issue of *Southern Folklore*, "Folklore Fieldwork: Sex, Sexuality, and Gender,"—have begun to address the ways in which gender and sexuality affect fieldwork relationships, as well as critiquing the ways in which ethnographers, in their write-ups of fieldwork, have eroticized the relationship between the ethnographer and the ethnographic subject. Among other things, they argue that older models of ethnography inscribed the erotics of colonialist conquest and penetration and that newer models explore the erotics of surrender and affiliation. Both models inscribe fantasies, and though the politics of metaphorical surrender may seem preferable to those of metaphorical rape, either fantasy may be appropriative of bodies other than one's own for one's own needs.

To the extent that the erotic (such as sexual bodies, genders, and sexualities) is a cultural construction, what is experienced as erotic, as well as the meanings attributed to erotic practices, may or may not cross cultural or historical boundaries. Furthermore, the erotic's representations of pleasure do not necessarily always translate as pleasurable when crossing gender, class, ethnic, racial, or religious registers even within the same culture—in part because such forms of representation and practice inevitably encode sociopolitical power relations and thus function as contestive sites of cultural production. In other words, what is pleasurable to one person in a particular performing context may be distasteful (or worse, if experienced as an expression of violence, dominance, and conquest) to another person in the same or a different performing context. Herein lies the dilemma in which arguments for censorship are embedded. The complexity of this issue is well illustrated by anthropologist Gayle Rubin, among others; from her groundbreaking 1979 essay on gender and sexuality, "The Traffic in Women," to her essay on hegemonic hierarchization of different sexualities, "Thinking Sex: Notes for a Radical Theory of the Politics of Sexuality," her work has consistently explored sexual and gender-based politics while defending the expression of sexual diversity.

Censorship—the product of conflicting class relations and changing constructions of gender, race, and diverse sexualities and nationalisms—involves the attempted public erasure and silencing of voices that are sometimes disruptive of traditional and emergent hegemonic interests. Inasmuch as theorists have argued that the public "production of specific forms of desire" creates and maintains "specific forms of political authority," the inscription of erotic folklore is imperative to our understanding of cultural differences and to our constructions of cultural and political histories.

Cathy Lynn Preston

See also Joke; Obscenity; Scatology.

✳✳✳✳✳✳✳✳✳✳✳✳✳✳✳✳✳

References

Babcock, Barbara. 1987. Taking Liberties, Writing from the Margins, and Doing It with a Difference. *Journal of American Folklore* 100:390–411.

Beck, Horace P. 1962. Say Something Dirty! *Journal of American Folklore* 75:195–199.

Foucalt, Michel. 1978. *The History of Sexuality*. Translated by Robert Hurley. New York: Pantheon.

Green, Rayna. 1990. "Magnolias Grow in Dirt": The Bawdy Lore of Southern Women. In *Calling Home: Working-Class Women's Writings, An Anthology*, ed. Janet Zandy. New Brunswick, NJ: Rutgers University Press.

Hoffmann, Frank. 1973. *An Analytical Survey of Traditional Anglo-American Erotica*. Bowling Green, OH: Bowling Green University Press.

Kodish, Debora. 1987. Absent Gender, Silent Encounter. *Journal of American Folklore* 100:573–578.

Laqueur, Thomas. 1990. *Making Sex: Body and Gender from the Greeks to Freud*. Cambridge, MA: Harvard University Press.

Legman, Gershon. 1990. Erotic Folksongs and Ballads: An International Bibliography. *Journal of American Folklore* 103:417–501.

Paros, Lawrence. 1984. *The Erotic Tongue*. Seattle, WA: Madrona.

Preston, Cathy Lynn. 1994. "Cinderella" as a Dirty Joke: Gender, Multivocality, and the Polysemic Text. *Western Folklore* 53:27–49.

ESCHATOLOGY

Mythic narratives about teachings concerning the last things, the end of the world, the destruction of the old world, and the creation of a new world. In the religious traditions of mankind, eschatological texts differ greatly. Eschatological myths, theories, and stories that deal with the end of the universe are to be found in almost every society. These works give descriptions of the developments of the universe after the final catastrophe in varying styles, either in imaginative mythic narrative or in scientific formulas or the language of physics. Eschatological myths lay the ground for the ethical requirements of human existence, describing the future expectations and destiny of both mankind and the universe.

In prophetic religions like Parsism, Judaism, Christianity, and Islam, the end of this world implies entering into the realm of God. Based on this model, world and human history are unified and based on a linear model. In contrast, the Hindu philosophy of religion espouses a cyclical concept of time. The destruction of the world is expected to take place several times: The world will return to chaos again but will be created anew. Eschatological myths (e.g., "The Revelation of St. John") characteristically tell about the collapse of the firmament, floods, universal conflagration, terribly cold winters, bloody wars, and other horrors.

Myths are central to the religions of the world. They usually are held sacred in their cultures and are considered to be true explanations of the origins of the cosmos as well as the events related to both the genesis and the collapse of culture. They relate in detail how the world, humans, the animal kingdom, and central elements of culture were created, thus establishing the world order. These myths are often incorporated into the present by means of rituals. In myths, religions offer provocatively different answers to people's "why questions." Myths, however, deal not only with the questions of origin but also with the end of the universe and destiny of man; therefore, a culture's cosmogonic and eschatological myths together form an essential fabric of the culture's worldview.

There is always a difference between reality as depicted in myths and the human, societal, cultural, and physical realities of the people that maintain these fundamental explanations about their human existence. The crucial difference between historical and mythic time interpretation is related to the model used for comprehending temporality. Historical time is linear, continuous, and composed of unique events, but mythic time is cyclical and repetitive. The latter encompasses and unites two temporal dimensions: the original time and the present. In traditional cultures, a wealth of myths are devoted to explaining the origin and destination of the universe. These myths can be categorized, respectively, as cosmogonic and eschatological myths that clarify the structure, function, and origin of time, as well as its end. The fundamental questions about the origin and destination of the universe are addressed in every human culture or community, without exception. Although the creation and the end of the universe and mankind are characteristically dealt with as elements of the myths of human cultures, very different promises and expectations are provided. In their efforts to locate the causes of variation, scholars have noted that there is a relationship among certain ecological settings or niches, worldview, and eschatological expectations and beliefs.

Juha Pentikäinen

See also Cosmology; Myth.

✳✳✳✳✳✳✳✳✳✳✳✳✳✳✳✳✳

References

Dundes, Alan, ed. 1984. *Sacred Narrative*. Berkeley: University of California Press.

Eliade, Mircea. 1971. *The Myth of the Eternal Return, or Cosmos and History*. Trans. Willard R. Trask. Princeton, NJ: Princeton University Press.

Long, Charles. H. 1963. *Alpha: The Myths of Creation*. New York: George Braziller.

Pentikäinen, Juha Y. 1989. *Kalevala Mythology*. Trans. Ritva Poon. Bloomington: Indiana University Press.

Sproul, Barbara C. 1979. *Primal Myths: Creating the World*. San Francisco: Harper & Row.

ESOTERIC/EXOTERIC FACTOR

Element in folklore that stresses a group's sense of its identity in relation to other groups. Coined by William Hugh Jansen, the set of contrasting terms has four dimensions. The esoteric factor in folklore refers both to a group's self-image and to its perception of what people from other groups think of it. The exoteric factor includes a group's image of another group and its notions of what that group believes that image to be. Examples of folklore evincing the esoteric factor are origin myths and legends that relate an ethnic community's beginnings (for instance, emergence myths among some Native American groups in the Southwest) and jokes told by African-Americans about white attitudes toward blacks. Folklore with strong exoteric tendencies is represented by ethnic jokes—those that offer actual characterizations of the targeted population and those that depict the population's alleged perception of the joketeller's attitudes.

Jansen believed that the esoteric/exoteric factor figures with particular prominence in the folklore of groups that demonstrate three features. Most important is isolation, whether the distancing factor be geography, religion, ethnicity and language, age, or some other marker of difference. A second contributor to a strong esoteric/exoteric component in a group's folklore is its being privy to knowledge and skills that seem especially arcane or specialized. Finally, Jansen suggested, groups that come to be regarded as especially prestigious or admirable may possess a pronounced esoteric/exoteric factor in their folklore.

Though Jansen himself viewed the esoteric/exoteric factor in folklore as pertinent to groups whose focus of identity might be occupational, religious, regional, or, in fact, related to any other distinguishing trait, most applications of his idea have occurred in the study of interethnic folklore, especially joking. Moreover, emphasis has most usually been directed at the exoteric member in the set of terms. Folklorists have, for example, defined a set of traits imputed to ethnic (and sometimes regional) others by mainstream culture in the United States: lack of efficiency, dirtiness, sexual promiscuity, inappropriate appetite, and laziness being some of the features that comprise a generic exoteric characterization. To these (and occasionally in place of some of them), particular features may be added to complete mainstream culture's exoteric view of a particular ethnic other. The Jew may be mercenary, the Scot may be stingy, the Italian may be cowardly, and the African-American may be criminally violent, for example. Occasional studies have focused on exoteric depictions of mainstream culture and its participants from the perspective of ethnic minorities, one of the most developed presentations being Keith Basso's treatment of Western Apache skits depicting the "whiteman."

Some folklorists have recognized that ethnic jokes have esoteric as well as exoteric significance since the qualities imputed exoterically to the ethnic outsider stand in direct contradistinction to how the joketeller would characterize his or her own group, at least ideally. Consequently, the joketeller who mocks the laziness and inefficiency of the ethnic other also may be asserting a sense of his or her own group's qualities of industry and efficiency.

William M. Clements

See also Blason Populaire; Ethnic Folklore; Joke.

✳✳✳✳✳✳✳✳✳✳✳✳✳✳✳✳✳

References
Basso, Keith A. 1979. *Portraits of "the Whiteman": Linguistic Play and Cultural Symbols among the Western Apache.* Cambridge: Cambridge University Press.
Clements, William M. 1986. The Ethnic Joke as Mirror of Culture. *New York Folklore* 12(3–4):87–97.
Davies, Christie. 1990. *Ethnic Humor around the World: A Comparative Analysis.* Bloomington: Indiana University Press.
Dundes, Alan. 1971. A Study of Ethnic Slurs: The Jew and the Polack in the United States. *Journal of American Folklore* 84:186–203.
———. 1975. Slurs International: Folk Comparisons of Ethnicity and National Character. *Southern Folklore Quarterly* 39:15–38.
Jansen, William Hugh. 1957. A Culture's Stereotypes and Their Expression in Folk Cliches. *Southwestern Journal of Anthropology* 13:184–200.
———. 1959. The Esoteric-Exoteric Factor in Folklore. In *The Study of Folklore*, ed. Alan Dundes. Englewood Cliffs, NJ: Prentice-Hall.

ETHNIC FOLKLORE

The traditional expressive behavior of ethnic groups as they migrate, resettle, and interact with other groups. Initially conceived of as the content of a distinctive ethnic identity—part of the constellation of cultural traits that together distinguish one group from another—ethnic folklore is now generally defined in terms of its role in the creation, maintenance, and negotiation of cultural boundaries between ethnic groups. A discussion of this shift in defining characteristics provides a theoretical history of ethnic folklore scholarship both in Europe and in the United States.

In Europe, the study of folklore actually originated in the political struggle of various groups for ethnic recognition even though they were affiliated with large empires. During the eighteenth and nineteenth centuries, ethnic groups used various folklore forms to bolster their claims for national independence, becoming instrumental in the establishment of modern nations. Wilhelm and Jacob Grimm, Johann Gottfried von Herder, and other romantic nationalists encouraged the rise of national pride through the reinforcement of ethnic identity and the perpetuation of values they defined as "ethnic."

237

In Europe, ethnic groups are the result of many centuries of an uninterrupted, slow process of oppression, relocation, and transplantation. As Linda Dégh has pointed out in her survey of European ethnic folklore scholarship, "The Study of Ethnicity in Modern European Ethnology," these groups have necessarily been studied by ethnologists as historical formations and as parts of a European cultural continuum. European ethnologists have tended to analyze the folklore of these ethnic groups either as the products of regional dialect groups comprising a general national culture or as the lore of alien minority groups, language islands, or colonies within nations. In the first instance, ethnographic field data are placed in the context of historical, geographical, ecological, and demographic factors believed to account for the specific combination of cultural elements that characterize the ethnicity of a regional group. Thus, *ethnic specifics*, local variations of national stereotypes, have been the focus of much of the research on the expressive culture of European ethnic groups.

Although research on the folklore of what Dégh has called "alien ethnic colonies" within larger European nations produced similar investigative strategies, the overall goal of that research was quite different. In fact, scholars often were completely disinterested in alien minorities such as itinerant Gypsy tribes or communities of eastern European Jews; the research of these scholars often supported assimilationist government policies. Historically oriented and profoundly influenced by Herderian nationalism, these ethnographers regarded the lore of emigrant colonies as the final vestiges of the national ideal. The Soviet school of ethnology provides one of the best examples of the justification of folklore research, especially research on ethnic folklore, for political reasons.

Likewise, in Germany, where World War I had both crippled the economy and deflated national pride, the study of ethnic folklore, grounded firmly in the heritage of the German romantic nationalists, became one of the most powerful tools of Nazi folk and race theorists. Focusing particularly on German ethnic groups in southeast Europe, agents of the Reich worked to organize individual communities as German nationals. Ethnic folklore research, then, was almost exclusively directed ideologically, toward imperialistic expansionism.

After World War II, a new generation of scholars finally came forward to critique the reconstructionism of traditional German *Volkskunde*. The postwar era provided these ethnographers with a rich variety of contexts for the study of German ethnic folklore as the resettlement of various groups began to take place. This focus on the processes of change that occur as ethnic groups interact became most prominent in European ethnology after the war, as ethnic group relocation between nations and internal migration became so widespread. In these contexts, studies of acculturation flourished, and folklore forms were analyzed as clear indicators of the acculturative process.

In Europe since the 1950s, the study of interethnic relations has grown into a special field. Community studies of areas in which several ethnic groups and/or nationalities interact have often included the analysis of folklore genres. In multiethnic regions of southeastern Europe, for example, a number of cooperative studies have produced careful folklore analyses of multilingual interethnic communities. Such studies have served to disturb the traditional definition of ethnic groups according to trait combinations since the research indicates that changing contextual factors continually disrupt the stability of those very combinations. The exploration of expressive culture in interethnic relations in Europe today focuses rather on the ways in which social interaction among ethnic groups and individuals produces a dynamic range of folklore forms that continually both maintain and create cultural traditions.

In the United States, many of the particular theoretical and methodological issues concerning ethnic folklore differ considerably from those of concern to European ethnologists. However, the folklore of ethnic groups has been a prominent concern of American folklorists since the very inception of the American Folklore Society (AFS). In fact, the 1888 AFS charter mentioned the traditions of Native Americans, African-Americans, and other ethnically distinct communities as particularly appropriate sources of data for folklorists.

Like their European precedents, the first studies of the folklore of American ethnic groups were collections of "survivals." The assumption behind these collections of songs, stories, superstitions, and other Old World forms was that these treasures would somehow be lost as soon as acculturation (specifically, linguistic acculturation) had taken place. The task of the folklorist, then, was to document these Old World traditions before they disappeared during the process of Americanization. Initially, British ballads, songs, and folktales were the foci of such studies, which concentrated on recovering these relics of British countryside traditions—especially in the upland South, New England, and the Ozarks. As Roger D. Abrahams has pointed out in his thorough discussion of the history of American ethnic folklore scholarship in the *Harvard Encyclopedia of Ethnicity*, a hierarchy of forms and even items was established in the late nineteenth and early twentieth centuries, but the actual collection of such items in North America was not carried out extensively until the 1920s and 1930s. These collections, several of them conducted under the auspices of the Works Progress Administration, focused primarily on determining the oldest and most widespread texts of ballads and folktales and estimating how widely they might be found and in what range of versions and variants.

A wide range of ethnic folklore research has been conducted employing this kind of antiquarian approach to the collection and analysis of ethnic lore of groups as diverse as Pennsylvania Germans, Louisiana French, and southwestern Mexican-Americans. Such studies have served primarily to document the conservative, traditional preservation of Old World ethnic traditions in these often isolated communities.

Studies of Native American folklore developed along somewhat similar lines. In the nineteenth century, the collection of Native American folklore, however, also was used to foster a kind of nationalistic sentiment. Native American lore was collected in order to identify distinctly "American" cultural roots that might serve to distinguish the young nation. These collections soon provided indexes of the rate of survival of Native American cultural forms since, unlike the study of the folklore of Euroamerican ethnic groups, no previous baseline studies of precontact narratives, songs, and rituals were available.

Other scholars, particularly those studying Euroamerican folklore, combined similar collecting techniques with a somewhat different analytic perspective. In these studies, the collected texts served to index not only the degree of preserved ethnicity but also the degree of "assimilation" of the particular ethnic group. Conducted primarily in culturally conservative communities where ethnic distinctiveness was highlighted, this kind of ethnic folklore research compared the collected material to Old World repertoires in order to gauge the various stages in the process of acculturation. The clear assumption was that the more Americanized an individual ethnic group became, the fewer vestiges of Old World forms would remain and that, in time, ethnic differences in American culture simply would disappear. Following the work of early-twentieth-century historians and social scientists interested in ethnicity, then, folklorists viewed ethnic communities as living laboratories in which the processes of assimilation and acculturation could be observed and analyzed firsthand. Such studies served to highlight the selective maintenance of traditional forms and practices within particular ethnic communities.

A similar perspective also has been used to suggest, however, that African and Native American repertoires or styles have been eliminated in the process of colonization. This deculturation perspective is most frequently identified with African-Americanists E. Franklin Frazier and Robert Park, although it was maintained by other collectors of African-American lore until well into the 1960s. Such a Eurocentric position has been rebutted easily by a number of prominent scholars, who have demonstrated a strong maintenance of African expressive forms, styles, and performance patterns in the United States. The work of Melville Herskovits has been particularly influential in formulating a more complex model of the ways ethnic folklore forms function as indicators of degree of acculturation. Herskovits has distinguished three modes of continuity and adaptation: straight *retention*; *reinterpretation*, in which forms are maintained in new environments with new uses and meanings; and *syncretism*, in which similar elements of two or more cultures merge. This attention to the cultural dynamics of intergroup contact in which expressive forms change and emerge redirected scholarly attention away from folklore items themselves and toward an analysis of the various factors affecting the use of these forms as displays of ethnicity.

Most twentieth-century folklore studies on ethnicity have focused on the changes in ethnic groups and their lore that came about as the result of culture contact. In 1959, in his influential *American Folklore*, Richard M. Dorson formulated a set of questions that served as guidelines for folklorists interested in the lore of ethnic groups for at least the next ten years: "What happens to the inherited traditions of European and Asiatic folk after they settle in the United States and learn a new language and new ways? How much of the old lore is retained and transmitted to their children? What parts are sloughed off, what intrusions appear, what accommodation is made between Old Country beliefs and the American physical scene? These are the large questions that confront the assessor of immigrant folk traditions."

Many folklorists took up Dorson's call for studies of immigrant traditions and answered these questions. A fine example of such acculturation studies is Robert Georges' work with the Tarpon Springs, Florida, Greek community, in which he analyzes the ways narratives, rites of passage, and holiday celebrations help to maintain the traditional belief system of these fairly isolated transplanted Greek fishermen. Georges demonstrates both the survival and reinforcement of Greek traditions in one small American community. Folklorists have continued to document both persistence and change in the ethnic traditions of immigrant groups. Barbara Kirshenblatt-Gimblett's study of traditional storytelling in a Toronto Jewish community, Robert Klymasz' study of Ukrainian folklore in Canada, and Elli Köngäs-Maranda's analysis of Finnish-American lore, for example, document the various factors effecting change in ethnic traditions in the New World.

European models of ethnological research have formed the basis for the "acculturation model" research of folklorists such as Linda Dégh, who has called for case studies that will provide an analysis of the assimilation process as it affects groups in contiguous and intermittent contact over a period of time. This process of "cultural adjustment" requires the observation of transgenerational folkloric expression as various ethnic groups come in contact with each other. Dégh has continually suggested that the determination of ethnic boundaries and the examination of intercultural borrowing should be the focus of research on ethnic folklore.

In this insistence on the analysis of the process of ethnic interaction, Dégh's work is representative of the ways in which American ethnic folklore scholarship since World War II has moved away from a concern with "survivals" of Old World forms as the cultural content of ethnic groups and toward an understanding of the processes of ethnic boundary maintenance or negotiation. Like their European colleagues, American folklorists have drawn extensively on the work of Norwegian ethnographer Fredrik Barth in making this shift in theoretical emphasis. Barth's 1969 *Ethnic Groups and Boundaries* proposed an understanding and definition of ethnic groups based not on the identification of a cluster of culture traits for each particular ethnic group but rather on the *process* that a group and others use to separate and define the group itself. Barth argued that the focus for the analysis of ethnicity should be "the ethnic *boundary* that defines the group, not the cultural stuff that it encloses." This simple but powerful notion of boundaries has proven to be one of the most theoretically useful concepts in clarifying the ways in which ethnic identity is articulated and actively negotiated in interaction within and between ethnic groups. Such a perspective points clearly to the influence of contextual variability on ethnic identity: As social, economic, and political conditions change, so may systems of ethnic identification.

Attention to the role of folklore in the process of boundary making was first articulated by William Hugh Jansen in his 1959 "The Esoteric-Exoteric Factor in Folklore." Jansen discussed the range of factors associated with boundary making and maintenance as they are revealed in oral narrative. His work suggested that by examining the folklore of a group's own self-image as well as that of its images of other groups, one might better understand the role folklore plays in the creation, negotiation, and maintenance of ethnic boundaries. Jansen's work focused primarily on the ways in which folklore operates as a "function of shared identity," binding groups together, but Richard Bauman has pointed out that differential identities and asymmetrical relationships also can be the basis for folklore performance. Américo Paredes has explored the relationship between "gringos" and "greasers" in the joking behavior of Mexican-Americans as dramatizations of real social inequities. Roger Abrahams also has suggested that folklore performances may additionally operate as a means of distinguishing separate or even antagonistic segments within the same ethnic community, as Alan Dundes' work on Jewish-American humor demonstrates.

As members of ethnic groups negotiate the construction, manipulation, and exploitation of boundaries between themselves and others, they draw on a wide range of cultural and linguistic resources in multiple cultural repertoires. In her 1983 essay "Studying Immigrant and Ethnic Folklore," Barbara Kirshenblatt-Gimblett suggested that a special feature of the folklore of ethnicity is a heightened awareness of cultural diversity and self-reflexivity, so that the relevant research questions become: "To what extent, how and to what effect is folklore used to make cultural comparisons and to mark cultural distinctiveness? How is folklore used to define cultural differences, incongruities and convergences? What are the nature and content of these comparisons, of this marking or foregrounding?" Attention to these questions required a shift from studying the lore of a particular named group to an examination of the settings, social occasions, and events in which boundary negotiation is an important activity.

Clearly, this shift in focus was at least partially a response to the new attention to folklore performance in the late 1960s and 1970s. With Dan Ben-Amos' 1971 redefinition of folklore as patterned expressive communication within a group meeting together face-to-face came an emphasis on the folk *group* rather than on solely text-centered analyses and on the folklore *process* rather than product. For scholars interested in ethnicity, this particular theoretical move opened the discipline in new ways to serious considerations of the manner in which ethnic group members use folklore in the creation and maintenance of cultural boundaries. In addition, the concept of emergence proposed by Dell Hymes and Richard Bauman—that folklore forms, contexts, and performances are constantly emerging— helped to undermine the long-held assumption that ethnic folklore traditions gradually and inevitably erode and disappear. Instead, folklorists now concentrated on the creative, ever-changing ways in which ethnic groups and individuals display their own ethnic identities.

At the same time, rising ethnic consciousness within the United States in the 1960s and 1970s created an increasing public interest in understanding the dynamics of ethnic interaction. Folklorists sometimes found themselves in the position of "ethnicity brokers" as they became involved in the public display of ethnicity in a variety of festival settings, ranging from the Festival of American Folklife in Washington, D.C., to small, local gatherings. Such festivals became means of dramatizing ethnic persistence in a particular region or community. The process of "going public" raised a whole new set of questions for both folklorists and members of ethnic groups, questions such as: What happens to folklore forms when they are performed within large heterogeneous groups that have come together only to be entertained, rather than within close, face-to-face, homogeneous communities with shared cultural values and expectations? What happens when ethnic identification becomes marketable? What is the effect on the ethnic community itself? Is the social base of ethnic folklore completely undermined in such performance contexts? Or are these festival situations simply different occasions on which boundary negotiation takes place, new responses to ethnic persistence in a truly pluralistic society?

During the late 1970s and 1980s, American folklore scholars began to extend their analyses of ethnic groups and their lore to consider the wide variety of contexts in which ethnicity is constantly negotiated and renegotiated. Many of the articles in the 1977 special issue of *Western Folklore*, "Studies in Folklore and Ethnicity," edited by Larry Danielson, demonstrated this range of concerns.

Acknowledging that ethnic meaning arises only out of the social interactions of individuals whose expressions of ethnicity may be affirmed, contested, and/or celebrated by other participants, researchers began to examine the interactions of particular ethnic individuals. As Shalom Staub pointed out in *Yemenis in New York City*, "Ethnicity is therefore an identity which resides not within the individual person, or even the particular group, but *between* individuals and *between* groups engaged in social interaction." The 1991 collection of essays on ethnic folklore edited by Stephen Stern and John Allan Cicala, *Creative Ethnicity*, represented this new direction in ethnic folklore scholarship. Through an examination of the forms, symbols, strategies, and stylistic resources of the folklore performances in a variety of ethnic contexts, the authors attempted to demonstrate the richness and diversity of ethnicity as it is experienced on a dynamic, personal level.

Today, scholars interested in the folklore of ethnic groups no longer confine themselves to the task of documenting survivals and chronicling acculturation patterns. Instead, folklorists around the world attempt to take into account both the broad historical conditions that influence ethnicity and the factors affecting specific individual negotiations of ethnic identity as they are played out within particular social interactions. The analysis of creative expressions of negotiations of ethnicity is crucial to an understanding of the ways in which groups and the individuals who comprise those groups continually articulate and reshape the meaning of their own ethnic identifications.

Margaret K. Brady

See also Blason Populaire; Esoteric/Exoteric Factor.

✳✳✳✳✳✳✳✳✳✳✳✳✳✳✳✳✳

References

Abrahams, Roger D. 1980. Folklore. In *Harvard Encyclopedia of American Ethnic Groups*, ed. Stephen Thernstron. Cambridge, MA: Harvard University Press.

Barth, Fredrik. 1969. *Ethnic Groups and Boundaries: The Social Organization of Cultural Difference*. Boston: Little, Brown.

Bauman, Richard. 1971. Differential Identity and the Social Base of Folklore. *Journal of American Folklore* 84:31–41.

Danielson, Larry, ed. 1977. *Studies in Folklore and Ethnicity*. Los Angeles: California Folklore Society.

Dégh, Linda. 1975. The Study of Ethnicity in Modern European Ethnology. *Journal of the Folklore Institute* 12:113–129.

Dorson, Richard M. 1959. *American Folklore*. Chicago: University of Chicago Press.

Georges, Robert A., and Stephen Stern. 1982. *American and Canadian Immigrant and Ethnic Folklore: An Annotated Bibliography*. New York: Garland.

Herskovits, Melville. 1942. *The Myth of the Negro Past*. New York: Harper.

Jansen, William Hugh. 1959. The Esoteric-Exoteric Factor in Folklore. In *The Study of Folklore*, ed. Alan Dundes. Englewood Cliffs, NJ: Prentice-Hall.

Kirshenblatt-Gimblett, Barbara. 1983. Studying Immigrant and Ethnic Folklore. In *The Handbook of American Folklore*, ed. Richard M. Dorson. Bloomington: Indiana University Press.

Klymasz, Robert B. 1973. From Immigrant to Ethnic Folklore: A Canadian View of Process and Transition. *Journal of the Folklore Institute* 10:131–139.

Paredes, Américo. 1959. *With His Pistol in His Hand*. Austin: University of Texas Press.

Royce, Anya Peterson. 1982. *Ethnic Identity: Strategies of Diversity*. Bloomington: Indiana University Press.

Stern, Stephen, and John Allan Cicala, eds. 1991. *Creative Ethnicity: Symbols and Strategies of Contemporary Ethnic Life*. Logan: University of Utah Press.

ETHNOAESTHETICS

Study of the artistic communication and human creativity of a culture or group, incorporating both individual and communal ideas about what is "good," "beautiful," "artistic," "appropriate," and/or "well made." As the term itself indicates, *ethnoaesthetics* is concerned with a group's own perceptions about what is pleasing or beautiful. Scholars who pursue this study generally reject the notion that such values are universally determined, attempting instead to discover the characteristic cultural qualities inherent in the artistic expression of particular groups. From this perspective, such forms of communication constitute eloquent statements about how certain people think, live, and behave in distinct places and times, demonstrating both continuity and change in the way they view the world. Although the approach is seldom used in this manner, it could refer as easily to the verbal arts as it does to the visual arts and would be quite productive in delineating the interrelationship between the two communicative processes.

Historically, the designation *ethnoaesthetics* has been employed more frequently by anthropologists than folklorists, indicating especially the cultural expressions of non-Western peoples, including those aptly described by Nelson Graburn as inhabiting "the fourth world," that is, native peoples without countries of their own whose art is seldom manufactured for their own use. Whether they specifically adopted this terminology or not, folklorists began to apply the methodology consonant with this concept as they became more concerned with context, performance, and dynamic process, giving less credence to their former emphasis on isolated objects and texts that were often regarded as if frozen in time and generated anonymously. This new direction in folklore scholarship reflected a major shift in the discipline that took place in the mid-1970s, entailing a concentration on the individual rather than on broad generalizations, classifications of types, delineations of groups, and regional trends.

In folk art studies, the behavioral orientation is well represented by Michael Owen Jones' wide variety of publications that demonstrate his inter-

245

est in individual motivation, focusing on the material object as a means by which to illuminate the mind of a particular maker and user. Significantly, Jones, like anthropologists who study tourist art, explores appreciation as well as creation, considering the attitudes of both the consumer and the traditional artist. Jones' influence is evident in a range of later publications whose authors began to question overarching assumptions about tradition and culture. John Vlach, for instance, directly acknowledges Jones' intellectual contribution to his own research. In *Charleston Blacksmith: The Work of Philip Simmons*, Vlach examines the perpetuation of tradition in the urban environment, stressing the ways in which this environment actually encourages the retention of folk aesthetics and creative processes. Many of Simon Bronner's numerous books and articles also situate studies of individual craftspersons within specific community, economic, and environmental contexts. Additionally, although his early regional and structural studies would hardly fall within this disciplinary shift, Henry Glassie's *Passing the Time in Ballymenone* is exemplary in its attention to context, as well as its interweaving of the multiple verbal and visual expressive performances that occur in this folk community.

All of these studies have been the subject of controversy as well as admiration. Their emphasis on individual creativity is laudable, but their lack of attention to the politics of production is highly problematic. Too frequently, folk art scholars underscore the importance of aesthetics while neglecting critical aspects of social conflict and power relationships. Issues of race, class, ethnicity, gender, and sexual identity have yet to become central to this area of academic concern.

An extensive overview would reveal that the canon in folk art or folk material culture scholarship is composed largely of the publications of male folklorists writing about male artists. The tacit assumption behind the existence and perpetuation of such an accepted body of scholarly works is that women neither study nor make the most significant forms of folk objects. Yet the most recent generation of folk art scholars comprises quite a number of women who have moved into the seemingly male-dominated and public realm of folk art study. But it is not the concentration on a specific category of folk art that distinguishes the scholarship of these women; rather, it is their endeavor to interrelate a variety of forms of artistic communication. Motivated by advances in feminist theory and performance theory, they have dissolved the traditional boundaries between verbal and visual expressive behavior, investigating the aesthetic principles that unite rather than separate these domains. It is this sort of research, conducted by scholars who sometimes designate themselves as folkloristic anthropologists, anthropological folklorists, or symbolic anthropologists, that fits most clearly within the ethnoaesthetic approach to human creativity. These innovative scholars include Barbara Babcock, Claire R. Farrer, Nancy Munn, and Barbara Tedlock, among others. They, in turn, have influenced their students and colleagues to analyze multidisciplinary, multivalent aspects of traditional artistic or symbolic behavior. Whether they explicitly describe this method as "ethnoaesthetic" or not, their approach constitutes one of the most productive directions in contemporary folk art studies.

M. Jane Young

See also Aesthetics; Texture; Tradition.

✳✳✳✳✳✳✳✳✳✳✳✳✳✳✳✳✳✳

References
Babcock, Barbara, Guy Monthan, and Doris Monthan. 1986. *The Pueblo Storyteller: Development of a Figurative Ceramic Tradition*. Tucson: University of Arizona Press.
Bronner, Simon. 1984. *Chain Carvers: Old Men Crafting Meaning*. Lexington: University Press of Kentucky.
Farrer, Claire R. 1991. *Living Life's Circle: Mescalero Apache Cosmovision*. Albuquerque: University of New Mexico Press.
Glassie, Henry. 1982. *Passing the Time in Ballymenone*. Philadelphia: University of Pennsylvania Press.
Graburn, Nelson H.H., ed. 1976. *Ethnic and Tourist Arts: Cultural Expressions from the Fourth World*. Berkeley: University of California Press.
Jones, Michael Owen. 1975. *The Hand Made Object and Its Maker*. Berkeley: University of California Press.
Munn, Nancy. 1973. *Walbiri Iconography*. Ithaca, NY, and London: Cornell University Press.
Tedlock, Barbara. 1992. *The Beautiful and the Dangerous: Encounters with the Zuni Indians*. New York: Viking.
Vlach, John M. 1981. *Charleston Blacksmith: The Work of Philip Simmons*. Athens: University of Georgia Press.

Ethnography

A method of studying cultures in which researchers immerse themselves in ways of life to perceive them as they are lived and then recount and interpret their fieldwork to help their readers understand what it is like to be a part of the cultures studied.

The four major types of ethnographies in the 1990s include the scientific, classical, and experimental ethnographies found within anthropology and folklore and ethnographies employed in research disciplines other than anthropology or folklore. The four approaches share a research methodology based on observing, recording, and, as fully as possible, participating in the daily activities of cultures and then writing accounts stressing descriptive detail. Each approach follows different literary conventions in reporting field experiences.

Scientific, classic, and experimental ethnography, the three primary approaches employed in folklore and anthropology in the 1990s, share an ancient history and method. Herodotus (484 B.C.–425 B.C.) wrote the first ethnography in anything like the modern sense, and in 1727, Joseph François Lafitau published his description of the Iroquois written from their point of view—the first modern field ethnography. Since Herodotus' time, many travelers, traders, missionaries, and government officials have conducted informal research among peoples and written about their experiences.

The word *ethnography* was first used in 1834 as a synonym for the then current term *anthropography*. Five years later, Harry R. Schoolcraft published his ethnography centering upon the folklore that he and his wife had collected from the Native American tribes of the eastern United States, and he published his best-known ethnography in 1848. This book, *The Indian in His Wigwam*, opened with an impressionistic account of Schoolcraft's first trip to the American West and ended with an Indian war song. Lewis Morgan wrote and published the first comprehensive field ethnography in 1851. Frank Hamilton Cushing, the first participant-observer in folklore and anthropology, lived in a Zuni pueblo from 1879 to 1884 and published a romantic account of the experience in *Century Magazine*. In 1888, Franz Boas published a field ethnography of the Baffin Island Eskimos. Alfred C. Haddon organized and led the first field ethnography team of trained observers in 1898.

All these early researchers were important in the development of ethnography, but Boas was arguably the most influential because, beyond his personal contributions to the field, he made Columbia University's Anthropology Department the most puissant training center for ethnographers in the United States during the first 30 years of the twentieth century. His students included Ruth Benedict, Ruth Bunzel, Melville Herskovits, Zora Neale Hurston, Alfred Kroeber, Robert H. Lowie, Margaret Mead, Paul Radin, and Leslie Spier; in 1926, every anthropology department in the United States was chaired by a former student of Franz Boas. During the same period, English anthropology produced its own set of ethnographers who affected the form, including A. R. Radcliffe-Brown, Bronislaw Malinowski, and Edward Evans-Pritchard. These British ethnographers tried to demonstrate the efficacy of functional theory, whereas the Americans attempted to salvage the past and accepted functionalism later. Both groups, however, produced classic ethnographies. Malinowski's 1922 description of the ethnography method as "an attempt to grasp the native's point of view and see his world through his eyes" characterized the approach of both groups.

These early, classic ethnographies—also called realistic ethnographies because of their similarities to the realist movement in literature—were far from uniform, and some of them were innovative and experimental. As time passed, however, ethnographers developed an inflexible set of genre conventions that included the use of a third-person, omniscient point of view to present a set of topics in a set sequence, as well as the elimination of any references to the investigator.

This predictable pattern was broken in the 1960s, 1970s, 1980s, and 1990s by pressures from different directions. In the 1960s and 1970s, ethnoscience argued that ethnographers should bring the rigor of the scientific method to ethnography, urged the replacement of the nonstandard selection of information of classic ethnography with a more precise framework for data collection and interpretation, and developed statistical tools to achieve these goals.

In the 1980s and 1990s, other voices argued for making ethnographies more personal and literary. *Reflexive, interactive, postmodern, experimental,* and *narrative* are all terms used to describe the varied attempts during these decades to restructure ethnography as a literary genre. Most ethnographers of this period included the field researcher as a part of the field, used the first-person voice, and did not follow chronological order, and many of them experimented with novelistic techniques. Drawing inspiration from Schoolcraft, Cushing, Hurston, James Agee, and Hunter S. Thompson and supported by the theoretical works of Clifford Geertz, David Schneider, Michael Owen Jones, Robert Georges, and many others, experimental ethnographers sought ways to include more direct representation of the experience of fieldwork itself into their written reports and to use writing to gain theoretical insights and more fully present the experience of other cultures.

Ethnography proliferated in the second half of the twentieth century in research fields other than folklore and anthropology. Nonanthropological, nonfolkloristic ethnographers adapted and developed methodologies to fit their needs from scientific, classical, and experimental ethnographies.

Various critics attacked both classical and experimental ethnographies in the 1980s and 1990s as unscientific and scientific ethnographies as too subjective and nonreflexive. It is impossible to predict the future directions the form may take with absolute certainty. Considering the long and useful history of ethnographies, however, it seems highly likely that ethnography will continue as a major research method and literary genre in some form—or forms—within folklore, anthropology, and other research fields.

Keith Cunningham

See also Anthropological Approach; Fieldwork.

✳✳✳✳✳✳✳✳✳✳✳✳✳✳✳✳✳

References

Georges, Robert A., and Michael O. Jones. 1980. *People Studying People.* Berkeley: University of California Press.

Marcus, George E., and Michael M.L. Fischer. 1986. *Anthropology as Cultural Critique.* Chicago: University of Chicago Press.

Oswalt, Wendell H. 1972. *Other People, Other Customs: World Ethnography and Its History*. New York: Holt, Rinehart, and Winston.

ETHNOMUSICOLOGY

The study of music that stresses the importance of music in and as culture. Ethnomusicology holds that music takes meaning from its cultural context. The term, which contracts *ethnology* with *musicology*, was first used to denote the discipline in 1950 by Jaap Kunst, replacing *comparative musicology* (from the German *vergleichende Musikwissenshaft*), the accepted name from the late nineteenth century. Kunst argued, along with others, that comparison neither distinguished nor sufficiently delineated the research in this discipline.

At the onset, studies focused on music outside the Western art music tradition. Early researchers came from a range of disciplines and geographic areas—ethnology and anthropology in the United States, musicology and music folklore in the United Kingdom, eastern Europe and Latin America, and psychology in Germany and Austria. The disparate academic backgrounds of the researchers imparted an interdisciplinary cast that persists in ethnomusicology, albeit with changing disciplinary shades.

Musics outside the Western tradition continue to hold an important position within ethnomusicology. However, the study of Western art music often has been implicit, through comparison, in the research. A few scholars explicitly have made Western music, even art music, a focus of their work. Moreover, research concerned with music in urban and complex societies has emerged as an important concern of ethnomusicologists. More generally, ethnomusicology seeks to explain and champion neglected and undervalued musics and to denounce ethnocentric attitudes toward the musics of other communities and cultures.

Ethnomusicology distinguishes itself from other academic disciplines through specific topics and issues of interest: origins and universals of music, musical change and conflict, the function of music within society, and relationships between language and music, to list a few historically prominent examples. Partly because of this issue-based orientation, scholars today most often define the discipline by means of a shared, if eclectic, corpus of research theory and methodology, rather than by geographic area.

Ethnomusicology can be characterized further by the persistent examination of the bounds and objectives of the discipline and by critical inquiry into its own definition. Charles Seeger argued that the most general term, *musicology*, would best describe this discipline that views all musics from all times with equal scholarly import, rather than restricting the general term to *historical musicology*, a discipline largely concerned with Western art music. And George List, writing in 1979, questioned if a single definition was even possible. Other writers have argued similarly. The inquiry into definitions stems, in part, from the divergent theoretical and methodological bases of the researchers seeking common modes of discourse. Another aspect of this questioning involves efforts to gain institutional support and position for ethnomusicology vis-à-vis other more established disciplines, especially anthropology and historical musicology.

Guido Adler, in his 1885 definition of musicology and its divisions, saw the focus of comparative musicology as the classification of the musics of the world. Thus, at Adler's christening of the discipline within academe, comparison was the discipline's central feature. Two technical developments made the comparison of oral-tradition musics feasible: the invention of the phonograph by Thomas Edison in 1877 and the development of a pitch measurement system by the English physicist and phonetician Alexander J. Ellis. The phonograph facilitated the collection of music data, previously a Herculean task limited by one's musical ear and access to cooperative performers. Ellis' cents system of measurement, outlined in his 1885 article "On the Musical Scales of Various Nations," made possible a more objective comparison of pitch elements based on the division of the octave into 1,200 equal units.

Comparison as practiced by Erich M. von Hornbostel of the Berlin Phonogramm-Archiv, along with his students and colleagues, was concerned largely with analysis of music elements such as scale tones, intervals, melodic movement, and rhythms. Based on analyses of recordings and musical instruments collected by colonial ethnologists, these studies produced grand, if not grandiose, classification schemes. The most renowned sought to illustrate global distribution of musical styles and artifacts. Important works of this period were Hornbostel's *Blasquinten* (blown fifths) theory relating the structure of musical scales, now discredited (see Kunst's "Around von Hornbostel's Theory of Cycle of Blown Fifths" for discussion), and Hornbostel and Curt Sachs' "Classification of Music Instruments," published in 1914, still a standard for musical instrument classification.

Comparison also infused much early ethnomusicological research in the United States. From the nineteenth century, scholars working on Native American music, most conspicuously Alice Cunningham Fletcher and Frances Densmore, created monographs on the music of individual Native American cultures. Stemming, in part, from the Austrian *Kulturhistorische Schule* (culture history school), students of Franz Boas, however, sought to organize Native American cultures into geographic areas established by shared cultural traits. George Herzog, who had worked with both Hornbostel and Boas, applied the notion of culture areas in his "The Yuman Musical Style" (1928). Helen

Roberts used this approach to classify Native American musical styles and instruments in her 1936 book, *Musical Areas in Aboriginal North America*.

Comparison was explicit in researching the relationships between African-American musical practices and those found in Africa, seen most notably in the work of Melville Herskovits and Richard Waterman. Alan Lomax's research methodology of cantometrics, exemplified in the 1968 publication *Folk Song Style and Culture*, linked musical style with social organization and took comparison as its central feature.

The use of the term *comparative musicology* declined in the 1940s, to be replaced eventually by *ethnomusicology*. The new term gained credence with Kunst's call to rename the discipline and was institutionalized with the establishment of the Society for Ethnomusicology in 1955. Coupled with this change in labels, there was a sharp decline in work concerned with cross-cultural comparison. In this new milieu, comparison was criticized and seen as premature until more detailed, accurate descriptions of individual cultures existed. Alan Merriam, in his 1964 book *The Anthropology of Music*, admonished much early research as considerably less than systematic in its use of comparison. In a 1966 review of Merriam's book, John Blacking added that comparison could yield spurious results in that superficial musical elements might seem similar but be based on different cultural models of behavior and belief. Such discussions corresponded to a realization that each culture's music deserved study in its own right, in terms appropriate to that culture and built around methods and theories that emerged from the study of that culture and its music.

Early comparative studies invariably focused on music expressions as artifacts, with little concern for the context of their existence. The shift toward the view of music as part of culture stressed methods of fieldwork, thereby making fieldwork a defining feature of ethnomusicology. Indeed, Bruno Nettl suggested in *The Study of Ethnomusicology* that a history of ethnomusicology could be written as a history of fieldwork. From the 1890s to about 1930, the collection of artifacts was accomplished with only short periods in the field. Data usually were collected by people other than the music researcher, with the exception of the fieldwork-based research by Americans on Native American music. During and beyond this period, some scholars were equally concerned with collecting and preserving entire music repertories. Scholars feared that much of the music of the world was on the verge of extinction, and as a result, major archives of recordings were begun in Germany and the United States. The next period, roughly from 1920 to 1960, stressed research for extended periods in small communities. Studies from this period took a broader concept of fieldwork, in which the collection of music artifacts was coupled with a concern for the complete context of any music's existence. Since the 1950s, parallel to the conviction that music expressions are important facets and indicators of a culture, there has been a further shift toward participant observation and more involvement with music. Moreover, interest in the music of complex and urban societies, where mediated forms of music such as radio broadcasts and sound records must be considered, has brought new methods of fieldwork while maintaining the significance of the participant observation method for ethnomusicology.

Since the late 1950s, ethnomusicological activity often has been characterized as oriented toward the methods and theories of either anthropology or historical musicology. Alan Merriam, the foremost champion of the anthropological orientation in ethnomusicology, suggested in *The Anthropology of Music* that the label *ethnomusicology*, combining ethnology with musicology, implies this division. Merriam drew upon methods and theories of anthropology, notably participant observation with extended periods of fieldwork and the theories of structuralism and functionalism. He argued as early as 1960 that ethnomusicology should be concerned with music in culture, later refined to music as culture, and he explicitly joined music to its cultural context in *The Anthropology of Music* through a definition of music that connected musical sound and musical behavior to a culture's beliefs and concepts of music. Mantle Hood, though sharing with Merriam a disapproval of the early comparative research and an endorsement of extended periods of fieldwork, was the strongest advocate for the musicological orientation to ethnomusicology. Hood's approach centered research around the mastery of non-Western music performance—what he called in 1960 "bi-musicality"—and he argued that training in performance, long basic to the European art music tradition, was equally applicable to the study of non-Western music. One component of this method was the development of a conservatory of music at the University of California, Los Angeles' Institute of Ethnomusicology, with artists representing cultures from around the world. Since the 1970s, there has been a general move away from interest in artifacts such as music compositions and genres toward an interest in processes. This change in emphasis has drawn the musicological and anthropological orientations within ethnomusicology closer together.

In Europe during the nineteenth century, research into local, oral traditions was driven by an interest in creating nationalist musics fortified and sustained through materials from peasant cultures. Composers such as Béla Bartók and Zoltán Kodály working in Hungary, Romania, and Transylvania and Percy Grainger in England drew upon indigenous folk music to create new art music compositions. Similarly, folk music enthusiasts, collectors, and analysts such as Cecil Sharp and Maud Karpeles researched the music of England and its immigrant offspring in the United States. Sharp's interest in melodic analysis and classification, as discussed in *English Folk Song: Some Conclusions*, is an important legacy, an antecedent of such work as Bertrand Bronson's research on the tunes of the Child ballads. Thanks in part to Karpeles, these and other folk music scholars gained an organized forum for their research with the founding, in 1947, of the International Folk Music Council, renamed the International Council for Traditional Music in 1981.

Ethnomusicology in Latin America displays the clearest correspondence to European folk music research. Comparable to their European counterparts, Latin American music scholars began to comprehend the relevance of local traditions as nationalizing forces. This recognition coincided with nationalist movements throughout Latin American—for instance, the Andean *indigenismo* and the Brazilian *modernismo* movements. In this context, such traditions were viewed as part of the opposition to dominant elite social classes who disregarded local traditions in favor of European-derived expressive forms. This research also paralleled European folk music scholarship in its emphasis on the study of the music artifact and its devaluation of performance and contextual issues. The trend was well represented by Isabel Aretz's *Síntesis de la etnomúsica en América Latina.*

Important as all this research is, its relationship with ethnomusicology is vague. Folk music scholarship rarely has drawn upon theory that relates music and its performance to performers and social contexts, although there are important exceptions, such as Philip Bohlman's *The Study of Folk Music in the Modern World.* The influence of folk music research in ethnomusicology has been circumscribed, too. The attention given to oral-tradition musics in ethnomusicology stems, in part, from early folk music research. However, with a theoretical framework that stresses comparison, folk music scholarship's import was more significant during the early periods of ethnomusicology, especially in the domains of melodic analysis and tune classification. This research did not fall neatly within or completely outside definitions of ethnomusicology.

The term *ethnomusicology* today has currency remote to the academic discipline. Activities such as the performance and dissemination of non-Western and oral-tradition musics and the teaching of such musics in primary and secondary schools are often linked with ethnomusicology. Moreover, the term often is invoked to describe the work of Western composers who make use of the musical possibilities of non-Western sources, as well as those people involved with non-Western musics as part of a global economic marketplace. Somewhat alarmed by these uses of the term, Alan Merriam in 1975 made the distinction between ethnomusicologists and others whose activities draw upon ethnomusicology.

In 1956, Willard Rhodes, arguing the importance of ethnomusicological scholarship for both the social sciences and humanities, warned against narrowing the discipline's scope and goals. His caveat evidently has been taken to heart, given the wide range of research and activities that now fall under the rubric *ethnomusicology.*

Leslie C. Gay Jr.

See also Ballad; Broadside Ballad; Cantometrics; Folk Music; Folksong, Lyric; Folksong, Narrative; Hymn, Folk; Lullaby; Musical Instrument, Folk.

✳✳✳✳✳✳✳✳✳✳✳✳✳✳✳✳

References

Adler, Guido. 1885. Umfang, Methode, und Ziel der Musikwissenschaft. *Vierteljahrschrift für Musikwissenshaft* 1:5–20. Translated in 1981 by Erica Muggelstone as Guido Adler's *The Scope, Method, and Aim of Musicology* [1885]: An English Translation with an Historico-Analytical Commentary. *Yearbook for Traditional Music* 13:1–21.

Aretz, Isabel. 1984. *Síntesis de la etnomúsica en América Latina*. Caracas: Monte Avila.

Béhague, Gerard. 1991. Reflections on the Ideological History of Latin American Ethnomusicology. In *Comparative Musicology and Anthropology of Music*, eds. B. Nettl and P. V. Bohlman. Chicago: University of Chicago Press.

Blacking, John. 1966. Review of *The Anthropology of Music*. *Current Anthropology* 7:218.

Bohlman, Philip V. 1988. *The Study of Folk Music in the Modern World*. Bloomington: Indiana University Press.

Bronson, Bertrand. 1959–1972. *The Traditional Tunes of the Child Ballads with their Texts According to the Extant Records of Great Britain and America*. Princeton, NJ: Princeton University Press.

Christensen, Dieter. 1991. Erich M. von Hornbostel, Carl Stumpf, and the Institutionalization of Comparative Musicology. In *Comparative Musicology and Anthropology of Music*, eds. B. Nettl and P. V. Bohlman. Chicago: University of Chicago Press.

Ellis, Alexander J. 1885. On the Musical Scales of Various Nations. *Journal of the Society of Arts* 33:485–527.

Herzog, George. 1928. The Yuman Musical Style. *Journal of American Folklore* 41:183–231.

Hood, Mantle. 1960. The Challenge of "Bi-musicology." *Ethnomusicology* 4:55–59.

———. 1963. Music, the Unknown. In *Musicology*, ed. Mantle Hood. Englewood Cliffs, NJ: Prentice-Hall.

Kunst, Jaap. 1948. Around von Hornbostel's Theory of Cycle of Blown Fifths. *Mededeling* 76:3-35.

———. [1950] 1959. *Ethnomusicology: A Study of Its Nature, Its Problems, Methods and Representative Personalities to Which Is Added a Bibliography*. The Hague: M. Nijhoff.

List, George. 1979. Ethnomusicology: A Discipline Defined. *Ethnomusicology* 23(1):1–4.

Lomax, Alan. 1968. *Folk Song Style and Culture*. Washington, DC: American Association for the Advancement of Science.

McAllester, David P. 1963. Ethnomusicology: The Field and the Society. *Ethnomusicology* 7(3):182–186.

Merriam, Alan P. 1960. Ethnomusicology: Discussion and Definition of the Field. *Ethnomusicology* 4(3):107–114.

———. 1964. *The Anthropology of Music*. Evanston, IL: Northwestern University Press.

———. 1975. Ethnomusicology Today. *Current Musicology* 20:50–66.

———. 1977. Definitions of "Comparative Musicology" and "Ethnomusicology": An Historical-Theoretical Perspective. *Ethnomusicology* 21(2):198–204.

Myers, Helen. 1992. Ethnomusicology. In *Ethnomusicology: An Introduction*, ed. H. Myers. New York: W. W. Norton.

Nettl, Bruno. 1975. The State of Research in Ethnomusicology and Recent Developments. *Current Musicology* 20:67–78.

———. 1983. *The Study of Ethnomusicology: Twenty-Nine Issues and Concepts*. Urbana: University of Illinois Press.

———. 1991. The Dual Nature of Ethnomusicology in North America: The Contributions of Charles Seeger and George Herzog. In *Comparative Musicology and Anthropology of Music*, eds. B. Nettl and P. V. Bohlman. Chicago: University of Chicago Press.

Porter, James. 1991. Muddying the Crystal Spring: From Idealism and Realism to Marxism in the Study of English and American Folk Song. In *Comparative Musicology and Anthropology of Music*, eds. B. Nettl and P. V. Bohlman. Chicago: University of Chicago Press.

Rhodes, Willard. 1956. Toward a Definition of Ethnomusicology. *American Anthropologist* 58:457–463.

Roberts, Helen H. [1936] 1970. *Musical Areas in Aboriginal North America*. New Haven, CT: Human Relations Area Files Press.

Seeger, Charles. 1965. Preface to the Critique of Music. *Inter-American Music Bulletin* 49:2–24.

———. 1970. Toward a Unitary Field Theory for Musicology. In *Selected Reports in Ethnomusicology*, ed. Department of Ethnomusicology. Los Angeles: Institute of Ethnomusicology, University of California.

Sharp, Cecil James. [1907] 1972. *English Folk Song: Some Conclusions*. London: E. P. Publishing.

von Hornbostel, Erich M., and Curt Sachs. 1961. Classification of Music Instruments. Trans. Anthony Baines and Klaus P. Wachsmann. *The Galpin Society Journal* 14:3–29. Originally published as Systematik der Musikinstrumente: Ein Versuch. *Zeitschrift für Ethnologie* 46:553–598.

Waterman, Richard A. 1952. African Influence on the Music of the Americas. In *Acculturation in the Americas*, ed. S. Tax. Chicago: University of Chicago Press.

Ethnopoetics

The study of aesthetic structures within oral performances. An outgrowth of the performance school, on the one hand, and structural linguistics, on the other, ethnopoetics seeks to discover and present the distinctive features of oral performances. Its aim is both descriptive and analytical. Although ethnopoetics was developed initially through the analysis of Native American narrative, it has been applied to a variety of other oral traditions and has influenced the ways folklorists present and interpret transcribed narrative in general. It offers valuable insights into such folkloristic issues as orality, literacy, translation, cultural change, and the relation of language and worldview (the Sapir-Whorf Hypothesis).

The study of ethnopoetics draws largely on the insights of two researchers, Dennis Tedlock and Dell Hymes, who have shaped the issues of the field. For Tedlock, oral performance differs from prose narrative in its reliance on the expressive capacities of the human voice. Through pauses and phonological cues (e.g., stress shift, intonation, amplitude, tone), the performer adds stylistic dimensions that become meaningful and entertaining to the native audience. Folklorists must find ways to express such oral texture in print through innovative use of visual signs. Even when presenting texts in translated form, folklorists can thus convey aesthetic features.

Proceeding from the realization that narratives in a number of Native American languages resemble poetry more than prose, Hymes and other researchers analyze texts to discover the formal means by which rhetorical structure and aesthetics find expression in oral narrative. Attention to details such as grammatical structures, parallelism, and repetition can help the researcher perceive not only poetic lines within the text but also grouping of lines into larger units, culminating in an overall aesthetic architecture of the performance itself. Often, the pattern number(s) of the culture in question plays a key role in determining the structure of a narrative.

Whereas folklorists working within Tedlock's framework stress the universal aspects of oral performance—its reliance on the voice—folklorists following Hymes' approach focus on the culture- and language-specific means by which aesthetic form is achieved. Assumptions of universality must be first tested cross-culturally. Both traditions represent important developments in folkloristics today.

Thomas A. DuBois

See also Aesthetics; Ethnoaesthetics; Performance; Texture.

✳✳✳✳✳✳✳✳✳✳✳✳✳✳✳✳✳

References

Fine, Elizabeth C. 1984. *The Folklore Text: From Performance to Print*. Bloomington: Indiana University Press.

Hymes, Dell. 1981. *"In Vain I Tried To Tell You": Essays in Native American Ethnopoetics*. Philadelphia: University of Pennsylvania Press.

———. 1992. Use All There Is to Use. In *On the Translation of Native American Literatures*, ed. Brian Swann. Washington DC: Smithsonian Institution Press.

Hymes, Virginia. 1987. Warm Springs Sahaptin Narrative Analysis. In *Native American Discourse: Poetics and Rhetoric*, eds. Joel Sherzer and Anthony C. Woodbury. Cambridge: Cambridge University Press.

Sherzer, Joel, and Anthony C. Woodbury. 1987. *Native American Discourse: Poetics and Rhetoric*. Cambridge: Cambridge University Press.

Tedlock, Dennis. 1983. *The Spoken Word and the Work of Interpretation*. Philadelphia: University of Pennsylvania Press.

———. 1990. From Voice and Ear to Hand and Eye. *Journal of American Folklore* 103(408):133–156.

Eᴛɪoʟoɢɪᴄᴀʟ NARRATIVE

An explanation of how things came to be the way they are or were at a given time or under certain conditions. The adjective *etiology* is derived from a late

Latin and Greek composite word: *aetiologia*, meaning "cause description" (*atia*, cause + *logia*, description); it is used in a number of fields to signify the science of causes or origins (e.g., in medicine to refer to the origins of a specific disease).

In folklore, the term *etiology* has been applied frequently in conjunction with other folkloristic concepts to designate the explanatory function of an item, commonly in narrative form. A story may belong to any of a number of genres, depending on the story's form, style, and contents, as well as on the narrator's intent for telling it (or the tale's function). Generally speaking, a traditional account of how a thing originated would be perceived as factual and taken seriously by narrator and listeners. Thus, etiological narratives are typically classified as falling within one of two main categories: belief (religious-sacred, mythological) and historical (legend, ethnic history, historical anecdotes). These two categories often overlap; such narratives also appear in instructional didactic roles (e.g., as moralistic fables or religious exempla). Laurits Bødker cites such Germanic terms as *Aetio fable*, *Åtiologische sage*, *Åtiologische märchen*, and *Åtiologische tierfabel*.

An etiological belief narrative may be labeled a myth or sacred story (e.g., biblical, Koranic)—myth being a belief whose validity is not accepted by the person applying the term. Consequently, Stith Thompson classifies the bulk of etiological themes as "Mythological"; Hasan El-Shamy expands the scope to "Mythological [and related belief] motifs."

Examples of such motifs include the following: A20, "Origin of the creator"; A110, "Origin of the gods"; A510, "Origin of the culture-hero (demigod)"; A980, "Origin of particular places"; A1335, "Origin of death"; A1370, "Origin of mental and moral characteristics"; A1610, "Origin of various tribes"; and A2221, "Animal characteristics reward for pious act." Examples of legendary (historically possible) motifs are: A1464.1.1, "First poetry composed in imitation of tone of hammer on anvil", and Z21.1. "Origin of chess." Meanwhile, the formulaic theme to which such a tale belongs has been recently designated as new Motif Z19.3§, "Etiological tales: 'that-is-why'-tales" (the sign § designates additions to Thompson's motifs).

A number of etiological tales appear cross-culturally as tale types. Among these are a few *animal tales*, such as "Why Dogs Look One Another under the Tail" (AT 200A) and "Why Dog Chases Hare" (AT 200C*). Infrequently, an etiological tale may be an *ordinary folktale* (compare with *Märchen*), such as "Why the Sea Is Salt: Magic Salt Mill" (AT 565); it may also appear as a *formula tale*, as in the case of "Origin of Chess" (AT 2009). The majority, however, are cited under the category of *religious tales* (AT 750–849), such as "Origin of Physical Defects among Mankind" (AT 758A), "Mushroom from Peter's Spittle" (AT 774L), and "Why Big Trees Have Small Fruit" (AT 774P).

Hasan El-Shamy

See also Belief Tale; Folktale; Legend; Myth.

✾✾✾✾✾✾✾✾✾✾✾✾✾✾✾✾

References

Bødker, Laurits. 1965. Folk Literature (Germanic). *International Dictionary of Regional European Ethnology and Folklore*. Vol. 2. Copenhagen: Rosenkilde.

Christiansen, Reidar Th. 1958. *The Migratory Legend*. Helsinki: Academia Scientiarum Fennica.

El-Shamy, Hasan. 1995. *Folk Traditions of the Arab World: A Guide to Motif Classification*. 2 vols. Bloomington: Indiana University Press.

Thompson, Stith. 1955–1958. *The Motif-Index of Folk-Literature*. 6 vols. Bloomington: Indiana University Press.

von Sydow, C. W. 1948. *Selected Papers on Folklore*. Copenhagen: Rosenkilde and Bagger.

EUHEMERISM

The practice of explaining folk narratives as oral records of actual, historical events. By extension, the term might be applied to similar explanations of other kinds of folk traditions, such as nursery rhymes. The term is taken from the name of a Greek philosopher of the third century B.C., Euhemerus, who argued that the gods had once been mortal heroes and royalty who had been deified. Hence, myths were accounts of the historical deeds of the gods. Euhemerists would argue that fantastic elements in folk narratives that cannot be taken literally are later accretions around a core of historical truth. Folklorists and historians most commonly conceive the term *euhemerism* as having negative connotations, as being applicable not to all attempts to uncover historical bases for folk traditions but only to such attempts that are naive and uncritical, at least by modern standards.

There has been a continuous tradition of euhemeristic interpretation, particularly in regard to myths, since ancient times. Early Christian writers found the concept appealing, for it gave them an intellectual tool with which to attack the sacredness of pagan narratives, reducing them to being considered distorted historical accounts involving mere mortals. However, in the Middle Ages, when it was no longer necessary to refute paganism, euhemeristic approaches allowed scholars writing universal history to use ancient myths as historical sources.

Medieval euhemerists eventually turned ancient gods and legendary heroes into human benefactors who had introduced knowledge and arts or who had been responsible for founding modern nations. These ideas continued into the Renaissance, with gods sometimes becoming historical progenitors of rising royal houses. As the age of rational inquiry evolved in the late seventeenth and the eighteenth centuries, some thinkers considering the nature of myth developed euhemeristic approaches. Antoine Banier (1675–1741), for example, argued that the ancient myths would not have been accorded respect had they not had historical substance.

More recently, euhemeristic approaches have had particular appeal for writers seeking to establish unorthodox theories. These authors have seen oral traditions as conveying information not found in more conventional sources. In the late nineteenth century, Ignatius Donnelly discussed oral traditions about great floods from numerous cultures to prove the existence of the lost continent of Atlantis; he also offered mythic and legendary accounts from many parts of the world to establish that in prehistoric times, a great comet had hit or come close to earth, causing calamities that were remembered in these oral traditions. In the 1960s, Erich von Daniken used myths and legends, among other materials, to argue that astronauts from outer space had visited the earth in ancient times.

In recent years, folklorists and others have carefully and critically examined the historical bases for folk traditions and the relationship between folklore and history. Richard Dorson stressed the need to understand American folklore in the context of American cultural history. Jan Vansina developed rigorous methods for examining African historical traditions, and Dorothy Vitaliano looked at ancient myths and legends in the light of modern geological knowledge.

Frank de Caro

See also Historical Analysis.

✳✳✳✳✳✳✳✳✳✳✳✳✳✳✳✳✳✳

References
Dorson, Richard M. 1971. *American Folklore and the Historian.* Chicago: University of Chicago Press.
Feldman, Burton, and Robert D. Richardson, eds. 1972. *The Rise of Modern Mythology, 1680–1860.* Bloomington: Indiana University Press.
Seznec, Jean. 1953. *The Survival of the Pagan Gods: The Mythological Tradition and Its Place in Renaissance Humanism and Art,* trans. Barbara F. Sessions. Princeton, NJ: Princeton University Press.
Vansina, Jan. 1965. *Oral Tradition: A Study in Historical Methodology.* Chicago: Aldine.
Vitaliano, Dorothy. 1973. *Legends of the Earth: Their Geologic Origins.* Bloomington: Indiana University Press.

EVIL EYE

An ancient belief, still commonly held, that certain people can cause damage to something valuable by gazing at it. In the third century A.D., Heliodorus wrote, "When anyone looks at what is excellent with envious eye he fills the surrounding atmosphere with a pernicious quality and transmits his own envenomed exhalations into whatever is nearest him." The common view, as illustrated here, has been that the eye is a source, rather than a receptor, of light and other emanations.

It is widely reported that envy is the motivating force behind the evil eye. That is, the malefactor sees something desirable, experiences envy, and emits a force from his or her eyes that damages the object. It is usually people (most often, a child or a bride), crops, or animals that are harmed, and it is the excellent or beautiful that is most at risk. Also, the damage is usually specific, not general; the evil eye is responsible for children failing to thrive or cows going dry, rather than for famines or droughts. The person who casts the evil eye, however, may not be aware that he or she has this power. Often, suspicion falls on particular individuals because they are outsiders or have a distinctive look to them, such as eyes of a color different from the norm or eyebrows that meet in the middle.

Because envy motivates the evil eye, expressions of admiration may be seen as dangerous and either be avoided or followed by reciting a formula (e.g., "God bless him") or committing an act intended to avert the evil, such as spitting on or touching the supposed victim (or even touching spit onto the victim) or perhaps giving the praised object to the person who praised it. Reversals are often reported: One may deliberately call a pretty child ugly or, in dressing a child, turn a sock inside out so as to ward off the evil eye.

Such protection takes many forms. Often, something is put near or on the enviable object to draw the gaze, such as a smudge of dirt or a colored ribbon or thread. The colors and objects vary by area: a black goat's tail or pot in Morocco, blue beads in rural Greece, the red *mano cornuta* (or horned hand) among Italian-Americans. Because the point of these objects is either to attract the gaze—thereby deflecting it from the vulnerable person or animal— or to ward off the evil, both the obscene (phalluses) and the holy (crucifixes) can serve for protection.

Paul Barber

See also Assault, Supernatural; Belief, Folk; Medicine, Folk.

✳✳✳✳✳✳✳✳✳✳✳✳✳✳✳✳✳

References

Blum, Richard, and Eva Blum. 1970. *The Dangerous Hour: The Lore of Crisis and Mystery in Rural Greece*. New York: Charles Scribner's Sons.

Dundes, Alan, ed. 1981. *The Evil Eye: A Folklore Casebook*. New York: Garland.

Elworthy, Frederick Thomas. [1895] 1989. *The Evil Eye*. Reprint. New York: Bell.

Heliodorus. *Aethiopicorum libri decem*. 1923. Translated into English as *An Aethiopian Romance* by T. H. Underdowne and revised by F. A. Wright. New York: Dutton.

Maloney, Clarence, ed. 1976. *The Evil Eye*. New York: Columbia University Press.

Westermarck, Edward. 1926. *Ritual and Belief in Morocco*. London: Macmillan.

EVOLUTIONARY THEORY

That theory that proposed that human culture evolved through stages over time according to a uniform and logical process. This theory was a mainstay of folklore and anthropological studies in the late nineteenth and early twentieth centuries, especially in Great Britain. It related to folklore in that folk traditions were seen as "survivals" from earlier times that could help in understanding earlier culture and the development of culture.

As the science of anthropology developed in the mid-nineteenth century, it adopted an evolutionary paradigm. Although Charles Darwin (1809–1882) did not originate thinking about evolution, his ideas in natural history were influential. Especially with his second landmark book, *The Descent of Man* (1871), Darwin—as well Thomas Henry Huxley (1825–1895), who played a key role in making known and defending Darwin—put human beings into the context of biological processes by establishing that humans did not remain apart from physical evolution. Knowledge of fossils and prehistory also was expanding in this period, and physical anthropology was developing as a field of study. The knowledge gained in these areas of study provided a new scientific basis for indicating not only the antiquity of the human race but also a continuous process of human advancement. As the science of anthropology took shape, its proponents logically looked to evolution (though evolution remained a controversial idea in society at large) as a theory that could unify their endeavors, for those who shaped the science of anthropology sought to understand the origin and historical development of humanity and of such social institutions as law, religion, and morality.

Anthropologists came to see human societies as evolving through stages, generally referred to as savagery, barbarism, and, finally, civilization. The American Lewis Henry Morgan (1818–1881) argued, for example, in *Ancient Society* (1877), that humans were a unitary group and followed certain logical steps in their advancement. He further divided the first two stages of development into lower, middle, and upper and associated particular developments with each stage (such as the use of pottery with the stage of lower barbarism).

Folklore became an aspect of evolutionary theory primarily through the writings of Sir Edward Burnett Tylor (1832–1917), commonly regarded as the principal founder of cultural anthropology, and his disciples, notably Andrew Lang (1844–1912). Tylor sought to show that culture evolved and to establish a comparative method for examining that process of development. In part, he was attempting to refute the positions of certain religiously oriented thinkers who argued that some humans had, in fact, devolved from a higher state to a lower one. This conception ultimately went back to the biblical story of a fall from grace but was primarily the result of an upsurge in the

European Christian missionary activity that followed upon the expansion of colonial empires. For missionary work, it became useful to believe not only that the "savages" who were being evangelized had degenerated but also that, as a result, they were incapable of spiritual progress without the help of the "superior" white race. Tylor relentlessly amassed evidence to prove the consistent evolution of culture and to bolster the optimism of those who believed in the inevitability of human progress.

Tylor thought that archaeology could fill in some of the gaps in the history of early humanity but that it could provide knowledge only about material culture, not about the mental and spiritual sides of human development. To fill in that particular gap, "survivals" were to be examined, compared, and analyzed. Like Morgan, he believed that nothing happens but in logical sequence. In terms of material culture, all evidence pointed to evolution. None of his contemporaries, he reasoned, would use an arrow as the ultimate weapon, and one could readily see how the bow was replaced by the gun and how simple tools were replaced by more complex ones. The same was true of nonmaterial aspects of culture, he asserted. Tylor began by asking how it was that a whole range of customs, beliefs, and processes that did not seem sensible for present-day culture nonetheless existed. The answer, he said, was because these were "survivals" from earlier cultural stages (just as antique bows and arrows were left over from earlier days). These beliefs and customs made perfect sense in their own historical context, and though society in effect evolved around them as a result of "sound judgment and practical reason," the beliefs and customs remained (because of some "efficient cause," such as psychological dependence) and could guide us in understanding that earlier context. According to Tylor, survivals were "processes, customs, opinions . . . which have been carried on by force of habit into a new state of society different from that in which they had their original home, and they thus remain as proofs of an older condition of culture out of which a newer has evolved" (from his 1871 work, *Primitive Culture*). Tylor probably took a clue from the work of earlier scholars and antiquarians who had established that folk traditions were "remains" or "relics" of earlier times and hence historical documents. Jacob and Wilhelm Grimm, for example, had argued that the folktales in their famous collection were among the last surviving pieces of an older Germanic culture. But Tylor established a more systematic and more informed and sophisticated conception within the grand framework of evolution.

Though Tylor looked at a wide range of cultural facts (particularly in *Primitive Culture*), many of the aspects of culture he examined were folkoric elements, for these often involved actions or ideas that seemed not to be fully rational in terms of the perspective of the educated elite of the late nineteenth century and that also could be presumed archaic. In looking at culture, Tylor developed a comparative method that involved fixing upon a particular presumed survival and then examining whatever information was available on manifestations of culture that appeared to be similar and related. Information might be drawn from older written materials, travel literature, the accounts of human behavior (which were multiplying as the result of observations made in colonial contexts), or other sources. The information might be about the mores of historical peoples, newly encountered, contemporary "primitives" (who had not yet evolved as fully as had civilized peoples), or European peasants (who, of course, were coming to be considered the prime repositories of folklore). Once the information had been amassed and compared, conclusions could be drawn as to what was revealed about earlier culture, how earlier humans thought and acted, and how certain aspects of culture had developed.

Tylor's best-known analysis, which explained a custom very widespread even today, aptly illustrates his method—his explanation of why we say "God bless you" (or something similar) when someone near us sneezes. Looking to a number of cultural contexts, he noted various similar customs. A member of the Zulu (who believe themselves surrounded by both good and evil spirits) said, when he sneezed, "I am now blessed; the ancestral sprit is with me," and asked for favors. He believed that a good sprit had entered his body. At one time in Guinea, when someone important sneezed, others would fall to their knees, kiss the earth, clap hands, and wish each other prosperity. Pacific islanders considered a sneeze a bad omen. Among the Amakosa, a sneeze was an occasion to call upon divine ancestor spirits. The Zulu also saw in repeated yawning a sign of approaching spirit possession. Persians ascribed yawning to demoniac possession, and modern Moslems, Tylor added, avoided yawning because the devil could leap into one's mouth when it was opened so wide. A Jewish proverb said, "Open not thy mouth to Satan," Celtic sneezers might be carried off by fairies, and members of a certain religious sect would spit and blow their noses to expel evil spirits that they might have breathed in. And the Zulu saw a sick person's sneeze as a sign of impending recovery. This compilation of information on oral lore, customs, and beliefs indicated to Tylor that at an earlier stage of culture, men and women believed that spirits could enter and leave the human body through the facial orifices. Though we have evolved beyond such a belief, its vestiges survive, enabling us to understand something of its former existence and nature. Tylor thought that, though culture evolved logically along certain lines in a progressive direction, not all individual cultures evolved at the same pace. Thus, even at the end of the nineteenth century, societies could be found where the older ideas persisted, not merely as isolated customs (as with European peasants) but also as more integrally related to a context. Hence, information about the "primitive" groups of the world was believed to be particularly valuable in understanding human development.

Tylor's ideas were used by the ethnologist John Lubbock (Lord Avebury) (1834–1913) and popularized by the writer James Anson Farrer (1849–1925), and they greatly influenced a generation of folklorists. Andrew Lang in particular sought to develop the study of folklore along the lines of Tylor's theories and methodology, and other folklorists of his day had their work shaped by Lang's interpretations of Tylor. Tylor had never suggested that folklore was necessarily always a survival or that all survivals fell into the realm of folklore, but Lang was to declare that folklore was the science of survivals and to argue that folkloric survivals were the virtual equivalents of geological fossils and archaeological artifacts. In *Custom and Myth* (1893), he insisted that the very motive for folkloric study was to look for an "irrational and anomalous custom" and to compare it to a context "where a similar practice is found . . . in harmony with the manners and ideas of the people among whom it prevails." If, for example, we could not understand why the ancient Greeks danced with serpents in their hands, we could look to Native Americans who still did so. We could understand why the Native Americans practiced the custom through ethnological investigation and thus "conjecture that similar motives once existed among the ancestors of the Greeks." In folklore, according to Lang, we would find "the remains of ideas as old as the stone elf-shots, older than the celt or bronze." And folklore was to be studied primarily because it could help us to understand the early state of mind from which we evolved.

Among other folklorists, Edwin Sidney Hartland (1848–1927) looked for traces of ancient religious rituals in later folk narratives, and Edward Clodd (1840–1930) examined the folktale best known by its German name—"Rumpelstiltskin"—to understand ancient name magic. The powerful influence of Tylor and Lang's evolutionary perspective is perhaps best seen in how matter of factly it was incorporated into Charlotte Burne's *Handbook of Folklore* (1914), intended as a basic introduction to the subject. The introduction emphasized that, through folklore, "the study of rudimentary economic and political forms should enable us to trace the *lines of development* of the several systems of civilized nations from their source" (emphasis added).

The evolutionary perspective was not without its critics, even among those who adhered to its basic tenets. Sir George Laurence Gomme (1853–1916) argued, in a number of publications, that his colleagues were not sufficiently tied to specific historical or geographic contexts, implying that to be concerned only with cultural evolution in the broadest terms was to deal with the development of human institutions too vaguely.

As the twentieth century moved ahead, the evolutionary perspective in folklore studies declined in interest and importance. Folklorists and anthropologists increasingly realized that the equivalences that had been drawn between customs and beliefs in widely diverse cultures had often been based on tenuous similarities. Careful fieldwork frequently showed that seemingly similar cultural practices had very different functions and meanings for different groups and thus really could not be compared to yield evolutionary explanations. Further, written sources that described various cultures had often been accepted uncritically and in fact presented very incomplete or misunderstood data. In general, particularly because of the trend toward fieldwork (which gave individual researchers profound insights into contemporary, whole societies), there was a move away from historical and genetic explanations and toward functional and symbolic ones.

Frank de Caro

See also Anthropological Approach; Comparative Mythology; Myth-Ritual Theory.

✳✳✳✳✳✳✳✳✳✳✳✳✳✳✳✳✳✳

References
Dorson, Richard M. 1968. *The British Folklorists: A History*. London: Routledge and Kegan Paul.
Dorson, Richard M., ed. 1968. *Peasant Customs and Savage Myths: Readings from the British Folklorists*. 2 vols. Chicago: University of Chicago Press.
Evans-Pritchard, Edward. 1981. *A History of Anthropological Thought*. New York: Basic Books.
Harris, Marvin. 1968. *The Rise of Anthropological Theory: A History of Theories of Culture*. New York: Thomas Y. Crowell.
Hodgen, Margaret T. 1936. *The Doctrine of Survivals*. London: Allenson.
Lowie, Robert H. 1937. *The History of Ethnological Theory*. New York: Holt, Rinehart, and Winston.
Voget, Fred W. 1975. *A History of Ethnology*. New York: Holt, Rinehart, and Winston.

EXEMPLUM

A short narrative using real or at least realistic events to illustrate a cultural belief. This type of story was recognized as one of the basic devices of rhetorical argument by Aristotle, who termed it *paradiegma* (paradigm). Roman rhetoricians such as Cicero and Quintilian termed such stories *exempla*, a word originally meaning "a clearing in the woods." The genre was based on historically verifiable incidents but often included frankly fictional narratives that involved animals (fables), comparisons drawn from ordinary life (parables), or realistic stories that were not verifiable but that *could* have happened.

Exempla became an important element in Christian homelitic writing, as preachers used such stories in sermons to lay audiences. As a guide, anthologies of such narratives circulated, beginning in the sixth century with Pope Gregory the Great's *Homiliae in Evangelia*. Such "example-books" enjoyed their greatest vogue from 1200 to 1400, when they circulated in Latin and many vernacular languages. The *Gesta Romanorum* was one of the most influential of these works in Latin, and several of Chaucer's *Canterbury Tales*, including the Pardoner's, Summoner's, and Monk's Tales, drew on vernacular versions from this genre.

Originally drawn from classical histories or saints' lives, these collections eventually included many traditional narratives. Hence, example-books have proven a useful guide to anecdotal oral narratives of the medieval and Renaissance periods. Exempla were used for a wide variety of purposes: Preachers could employ historical figures as good or bad examples to exhort listeners to practice virtue and avoid sin. But many more contemporaneous examples were used to frighten them with the wages of blasphemy.

One such exemplum was "The Dancers of Kolbeck," about individuals who insisted on dancing and singing outside a church during mass and were punished by being compelled to dance without stop for an entire year. Word of this event, which allegedly occurred in 1012, spread rapidly through Europe as a sermon exemplum, and beggars even carried letters claiming to prove that they had themselves been participants in the event. A number of other horrific events, such as accounts of bleeding hosts, accidental cannibalism, ritual sacrifice, and *penis captivus* (imprisoned penis), also are found in collections of exempla.

As time passed, however, these collections began to emphasize stories intended to amuse rather than scare. Hence, many examples in later collections resemble jokes or fabliaux, illustrating the sexual lapses of monks or priests and their parishioners. However, traditional narratives remain an integral part of folk preaching, and Véronique Campion-Vincent, in fact, has argued that contemporary legends are best understood as the historical descendants of exempla. Indeed, many such legends continue to circulate as sermon illustrations: Televangelist Oral Roberts recently used a version of "The Vanishing Hitchhiker" as an exemplum.

Bill Ellis

See also Belief Tale; Legend.

✳✳✳✳✳✳✳✳✳✳✳✳✳✳✳✳

References

Campion-Vincent, Véronique. 1976. Les Histoires exemplaires. *Contrepoint* 22–23 (December):217–232.

Keller, John Esten. 1949. *Motif-Index of Mediaeval Spanish Exempla*. Knoxville: University of Tennessee Press.

Lyons, John D. 1989. *Exemplum: The Rhetoric of Example in Early Modern France and Italy*. Princeton, NJ: Princeton University Press.

Mosher, Joseph Albert. 1911. *The Exemplum in the Early Religious and Didactic Literature of England*. New York: Columbia University Press.

Tubach, F. C. 1969. *Index Exemplorum: A Handbook of Medieval Tales*. FFC 204. Helsinki: Academia Scientiarum Fennica.

EXORCISM

The practice of dislodging an evil spirit from a person, often by prayers or charms. Sickness may be seen as the entrance of a malevolent spirit into the afflicted person, and this spirit may be removed to the exorcist (via transference), who temporarily suffers the pain of the patient. Commonly, the process begins with some type of divination, which identifies the spirit and determines propitious signs for a cure. Both exorcist and patient typically put themselves into a hypnotic state by means of drumming, dancing, and various other forms of either sensory stimulus or sensory deprivation.

The exorcist expels the spirit not through his or her own efforts but through an appeal to a higher authority. He or she typically talks to the demon rather than the patient and tries to induce it, by threats or commands and in the name of the friendly deity or spirit, to leave the possessed person. The demon (or demons) may balk or even strike a deal, demanding something in return for leaving the victim, and it is not uncommon for the exorcist to profit from such transactions. Cures by exorcism may be quick and efficient, although in the Christian church, cures by a single application of exorcism appear to have been rare; more often, exorcisms have lasted days, weeks, months, and even years. If the first attempt at exorcism is unsuccessful, the methods used may become more extreme. Sometimes, patient and healer negotiate the cure. Carmen Blacker describes a Japanese healer telling a patient that she will have to undergo the "cold water austerity" night and morning for 21 days; then, when the patient rejects this solution, the healer proposes the recitation of the Heart Sutra every night at half past midnight.

Often, the exorcism ceremony involves a laying on of hands. In the Japanese Mahikari cult, the hands are held up, palms out, and thought to exert a curing force on the subject. Here, as in many other belief systems, if the subject becomes physically sick and vomits, a purification is believed to be taking place.

Historically, outside observers have often viewed curing rituals by exorcism as a kind of flimflam intended to bedazzle gullible subjects and spectators. Such a view supposes the curer to exist in another belief system than the audience. As Seth and Ruth Leacock have pointed out in their study of an Afro-Brazilian cult, "Far from being a ceremony designed to mystify the uninitiated, a curing ritual is a performance before a knowledgeable and critical audience." Moreover, some contemporary scholars have recognized that, just as modern medicine has advantages over traditional medicine, the converse is also true. Winston Davis has observed that "although [modern medicine] can diagnose terminal illnesses with terrifying accuracy, it may offer no hope at all for their cure." Traditional curing, involving the exorcism of spirits, virtually always offers the possibility of a cure; it is steadfastly optimistic. And

An exorcism in Siberia. The ghost of Amo enters a house, called by the bound exorcist. Exorcism is common to many religions, from shamanism to Christianity.

it is difficult to deny the evidence from modern scholars, such as William Sargant, that a good deal of real curing, in particular of psychological trauma, does take place in curing ceremonies.

Paul Barber

See also Assault, Supernatural; Medicine, Folk; Possession; Shamanism.

✳✳✳✳✳✳✳✳✳✳✳✳✳✳✳✳✳

References

Blacker, Carmen. [1975] 1986. *The Catalpa Bow: A Study of Shamanistic Practices in Japan.* London: Unwin Paperbacks.

Davis, Winston Bradley. 1980. *Dojo: Magic and Exorcism in Modern Japan.* Stanford, CA: Stanford University Press.

Kemp, Patience. 1935. *Healing Ritual: Studies in the Technique and Tradition of the Southern Slavs.* London: Faber and Faber.

Leacock, Seth, and Ruth Leacock. 1972. *Spirits of the Deep: A Study of an Afro-Brazilian Cult.* Garden City, NY: Doubleday Natural History Press.

Sargant, William. 1974. *The Mind Possessed: A Physiology of Possession, Mysticism and Faith Healing.* New York: Lippincott.

Walker, Sheila S. 1972. *Ceremonial Spirit Possession in Africa and Afro-America.* Leiden, Netherlands: E. J. Brill.

F

FABLIAU

A humorous narrative treating a sexual or obscene theme. Originally a medieval French dialect variant of *fable* (meaning story or folktale), the term *fabliau* first appeared as a self-descriptive label in a series of verse poems at the end of the twelfth century. Though literary in nature, these works may have been intended for oral performance; in any case, they incorporated themes from contemporary oral tradition. About 125 poetic versions of fabliaux survive from medieval French, and the genre was also used in Boccaccio's *Decameron* (circa 1350) and Chaucer's *Canterbury Tales* (circa 1380), two literary works that mimic oral storytelling sessions.

Critics of the literary fabliaux agree that their distinctive style and structure reflect awareness of an underlying folk narrative aesthetic. Fabliaux tend to be brief, focusing on an intrigue that is usually erotic in nature. The typical plot structure involves some kind of deception or ruse perpetrated by the main figure, who uses the ruse as license to commit some kind of cultural misdeed. In medieval examples, the story presents women as unfaithful and sexually unrestrained (modern examples often invert this stereotype). The story's style is characterized by irony, both in its commentary on events and in its use of elevated, "courtly" language to describe sexually explicit or scatological events. Many narrative themes found in the literary fabliaux have since been collected from oral tradition in many cultures.

In contemporary American folklore, fabliau-type narratives survive in several distinct formal genres. Themes of female infidelity appear in ballads such as "Our Goodman" (Child 274), in which a husband finds more and more evidence of his wife's infidelity, such as "a head lying on my pillow." He is, however, pacified by her witty explanations of the incriminating items as common household objects, such as "a cabbage head." Many folktales and jokes also continue fabliau themes: the widespread "Rabbit Herd" (AT 570), for instance, shows the hero using a magical object to seduce a king's daughters and wife and humiliate the king, often by having him kiss his donkey's rump.

Some medieval fabliaux begin by asserting the "truth" of the story that follows; hence, it is interesting that some contemporary legends relate fabliau-like plots that "really happened." In "The Nude Birthday Party," for example, a would-be philanderer is taken home by his secretary. Assuming a conquest is forthcoming, he strips naked and jumps through a doorway, only to find that his wife and friends have arranged a surprise party for him there.

The fabliau in the modern sense is best characterized as a narrative that plays with the bounds of public decency, both in its subject and in its style. Most of the modern examples deal with potentially obscene themes but in ways that leave them suitable for "polite" mixed audiences. Thus, perhaps the hallmark of the genre is its ability to deal with sexual or scatological topics through clever indirection rather than directly through vulgarity.

Bill Ellis

See also Erotic Folklore; Joke; Obscenity; Scatology.

✳✳✳✳✳✳✳✳✳✳✳✳✳✳✳✳✳

References

Bédier, Joseph. 1894. *Les Fabliaux: Études de littérature populaire et d'histoire littéraire du moyen âge.* Paris: E. Bouillon.

Hines, John. 1993. *The Fabliau in English.* London: Longman.

Lacy, Norris J. 1993. *Reading Fabliaux.* New York: Garland.

McCarthy, William Bernard. 1993. Sexual Symbol and Innuendo in "The Rabbit Herd" (AT 570). *Southern Folklore* 50:143–154.

Randolph, Vance. 1976. *Pissing in the Snow and Other Ozark Folktales.* Urbana: University of Illinois Press.

Shenck, Mary Jane Stearns. 1987. *The Fabliaux: Tales of Wit and Deception.* Amsterdam: John Benjamins.

Fabulate

A migratory legend that does not reflect personal experience but instead is told principally for entertainment. Coined in 1934 by C. W. von Sydow, the term *fabulate* was intended as a contrast to *memorate*, a narrative reflecting an individual's contact with the supernatural. Fabulates, Sydow said, may have some elements based in experience, "yet they do not immediately come from these, but from a mental image that has originated from elements of this type in which they, so-to-say, crystallized." To this extent, he concluded, the events narrated in the fabulate "could not have actually happened in the form that they take in the telling; they were shaped much more by the creative art of the folk."

Sydow used the term *fabulate* to refer to a variety of narratives, many of which would be classified as legends in the Anglo- American system. But his sense of the term extended beyond the belief legend to jocular narratives, such as the "person fabulates" told about Germanic trickster Till Eulenspiegel: These would more likely be termed *Schwanks* or jocular tales today. Sydow's vague sense of the concept's defining trait, Juha Pentikäinen has noted, led succeeding folklorists to use the term in confusingly diverse senses. It has been used as everything from a global term for *all* prose narration to a more judgmental label for a story that "clearly contains invented, empirically unbeliev-able elements."

This emphasis on the notion that fabulates were objectively untrue has raised opposition. Such a claim assumes that truth-falsehood claims, particularly about supernatural events, can be resolved objectively by folklorists. So the term *fabulate* (like the related term *urban legend*) may imply the collector's belief that the teller is ignorant or irrational.

But Sydow's essential distinction between stories as stories and stories as evidence for belief has some basis. Gillian Bennett has contrasted urban legends told with conviction and those told more for their value as narratives, and she found a large number of rhetorical differences. For her, legends told "for laughs" may be morphologically identical to folktales, and so there is value to identifying them and considering them separately from narratives told "for true." However, the term *fabulate* then becomes a descriptive term appropriate only to a given performed text; given changes in context, the same informant may relate the same events "for laughs" or "for true." Judgments about the empirical truth behind the narrative simply become irrelevant.

Pentikäinen, like most European scholars, restricts the term *fabulate* to narratives that subordinate matters of belief to the artistic form of the performance itself. Hence, the fabulate is essentially a narrative developed and standardized by the narrator's desire to tell an entertaining story. Characters included may take roles or perform actions that are more in line with characters in *Märchen* than in belief legends. Consequently, the fabulate is a better guide to a culture's storytelling aesthetic than to living folk belief.

Bill Ellis

See also Legend.

✳✳✳✳✳✳✳✳✳✳✳✳✳✳✳✳✳

References

Bennett, Gillian. 1988. Legend: Performance and Truth. In *Monsters with Iron Teeth*, eds. Gillian Bennett and Paul Smith. Sheffield, England: Sheffield Academic Press.

Hand, Wayland D., ed. 1971. *American Folk Legend: A Symposium*. Berkeley: University of California Press.

Pentikäinen, Juha. 1973. Belief, Memorate, and Legend. *Folklore Forum* 6:217–241.

von Sydow, Carl Wilhelm. [1948] 1978. *Selected Papers on Folklore*. New York: Arno Press.

FAKELORE

Fabrication claiming to be authentic folklore; also called *pseudofolklore*. Richard M. Dorson introduced the concept in an article in the *American*

Mercury in 1950. For more than two decades, Dorson remained the principal American academic voice fighting against the spread of fakelore. He wrote against literary, commercial, and political producers of fakelore, and within folkloristics both his definition of fakelore and his often polemical broadsides against what he perceived as dishonest popularization and distortion remained largely uncontested. Only during the 1980s did the reflexive examination of folklore's history lead to a theoretical examination of the concept, as well as to an effort to integrate "fakelore" into the larger European discourse on "folklorismus."

Fakelore was subsumed into a number of emergent discussions on the ways in which folklore, politics, and commerce intertwine. Folklore has always been a powerful agent in nationalistic attempts at cultural legitimation, and similarly, ethnic groups have revived and invented traditional heritage to enhance their cultural identity in multicultural societies or to bolster their claims for political independence. The globalization of the Western market economy has led to the further commodification of folklore, that is, the preparation of seemingly unique cultural goods or performances for mass consumption. Given the pervasive nature of the politics of culture, labeling such processes as "fakelore" and excluding them from study could eventually no longer be upheld.

Dorson's initial targets were Paul Bunyan stories, which he portrayed as not based on oral tradition but as literary fabrications potentially designed to boost the image of the lumber industry. Next, Dorson attacked Benjamin A. Botkin's highly successful *Treasury of American Folklore* and its regional spin-offs. Using the treasuries as an example of fakelore, Dorson postulated a distinction between properly documented oral folklore collected from real people in the field and rewritten materials that, from Dorson's point of view, misled the gullible public. During the Cold War period (1960s through 1970s), Dorson expanded his attack to include not only commercial fakelore but also the ideological manipulation of folklore, targeting in particular Communist creations of workers' lore. He also used his arguments in an unsuccessful attempt to forestall a legislative cut of federal funding for folklore research by presenting the properly trained folklorist as an important servant of democracy, capable of obtaining genuine knowledge of the traditional ideas of the anonymous millions.

Dorson's formulation made manifest the latent authentic-versus-fake dichotomy in folklore studies and put it to use in solidifying folklore's place in academe. He portrayed folklorists as the only academics capable of recognizing, documenting, and analyzing folklore: Subjected to interpretation by the untrained, authentic folk materials would be spoiled. In the 1980s, the analytic attention paid to the notion of tradition seriously undermined the assumed dichotomy between the genuine and the fake. This debate has brought forth an appreciation for the created, invented aspects and the often consciously strategic deployment of all expressive culture in settings such as ethnic festivals, political propaganda, and, most pervasively, market settings such as the tourist trade.

Regina Bendix

See also Authenticity; Folklorismus/Folklorism; Invented Tradition.

✳✳✳✳✳✳✳✳✳✳✳✳✳✳✳✳✳✳✳

References

Bendix, Regina. 1988. Folklorismus: The Challenge of a Concept. *International Folklore Review* 6:5–15.

Dégh, Linda. 1977–1978. Grape-Harvest Festival of Strawberry Farmers: Folklore or Fake? *Ethnologia Europaea* 10:114–131.

Dorson, Richard M. 1950. Folklore and Fakelore. *American Mercury* 70:335–343.

———. 1962. Folklore and the NDEA. *Journal of American Folklore* 75:160–164.

———. 1976. *Folklore and Fakelore: Essays toward a Discipline of Folk Studies.* Cambridge, MA: Harvard University Press.

Dundes, Alan. 1985. Nationalistic Inferiority Complexes and the Fabrication of Folklore. *Journal of Folklore Research* 22:5–18.

Fox, William. 1980. Folklore and Fakelore. *Journal of the Folklore Institute* 17:244–261.

Handler, Richard, and Jocelyn Linnekin. 1984. Tradition, Genuine or Spurious. *Journal of American Folklore* 97:273–290.

Miller, Frank J. 1991. *Folklore for Stalin: Russian Folklore and Pseudofolklore of the Stalin Era.* New York: Sharpe.

FAMILIAR

A theological designation for an auxiliary spirit used by a witch. Familiars usually appeared in animal form, and in the learned view, they were quite simply demons. The familiar was supposed to have been either given to the witch by the Devil himself or purchased from another witch. The notion of the familiar is not, as has been claimed, peculiar to England; indeed, it is so widespread that it must be said to be one of the regular elements in the belief in witches. In Scandinavia, there was a particular type of familiar that sucked the udders of cows and afterward regurgitated the milk for the witch; this familiar took the shape of a hare. Familiars are depicted in medieval church murals, testifying both to the popular nature and the age of the belief.

One special popular feature was that one did not need to be a witch to have such a demon in one's service; one simply had to make sure to be rid of the familiar before one died, as one's soul was otherwise lost. Familiars also played a prominent role in learned magic, where they often constituted a salable commodity. Indeed, Adam Squire, master of Balliol College in Oxford

Familiars were believed to be demons in disguise. Appearing primarily in animal form, these auxiliary spirits were thought to be given to witches to by the devil himself.

in the 1570s, almost lost his job for allegedly selling gamblers a "fly" that would guarantee success at dice.

Gustav Henningsen

See also Witchcraft.

❀❀❀❀❀❀❀❀❀❀❀❀❀❀❀

References

Parrinder, Geoffrey. 1958. *Witchcraft*. Harmondsworth, England: Penguin.

Thomas, Keith. 1971. *Religion and the Decline of Magic*. New York: Scribner.

FAMILY FOLKLORE

Traditional expressive behavior and its products that are transmitted by family members to family members and that pertain to relatives, family events, and family ways of being and doing. Family folklore includes stories, jokes, and songs about family members and events, as well as the ways relatives share those items with one another; festivals the family celebrates, such as religious and national holidays; festivals that celebrate family, such as weddings, reunions, and funerals; foods, cooking instruction, ways of eating, and ways of gathering to eat within a family; family naming traditions; a family's ways of dancing; expressions and gestures a family uses; visual records of family life, such as arrangements of items inside and outside the home, photographs, photograph albums, videotapes, embroideries, and quilts; occupational, song, story, and craft traditions carried on within a family; and fieldwork methods used within family settings.

A review of folklore studies shows that folklorists have long been welcome in the homes of families. Once back at their desks, however, most professional and amateur folklorists before the 1970s discussed the rich material they collected in families as regional or ethnic, religious or occupational folklore. They approached the family as a source of folklore materials, not as the subject of their study.

Several folklorists, though, published a family story or two as "family folklore," usually without analysis, in state journals. Then, in 1958, Mody Boatright put out the call to folklorists to collect "an important source of living folklore"—the "family saga," featuring individual stories with a variety of themes that preserved a family's way of seeing itself in history. Interested in a generic approach, Boatright asked what forms and motifs made up the family saga. A second mode of inquiry, a small-group approach, came in 1961 when Kim Garrett suggested that every family that recognizes itself as a unit has its own traditions, including stories, taboos, and expressions.

In the mid-1970s, the study of family folklore burgeoned. Folklorists' growing interest in folklore as communication within and between small groups, their continuing interest in contextual studies, the focus of feminist scholarship on women's lives and concerns, the consideration of more privatized forms of folklore such as personal experience narratives, and the airing of Alex Haley's television series *Roots* exploring his African-American family's history, all contributed to an increased interest in studying the family as the subject of its own folklore.

FAMILY AS A FOLK GROUP

Many family folklorists follow the lead of L. Karen Baldwin, who suggested in 1975 that the family is not just a group that generates its own traditions but rather is the "first folk group, the group in which important primary folkloric socialization takes place and individual aesthetic preference patterns for folkloric exchange are set." The family, then, is the social base of folklore.

FAMILY GROUP AND DIFFERENTIAL IDENTITY

Families offer the opportunity to study how folklore differs within a group since most families exist as conglomerates of subgroups—as households and "branches," as gender and age subgroups, as subgroups of individuals who resemble or act like each other, and as other subgroups that families identify as important to themselves. Family members often tell different versions of the same story for their own, compelling reasons. Age groups within families have differing traditions. And families constantly change as they add in the traditions of other families through marriage. Thus, different racial, ethnic, and class traditions must be negotiated as newlyweds from two different ethnic groups, for example, prepare to celebrate Christmas or Hanukkah for the first time. When children are born, all titles and some nicknames in the family— father, mother, sister, and brother—shift in one great generational wave to grandfather, grandmother, aunt, and uncle. Hugo Freund's work with one family's Thanksgiving reveals how relatives' differing perceptions of celebration create different meanings for the same family event.

FAMILY FOLKLORE AND IDIOSYNCRATIC FORMS

Much of folklore is identified by its transmission and variation through time and space. One family's folklore, though, includes much material that does not resemble any other family's material in content, though it may be similar in structure. For example, most families have words they use for taboo subjects, such as the words a child may use to indicate a need to go to the bathroom. One family's word may never occur in any other family, but structurally, most families have such words. Thus, family folklore offers the chance to study materials in this more individualistic, privatized sphere.

ADDING NEW TOPICS TO FAMILY FOLKLORE STUDY

Because many of the first family folklorists worked with their own families and were bound by family requests for privacy, little discussion of the painful side of family life emerged until researchers turned to studies of many different families outside of their own. The work of Steven Zeitlin and others in the Family Folklore Section of the Smithsonian Institution's Festival of American Folklife, for example, shows how families experiencing divorce or the abandonment of the family by one parent used ritual and storytelling in the reconstruction of their single-parent family. Elizabeth Stone, interviewing families across the United States, records family members' stories of abuse and abandonment and how individuals transformed stories about hurtful relatives into stories that could lead them down new and healthier paths of life.

INCORPORATING NEW MATERIALS
INTO FAMILY STUDIES

In addition to photographs, videotapes, embroideries, quilts, and other documents of family history and tradition, family folklorists in the last few years have studied newspaper obituary poems, miscarriage announcements in African-American newspapers, and narratives about family pets.

WIDENING THE DEFINITION OF FAMILY

Although most published family folklore studies to date concern extended families made up of heterosexual, married couples and their children, all families are open for study, including one-person families with support systems, two-person families, single-parent families, blended families, households of nonrelated friends, and gay and lesbian families. Joseph Goodwin's research on gay male families, for example, discusses the structure of gay families as that based almost totally on levels of closeness, in addition to the families' use of nicknames, jokes, stories, and ritual. Increased study of family and homosexual folklore may bring explorations of ceremonies of commitment and now-legal marriage ceremonies in Denmark and Norway, as well as work on the effect of AIDS on homosexual and heterosexual family traditions. Artificial insemination, egg-donor programs, surrogate mothers, and increasingly complicated adoption cases also may affect family folklore discussions.

Scholars of family folklore have much to contribute to the current national melee over "family values," a phrase used to signal "conventional, heterosexual family" rather than a discussion of any family's moral and ethical foundations. Family sociologist Jan Dizard discusses the debate—and its underlying paradox—well:

> On the one hand, unconventional families are accused of threatening the values and commitments for which families stand. On the other hand, when they attempt to demonstrate those very same commitments and values, they are denied the opportunity to incorporate them into their lives. For most Americans, familism and the conventional family are so strongly associated that efforts to infuse nontraditional living arrangements with the values and commitments of familism seem like yet another assault on the already fragile family. Thus cohabitation, communal and group living arrangements, and homosexual couples, no matter how deep and conventional the sentiments and commitments that bind them, are judged by many as a threat to the very idea of family.

Future scholarship may see more family folklorists writing of the traditions alive in all forms of committed relationships.

INDICATORS OF SOCIETAL CONCERNS

Many folklorists see family traditions, especially stories, as indicators of broader, societal concerns. Stanley Brandes has studied family narratives of lost fortunes that are told by white, lower-middle and working-class citizens of the United States. He finds that the tellers of such stories are seeking to deflect onto ancestors the anxiety they feel for not achieving top economic success in a capitalist country that maintains that all individuals can become economically successful. Alan Dundes, Ed Walraven, and Janet Langlois have considered parent-child interaction as it is configured in dead-baby jokes, stories of child throwaways, and legends of La Llorona in a garbage dump. Kathryn Morgan has discussed her African-American family's use of their stories as "buffers" to protect the family from the ravages of racism. And Marilyn White has used her African-American family stories to describe interracial and intraracial relationships in rural Virginia from 1865 to 1940.

TRANSMISSION

How traditional materials are passed down through extended families has been the subject of several studies. Lucille Burdine and William McCarthy, for example, show how folklore is not handed down "en bloc" from person to person, generation to generation; rather, each element of folklore finds its own sympathetic channel of transmission in different members of a family. Other studies by Baldwin, Margaret Yocom, and Jane Beck discuss gender differences in transmission, as well as attitudes of ownership and deference between generations.

GENDER STUDIES

Folklorists have been concerned about the ways in which gender intersects with family folklore. Some have turned to evidence of gender-role stratification in stories. Others have explored how gender difference influences folkloric forms and processes. Baldwin and Yocom, for example, have studied how family stories and storytelling differ among men and women in their Anglo-American and Pennsylvania-German families. They found women's telling to be more collaborative, interruptable, and filled with information and genealogy; men's telling, by contrast, is often uninterrupted and more competitive, the story beginnings and endings are formally marked, and the men's stories "make a point worth telling." Yocom has explored gender differences in the transmission of woodcarving and knitting skills in an extended Anglo- and French-Acadian family in Maine. And Thomas Adler's study of gender and family food preparation shows that men's cooking traditions in the family are often limited to one or two celebratory meals a week—often Sunday breakfast—or to outdoor meals with meat; women cook the mundane, every-day, diversified meals.

PROCESSES WITHIN ONE FAMILY

Studies that look closely at how one particular family performs its traditions have interested scholars such as Patrick Mullen and Susan Roach, who have looked at how a couple encounters and resolves conflicts within family story-telling and how quilting reveals the cultural and familial values of the family. Many studies already mentioned, such as those by Baldwin, Freund, White, and Yocom, also explore traditions and traditional processes within one family.

GENRE STUDIES

Folklorists have puzzled over the generic nature of family stories and how the individual stories relate to the whole of a family's repertoire. Family stories, often brief and elliptically told, usually do not take the form of legend, folk-tale, or memorate. Boatright and William Wilson see family stories as anec-dotes that together comprise a larger "saga" or "novel" and emphasize that each anecdote must be heard in light of other anecdotes for the larger story to be understood. Baldwin stresses that a family's "narrative" is a "composite of changing and interchangeable parts" and that since no one person is the ulti-mate source, many people must be heard so their "piece" of the "narrative composite" can be included. Zeitlin details the similar themes that sweep through family stories in the United States, themes that revolve around the characters of family members (heroes or heroines, survivors) and the transi-tions in family histories (migrations, courtships).

FAMILY AS CONTEXT

Folklorists primarily interested in craft, occupation, and storytelling have turned to families as sources of information. Though family folklore is not the subject of their studies, much about the family context of tradition can be seen in their work. Beck's work with the last basketmaker in Vermont's Sweetser family and John Burrison's study of the pottery families in Georgia show how families amassed and passed on their skills.

FAMILY FOLKLORE FIELDWORK

Discipline-wide and regional fieldwork guides have often described family folklore fieldwork as ideal for the novice folklorist because it is easily gathered. As more and more folklorists began working with their own families, however, the discussion about such personal-family fieldwork deepened. Baldwin, Yocom, and Susan Sherman have detailed concerns particular to such fieldwork; they and others also have challenged the notion of "objectivity" as an impossible goal for anyone and a counterproductive one for personal-family fieldworkers in particular. These scholars have discussed the importance of including one's self in family activities as a member of the group, as well as the necessity of exploring and using one's "involvements"; anthropological discussions of reflexivity and reciprocity and feminist reminders that the personal is political reinforce family fieldworkers' positions.

FICTION WRITING, NONFICTION WRITING, AND NEOTRADITIONAL STORYTELLING

Fiction writers, writers of biography and autobiography, and, more recently, neotraditional storytellers who perform for paying audiences incorporate family folklore in their presentations. Michael Ondaatje's description of a day's storytelling in his Ceylonese family provides a taste of the riches to be found in such creations:

> We will trade anecdotes and faint memories, trying to swell them with the order of dates and asides, interlocking them all as if assembling the hull of a ship. No story is ever told just once. Whether a memory or funny hideous scandal, we will return to it an hour later and retell the story with additions and this time a few judgements thrown in. . . . All day my Aunt Phyllis presides over the history of good and bad Ondaatjes and the people they came in contact with. Her eye . . . will suddenly sparkle and she will turn to us with delight and begin "and there is another terrible story."

Studying family folklore, then, offers researchers the opportunity to preserve and enjoy family traditions and to question the concept of family and the nature of folkloric creations.

Margaret R. Yocom

See also Feminist Perspectives on Folklore Scholarship; Gay and Lesbian Studies and Queer Theory; Gender.

✵✵✵✵✵✵✵✵✵✵✵✵✵✵✵✵

References

Baldwin, L. Karen. 1985. "Woof!" A Word of Women's Roles in Family Storytelling. In *Women's Folklore, Women's Culture*, eds. Susan Kalcik and Rosan Jordan. Philadelphia: University of Pennsylvania Press.

Beck, Jane. 1983. Newton Washburn: Traditional Basket Maker. In *Traditional*

Craftsmanship in America, ed. Charles Camp. Washington, DC: National Council for the Traditional Arts.

Boatright, Mody C. 1958. The Family Saga as a Form of Folklore. In *The Family Saga and Other Phases of American Folklore*, eds. Mody C. Boatright, Robert B. Downs, and John T. Flanagan. Urbana: University of Illinois Press.

Brandes, Stanley. 1975. Family Misfortune Stories in American Folklore. *Journal of the Folklore Institute* 12:5–17.

Burdine, Lucille, and William B. McCarthy. 1990. Sister Singers. *Western Folklore* 49:406–417.

Dizard, Jan E., and Howard Gadlin. 1990. *The Minimal Family*. Amherst: University of Massachusetts.

Goodwin, Joseph P. 1994. My First Ex-Lover-in-Law: You Can Choose Your Family. *Southern Folklore* 51:35–47.

Morgan, Kathryn L. 1980. *Children of Strangers: The Stories of a Black Family*. Philadelphia: Temple University Press.

Ondaatje, Michael. 1984. *Running in the Family*. London: Picador.

Sherman, Sharon R. 1986. "That's How the Seder Looks": A Fieldwork Account of Videotaping Family Folklore. *Journal of Folklore Research* 23:53–70.

Stone, Elizabeth. 1988. *Black Sheep and Kissing Cousins: How Our Family Stories Shape Us*. New York: Penguin.

Wilson, William A. 1991. Personal Narratives: The Family Novel. *Western Folklore* 50:127–149.

Yocom, Margaret R. 1982. Family Folklore and Oral History Interviews: Strategies for Introducing a Project to One's Own Relatives. *Western Folklore* 41:251–274.

Zeitlin, Steven J., Amy J. Kotkin, and Holly Cutting Baker. 1993. *A Celebration of American Family Folklore: Tales and Traditions from the Smithsonian Collection*. Cambridge, MA: Yellow Moon.

Feast

Ceremonial meal that reaffirms social solidarity while providing culinary gratification to an assembly of individuals. Feast is the sensuous and symbolic display of food and a quintessential metaphor for a surfeit of consumption. As eating beyond the point of satiation, feasting is forever shadowed by its obverse: socially mediated hunger, food asceticism, or fasting. In addition, feasting often has sacrificial connotations. Humans may share with deity in the consumption of specially consecrated foods and ritually slain divine victims.

Although food customs and habits vary significantly from culture to culture, feasting often occurs at key points in a community's food supply cycle: sowing, first fruits, harvest, beginning of the hunting season, and so on. Cosmic events relating to the agricultural cycle also may cause feasting: the change of seasons, the new year, or the appearance of moon, sun, or stars. As symbolic imitation of hypertrophy, bountiful feasting provides a means for redistributing an abundant harvest or kill in the spirit of celebration and thanksgiving. Mundane work responsibilities usually are suspended on feast days, during which hard work is compensated by the meal.

Feasts often are scheduled to mark special periods in the life of the individual. Here, banqueting is one element in a complex of celebratory events, including ceremony, procession, or dance. Birth/circumcision/naming, weaning, confirmation/initiation, marriage, retirement, anniversaries, or funerals are some of these life-passage events. Solidarity between social groups may be invoked through exchanges that include food sharing, as in the case of potlatch funerary feasts of the Native American cultures of the Northwest.

The term *feast* (from the Latin *festum*) has a specialized use to describe major celebrations in organized religion and is often used interchangeably with *festival*. Feast days are devoted to celebrations of faith and are times to refrain from profane work (aside from the work of food preparation). Feasts usually occur in relationship to fasts or other penitential observances in the religious calendar.

Until the latter part of the twentieth century, writers on Jewish tradition used *feast* to discuss the weekly Sabbath, the first day of the new lunar month, and a number of annual calendar celebrations: Rosh Hashanah, Sukkoth, Pesach, Shavout, Hannukah, and Purim.

Agape, or love feast, is the shared celebration of early Christians that is connected with Eucharist practices today. The Western Christian church distinguishes several festal cycles. Sanctoral or movable feasts such as Easter or Pentecost fall on different dates each year. Temporal feasts, also called feasts of obligation, occur on fixed calendar dates. These include Sundays; the feasts of: Nativity (Christmas), Circumcision, Epiphany, Ascension, Holy Trinity, and Corpus Christi; and the five official saint's feasts: St. Joseph, Sts. Peter and Paul, Assumption, All Saints, and the Immaculate Conception. Localities celebrate feast days for their patron saints; families may celebrate on individual members' name days. Other feasts in world religions are scheduled at the conclusion of the fast of Ramadan (Islam), at key points in the life of Buddha (Buddhism), and during Holi (Hindu).

Feasting emphasizes excess and bodily processes and is usually a feature of festival representations and allegories. The medieval feast of Fools coincided with the feast of Circumcision. This temporary inversion of social strata burlesqued ecclesiastical procedures, often featuring the election of a Lord of Misrule, Pope of Fools, or Boy Bishop.

Recent scholars have highlighted the importance of gender in food practices. Food is often controlled by women and may be used by women to control and transform the self and effect change within a community.

Emily Socolov

See also Custom; Festival.

✳✳✳✳✳✳✳✳✳✳✳✳✳✳✳✳✳✳

References

Bakhtin, Mikhail. 1984. *Rabelais and His World.* Bloomington: Indiana University Press. Originally published as *Tvorchestvo Fransua Rable*, Moscow, 1965.

Bynum, Caroline Walker. 1987. *Holy Feast and Holy Fast: The Religious Significance of Food to Medieval Women.* Berkeley: University of California Press.

Kan, Sergei. 1989. *Symbolic Immortality: The Tlingit Potlatch of the Nineteenth Century.* Washington, DC: Smithsonian Institution Press.

MacCulloch, J. A. 1925. Feasting. In *Encyclopaedia of Religion and Ethics*, ed. James Hastings, pp. 801–805. New York: Charles Scribner's Sons.

Weiser, Francis X. 1958. *Handbook of Christian Feasts and Customs: The Year of the Lord in Liturgy and Folklore.* New York: Harcourt, Brace.

FEMINIST PERSPECTIVES ON FOLKLORE SCHOLARSHIP

A theoretical reorientation of the discipline that encompasses the gendered nature of all aspects of this academic pursuit, bringing to light the hitherto neglected area of women's expressive behavior and entailing the construction of new paradigms centered on women's experience both as folklorists and as folk.

Conscious and unconscious gender biases, especially biases against women, have pervaded the discipline of folklore since its inception. Such a statement could be made about many academic disciplines. This is quite likely a reflection of the patriarchal nature of Eurocentric society more generally, but it is a particularly disturbing commentary on a field of study that purports to pay scholarly attention to individuals and groups who have been marginalized or entirely omitted from historical and contemporary written records. Gender as a particular area of theoretical discourse usually has been neglected by folklorists, both male and female, but a few folklorists, mostly women, have begun to rectify this imbalance in their research, scholarly writing, and teaching. Although gender and women's studies are not synonymous, feminist theory's emphasis on women's roles can be employed to highlight men's roles as well. For instance, emphasizing the distinction between the traditional expressive behaviors of women and men illuminates a folk group's particular ideas about gender as a whole. In contrast, the virtual equation of men with culture in folklore theory leads not just to the absence of folklore *about* women and performed *by* women but also to the omission of that which is specifically men's lore. The solution to this dilemma from the perspective of feminist scholarship entails challenging implicitly male-oriented paradigms and constructing alternative and oppositional models that incorporate women's experience within the realm of folk culture and performance.

It has been a slow and arduous task to change the historical orientation of the discipline: Few publications focusing on gender and folklore appeared between 1975 and 1995, and those that have seen print frequently have been subjected to such extensive revision and scrutiny that their timely publication has been impossible. Furthermore, such scholarly writings—and more specifically those produced by women—are largely missing from the "folklore canon," that is, the academic books and articles accepted by folklorists as most significant to the field, such as those that appear on the Ph.D. reading lists of major folklore departments, those that receive major disciplinary awards, or those that are included in histories and overviews of the field. Courses on gender and folklore, women and folklore, and/or men's folklore are not regarded as standard offerings for most folklore curricula, and the number of female faculty hired by the major folklore departments and programs is insufficient. Not only do the majority of folklorists neglect the gendered aspects of folklore but folklorists who are women also find themselves in situations that involve the unequal distribution of status and power.

It is of special note that this disciplinary gap persists at a time when most folklorists are proudly discussing new directions in the theoretical underpinnings of the discipline, explicitly questioning who they are and what they study. Edited volumes with titles containing phrases such as "new perspectives," "frontiers of folklore," and "urban folklore" and consisting mostly of contributions by men have been partially responsible for changing the shape of the field. Academic discourse during the early and mid-1970s gave rise to an innovative approach to the study of folklore—one that emphasized performance and context, behavior, communication, and process, bringing about more dynamic definitions of "the folk" and "folklore" and breaking down rigid traditional genres so that they became regarded as emergent, flexible social phenomena rather than normative, mutually exclusive categories. Still, although this new perspective has greatly benefited the practical and theoretical study of folklore in general, it has done little to give the folklore of and about women its proper place in folklore scholarship. An exciting new concept of social group now characterizes the discipline, but attention to gender and related concerns is often lacking; the voices of women, both folklorists and folk, remain largely unheard, and their presence goes unnoticed in this reexamination of the field.

Nevertheless, some academics have developed gender-oriented scholarship in folklore and in other related disciplines, such as anthropology and literary studies. The recent evolution of feminist folklore scholarship was initiated by the concerted and successful attempt to identify and validate women's traditions, leading to the political interpretation and reinterpretation of these gender-based materials and paving the way for the utilization of feminist theory at all levels of data collection and analysis.

Folklorists who employ feminist theory and methodology have incorporated these advances in their research, promoting new ways of thinking that have radically changed their disciplinary outlook. Although genre theory and the performance perspective enriched the discipline with their event-centered focus, feminist theory examines a broader range of materials and acknowledges a greater time depth in the generation of folklore. For feminist folklorists, the study of folklore begins when a member of a folk group initially learns how to produce or perform an item of expressive behavior, and it continues as this individual decides to actively engage in artistic communication and, later, to transmit this traditional knowledge to others. A feminist folklore perspective thus explores the initial production of folklore and its subsequent reproduction. Moreover, it includes the criticism of the final product and/or performance, as well as a critique of the entire procedure by the folk community and the folklorist. This approach also entails an investigation of the creation and/or re-creation of particular forms of folklore by various performers in different time periods. It is, therefore, significant to recognize that, in addition to highlighting the role of women in the study of folklore, bringing to light entire areas that have been neglected, feminist folklorists have also significantly changed the theoretical orientation of the discipline.

Earlier folklore publications had indirectly addressed the omission of gender and women, but it was not until the 1975 publication of *Women and Folklore* (initially a special issue of the *Journal of American Folklore*) that women's folklore began to be explicitly regarded as a legitimate area of academic focus. Challenging inflexible boundaries and predetermined dichotomies such as those promoting the oppositions of male/female, public/private, culture/nature, and powerful/powerless, the various authors in this volume examine the prevalent images of women and the subsequent genres through which women's creativity has been viewed, suggesting that new images, genres, and disciplinary directions need to be developed in the study of women and folklore. This collection of exploratory essays falls short of providing a theoretical basis for the study of women's expressive behavior, but it does serve to focus attention on an emergent area of folklore research. Unfortunately, this book was not followed by the spate of scholarly articles on gender theory or women's expressive behavior that the volume editor, Claire R. Farrer, and the other essayists had hoped to spark; few articles or books providing a theoretical framework for an approach to women's or men's expressive behavior specifically or artistic communication between men and women more generally have been published to date. The twenty years following Farrer's 1975 publication, however, witnessed the formal establishment of the women's section within the American Folklore Society and the subsequent publication of a newsletter devoted to furthering gender awareness within the discipline. Furthermore, conferences, symposia, books, and scholarly articles specifically addressing gender, women's folklore, and feminist perspectives are beginning to become recognized components of the study of folklore, both nationally and internationally.

Published in 1982, *Spiders and Spinsters: Women and Mythology*, written by Marta Weigle, details the images of women in men's myths and rituals in Eurocentric societies, calling for further research that would look to different cultural traditions and women's mythologies within those traditions. There is a wealth of fascinating material in this book, but it suffers from the lack of both critical commentary and an overall synthesis. Echoing the earlier assertions of the essayists in Claire R. Farrer's edited volume, Weigle's writings, including her subsequent 1989 volume, emphasize the need for a reevaluation of traditional categories and the establishment of new and more flexible paradigms that would give women a significant role in the symbolic realm of cultural mythologies and folklore. In fact, this latter point illustrates a major contribution of feminist theory to folklore scholarship in general and is characteristic of all of the publications and conferences discussed in this essay; they are solidly situated within the contemporary, "postmodern" discourse that eschews arbitrary divisions in all areas of knowledge, affirming instead the multidimensional aspects of experience.

Frank A. de Caro's *Women and Folklore: A Bibliographic Survey* (1983) is a useful compilation of publications on women's folklore, folklore about women, and related topics, taking great strides in the task of reclaiming this body of lore for serious consideration and study. Similarly, "Women and the Study of Folklore" (1986), written by Rosan A. Jordan and Frank A. de Caro, provides an excellent overview of this topic, although it is limited primarily to verbal art. This article locates discussions of women and folklore in the public arena, appearing in *Signs*, a well-respected journal that incorporates academic perspectives from diverse disciplines. Although most of the material included in these two publications is not distinctive from a theoretical or methodological perspective, there are far-reaching philosophical implications in such attempts to create and validate the scholarship of gender, discovering differences not *between* folk groups and genres but *within* such groups and preestablished expressive categories.

Recently, other folklore scholars, primarily women, have published articles that highlight women's roles as folk performers and practitioners of artistic communication, whether the communicative mode is verbal or visual. They have challenged the idea that domestic implies insignificant, revealing the considerable power women wield in the private domain, as well as the way in which women's forms of folklore reflect the serious concerns of community life. Furthermore, they discuss situations in which women are effective performers in the public sphere and focus on material items created by women that serve as symbols of cultural identity and social continuity. Finally, these scholars point out that women's humor is not only distinctive but also artfully used to negotiate gender interactions, often in a manner that is oppositional or contestational.

Ten years after the publication of Farrer's groundbreaking edited volume, *Women's Folklore, Women's Culture*, edited by Rosan A. Jordan and Susan Kalcik, appeared. The various articles included in this book serve to describe women's expressive behavior in a variety of situations, emphasizing its frequently collaborative nature. This volume is divided into sections that portray the private world of women and discuss performances within the intimate circle of family and friends, as well as outlining the neglected areas of women's folklore in the public arena. Additionally, the essayists examine the dynamic interactions between public and private spheres and between male and female activities. The book as a whole, however, neither characterizes "new genres" that are exclusively women's genres nor provides a coherent theoretical framework within which to analyze these genres. A number of significant categories of women's folk performances are missing from this book, as is serious attention to the claim that "studying women makes a difference." This volume achieves significance by focusing scholarly attention on women and folklore, pointing to the need for the development of a theoretical framework that would give the folklore of and about women its proper place in folklore scholarship and laying the foundation for new orientations in data collection and analysis.

In 1985, concerned that feminist theory was not being adequately addressed or developed within contemporary folkloristics, a group of women scholars associated with the Folklore Program at the University of Texas, Austin, with the help of many other folklorists, formulated and organized an all-day symposium on folklore and feminist theory. This conference stemmed from the belief that folklore, like all academic disciplines, operates within certain paradigms that reflect the ideologies of the intellectual climate in which they originate. Thus, in the mid-1980s, gender bias in all forms of folklore scholarship—publication, fieldwork, research, teaching—was reflected in the absence of the female and/or the dominance of the male, or it appeared as the denigration of female experience, all of which served the interest of male privilege. The need to address specifically such biases within the formal organization of folklore as a discipline was regarded as a necessary step in reorienting disciplinary concerns. The conference, officially entitled "A Feminist Retrospective on Folklore and Folkloristics," was part of the 1986 annual meeting of the American Folklore Society in Baltimore, Maryland. The purpose of the symposium was to discuss and debate not only women's folklore (as had a 1979 women and folklore conference held at the University of Pennsylvania and several earlier publications on women's folklore) but also and more importantly to introduce feminist theory into the study of folklore and bring folklore scholarship to bear on feminist theory. This included the consideration of why and how the analysis of women's lore changes the study of all folklore, why studying any folklore with a feminist eye makes a difference, and how folklorists can contribute to the growing body of feminist scholarship that is developing in many disciplines.

Several publications directly or indirectly arose from this conference: special issues of the *Journal of American Folklore* ("Folklore and Feminism," edited by Bruce Jackson) and the *Journal of Folklore Research* ("Feminist Revisions in Folklore Studies," edited by Beverly J. Stoeltje) and two edited volumes, *Feminist Theory and the Study of Folklore* and *Feminist Messages: Coding in Woman's Folk Culture*. The conference and these publications have been variously successful in meeting the challenges as noted above.

Published in 1993, *Feminist Theory and the Study of Folklore*, edited by Susan Hollis, Linda Pershing, and M. Jane Young, is a collection of essays that achieves a new degree of sophistication in feminist approaches to the study of folklore, calling into question not only case studies but also any theoretical formulations that fail to take into account women's experiences and perceptions. This book is an attempt to provide a resource for those seeking a more comprehensive view of the contemporary research being conducted on the intersection of feminist theory and folklore. Additionally, many of the authors in this volume focus on women's expressive genres to further an understanding of symbolic modes that serve women's own interests, distinguished by a process-centered female aesthetic. The book is divided into three parts, each addressing a specific theme and beginning with a theoretical introduction to that theme: feminist reexaminations of folklore theory and the development of the discipline, new ways of looking at the types of materials conventionally studied by folklorists, and the exploration of hitherto unapproached or little recognized materials in folklore and feminism.

Joan Radner's edited volume, *Feminist Messages: Coding in Women's Folk Culture*, also published in 1993, takes a somewhat different direction, specifically addressing the coding of women's folklore forms rather than the more general application of gender-related concepts to the study of folklore. The articles in this volume draw extensively on feminist theory, pointing to a need for increased communication with feminist theorists across a variety of disciplines and conducting research in diverse cross-cultural areas. Coding, as it is defined by these authors, refers to women's frequently disturbing or subversive expressions of resistance, necessitated by the fact that their lives often have been controlled, dominated, or made peripheral by men. Such coding—sometimes deliberate, sometimes unconscious—is essentially ambiguous, conveying diverse messages and thus serving to protect women from those who might find such messages rebellious, and, therefore, threatening. Radner's book is especially significant in providing a framework within which to interpret women's creative practices that have conventionally gone unnoticed or have been devalued by the dominant culture.

All of the conferences and publications mentioned since the appearance of Farrer's 1975 edited volume concentrated primarily on folklore of and about women in cross-cultural contexts; the need for new images, genres, and approaches; and the significance of using feminist theory to illuminate this area of inquiry. Although the political implications of the analysis and interpretation of women's folklore was central to these discussions, the political nature of the fieldwork conducted by folklorists remained largely ignored until the 1990 publication of "Folklore Fieldwork: Sex, Sexuality, and Gender," a special issue of *Southern Folklore* edited by Camilla A. Collins. As indicated by the title of this particular issue, the authors emphasize gender in general and from a number of perspectives rather than choosing only to highlight women's traditional artistic behavior. Furthermore, this publication delineates the way in which folklorists discuss gender issues in their fieldwork, constructing personal anecdotes frequently passed on informally. Thus, the distinction between "folk" and "folklorist" becomes blurred as the folklorists create their own folk narratives to describe their experiences doing fieldwork. The various essays make it clear that sex, sexuality, and gender influence the methods employed by folklorists to collect data, as well as the sorts of phenomena that they choose to investigate. Here, too, rigid categories and boundaries are discarded so that the divisions between subject and object or folklore and folklorist become more fluid as fieldwork is characterized as made up of conversations rather than formal interviews and the establishment of friendships rather than reserved relationships. These authors stress the subjectivity of such interactions, pointing out the necessity for folklorists to recognize their own feelings and perceptions, as well as those of their interviewees. They also insist that folklorists give more thought to the attitudes and perspectives generated by the gendered aspects of all fieldwork, recognizing the need to negotiate and interconnect both men's and women's domains in the field.

Fieldwork that incorporates the perspective of "the other" is crucial to contemporary folklore scholarship, just as it is to the "new ethnography" in anthropology. Certainly folklorists must revise the authoritative way in which they write about "the folk," but first they must examine the biases inherent in their fieldwork. Too often, perhaps because of their academic status, folklorists are blinded by their own perceptions of their importance, entirely unable to perceive the frequently negative manner in which they are regarded by those they presume to study. Seen from this viewpoint, folklorists take on a more marginal position; rather than valiant discoverers of folk performances— usually male "heroes" who compose romantic tales of their fieldwork exploits—they are sometimes unwanted intruders who are skillfully managed in the everyday lives of the folk who themselves are fully aware of the value and power of their artistic behavior. Feminist scholars suggest that folklorists listen more carefully to what their informants say about the interrelationship of form, function, and audience in their expressive behavior—a point that is significant to the discipline in general, over and above gender considerations.

The volumes on gender or women and folklore published since the mid-1970s demonstrate that folklore and feminism can contribute a new understanding of women's marginal status in defined cultural contexts. On the one hand, women's marginality in male-dominated cultures is imposed; patriarchy enforces the rule of men from the very center of a society's organization (i.e., through the formation of laws, customs, and institutions that promote and preserve male domination) and leave women at its periphery. On the other hand, marginality encourages women to remain detached from the status quo. Their peripheral position may point to an incompatibility with established norms, leading to innovation, especially in expressive domains, and the development of alternative theories of knowledge. In reviewing women's expressive culture from a feminist stance, it is particularly important to look for ways in which women use their marginal status to creatively undermine the prevailing system by the invention or maintenance of traditions that signal the viability and appropriateness of a different way of thinking and behaving.

The feminist lens has given folklorists a new way of looking at the gendered nature of their endeavors. It is, however, important to recognize that other sorts of social concerns have remained largely unaddressed. For instance, none of the publications discussed here sufficiently incorporate feminist approaches to the folklore of women who are often doubly marginalized in our society by virtue of other factors in addition to their gender; these include women of color, lesbians, women with disabilities, and older women, who seldom have been the focus of folklore research. Although attempts have been made to fill this gap, it remains an area of folklore scholarship that deserves considerable attention in the near future. Furthermore, the broader focus on gender that feminism brings to folklore also points to the necessary inclusion of other critical concerns, such as the intersection of gender with race, class, ethnicity, and sexual identity.

Although feminist theory can expand and enhance folklore theory by generating new analytical models, this is not a one-way process. Women's folklore also can supply new data for and encourage the development of theories that define feminist scholarship. By providing a cross-cultural spectrum of traditional texts in various aesthetic media that address gender-related difference, women's folklore significantly enriches the examination of sexual difference in regard to hierarchy, power differentials, and the political imagination. A claim for the value of traditions that formulate female-centered considerations presupposes a need to allow folklore to speak for and about the traditions of women's difference as this is manifested in their material life activities and then given voice through a range of expressive means. These specific features of women's material life activity carry important consequences for understanding and constructing all social relations, not just those that pertain to a particular arena of traditional production or performance. Thus, both folklore and feminism conjoin in their mutual validation of the regenerative aspects of social and cultural life, augmenting relationships of power with humanistic insights.

M. Jane Young

See also Family Folklore; Gender.

✳✳✳✳✳✳✳✳✳✳✳✳✳✳✳✳✳

References

Collins, Camilla A., ed. 1990. Folklore Fieldwork: Sex, Sexuality, and Gender. *Southern Folklore* 47(1).

de Caro, Frank A. 1983. *Women and Folklore: A Bibliographical Survey*. Westport, CT: Greenwood.

Farrer, Claire R., ed. 1975. *Women and Folklore*. Austin: University of Texas Press.

Hollis, Susan, Linda Pershing, and M. Jane Young, eds. 1993. *Feminist Theory and the Study of Folklore*. Chicago: University of Illinois Press.

Jackson, Bruce, ed. 1987. Folklore and Feminism. *Journal of American Folklore* 100(938).

Jordan, Rosan A., and Frank A. de Caro. 1986. Women and the Study of Folklore. *Signs: Journal of Women in Culture and Society* 11(3):500–518.

Jordan, Rosan A., and Susan J. Kalcik, eds. 1985. *Women's Folklore, Women's Culture*. Philadelphia: University of Pennsylvania Press.

Radner, Joan N., ed. 1993. *Feminist Messages: Coding in Women's Folk Culture*. Chicago: University of Illinois Press.

Stoeltje, Beverly J., ed. 1988. Feminist Revisions in Folklore Studies. *Journal of Folklore Research* 25(3).

Festival

A periodic celebration representing through traditional observances, performances, rituals, and games the worldview of a culture or social group. Virtually universal, festival may be the most complex social and symbolic event to persist in tradition. The etymology of the term goes back to the Latin word *festum*, originally meaning "public joy, merriment, revelry" and used commonly in the plural form, which suggests that a plurality of activities and celebrations characterized the festival from ancient times.

From the Latin *festa* derive the Italian *festa* (singular), the Spanish *fiesta*, the French *fête*, the Portuguese *festa*, and the Middle English *feste*, *feste dai*, *festial*. The word *festival* was originally in English (and in French) an adjective indicating the quality of certain events, before it became the noun for the celebrations themselves. Secondary meanings of the term in different languages indicate single structural elements of the festival or forms of it. *Festa* were sacred offerings in Latin, a *feast* in English is a very abundant and joyful meal, a *fiesta* in Spanish is a public combat to show ability and bravery, a *festa* in Romanian is a malicious and humorous prank, and a *fête* in French is also a birthday celebration or simply a rather formal party. In current usage, *festival* may mean: a time of celebration, sacred and/or secular; the annual celebration of a special person or a memorable event; the harvest of a particular crop; a series of performances in the fine arts, dedicated to an author or genre or mass medium (i.e., Shakespeare, music, cinema); or generic gaiety and cheerfulness.

In the social sciences, *festival* commonly means a periodic celebration composed of a multiplicity of ritual forms and events, directly or indirectly affecting all members of a community and explicitly or implicitly showing the basic values, the ideology, and the worldview that are shared by community members and are the basis of their social identity.

Festivals traditionally have been classified as either secular or religious. This conventional dichotomy, made popular by Émile Durkheim, is currently maintained in the social sciences, despite the fact that each type of festival usually includes several elements of the other. Secular festivals resort to religion and metaphysics to deepen their impact and social significance; religious festivities always have political and economic aspects.

An equally widespread classification opposes rural and urban festivals. The former are commonly considered older, celebrating fertility and based on myths; the latter are conceived to be more recent, celebrating prosperity and based on history and legend.

A recent classification based on social and class structure tries to distinguish among festivals given by the people for themselves, those given by the establishment for its own sake, those given by the people for the establishment, and finally, those given by the establishment for the people. The latter category, by far the largest, is the modern counterpart of the *panem et circenses* (bread and circuses) of Roman times.

Festive behavior has been studied as a social phenomenon having one basic characteristic. Most scholars have underlined transgression and symbolic inversion as typical of social behavior at festival times; others have remarked that festival finally confirms the world-as-it-is, and festive behavior parallels daily behavior, although in a more stylized form and with greater symbolic meaning.

Both approaches appear correct, albeit incomplete. Since festival periodically renews culture by representing chaos and cosmos, nature and culture, disorder and order, it requires the simultaneous presence of all basic behavioral models of daily life (even if inverted, stylized, disguised, or distorted by the

Enactments of ritual drama are part of many festivals. Actors often wear elaborate masks and costumes to represent mythological characters, as in this depiction of an Indonesian festival demon.

festive scenery). In fact, both symbolic inversion and intensification are present in festive behavior, together with the element of symbolic abstinence from work, play, study, or daily habits. During festival times, people who participate do something they usually do not, abstain from something they normally do, carry to the extreme consequences behaviors regulated by measure and common sense in daily life, and invert standard patterns of social life. Abstinence, reversal, intensification, and trespassing are all basic facets of festive behavior.

A morphology of festivals must indicate their minimal units and the possible sequences of these units. Such a theoretical operation, analogous to what Russian folklorist Vladimir Propp did for the constituent parts of the folktale, may aim at an archetype accounting for all festivals or, more accurately, at "oicotypes" accounting for a class of festivals of the same kind or from the same cultural area. Studies have indicated that several constituent parts seem to be quantitatively recurrent and qualitatively important in festive events. These units, building blocks of festivals, can all be considered ritual acts or "rites" since they happen within an exceptional frame of time and space, and their meaning is considered to go beyond their literal and explicit aspects.

The framing ritual that opens the festival is one of *valorization* (or for religious events, *sacralization*), which modifies the usual and daily function and meaning of time and space. To serve as the theater of the festive events, an area is reclaimed, cleared, delimited, blessed, adorned, and forbidden to normal activities.

Similarly, daily time is modified by a gradual or sudden interruption that introduces "time out of time," a special temporal dimension devoted to special activities. Festival time imposes itself as an autonomous duration, not so much to be perceived and measured in days or hours but to be divided internally by what happens within it from its beginning to its end, as in the "movements" of mythical narratives or musical scores. The opening rite is followed by a number of events that belong to a limited group of general ritual types. There are *rites of purification* and cleansing by means of fire, water, or air or those rites that are centered around the solemn expulsion of some sort of scapegoat, carrying the "evil" and "negative" out of the community. If the rationale of these rites is to expel the evil that is already within, as in exorcisms, other complementary rites aim at keeping away the evil perceived as a threat coming from outside. These rites of safeguard include various forms of benediction and procession of sacred objects around and through significant points of the festival space setting, in order to renew the magical defenses of the community against natural and supernatural enemies.

Rites of passage, in the form described by Arnold van Gennep, mark the transition from one life stage to the next. They may be given special relevance by being part of a festive event. These may include forms of initiation into age groups, such as childhood, youth, and adulthood, or initiation into occupational, military, or religious groups and even public execution of criminals.

Rites of reversal through symbolic inversion drastically represent the mutability of people, culture, and life itself. Significant terms that are in binary opposition in the "normal" life of a culture are inverted. Sex roles are inverted in masquerade, with males dressing as females and females dressing as males; social roles are inverted as well, with masters serving their serfs. Sacred and profane spaces also are used in reverse.

Rites of conspicuous display permit the most important symbolic elements of the community to be seen, touched, adored, or worshipped; their communicative function is "phatic," of contact. Sacred shrines, relics, and magic objects are solemnly displayed and are visited by individuals from within the immediate boundaries of the festival or pilgrims from faraway places. In sacred processions and secular parades, the icons and symbolic elements are instead moved through space specifically adorned with ephemeral festive decorations, such as festoons, flower arrangements, hangings, lights, and flags. In such perambulatory events, along with the community icons, the ruling groups typically display themselves as guardians and keepers and as depositories of religious or secular power, authority, and military might.

Rites of conspicuous consumption usually involve food and drink. These are prepared in abundance and even excess, made generously available, and solemnly consumed in various forms of feasts, banquets, or symposia. Traditional meals or blessed foods are among the most frequent and typical features of festival since they are a very eloquent way to represent and enjoy abundance, fertility, and prosperity. Ritual food is also a means to communicate with gods and ancestors, as expressed in the Christian belief that Christ is present in the sacred meal of Communion, the Greek tradition that Zeus was invisibly present at the ritual banquets of the Olympic Games, or the practice of the Tsembanga Maring people of New Guinea who raise, slaughter, and eat pigs for and with the ancestors. In far less frequent cases, as in the Native American potlatch, objects with special material and symbolic value are ritually consumed, wasted, or destroyed.

Ritual dramas are usually staged at festival sites, as rites have a strong tie to myths. Their subject matter is often a creation myth, a foundation or migratory legend, or a military success particularly relevant in the mythical or historical memory of the community staging the festival. By means of the drama, the community members are reminded of their golden age, the trials and tribulations of their founding members in reaching the present location of the community, the miracles of a saint, or the periodic visit of a deity to whom the festival is dedicated. When the sacred story is not directly staged, it is very often hinted at or referred to in some segments or events of the festival.

Rites of exchange express the abstract equality of the community members, their theoretical status as equally relevant members of a *communitas*, a community of equals under certain shared laws of reciprocity. At the *fair*, money and goods are exchanged at an economic level. At more abstract and symbolic levels, information, ritual gifts, or visits may be exchanged; public acts of pacification, symbolic *remissio debitum* (remission of debt) or thanksgiving for a grace received may take place in various forms of redistribution, sponsored by the community or a privileged individual who thus repays the community or the gods for what has been received in excess.

Festival typically includes *rites of competition*, which often constitute its cathartic moment in the form of games. Even if games are commonly defined as competitions regulated by special rules and with uncertain outcomes (as opposed to rituals, the outcomes of which are known in advance), the logic of festival is concerned with the competition and the awards for the winner; the rules of the game are canonic, and its paradigm is ritual. The parts or roles are assigned at the beginning to individuals as equal and undifferentiated "contestants," "hopefuls," or "candidates." Then, the development and the result of the game create among them a final hierarchical order—either binary (winners and losers) or by rank (from first to last). Games show how equality may be turned into hierarchy. Besides games in the strict sense, festival competitions include various forms of contests and prize giving: electing the beauty queen; selecting the best musician, player, singer, or dancer, individual or group; or giving an award for a newly improvised narrative or work of art of any kind or for the best festive decorations. By singling out its outstanding members and giving them prizes, the group implicitly reaffirms some of its most important values.

Athletic or competitive sporting events include individual or collective games of luck, strength, or ability. These have been considered "corruptions" of older plays of ritual combats with fixed routine and obligatory ending, such as the fight between Light and Darkness representing cosmogony; fights of this type were then progressively historicized and territorialized into combats between, for example, the Christians and the Moors or representative individuals, with the champion (literally meaning the sample) carrying the colors of the whole group.

In their functional aspects, these types of games may be seen as display and encouragement of skills, such as strength, endurance, and precision, that were required in daily work and military occupations; this was, for instance, the rationale of medieval mock battles. In their symbolic aspect, festival competitions may be seen as a metaphor for the emergence and establishment of power, as occurs when the "winner takes all" or the winning faction symbolically takes over the arena (or the city) in triumph.

At the end of the festival, a *rite of devalorization*, symmetrical to the opening rite, marks the conclusion of the festive activities and the return to the normal spatial and temporal dimension of daily life.

It is obvious that one should not expect to find all the morphological elements listed here in each festival, just as one should not expect to find all of Vladimir Propp's "functions" present in every fairy tale. A complete festival morphology will correspond to the complete festive cycle, and several of its parts will form the configuration of each of the actual festive events. This fragmentation of the festive complex into events distributed all along the calendrical cycle follows the course of history and its trends of centralization and decentralization in social life, as well as the interplay of religious and secular powers and their division in the running of social and symbolic life and its "collective rituals." Furthermore, in today's Western and Westernized cultures, larger and often more abstract and distant entities try to substitute themselves for the older, smaller, tightly woven communities as reference groups and centers of the symbolic life of the people. Today, we try to bring the audience close to the event by means of the mass media or to bring the event close to the audience by delegating smaller entities, such as the family, to administer the event everywhere at the same time; we also may try to fragment the old festivals into simpler festive events centered on one highly significant ritual. Such fragmentation is seen in the United States, where the ritual meal is the focus of Thanksgiving, the exchange of gifts is the highlight of Christmas, and excess is the hallmark of New Year's. Military might and victories are celebrated on the Fourth of July, and civic pride is championed at the Rose Parade. Carnivalesque aspects underlie Mardi Gras and Halloween. And symbolic reversal is nowhere more evident than in the demolition derby. Even the tradition of dynastic anniversaries is present, modified though it may be, in celebrations of George Washington's and Abraham Lincoln's birthdays; competitions are perfectly typified by the Indianapolis 500, the Superbowl, and the Kentucky Derby. Even the archaic tendency to consider the ritual games of the festival as cosmic events may be surfacing in the use of the term *world championship*, obstinately applied to events that, in the strict sense, are really encounters of local teams playing a culture-bound and territorially limited game, such as American football or baseball. Festive rites of passage take place on Valentine's Day, at debutantes' balls, and in drinking celebrations on one's twenty-first birthday and at fraternity and sorority rushes. Rites of deference and confirmation of status include presidential inaugurations, Father's Day, and Mother's Day. The archaic Kings and Queens of the May have their functional equivalents in the yearly beauty pageants of Miss, Mister, and Mrs. America. Plays have been grouped in various yearly festivals of the arts that range from Shakespeare festivals to the Oscars ceremonies in Los Angeles, through symphonies, jazz festivals, and fiddling contests. And the modern *ferias*, the county fairs, are numerous and ever present.

If not festival proper, such events are part of a festive cycle, a series of events that in other times and cultures would fall within tighter boundaries of time, space, and action. This festive complex is constantly changing and evolving. But with all its modifications, festival has retained its primary importance and continues to celebrate life, remaining the most important showcase for culture's values and worldview.

Alessandro Falassi

See also Carnival; Custom; Feast; Fool.

✳✳✳✳✳✳✳✳✳✳✳✳✳✳✳✳✳

References

Bercé, Yves-Marie. 1976. *Fête et révolte*. Paris: Hachette.
Caillois, Roger. [1939] 1940. Théorie de la fête. *Nouvelle revue française* 28:49–59 and 27:863–882.
Cox, Harvey. 1969. The Feast of Fools: A *Theological Essay on Festival and Fantasy*. Cambridge, MA: Harvard University Press.
Falassi, Alessandro, ed. 1987. *Time Out of Time: Essays on the Festival*. Albuquerque: University of New Mexico Press.
Hatch, Jane M. 1978. *The American Book of Days*. 3rd edition. New York: Wilson.
Lloyd, Warner W. 1959. *The Living and the Dead: A Study of the Symbolic Life of the Americans*. New Haven, CT: Yale University Press.
Ludwig, Jack Barry. 1976. *The Great American Spectaculars: The Kentucky Derby, Mardi Gras, and Other Days of Celebration*. Garden City, NY: Doubleday.
MacAloon, John J. 1983. Rite, Drama, Festival, Spectacle. Philadelphia: Ishi.
Pieper, Joseph. 1965. *In Tune with the World: A Theory of Festivity*. New York: Harcourt.
Stearns, Peter, ed. 1994. *Encyclopedia of Social History*. New York: Garland.
Stoeltje, Beverly. 1983. Festival in America. In *Handbook of American Folklore*, ed. Richard Dorson. Bloomington: Indiana University Press.
Turner, Victor, ed. 1982. *Celebration: Studies in Festivity and Ritual*. Washington, DC: Smithsonian Institution.
Wilson, Joe, and Lee Udall. 1982. Folk Festivals: A *Handbook for Organization and Management*. Knoxville: University of Tennessee Press.

FIELDWORK

Firsthand observation and documentation of folklore. Fieldwork is the key research act for most scholarship in folklore, anthropology, and oral history. In 1964, Richard M. Dorson wrote, "What the state paper is to the historian and creative work to the literary scholar, the oral traditional text is—or should be—to the student of folklore." Today, few folklorists would limit the field-gathered information to "texts," and many could not even agree on what the word *text* means, yet Dorson's observation still holds true.

Fieldwork consists of observing and documenting people where they are and doing what they do. It is one of the three major modes of acquiring primary information in the social sciences. (The other two—statistical surveys and decontextualized interviews or performances—are rarely used in primary folklore studies.) Fieldwork information is gathered with various media: notebooks, film and video cameras, and audio recorders. Fieldworkers may seek items in active tradition (things people do now) or things in passive tradition (things they know and recognize and may even have an aesthetic for but wouldn't, unless solicited, perform or utter). Fieldworkers may join in the events going on (*participant observation*), or they may pretend to be totally outside those events (except in large community events, such as festivals and parades, it is difficult for a fieldworker to be totally invisible). They may be active in their pursuit of information (interviewing, asking for items, asking for explanations), or they may be passive (waiting, observing, recording).

Some folklore researchers use preexisting print or electronic media as the sources of primary information (for example, studies of the apparent scope, character, and function of folklore materials in commercial advertising or political speeches or folklore in the works of Homer, Shakespeare, and Mark Twain or folklore on the Internet). But such studies are predicated on ideas of folklore derived from fieldwork. Milman Parry and Albert Lord's hypothetical and theoretical work on the nature of Homeric performance and composition was extrapolated from their extensive fieldwork among Serbian epic singers. They were able to assert that certain materials in classical texts were grounded in folklore performance and transmission only because their fieldwork let them understand the character of such performance and transmission.

Even folklore scholars whose work is totally theoretical are dependent for the substance underlying their generalizations and speculation on the fieldwork of others. It would be difficult, if not impossible, to theorize cogently and relevantly about the meaning of folklore in a community unless someone had first gathered information about what folklore exists in that community and what functions the folklore performs. Comparative folklore studies (texts or behaviors from different places or times compared for differences in aesthetic or functional aspects) is predicated on the quality and scope of the field-gathered material.

Folklorists doing fieldwork may be looking for specific genres or kinds of folk behavior: ballads, recipes, survivals of older traditions in modern communities, modern folkways in technological communities, or the nature of folk performance. It is difficult to know the social meaning of an item of performance without knowing about the conditions of performance. For example, the place and function of ballads in a community are interpreted differently if many people in that community sing many long ballads on a regular basis to a wide local audience that knows and enjoys such ballads or if, by contrast, the performers sing their songs only when collectors come in from the outside to solicit them. The words and tunes may be the same, but what we make of them may vary. One may analyze a particular ballad text differently if it was learned from a book, a recording, a school chum, or a grandparent.

In the nineteenth and early twentieth centuries, scholars often examined texts alone, much as literary scholars examined texts of poems as freestanding items. Today, however, folklore texts are rarely examined without consideration of collateral information. Only through fieldwork can researchers gather the items, provide information for identifying folk genres, and locate the nature of folklore performance in ordinary life.

It is not just that scholars are more sophisticated now about the questions that might be asked; it is also that the equipment available today frees the fieldworker to ask more sophisticated or multidimensional questions. When fieldworkers had to take down all words by hand, approximations of narratives or tunes were sufficient. Now that machines capture the words and music, fieldworkers can examine context—not just context of performance but also context of recording, the relation between scholar and source. Put another way, it is no longer just the joke that is investigated. Rather, modern researchers ask a host of question: Who tells which jokes to whom and under what circumstances? How are the jokes interpreted? Who laughs, and who does not laugh? What part do those jokes play in the social event going on? How does that redaction of that joke relate to others made of the same words? Is the meaning the same if the context is different? What is the relation between observer and observed? The whole reflexive movement in field sciences in recent years (see, for example., Clifford and Marcus' 1986 work, *Writing Culture*) is predicated on a technology that can document the observer at the same time that it documents the observed.

Fieldwork is a technology-driven endeavor. The kinds of questions one asks of field-gathered material are based on the kinds of information that can be gathered in or brought home from the field. Fieldworkers approaching complex events will define their options differently if they have access to various kinds of image and sound recorders and know how to use them effectively and efficiently. Fieldworkers studying material culture have different questions and therefore may incorporate different technologies than fieldworkers interested in narrative tradition or matters of custom or belief. Fieldworkers trying to document the folklife of a community may need a wider range of technical expertise than fieldworkers focusing on genres or items.

Nineteenth-and early-twentieth-century folklorists depended on simple recording devices and techniques, including notebooks and memory. They used bulky machinery to record musical performances on cylinders and then on large flat disks. These machines were capable of recording only a few minutes of performance before they had to be wound up and supplied with a new recording surface. Furthermore, unless the recordist struck a tuning fork or other device of known frequency at the beginning or ending of the recording, there was no way for a listener to know exactly at what speed these recordings were to be played. That meant listeners never knew if they were hearing the recordings at the right tempo or pitch. Because the equipment was so bulky, movement was difficult, and performers often had to be brought to where the machine was located. Cameras used large glass plates and required a great deal of light, either natural or flash powder.

What the great folklorists of the nineteenth and early twentieth centuries provided us were not so much records of performances but rather interpretations or versions of performances: They were not only editors of what they found but also participants in the line of performers they documented. When, for example, folklorist Vance Randolph spent an evening listening to stories or songs and then went home and wrote up the stories he had heard or sat at the piano and worked out songs he had heard, he was doing exactly what many folk performers do.

Folklorists now can gather more complex field documents because they have at their disposal instruments that provide a record of transient detail that was impossible to obtain a half century ago, such as: small, automated, 35mm cameras weighing less than a pound that zoom from wide-angle to telephoto shots and focus and set apertures automatically, using film capable of making images in moonlight; video cameras easily held in one hand that record high-quality images in low light and high-fidelity stereo sound on tape, using rechargeable batteries that last two hours each; audio recorders controlled by crystals, with tapes that are therefore replicable on any crystal-controlled machine anywhere; and, for the truly sophisticated user, digital audiotape (DAT) machines with real-time coding. A fieldworker can carry a full complement of this new equipment—video camera, still camera, crystal-controlled audio recorder, enough tape for a dozen hours of video and sound recording and enough film for hundreds of separate images—in a shoulder bag. The effects of all this technology are multifold.

First, the fieldworker is capable of acquiring an enormous amount of information—far more than was ever possible previously. Before mechanical means of reproduction were available, documentation of even the simplest text was at best an approximation, limited to what someone could write down in the midst of an event that could never be redone exactly. With early means of reproduction, it was possible to make crude recordings and obtain still photographic images in a narrow range of situations. With modern equipment, it is possible to get extremely accurate sounds and images in a wide range of situations. Second, the fieldworker has been freed of the need to concentrate on capturing items (the machines do that) and allowed to consider more complex questions, such as the way various parts of performance or enactment interrelate or minute complexities of performance itself. The performance analyses of Dennis Tedlock, for example, would be impossible without accurate recordings that can be listened to again and again with equipment that lets the analyst find exact moments in performance. Third, the problem of how to get information has been replaced by what is to be done with the great mass of information so easily acquired. A nineteenth-century collector of ballads or animal narratives had no difficulty managing his information; it was easy enough to organize the songs and stories and provide simple annotations giving the specifics of performance. A twentieth-century fieldworker coming home with videotapes, audiotapes, and photographs of a complex event has a far more difficult job of documentation, storage, and analysis.

In the field, the researcher looks at a world of nearly infinite possibilities: so many songs, dances, stories, images, recipes, redactions, processes, interactions, moments, movements, facial expressions, and body postures. Once home, the researcher deals with a world of specific and limited possibility: the kind, quality, and range of information brought home, no more and no less. What is not in the notes, on the film or tapes, or in memory is gone. Subsequent analysis will be predicated not on what existed out there in real life but on what made it back. Since field documents may be used in studies never envisioned by the fieldworker at the time of the fieldwork and since analysis may occur long after memory has had time to impose its confusions, proper documentation is of key importance in all fieldwork projects. Without notes on who was doing what and under what conditions the documentation and event occurred, sound recordings, videotapes, and photographs may, in time, be nearly useless.

Fieldworkers also deal with the problem of preservation. A large portion of the audio cylinders made early in the twentieth century, for instance, have already turned to carbon dust, and no one knows how long information on audiotapes and videotapes will last. Audiotapes made in the 1960s often present problems today because the recording material has pulled away from the backing. And notes made with felt-tip pens fade. The most lasting form of documentation is graphite pencil on acid-free paper. Such paper is enormously resistant to decay (it lasts centuries), and the graphite particles, imbedded in the paper fiber, are not subject to fading or oxidation.

The immediate result of fieldwork is the acquisition of various kinds of documentary materials. A long-term result is involvement in a range of ethical questions and responsibilities. To whom does the material one brings home from the field belong? What obligations are there regarding privacy and ownership issues? Who is owed what if material is used in a book or a recording or a documentary film? What obligations obtain toward other researchers working in the same area or on the same materials? Fieldwork is only one part of a complex series of personal, intellectual, and ethical acts and decisions.

Bruce Jackson

See also Participant-Observation Method.

✳✳✳✳✳✳✳✳✳✳✳✳✳✳✳✳✳

References

Clifford, James, and George Marcus, eds. 1986. *Writing Culture: The Poetics and Politics of Ethnography.* Berkeley: University of California Press.

Dorson, Richard M. 1964. Collecting Oral Folklore in the United States. In *Buying the Wind: Regional Folklore in the United States,* ed. Richard M. Dorson. Chicago: University Chicago Press

Finnegan, Ruth. 1992. *Oral Traditions and the Verbal Arts: A Guide to Research Practices.* New York: Routledge.

Georges, Robert A., and Michael O. Jones. 1980. *People Studying People: The Human Element in Fieldwork.* Berkeley: University of California Press.

Goldstein, Kenneth S. 1964. *A Guide for Field Workers in Folklore.* Hatboro, PA: Folklore Associates.

Ives, Edward E. 1964. *The Tape-Recorded Interview: A Manual for Field Workers in Folklore and Oral History.* Knoxville: University of Tennessee Press.

Jackson, Bruce. 1987. *Fieldwork.* Urbana: University of Illinois Press.

Jackson, Bruce, and Edward D. Ives, eds. 1996. *The World Observed: Reflections on the Fieldwork Process.* Urbana: University of Illinois Press.

Lord, Albert. 1960. *The Singer of Tales.* Cambridge, MA: Harvard University Press.

Tedlock, Dennis. 1983. *The Spoken Word and the Work of Interpretation.* Philadelphia: University of Pennsylvania Press.

FILM, FOLKLORE

A term commonly applied to a film that documents folklore for research and other purposes. Such films, when edited to be shown to an audience, are called, in the term coined by Sharon Sherman, *folkloric films.* The terms *folkloric film* and *film and folklore* also refer to nonacademic or so-called Hollywood films that use folklore as a major theme. Videotape use and production often are encompassed in the larger term of *film and folklore.* As the scope of videography increases and its use continues to grow, video has become the medium of choice (at least until the next major technological development), and *folklore and video*—or, preferably, *folkloric videos*—will become the commonplace term, incorporating film within its definition, much as the current term incorporates video.

Compared to their contemporaries in the social sciences and other fields, folklorists began to use film as a tool at a much later date, but the film movement in folklore reflects all of the techniques and preoccupations of earlier filmmakers who created the field of documentary film. Like the "films of fact" shot in the early 1900s, folkloric films are often made up of short clips of interesting phenomena captured for posterity. The earliest such documentation of folklore on celluloid is a *March of Time* series film made in 1935, which depicts John Lomax interviewing musician Leadbelly (Huddie Ledbetter) and recording his folksongs for the folksong archive of the Library of Congress; a second film on Leadbelly appeared in 1945. American folkloric films were not produced again until the late 1950s. The first call for film reviews in the *Journal of American Folklore* (published by the American Folklore Society) did not appear until 1974. Despite this somewhat late acknowledgment of the importance of film, these reviews demonstrate the growing interest in film among folklorists during the 1970s when new theories about performance began to gain acceptance.

In Europe, short, straightforward camera shots of folkloric subjects were taken for documentation purposes by the Institute für den Wissenschaftlichen Film. After World War II, the institute sponsored a program in fieldwork to train ethnologists in the use of film equipment. In 1959, the institute published its own rules for documenting ethnology and folklore and demanded that fieldworkers document only authentic events filmed without elaborate camera work. The institute organized a film archive in 1952 and began editing the *Encyclopaedia Cinematographia*. The ethnological films, which are categorized first by world region, then by country, and finally by region within each country, are of great value for comparative folklore research. They are short and unnarrated and deal with only one subject, such as a children's game from West Africa, a festival dance in South Africa, or the performance of an epic heroic song in Romania.

Other folkloric films have a heavily narrated and expository style similar to those documentaries made prior to World War II and on through the 1960s. Certain folkloric films utilize either a cinema verité or post-verité approach, which combines synchronous sound or voice-over with linear depictions for the recording of complex expressive events (including interactions, performances, and the many facets of creative processes) in their entirety. Yet others are reflexive and intersubjective, incorporating the film-maker as one of the subjects. In the realm of nonfiction film, certain trends have become firmly established. Stylistically, then, the folkloric film does not differ from documentary and ethnodocumentary film.

On a theoretical level, many folklorists who use film are tied both to the models used by their documentary film forerunners and to the conceptual premises of early folklore scholars. Some folkloric filmmakers tend to focus on romantic visions of the noble savage or preindustrial folk. Just as this bias on the part of folklorists gave way to more enlightened notions of the folk as any people with a common tradition, filmmakers also shifted their attention from romanticism to examine present-day issues involving diverse groups of people. In folkloric films, one can find both attitudes existing side by side.

In *Nanook of the North* (1922), Robert J. Flaherty's romanticization of native Arctic life, the focus on the individual as a representative figure for a culture that Flaherty saw fading and the involvement of Nanook and the

Inuit in the filming process are elements of a filmic model that folklore documentary filmmakers emulated. In folkloric films, the rural often takes precedence over the urban and the past assumes greater importance than the contemporary. John Cohen's search for Child ballads in Appalachia, documented in *The High Lonesome Sound*, Jorge Preloran's documentation of little-known peoples in the isolated regions of Argentina, and Les Blank's depiction of Cajun and Creole culture in the Louisiana bayou all fit this pattern. Yet none of these filmmakers is locked into this pattern. All of them have examined very contemporary activities and the urban scene as well. Often, like Flaherty, they begin with a romantic, stereotypic notion of the folk for their initial films and then recognize a need to broaden the definition of their work as their film corpus grows.

Just as Flaherty selected Nanook, folklore filmmakers often choose a biographical "everyman" to represent the group. Les Blank, in several films, has Marc Savoy explain aspects of being a Cajun; Jorge Preloran looks at Hermogenes Cajo as an exemplar of religious folk artists; Bill Ferris documents James Thomas as a bluesman and storyteller; and Sharon Sherman presents quiltmaker Kathleen Ware and chainsaw sculptor Skip Armstrong. As one might expect with the passage of time and the changes in techniques and styles, such folklore filmmakers have taken Flaherty's approach a step further by documenting people both as cultural or artistic representatives and as unique personalities. Having film subjects participate in the filming process, as Nanook did, is only now becoming a common means of sharing the authority for the film, as is evidenced by Zulay Saravino and Jorge and Mabel Preloran in *Zulay, Facing the 21st Century*.

Folklore filmmakers most interested in texts will often employ the techniques of montage inspired by Russian filmmaker Dziga Vertov. Like folklorist Vladimir Propp, Vertov was primarily interested in form. He thought that the recombination of filmic elements could create a new "truth," which he called *Kino-Pravda* (film truth). In *Man with a Movie Camera* (1928), he not only shows a day in the life of Moscow, he also edits the material to demonstrate what he thinks about the subject he has filmed. Vertov reveals how film operates by showing himself at the editing table with the images he has shot tumbling into various places to create new meaning, thus anticipating a post-modern view of film.

Accused of concentrating on form rather than content by the Stalinists of the 1930s, Vertov lost favor with his government. His influence can best be seen in the work of avant-garde filmmakers such as Jean Luc Godard. In addition, Vertov's Kino-Eye, which must "document from life," is the precursor of cinema verité, a technique aiming at film truth that was made popular in the 1960s with the advent of portable sync-sound equipment. French anthropological filmmaker Jean Rouch deliberately uses the term as homage to Vertov.

Vertov establishes reflexivity in film, showing the viewer the means by which representation is achieved. But unlike Flaherty and Rouch, who tried to incorporate the reactions of those being documented, Vertov's film "truth" is solely the filmmaker's own truth as he or she constructs it. In contrast, Flaherty wished to present the worldview of those he documented. These two approaches, that of Vertov and that of Flaherty, dominate documentary practices today. Neither practice is easily bounded or that distinct, except perhaps in terms of form. Whereas those who "play with" form are overtly providing viewers with their vision, other filmmakers still present their own stamp of authority while deluding themselves into thinking they are allowing their subjects to shape the film. Although one might suppose that Flaherty was reproducing the natives' attitudes because he tried to include his subjects' ideas, his methods for *Man of Aran* and *Moana* indicate otherwise. Vertov, despite his domination of the film, does reveal how his authority is constructed. Both styles underscore how subjective film is, but Vertov's work is more blatant about the impossibility of objectivity. Likewise, the admonition of British filmmaker John Grierson that documentary must expose social problems has led to a number of films whose editing styles reveal the ideologies of their makers. In folkloric film, the montage structure employed in such films as Ferris's *I Ain't Lying* and *Made in Mississippi* and Blank's food films (e.g., *Garlic Is as Good as Ten Mothers*) provides a means for discovering what the filmmaker thinks about the subject being documented.

For folklorists, cinema verité provided the first real opportunity to document events from beginning to end and to allow fieldwork tools to match the new theoretical perspectives about folklore as human behavior established in the late 1960s. Long takes and sync-sound filming became the rage. At last, the people being studied could speak for themselves in sync-sound and provide their own functional analyses without the imposition of a narrator or scholar. A number of documentary films demonstrated to folklorists how filmmakers might focus on and document individuals to arrive at a "truth"; such films included: *Salesman* (1969), which pictured the life of a door-to-door Bible salesman, and *Showman* (1962), a portrait of movie mogul Joseph E. Levine, by Charlotte Zwerin and Albert and David Maysles'; *Lonely Boy* (1961) by Wolf Koenig and Roman Kroiter, about teenage idol Paul Anka; and *Don't Look Back* (1967), D. A. Pennebaker's film on Bob Dylan.

The problem was that cinema verité did not provide "the answer" folklorists wanted. If anything, it raised more questions. Films are edited to suit filmmakers' theories. Those films that seem most appropriate for documentary in general and folklore in particular acknowledge their power to seemingly represent experience *and* reveal the means by which they do so. Such films go beyond the ideals of cinema verité into the openly subjective realm of what Sharon Sherman terms *post-verité*, in which the art form of the documentary is a given. Whereas cinema verité was art masquerading as objectivity, post-verité unmasks the illusion of objectivity and displays it. For example, in *Gimme Shelter*, flashbacks confuse what is "real"; in *Woodstock*, an observational camera style is fused with split-screen images, sound mixes, and rhythmic shots chosen for their balance with the audio track. The long takes disappear into edited rhythms, as they do in Roberta Cantow's folkloric film *Clotheslines*. The interview, abhorred by cinema verité for proclaiming the constructed nature of film, may occupy a central role in post-verité, as in such folkloric films as Tom Davenport's *A Singing Stream*, Judy Peiser's *All Day, All Night: Memories from Beale Street Musicians*, and Paul Wagner's *The Grand Generation*. For *Paris Is Burning*, Jennie Livingston creates a post-verité film from a mélange of interviews, cinema verité, and intertitles.

In the United States, for the most part, cinema verité films were used to tell the stories of the "other people," those without access to media production. With post-verité, the "others" may become the cinematic weavers of their own stories, directly addressing the camera as the "experts." In recognizing the blatancy of film as art, post-verité films may also cross into the realm of reflexivity. Zulay Saravino takes over the making of a film about her culture and turns it into one about her transcultural experiences in *Zulay, Facing the 21st Century*. Akin to Vertov, Saravino shows herself editing the film about herself. The window for objectifying people becomes a dialogue with and in film. In *Carnival in Qeros*, the carnival becomes secondary as the Qeros interact with John Cohen, striking a bargain for payment in alpacas in exchange for Cohen's right to film the villagers.

Unlike documentaries, which look at people within the filmmaker's own society, films that Sharon Sherman calls *ethnodocumentaries* tend to document the "other"—people who are conceptualized as being unlike the film team or ethnographer. Examples include Gregory Bateson and Margaret Mead's *Trance and Dance in Bali*, one of the first films to document a single event; John Marshall's many films on the !Kung bushmen; Robert Gardner's interpretative *Dead Birds* on the Dani of West Irian; Jorge Preloran's film on the Warao; and Timothy Asch's work on the Yanomamö and the Balinese. Folkloric films combine the goal of the documentary to record unstaged events with the goal of the ethnodocumentary to provide information about culture. As ethnographers have become less concerned with cultural overviews and more interested in *events* in culture (such as a feast, a funeral, a festival), their films have become more like folkloric films. The folkloric film focuses primarily on traditional behavior, documenting many of the most fundamental features of our lives, ranging widely from rituals, ceremonies, folk art and material culture to folk narrative and folksong and to the lore of various peoples bonded by ethnicity, age, gender, family, occupation, recreation, religion, and region.

Unlike most ethnodocumentary filmmakers, the folkloristic filmmaker does not limit himself or herself to so-called exotic, primitive, Third World, or aboriginal peoples. In contrast, the folklorist, as Richard M. Dorson has pointed out, need not travel far to discover folklore being generated and can conduct fieldwork at the folklorist's "back door." It can be argued that those folkloristic filmmakers who are the most successful have, in fact, examined traditions in their own locales, sometimes even among their own families.

These differences of major focus and locale set the folkloric film apart from other documentary film traditions. Both documentary and ethnodocumentary filmmakers have included footage whose content is of interest to folklorists, e.g., a Wolof woman making pottery, two Yanomamö narrators telling a myth, Bert Haanstra's segments of hand glass blowing in *Glass*, and Vertov's use of folksong in *Three Songs of Lenin*. Such films represent the precursors of the folkloric film, for they include folkloric material and predate the use of film by folklorists per se. Any film having folklore content might aptly be called a *folkloric film*. Just as anthropologists define certain films as ethnographic when they successfully elucidate anthropological approaches or lend themselves to the dictates of anthropological research or teaching, the true folkloric film may be defined as one whose content deals primarily with topics that folklorists study and whose intent is to meet the dictates of folkloristic research and teaching. Such films include ones created about folklore by folklorists themselves or by nonfolklorists who are filmmakers or videographers recording folklore. Put simply, the point of these films is to document folklore.

The filmmaker's theoretical assumptions about folklore are disclosed by and determine the techniques that the filmmaker uses. Those films that purport to deal with folklore (in the broadest sense of creative expression) generally focus upon either (1) the individual performer or artists; (2) the community (region, family, occupational group) or the "culture"; or (3) texts, technological processes, or artifacts. Furthermore, notions of folklore as having a space-time continuum often generate films with a historical or topological focus.

Analyzing how filmmakers apply form to content offers a method for revealing their intent. Films that profile individuals or community members tend to demonstrate creative interactional processes and events. Such films are most often not narrated and are shot and presented in a verité or observational style, with sync-sound or the sound-over voices of the participants. Occasionally, a single event—as seen in the work of wartime documentarians and television films such as *The Murrow-McCarthy Debate*, as well as in the ethnodocumentary films of Bateson and Mead, Marshall, and Asch—has served as the organizing principle for certain works of folkloric filmmakers: John Cohen's *Carnival in Qeros*, Tom Davenport's *It Ain't City Music*, Bess Hawes' *Pizza, Pizza, Daddy-O*, and Sharon Sherman's *Passover, A Celebration* and *Tales of the Supernatural*. On the other hand, films that attempt to demonstrate technological processes, examine texts and artifacts, and set up typologies or reconstruct the historicity of folklore productions generally make use of narration and a montage of images that are unrelated in filmic time to actual events. This style also predominates in interpretative films in which a narrator explains either the action on the screen or the thoughts of the filmmaker (or the people in the film). For historic reconstruction, such as Pat Ferrero's *Hearts and Hands*, the narration may be assembled from the words of journal, diary, and letter writers. Such films are edited to convey the ideas of the filmmaker about the subject.

The reasons for these methodologies are readily apparent. If the filmmaker's concentration is upon people and their creative processes, then the film generally will allow these people to convey their own tastes and aesthetics to the audience. Narration may be used as a complement to add information lacking on the audio track, but individuals will speak for themselves. In this way, the individual shapes the work of the filmmaker, who must structure the film around a sequence of linear events in which the individual is engaged. Occasionally, that structure is determined openly by both the filmmaker and the persons being filmed, and the process of the negotiation becomes part of the completed film.

A unique twist to the study of film and folklore is the popular use of folklore as the primary plotline or unifying thread for feature films. *The Serpent and the Rainbow*, for example, exploits the practices of voodoo. The urban legend about a babysitter frightened by a telephone caller is the basis for *When a Stranger Calls*. *Avalon* plays upon family and ethnic narratives to structure the larger narrative of family and ethnic neighborhood dissolution in the United States of the 1940s through the 1960s, using one family as exemplar. *When Harry Met Sally* relies on the courtship narratives of many different couples as a transition device.

Memorable in its re-creation of folklore is *Candyman*, in which a folklore graduate student conducts research on the legend or horror tale of "the hooked-arm man," who has scared teenagers in lovers' lanes for decades. In this film, the legend comes to life, and the man with the hook torments the graduate student. That which is being studied within the film becomes the framework for the film. With the popularity of Jan Brunvand's books on urban legends, this genre of folklore is familiar to a vast audience, and thus viewers have undoubtedly seen the irony.

Nonacademic feature films in general release often incorporate folklore as a detail—for example, a woman singing "Barbara Allan" (Child 84) in *The Piano*. Animated films, such as *Anansi the Spider* and *John Henry*, are targeted at the educational market, but the folkloric films perhaps the most popular with general audiences are Walt Disney's animated *Märchen*. From *Cinderella* to *Snow White and the Seven Dwarfs* and *Beauty and the Beast*, the Disney studio has presented a number of "Disneyized" folktales to huge audiences. The viewers may accept these renditions as the original tales, an idea reinforced by "spin-off" products such as books, dolls, games, and other toys.

On a thematic level, a similar process occurs. Folk beliefs about vampires and werewolves have spawned a whole genre of horror films. Folklike heroes and plots emerge in stories created or adapted from books by screenwriters, such as *The Never-Ending Story, The Princess Bride*, and *Friday, the 13th*. Other visual forms of popular culture appropriate themes such as "the quest," "journey," or "adventure" found in folktale and epic, reconfiguring them in video and computer games. In these ways, popular culture "swallows" folklore, reinterprets it, and spits it out in a new form. The facile quality of video cameras has encouraged people everywhere to become videographers who document their lives. In essence, what filmmakers and videographers choose to record in both professional films and home movies or amateur videos often involves presenting a vision of the self by documenting the central aspects of life, such as rites of passage (birthdays, bar mitzvahs, sweet sixteens, graduations, weddings); calendrical and religious holidays (Christmas, Passover, Mardi Gras); and performance events (from children's sports to ethnic festivals). Folkloric films also create biographies of individual folk artists, documenting the traditional processes in which they are engaged (for example, play activities, folk singing, craft creation). These subjects form the key narratives of the folkloric film and the folkloric video, which build upon these "narratives of life" by explaining how such events and processes function in the lives of those depicted. At the same time, filmmakers who document, interpret, and present folkloristic themes actually use such themes to present self-images. Thus, film not only offers a multilevel means of capturing facets of a culture, an ethnic community, a family, and/or an individual folk artist or performer, it also constructs a comprehensive image of the self.

Sharon R. Sherman

See also Fieldwork; Popular Culture.

✳✳✳✳✳✳✳✳✳✳✳✳✳✳✳✳✳

General References

Barsam, Richard. 1988. *The Vision of Robert Flaherty: The Artist as Myth and Filmmaker.* Bloomington: Indiana University Press.

Collier, John, Jr. [1967] 1986. *Visual Anthropology: Photography as a Research Method.* Revised and expanded, with Malcolm Collier. Albuquerque: University of New Mexico Press.

Dorson, Richard M., ed. 1983. *Handbook of American Folklore.* Bloomington: Indiana University Press.

Heider, Karl. 1976. *Ethnographic Film.* Austin: University of Texas Press.

Hockings, Paul, ed. 1975. *Principles of Visual Anthropology.* The Hague: Mouton.

Jackson, Bruce. 1987. *Fieldwork.* Urbana: University of Illinois Press.

Jacobs, Lewis, ed. [1971] 1979. *The Documentary Tradition,* Second edition. New York: W. W. Norton.

Nichols, Bill. 1991. *Representing Reality: Issues and Concepts in Documentary.* Bloomington: Indiana University Press.

Rollwagen, Jack R., ed. 1988. *Anthropological Filmmaking: Anthropological Perspectives on the Production of Film and Video for General Audiences.* New York: Harwood.

Rosenthal, Alan, ed. 1988. *New Challenges for Documentary.* Berkeley: University of California Press.

Rotha, Paul. [1952] 1963. Documentary Film. Third edition, with Sinclair Road and Richard Griffith. London: Faber and Faber.

Ruby, Jay, ed. 1982. *A Crack in the Mirror: Reflexive Perspectives in Anthropology.* Philadelphia: University of Pennsylvania Press.

Sherman, Sharon R. 1977. The Folkloric Film: The Relevance of Film for Understanding Folkloric Events. Ph. D. dissertation, Indiana University, Bloomington.

Waugh, Thomas, ed. 1984. *"Show Us Life": Toward a History and Aesthetics of the Committed Documentary.* Methuchen, NJ: Scarecrow Press.

Nonfeature Folkloric Film References

Blank, Les. 1980. *Garlic Is as Good as Ten Mothers.* 16mm, color, 51 min. El Cerrito, CA: Flower Films.

———. 1990. *Yum, Yum, Yum: A Taste of Cajun and Creole Cooking.* 16mm, color, 31 min. El Cerrito, CA: Flower Films.

Cantow, Roberta. 1981. *Clotheslines.* 16mm, color, 30 min. New York: Buffalo Rose Productions.

Cohen, John. 1990. *Carnival in Qeros: Where the Mountains Meet the Jungle.* 16mm, color, 35 min. Berkeley: University of California Media Center.

———. 1962. *The High Lonesome Sound: Music Making in the Kentucky Mountains.* 16mm, B&W, 29 min. New York: Cinema Guild.

Davenport, Tom. 1974. *It Ain't City Music.* 16mm and video formats, color, 14 min. Delaplane, VA: Davenport Films.

Davenport, Tom, and Daniel Patterson. 1987. *A Singing Stream.* 16mm, color, 50 min. Delaplane: Davenport Films.

Ferrero, Pat. 1987. *Hearts and Hands: A Social History of Nineteenth-Century Women and Quilts.* 16mm, color, 63 min. San Francisco: Ferrero Films/New Day Films.

Ferris, William. 1969. *Delta Blues Singer: James "Sonny Ford" Thomas.* 16mm, B&W, 45 min. Memphis, TN: Center for Southern Folklore.

———. 1975. *I Ain't Lying: Folktales from Mississippi.* 16mm, color, 25 min. Memphis, TN: Center for Southern Folklore.

———. 1975. *Made in Mississippi.* 16mm, color, 25 min. Memphis, TN: Center for Southern Folklore.

Hawes, Bess. 1969. *Pizza, Pizza, Daddy-O.* 16mm, B&W, 18 min. Berkeley: University of California Media Center.

Livingston, Jennie. 1991. *Paris Is Burning.* 16mm, color, 76 min. Los Angeles: Miramax Films.

Peiser, Judy. 1990. *All Day, All Night: Memories from Beale Street Musicians.* 16mm, color, 30 min. Memphis, TN: Center for Southern Folklore.

Preloran, Jorge. 1969. *Imaginero.* 16mm, color, 59 min. New York: Phoenix Films.

Preloran, Jorge, Mabel Preloran, and Zulay Saravino. 1993. *Zulay, Facing the 21st Century.* 16mm, color, 108 min. Culver City, CA: Preloran.

Sherman, Sharon R. 1970. *Tales of the Supernatural.* 16mm, B&W, 29 min. Eugene: Folklore Program, University of Oregon.

———. 1979. *Kathleen Ware: Quiltmaker.* 16mm, color, 33 min. Eugene: Folklore Program, University of Oregon.

———. 1983. *Passover: A Celebration*. Video, B&W, 28 min. Eugene: Folklore Program, University of Oregon.

———. 1991. *Spirits in the Wood: The Chainsaw Art of Skip Armstrong*. Video, color, 28 min. Eugene: Folklore Program, University of Oregon.

Wagner, Paul. 1993. *The Grand Generation*. 16mm, color, 28 min. Charlottesville, VA: American Focus.

FOLK CULTURE

The customary beliefs, social forms, and material constructions of specific folk groups. Folk culture includes the totality of associated elements such as speech patterns, social actions and activities, beliefs, behaviors, ideology, and artifacts specific to the group. It arises out of the organizational core of the group's identity to reflect the particular aims, interests, standards, and activities of the group. As opposed to more academic forms of culture, it is learned by interaction and participation within the group rather than through formal channels.

Culture can be defined in terms of the learned patterns of behavior, beliefs, art, rituals, institutions, and expressions characteristic of a particular group and how these elements are expressed. This pattern of learning and transmission is not limited to strictly oral or strictly written forms of transmission: Either or both may be employed in the learning process. Folk culture is both a representation and a reaffirmation of the total identity of a particular group, and it is learned by way of membership and interaction within the group.

Folk culture is usually viewed in contrast to elite culture. Some of the early definitions of folk culture focused on the idea that it was something separate from *urban* or *mass* culture, and that is representative of the beginnings of civilized culture. Folk culture was considered something that existed only within small, isolated, homogeneous, nontechnological groups, whose members were generally illiterate or nonliterate and lived in some form of preurban society. Early studies focused their attention on groups considered to be representative of preurban culture: peasants, aboriginal groups, or ethnic minorities, for example. Since the 1960s, studies of folk groups have broadened the scope of folk culture to include groups of any level on the folk-to-urban continuum and recognize that the folk culture of "rural" groups can and does manifest itself in new forms in an urban setting.

Closely allied with the concept of folk culture is the notion of *folk society*, a group of individuals who are organized around some common interest, shared institutions, and a common culture. The folk society is a self-perpetuating entity that bases its identity on shared institutions and culture. There is generally a dichotomy between folk culture and folk society, which views culture as the values, ideas, and symbols of the group and society as the actual mechanics, the way culture is represented through the social interaction of the group's members. Some scholars and studies have and do use the terms interchangeably and consider the distinction a moot point. To some extent, there is very little difference between the concept of folk culture and folk society, for the two do not exist in singular and separate states. However, the distinction between folk culture and folk society is beneficial for distinguishing between a study that focuses on the ideological constructs of a group versus one that focuses on how those constructs are manifested through group interaction.

The study of folk culture may encompass such diverse methodological tools as ethnography, folklore theory, cross-cultural comparisons, historical documentation, historic-geographic corollaries, psychological analyses, economic impact analyses, and a host of other methodologies. Folk culture studies also occur in a "hyphenated" form, in which one particular feature of the culture is the focus. For example, studies of material folk culture (alternately, folk material culture) focus on the material constructs of a particular group as representations of the group's culture.

As noted earlier, the definition of folk culture and the focus of its study has changed. Early ideas of folk culture tended to be based on romantic ideas of antiquarian survivals, wherein the folk culture of peasants, whether their own or borrowed from their "betters" (*gesunkenes kulturgut*) could be viewed as vignettes of our more civilized culture in its earlier stages. Some early ideas and studies focused on folk culture in nationalistic terms in an attempt to trace cultural lineage and establish ethnic superiority and like reasoning. Though the views of romantic nationalism are not in the fore of modern folklore theory, there are some applications in which such a study of folk culture has been used to establish tribal claims on property or recognition as a truly distinct group.

Richard Dorson pointed to the 1960s as the period in which folk culture studies were broadened by what he called a new type of folklorist. These changes are identified by a shift from concentrating strictly on rural groups and looking for romantic survivals to an acceptance of modern realities and a search for reinterpreted traditions in the urban setting and even emergent traditions. Studies have included changes and retentions in folk culture among urban immigrant groups, such as Hungarian steelworkers and Hmong and Vietnamese shop owners, as well as the uses of new technologies to carry on old traditions and even emergent traditions in gay and lesbian groups, occupational groups, avocational groups, and so on. As with earlier definitions and studies of folk culture, there is an interest in finding the continuities within which to identify the culture of the group.

Randal S. Allison

See also Anthropological Approach; Folk Group; Folklife; Folklore.

❊❊❊❊❊❊❊❊❊❊❊❊❊❊❊❊

References

Bronner, Simon J. 1986. *Grasping Things: Folk Material Culture and Mass Society in America.* Lexington: University Press of Kentucky.

Dorson, Richard M., ed. 1972. *Folklore and Folklife: An Introduction.* Chicago: University of Chicago Press.

———. 1983. *Handbook of American Folklore.* Bloomington: Indiana University Press.

Silverman, Eric Kline. 1990. Clifford Geertz: Towards a More "Thick" Understanding? In *Reading Material Culture: Structuralism, Hermeneutics and Post-Structuralism,* ed. Christopher Tilley. Cambridge, England: Basil Blackwell.

Vlach, John Michael. 1985. The Concept of Community and Folklife Study. In *American Material Culture and Folklife: A Prologue and Dialogue,* ed. Simon J. Bronner. Ann Arbor, MI: UMI Research.

FOLK GROUP

Usually referred to in academic literature as "the folk" (plural, "folk groups"), a social group whose members share a traditional culture; also known as the "common people." From a sociological viewpoint, the term *folk* designates a group of persons whose relations are characterized by cohesion and a primary group's patterns of social interaction.

A *primary group* (compare *Gemeinschaft,* or community) is differentiated from a *secondary group* (compare *Gesellschaft,* or society) according to certain criteria, including: size, purpose, duration, patterns of communication (interaction), type of social control, and degree of inclusiveness (or how much of the individual's life is involved in the group's activities).

Typically, a primary group is small in number, of multiple and varied purposes, and formed with the intent of being long-lasting; within a primary group, members usually interact via unrestrictive media and all available patterns of communication, typically face to face. Conformity to group rules of conduct (mores, folkways, and other social norms) is achieved through informal but very effective means (e.g., by generating a sense of shame, sin, or honor; by gossip; by fear of the supernatural), and group activities involve "the whole person" (from familial, economic, political, and related standpoints in both the personal as well as the impersonal aspects of life). For a member, life within the primary group is usually satisfying. By contrast, a secondary group is typically large in number and of specified and limited purpose(s), and it may be either transient or long-lasting. Within a secondary group, members interact via restrictive media and limited bureaucratic channels and modes (usually in writing). Social conformity is imposed on members by means of formal laws and bureaucratic regulations affecting only facets of the individual contractually involved with the secondary group (e.g., knowledge of electronics in a large electronics-manufacturing corporation). For the individual, life within a secondary group lacks a sense of satisfaction and belonging.

Naturally, due to recent accelerated rates of social and cultural changes, only a few social groups will manifest all these criteria at once. Whether a social group may be viewed as primary or secondary is determined by a patterned combination of a number of these factors (e.g., a tribe may count the number of its members in the thousands or even hundreds of thousands, but other factors such as a stronger sense of belonging would compensate for this potential impersonality). Within a secondary group setting, primary groups characteristically develop and prevail. A folk group may be viewed as a primary group.

The term *folk* has been used in a variety of academic fields and over a period of more than one and a half centuries. Various nationalistic and political ideologies, in addition to recent academic orientations, have contributed to the development of a variety of interpretations of that term and have generated a number of controversies about who the folk may be.

As a discipline, folklore is historically a European science, emerging out of elite intellectual developments subsequent to the eighteenth and nineteenth centuries' philosophy of romanticism. Following the postulates advanced by the French philosopher Jean-Jacques Rousseau (1712–1778), romanticists believed that human beings came into this world in a state of savagery, yet it was a noble state because nature accorded everyone freedom and equality. They also viewed "civilization" as corruptive, for it robbed individuals of nature's gifts of freedom and equality, as exemplified at that point in history by life under European imperial governmental systems. Longing for that past "state of nature," romanticists began a search for the "noble savage" overseas, beyond the geographic and cultural boundaries of civilized Europe and its extensions in the new (colonized) world. Romanticists focused their attention on the tales, proverbs, riddles, songs, manners, customs, beliefs, and related traditions of peoples perceived then to be living at stages of human development closer to savagery and not yet corrupted by civilization. They also reflected on the meanings and inherent goodness of these "savage" forms of expression but discovered that inequality and loss of freedom already had marred the lives of those nations thought to be free of the evils of civilization.

The failure to locate the philosophical ideal of the noble savage gave rise to disillusionment and futility in the works of the romanticists. Yet they became aware of the cultural creations of the non-European peoples within whose cultures they had searched for purity, equality, and freedom. Subsequent reflections on residuals of the "noble state of savagery" led Romanticists to theorize that such a state also must have existed in Europe prior to onset of and consequent corruption by civilization. This evolutionary notion led to the discovery in Europe of forms of cultural expressions similar to those gleaned overseas and thought to date back to the ancient past and its noble savage.

These materials characteristically were sought among the least "civilized" groups in Europe. Consequently, the association was made between a certain social group of lower-class standing and the cultural data resembling those gleaned from non-European groups. In England, such materials were labeled *popular antiquities* until William Thoms, in 1846, offered the term *folk-lore* as a substitute.

The word *folk* first appeared in ethnological studies in Germany as an adjective in such composite terms as *Volksleben* (folklife), *Volkslied* (folksong), and *Volksglaube* (folk-belief). In the English language, it was used first by William Thoms for the purpose cited earlier. Thus, from the time of its emergence on the academic stage, the term *folk* has been used to denote social groups other than the cultural elite and similar social and cultural categories of a population; typically, it referred to the segment of the population whose members were perceived to have not been corrupted by civilization. However, with the fading of the romantic glorification of savagery, the introduction of the evolutionary theory, and the application by Sir Edward B. Tylor of that theory to the realm of culture, the term *folk* lost its connection with nobility and acquired new connotations. Among these are the following, identified by Åke Hultkranz:

1. *Folk* refers to the nation. This definition is quite adequate in certain languages such as German (*Volk*), French (*pueble*), Spanish (*pueblo*), and Arabic (*sha`b*); however, it is impossible in English.

2. *Folk* designates the lower stratum (*Unterschicht*). This interpretation, given by M. Manhardt, Eduard Hoffmann-Krayer, and Hans Naumann, played a major role in German *Volkskunde*. It designated social masses who were unsophisticated and unanalytic. Since the 1920s, this distinction between the "elite" and the "folk" has been severely criticized.

3. *Folk* refers to an old-fashioned segment within a complex civilization—civilization being "complex and usually wide-spread culture characterized by advanced technological resources and spiritual achievements of high order (in science and art)." In Europe and Latin America, the lower stratum was considered identical with peasant society and rural social groups. Robert Redfield described the "folk" as including "peasants and rustic people who are not wholly independent of cities." In this respect, reference is to the concept of a dependent society or "half society," which, unlike a "primitive" community, does not stand in isolation from the rest of the nation. By contrast, primitive cultures are excluded from the folk category because they are, at least theoretically, complete in themselves and are isolates.

4. *Folk* labels the basic culture-carrying social stratum within a complex society. This viewpoint has been particularly emphasized by the American sociologists. It is especially applicable to large societies with a population composed of diverse ethnic groups, each with its corresponding culture (e.g., Italian-, French-, Japanese-, and African-American). One "culture" is perceived as the basic one; others are not.

5. *Folk* denotes a social group connected by a common tradition and a peculiar feeling of communion, the basis of which is a common historical background. This mystical definition is based on a group's esprit de corps; it allows for a very flexible view of the criteria according to which a primary group is reckoned, with an individual's sense of belonging playing the decisive role.

More recently, folklorists and anthropologists have found these and similar descriptions of the "folk" unsatisfactory in light of a number of theoretical considerations. The most dissonant of these is the fact that certain non-European social groups that could not be characterized as "folk groups" possessed folklore and that individuals from all walks of life—including the most sophisticated—use folklore during the course of their daily living.

Anthropologists sought to eschew the term *folk* altogether; consequently, such labels as *oral literature* (Robert Redfield) and *verbal art* (William Bascom) were proposed as substitutes. Some anthropologists (e.g., Ruth Finnegan) adamantly refuse to consider "oral Literature" (in Africa) as folklore.

Seeking to provide a rationale for a folklorist's presence among nonfolk groups, folklorist Richard Dorson adopted a radical form of the viewpoint expressed in Hultkrantz' third definition, cited earlier. He stated that two conditions for the study of folklore were then, in the 1970s, being realized in sub-Saharan Africa. These were "the appearance of an intellectual class with a culture partly different from that of the mass of the people" and "the emergence of a national state." Dorson explained that "in the tribal culture all the members share the values, participate in the rituals, and belong fully to the culture, even if some hold privileged positions as chiefs or diviners." Meanwhile, "in the national culture a schism divides the society." Dorson concluded that "at this stage of development the concept of *folk* becomes useful. Tribal culture, as it fragments under the impact of modern ways, turns into submerged folk culture in the new nation."

Previously, in 1965, Alan Dundes had sought to redefine the term *folk* in a manner that would allow for the presence of lore among those who, according to academic definitions, may not be viewed as "folk." He stated that the term "can refer to any group of people whatsoever who share at least one common factor. It does not matter what the linking factor is."

Bold as these and other justifications may be, students of folklore should remember that "lore" is a category of culture, whereas "folk" is a sociological entity. Although it is believed that there is no folk without "lore," it should be stressed that there is no person who is lore free. The likelihood that the presence of folkloric components in the culture that an individual shares with other members of the community would not automatically transform that individual into one of the "folk" is equal to the likelihood that the presence of an academic component in the culture of a genuine member of a folk group would transform that individual into a member of the elite.

Hasan El-Shamy

See also Folk Culture; Great Tradition/Little Tradition.

✳✳✳✳✳✳✳✳✳✳✳✳✳✳✳✳✳✳

References

Dorson, Richard M., ed. 1972. *African Folklore*. New York: Doubleday.
Dundes, Alan. 1965. *The Study of Folklore*. Englewood Cliffs, NJ: Prentice-Hall.
Finnegan, Ruth. 1970. *Oral Literature in Africa*. Oxford: Oxford University Press.
Hultkrantz, Åke. 1960. *General Ethnological Concepts, International Dictionary of Regional European Ethnology and Folklore*, vol. 1. Copenhagen: Rosenhilde and Bagger.
Oring, Elliott, ed. 1986. *Folk Groups and Folklore Genres: An Introduction*. Logan: Utah State University Press.
Tönnies, Ferdinand. 1887. *Gemeinschaft und Gesellschaft*. Trans. and ed. by C. P. Loomis as *Fundamental Concepts of Sociology*. New York: American Book, 1940.

FOLKLIFE

The total lifeways of any human community, including its artifacts, art, craft, architecture, belief, customs, habits, foodways, costume, narrative, dance, and song, among other cultural expressions. In this sense, folklife means specific cultural creations, as well as the discipline for the study of the process and form of such creativity. *Folklife studies* refers to the discipline or scholarly movement and its sensibility for appreciating the culture of everyday life in complex societies. It also evokes the long-standing disciplinary dichotomy between oral culture and material culture that represents a major intellectual fissure within world folkloristics. The contemporary folklife studies movement asks its own scholars to be as attentive to the documentation and analysis of contemporary culture as they have been to rural, agricultural, and peasant historical and traditional life. Folklife studies challenges both academic and nonacademic sectors to appreciate, learn from, and analyze the cultural production of all people and communities within a society, not just the socially elite, academically trained, or politically powerful. Folklife especially emphasizes that scholarly attention be paid to all those cultures found within the context of the local region.

Within the European context, the foundation of the discipline of folklife studies can be observed in a long history of antiquarian interest evidenced in Latin and vernacular texts and in a series of royal questionnaires sent to municipalities essentially as inventories of the geography, buildings, trades, shrines, relics, customs, honors, and so forth of those territories, with an eye to their value as economic or political resources. There are several important sources in this regard. In the 1200s, Saxo Grammaticus' *Gesta Danorum* (The tales of the Danish people) described legendary accounts of Danish kings, as well as religious practices of the people. Olaus Magnus' *Historia de gentibus septentrionalibus* (History of the northern peoples) recorded a 1555 view of the countryside and people of Sweden. Philip II's 1575–1580 questionnaires (*Relaciones geograficas*) concerned the cultural and regional history of all elements of his Spanish empire (including Latin America). Swedish King Gustavus Adolphus' Council on Antiquities in 1630 commissioned its representatives to conduct comprehensive research on the old objects, ideas, and practices of the king's subjects, as well as the geography of their regions. A 1789 questionnaire administered only to Catalonia by an official of the Spanish Crown inquired about cultural geography, agricultural practices, games and pastimes, labor organization, behavior during public festivals, and other similar matters. The questionnaires of 1811 sent to many of Napoleon's possessions also asked about diverse dialects, customs, and practices of countryside inhabitants. The Napoleonic example served as a transition point between the old-style royal surveys of local resources and the romantic nationalist concern with the particularities of cultural difference. Such writings suggest an early attention to recording historical and contemporary regional culture, with the idea of custom being specifically bound up in place and material life.

Folklife developed as a scholarly discipline in Scandinavia and Germany. Folklife studies was conceived within the context of a number of influential movements and ideas. European romanticism had great enthusiasm for examining the lives of the peasant class, who, it was believed, maintained a simpler and less complicated style of life evocative of a cherished rural past. These qualities, according to the romantics, were eroded by industrial changes, and they needed to be salvaged and documented. Folklife, therefore, developed because of the feared disappearance of the essential culture that scholars wished to study. Another major influence was the fervor of European nationalism, in which the identification of distinctive forms of culture could be used to help bolster national identity.

The primary genesis of the English word *folklife* comes from the Swedish *folkliv*, a term formulated in the nineteenth century and defined as the life and ways of the folk (the common people or, more specifically, the peasant class) as subject to rigorous, empirical scholarly investigation. In 1909, the term *folklife research* (in French, *étude de la vie populaire*; in Spanish, *estudio de la vida del pueblo*; in Greek, *laographeia*; and in Norwegian, *folkelivsgransking*) was coined at the University of Lund when lectures in *Svensk folklivsforskning* (Swedish folklife research) were begun by Sven Lampa. This term was an equivalent of the German term *Volkskunde* (the knowledge of the folk, folklore), which first appeared in 1805–1808 when Clemens Brentano and Achim von Arnim edited and published their folksong collection, *Des Knaben Wunderhorn* (The boy's magic horn).

Volkskunde has been defined and explained in many different ways by scholars in Germany, Switzerland, and Austria since that time. As *Volkskunde* developed, the emphasis was on the collection and preservation of the oral and material life of the German "Volk." Attention usually fell on the rural peasantry as the "Volk" or "people" in question, but scholars did not investigate the traditions of this group solely to gain a historical or cultural understanding of this perceived "lower level" of German society. Rather, *Volkskunde* scholars strove to understand something about the essential nature of the German people as a whole, and the study of peasants and their narratives and customs was seen as the key to this understanding. Their research produced rich studies, with folk art and architecture as well as folk religion of the Roman Catholic and Protestant regions given special attention. *Volkskunde* developed into a complex discipline, and it experienced many challenges, changes, and crises. The most disturbing development was its use by the National Socialists prior to and during World War II for furthering their agenda of Germanic biological determinism and racial superiority. The discipline was used during this time to discern what was perceived as the true and false characteristics of German culture as evidenced in the pure German *Volkskunde* of the peasant. Today, German *Volkskunde* could best be described as the discipline that studies the variety of cultural traditions found within German-speaking countries. It is a vital field focusing scholarly concern on the central issue of culture and its empirical analysis as related to all segments of society, with a specific interest in contemporary issues such as the impact of mass media, representations and falsifications of the traditional, tourism, ethnic relations, and the culture of everyday life.

Folklife studies was greatly influenced by theories of history and culture current during the early twentieth century in Germany and Scandinavia. The philological and historical orientation of folklore studies, affected as it was by evolutionist and diffusionist theories of culture, had a profound influence on the work of the early folklife scholars. The historical-geographical mapping employed as a way to show the development of oral forms and the illustration of regional variations were applied to material culture as well. Peasant culture continued to be the source for discoveries of ancient remnants of history evidenced in the peasants' simple, pastoral lives. Scandinavian folklife research was influenced by the German ethnology of the pre-1914 period to follow a cultural-historical approach. This meant that it usually opposed evolutionary explanations of cultural transformation emphasizing diffusionary explanations of cultural movement and dispersion. Like the German-speaking scholars, the Scandinavian and Nordic folklife scholars emphasized the study of the culture area as central to typologizing a region's elements of material culture, such as houses, barns, carts, or farm implements. The distribution and relation of these elements to traditional peasant culture could then be plotted onto cultural maps to see evidence of development, similarity, and survival. After this was accomplished, it was the scholar's task to turn to well-documented archives and historical sources for purposes of comparison and assessment. This cartological and research method for studying all aspects of folk culture and their historical development became a hallmark of European folklife methodology, and folk cultural atlases were produced as evidence of this meticulous research.

Sigurd Erixon (1888–1968), an influential leader of Swedish folklife research (and the second professor of Nordic and comparative ethnology at the University of Stockholm), saw *folkliv* as a regional branch of general anthropology. In his conceptualization, regional ethnology was comparative cultural research on a regional basis with a sociological and historical orientation and certain psychological implications. It emphasized the study of material life, custom, and belief, but Erixon also included oral folklore as a part of the overall picture. Erixon believed in the importance of collecting traditional resources, preserving them in archives, and seeing how they functioned for individuals, families, and small communities. German and Swedish folklife scholars promoted methods of empirical and data-based research, such as personal visits, extended field interaction, field interviews, questionnaires, indexes of materials collected, and direct correspondence for the study of still existing cultural expressions, as well as the examination of newspapers, travel accounts, wills, memoirs, diaries, autobiographies, collections of letters, and account books to assist historical work.

Gradually, especially after World War II, many scholars of European folklife began to expand the scope of their work away from survivalistic, static, peasant-based studies. Regional groups were no longer perceived as permanent static culture-bearers. Erixon himself felt that, by this time, the phase of folklife collection was coming to an end due to the gradual dilution of traditional material among rural informants. Under the influence of functionalist theory in the 1940s and 1950s and a more sophisticated view of cultural systems, the focus of folklife research shifted away from the historical and developmental concerns of the researchers and their culture and toward the complexity of the informants' cultural context. As the twentieth century progressed, the objective, positivist research that emphasized elements in life (the hammer, the sled, the patchwork quilt, the song, the memorate) over the context and process of living (work, play, craft, speech, belief) gave way to a focus on research with humans as subjects. Scandinavian and Nordic ethnologists, like their German-speaking counterparts, still engage in historical research, but they also recognize the potential for folklife research in varying contexts of contemporary culture, including urban life, social class dynamics, and cultural transformation due to immigration and emigration.

An important corollary to the agenda of folklife research in Sweden was the development of a new type of museum. Beginning in 1891, Artur Hazelius (1833–1901) founded, near Stockholm, the first open-air folklife museum and called it "Skansen." (Hazelius had previously opened the Nordic Museum [*Nordiska Museet*] to study Swedish peasant culture.) Skansen served as the public access to rural and town vernacular architecture from all parts of the country, placed on display in re-created natural settings. These rebuilt structures (e.g., farmhouses, manor houses, barns, a church) were complemented by furnishings brought from many areas to represent the variety and excellence of regional types. This museum concept presented the results of ethnological research of the material and social aspects of national and regional culture. Such research could represent everything from investigations of past methods of bee-keeping in Wales and funeral customs in the Romanian countryside to the making of fish spears in coastal Norway and sickles, hooks, and scythes in Bavaria. These institutions exist to teach visitors about the past as well as to conserve significant examples of cultural history. They maintain agendas of research, as well as being repositories of tape recordings, photographs, tools, furniture, clothing, decorative arts, paintings, and religious material culture—from silver votive offerings to carved wooden statues to hand-colored religious chromolithographs. Open-air museums, or outdoor museums of folklife, vary in size and quality, and they spread from Scandinavia to other locations throughout continental Europe, Great Britain, and North America. The folklife museum concept continues to exist in every size and international context, from sixteen different open-air museums in Romania to unmarked, even clandestine museums of revolutionary culture in Central America.

Folklife studies in Great Britain can be traced to eighteenth-century antiquarianism, but it was more specifically influenced by the *Volkskunde* and *Folklivesforskning* movements and their historical-cultural approach to ethnological research. Retaining a strong tie to the study of traditional life—that is, rural, preindustrial life—the documenting and analysis of material culture forms continue to be central concerns of folklife studies in Wales, Scotland, Ireland, and England. Work also has been conducted on calendar customs, festival, occupation, leisure, and systems of belief. The first institutionalized folklore and folklife research in the British Isles was conducted by the Irish Folklore Institute, commissioned by the Irish government in 1930. This development occurred because the Folklore of Ireland Society (formed in 1927 on a voluntary basis), with its aim of collecting folklore, became overwhelmed and appealed to the government for assistance. The Irish Folklore Institute became a larger and better equipped organization and was renamed the Irish Folklore Commission in 1935 under the leadership of James H. Delargy (1899–1980). In 1971, it became the Department of Irish Folklore at University College, Dublin. In Great Britain, the center for folklife research has not been university-based departments, of which there are few, but folklore institutes and museums, such as the Welsh Folk Museum at St. Fagan's, outside of Cardiff (opened to the public in 1948 and started by Iorwerth C. Peate [1901–1982]), and the Ulster Folk and Transport Museum (started in 1958 by E. Estyn Evans [1905–1989]).

As in Great Britain, there has been a historical division between folklife and folklore as applied in the United States. Folklore emphasizing the study of oral forms, especially narrative and song, was stressed, whereas the study of material culture, for example, was excluded from scholarly concern. Starting in the 1950s under the influence of U.S.-trained but European-influenced scholars Alfred L. Shoemaker (1913–) and Don Yoder (1921–), the concept of folklife studies was introduced to the American academic environment. Centering their interest on the ethnic, regional, and sectarian cultures of Pennsylvania, scholars of American folklife (as Yoder called it) concentrated on rich traditions of material culture, religious and medical belief, custom, festival, food, costume, and so forth. Yoder saw this approach as applicable and necessary throughout the American context, and he was especially interested in how the approach would add new dimensions to the study of U.S. history and the preservation of vernacular heritage. He conceived of this approach as part of a movement for the study of American historical and contemporary ethnography. Yoder also subsumed folklore—that is, the oral components of a culture—into his conceptualization of folklife, in agreement with the holistic understanding of traditional culture conceived of by his European counterparts. Among his diverse research interests were folk art and architecture, folk religion, folk medicine, folk cookery, and folk costume. American folklife's emphasis on all the elements of local culture and environment as keys to understanding the total picture of American civilization influenced the study of geography, art history, history, museum studies, anthropology, religious studies, historic preservation, and American studies.

Folklife as a discipline and movement has developed slowly throughout the world in a variety of professional and nonprofessional ways. Folklife institutes with extensive research libraries and archives are connected to universities or stand alone with state or private support. Elaborate and modest museums exhibit aspects of everyday life. Government-supported, public sector folklife research and festival presentation has become an important means of presenting folk arts and folk artists within a region, state, or country, as well as encouraging the financial support and academic study of such expressive culture. Regional folklife societies, clubs, and voluntary associations have been organized with a focus on local traditional culture. Individuals interested in their own regions may lack a theoretical focus but enjoy the investigation of their own past and present cultural forms.

The multiplicity of regional names representing the expressions of traditional culture and the study of those expressions—folklore, folklife, ethnology, *folklivsforskning, Volkskunde*—has not assisted the discipline of folklife and its search for an acceptable identity and presence in the academic world. Sigurd Erixon preferred to call *folkliv* research *regional ethnology,* which he proposed as an international designation for the discipline that studies national folk cultures or folk culture in general. He also worked to achieve a uniform notion of European folklife research, or "European ethnology," among the diverse European academic communities. Participants at two meetings of folk culture scholars attempted to resolve this terminological issue. The first was the Arnhem Congress, which met at the Dutch Open-Air Museum at Arnhem in Gelderland in 1955 for the specific purpose of determining disciplinary terminology for folklore/folklife research. Certain delegates favored *ethnology* or *European ethnology* for the international name of the discipline. The German-speaking contingent opposed the decision to stop using *Volkskunde* because of its established presence in academics and government in their countries. In 1969, Scandinavian and Finnish scholars met jointly in Jyväskylä, Finland, and agreed that *etnologi* should replace *folkliv* as the official name for their academic subject. By 1970, German scholars also were agreeing with the change as a positive response to the search for an international term. Most contemporary academics in Western Europe now refer to the study of folklife as *ethnology,* with the thought of emphasizing its international aspect. Still, multiple names and institutional auspices responsible for what could be called *folklife* abound in various regions in European nations. For example, for local historians or individuals working in the public sector in the Romance-language-speaking countries, *folklore* or *culture populaire* are used, especially if the individuals are openly engaged in local promotion, preservation, or resistance. In France, *ethnology,* along with *ethnography* and *anthropology,* are seen as stages in the overall process of research into human cultures, whether at home or elsewhere. In Canada and the United States, contemporary terminological usage and conceptual understanding of "folklife studies" maintains its close association with folklore studies, and the two scholarly fields are understood as one discipline, referred to as *folklore and folklife.*

The term *ethnology* may exist, but it still stands for two disciplinary orientations: one with a material and social outlook (folklife) and the other with an oral folkloristic character (folklore). Standard European and North

American conceptualizations of folklife describe it as the total traditional lore, behavior, and material culture of any folk group, with particular emphasis on the customary and material categories. In reality, folklife has represented the study of material aspects of folk culture, especially rural, agricultural, and peasant culture, in the face of a predominant emphasis by scholars on oral and text-centered products of a community. This division can be best exemplified by the two contemporary academic journals of ethnology in Sweden, *Etnologia Scandanavica* and *ARV-: Nordic Yearbook of Folklore*, or by the journals *Folk Life* and *Folklore* that serve folkloristic interests in Great Britain. This disciplinary split personality makes little difference to some academic communities and is a point of contention for other groups of scholars, especially those competing for meager financial resources or academic positions. Such divisions manifest themselves in the composition and direction of academic departments, museums, and government agencies; in the contents of scholarly journals, books, and other community publications; and in the funding of programs for the preservation and maintenance of living but sometimes barely surviving or visible traditional ways of life.

Folklife remains an autonomous discipline in the sense that it is not a composite of various disciplines concerned with the study of regional culture; however, it has not become a theoretically self-sufficient discipline. In this sense, folklife's greatest strength has been phenomenological, but it has provided little epistemology for its students. It continues to depend heavily on theory and analytical studies of history, material culture, architecture, performance, language, religion, culture, and society. Among the other disciplines that are related to folklife studies in sharing subject matter and a kinship with examining regional culture and that the folklife approach may have directly or inadvertently influenced are: agricultural history, rural and urban sociology, human relations, ethnohistory, oral history, ethnomusicology, social psychology, medical history, art history, architectural history, history of diet and nutrition, cultural geography, medieval studies, historical archaeology, historical preservation, local history, maritime history, industrial archaeology, history of technology, dialectology and linguistic geography, and cultural studies.

More than a field of otherwise excluded categories of expressive culture, the past and present folklife sensibility represents an integral approach to noticing, collecting, mapping, preserving, archiving, displaying, analyzing, protecting, and promoting the entire traditional creative and/or utilitarian output of the individual, family, community, region, or nation. These traditions may be transmitted by face-to-face communication, imitation, or various forms of media, such as print, film, computer, audio tape, telephone, or facsimile. Some folklife scholars also are working on the dynamic nature of the culture of the individual as an important corollary to studies of community tradition.

Contemporary folklife studies shares with folklore studies a common interest in describing, analyzing, and comparing the culture of small communities and the variety of traditional cultural systems interacting within such communities. These communities can be defined through shared geography; age; gender; occupation; leisure; and religious, medical, political, or other belief system. Both contemporary folklife and folklore emphasize aesthetic or artistic creation; historical process; the construction of mental, verbal, or material forms; and the relationship and balance of utility and creativity to such forms within a particular culture. Their methodology emphasizes intensive historical research using all available sources and field studies in which people speak for themselves and use their own aesthetic and classificatory systems to explain themselves and influence those scholars who have been allowed to understand, appreciate, and learn from their lives.

Leonard Norman Primiano

See also Art, Folk; Craft, Folk; Folklore; Material Culture; Volkskunde.

✳✳✳✳✳✳✳✳✳✳✳✳✳✳✳✳✳✳

References

Buchanan, Ronald H. 1965. A Decade of Folklife Study. *Ulster Folklife* 10:63–75.

Chiva, Isac, and Utz Jeggle, eds. 1987. *Deutsche Volkskunde—Franzosische Ethnologie: Zwei Standortbestimmungen* (German folklore—French ethnology: Two dispositions). Frankfurt: Campus Verlag and Paris: Editions de la Maison des Sciences de l'Homme.

Dorson, Richard, ed. 1972. *Folklore and Folklife: An Introduction*. Chicago: University of Chicago Press.

Dow, James R., and Hannjost Lixfeld, ed. and trans. 1986. *German Volkskunde: A Decade of Theoretical Confrontation, Debate, and Reorientation* (1967–1977). Bloomington: Indiana University Press.

Erixon, Sigurd. 1962. Folk-Life Research in Our Time: From a Swedish Point of View. *Gwerin* 3:275–291.

———. 1967. European Ethnology in Our Time, *Ethnologia Europaea* 1:3–11.

Fenton, Alexander. 1985. *The Shape of the Past: Essays in Scottish Ethnology*, vol. 1. Edinburgh: John Donald.

———. 1993. Folklore and Ethnology: Past, Present, and Future in British Universities. *Folklore* 104:4–12.

Gailey, Alan. 1990. "...such as pass by us daily,...": The Study of Folklife. *Ulster Folklife* 36:4–22.

Hall, Patricia, and Charlie Seemann. 1987. *Folklife and Museums: Selected Readings*. Nashville, TN: American Association for State and Local History.

Higgs, J.W.Y. 1963. *Folk Life Collection and Classification*. London: Museums Association.

Honko, Lauri, and Pekka Laaksonen, eds. 1983. Trends in Nordic Tradition Research. In *Studia Fennica: Review of Finnish Linguistics and Ethnology* 27.

Jacobeit, Wolfgang, Hannjost Lixfeld, and Olaf Bockhorn, eds. 1994. *Volkische Wissenschaft* (Nationalistic folklore studies [of the Third Reich]). Vienna: Bohlau Pub.

Kavanagh, Gaynor. 1983–1984. Folk Life: Present and Future Tenses. *Folk Life* 22:5–16.

Lindqvist, Mats. 1992. Between Realism and Relativism: A Consideration of History in Modern Ethnology. *Ethnologia Scandinavica* 22:3–16.

Owen, Trefor M. 1981. Folk Life Studies: Some Problems and Perspectives. *Folk Life* 19:5–16.

Paredes, Américo. 1969. Concepts about Folklore in Latin America and the United States. *Journal of the Folklore Institute* 6:20–38.

Reiakvam, Oddlaug. 1994. Norwegian Ethnology: Sketches for the Ancestors' Gallery. *Ethnologia Scandinavica* 24:9–21.

Segalen, Martine. 1988–1989. Current Trends in French Ethnology. *Folk Life* 27:5–25.

Tokarev, Sergei Aleksandrovich. 1966. *Istoriya russkoi etnografii* (The history of Russian ethnography). Moscow: Hauka.

Weber-Kellermann, Ingeborg. 1969. *Deutsche Volkskunde zwischen Germanistik und Sozialwissenschaften* (German folklore between the study of German language and literature and the social sciences). Stuttgart: J. B. Metzlersche Verlagsbuchhandlung.

Yoder, Don. 1963. The Folklife Studies Movement. *Pennsylvania Folklife*. 13:43–56. Reprinted in Don Yoder, *Discovering American Folklife: Studies in Ethnic, Religious, and Regional Culture*. Ann Arbor, MI: UMI, 1990.

———. 1976. Folklife Studies in American Scholarship. In Don Yoder, ed., *American Folklife*. Austin: University of Texas Press. Reprinted in Don Yoder, *Discovering American Folklife: Studies in Ethnic, Religious, and Regional Culture*. Ann Arbor, MI: UMI, 1990.

FOLKLORE

Term coined by Briton William John Thoms who, in 1846, proposed that the Anglo-Saxon compound *folklore* be used instead of the Latinate *popular antiquities* to describe "the manners, customs, observances, superstitions, ballads, proverbs" and other materials "of the olden time." Although the word *folklore* appears to have been new at that time, an interest in the phenomena of the field was not. Rulers in different parts of the world had long ordered the collecting of heroic songs and other traditions through which they could glorify themselves. Religious leaders and learned scholars periodically gathered superstitions in order to expose them and weed them out. However, during the romantic currents in late-eighteenth- and early-nineteenth-century Europe, intellectuals insisted that the traditions of peasants were valuable remnants from a remote past and should be collected before they disappeared. Thoms himself was inspired by the works of the brothers Jacob and Wilhelm Grimm. They in turn were indebted to Johann Gottfried von Herder (1744–1803) who saw in the arts of common people (*das Volk*) a reflection of the true spirit of a nation. It is not astonishing that the idea of folklore as a priceless national or panhuman testimony from antiquity gained force at a time when industrialization caused rapid transformations of traditional landscapes and ways of life. Also today, both the formal study of folklore (*folkloristics*) and the informal interest in it are linked to nostalgia for the past and uneasiness with modernity.

Long used primarily by English speakers, the word *folklore* is now accepted internationally. In some countries, it has replaced native terms; in others, it is used alongside them. But though nineteenth- and early-twentieth-century scholars often investigated the origin and distribution of selected tales, songs, or games, folklorists today employ a wide range of approaches to study an impressive variety of verbal, material, and other expressive practices, including funeral laments, quilt making, and vernacular house building. Some investigate traditional tales to understand the structures of human thought. Others study storytelling as a social accomplishment, paying attention to the relationship between folklore forms, the people creating them, and other contexts. Many scholars, among them feminists and representatives of formerly colonized peoples, also are engaged in changing the biases that in the view of many contemporaries have been inherent in folklore research.

FOLKLORISTIC PERSPECTIVES

It has, not unexpectedly, proven difficult to define the term *folklore*. Recent attempts range from suggestions that *folklore* stands for "traditional cultural forms that are communicated between individuals through words or actions and tend to exist in variation" (Bengt af Klintberg) to the idea that it is "artistic communication in small groups" (Dan Ben-Amos). Many folklorists, however, dispense with definitions. Concerned that folklore not be regarded as lists of things, they prefer to look at it as one of several perspectives from which "a number of forms, behaviors, and events may be examined" (Elliott Oring). Among the many words used to characterize such perspectives, the following will be considered here: *folk*, *medium of communication*, *tradition*, *genre*, and *aesthetic processes*.

Folklorists around the world long took it for granted that the word *folk* connoted illiterate peasants and other groups that from the folklorists' standpoints were old-fashioned or exotic. It was self-evident that these groups would be more tradition bound and would carry more folklore than the elites, who were believed to shun the yokes of tradition. However, during the last few decades, folklorists have increasingly come to think that the folk are all human beings. All people are involved in folklore processes, regardless of group—sometimes as performers, often as audiences. During their lifetimes, all people come to share the folklore of many groups, often cross-cutting social and territorial boundaries.

Yet despite their conviction that all humans partake in folklore processes, folklorists continue to study some humans more than others. Some critics argue that folklorists privilege male informants and masculine forms, and others point out that folklorists continue to study and celebrate the creative expressions of poor and marginal peoples even as they ignore the deplorable living conditions of these individuals. The ways in which researchers come to terms with such issues are of central importance to the future of folklore study.

Mode of communication is another phrase that recurs in discussions of folkloristic perspectives. Scholars long emphasized that folklore is primarily communicated orally or in the practices of everyday life. They also stressed that, largely due to such informal channels of communication, folklore forms exhibit variations within standardized structures or plot outlines. Each time a traditional log house is built, there are changes of a kind that do not occur in industrially produced houses. In oral tradition, there are as many versions of the Cinderella story as there are narrators, whereas the wording of a poem written to be printed is not changed even if it is read aloud.

However, informal channels cannot be seen as the sole modes of communication because folklore has long been transmitted in numerous other ways, not least in legal or religious documents, in newspapers, or, recently, via television, video, and all the electronic media. Furthermore, traditional themes and structures have long been communicated through the works of well-known artists and authors. Western classical ballet shares some of its stylized and repetitive character with the European folktale, and Shakespeare often built his plays on folklore. Paradoxically, folklorists say that they study orally communicated forms, yet these forms are available for investigation thanks to various media, including print.

Some of the success of many films, comic books, and advertisements can be attributed to the fact that they are based upon ancient and widely circulating themes. Superman travels through space in a womblike vessel, only to be found and raised by a poor North American couple. His story has parallels in the stories of Moses, Cyros, and other heroes who are similarly found as children floating around in small containers. Furthermore, identity changes are characteristic not only of Superman but also of most heroes and heroines of tradition. The transformation of the poor and orphaned fairy-tale heroine into a rich and beautiful queen is reenacted over and over in films, magazines, and real-life stories. Some folklore themes have a psychological force that makes people re-create them century after century in different modes and media.

This brings us to *tradition*, a slippery key word in discussions of folkloristic perspectives. Basically, folklorists long regarded tradition as a store of standardized themes, structures, and forms of knowledge, more or less widely distributed in the world and at the same time adapted to diverse cultures. These themes, structures, and forms were said to have been passed on from generation to generation in tradition-directed groups.

Recently, however, folklorists have begun to think of tradition less naturalistically and more as a construction in which the past is always interpreted in a given present. In that sense, all tradition involves change. The interpretations of the past may be unconscious or conscious, unintentional or intentional. National symbols all over the world tend to be inventions based upon traditional forms that people perceive to be particularly valuable. The invention and selection of national symbols, therefore, involve important issues of cultural politics. This is true also of many other phenomena, such as those traditions that people select as the genuinely representative ones to be displayed in museums or presented to tourists.

Genre is another concept that has long been central to discussions of folkloristic perspectives. A genre may be seen as a bounded, distinguishable form characterized by a specific combination of stylistic traits and elements of content. People tend to make all kinds of culture-specific distinctions between expressive forms in their repertoires. At the same time, some stylistic or structural elements recur in the folklore genres of many cultures, among them symmetries, alliterations, parallelisms, and all kinds of repetitions. The tendency toward tripartite repetitions, for example, can be found in a variety of Western genres: fairy tales, textile patterns, interior decoration, houses, ballads, jokes, or games. In the traditions of some Native American peoples, on the other hand, four is a more common unit of repetition. But regardless of the specific numbers, repetitions help performers to achieve control over their materials. A firm, repetitive structure aids memory at the same time as it frees fantasy and improvisation. The given patterns simultaneously offer restrictions and creative freedom.

Some genres, such as proverbs and riddles, were long called "fixed" because they were believed to change less than "unfixed" forms, such as narratives. However, recent studies of folklore in social interaction make such distinctions untenable. Fixed forms change, too, since people in daily life often do not cite them in full but merely hint at them through tone of voice. More recently, folklorists have increasingly observed that genres are malleable social phenomena that people often blend and mix so that artful hybrids emerge.

Aesthetic process, finally, is a notion combining two important words in recent discussions of folkloristic perspectives. Although some scholars argue that the word *aesthetic* has become overemphasized in folkloristics, many others stress that not only are folklore genres aesthetically or poetically shaped but also that folklore is an artful way to affect social life. Indeed, it is because of its aesthetic force that folklore becomes a powerful vehicle through which people can examine or critique the lives they lead.

PARADOXES, NATIONAL PATHS, AND INTERNATIONAL TRAJECTORIES

In folklore, people thus create or challenge, mirror or express, maintain or disprove values that are central to them. Even the simplest anecdote may articulate profound existential questions. Here, we touch upon some perplexing paradoxes. One is that people articulate both the best and the worst in their lives in folklore. To those who have fled from one part of the world to another, a few beloved songs, stories, or dishes become symbols of a precious inheritance that must be preserved in order to be reconstituted. Conversely, folklore can incarnate some of the worst aspects of life, such as detested symbols of racism and humiliating jokes directed at one's own group. Folklore can be invoked to hold communities together or cruelly separate them from one another.

Another paradox is that folklore materials, at one and the same time, can be international and national, global and regional, local and deeply personal. The patterns of a hero tale may be spread across the earth at the same time as one special hero incarnates the fate of a nation. The guessing game "how many horns has the buck" is ancient and widely distributed, but it lives in the fleeting moments when it is played; a simple, mundane event is thus placed in a vast comparative perspective.

Some of the paradoxes of folklore materials and processes are true also of the study of them. Folkloristics regards itself as an international field. At the same time, it is almost everywhere a construction in service of national or other political interests. The vagaries in the designations of the field are indications of this. In post–World War II Germany, the previously used term *Volkskunde* has increasingly been avoided because Hitler used it for propaganda reasons. Many Latin American scholars prefer *popular antiquities* over *folklore* because they associate folklore with colonial imperialism. In India, various native terms, among them the south Indian *janapada*, have been proposed as translations of *folklore*, a word that was introduced by the British during the occupation. In Sweden, *etnologi* is now used instead of the older term *folklivsforskning* (folklife research) because the component *folk* is regarded as a tainted leftover from the class-biased days when the objects of study were peasants and manual laborers.

Folklorists everywhere have been involved in nation building and concomitant class and power struggles. In the nineteenth century, when Finland was freeing herself from Sweden and Russia, the *Kalevala* epic, which scholars pieced together from songs collected in oral tradition became the first example of literature in the native language. At that time, the field of folkloristics was a matter of national concern in Finland, just as it is today. And in recently reestablished nations, folkloristics plays an important part in efforts to recapture a national identity. In post-Soviet Latvia, for example, the most up-to-date scholarly methods are applied to reconstitute the country's folksong tradition.

In other previously colonized nations, the study of native folklore by native scholars is a way of self-assertion not only vis-à-vis colonial occupants but also vis-à-vis anthropology, in the sense that the scholars themselves or their fore-bears have been the perpetual "others" in studies by Western anthropologists. In the views of some contemporary Asian and African folklorists, anthropology is even more of a colonialist creation than folkloristics. Although there are well-established folklore departments in such large countries as Japan, India, or Nigeria, the folklore of other African and Asian nations is still primarily studied by Westerners. But many scholars who now wish to investigate the folklore of their own countries face obstacles. Which of the many ethnic or tribal groups inside the borders are to study which other groups? To what extent is it possible or desirable to establish unifying folklore archives and folklore centers?

Over and over, folklorists have set out to collect, preserve, and protect national folklore heritages that have been seen as vanishing. Over and over, they have established national institutions, ranging from the impressive Folklore Archives in Helsinki to the American Folklife Center at the Library of Congress in Washington, D.C. However, in recent years, some folklorists have worked to expand the national confines, calling for the safeguarding of folklore everywhere under the auspices of the United Nations Educational, Scientific, and Cultural Organization (UNESCO). Yet such efforts raise many questions. Whose heritages and what materials should be safeguarded by whom? Will the peoples with power preserve and protect the traditions of the powerless? Future understandings of folklore depend to a great extent on how issues such as these are resolved.

Barbro Klein

See also Folk Group; Folklife; Genre; Tradition.

✽✽✽✽✽✽✽✽✽✽✽✽✽✽✽✽

References

Bausinger, Hermann. 1990. *Folk Culture in a World of Technology*. Trans. Elke Dettmer. Bloomington: Indiana University Press.

Briggs, Charles, and Amy Shuman, eds. 1993. Theorizing Folklore: Toward New Perspectives on the Politics of Culture. *Western Folklore* 52:109–400.

Cocchiara, Giuseppe. 1981. *The History of Folklore in Europe*. Trans. John N. McDaniel. Philadelphia: ISHI.

Dundes, Alan, ed. 1965. *The Study of Folklore*. Englewood Cliffs, NJ: Prentice-Hall.

Frykman, Jonas, and Orvar Löfgren. 1987. *Culture Builders: A Historical Anthropology of Middle Class Life*. Trans. Alan Crozier. New Brunswick, NJ: Rutgers University Press.

Khan, Shamsuzzaman, ed. 1987. *Folklore of Bangladesh*. Dhaka, Bangladesh: Bangla Academy.

Oring, Elliott, ed. 1986. *Folk Groups and Folklore Genres: An Introduction*. Logan: Utah State University Press.

Paredes, Américo, and Richard Bauman, eds. 1972. *Toward New Perspectives in Folklore*. Austin: University of Texas Press.

Radner, Joan Newlon, ed. 1993. *Feminist Messages: Coding in Women's Folk Culture*. Urbana: University of Illinois Press.

Siikala, Anna-Leena, and Sinikka Vakimo, eds. 1994. *Songs beyond the* Kalevala: *Transformations of Oral Poetry*. Helsinki: Suamalaisen Kirjallisuuden Seura.
Toelken, Barre. 1979. *The Dynamics of Folklore*. Boston: Houghton Mifflin.

FOLKLORISMUS/FOLKLORISM

Folklore outside its primary context, or spurious folklore. The term *folklorismus* has been applied to visually and aurally striking or aesthetically pleasing folk materials, such as costume, festive performance, music, and art (but also foods) that lend themselves to being extracted from their initial contexts and put to new uses for different, often larger audiences. The term surfaced first at the turn of the twentieth century as an analogy to *primitivism* when avant-garde circles took an interest in the expressive visual and musical forms of both "primitive" and Western folk cultures. Before the 1960s, the term appeared as *neofolklorism* in French and Russian discussions, referring particularly to the adaptation of folkloric materials in the high cultural contexts of music, art, and literature. In the German discourse, the term appeared in a sociological lexicon in 1958, but it was the folklorist Hans Moser who introduced it into German *Volkskunde* in 1962 and who urged his colleagues to study the seemingly fake in addition to "real" folklore and folk cultures. Over the course of nearly three decades and against much initial resistance, the discourse about and study of folklorism contributed to a thorough revision of *Volkskunde*'s canon, and it broadened the interdisciplinary scope and relevance of the discipline. Although the term itself is now rarely used, the issues originally addressed under the label have become major foci of research. For instance, the staging of folk dance or festivals for tourists, previously shunned as commercial and hence spurious, is now an important area of study. The same holds true for political applications of folklore, be this in historical eras, such as romantic nationalism or Stalinist communism, or in contemporaneous settings, such as ethnic territories struggling for political independence. Less contested but equally vigorous was the folklorism discourse in the Soviet Union and the former Eastern Bloc countries. Communist cultural policy openly valued the use of folk materials for altering societal patterns, and depending on the particular situation of academe in a given state, applied folkloristics and sophisticated analyses of folklorism-related processes occurred side by side. From 1979 until the mid-1980s, the Hungarian scholar Vilmos Voigt sporadically organized conferences on the theme and published the *Folklorismus Bulletin*, which offered ready access and overviews to these otherwise difficult-to-trace developments. In the United States, a similar but more narrow discussion centered on the term *fakelore*.

The German folklorism discourse unraveled the dichotomous premise underlying the definition of folklore that had confined true folklore to communal, preferably peasant settings and excluded materials and groups tainted by the forces of modernity, such as industry or media. This eventually led to a differentiated view of cultural processes, involving folklore in modernity. Moser suggested *folklorism* as a term for the journalistic promotion of culture and the propagandistic use of folklore in branches of the economy. The term was purposely conceived broadly: On the one hand, it addressed the interest in and nostalgia for things folk in an age in which mass communication and industrialization seemed to lead to a loss of cultural distinctiveness; and on the other hand, it encompassed the ways in which the need for distinctiveness was satisfied, strengthened, or awakened. Moser isolated three forms of folklorism: the performance of traditionally and functionally determined elements of folk culture outside that culture's communal context; the performance of folk motifs in another social stratum; and the purposeful imitation and creation of folklike elements outside any tradition. Moser also acknowledged differences in folklorism arising from political economies. In Western capitalist nations, he saw a preponderance of folklorism due to the expansion of industrial markets, ranging from tourism to commodity goods. In communist states, the cultural-political mission of folklorism was emphasized. And in developing, postcolonial nations, folklorism seemed to be used as a shield against radical progress.

Most productive for an introspective turn in *Volkskunde* was Moser's discussion of folklorism and *Rücklauf* (literally, flowing-back) of academic theories and studies into communities and voluntary organizations. This necessitated an examination of the history and present of the cultural and political roles of public sector *Volkskunde* and opened up the way toward recognizing the discipline's interrelationship with nationalism. More fundamentally, such introspection revealed the dichotomous bias in the way "authentic" folklore was defined as separate from spurious cultural materials.

Although a majority of scholars throughout the 1960s and 1970s preferred to use *folklorism* as a descriptive label for everything not included in their discipline, a vigorous minority pressed for a complete revision of *Volkskunde*'s canon. Hermann Bausinger argued that contrasting folklorism with "genuine folk culture" drew the latter into a closed circle in which it inevitably mutated toward folklorism, that so-called first- and secondhand traditions merged in many respects, and that, by excluding one realm from research, scholarly results were inevitably falsified. Bausinger and Konrad Köstlin linked folklorism to processes of modernization and globalization that increasingly rendered identity into a consciously molded rather than a traditionally provided set of practices and symbols—a dynamic that has been closely documented for ethnic groups in the United States. Furthermore, industrialization had made possible the mechanical reproduction of what had formerly been unique items of expressive culture embedded in communal contexts. Rather than confining themselves to vanishing cultural enclaves untouched by modernity, German scholars recognized the need to study folklore's altering roles through time in settings such as political displays, tourism, and arts, crafts, and music markets.

The term *folklorism* has been increasingly abandoned because it lacks specificity. In its stead, more accurate explanatory concepts have been sought. The preparation and presentation of folkloric materials in emblems representing a more wholesome age or way of life has been called *cultural therapy*, the medicinal effect likened to that of a placebo. The English terms *invention of tradition* and, more frequently, *revitalization* have been adopted to describe the use or manipulation of isolated folkloric materials for anything from efforts at regional promotion to politically inspired movements. The Hungarian Tamas Hofer has labeled the emergence of the discipline at the turn of the nineteenth century—intertwined as it was with the rise of nation-states—a revitalization movement whose ideology simmers latently in folkloristic theory and practice. The discourse on folklorism has contributed substantially to making folklorists conscious of these legacies.

Regina Bendix

See also Authenticity; Fakelore; Invented Tradition.

✳✳✳✳✳✳✳✳✳✳✳✳✳✳✳✳✳✳

References

Bausinger, Hermann. [1966] 1986. Toward a Critique of Folklorism Criticism. In *German Volkskunde: A Decade of Theoretical Confrontation, Debate, and Reorientation* (1967–1977), eds. J. Dow and H. Lixfeld. Bloomington: Indiana University Press.

———. 1990. *Folk Culture in a World of Technology*. Trans. Elke Dettmer. Bloomington: Indiana University Press.

———. [1982] 1991. Zum Begriff des Folklorismus. In *Der blinde Hund*, ed. H. Bausinger. Tübingen, Germany: Verlag Schwäbisches Taglatt.

Bendix, Regina. 1988. Folklorism: The Challenge of a Concept. *International Folklore Review* 6:5–15.

Hrander, Edith, and Hans Lunzer, eds. 1982. *Folklorismus*. Neusiedl/See, Austria: Verein Volkskultur am Neusiedl See.

Köstlin, Konrad. 1969. Folklorismus und Ben-Akiba. *Rheinisches Jahrbuch für Volkskunde* 20:234–256.

Moser, Hans. 1962. Vom Folklorismus in unserer Zeit. *Zeitschrift für Volkskunde* 58:177–209.

———. 1964. Der Folklorismus als Forschungsproblem der Volkskunde. *Hessische Blätter für Volkskunde* 55:9–57.

Newell, Venetia J. 1987. The Adaptation of Folklore and Tradition (Folklorismus). *Folklore* 98:131–151.

Rihtman-Augustin, Dunja. 1978. Tradition, Folklore, and Mass Culture in Yugoslavia. In *Folklore in the Modern World*, ed. Richard M. Dorson. The Hague: Mouton.

Voigt, Vilmos. 1979–1980. Confines of Literature, Folklore, and Folklorism. *Neohelikon* 7:123–140.

FOLK MUSIC

Tunes sung, with or without verbal texts, or played on instruments in folkloric performance settings. Contemporary perspectives stress the idea that such music, whatever its origins and previous usages, can be considered folk music when its use is primarily for the enjoyment of performers and listeners in noncommercial settings. This definition, like many recent definitions of folklore in general, stresses *behaviors* in *contexts*—in particular those that are more informal than formal—that exist outside performance settings typically associated with popular and elite or art music in Western cultures.

Earlier definitions of folk music stressed *textual* aspects. Thus, the often quoted definition promulgated by the International Folk Music Council (IFMC) in 1954 described folk music as "the product of a musical tradition that has been evolved through the process of oral transmission," a process entailing continuity, variation, and communal selection. This definition views folk music as a special kind of text, shaped unconsciously in a Darwinian manner by a community to fit its own needs and values. Here, melodies are considered as texts, too, and those that are transmitted aurally are privileged over sight-readable music "texts." The formative scholarship on folk music stressed its value as a representation of a special kind of community, one imagined to exist among a homogeneous group of nonelite people within a peasant, working-class, ethnic, or regional community. These types of communities were held to be particularly important by early folklore scholars who were strongly influenced by populist cultural nationalist agendas. Thus, through processes of borrowing, co-optation, and canon formation, the music associated with nonelite communities became an important symbol of identity for intellectual elites involved in nationalist enterprises.

Consequently, folk music was analyzed in terms of musical elements thought to be characteristic of such national/communal settings. Because one type of verbal folksong text, the ballad, was recognized in the eighteenth century as having important connections with elite literature, its musical aspects received considerable scholarly attention. The ballad, as performed in western Europe and in other parts of the world colonized from this region, was typically performed solo and a cappella. Consequently, musicologists who focused upon folksong generally concerned themselves with monophonic sound. This concern reflected, as well, the limitations of data collection in the era prior to the widespread use of sound recordings, for at that time, it was rarely possible to accurately notate more than a single line of melody. In this context, certain aspects of melody—particularly scale and, to a lesser extent, melodic contour—were thought by influential scholars such as Cecil Sharp to be diagnostic of cultural *geists* (spirits). So, for example, considerable weight was given to tunes with scales that, because they had less than a full octave or were modal rather than harmonic, might be considered to be survivals of very old music practices. Considerable attention was also paid to developing the idea of the "tune family," utilizing selected aspects of melody for comparative analysis that paralleled the research into the history of verbal folksong texts that led to schemes of classification and typology, such as those of Francis James Child and Malcolm Laws.

The growth of the discipline of ethnomusicology in the twentieth century, coupled with the advent of convenient sound-recording technology, led to a broadening of perspective. Alan Lomax, studying the relationships between folksong style and culture, developed cantometrics, a system of analysis designed to describe recorded musical performances using standardized terminology. Cantometrics' 37 different parameters encompass a variety of factors, including: the social organization of vocal groups and orchestras, levels of cohesiveness and explicitness, rhythmic organization, melodic complexity, embellishment, and vocal stance. Lomax sought to describe aspects of *texture* as well as text.

As a descriptive system, cantometrics is much more inclusive than previous musical analysis systems, most of which have suffered from the fact that they utilize the prescriptive notation developed by Western art music, which biases the description. Lomax's analytic uses of his descriptive system, however, also have proven contentious. Utilizing Freudian ideas about human behavior, he suggested certain relationships between aspects of sound and musical organization, on the one hand, and broadly conceived cultural patterns, on the other. This reflected Lomax's own preference for theory-driven survey research rather than in-depth, data-driven field studies.

Nevertheless, Lomax's work served to broaden the scope of musical description, something that was necessary given the contemporary approach described at the beginning of this entry. Indeed, the problem folk music scholars now face is one of the boundaries of their field. Is, for example, the music made by of a group of friends who gather occasionally to play Bach or Beethoven for their own enjoyment to be considered folk music? One argument against calling such performances folk music is that in these performances the musicians intend to follow closely the composer's original score; the emphasis in folk music, by contrast, is upon a variety of intentions related to the perceived history, meaning, and uses of the music. Clearly, though, the differences between these intentions are a matter of degree rather than of opposition, for folklorists have shown that noncommercial musical traditions such as fiddling and Sacred Harp religious singing often place considerable emphasis upon the score as a document of the intention of the composer. However, such musics tend to fall outside the realm of elite art music, which is perpetuated through formal training based not just upon scores but also upon an extensive interpretive literature.

A second parallel dilemma is raised by the fact that there are many examples of musical performance that are called folk music but that take place in commercial or formal settings. These examples may reflect an understanding of folk music in cultural nationalist terms. Or they may be using folk music as a metaphor for the values associated with informality and noncommercialism. Whatever the case, when one analyzes the musical aspects of such performances, one usually finds considerable differences, particularly in terms of textures, in comparison with the same musics in noncommercial and informal settings. So, for example, when folklorist MacEdward Leach collected "The Blue Velvet Band" from folksinger William Riley of Lance au Loup, Labrador, in 1960, Riley closely followed the lyrics and melody of the song as first recorded by its author—professional country music singer Hank Snow—in 1937. But in terms of texture, there is a world of difference: Riley sings a cappella in a rubato parlando style; Snow accompanies himself with a guitar to a faster fixed tempo. Further, Riley's performance omits both Snow's opening spoken introduction, which contextualizes the song as a fictional cowboy bunkhouse performance, and Snow's closing yodel, an ornamental feature characteristic of his commercial musical domain.

This example reminds us that folk music researchers continue to focus upon issues of variation—whether in text, texture, or context—reflecting an underlying assumption that individual folk music pieces are, to a greater extent than other forms of music, constantly changing. The idea of viewing folk music as a mode of expression that frees singers and instrumentalists to re-create and improvise within the arena of a collective or shared *music-culture* (a term coined by Mark Slobin and Jeff Titon) recalls the IFMC's communalist definition mentioned earlier and suggests the importance of a perspective that moves beyond individual items and performances to consider entire repertoires.

Many studies of individual folk tunes exist, but folk music is nonetheless conventionally thought of in a plural sense as an aggregation of tunes. Although contemporary scholars tend to follow the strategy of viewing folk music in terms of individual behaviors in specific contexts (as suggested in the definition offered at the outset), a considerable number of those who speak of folk music think of it in these aggregational terms. It is useful to think of such aggregations as *canons*. Philip Bohlman suggests that canon formation is an essential aspect of folk music in the modern world. He offers several models of canon formation, ranging from local to national, in his discussion of the ways in which groups of people participating in folk music performances perceive their repertoire. Such canon formation is assessed critically and analytically by contemporary scholars as a source for data about the realities of folk music from a contextual point of view. Beyond this, however, it must be recognized that the entire body of writing about folk music, scholarly and otherwise, constitutes the most important and influential canon that shapes perceptions about what is and what is not folk music.

Neil V. Rosenberg

See also Ballad; Broadside Ballad; Cantometrics; Ethnomusicology; Folk Song, Lyric; Folk Song, Narrative.

✳✳✳✳✳✳✳✳✳✳✳✳✳✳✳✳✳

References

Bohlman, Philip V. 1988. *Folk Music in the Modern World.* Bloomington: Indiana University Press.

Child, Francis James. 1965. *The English and Scottish Popular Ballads.* New York: Dover.

International Folk Music Council. 1955. Resolutions: Definition of Folk Music. *International Folk Music Journal* 7:23.

Laws, G. Malcolm. 1957. *American Balladry from British Broadsides.* Philadelphia: American Folklore Society.

———. 1964. *Native American Balladry.* Philadelphia: American Folklore Society.

Leach, MacEdward. 1965. *Folk Ballads and Songs of the Lower Labrador Coast.* Ottawa: National Museum.

Lomax, Alan. 1968. *Folk Song Style and Culture.* Washington, DC: American Association for the Advancement of Science.

Slobin, Mark, and Jeff Todd Titon. 1992. The Music-Culture as a World of Music. In *Worlds of Music,* ed. Jeff Todd Titon, et al. New York: Schirmer.

FOLKSONG, LYRIC

Traditional song type that "expresses" rather than "depicts" or "narrates." A lyric folksong does not so much examine a situation by listing salient component parts (as catalog folksongs, often called just *songs,* do) or re-create an event by recounting the sequence of its stages from beginning, through middle, to end (as ballads do) as it expresses an emotional reaction to a significant experience. Religious lyric folksongs, for example, often look forward eagerly to the release from earthly travail that death will bring when the individual is finally united with the heavenly family in a joyful, eternal afterlife:

> O when shall I see Jesus and dwell with him above;
> And from the flowing fountain drink everlasting love?
> When shall I be deliver'd from this vain world of sin?
> And with my blessed Jesus drink endless pleasures in?

In contrast, secular lyric songs more often look backward and lament rather than rejoice, as does this Irish emigration song from the nineteenth century that expresses grief at forced departure from a beloved native land:

> The morning was bright,
> But my heart is now low,
> For far from those dear hills

> I'll soon have to go
> Across the wide ocean,
> Forever to roam,
> And leave far behind me
> The hills of Tyrone.
>
> My poor heart is breaking
> With sorrow and pain
> For friends and companions
> I'll ne'er see again.
> I'm bidding farewell
> To the friends I have known,
> And adieu to the wee lass
> I leave in Tyrone.

However, religious lyric songs such as "O When Shall I See Jesus" that treat our relationship with a deity and even those secular lyric songs such as "Hills of Tyrone" that treat our relationship with social conditions, institutions, or habitations are in a distinct minority in British and American folksong repertoires, as they almost certainly are in other cultures as well. By far the most common kind of lyric folksong is that which treats interpersonal relationships with "significant others," particularly male/female romantic entanglements. Indeed, such a topic is so dominant within the genre that many folklorists would consider "love song" virtually the equivalent of "lyric song"—or at the very least, definitive of the type.

As epitomized in love songs, the most striking feature of a lyric folksong (or just *lyric*) is the aforementioned quality of its appeal to affect. The lyric song is more directly about the feelings it expresses—regret, longing, despair, ecstasy—than it is about a lengthy sea voyage to a new country or about a lover who, despite vows of fidelity, soon abandons one for another. These feelings are not so much *implied* by the topic as they *are* the topic, and they cluster around the two poles of joy and sorrow, often represented textually in images of life and death:

> Come, all young maidens, take a warning from me
> Never build your nest on the top of the tree
> The roots they will wither, the branches decay
> Like that false-hearted young man, they will soon fade
>   away.

Other features common to lyric songs seem to be logical extensions of the primary trait. For instance, lyric folksongs almost always adopt the first-person

344

point of view, so that the circumstances, the worldview, and most prominently of course, the feelings are all offered from the perspective of the speaker himself or herself, as in this ancient Chinese example:

> The meadow grasshopper chirps
> And the hillside grasshopper leaps.
> Until I have seen my lord,
> My anxious heart is disturbed.
> But as soon as I shall see him,
> As soon as I shall join him,
> My heart will have peace.
>
> I climb that southern hill
> There to gather the ferns.
> Until I have seen my lord,
> My anxious heart is tortured.
> But as soon as I shall see him,
> As soon as I shall join him,
> My heart will be gay.

A third characteristic is lack of concreteness. Lyric love songs in particular give almost no details of the journalistic sort, seldom specifying where or when circumstances to which the song alludes took place. Names of protagonists are invariably absent, as are specific identities—rich ladies from London, Turkish damsels, bold lieutenants. Medieval (or "Child") ballads too are vague in detail but in a stylized, adumbrated way; lyric songs carry this trait to an extreme, so that details are not just stylized but generic and universal. Males are "young men," females are "maidens," place is a generalized outdoors, time is an implied spring or summer, and character and motives are predetermined. Even the circumstances that contributed to the condition lamented are but barely sketched since presumably they are typical and so already well known to all:

> I once had a sweetheart but now I have none,
> And since he has left me I care for none;
> And since he has left me, I'll have you all know
> That men are deceitful, wherever they go.

A fourth characteristic of the lyric love song folklorists often stress in describing the type is its heavy employment of verbal formulas. This feature is found in all folklore that depends extensively on oral composition, acquisition, retention, and transmission, but it is, once again, especially prominent in the lyric. Thus, the Anglo-American folksinger has lamented in song after song that "if I had wings like an eagle I'd fly" or that "I wish, I wish, but I wish in vain / I wish I were a maid again," and the African-American blues singer has claimed over and over that he or she "woke up this morning feeling sad and blue / Woke up this morning, didn't hardly know what to do." Such set pieces have been called "floating stanzas" by some folksong scholars because they seem to fit comfortably into quite distinct songs.

A fifth trait is the lyric's consistent employment of figurative imagery. Favored images are those of the natural environment: topographical features of the landscape, such as mountains and valleys; birds, such as larks, nightingales, and linnets; and a wide range of botanical phenomena, especially flowers—roses, for instance, or lilies. In other types of folksong, such natural imagery is basically just setting, but in lyric songs, nature enjoys a far more prominent role and far more semiotic significance:

> I thrust my hand into some young bush
> Thinking there the sweetest flower to find
> I pricked my finger to the bone
> And left the sweetest flower alone.
>
> I leaned my back up against some young oak
> Thinking it was a trusty tree
> But first it bended and then it broke
> And so my true love did to me.

Perhaps the most complex trait of lyric songs is their semantic structure, by which we mean the particular kind of relationships the essential images in the text bear to each other. In other genres of song, this structure is quite straightforward: In the ballad, for example, relationships are causal and sequential; in catalog songs—such as lullabies, worksongs, ritual songs, and play songs—images are related by part/whole correspondences, by physical propinquity, or by some other shared empirical characteristic. In lyric song, however, the dominant relationship is what might be called thematic resonance; for example, there is clear association in the vitality of soaring birds, burning sun, frolicking lambs, or a girl running through meadows gathering flowers indiscriminately, as there is in the immobility of a dead lover, a marble tombstone, or a hushed cuckoo. These images can truly be called symbols; they signify such concepts as amplification, intensity, profusion, verticality, activity, and their opposites—silence, stillness, singleness, and so on—that cluster around the two paradigmatic themes of life and death, with their associated emotions of joy and sorrow, as in this Russian example:

346

"Ah, why, little dove, are you sitting so unhappy
So unhappy are you sitting and so sad?"
"How can I, a little dove, be happy,
Be happy and joyful?
Last evening a pretty dove was with me,
A pretty dove who sat by me,
In the morning my dove lay slain,
Lay slain, shot!"

Although enough songs in folk tradition exhibit the features here enumerated to gain them recognition as a type, none of the traits, not even the type's most essential ingredient—that it treats emotional effects of a significant experience—is necessarily restricted to lyric songs. Employment of an emotional perspective is only one way of representing and communicating about human affairs; recounting their evolution over time is another way, and anatomizing their constituent parts (the approach taken here in elucidating lyric song itself, for instance) is yet another. These three ways of articulating experience in sung verse are the most common in British and Anglo-American tradition, and any single song will invariably draw upon the conventions of more than one method. Thus, a narrative stanza or two will often appear in a lyric song, telling at least a bit of the lovers' original meeting, for instance, but ballads will frequently arrest the progress of their narratives to express affective response to the events so far recounted. Indeed, some songs may so vary from singer to singer that ballad stanzas may be dropped wholesale and lyric stanzas may be augmented—or the other way round—so that genetically related versions of the same song may be categorized differently, one as ballad, another as lyric. When we categorize any version of a song, then, whether as a lyric or as something else, we are saying only that it draws upon certain formal conventions more than on others.

Roger deV. Renwick

See also Folk Music; Hymn, Folk; Lullaby; Worksong.

✳✳✳✳✳✳✳✳✳✳✳✳✳✳✳✳✳

References
Belden, Henry M., and Arthur Palmer Hudson, eds. 1952. *The Frank C. Brown Collection of North Carolina Folklore.* Vol. 3. Durham, NC: Duke University Press.
de V. Renwick, Roger 1980. *English Folk Poetry: Structure and Meaning.* Philadelphia: University of Pennsylvania Press.
Granet, Marcel. 1932. *Festivals and Songs of Ancient China.* New York: E. P. Dutton.
Reeder, Roberta, trans. and ed. 1993. *Russian Folk Lyrics.* With an Introduction by V. Ja. Propp. Bloomington: Indiana University Press.

FOLKSONG, NARRATIVE

A concept that assumes two things: first, that the item or complex in question is linked to the repertoire of a particular group (that is, it must have entered tradition at some level), and second, that its textual material is rooted in a sequence of past actions of dynamically involved characters, normally progressing through stages of stasis, disequilibrium, and resolution.

The recognition of narrative as a significant category of folksong has a long-standing history, dating in British scholarship to correspondence between Thomas Percy and the poet William Shenstone in the 1760s. On at least two occasions, Shenstone proposed a distinction between ballads, whose defining feature was action, and songs, which expressed emotion. To eighteenth-century neoclassicists, it made perfect sense to conscript two of Aristotle's divisions of poetry—epic and lyric—as frames for sung verse. It is perhaps more surprising that this literary generic construct remains accepted in today's more ethnographically oriented studies. Indeed, constituting genres solely on the basis of textual features may seem regressively item oriented, possibly obscuring relationships between songs within particular contexts and distorting our view of the cultural function of song. In some cases, however, ethnographic research reveals corresponding native distinctions: In Scotland, the concept of *muckle sang* corresponds generally to the notion of ballad, and in Newfoundland, a distinction between songs and ditties or, in some areas, between stories, songs, and ditties embodies a separation of narrative and lyric. So the categories are not completely analytic, but as with any generic frame, they must not be adopted in a way that prioritizes one group or the other or in a way that fails to account for how the various categories interrelate in practice. Conversely, researchers should be alive to formal, thematic, and poetic differences within categories, as they too may contain clues for the interpretation of cultural processes.

An apposition between the narrative and the emotive, unfortunately, does not pave the way to a clear and easy means of classifying songs. With the broadening of the term *folksong* as an intellectual concept in the twentieth century, not only has the bipartite division proven insufficient but there also has been little progress toward the development of a system of classification that is both comprehensive and based on truly logical principles. Folklorists have expanded the literary model to include descriptive songs, which are purely expository and document certain aspects of a situation without weaving them into a story or presenting one's opinion of them one way or another. Moniker songs, which name and then briefly characterize members of a group, are good examples. But the model leaves little room for songs in which mode of expression is secondary to function, as, for example, in some work songs or in dance or game accompaniments. Further, beyond the difficulty of establishing suitable categories, there is the equally problematic question of deciding where a specific song might fit. If a moniker song characterizes through action or dialogue, it is difficult to ignore the narrative component. Likewise, many nineteenth-century lyric songs contain at least the essence of a narrative, and often, the singer's attention is divided equally between telling a story and expressing his or her feelings about it. Further complications arise if one stops to ask what constitutes the song? Is it bounded solely by the text and melody? What other types of cultural and/or aesthetic information are applied in the interpretation of a song performance? Anna Caraveli's crucial revelation of "the song beyond the song" demonstrates that all sorts of satellite knowledge attaches itself to songs in particular situations. This can include oral narratives that explain or give grounds for a lyric evocation. Hugh Shields, writing of the predominantly lyric tradition in Gaelic Ireland, and Vladimir Propp, discussing lyric songs in Russia, have both noted the importance of an implied or assigned narrative to their respective materials. Even when narrative has little or no overt influence at the level of text, tradition nonetheless may hold it as an integral aspect of the song.

Bearing such difficulties in mind, we can say that as an intrinsic concept, narrative folksongs are oriented, at a textual level, toward the specific past actions of one or more characters and follow a conflict through to its resolution. In broad stroke, it includes everything from oral epics to *cante fable* (singing tale) and narrative obituary verse, though the most prevalent form in the recorded song traditions of western Europe and the Americas is the ballad, which consists of several subgenres: (1) the classical ballad, (2) the print-generated broadside ballad, (3) the native American ballad, and (4) the blues ballad. The underpinnings of these categories are complex and not always consistently applied, for they are founded on certain assumptions about context of production that do not coincide well with the repertoires either recovered from oral singers or assembled in the broadside collections of antiquarians. Formally, all ballads are stanzaic, except for some southern and eastern European traditions, which are stichic but molded by a strophic melody, and though specific forms differ, in Teutonic balladry (of which the Anglo-American tradition is a part), the most common is a quatrain of alternating tetrameter and trimeter lines, rhyming *abcb*. Where melody demands, this basic form can be rendered as a "double stanza" of four seven-stress lines rhyming *aabb*, a pattern common in broadsides. In terms of isolating subgenres, however, the key elements are differences in narrative method and poetic style, and the ethnographic validation of maintaining subgeneric divisions hinges on the assumption that each particular style is rooted in a specific set of cultural circumstances. For historical reasons, it makes sense to deal first with the classical and broadside varieties.

The classical ballad, on the basis of its thematic substance alone—its grounding in traditional belief systems, its emphasis on kinship, and its setting in a world that is at once aristocratic yet characteristically rural—suggests a cultural environment that is if not strictly medieval as some propose then at least premodern. Although there are manuscript texts in ballad form dating as far back as the thirteenth century, it does not logically follow that all ballads are medieval, as was the tacit assumption in earlier scholarship. Contemporary approaches urge that ballads be treated as coterminous with the lives of the singers, even if chivalric themes suggest a more antiquated setting and despite purported links with such late-medieval literary genres as metrical romance. Within this framework, the cultural trait overarching classical ballad style is orality, that is, the genre appears to emanate from nonliterate culture. Emphasis on orality avoids grounding the ballad in a specific historical era, linking it instead to a cultural condition extant in at least parts of Europe and America until well into the nineteenth century. Stylistically, the oral nature of the classical ballad is evidenced by formulaic diction and stanzaic sequencing based on repetition and chiastic structuring, resulting in a condensed, "gapped" method of narration often described as "leaping and lingering." Other conventionally cited narrative traits—concentration on a single narrative episode, dramatic development through dialogue and action, and impersonal or objective tone—are not of themselves markers of orality, but they do echo Axel Olrik's Epic Law of Single-Stranded Plot and his insistence that, in oral narrative, action is everything. They also highlight the degree to which the story takes center stage in the classical ballad, leaving most other common features of narration—description, characterization, and evaluation—to be inferred subtextually.

The broadside ballads, printed on single sheets of paper and hawked in the streets and at fairs, developed with the rapid expansion of cheap, popular literature in the wake of the invention of the press (in 1454). The earliest broadside poetry mimicked elite forms of the day, but by the mid-sixteenth century, the ballad form had become a common medium for broadside writers, probably due to its popularity among the reading public. Formally and to a lesser extent thematically, the broadsides and the classical ballads share common ground, but the former's literary provenance shows stylistically in a greater emphasis on description, idiosyncratic language, and linear structure. Where formulas appear, they are conventional rather than intrinsic, found, for example, as convenient opening or closing stanzas, not as part of a totalizing poetic language. Natascha Würzbach has argued that the most prevalent broadside commonplaces are the "come-all-ye" formulas directing the audience's attention to the singer/seller, thus highlighting the commercial basis of the genre.

The subject matter of the broadsides also tends to grab one's attention in very obvious ways; in fact the comparison between broadsides and contemporary tabloids has been made often. The early "black letter" ballads, so-called because of their gothic typeface, revel in bawdy tales, rustic humor, and accounts of the fantastic, as well as in political and religious issues. By the late eighteenth century, by which time roman "white letter" type replaces black letter, crime and punishment become the mainstays of the trade, coupled with a tendency for romantic narratives to emphasize class difference and emigration as the greatest obstacles to a happy union, such that tales of love are played out in response to emergent social pressures of the times. Thus, the broadsides, in contrast to the classical ballads, are fundamentally modern and urban, resulting in shifts not only in theme but also in attitude. First, they are rational, depicting a world much more in line with the empirical surroundings of the singers and their audience. The supernatural occupies only a very small place in broadside narratives, and otherworld figures tend to be confined to those sanctioned, however equivocally, within modern ideology, mainly ghosts and the sacred. For the most part, the marvelous in broadsides consists of natural curiosities that challenge credulity rather than reinforce belief, and one might even allow that its components include extraordinary social roles filled by human characters, such as warrior women and laborer heroes who achieve dramatic rises in wealth and class standing. Second, the broadsides are more subjective than classical ballads, often stating the moral to be drawn from the narrative through conventionalized warnings to the audience. This, coupled with frequent metanarration and asides to the audience, gives the narrator's voice a dynamic presence in the text, and it is not uncommon for the narrator to appear as a character, either as a witness to the events or even as the protagonist.

These generic descriptions and distinctions, however, must be accepted in the abstract, for even though any number of texts can be put forward as representative of one subgenre or another, attempts to construct concrete boundaries are destined to fail. As stated at the outset, the division assumes particular styles emanating from particular cultural contexts, leaving to one side the fact that individual items are highly capable of flourishing outside their matrices. To approach the topic diachronically, a concomitant distinction between oral versus literate, vis-à-vis context of production, and oral versus print (or recording) vis-à-vis medium of transmission, is essential, for in reality, the classical and broadside ballads constitute parallel traditions that existed in immediate proximity for almost four centuries; traces of interchange and mutual influence are extensive. Broadsides have been disseminated widely through oral transmission, and several "oral" ballads owe at least part of their circulation to print. Where such exchanges occur, it has been widely demonstrated that songs can become shaped by the aesthetic conventions of the adopted milieu. Emendations to classical ballad stories reworked for the broadside press commonly include the addition of descriptive detail, nonformulaic language, subjective interpolation by the narrator, and other typically broadside traits. Similar processes are operative in oral transmission in later stages of tradition, as, for example, the tendency toward the lyrification of classical ballads in the nineteenth century, noted by Tristram Coffin.

Coping with the sheer dynamism of tradition has proven the greatest obstacle to a clear definition of balladry at any level or in any form, which, coupled with the divergent intellectual and cultural interests of those who have studied the form, has meant that virtually all efforts toward ballad classification and analysis have been open to challenge. Understanding something of the history of the scholarship may at least put some of the debate in perspective, even if it resolves nothing completely. Much of the early antiquarian writing probably was based on a familiarity with the urban broadsides, as is evidenced by the general adoption of the term *ballad*, or *ballet* as it was frequently spelled, which in the seventeenth and early eighteenth centuries normally indicated a song printed or written on a sheet of paper. Ongoing antiquarian research, particularly in the wake of Percy's *Reliques of Ancient English Poetry* (1765), led to the "discovery" of the traditional (classical) ballad, then still common in rural areas of Britain, especially in northern England and lowland Scotland. Subsequent collectors, influenced by national-romantic conceptions of *das Volk*, became increasingly drawn to the ballad as folk poetry, and by the time William Motherwell collected in the 1820s, there was at least an intuitive understanding of the difference between the classical and broadside forms. During roughly the same period, the Grimms formulated their notion of *das Volke dichtet* to account for the esoteric features stamped on the products of oral tradition.

The central figure of late-nineteenth-century Anglo-Scots ballad studies was Harvard professor Francis James Child, whose monumental anthology, *The English and Scottish Popular Ballads*, appeared between 1882 and 1898. Years earlier, his curiosity about the nature of ballads had been piqued while preparing an edition for a general series on British poets, and in subsequent research, conducted in collaboration with the Danish folklorist Svend Grundtvig, he attempted to concentrate solely on the traditional form, which he termed "popular." What he could not ignore, of course, was the degree of mutual exchange between the popular and the "vulgar" (broadside) forms, and he often gave the nod to print material that possibly had traditional roots or parallels. It is also quite possible that he was unable to break completely free of the antiquarians, who had derived their understanding of the ballads largely from broadsides. Several of the most famous ballad types—"The Chevy Chase" and much of the Robin Hood material, for example—existed only in versions that displayed greater stylistic affinity with the broadside than with the oral form. Unfortunately, Child died before writing the essay explaining the process that guided his specific choices, and in the absence of this state-ment, the collection was left to speak for itself.

Where Child's erudition carried the voice of authority, *The English and Scottish Popular Ballads* stood as a five-volume definition of *the* ballad, and more ardent disciples granted traditional status only to versions of Child ballads. Broadsides were regarded as, at best, poor cousins, and those that Child himself included were assumed coarse vestiges of once pristine traditional compositions. Critics, on the other hand, insisted that the collection be taken at face value, and because of the multiformity of its content, they argued that a distinction between broadside and traditional forms was if not arbitrary then virtually impossible to define, concluding, as Thelma James did, that a Child ballad was little more than a ballad selected and anthologized by Child. This position became increasingly tenable in light of renewed song collection, which revealed traditions in which classical ballads mingled freely with broad-sides and singers who rarely made any palpable distinction between them. Even though most song collections deferred to the influence of Child by plac-ing classical ballads first, a practice D. K. Wilgus criticized as constituting a "Child and other" approach, the bulk of the narrative material in tradition in the twentieth century consisted of either broadside versions or the two other forms of modern balladry—the so-called native American ballad and the "blues" ballad.

The native American ballad (NAB) is very closely related to the broad-side; many types within this subgenre are, in fact, products of the American broadside trade and are, at times, stylistically indistinguishable from British broadsides. As a subgenre in its own right, however, the NAB brings to the fore three elements that either are not apparent or exist as secondary consid-erations in the print ballads: (1) a concern for occupation, (2) journalistic style, and (3) in contrast to the ribaldry and moralization of the broadsides, a focus on puritanism, sentimentalism, and an often fatalistic resignation to the hand of providence. It should be pointed out that none of these characteris-tics make the NAB a distinctly American form, for contemporaneous songs in Europe—Scottish bothy ballads, Norwegian *rallarviser*, Irish street ballads, and even many Victorian broadsides—reveal similar influences, which high-lights one problem in discussing this form—the inadequacy of the term that defines it. Moreover, the current understanding of the NAB tends to exclude non-English-American parallels, such as the Mexican/Chicano *corrido* in the Southwest and the francophone *complaintes* in Canada. Proposing a term that successfully encompasses all these traditions is no easy task, but it is possible to account briefly for some of the features common to many, if not all of them. The style appears to be a logical evolution of the broadsides, conditioned by a number of social developments of the late eighteenth and the nineteenth centuries. The concern for occupation can be correlated to the transition from petty production to industrial labor as the basis of rural working-class economy, particularly in resource-based industries (such as mining, lumbering, offshore fishing, transportation industries, and others) with which the NAB is so strongly associated. Details of occupational life and work technique receive a great deal of attention, and many narratives are set against a background of harsh working conditions, especially in inherently dangerous trades. Employer/worker relations are a prevalent theme, though they are not always expressed antagonistically; if social differences between worker and boss are not immediately relevant to the narrative, they are likely to be ignored.

The late nineteenth century marks the first period in history in which literacy rates in Western, industrialized countries approached the 100 percent level, and in addition to the varieties of chap literature purchased for entertainment, one of the more prevalent sources of reading material was the newspaper. It is therefore not surprising that ballads of the time should exhibit journalistic influences, among them a pronounced concern for details relating to time and place, an increased tendency toward reportage as opposed to dramatic narration, and a notable reliance on actual events, especially murders and disasters, for subject matter. Anne B. Cohen's study of the journalistic and balladic responses to the murder of Pearl Bryan in 1896 shows clearly the ballads' reliance on news reports not only for specific details but also for viewpoints and thematic formulas. Journalism, as a prominent arbiter of Victorian ethos, may also account to some degree for the puritanical and sentimental quality of the NAB, though there are likely other influences operating here, including religious and temperance movements and the rapidly expanding popular music industry, all of which relied heavily on sentimental and moralistic material to attract audiences. From a stylistic perspective, one of the main outgrowths of the infusion of sentiment is a drift away from the focus on a single episode toward a presentation not only of the event itself but also of its reverberations. A narrative of disaster will generally move quickly past the scene of the tragedy to its impact on relatives, giving full vent to their grief and the uncertainty of their future.

The blues ballad, although its name suggests a strictly Afro-American form, has been shown by D. K. Wilgus to constitute a syncretism of black and Irish traditions, one of a number of prominent nineteenth-century forms resulting from this particular cultural fusion. Thematically, though it responds to many of the same occupational impulses as the NAB, focusing on the worker or strong man as modern hero, it deals bluntly and at times sardonically with the topics of crime, violence, and sex. Its protagonists are commonly antiheroes and almost never passive. Perhaps its most notable feature is the degree to which it emphasizes character over narrative sequence, maintaining as the primary objective the praise or satirization of its human subject. Like the NAB, much of its subject matter derives ostensibly from actual events, but rather than re-create the narrative in verse, the blues ballad assumes the audience's familiarity with the details of the incident and offers instead brief, highly formulaic, and often stylized allusions to events and character reactions, generally weaving a pastiche of commentary around an implied narrative; it leaps but rarely lingers. In addition to textual features, a crucial element of blues ballad style is the accompaniment, provided by guitar or banjo, that, as in the blues proper, acts as an independent voice within the song, providing a textural response to the vocal line and, through the placement of instrumental breaks, structures groups of stanza into thematically connected units.

To varying degrees, collectors and analysts in the twentieth century have been confronted with all the styles simultaneously, and no ethnographically sound study of modern tradition should regard them as discrete but should explore their many interconnections in all their richness. Nor will such a study find that the interrelationships fall neatly into a historical model, with one form evolving into another. If the stanzaic form of the classical ballad turns up in the blues ballad, it is equally true that the instrumental component of the blues ballad, by virtue of its broad influence on contemporary popular music, has ultimately shaped the performance of classical ballads in the folksong revival. From an ethnohistorical perspective, however, individual styles can remain the subject of focused analyses. The development of the oral-formulaic theory and other approaches to the study of formulaic poetry have reawakened scholarly interest in the classical ballad, which remains the most broadly documented example of oral literature in anglophone culture and offers great potential for research into our preliterate past. Likewise, a number of recent works have examined the broadside as a dominant form of early popular culture. Regardless of perspective, the study of both theme and style in narrative folksong can contribute to the understanding of tradition, for there is as much to learn from the way a story is told as from the tale itself.

James Moreira

See also Ballad; Broadside Ballad; Epic Laws; Folk Music; Incremental Repetition; Oral-Formulaic Theory.

✳✳✳✳✳✳✳✳✳✳✳✳✳✳✳✳

References

Cohen, Anne B. 1973. *Poor Pearl, Poor Girl!: The Murdered-Girl Stereotype in Ballad and Newspaper*. American Folklore Society, Memoir Series, vol. 58. Austin: University of Texas Press.

Dugaw, Diane. 1989. *Warrior Women and Popular Balladry, 1650–1850*. Cambridge Studies in Eighteenth-Century English Literature and Thought 4. Cambridge: Cambridge University Press.

Green, Archie. 1972. *Only a Miner*. Urbana: University of Illinois Press.

Ives, Edward D. 1978. *Joe Scott, The Woodsman-Songmaker*. Urbana: University of Illinois Press.

Laws, G. Malcolm. 1957. *American Ballads from British Broadsides*. American Folklore Society, Bibliographic and Special Series, vol. 8. Philadelphia: American Folklore Society.

———. 1950. *Native American Balladry*. American Folklore Society, Bibliographic and Special Series, vol. 1. Philadelphia: American Folklore Society.

Shepard, Leslie. [1962] 1978. *The Broadside Ballad*. Hatboro, PA: Legacy Books.

Watt, Tessa. 1991. *Cheap Print and Popular Piety, 1550–1640*. Cambridge: Cambridge University Press.

Wilgus, D. K. 1959. *Anglo-American Folksong Scholarship Since 1898*. New Brunswick, NJ: Rutgers University Press.

Wilgus, D. K., and Eleanor Long. 1985. The *Blues Ballad* and the Genesis of Style in Traditional Narrative Song. In *Narrative Folksong: New Directions—Essays in Appreciation of Edson Richmond*, eds. Carol L. Edwards and Kathleen B. Manley. Boulder, CO: Westview Press.

Würzbach, Natascha. 1990. *The Rise of the English Street Ballad, 1550–1650*. Cambridge and New York: Cambridge University Press.

FOLKTALE

A traditional narrative; more narrowly, a traditional fictional story in prose. Fictional folktales, told as entertainment, can be distinguished from myths and legends, which are intended to convey information or at least a point of view. Even fictional folktales, however, educate by illustrating or explaining particular cultural ideas and especially by cautioning against undesirable behavior. *Traditional* means handed down or passed on; traditionality is most obvious in folktales that are manifested in many more or less different versions (or variants). The tale types most common in Europe, the Middle East, and India are listed in *The Types of the Folktale,* an index introduced in 1910 by Antti Aarne and enlarged twice (in 1928 and 1961) by Stith Thompson. Each tale type is assigned a number designated by AT (in honor of the compilers) or Type.

The shortest and most numerous tales are the *humorous anecdotes* (AT 1200–1874), most of which deal with cleverness, stupidity, or both. As with jokes, these anecdotes often use stereotypes to ridicule broad classes of people: numskulls, con artists and their dupes, unfaithful and otherwise disagreeable spouses, ungodly parsons. The subjects of some of these anecdotes, many of which were found in early written sources, are now archaic, but others remain current in oral tradition. Of course, numerous anecdotes exist that have not been indexed. Gershon Legman's work compensates for the habitual scholarly neglect of erotic material.

Animal tales (AT 1–299) are much like anecdotes in that they tell of tricksters and their victims. These tales, which are generally satirical, are popular throughout the world, but in different cultures, they tend to follow different patterns. The animals talk and act like humans, and some of the tales correspond exactly to anecdotes with human agents. For example, in AT 43, "The Bear Builds a House of Wood, the Fox, of Ice," corresponds to AT 1097, "The Ice Mill"; AT 153, "The Gelding of the Bear and the Fetching of Salve," corresponds to AT 1133, "Making the Ogre Strong (by Castration)." Many other animal tales duplicate or reflect on motifs in human-populated tales. For example, in AT 50, "The Sick Lion," and AT 91, "Monkey Who Left His Heart at Home," victims are to be sacrificed for the alleged curative properties of parts of their bodies, just as in human-populated tales, a diseased character hopes or pretends to hope to be cured at the expense of a sacrificial victim. Animal judges mock corrupt and foolish human judges. Animal tales make use of stock characters, and different animals assume some of the same roles: the fox, the jackal, the monkey, or the coyote is clever, as are the rabbit and the hare; the bear, the wolf, or even the human is stupid. Other objects, even inanimate ones, occasionally appear as folktale characters. In an African tale that was carried to the New World, one or two people are terrified by objects and animals that speak (Motif B210.1).

Tall tales (tales of lying, AT 1875–1999) are anecdotes that begin realistically but culminate in the incredible. When they are performed, the narrator takes the role of the con artist, and the audience becomes the dupe. Tall tales, especially about hunting and farming, have flourished in the New World in response to its promise of abundance. *Formula tales* (AT 2000–2399), which rely on a firm structure, are similar to formulaic prayers. Some of these tales, evidently honed on audiences of young children, are silly; others explore sacred subjects. This affinity of the sacred and the profane is expressed overtly in a tale in which a man, reproved for playing cards, assigns to each a symbolic, religious significance (AT 1613, "Playing-Cards Are My Calendar and Prayerbook"). *Cumulative tales*, such as "The House That Jack Built" (AT 2035), add one phrase at a time and require the narrator to rattle off a series of events, often in reverse order. In an *endless tale*, numerous sheep have to cross a bridge or ants have to move a heap of sand; a *round* (AT 2320) is a story that ends where it began and then begins again.

Some folktales depend on the response of an audience. *Dilemma tales*, which are popular in Africa, involve the audience in a particularly important role: The story sets up a situation with no easy answer, such as one in which various characters must share an indivisible reward, and the audience discusses the merits of the possible solutions (e.g., AT 653, 945 II). In *catch tales* (AT 2200–2205), also called *hoax stories*, the audience is asked what it thinks will happen next, and it responds with a well-known folktale convention ("The lost object is in the fish's stomach" [Motif N211.1], "The attic is full of horrors"). But in the end, all is mundane (the fish's stomach contains only guts).

Children listen captivated to the gypsy tales of this storyteller in 1989.

Tales with divine characters, such as God, Jesus, St. Peter, or an angel, are grouped together (AT 750–849). These naturally tend to be didactic, but even here, some are humorous.

Tales composed of more than a single episode are called *complex*. The best-known complex folktales are those with magical motifs (AT 300–749). Realistic complex tales are called *novellas* or *novelle* (AT 850–999). Many depict cleverness and wisdom: A clever hero wins the hand of the princess, a clever woman proves herself worthy of her husband, or a wise peasant out-riddles the king. Sage advice leads either to success or, just as often, to disaster. Some novelle describe social and marital problems: A poor peasant obtains the property of the rich man; an innocent woman suffers unjustly; a haughty wife is reformed. Others testify to the inevitability of fate.

Traditional tales and episodes are combined in various ways. Many complex tale types are composed of a string of episodes that relate to a particular theme, such as persecution, separation, or heroism. Animal tales and humorous anecdotes are sometimes joined together on the basis of a similar cast of characters: the fox and the wolf or the rogue and the dupe. Such combinations can become traditional. Other humorous complex tales consist of a frame into which various short tales are set: for example, "The Bargain Not To Become Angry," AT 1000; "The Husband Hunts Three Persons as Stupid as His Wife," AT 1384; and "Clever Elsie," AT 1450. Frame tales are also noteworthy features that lend unity to several literary collections of folktales: the pilgrimage in Chaucer's *Canterbury Tales*; the house party in Straparola's *Pleasant Nights*; the storytelling session set into a magic tale (a version of "The Needle Prince," AT 437) in Basile's *Pentamerone*; Shahrazad in *The Thousand and One Nights*. Modern literary authors, balancing a need for realism with a desire to tell a good story, occasionally employ embedded narrative, establishing a situation in which a character narrates a folktale. The same device, which distances the author from the tale, has been used in films (for example, *Dead of Night* [1945]).

The categories that Aarne devised for *The Types of the Folktale* represent qualities that are not exclusive to the tales listed for each. For example, the clever cat in "Puss in Boots" (AT 545B) is a close relative of the clever fox in animal tales. Many tales not classed as formula tales depend on accumulations of events. The hero meets a series of strong men with special abilities, all of whom, usually in order, help with the quest or task ("The Helpers," AT 533), or traveling companions learn a few words of a new language that, recited in order, convict them of a crime they did not commit ("We Three, for Money," AT 1697). Magic tales can include religious motifs: The foster parent in "Our Lady's Child" (AT 710) can be either a religious character (the Virgin Mary), a demonic woman, or a male ghoul.

Humor is not confined to anecdotes but is important in both magic tales and novelle. In several tale types, in which the hero must make the melancholy princess laugh or speak, the audience too will be amused (AT 559, 571–574, 945). In "The Rabbit Herd," AT 570, and in "The Birthmarks of the Princess," AT 850, members of the royal family put themselves in compromising positions in an effort to obtain some special object from the hero, and then they have to give him whatever he wants to prevent him from broadcasting what they did. The humor of "The Hero Catches the Princess with Her Own Words," AT 853, comes from conversational double entendre.

Puns and verbal misunderstandings are common sources of folktale humor. Often, a misunderstood statement leads to surprising success (AT 1641, "Doctor Know-All"; AT 1563, "Both?"). Other misunderstandings are unfortunate. A fool, thinking that a messenger has come from heaven, gives the messenger valuables to take to a dead relative (AT 1540, "The Student from Paradise"), or another fool gives away the family savings, earmarked for "Hard Times," to someone who claims to be just that (AT 1541, "The Long Winter"). Anecdotes about the misunderstandings of deaf people (AT 1698) are very much current in oral tradition, as are dialect stories that make fun of heavily accented speech.

The Types of the Folktale is intended to be a finding list (an index), not a logical classification. However, Aarne's arrangement corresponds in a general way to the noteworthy aspects of the tales: animal or supernatural characters, magic objects, wise answers, and so forth. In many cases, the purpose of a tale seems to be to permit the expression of a particular, interesting episode or motif. Rhymes or songs are also memorable features that help to stabilize tales: Any reader of the Grimms' collection recognizes "mirror, mirror, on the wall" and "flounder, flounder in the sea." The plaints of murdered or transformed souls are often versified (AT 403, 720, 780), as are riddles (AT 851, 927) and warnings (AT 955, 1360C). Prose tales interspersed with songs or rhymes, called *cante fables*, are known from Indian, Arabian, Persian, and medieval European literary traditions.

Cross-references in *The Types of the Folktale* show that, although by definition each is supposed to stand for an independent tale, some tale types are not entirely separate from each other. In several cases, a single number covers separate tales. For example, "The Ungrateful Serpent Returned to Captivity" (AT 155) includes the tale summarized there, in which the villain is tricked back into a trap, a longer form in which a series of judges initially condemns the man for his own ingratitude, and also an Aesopic fable in which the snake bites the man and the man dies. The references to "The Ghoulish Schoolmaster and the Stone of Pity," AT 894, contain three separate tale types, all of which end with the same episode with the stone that swells in sympathy. Tale types that share their contents are said to belong to the same cycle of tales or to have an affinity for each other. There is, for example, a cycle of magic tales and novelle in which a villain makes away with the heroine's newborn children and another of stories with cruel stepmothers. Gordon Hall Gerould observed that initially separate tales join together because they share a "point of contact." The references, summaries, and divisions between tale types in *The Types of the Folktale* represent the tales from northern Europe better than they do those from the south. To defend against this bias, confirmation can be sought in such sources as R. M. Dawkins study of Greek tales and Aurelio Espinosa's Spanish tale collection.

As much as we would like everything to be neatly organized, folktales have too many dimensions to permit them to be classified to everyone's satisfaction. This is true even of the definition of the folktale. The same story can be told in different genres—for example, as a legend and a fictional folktale, a folktale and a ballad ("The Singing Bone," AT 780; "The King and the Abbot," AT 922), a folktale and a myth, or a folktale and a riddle ("The Princess Who Cannot Solve the Riddle," AT 851; "Out-Riddling the Judge," AT 927). In such a case, the genre naturally affects the form of the story. And if a tale is known in two forms, in different genres or even as different subtypes within the same genre, these are likely to affect each other. Legends are turned into magic tales when their aesthetic impact outweighs their belief component ("The Juniper Tree," AT 720; "The Girl as Flower," AT 407). Novelle and anecdotes have long been incorporated into plays (e.g., Shakespeare's *The Taming of the Shrew*, AT 901). Dramatic productions also have suggested or reinforced characters and scenes for folktales. An impostor disguised as a doctor or other learned man (Motifs K1825, K1955–1956) is such a figure, as is the commonplace farcical situation of illicit lovers who are threatened with discovery.

Some of the tales or components of tales found in Europe and the Middle East also are known in other parts of the world, but the European-centered tale type index is unsuitable for global research. Nevertheless, there are both motifs and whole folktales that are found throughout great regions. In order to facilitate access to all traditional literature, Stith Thompson created *The Motif-Index of Folk-Literature*. Complete tales are identifiable through the numbered motifs that refer to incidents. Some of these are known, as independent tales or as components of longer tales, throughout most of the world.

One ubiquitous episode is the "Obstacle flight" (Motif D672), in which objects thrown to hinder pursuit grow into obstacles: a twig into a forest, a stone into a mountain, a flask of water into a lake. In Europe and Asia Minor, this motif appears sporadically in several different magic tales and regularly in AT 313, "The Girl as Helper in the Hero's Flight." The oldest example of the "Obstacle flight" motif comes from eighth- century Japan in a myth about an escape from the land of the dead. The motif is also known in Polynesia and Africa. In the Americas, it has come from prehistoric Asia and, more recently, from Europe. There is an analogous episode of a "Transformation flight" (Motif D671), in which the fugitives disguise themselves in other forms, such as a church and a priest or a lake and a duck. In the ancient Greek story of Jason and the Argonauts, objects are thrown to hinder pursuit, with no transformations (Motif R231, "Obstacle flight—Atalanta type"): Medea scatters pieces of the dismembered body of her brother, which her father, who is pursuing her ship, stops to gather.

Another such episode is the "Mysterious housekeeper" (Motif N831.1), in which a woman emerges, unobserved, from an object (such as an animal or a chip of wood) and secretly does the housework. The fortunate resident, puzzled, hides and spies to see what is happening and then disenchants the housekeeper. This is part of AT 408, "The Three Oranges," in the Middle East, Europe, and India and is an independent tale or a part of other tales in Africa, Southeast Asia, China, and the Americas.

"The disguised flayer" (Motif K1941) is also widespread. The idea of putting on a skin disguise may not be distinctive enough to warrant being called a tale type, but, in places as far apart as northern Africa (Berber), Madagascar, Japan, and (native) America, this happens just after a particular scene in which a character discovers someone hiding in a tree that hangs over a well, and one of them kills the other. Widespread, presumably ancient episodes such as these can be found by looking for large blocks of references in the *Motif-Index*.

In addition to motifs and episodes, there are other characteristics of folktales that warrant cross-cultural investigation. A significant part of folktale humor is not bound to any single culture: Paul Radin noticed qualities of the trickster (which he identified in the tales of the Winnebago Indians) in clowns and in Punch-and-Judy shows, both of which come from *commedia dell'arte* tradition. Quests, too, are universal: This common pattern in hero tales and myths has long been recognized. Other patterns that describe other broad genres of tales—for example, stories in which the protagonist is a victim of persecution—can be identified. Oral-formulaic theory is investigating, among other things, the idea that there are general principles such as those expressed in Axel Olrik's Epic Laws of Folk Narrative. Poetic devices such as contrast and exaggeration are common in folktales. Rhythmic properties, not only repetition and replication but also framing, anticipation, and recapitulation, are quite general. People use narrative to give form to both real and imaginary events, and folktales are an important source of material that shows how this happens.

Thompson developed his expertise at motif classification using material from Native Americans and Europeans. Folktales from other continents were not so well indexed. Fortunately, since the motif index was last revised in six volumes (1955–1958), a considerable amount of additional narrative material from underrepresented regions has been published and indexed. The South American collections of Johannes Wilbert and Karen Simoneau are indexed with motif numbers, and several indexes are now available for Africa. Recent indexes in the Folklore Fellows Communications series include Lee Haring's for Madagascar (FFC 231, 1982), Nai-tung Ting's for China (FFC 223, 1978), Hiroko Ikeda's for Japan (FFC 209, 1971), and Patricia Waterman's for aboriginal Australia (FFC 238, 1987).

Genres of narrative defined according to European concepts are not always generalizable: For example, in Asia, Africa, Australia, and the Americas, there are mythical folktales, cosmogony used for entertainment. Two such examples are "Snaring the sun" (Motif A728), in which the sun is caught with ropes, and the "Earth diver" (Motif A812), in which, when the world is flooded, an animal brings some earth to the surface and thus creates the land. Certain tales have been shown to have migrated from Asia to (prehistoric) America or from Africa to the Americas. This latter migration is recent enough that tales of the same type can be identified with certainty.

Although they also can be dramatized or written, folktales are most often manifested as oral performances. Almost anyone who can understand the simplest folktales can narrate those, but elaborate stories require special expertise to be told properly (that is, not just as a summary). Accomplished narrators are able to animate a bald plot, turning it into a fascinating story. They can add to and delete from traditional tales, but, in Europe at least, the continuation of the same tale types proves that narrators are often happy to retell the same old story. Depending on social expectations and the personality of the individual narrator, folktale performance can be understated or highly dramatic (see Performance). Dialogues between the characters alternate with descriptive passages. Like the product of any traditional artist, a version of a folktale belongs both to tradition and to its narrator. Occasionally, a narrator creates a new tale from traditional structures and motifs. It has sometimes been difficult to separate traditional tales (folktales) from idiosyncratic, individual tales, especially outside of Europe, but as more and better indexes have become available, it becomes easier to identify traditional elements.

The apt term *Homo narrans* was coined by Kurt Ranke to remind us how peculiarly human is the ability to tell stories. Tale telling is undoubtedly as old as humankind, and written examples of folktales begin early. The oldest magic tale, "The Two Brothers or Bata and Anubis," from ancient Egypt (1250 B.C.), is described as a composite of AT 302B, 318, 516B, and 870C*. There are Sumerian fables, with the usual characters such as the fox, the wolf, the sheep, and the dog, from the sixth century B.C., and the Gilgamesh epic, which is Sumerian and Babylonian, contains a number of important folktale motifs. Stories of the Assyrian sage Achikar (circa 420 B.C.) come from the same mold as do modern wisdom tales. Written folktales from ancient times seldom are the same as later complex tales, but simple tales are easily recognizable as identical to modern ones. Odysseus' blinding of the Cyclops (in book 9 of *The Odyssey*) is now told as an oral tale (AT 1137), as is the idea that a sailor should walk inland until no one recognizes his oar (in book 11). Apuleius' *Metamorphoses* (also called *The Golden Ass*, from the second century A.D.), contains several witch legends and the earliest version of a magic tale corresponding to a complete modern tale type ("Cupid and Psyche," AT 425B). The tradition of Aesopic fables has long been both oral and written; in addition to Greek and Roman texts, there are fables in the Sanskrit *Pañchatantra* (before 500 A.D.). The beast epics (Reynard the Fox) of the Middle Ages reveal the satirical potential of animal tales.

Another Eastern source of early tales, in addition to the *Pañchatantra*, are the *Jatakas*, describing the former lives of the Buddha, which are replete with magical transformations. Some of these motifs and tales exist in oral tradition—for example, one in which a self-sacrificing hare, who immolated himself to feed a beggar, is sent to the moon, where he can still be seen (no. 316; compare Motif A751.2, "Man in the moon a rabbit"). An eleventh-century Indian collection, Somadeva's *Ocean of the Streams of Story*, is an early source for many of the motifs in European magic tales. The *Arabian Nights* was first published in French as *Mille et Une Nuit* (1703–1713), but part of it is as old as the ninth century; it includes tales from Persia (tenth century), from Baghdad (tenth and twelfth centuries), and from Egypt (eleventh to fourteenth centuries), as well as contemporary material.

Anecdotes and novelle are present in the works of Boccaccio and Chaucer (fourteenth century). Collections of humorous anecdotes were made in Germany, beginning in the thirteenth century and continuing, there and elsewhere in Europe, through the eighteenth century. There are anecdotes, magic tales, and novelle in Straparola's *Pleasant Nights* (1550–1553) and magic tales in Basile's *Pentamerone* (1634–1636). Collections of fairy tales were popular in France in the eighteenth century. In contrast to the Enlightenment belief in the superior virtue of reason, magic tales represent fantasy. Beginning in the 1760s, folktales were the basis of dramatic entertainments, homely subjects chosen for their contrast with the pretentious ones favored by aristocratic culture. Spectacular entertainments (films, musicals, operas, puppet shows, and British Christmas pantomimes) continue to employ folktale plots in this manner.

In the modern world of mass culture, anecdotes are still oral, but longer folktales are more often printed or filmed. Traditional tales are rewritten and illustrated for children and occasionally also for adults. Children hear a variety of folktales from parents, teachers, and librarians and are encouraged to discuss the precepts therein. "The Three Bears," which is easy to narrate, is one of these juvenile mainstays, as is "The Little Red Hen," which is also easy to tell and in addition endorses a work ethic. Folktales from foreign countries are used in schools to teach geography and multiculturalism. In spite of a general feeling that folktales (as opposed to jokes) have been relegated to the nursery, many adults still appreciate them. Cartoons in magazines and newspapers refer to well-known nursery tales. Storytellers tell folktales even to adult audiences, and some psychotherapists use them with their patients. Fables are sustained by proverbial references: for example, to sour grapes and putting all the eggs in one basket. In the scholarly realm, anthropologists utilize folktales to elucidate subtle aspects of the cultures they seek to describe, and the idea of using folktales to explore the human psyche was legitimized by Sigmund Freud and C. G. Jung.

Folktales have long been central to folklore scholarship, which is often said to have begun with Jacob and Wilhelm Grimm. In their *Kinder- und Hausmärchen* (Children's and household folktales) (1812–1815 and later editions), they identified many of the narrators who told them the tales and included references to other oral and written variants. Although they did not believe that variants of the same tale had developed from an identifiable original form, later scholars did. The comparative method, adapted from philology, was applied to folktales in the belief that the tale's original form and original home could be identified.

Regardless of its sometimes questionable ability to establish an original form, a comparative study, which identifies the amount of variation present in a tale, its region, and its oldest known variants, is the only way to determine the extent of the tradition of a tale. But geography is only one source of social separation. In Europe, judging by studies of folktale narrators and by the names of narrators published in folktale collections, men tend to narrate tales with a male hero, and women tell those with a female; however, this is only a preference, and there is considerable crossover so that people of both sexes narrate tales with male and female protagonists. In societies where the sexes are more separated, strong sex-linked traditions develop, with separate repertoires. Chief characters also give some indication of the groups of people who are likely to appreciate certain tales: farmers, soldiers, travelers, spouses, and children.

Analyses of modern folktales (including jokes), which emphasize the narratives' ability to express social tensions, are able to take into account the relevant aspects (sex, ethnicity, social class) of the narrator and the audience. Intensive collecting from limited areas, which is able to identify the contributions of certain individuals to the folktale tradition there, proves that tradition is nothing other than the cumulative result of individuals' efforts. Folklorists refer to the "logical composition" of tales and even describe tales as living organisms. Stith Thompson and others used the phrase "life history of a tale." "Folktale biology" (from Max Lüthi) refers to the study of tales as they fit into their social and cultural contexts, and the "oikotype" (from C. W. von Sydow, formed from the Greek root of the English word *ecology*) refers to subtypes that have been specially adapted to conform to local folk belief.

European folktale scholarship developed in the nineteenth century, partly in the tradition of Indo-European philology; coupled with the scholarship's strong emphasis on cultural geography, this has resulted in a tendency toward racism. Some early folklorists maintained that tales were inherited, much as words were, in forms that changed in rather regular ways. Others emphasized diffusion: The tale was thought to have traveled from one country to its neighbors. Such notions can be very helpful to describe the pattern of a tale's variations, but they are hypothetical, not proven facts, and thus not strong foundations for further argument. In particular, most so-called Indo-European tales are known to neighboring peoples who speak other kinds of languages (Semitic, Uralic, and Altaic, for example). Especially as more Middle Eastern, African, and Asian variants become known, racial theories of the origin of well-known folktales become difficult to maintain. Rather, scholars must attend to the overall stability of the tales and look for culturally, psychologically, and aesthetically based explanations of their variations.

Johann Gottfried von Herder, reacting against the universality envisioned by philosophers of the Enlightenment, called attention to the uniqueness of each culture, and soon after, the Grimms were pointing to mythology and folklore as expressions of the German spirit. This attitude is untenable when the folklore in question is also found in other cultures. Most collections of folktales are intended to represent particular countries or regions—many books are titled something like *Folktales of [wherever]*, or *[African/Italian/Mayan/etc.] Folktales*, and folklore archives are regional or national. But most of the tales in such books and archives are told in other places as well. The borders between cultures are indistinct and constantly shifting because contact between neighbors and traders is and always has been very common, and folktales, which can be given away for nothing or swapped for a drink or a meal, are among the most often-traded commodities.

The romantic attitude of the Grimms is still present in the idea that an appreciation of cultural and social context is important for understanding why a particular tale (or a particular joke or song) is performed. (This idea is not very different from that of the historic-geographic scholars regarding the importance of establishing the period and place of origin of each folktale, in order that its origins, history, and prehistory could be determined.) But the same tale, if it is at all popular, is also performed in other, quite different social and cultural contexts. Thus, a tale is able, to some extent, to transcend its context. It is this property that justifies comparative folktale scholarship. It is to be hoped that, as more tales are collected as performed in their natural contexts, the extra information thus obtained will be used along with the knowledge about the forms of the tale that only a comparative study can provide, thereby enhancing our understanding of the tradition.

Christine Goldberg

See also Dilemma Tales; Epic Laws; Fabliau; Fabulate; Historic-Geographic Method; Legend; Legend, Contemporary; Legend, Urban; Magic Tale; Motif; Myth; Oral-Formulaic Theory; Romantic Nationalism; Tale Type.

✳✳✳✳✳✳✳✳✳✳✳✳✳✳✳✳✳✳✳

References
Aarne, Antti, and Stith Thompson. 1961. *The Types of the Folktale.* Helsinki: Academia Scientiarum Fennica.
Bascom, William R. 1975. *African Dilemma Tales.* Chicago: Aldine.
———. 1992. African Folktales in the New World. Bloomington: Indiana University Press.
Bolte, Johannes, and Georg Polívka. 1913–1932. *Anmerkungen zu den Kinder- und Hausmärchen der Brüder Grimm.* 5 vols. Leipzig, Germany: Dieterich.
Dawkins, R. M. 1953. *Modern Greek Folktales.* Oxford: Clarendon.
Espinosa, Aurelio M. 1946–1947. *Cuentos populares españoles.* 3 vols. Madrid: S. Aguirre.
Klipple, May Augusta. 1992. *African Folktales with Foreign Analogues.* New York: Garland.
Radin, Paul. 1955. *The Trickster: A Study in American Indian Mythology.* London: Routledge and Kegan Paul.
Ranke, Kurt, ed. 1977. *Enzyklopädie des Märchens.* Berlin: Walter de Gruyter.
Thompson, Stith. 1955–1958. *Motif-Index of Folk-Literature.* 6 vols. Bloomington: Indiana University Press.
———. 1977. *The Folktale.* Berkeley: University of California Press.
von Sydow, C. W. 1948. *Selected Papers on Folklore.* Copenhagen: Rosenkilde and Bagger.
Wilbert, Johannes, and Karen Simoneau. 1992. *Folk Literature of South American Indians: General Index.* Los Angeles: UCLA Latin American Center Publications.

FOODWAYS

The culture-based definition of the edible and the body of customary, verbal, and material traditions that pertain to the utility of food as an instrument of cultural continuity, a sign of group identity, and a significant aspect of folk culture.

The term *foodways* is more unique among the lexicon of folklore and folk-life than the concept behind it. When William Graham Sumner introduced the term *folkways* in 1906, he intended to provide a way of describing the knitted wholeness of folk culture—the way in which custom, belief, and expression yield a unique imprint for each of the world's observably different societies. Among the many kinds of things folklorists study, only food approaches the broad vision of Sumner's coinage—an attribution that holds interesting clues to the oddly tangential position foodways has held within the range of folk expression.

Foodways means nothing less than the full consideration of how food and culture intersect—what food says about the people who prepare and consume it and how culture shapes the dietary choices people make.

The first of these areas has more often been the province of popular and academic ethnographers, for whom the observation of eating habits has provided a primary means of differentiating between peoples, often according to the locales they inhabit. The most basic and stereotypical of cultural characterizations—the stuff of elementary school geographies and popular travelogues—make primary reference to the specific foods various peoples eat and often describe the physical or cultural attributes of whole societies in terms of these foods.

Whatever the accuracy of statements about the foods particular people subsist upon, folklore's relatively late coming to the study of food and culture has meant that folklorists are more likely to focus upon particular foods as significant *choices*, implicitly rejecting physical determinism in favor of a cultural model—one in which the foods that people eat are believed to say more about who they are than about the edible stuff they have at hand.

In this sense, foodways is a tacitly modern way of looking at some very old traditions, a view informed more by the consumerist decision making of Western market economies than anthropological or archaeological precepts. Therein lies the basis for both the departure of folklorists who study food from the ranks of other social scientists and the appeal of the term *foodways*.

The significant predispositions of pioneer American folklorists toward spoken, sung, or performed expression were confirmed and energized by international folksong revival movements in the postwar era. As a result, emerging western European configurations of folklife, including the so-called material culture areas of architecture, craft, and costume, entered American folklore scholarship more quietly than they might have. Anthropological interest in the intersection of food and culture had been focused upon during the two decades preceding the folksong revival by the National Research Council's Committee on Food Habits. Under the leadership of Margaret Mead, the committee focused anthropology's prevailing internationalism upon American ethnicity, finding in "food habits" an evident, tangible link between ethnic identity and patterns of commerce, between cookery and community.

The Committee on Food Habits was created in response to wartime concerns about the acceptability of food rationing, the effects of embargoes limiting international commerce in foodstuffs, and the loyalty of immigrant "nationality" groups to the U.S. war effort. Thus, adherence to deeply held traditions, usually considered by folklorists to be a positive cultural indicator, instead designated several American ethnic groups as potential "soft spots" in regard to wartime morale and national security. Despite this odd and unfortunate application of research, the Committee on Food Habits performed an essential transition in the study of foodways. By bringing social scientific rigor to bear upon the everyday eating habits of ordinary Americans, Mead and her colleagues established scholarly precedent for ethnological interest in the social meanings, functions, and values of food, particularly as an accessible marker of cultural community.

To a comparable degree, Don Yoder was instrumental in translating European scholarship into American practice, principally by illustrating European ethnological theory with ongoing fieldwork and historical analysis of Pennsylvania's Old Order Amish and Mennonite communities. The quiet integrity of Yoder's scholarship on recognized folk communities enabled the larger and more challenging theoretical assumptions at the heart of this scholarship to pass into American folkloristic usage almost unnoticed. What was noticed and marginalized at first was the term *folklife*, which seemed from its first American usage in the late 1950s to denote a concept too broad and holistic to coexist peaceably with the more established and accepted *folklore*.

But it was not so much the grand interdisciplinary purpose of folklife studies—to identify and document tradition wherever and however it expressed itself in community life—that opened the door for folklorists' study of food. Rather, it was the specific attention Yoder, Warren Roberts, Louis Jones, and others devoted to activities less frequently regarded by folklorists as culturally significant—most notably, cookery and costume.

The entry of foodways into the canon of traditional expression had the unintended effect of making the methods and materials of narrowly focused European folklife studies the means to a more inclusive view of tradition in contemporary American society. Foodways rendered moot standing distinctions between "the folk" and "nonfolk" based upon individual repertoires of traditional expression. Since these distinctions were in turn based upon well-established folklore genres of considerable tenure, the folklife movement, with foodways at its ideological bow, succeeded where the folksong revival had failed in reconnecting the notion of tradition to ordinary people and the communities they constituted. Today, foodways and its fellow folklife *émigrés* suggest a domestic, conservative profile of an established discipline against which the idiosyncratic folk artist or protest singer departs. The fact that these contemporary impressions vary so greatly from historical and ideological realities confirms both the infusive effects of folklife studies and American cultural predispositions toward hearth and home.

Even as foodways came to be recognized in American society at large as properly belonging in the niche created for the handmade, the old-fashioned, and the homespun, the ubiquity of the edible made the topic an odd fit for academic taxonomies and nomenclature. Whereas terms like *folk art*, *folksong*, and *folk craft* had come to refer as much to the formal (i.e., *in*formal) character of these expressions than the people who produce or understand them, *folk foods* or even *folk cookery* failed to register a comparable degree of recognition or usage. In this regard, foodways benefited considerably from those theoretical advances in folklore studies during the 1970s and 1980s that pushed performance to the forefront of analysis. Proponents of performance theory were not particularly concerned with using its precepts to expand the canon of folk expression, but foodways studies benefited from the introduction of larger units of study, including events that display skill, symbol, and strategy.

If the American vocabulary used to describe culture-as-food and food-as-culture has lagged, foodways by any name has advanced in less than one generation from import to export. Folklorists have laid claim to foodways. In a real sense, foodways seems equally at home in a discipline concerned with how communities express and (in so doing) sustain identity. A five-part division of both the subject and its scholarship reveals what one might expect from a relatively young discipline: a little theory, a great deal of description, efforts toward definition, and a refreshingly high degree of respect for the work of journalists, nutritionists, historians, critics, and social scientists of every stripe.

PRODUCTION AND GATHERING OF FOODSTUFFS

Focusing on hunting, agriculture, fishing, gardening—from the lore of determining when to plant potatoes or where the blue crabs are running to the preservation of exotic seed stock—this category groups traditions that thread among issues and enterprises as varied as deciding what is edible and songs that synchronize a dozen hands drawing a fishnet against the current. Folklore's deep chronicles of challenging occupations—cowboys, commercial fishers, migrant farm workers—yield fresh insight when viewed in the context of the long processes they set in motion.

DISTRIBUTION OF FOODSTUFFS

This area of foodways study considers how the products of farm and stockyard find their way to the cooks who transform them into food. Calls of street vendors and tobacco auctioneers, pyramids of grapefruit meticulously arranged

369

for market display—these are the artistic evidence of a culture of commerce. Underpinning this culture are assumptions about regions and regionalism that inform a large part of American folklore scholarship. Boundaries observed and crossed construct patterns of place, as specific as a roadside stand in corn country and as general as the custom of giving fruit baskets as a sign of hospitality or sympathy.

COOKERY

For much of the relatively brief history of American foodways, cookery has held the high ground, subjugating all else to context. Most apt for performance studies, the centrality of cooking as transformation focuses attention on skills as well as secrets. Unfairly reduced to the brief notation of recipes, cooking is, by definition, individuated and nonreproducible. The traditions associated with cooking range from gender-specified roles and settings to elaborate "scripts" that contain, enact, and signify the relationship between master and apprentice, mother and daughter.

DISTRIBUTION OF FOODS

What people do with food when it is ready to be eaten is simply to express with it and through it the substance of identity, sentiment, and community. Such matters as why homemade cakes are being sold at a church bazaar or how the individual bakers who prepared them are identified may matter more than recipes or taste. Yet virtually everything a potluck casserole, table for two, or clambake signifies is allusive and implicit. By examining the array of events in which food is sold or shared, folklorists connect the descriptions of food and travel writers to basic tenets of social science. Image and action are complementary—the groaning table and the feast.

CONSUMPTION OF FOODS

Because we are dominated by an obsessive self-consciousness about what we eat, such matters as when, where, and how food is taken have been largely overlooked. Yet the rules that govern a child's behavior at mealtime or the custom of eating Thanksgiving dinner in midafternoon are as fixed in most American households as preferences for particular foods (enjoyed or forbidden). Oreo cookies consumed filling first or pie-eating contests are obvious examples of how well food serves other needs beyond nourishment—to play, to compete—and a confirmation of how seldom the consumption of food is driven and determined by hunger alone.

Foodways provides a vocabulary of experience that demonstrates the presence and power of tradition in everyday life. The variety of this vocabulary is ample evidence of cultural continuities and identities that are not always easy to exemplify by other means. However, the degree to which food and culture are intertwined renders much of what may be gleaned from the arrangement of a place setting or the clientele of an ethnic food store too common to matter. In this regard, foodways presses a point about which much is assumed but little is said: Is tradition cause or consequence? Is the observable fact that people express themselves—who they are, what they value—through food an imperative for further inquiry or a truism too trite to pursue?

Foodways foregrounds the ordinary in a rhetorical sense but enables, as do other kinds of expression, the extraordinary to become distinguished as the consequence of reasonable comparison. People who do not sing, whistle, or play a musical instrument every day may consider themselves uninvolved in musical traditions. Such people are often gladdened by reminders of the lullabies they have sung to their children or the evening in a tavern when verses of popular songs rose unexpectedly in their throats. In the same sense, it is not the fact that all people eat that makes foodways culturally significant. Many people do not cook, are not choosy, and eat alone. Such people are involved in foodways when food enables them to connect with family members or friends, practice their faith, or assist someone less fortunate.

Special occasions in which food plays a prominent role, such as Thanksgiving dinner or a country fair, are of particular interest because they are invested by those who participate with a high degree of significance and importance. What has been too frequently overlooked is the less conspicuous role food plays in other sorts of social commerce—from courtship to wedding cake, from potluck to potlatch. Locating significance in this muddy mix of subject, appetite, science, symbol, currency, and taste is a daunting but engaging task. The need to ask (and to know) how people express themselves through food demands attention to circumstance and process, intention and outcome. The contexts in which food assumes significance are as many and as varied as songs and singers, but they often lack the recognizable features that signal a performance in progress. So it is that foodways is perhaps the most common and least comprehended of traditional expressions.

Charles Camp

See also Custom; Feast; Festival; Folklife.

✳✳✳✳✳✳✳✳✳✳✳✳✳✳✳✳

References

Arnott, Margaret L., ed. 1975. *Gastronomy: The Anthropology of Food and Food Habits.* Paris: Mouton.

Camp, Charles. 1989. *American Foodways.* Little Rock, AR: August House.

Cussler, Margaret, and Mary L. de Give. 1952. *'Twixt the Cup and the Lip: Psychological and Socio-Cultural Factors Affecting Food Habits.* New York: Twayne.

Gutierrez, C. Paige. 1992. *Cajun Foodways*. Jackson: University Press of Mississippi.

Jones, Michael Owen, Bruce Giuliano, and Robert Krell, eds. 1983. *Foodways & Eating Habits: Directions for Research*. Los Angeles: California Folklore Society.

Mintz, Sidney W. 1986. *Sweetness and Power*. New York: Penguin Books.

Neustadt, Kathy. 1992. *Clambake: A History & Celebration of an American Tradition*. Amherst: University of Massachusetts Press.

Vennum, Thomas, Jr. 1988. *Wild Rice and the Ojibway People*. St. Paul: Minnesota Historical Society Press.

Fool

A stock character in folk literature, seasonal festivities, and traditional performances and representations, usually associated with the European Middle Ages and Renaissance but displaying characteristics with parallels among diverse figures over great historical and cultural range. Basic to the fool role is actual or performed madness or idiocy. Due to a mental deficiency and consequent inability to function in ordinary society, the fool occupies the margins of culture. Here, the fool gains license to speak freely and to reflect on the foibles of others. The familiar costume and cliché antics of the fool frame this "free speech" so that it seems to be mere playful babble or nonsense. However, many cultures perceive a certain wisdom or at least alternative view of the world underlying the contrary, topsy-turvy behavior of the fool. This ability to see the world differently than others and to remain isolated from the mainstream invests the fool with considerable ambiguity, which is sometimes believed to afford this individual divine or clairvoyant powers.

The specifically European fool role and imagery have rather limited historical contexts and, in some cases, very specific allegory. Yet many characteristics of the fool resonate widely with other figures. Inversion, antiauthoritarianism, parody, sexuality, ambiguity, and earthiness are essential to fools, tricksters, shamans, and clowns. On the one hand, these figures are essential to their cultural contexts; on the other hand, they reveal the weakness and limits of their cultures by burlesquing and debasing sacred ceremonies and objects, highlighting the foreign, playing with language, and associating with misfortune. The linguistic play of Groucho Marx may be worlds away from Zuni clowns speaking Spanish or English to the gods, but both demonstrate the power of foolery.

Costume and Symbolism of the Fool

Traditional European fools utilize a fairly consistent repertoire of costume elements and implements that draw attention to their special status. These costume motifs, which developed over hundreds of years but became fairly stable by the early modern period, assist the fools in their commentary on society and are themselves open to diverse interpretations. On the head, the typical fool wears a cap topped with bell-tipped ass ears. Fools often tote bells on their scepters, shoes, or belts as well. In addition to serving as audible attention-getters for the fool, bells on the costume may have originated as a satire of a medieval fashion element that began among the elite and then became a veritable fad among citizens. The prominent ass ears in representations of the fool suggest that the fool is as obstinate as this notorious beast. The ears perhaps also indicate the pronounced and unrestrained sexuality common to the animal and the fool. Some fools also feature a rooster's comb on their heads. At times, the behavior of fools can be likened to the crowing, masculine boasting of the cock. Many implements carried by fools reinforce the phallic imagery of the fool: stretching shears that extend to pinch women, fur-tipped poles also used to taunt female bystanders, and handheld sausages. In festivals, fools frequently grab and harass women. The plowing fool who spreads seeds or even tiny images of the fool is also a familiar character in festivals and traditional pictorial representations. Contemporary folklore in areas where fools inhabit carnival celebrations tells of masked fools seducing and impregnating young women, who must bear the children out of wedlock when the fathers remains anonymous. These and other children born in late fall as a result of the heightened sexuality and increased license associated with fools and their springtime rites are sometimes referred to as carnival children.

The dress of fools consists of a motley of colors and fabrics. A patchwork of rags or other material commonly covers the body of the fool. This apparel might owe its origin to the lowly status of the fool, who must make do with available materials. Some interpreters see the patches as Christian allegory of the sins committed by fools and others distant from the teachings of the church. Another view holds that this costume derives from earlier representations of wild men and creatures believed to live on the periphery of towns and villages. The colorful, patchwork apparel does bear resemblance to more mystical figures, such as the pied piper of Hamelin and shamanic figures in many cultures. Whether or not these similarities are historical, all of these figures do embody the mysterious power of ambiguity.

An alternate dress for the fool features the more refined tights and bicolor scheme of the harlequin. Here, theatrical stylization has replaced elements of folk belief, but traces of duality and ambiguity remain in the binary pattern.

Items fools hold in their hands include mirrors, books, scepters, baubles, and animal bladders. Mirrors and books can symbolize both the vanity of the fools themselves and their propensity to depict and document the foolishness of others. A fool gazing into a mirror differs little from a fool standing face to face with a scepter adorned with a fool's head. In either case, the fool admires its own external features and prefers them to those of ordinary folk. Likewise,

The character of the fool can be found throughout history and across cultures. Fools play a variety of roles in culture, depending on the context in which they appear.

a glass bauble can serve as a distorting mirror, reflecting the image of the fool. The scepter or bauble also serves as a parody of the paraphernalia of the royals who frequently employed fools. A pig's bladder, often attached to a stick made from a dried ox phallus, resembles a glass bauble but is used instead to beat the ground. This behavior shows the impishness of fools, while also linking them to fertility rites that involve pounding and stomping the soil.

CONTEXTS OF THE FOOL

In European tradition, we can distinguish among professional fools, actors playing the role of fool, and literary fools. Professional fools are those who earn a living on the basis of their recognized mental and social deficiencies. Their profession dates to ancient Greece and Rome and appears in Italy, France, Germany, and England from the Middle Ages and Renaissance. The European court fool is the best-known incarnation of the professional fool. References to this figure date from the twelfth century, but some evidence suggests this fool is derived from Eastern, Celtic, and Roman predecessors. Court fools often had physical deformities, which, like mental flaws, prevented them from participating in ordinary social roles. In this regard, they are similar to the "freaks" (e.g., dwarfs and grotesques) and exotics who appeared at carnivals and fairs. The activities of court fools ranged from serving as a sort of lap dog accompanying royalty or roaming in and out of the court and into local taverns and establishments (much like a village idiot) to more formal performances at feasts and gatherings. Some court jesters would regularly read the news to the court, much like contemporary comics such as Jay Leno or Howard Stern who base their routines on reading and commenting on news stories.

Mimetic fool performances occur in the theater, folk dramas, and festivals. Numerous playwrights, Shakespeare foremost among them, have relied on the characteristics of fools for dramatic effect. Often, fool figures serve to point out the foolishness in all people, that is, they provide a mirror in which other characters and the audience may see themselves so that they may correct their weaknesses. In act 1, scene 2 of *As You Like It*, Celia remarks to Touchstone, the fool: "By my troth, thou sayest true; for, since the little wit that fools have was silenced, the little foolery that wise men have makes a great show." Until the late sixteenth century, theatrical fools were modeled primarily on the existing social type of the fool. By the seventeenth century, a purely theatrical creation, the harlequin, began to provide the model. The harlequin role emphasizes physical agility rather than the traditional symbolism associated with the fool. Although retaining the fool's lack of moral sense, the harlequin does not derive from social ideology and therefore has no mystical or subversive tendencies.

A variety of traditional plays also feature fools in important roles. Among these plays are the sketches performed by traveling troupes that thrived prior to the Enlightenment. These skits often revolve around jest figures, such as Hans Wurst (John Sausage), who fail to perceive basic realities of everyday life properly, thus finding themselves in all manner of laughable predicaments. Similar sketches are featured at local celebrations where town residents become amateur performers to stage humorous plays, such as "The Old Wives' Mill" in which a series of farmers rejuvenate their haggard wives until the fool causes the mill to malfunction and produce an even less desirable mate. These amateur comic plays provide a counterpoint to local productions of religious plays (such as reenactments of the Passion of Christ).

Certain calendrical festivals, such as carnival or the Feast of Fools (December 28), have given rise to special groups of fools (fools' guilds, *sociétés joyeuses*) that perform their antics in public. Unlike professional fools, these actors do not take their roles because of their physical or mental disabilities but rather because of the license provided them—often as one of various rights given to trade guilds—by civic authorities. Festival fools draw on the same costume elements, behavior, and symbolism as other fools. They also go beyond these specific motifs and engage more generally in the inversion of the ordinary by constructing entire worlds in the mirror image of the normal, thus criticizing and satirizing ordinary society and engaging in licentious behavior. These fools do not provide an ongoing voice opposed to the mainstream but rather engage themselves and their audiences in a periodic release of the tensions of the everyday and offer alternative visions of social organization.

Fools also appear as central characters in European popular literature, beginning in the late Middle Ages. Works such as *The Ship of Fools* and *Till Eulenspiegel* continue to be widely translated and read and to provide inspiration for new representations. The former recounts, in rhyming verse, many of the features of the fool and relates how these characteristics afflict many of us. The latter follows the life of a rogue. Although Eulenspiegel does not dress like a typical fool, his adventures come about because his limited wisdom and understanding lead him to perceive situations and language incorrectly or literally. For example, he mistakes a kitchen mustard plant for hemp and defecates on it as he was instructed to do when encountering the latter plant. In some episodes, Eulenspiegel is downright malicious rather than ignorant. His antics resemble those of tricksters found in various oral traditions as much as those of traditional fools. Despite their differences, both of these character types share an emphasis on lower bodily strata—sexuality, excretion, exhibitionism—and antiauthoritarian tendencies. Audiences for these works in different eras and cultures certainly have different understandings of the motifs depicted, but these general tendencies seem to have universal appeal.

Peter Tokofsky

See also Carnival; Drama, Folk; Festival; Trickster.

✻✻✻✻✻✻✻✻✻✻✻✻✻✻✻✻

References

[Bote, Hermann?]. [1515] 1994. *Till Eulenspiegel: His Adventures*. Trans. Paul Oppenheimer. Oxford: Oxford University Press.

Brant, Sebastian. [1494] 1944. *The Ship of Fools*. Trans. Edwin H. Zeydel. New York: Columbia University Press.

Erasmus, Desiderius. [1511] 1958. *In Praise of Folly*. Trans. John Wilson. Ann Arbor: University of Michigan Press.

Foucault, Michel. 1965. *Madness and Civilization: A History of Insanity in the Age of Reason*. Trans. Richard Howard. New York: Vintage.

Steward, Julian. 1931. The Ceremonial Buffoon of the American Indian. *Papers of the Michigan Academy of Science, Arts and Letters* 14:189–198.

Sypher, Wylie, ed. 1956. *Comedy*. Garden City, NY: Doubleday.

Welsford, Enid. 1966. *The Fool: His Social and Literary History*. Gloucester, England: Peter Smith.

Willeford, William. 1969. *The Fool and His Scepter: A Study in Clowns and Jesters and Their Audience*. Evanston, IL: Northwestern University Press.

FORMULA

Smallest functional "word" or unit of phraseology in oral-formulaic theory, defined by Milman Parry as "an expression regularly used, under the same metrical conditions, to express an essential idea." First investigated in the ancient Greek *Iliad* and *Odyssey*, the formula was initially understood as a symptom of traditional diction, of a compositional idiom fashioned over generations and passed down to Homer. Primary examples include noun-epithet formulas (e.g., "swift-footed Achilleus," "white-armed Hera") and complementary, line-filling verbal phrases (e.g., "he/she spoke"). Parry later concluded that traditional formulaic language also must be oral, furnishing the bard with a ready means of composing in performance, and he consequently undertook textual analyses of passages from the Homeric epics to illustrate the density of formulas and the poet's dependence upon them.

The first expansion in the concept arose from Parry's and Albert Lord's fieldwork on still extant oral epic poetry in the former Yugoslavia. On the basis of correspondences between ancient Greek, known only in manuscript texts, and south Slavic, which they were able to experience and record firsthand, Parry and Lord argued by analogy that Homer's poems were oral and traditional. Both poetries revealed many examples of phrases repeated either verbatim or with patterned variation, with individual formulas composed of "formulaic systems," or groups of phrases related by their metrical and syntactic identity. The phraseology also showed extension (in the number of formula within a given system) and thrift ("the degree in which [a formulaic system] is free of phrases which, having the same metrical value and expressing the same idea, could replace one another").

From this basis, scholars pursued the phenomenon of formulaic phraseology in numerous different traditions, many of them manuscript-based poetries—Old and Middle English, Old French, medieval and later Spanish, and medieval German—and the method was extended to biblical studies, Chinese, international ballad studies, Finnish, central Asian epic, Russian, medieval and modern music, and numerous other areas. In many cases, the object was to demonstrate a certain percentage of formulaic density and then to pronounce the given text "oral" or "written" on that criterion alone. In recent years, the reliability of the quantitative approach as a litmus test has been strongly questioned, and universal definitions and concepts have been pluralized to reflect inherent differences among traditions.

Formula studies have consistently raised the issue of whether a performer dependent on this idiom was also its prisoner, that is, whether the compositional method was so constricting as to hamper artistic expression. Another problem that has arisen is the unpredicted persistence of this originally oral-traditional diction after the introduction of writing and in fact its actual use by literate authors. Both issues may be addressed by observing that formulas activate a metonymic network of meaning, the concrete part standing for the untextualized whole, and that this network persists after the advent of texts as long as there is an audience able to "speak the language." Phrases such as "swift-footed Achilleus" are neither merely mechanistic nor uniquely appropriate to each context; rather, they use a telltale detail to summon the named character, object, or situation in its full traditional resonance. Formulas do much more than provide ready metrical solutions for compositional challenges, then; they amount to keys to the implicit word-hoard of tradition.

John Miles Foley

See also Bard; Oral-Formulaic Theory.

✼✼✼✼✼✼✼✼✼✼✼✼✼✼✼✼✼✼

References

Foley, John Miles. 1985. *Oral-Formulaic Theory and Research: An Introduction and Annotated Bibliography*. New York: Garland.

———. 1988. *The Theory of Oral Composition: History and Methodology*. Bloomington: Indiana University Press.

———. 1990. *Traditional Oral Epic: "The Odyssey," "Beowulf," and the Serbo-Croatian Return Song*. Berkeley: University of California Press.

———. 1991. *Immanent Art: From Structure to Meaning in Traditional Oral Epic*. Bloomington: Indiana University Press.

———. 1995. *The Singer of Tales in Performance*. Bloomington: Indiana University Press.

Lord, Albert B. 1960. *The Singer of Tales*. Cambridge, MA: Harvard University Press.

———. 1991. *Epic Singers and Oral Tradition*. Ithaca, NY: Cornell University Press.

Parry, Milman. 1971. *The Making of Homeric Verse: The Collected Papers of Milman Parry*. Ed. by Adam Parry. Oxford: Clarendon Press.

FRAME

A set of metacommunicative premises or expectations guiding the exercise and interpretation of activity and perception. A frame can be explicitly or implicitly signaled by *framing devices* (i.e., a type of extant metacommunicative cue) that suggest the relevant premise set as well as the boundaries of the message set to which those premises should be applied. In short, a frame provides information about how messages "contained within" the frame (i.e., delimited by the frame's signaling devices) are intended to be understood.

In 1955, Gregory Bateson introduced the concept of the "psychological frame" to account for the ways in which individuals indicate to one another the level of abstraction at which messages are intended. Bateson based his insights in part on his observation of monkeys interacting with one another at the zoo. The monkeys employed seemingly hostile signals resembling those typically associated with combat in order to indicate that their actions were actually to be understood as noncombat—specifically, as play. Bateson concluded that the monkeys had engaged in a type of *metacommunication* (i.e., communication about communication): The monkeys had signaled the frame-indicating message "This is play."

Drawing in part on Bateson, sociologist Erving Goffman developed the transituational analysis of frame in terms of the domain of social ritual he called the *interaction order*. With this term, Goffman referred to participants' structuring, process coordination, and interpretation of their own and each other's involvement in face-to-face interaction. For Goffman, social meaning was situated; thus, his basic unit of study was the social situation. In his 1982 American Sociological Association presidential address, Goffman described the social situation as providing a "natural theater" whose achieved orderliness resulted from its participants' application of "systems of enabling conventions."

To Goffman, one of the more important of these enabling conventions was the idea of frame. In *Frame Analysis* and *Forms of Talk*, Goffman treated frame as both a cognitive resource and a socially emergent and indicatable tool by which participants organize their interactional experience. He began his analysis by discussing *primary frameworks*: schemas of interpretation by which people understand the "basic facts" of (1) natural activity (e.g., the assumption that time is singular and irreversible), and (2) social activity (e.g., the assumption that the sounds emitted from an individual's mouth constitute speech or the interpretation that two individuals are "actually" fighting as opposed to "just" play-fighting). Goffman then turned to two major ways in which primary frameworks can be transformed (i.e., framed): keyings and fabrications. A *keyed* frame patterns activity—in whole or in part—on some primary framework, but its participants share an implicit understanding that another type of activity (other than that of a primary framework) is occurring.

Events that are keyed to varying degrees include: animal play, human play (including ludic folklore, such as riddling or the telling of narrative jokes), daydreaming, dramatic scriptings (such as folk and theatrical plays and televised dramas and situation comedies), sporting contests, and instrumental demonstrations. Keyings are themselves vulnerable to the transformation of *rekeying* (i.e., reframing), as in instances of mimicry or parody (e.g., anti- [or catch] legends that poke fun at scary story legends). In contrast to keyed frames, fabrication frames are transformations of unequal *footing* (i.e., of unequal alignment in participants' relationships to their own and their coparticipants' involvement and to the messages contained within the frame). In short, in a *fabrication*, one or more participants manage activity such that other participants are encouraged to have a false idea about what is going on. Examples of *benign fabrications* (in which the dupe's personal interests are not seriously jeopardized) include surprise parties, benign practical jokes, and experiments in which subjects are hoaxed into a false understanding of what the experiment is testing. Examples of *exploitative fabrications* (in which the construction is inimical to the dupe's personal interests) include undercover spying, false witnessing, and financial cons and scams.

Goffman also raised the issues of frame anchoring, frame clarity, frame involvement, and out-of-frame activity. According to Goffman, framed activity is anchored to (i.e., grounded in) the environing world in several ways, among them: (1) through participants' use of initial, medial, and/or terminal framing devices called *brackets* (e.g., the chairman's gavel calling a meeting to order and later adjourning it; narrative beginning and ending formulas, such as "once upon a time" and "they lived happily ever after"; or the signals given for time-outs during a football game), and (2) through the fact of participants' bodily presence in the interaction (e.g., the physical relationship of person to adopted interactional role is said to be in balance when an actor is hired to play the role of a villain in part because the actor can sneer in a particularly effective manner; alternatively, in Goffman's words, "role gives way to person" when, for instance, a performer must cancel a performance due to personal illness). *Frame clarity* (i.e., the arrangement obtaining when all participants share a working consensus as to what is going on) can become ambiguous during instances of (1) *misframing* (as when the sound of a car backfiring is mistaken for the sound of a gunshot), or (2) *frame disputes* (e.g., husband-wife arguments about who did what to whom and why). A participant's *frame involvement* (i.e., the level of engrossment in a framed activity) is held up to question when the participant *breaks frame* (i.e., he or she engages in activity to which the official frame cannot be applied). Examples include: (1) *flooding-out* (e.g., when an individual dissolves into laughter or anger at an inappropriate moment), and (2) *downkeying*—that is, frame movement toward or into a primary framework (e.g., when playfulness gets out of hand—perhaps during the use of ritual insults—and a participant becomes angry, feeling that his or her personal interests have been violated). Finally, Goffman argued that multiple *laminations* (i.e., layers of frame) can be developed in any situation and that information from multiple channels can become available during any given interaction. Some of this latter information can result from *out-of-frame* activity (i.e., activity that is alternate to the interaction's official focus and to which participants either only partially attend or try officially to ignore). Examples include information presented (1) through an *overlay channel* (e.g., the announcement of a storm warning that runs across [i.e., overlays] the bottom of one's television screen while another program is in progress), or (2) in sounds that participants relegate to the *disattend track* (e.g., participants' trying to ignore the sound of a baby crying during a church service).

In contrast to Goffman, who often based his consideration of frame on anecdotes of behavioral situations drawn from mainstream American life, sociolinguist John Gumperz treated frame in light of conversational discourse obtained from members of culturally heterogeneous, urbanized communities. Gumperz argued that cultures can differ markedly in their expectations for *communicative competence*, which (when viewed in interactional terms) includes knowledge not only of linguistic grammar and the lexicon but also of the social conventions by which speakers signal information about communicative intent and conversational cooperation. During conversations, a speaker uses such conventions to prompt his or her hearer to make *conversational inferences*—that is, to develop situated or context-bound interpretations of the speaker's current intent as well as to formulate expectations of what is to come. Such inferences contribute to the listener's development of frames (in the Bateson-Goffman sense of the interactive frame—that is, frames developed during social interaction) for understanding the conversation. At this level of interpretation, participants attend to what Gumperz called *contextualization cues*—that is, message signals (usually culturally learned) that acquire implicit but context-specific meaning by virtue of their use in actual conversations. Such cues function as framing devices, but they also often occur in sets and can operate at a greater degree of interactional subtlety than devices typically discussed by Goffman. Examples of contextualization cues include: the speaker's use of code, dialect, and/or style switching (as in bilingual joke telling among ethnic participants or a non-Brooklyn-raised storyteller switching to a Brooklyn dialect to represent the speech of a story character), prosody (including intonation, changes in loudness, and utterance chunking through pauses), lexical and syntactic choice (e.g., a storyteller's simplifying of vocabulary and syntax to represent the speech of a child character), formulaic expressions (such as "in-group" language), and conversational opening, closing, and sequencing strategies. Nonverbal cues include facial and kinesic signs (e.g., a listener's frowning to indicate displeasure, a speaker's snapping his or her fingers to reinforce the meaning "just like that!"

or a storyteller's flexing a bicep to indicate a character's strength), body postures (e.g., a storyteller's bowing the shoulders to indicate the advanced age of a character or, in social interaction, the turning of one's back on a coparticipant to indicate one's disgust with that person), proxemic distance (e.g., a speaker moving in close to a coparticipant during the sharing of a secret), and gaze direction (e.g., looking one's coparticipant straight in the eye to suggest the truth of what one is saying). Contextualization cues can be ambiguous or even uninterpretable if considered individually. Therefore, in interpreting conversational utterances in situ, competent listeners look for multiple cues that fit culturally learned *co-occurrence expectations*; in other words, the cues co-occur at various levels of communication within the same stretch of the speaker's talk, and the cues reinforce each other such that the constellation (or set) they form is interpreted as indicating meaning. A constellation of contextualization cues can be used to signal, for example, the speaker's membership in some group (e.g., one's smiling and employing hugs or slaps on the back when joining a group of friends), the speaker's attitude (Goffman's "footing"—for example, a listener's raising the eyebrows and mouthing "Wow!" to indicate surprise at a speaker's message), or the conclusion of the speaker's turn at talking (e.g., a speaker's extended pausing coupled with a direct and anticipatory gaze at the coparticipant). Gumperz also used *frame* in terms more recently associated with the concept of *schemata*—that is, as "a set of expectations that rests on previous experience." To Gumperz, the interpretive process in a conversation begins with the participants' making implicit but culturally informed guesses about the type of speech activity being developed—for example, "chatting about the weather" or "telling a story." Participants base their guesses on their previous experience with similar situations and on cultural knowledge. Informed guesses allow participants to anticipate, for instance, the turn-taking procedures, overall themes, and possible outcomes of the conversation. Whether treating frame in the sense of schemata or of interactive frame, Gumperz pointed out that frames relevant later in a conversation are subject to interpretation in terms of frames that were pertinent earlier in the same conversation. Alternatively, frames pertinent later in a conversation can be used to reframe understandings believed to be relevant earlier in the same conversation. Gumperz emphasized that the development of meaning in and throughout a conversation is not a matter of unilateral action but is "rather [one] of speaker-listener coordination involving [the] rhythmic interchange of both verbal and nonverbal signs."

Sociolinguist Deborah Tannen has distinguished between the concept of *interactive frame* (based on Bateson's and Goffman's work) and the frame-related concepts of *schemata* and *script*.

Since much verbal folklore (story and joke telling, riddling, ballad singing, and so forth) and nonverbal folklore(such as folk gestures) constitute either framed activity or behavior that can frame other activity, the consideration of contextualization cues and frame use is especially pertinent to folklore study. Many contextualization cues (such as the shrugging of one's shoulders to indicate doubt) are culturally learned and thus traditional. Some, though, are emergent within their context of use (e.g., a storyteller's marked [perhaps sarcastic or exaggerated] reuse of a particular phrase or gesture in order to suggest narrative continuity or to encourage audience participation). Whether the cueing devices are traditional or emergent, participants' use and understanding of them represent valuable information for the fieldworker, signaling the participants' commitment to the interaction as well as the participants' attitudes toward each other.

Danielle M. Roemer

See also Discourse Analysis; Linguistic Approaches; Performance.

✳✳✳✳✳✳✳✳✳✳✳✳✳✳✳✳✳✳

References

Bateson, Gregory. [1955] 1972. A Theory of Play and Fantasy. In *Steps to an Ecology of Mind*, ed. Gregory Bateson. San Francisco: Chandler.

Goffman, Erving. 1974. *Frame Analysis: An Essay on the Organization of Experience*. New York: Harper & Row.

———. 1981. *Forms of Talk*. Philadelphia: University of Pennsylvania Press.

Gumperz, John J. 1982. *Discourse Strategies*. Cambridge: Cambridge University Press.

Tannen, Deborah, ed. 1993. *Framing in Discourse*. New York: Oxford University Press.

FREUDIAN PSYCHOLOGY

The theory and techniques developed by Sigmund Freud (1856–1939), the founder of psychoanalysis. The term is also applied liberally by nonspecialists to label approaches of "depth psychology" investigating unconscious mental processes and to certain methods of psychotherapy that are attributable, directly or indirectly, to Freud. Such approaches and methods are so characterized when they address data that are erotic, incestuous along parent-child lines, noncognitive, and symbolic.

Freud was born in Freiberg, Moravia (now in Příbor, Czech Republic), and raised in Vienna. He was considered the brightest of the eight children of a Jewish businessman of modest means and given preferential treatment; he was trained as a medical doctor and began his professional life as a clinical neurologist. He soon became aware of the profound impact that sexual experiences had exerted on the minds and bodies of certain patients, and his search for explanations to this phenomenon led him gradually to the components of his theories. The cornerstones of Freud's psychoanalytic approach are the interplay between unconscious and conscious psychological processes, the hereditary nature of instinctual drives, and the three-level systemic structure of the mind (or psyche).

One of Freud's cardinal contributions to the study of human psychology was his identification of the unconscious as a psychic entity controlled by considerations and forces different than those governing the conscious mind. Within the unconscious, feelings and ideas assume ever shifting patterns—combinations and configurations of the concrete and the abstract, the tangible and the intangible, the known and the unknown, the logical and the illogical, and so on—all under symbolic guises. Thus, two dissimilar ideas or images may be fused into one; experiences that are interconnected may be shifted or displaced out of context; feelings and thoughts may be portrayed in the form of dramatic images rather than expressed as abstract concepts; and certain objects may be represented in symbolic guise by images of other entities, although the resemblance between the symbol and the original object may be incomprehensible.

Recognition of these unconscious mental modes of operation made possible the understanding of such previously mystifying psychological phenomena as dreaming and, by extension, such cultural phenomena as myth making, and similar group experiences.

A basic premise of Freudian theory is that instinctual impulses (drives), especially the sexual, which originate in childhood, trigger unconscious conflicts. Thus, adult sexuality is a product of a complex process of biological development beginning in childhood; this development goes through stages determined by a variety of body functions or areas (zones) and the child's relation to adults, especially to parents. These psychosexual stages are: the oral, the anal, and the phallic or genital.

According to Freud, the child becomes capable of an emotional attachment to the parent of the opposite sex for the first time during the *Oedipal stage* (four to six years of age). However, physical and intellectual immaturity prevent the child from satisfying these desires (that is, they frustrate realization of fantasies); consequently, the desires are unconsciously associated with failure and suppressed. These early patterns of conflict serve as prototypes for an individual's development (and conflicts) during later stages of life, especially in such situations as relationships to parental figures and authority and dependency on others.

The structure of the psychic system is designated in a three-level hierarchy: the *id*, *ego*, and *superego*. The id signifies the sexual and aggressive tendencies that arise from the *Triebe* (primary or biological drives, libido, and so forth); it is primitive and pleasure oriented. The superego refers to internalized standards initially imposed by parental figures and subsequently by all acquired religious, ethical, and moral rules of conduct; the superego controls the ego in accordance with these rules. If the person fails to conform to the admonitions of the superego, he or she may feel shame or guilt (compare with anxiety). The ego is the domain of such functions as perception, thinking, and motor control that can accurately assess environmental conditions. It mediates between the dictates of the id and the constraints of the superego. Defensive mechanisms (e.g., repression, projection, rationalization, identification) protect the ego against the injurious effects of these early experiences and similar unacceptable impulses. Nonetheless, like water in an earthenware jar that filters out through its porous wall (weak points), the contents of the unconscious are externalized through dreams and folk narratives (Freud's critics facetiously labeled this aspect of his theory *hydraulic*).

Evolutionary postulates about the human "primordial horde" presupposing the genetic transmission (biological inheritance) of historical experiences provide the rationale for the origins of the Freudian theoretical model and also argue for the universality of its constituents (e.g., the Oedipus complex). Adjustments introduced into this biologically determined Freudian model are referred to as neopsychoanalytic (neo-Freudian). Typically, revisions place more emphasis on social and cultural considerations.

In folklore and anthropology, drastic criticism has been leveled at Freudian approaches, ranging from their blindness to social and cultural factors to their sensationalism, and they have been attacked as comprising "a non-theistic" belief system (i.e., a matter of unquestioning faith) whose dogmas lie beyond verification. Yet the various Freudian approaches have been dominant in the study of learned traditions—to the detriment of other cognitive types of psychological systems, especially those dealing with the psychology of learning.

Hasan El-Shamy

See also Jungian Psychology; Psychoanalytic Interpretations of Folklore; Psychological Approach.

✻✻✻✻✻✻✻✻✻✻✻✻✻✻✻✻

References

Adler, Alfred. 1925. *The Practice and Theory of Individual Psychology*. New York: Harcourt, Brace, and World.

Brill, A. A., tr. ed. 1938. *The Basic Writings of Sigmund Freud*. New York: Modern Library.

Dundes, Alan. 1975. *Analytic Essays in Folklore*. The Hague: Mouton.

Freud, Sigmund. 1938 [1913]. *Totem and Taboo*. New York: New Republic.

———. 1939. *Moses and Monotheism*. New York: A. A. Knopf.

———. 1950. *The Interpretation of Dreams*. New York: Modern Library.

Fromm, Erich. 1955. *The Sane Society*. New York: Holt.

Horney, Karen. 1939. *New Ways in Psychoanalysis*. New York: Horton.

Schultz, Duane. 1987. *A History of Modern Psychology*. New York: Academic.

El-Shamy, Hasan. 1981. Emotionskomponente. In Kurt Ranke, ed., *Enzyklopädie des Märchens*, vol. 3. Berlin: Walter de Gruyter, pp. 1391–1395.

Spiro, Melford E. 1982. *Oedipus in the Trobriands*. Chicago: University of Chicago.

Functionalism

In folklore studies, the view that every folklore item must have a function. Here, the expectation is that every proverb, tale, folk belief, or ballad must satisfy some important cultural, social, or psychological function. This view of the functional in folklore is parallel to Bronislaw Malinowski's position that everything in human life must have a function.

On a more theoretical level, three kinds of functionalism play an important role in social sciences literature on the topic. The first posits that it is the needs of the psychobiological human entity that are at center stage, the second emphasizes the roles and functions of social structures within the group, and the third approach to functionalism argues for social cohesion through the shared mental structures of the "conscience collective." The first of these is represented by the work of Bronislaw Malinowski, the second by the writings of Reginald Radcliffe-Brown, and the third by writings of Émile Durkheim and Marcel Mauss. Given that a great deal of folklore consists of either beliefs or the oral aspects of culture, it would seem that the works of Durkheim and Mauss are the most significant for many folklorists. Malinowski's biopsychological work, however, is relevant for folklorists who are interested in material folklore.

As one of the great fieldworkers of all time, Malinowski was convinced that every detail of a culture (and this most certainly would include its folklore) had a function. If any social scientist would have the exclusive rights to be called an archfunctionalist, that would certainly be Bronislaw Malinowski. In anthropology, he and Radcliffe-Brown are viewed as the founders of modern functionalism. However, their functionalisms are dramatically different. Radcliffe-Brown's is a structural functionalism, whereas Malinowski's functionalism is based on human biology and psychology. It must be noted that this biopsychological approach pays close attention to the individual and de-emphasizes the importance of the social system as having a reason of existence beyond that of the individual; for Malinowski, functionalism is a metamorphosis of the seven needs of the individual: nutrition, reproduction, bodily comforts, safety, relation, movement, and growth into the secondary needs of society. The needs of the individual are satisfied by the social structure of his or her culture, whose function it is to satisfy those human needs. In other words, every social institution has a need to satisfy, and so does every item in a culture. For folklorists, this means that even the smallest item one collects, such as a single folk belief, has a function to perform both at the level of the individual and at the level of the society and the culture. Malinowski gives us the ultimate in a functional approach. In contrast to Malinowski's interest in the individual and biopsychological approaches, Radcliffe-Brown was interested in the functioning of the social structure.

Radcliffe-Brown has had significant influence in both anthropology and sociology. The functionalist dimension of his work and its structural underpinnings constitute the foundation of structural functionalism in social anthropology as well as in sociological thought. In a period when American anthropology under Franz Boas' influence was putting increasing emphasis on fieldwork, Radcliffe-Brown's main interests remained in generalization and theory. His two major methodological positions were (1) that the individual is of no account and that it is only the social system that matters, and (2) that the organic analogy should be used. Both these points have often been rejected in American anthropology.

Radcliffe-Brown derived his concept of function from physiology. He believed that the term *function* in the social sciences meant the same process as in biology. A different way of putting this is to say that function is the contribution an element makes to the whole social system. The difference between Radcliffe-Brown and Malinowski is, then, that Malinowski started with the individual, whereas individual needs were incidental to Radcliffe-Brown, who regarded the system of human interactions rather than human beings as being central in a functionalist approach to society.

Structure refers to a system of organized parts. These parts are individual persons who participate in social life, occupying statuses within the system. The social network is made up of social relationships between individuals of a society. The individual is in turn controlled by norms or patterns. Folklore's function is to maintain these norms and patterns. It is in his use of the concept of structure and its maintenance that Radcliffe-Brown made his major contribution to functionalism. His approach is markedly different than Durkheim's or Mauss' view.

The work of Durkheim has had a profound influence on the social sciences; his views on why and how society functions have become an integral part of our intellectual heritage. The main subject that preoccupied Durkheim on this topic throughout his life was that of social solidarity or cohesion. He wanted to understand, more than anything else, how a social unit holds its members together. He used concepts such as *organic solidarity* and *conscience connective* to address this issue.

In "The Division of Labor in Society" (1893), Durkheim concentrated on increased specialization of individuals as the key to social solidarity. Societies that have a great amount of specialization possess *organic solidarity*; each individual must work with others to survive. On the other hand, societies that have no differentiation of this type are held together by *mechanical solidarity*. Individuals in such societies have a strong sense of sharing common experiences, but cooperation with others is not necessary. What binds the group together is the cohesion of common experiences. Folklore is a very important part of this common experience, as every group and subgroup shares a folklore that helps cement the solidarity of the group. An aspect of this can be seen in internally undifferentiated occupational groups in contemporary culture where such groups have their own lore.

Later, Durkheim added another explication of social solidarity: that which centers around the conscience collective. The meaning of this phrase in English is something like "shared awareness" or "common understanding." Society must be studied by studying *social facts*, which are parts of the shared awareness in a society. For Durkheim, social facts were what anthropologists understand to be culture. An example of this can be seen in the *Elementary Forms of the Religious Life* in which Durkheim claimed that the totem, the sacred object, is a representation by which society symbolizes itself. The totem is the society rationalized through religion. Such a belief implies that a totem, like any other symbol, is a *collective representation*. This value is given to the representation by the society itself. This results in an epistemology that claims that individual knowledge results neither from the "mind" nor from the senses; rather, we know what we know because we learn socially devised "collective representations." Folklore encompasses a group of these representations that comprise social knowledge and social facts. Durkheim contributed further on this topic with Marcel Mauss.

Two aspects of Mauss' works that have had a major influence on social scientists are his analysis of gift giving and his analysis, with Durkheim, of "primitive" classifications. Mauss and Durkheim saw primitive classifications of categories of phenomena as being the first scientific classifications known to man—a view not very different from contemporary views about folk belief. They regarded such classificatory systems as systems of cognitive categories. The main function of these classifications was to make the relationship between phenomena understandable. As to gifts, Mauss recognized that gifts are obligatory and a part of a network of social obligations. In other words, gift giving and the repayment of gifts represent responsibilities within the social fabric that contribute to cohesion and social solidarity. The underlying importance of functional approaches for folklore studies is the theoretical contextualization of folklore materials within a conceptual framework that folklorists generally assume but do not attempt to cultivate. In this perspective, all folklore materials are a function of a human need, a social and structural necessity, or a device for social cohesion.

Functionalism—viewed as Malinowski's biological and psychological given, Radcliffe-Brown's interplay between the structures of society, and Durkheim and Mauss' social cohesiveness or cultural matrix—provides folkloristics with a multifaceted theoretical matrix for any item in folklore.

Mark Glazer

See also Anthropological Approach.

✹✹✹✹✹✹✹✹✹✹✹✹✹✹✹✹

References

Durkheim, Émile. 1915. *The Elementary Forms of Religious Life*. Trans. J. W. Swain. London: Allen & Unwin.

———. [1893] 1933. *Division of Labor in Society*. Trans. G. Simpson. New York: Macmillan.

———. 1951. *Suicide*. Trans. J. Spaulding and G. Simpson. New York: Free Press.

Jarvie, I. C. 1973. *Functionalism*. Minneapolis, MN: Burgess.

Malinowski, Bronislaw. 1922. *Argonauts of the Western Pacific*. New York: Dutton.

———. 1939. The Group and the Individual in Functionalist Analysis. *American Journal of Sociology* 44:938–964.

———. 1944. *A Scientific Theory of Culture*. Chapel Hill: University of North Carolina Press.

Parsons, Talcott. 1951. *The Social System*. Glencoe, IL: Free Press.

Radcliffe-Brown, Reginald. 1935. On the Concept of Function in Social Science. *American Anthropologist* 37:394–402.

———. 1952. *Structure and Function in Primitive Society*. New York: Free Press.

G

GAMES, FOLK

Play forms, usually with explicit rules, known to a particular group of people. Although artifacts recognizable as games have been among the archaeological finds of ancient Sumer, Egypt, Persia, Greece, Rome, and China, scholars continue to disagree over definitions of the genre. Games range from the covert, xeroxed visual riddles in office folklore, baby tickling styles, and adolescent courtship rituals to the large-scale painted games within urban graffiti and performances at public festivals.

Games are both observable and, simultaneously, inside the minds of the players. Perhaps the most profound paradox in game scholarship was framed by William Wells Newell, collector of children's folklore, who noted that players were simultaneously conservative and inventive with their games. Games are a solid and collectible—yet slippery and evolving—phenomenon.

The Study of Games, by Elliot M. Avedon and Brian Sutton-Smith, contains historical references for specific forms of games and traces the word *game* to its Indo-European root—*ghem*, meaning "to leap joyfully, to spring." The study isolates the three most familiar usages for the word: first, "a form of play, amusement, recreation, sport, or frolic involving specific rules, sometimes utilizing a set of equipment, sometimes requiring skill, knowledge, and endurance"; second, "a condition of a leg, when someone is lame or injured and they limp"; and third, "wild animals, birds, or fish that are hunted for sport, or for use as food." A game as folklore genre combines the notion of the form, condition, and object.

The prominence of rules in game definitions serves as the game's primary marker. Lev Semyonovich Vygotsky noted that in games, there are overt or revealed rules and concealed drama, whereas in other forms of play, there is revealed drama and concealed rules. As there are layers of rules to each game, one could argue, so there are layers of drama. Historically, the overt thematic dramas of the games were given research priority, with the emphasis on the game's spoken texts. Recently, it is the covert dramas that are being written about, with the emphasis on the game's symbolism and its connection to context and larger cultural patterns.

The more popular phenomena for game research have been: the verbal play of jump-rope rhymes, singing games, ball-bouncing rhymes, and riddles; board games such as chess, backgammon, and go; chasing and fighting games; and games focused on objects, such as string games and doll plays. Typically, in the collections of games, the texts are of a specific genre cross-culturally,

Dutch girls enjoying hopscotch, a folk game that is found throughout the world, from New York to New Delhi.

such as singing games, or of a particular genre prominent in one place, as in stylized ball play.

All games in active traditional circulation among players are considered folk games, yet some games are traditionally associated with certain peoples and often highlighted in game study, such as hunting games associated with a particular hunting-and-gathering culture. Even the highly regulated popular sport of basketball has its own folk variations, which themselves can be considered folk games. Although adults and children alike play games, the folklore literature has emphasized either the festival games of adults or the vast repertoires of the most prolific of game players—elementary-school-age children.

The most comprehensive cross-cultural collection of folk game studies to date is Helen Schwartzman's *Transformations: The Anthropology of Children's Play*. Cross-referenced by specific game genre and locale, this volume serves as an encyclopedia of game types and play lore, as well as a catalog of films on folk games. A reference book for both ethnographic and psychological studies, *Transformations* serves as a reminder that alongside the history of specific games, the study of games in general has had its own traditions.

The main thrust of much nineteenth- and mid-twentieth-century game lore research was directed to finding early, if not "original," versions of games. There is a certain adventure in following a game's historical path as we trace chess, according to E. B. Tylor, from its likely start as an eighth-century Indian war game of *draughts*, through Persia and its acquisition of the name of the *shah* (or king), to the name's transformation to *schach*, *eschees*, and *chess*. There is romance in connecting the marital lyrics of girl's circle dances to biblical courtship rites, as Iona and Peter Opie have done, and mystery in postulating the possible meanings of the nonsense words of verbal play. This retrospective process sheds light on the history and the migration of the game, but it tells us little of what the games actually mean or meant to the human players.

Although histories of specific games were attempted in the seventeenth and eighteenth centuries, games were not collected formally in Europe until the 1800s, when the folklore societies began to search for survivals of early cultural rituals and traditional forms that embodied national character. Pioneered by Alice Bertha Gomme in England, Scotland, and Ireland and by William Wells Newell in the United States, the first collections of games were focused on region. Like the folktale or folksong, games were examined historically and geographically as artifacts from a passing time and initially were gathered through the sifting of a tremendous number of written sources. For example, François Rabelais' sixteenth-century French tale of *Garganatua and Pantagruel* contains perhaps the earliest categorization of folk games, thus making it a classic resource comparable to Pieter Breughel's sixteenth-century painting of Flemish village games, circa 1560.

In the mid-twentieth century, Iona and Peter Opie expanded upon the earlier, primarily literary tradition of game collection with their direct observations in *Children's Games in Street and Playground*. Like Newell, the Opies gathered and categorized texts of songs and games and printed them verbatim based upon fieldnotes. Musical notation was included in this as in earlier studies, but there was a great elaboration upon the comparative footnotes. Unlike the overt evolutionism of the nineteenth-century cross-cultural game histories represented by the work of E. B. Tylor, the works of the mid-twentieth-century folklorists tended to emphasize one region in detail. Brian Sutton-Smith's *A History of Children's Play: The New Zealand Playground, 1840–1950* exemplified this later focus. His study further expanded upon the historical emphasis of earlier studies and introduced a new research technique: the collection of games by means of the methodology of oral history as well as through written documentation. In Sutton-Smith's work, the recording of individuals' game recollections gracefully demonstrated the significance of historical context in the development of the games themselves.

In the 1970s, Rivka Eifermann expanded upon the concept of geographic mapping developed in the earlier English works by surveying Israel's games and comparing groups of players and their games by age, game size, physical context, and ethnic variation. Unlike folklorists who conducted other psychological studies that had appeared around this time, studies in which the game was examined in order to understand some other process (e.g., cognition or moral judgment), Eifermann, like Sutton-Smith, examined the game as a cultural form. The assumption behind Eifermann's study was that the games, like other cultural phenomena, served some purpose: child training, subversive expression, or physical pleasure, for example. The study of games in their varying contexts could then reflect and legitimate the differing needs of the cultural communities in which the games were played.

The author of each of the classic works on games cited in the preceding passages attempted to categorize play forms in a particular way. The Opies categorized by motion: "chasing" versus "catching," or "seeking." For Newell, the categories were romance and survivalism: games of "love," "histories," and "mythology." Categorization by action in general becomes difficult since the same text may be a hand-clapping game in one area, a jump-rope rhyme in another, and a verbal taunt in a third. Similarly, a soccer game may be played with a ball in one country but with bottle caps in another. Categorization by theme, on the one hand, provides too little latitude for textual variation and, on the other, allows too many opportunities for theoretical bias (e.g., game texts as "broken-down" myths). Sutton-Smith examined a century's worth of games in his ethnographic research and offered thematic patterns by era and indexed them by game name. The alphabetical approach of the Gomme collection was an attempt to avoid the classification problem by merely listing titles; however, even titles or first lines of games are subject to change. Asking the participants in a specific study for their own terms and classification often proves to be the most useful approach, as we recognize that classification is in itself a game tradition, either imposed or brought out by the players themselves.

Games also have been classified by occasion, and this raises questions regarding the significance of spatial and temporal context in folk game research. Some games only appear during certain seasons, over certain holidays, and among certain age groups (e.g., snowball fights, April Fool's pranks on April 1, bobbing for apples at Halloween, and adolescent kissing games). Even these patterns will generally shift over time in any given place and across contexts.

For Roger Caillois, in *Man, Play and Games*, there were four basic categorical elements in game play: *agon* (competition), *alea* (chance), *mimicry* (simulation), and *ilinx* (vertigo). Caillois' scheme remains a popular model among researchers, despite the fact that though many games emphasize one of these elements, most combine many. Categorizations, like any set of lenses, are useful in that they allow new ways of seeing phenomena, but categories also can serve as blinders as observations are placed into analytic boxes.

Dorothy Howard, in her introduction to Alice Bertha Gomme's collection *The Traditional Games of England, Scotland, and Ireland*, noted that methodologies of game research have to be examined in their own historical context. In the late nineteenth century, Lady Gomme was not allowed to watch the playing of the games she described, given her gender and nobility; therefore, her skills and interests had to be limited to the antiquarian's armchair. Collectors through the first half of the twentieth century, although utilizing direct observation and fieldnotes, could not capture as much detail as those who did fieldwork in the day of the audiotape player. Currently, with the availability of film and videotape, subtleties in the performance of games are recordable in a manner not possible a generation ago.

Pioneered by both anthropologists and psychologists in the 1940s and 1950s, the use of ethnographic film and video is both highly valued and underutilized in game study. *Trobriander Cricket: An Ingenious Response to Colonialism*, a 1973 film by Jerry Leach and Gary Kildea, was able to capture not only the formal game rule adaptation of the colonial game among Melanesian Trobriander tribes but also the joking, dancing, costumed midgame ceremonies that were their own play forms, parades, and parodies. *Pizza, Pizza, Daddy-O*, a 1969 film by Bess Lomax Hawes and Robert Eberlein, demonstrated the style, rhythm, formation, and mood of the singing games of African-American girls in a manner not tenable on the written page.

As ethnographic methodology became more accepted and recording technology became more precise, the emphasis in game study shifted to the processes involved in the playing of the game. Based upon his ethnographic study of the Balinese cockfight, Clifford Geertz developed the notion of "deep play," a model in which the game serves as an icon for a culture's basic character. Geertz made the case for the significance of folk games in understanding the values of the larger culture, and by doing so, he elevated the game's status from the peripheral to the central. B. Whitney Azoy's study *Buzkashi: Game and Power in Afghanistan* made a similar argument and expanded the anthropology of gaming to a book-length ethnography. For these researchers, the study of the game was synonymous with the study of the larger culture, and the games were stylized models of that society.

The variety of research on folk games ranges from sociological and geographical surveys to psychological small-group studies, from sociolinguistic studies of riddling and joking games to layered ethnographies of games and sports. In 1974, the Anthropological Association for the Study of Play formed and soon reorganized as the Association for the Study of Play in order to incorporate a diversity of disciplines involved in the study of folk games. The types of questions asked now vary almost as much as the forms of games themselves.

Work focusing on the highly studied, international game of hopscotch provides a useful example of the range of folk game research and also of the significance of audiovisual recording. Known in Australia as "hoppy," in New York City as "potsie," and in French Switzerland as "*la marelle*," hopscotch has a sizable but limited literature, in that the literature emphasizes almost exclusively the physical construction of the hopscotch form. In this slow-paced game of physical skill, each player typically tosses a marker, such as a stone, onto the chalked hopscotch board, which contains squares in a pattern, each with a number from 1 to 10 or more. Then, the players sequentially hop from square to square, alternately land on one foot and then two feet, and then attempt to pick up the stone without falling. It is a competitive game in which the player who progresses the farthest, without erring in either tossing or hopping, wins.

Sometimes drawn in a spiral, sometimes as a large rectangle, and sometimes in a circle, the form itself varies and is the most discussed variation in the game literature. According to Newell, "This is one of the universal games, common from England to Hindostan." He noted it was called "The Bell" in Italy and "The Temple" in Austria, and in Italy, the last three divisions of the chalk patterns are the *Inferno*, *Purgatoria*, and *Paradiso*. The Opies found English references to the game in eighteenth-century documents, and American folklorists Mary and Herbert Knapp claimed that a hopscotch diagram is still visible on the pavement of the Roman Forum. Yet all this description in the literature, although significant in our understanding of the game's popularity in general, tells us nothing of how the game has actually been played. For this, we need real voices in transcription, stories about rules and the breaking of rules, and the ethnographic description of real times and places where real people get to play.

Among European-American and African-American girls in an urban elementary schoolyard in Pennsylvania, the folk variation lay not in the form or in the labels of the boxes but in the rules themselves. In one study, carried out in 1991–1992 by Ann Richman Beresin, children watched videotapes of themselves at play and gave their own commentary on game meaning, rules, and style and on the interconnection between game rules and power. Since the form of their hopscotch was a rectangle with a rounded top, numbered and drawn in paint by the elementary school officials, their folk variation was in the terminology and rule flexibility. For example, they used rules such as "walksies" and "no walksies" or "helpsies" and "no helpsies," meaning forms of acceptable movement in the game. All of these stylized movements had to be "called" at the beginning of a game, and it was the calling that shaped the game. The fixing of the game in paint by the school officials, as opposed to the more studied child-drawn chalk game, implicated larger historical trends visible in Western children's folklore—namely, the subtle control exerted by adults over what had been a children's domain. It can be said that the new rules invented by the children were a direct response to such control.

Nowhere in the English-language folk game literature are such rule variations examined, making one wonder how we can know a game without knowing the players or the plays. The variations have been skipped over in most collections—one could say, across the board. Audiovisual technology makes possible the expansion of questions about the game process, and the opportunity for observation over time, in one place, allows for the examining of larger cultural patterns related to the players, the school, and the larger society.

Descriptions of playful bodies and studies of their games, as in wrestling, chasing, stunts, or pranks, are still rare, due in part to the underutilization of audiovisual recording as a methodological tool and in part to the blinders of Western culture's romanticism. Speech and rhyme have been given priority, even in the very physical games of rope jumping and hand clapping and ball bouncing. Large-scale ethnographic studies of game genres and game processes are needed, especially in this time of increased adult control over children's play (particularly in Western culture) and emphasis on official sports and generalized rules.

Also underrepresented in the English-language literature are the games of non-Western countries and games of Western minorities. As Helen Schwartzman pointed out, in the early ethnographic reports of tribal cultures listed in the Human Relations Area Files, as well as in the modern psychological literature on minority groups, peoples mistakenly have been described as not having any games at all. The fallacy of such a notion lies in the complexity of fieldwork in unfamiliar cultures, the misdirection of the questions asked about play and games, the lack of time depth in most studies, and the secrecy often surrounding a folk group's customs.

Another neglected area involves the pre- and postgame rituals that may be significant to the playing of the game itself. Rituals and minigames—such as the opening anthem before the ball game or the chanting and hand pointing of "Eeny, Meeny, Miny, Moe," and the making of a tower of fists in "One Potato, Two Potato" as players set the terms of the game—often precede the full games and begin the competition, drama, or performance. Real players of real games can attest that the boundaries researchers have made around the games listed in books are often neat and artificial ones, as games often blend into one another or cross genres during play.

Seekers of information on other forms of folk games not readily found in the game text literature need to comb ethnographies of particular populations, daily life histories, and fictional and nonfictional films and narratives, as well as the treasures hidden in the related areas of folk gesture, folk drama, dance, and ritual. Students of adult festivals and observers of animal play will find games and a corresponding relevant literature in these areas as well. Many games are listed as songs, both in educational instructional publications as well as in ethnographic reports, and sometimes a game description can be found hidden behind the folk toy in a collection of material culture. For the most authoritative resource on folk games, one should seek out the players. Through incorporating their views, the folk game literature can be verified or challenged.

Ann Richman Beresin

See also Children's Folklore; Toy, Folk.

✻✻✻✻✻✻✻✻✻✻✻✻✻✻✻✻✻

References

Avedon, Elliot M., and Brian Sutton-Smith, eds. 1971. *The Study of Games*. New York: Wiley.

Azoy, G. Whitney. 1982. *Buzkashi: Game and Power in Afghanistan*. Philadelphia: University of Pennsylvania Press.

Caillois, Roger. 1961. *Man, Play, and Games*. New York: Free Press.

Eifermann, Rivka. 1968. *School Children's Games*. U.S. Department of Health, Education, and Welfare. Office of Education, Bureau of Research, Washington, DC.

Geertz, Clifford. 1973. Deep Play: Notes on the Balinese Cockfight. In Clifford Geertz, *The Interpretation of Cultures*. New York: Basic Books.

Howard, Dorothy. [1884–1889] 1964. Introduction. *The Traditional Games of England, Scotland, and Ireland with Tunes, Singing-Rhymes, and Methods of Playing According to the Variants Extant and Recorded in Different Parts of the Kingdom*. Collected and annotated by Alice Bertha Gomme. New York: Dover.

Knapp, Mary, and Herbert Knapp. 1976. *One Potato, Two Potato: The Folklore of American Children*. New York: W. W. Norton.

Newell, William Wells. [1883] 1963. *Games and Songs of American Children*. New York: Dover.

Opie, Iona, and Peter Opie. 1969. *Children's Games in Street and Playground*. Oxford: Oxford University Press.

Schwartzman, Helen. 1978. *Transformations: The Anthropology of Children's Play*. New York: Plenum.

Sutton-Smith, Brian. 1981. *A History of Children's Play: The New Zealand Playground, 1840–1950*. Wellington: New Zealand Council on Educational Research and Philadelphia: University of Pennsylvania Press.

Vygotsky, Lev Semyonovich. Mind in Society: *The Development of Higher Psychological Processes*. Edited by Michael Cole et al. Cambridge, MA: Harvard University Press.

GAY AND LESBIAN STUDIES AND QUEER THEORY

The study of the cultures of homosexual men and women and a theoretical approach that considers these cultures on their own terms. In 1869, Károly Mária Kertbeny first used the term *homosexualität* (homosexuality) in his writing opposing the German Confederation's plan to adopt Prussia's antisodomy law. Other opponents of such laws, including Karl Heinrich Ulrichs, K.F.O. Westphal, and Richard von Krafft-Ebing, proposed other, less enduring terms to designate sexual acts and attraction between people of the same sex. Magnus Hirschfield founded the Scientific-Humanitarian Committee in Berlin in 1897 and established an extensive library of material pertaining to homosexuality. He eventually had to flee Germany; his collection was burned by the Nazis. These men, through their interest in the origins of homosexuality and their opposition to legislation against same-sex relations, laid the groundwork for what became the modern gay rights movement.

The early twentieth century saw the spread of homophile organizations to other parts of Europe and to the United States. Henry Gerber established the Society for Human Rights in Chicago in 1924. Activity declined during the years of the Great Depression, only to resume after World War II—perhaps encouraged by Alfred C. Kinsey's monumental studies *Sexual Behavior in the Human Male* (1948) and *Sexual Behavior in the Human Female* (1953). In response to Sen. Joseph McCarthy's attempts to identify and prosecute homosexuals, Harry Hay founded the Mattachine Society in Los Angeles in 1950. Five years later, Del Martin and Phyllis Lyon organized the Daughters of Bilitis in San Francisco. These two groups sought acceptance for gay men and lesbians. Their respective journals, *One* and *The Ladder*, contain some of the earliest contributions to gay and lesbian studies.

Emboldened by the social upheaval of the 1960s—the civil rights movement, the Vietnam War protests, the women's movement, and the sexual revolution—homosexual people began to become more visible and to demand an end to discrimination based on sexual orientation. The fledgling gay liberation movement received a significant boost from the Stonewall

Rebellion in 1969–100 years after Kertbeny's first published use of the term *homosexual*. Frustrated by police harassment, patrons of the Stonewall Inn in New York City's Greenwich Village fought back when the police raided the bar on the night of June 26, 1969. The struggle continued for the rest of that month.

Seemingly overnight, gay and lesbian organizations sprang up, and with them came a significant increase in the attention paid by scholars to homosexuality. The medical and psychological studies that had predominated in the field gave way to more ethnographic depictions of lesbian and gay life published throughout the 1970s. The latest Kinsey studies documented a variety of lifestyles, embodied in the title of one of the volumes: *Homosexualities*.

In the 1980s, gay and lesbian studies exploded. The existence of a gay and lesbian culture—or cultures—became irrefutable. In 1980, one could have read virtually everything published in the field; by 1990, however, one would have been hard pressed to read most of the titles on a single aspect of homosexuality. Corey Creekmur and Alexander Doty's 1995 *Out in Culture* included a 24-page bibliography of publications on lesbian and gay popular culture alone.

Although Christopher Isherwood made a foray into lesbian and gay studies in *The World in the Evening* (1956) by mentioning camp—a prototypical gay sensibility—Susan Sontag might be credited with making the first theoretical contribution to the field with her 1964 essay "Notes on Camp." (Camp is a style of humor that inverts and subverts values, often by playing with stereotypes. It frequently has a serious edge, serving to mock heterosexual norms.) Several writers contributed articles on gay men's language to both popular magazines and scholarly journals during the 1960s and 1970s. Esther Newton's 1972 volume *Mother Camp: Female Impersonation in America* was a cultural anthropological study of drag queens. Michael Bronski, in his 1984 book *Culture Clash: The Making of Gay Sensibility*, documented the impact of gay culture on popular culture. Another 1984 volume, Judy Grahn's *Another Mother Tongue: Gay Words, Gay Worlds*, offered an interesting but largely unsubstantiated speculation about the origins of gay and lesbian traditional culture. Many homosexual people embraced Grahn's book because it proposed a gay and lesbian mythos. The first book on gay men's folklore, Joseph P. Goodwin's *More Man than You'll Ever Be: Gay Folklore and Acculturation in Middle America*, appeared in 1989. Comparable lesbian studies are yet to be published, although some progress was made with the publication in 1994 of *Prejudice and Pride: Lesbian and Gay Traditions in America*, a special issue of *New York Folklore*.

As the field of lesbian and gay studies has grown, the terminology has changed. *Homosexual* gave way to *gay*, which in turn was expanded to *gay and lesbian*. In the late 1980s, homosexual people increasingly began to appropriate the term *queer*, which had been used as a tool of oppression for decades by the majority culture. Adapting the term as an emic concept (a name the community applied to itself) imbued it with pride, inverted it, denied the conflation of sex acts with homosexuality, pointed out the ridiculous aspects of the stereotypes the word referred to, and threw the term back into the faces of those who opposed equal rights for queers. But the word has a more mundane value, as well: It subsumes not only *gay* and *lesbian*, but also *bisexual*, *transsexual*, and *transgendered*, offering a succinct term for several categories of outsiders. Queer is a subversive concept since it calls into question traditional gender roles and ideas of what constitutes appropriate behavior. The study of queer culture contradicts traditional notions of homosexuality as sin or illness. It documents the existence of a dynamic, widespread, living culture.

About 1990, gay and lesbian studies gave rise to queer theory. Although not yet codified, queer theory has had a great impact on recent studies of lesbian and gay culture. (Studies on the culture of bisexual, transsexual, and transgendered people only began to appear in the mid-1990s.) Drawing from rhetoric and discourse, philosophy, deconstruction, postmodernism, rereadings of psychoanalytic theory, and especially feminist theory, queer theorists seek to reframe issues. The "white heterosexual male" is no longer the benchmark against which everything else is measured. Thus, gay, lesbian, and queer cultures are not defined in relationship to heterosexuality. Instead, they are documented and analyzed as inherently valid manifestations of ways of being.

One of the continuing debates in gay and lesbian studies is whether homosexuality is innate (the essentialist point of view) or the result of social forces arising fairly recently (the social construction theory). Social constructionists maintain that sexuality takes its meaning from its culture, just as feminist theory holds that gender roles are socially constructed. To interpret homosexual acts in ancient Greece using contemporary American gay male culture as a frame of reference, therefore, is anachronistic. According to some proponents of this point of view, gay and lesbian culture could not have existed until homosexuality was labeled in the nineteenth century. Michel Foucault has suggested that the beginning of the social construction of homosexuality can be traced to Westphal's 1870 writing on "contrary sexual feelings."

In covert novels and short stories written for homosexual people before Stonewall (and even since), coding allowed the audience to read queerness into the texts. The readers were adept at deciphering ambiguous diction and esoteric symbols. In recent years, queer people have begun reading texts as queer even when the messages were not (consciously) encrypted by their authors. This kind of "cross-reading," according to Creekmur and Doty in their introduction to *Out in Culture*, depends on camp. They explained the queer resonance that the movie *The Wizard of Oz* has for gay men and lesbians by pointing out that almost everyone in the film lives a double life: "Its emotionally confused and oppressed teenage heroine longs for a world in which her inner desires can be expressed freely and fully. Dorothy finds this world in a Technicolor land 'over the rainbow' inhabited by a sissy lion, an artificial man who cannot stop crying, and a butch-femme couple of witches."

Authors can invert coding as a subversive queer act. Michèle Aina Barale, in her essay in *The Lesbian and Gay Studies Reader*, offered an example of a queer reading of a queer text. In considering Ann Bannon's 1962 novel *Beebo Brinker* from a queer point of view, Barale demonstrated how a lesbian novel ostensibly written for heterosexual men is actually a subversive text that forces the straight male reader into a complicit acceptance of the homosexuality of the characters in the book.

Like words, appearances have been coded in gay and lesbian culture. Various "types" have been common during the twentieth century. The most familiar types may be the lesbian presentations of self as *butch* or *femme* (conforming to visual and sometimes behavioral stereotypes of masculine or feminine). Sue-Ellen Case, in *The Lesbian and Gay Studies Reader*, used a study of the "butch-femme aesthetic" to support Teresa de Lauretis' concept of a feminist subject, as distinct from a female subject. According to de Lauretis, the postmodern concept of the female subject is described in (and locked into) heterosexual terms and cannot escape from that ideology. The feminist subject (butch and femme lesbians in Case's essay) is not restricted in this way. She can take action and move beyond heterosexual ideology.

Queer theory can challenge folklorists to question their assumptions and to look at their subject from new points of view. Although folklorists have traditionally worked with marginalized groups, people who are outside the official power structure, they are just beginning to explore the richness of gay and lesbian culture; they have not even begun to consider the possibilities of bisexual, transsexual, and transgendered cultures. If these groups are socially constructed, their cultures are perhaps just being born. Researchers should begin documenting them now.

Joseph P. Goodwin

See also Family Folklore; Feminist Perspectives on Folklore Scholarship; Gender.

✳✳✳✳✳✳✳✳✳✳✳✳✳✳✳✳✳

References
Abelove, Henry, Michèle Aina Barale, and David M. Halperin. 1993. *The Lesbian and Gay Studies Reader*. New York: Routledge.
Butler, Judith. 1990. *Gender Trouble: Feminism and the Subversion of Identity*. New York: Routledge.
Case, Sue-Ellen, Philip Brett, and Susan Leigh Foster. 1995. *Cruising the Performative: Interventions into the Representation of Ethnicity, Nationality, and Sexuality*. Bloomington: Indiana University Press.
Creekmur, Corey K., and Alexander Doty. 1995. *Out in Culture: Gay, Lesbian, and Queer Essays on Popular Culture*. Durham, NC: Duke University Press.

de Lauretis, Teresa, ed. 1991. Queer Theory: Lesbian and Gay Sexualities. *differences: A Journal of Feminist Cultural Studies*, vol. 3.

Dynes, Wayne, ed. 1990. *Encyclopedia of Homosexuality*. New York: Garland.

Foucault, Michel. 1978. *The History of Sexuality, Volume 1: An Introduction*. Trans. Robert Hurley. New York: Pantheon Books.

Goodwin, Joseph P. 1989. *More Man than You'll Ever Be: Gay Folklore and Acculturation in Middle America*. Bloomington: Indiana University Press.

Sontag, Susan. 1964. Notes on Camp. *Partisan Review* 31:515–530.

Summers, Claude J., ed. 1995. *The Gay and Lesbian Literary Heritage: A Reader's Companion to the Writers and Their Works, from Antiquity to the Present*. New York: Henry Holt.

GENDER

Identification of a person as male or female according to culture-specific criteria. In everyday speech, the terms *sex* and *gender* tend to be employed interchangeably to indicate the aggregate of structural, functional, and behavioral differences that distinguish females and males from each other. Folklorists and other social scientists, however, draw a significant distinction between these two concepts. In their more precise terminology, *sex* denotes only those physiological and functional features that are direct manifestations of one's genetic endowment with two X chromosomes (female in humans) or one X and one Y chromosome (male in humans). *Gender* denotes that much larger body of behaviors, roles, and expectations that, although regarded by members of a society as appropriate only for members of one biological sex or the other, vary considerably across cultures and historical periods and hence must be culturally conditioned rather than biologically determined. Though it is common if not universal to make the male/female distinction the first and most crucial division among people, this does not mean that the concepts "woman" and "man" are universal categories since what it means to behave appropriately for one's gender may be radically different in different societies.

In most if not all societies and cultural traditions, including the Euroamerican cultural and philosophical tradition from which the discipline of folklore emerged, those distinct roles seen as proper for men and women are believed to be natural, that is, biologically determined and/or divinely ordained. These roles are not only in specifically sexual activity but also in work, family, religion, government, recreation, expressive culture, and other aspects of social interaction. A gender perspective decouples the biological structure and function of the male or female body from the behaviors, feelings, and roles deemed appropriate to that body. Thus, a gender-informed perspective is often linked with a critical feminist philosophy that seeks to free women from the (generally devalued and limited) social roles to which they were formerly restricted, although the study of how to be a (cultural) man is as significant as, if less common than, the study of how to be a (cultural) woman. The study of gender likewise implicates the study of sexuality since the structure/behavior decoupling fundamental to this perspective argues that even the apparently inevitable roles within intimate sexual relationships and an individual's sexual attraction to persons of the same or opposite gender are substantially influenced by cultural attitudes. A gender-informed approach to folklore thus has strong connections to gay and lesbian theory and serves as a counterbalance to psychoanalytic approaches to the extent that they posit universal and distinct psychosexual developmental pathways for women and men.

Both biology and culture may contribute to those behaviors seen as gender-specific, but it is rarely possible to determine the exact extent of their relative contributions. Empirical research and philosophical debate continue. The crucial contribution of a gender perspective is to recognize that there is a separation, not a complete congruence, between biological and cultural factors and that consequently the question must always be asked about the extent and nature of possible connections between them. This inherently cultural-constructivist perspective also makes it clear that the very perception of a characteristic as natural, biological, or hormonal can itself be a social expectation. For example, those societies that attribute greater aggressiveness to males may perceive aggression as an essential, hormonally determined male trait, but other cultures see aggressiveness and the willingness to fight fiercely (usually to protect the young rather than to acquire territory) as an essential female trait.

The study of gender in folklore has historical roots extending back as far as the 1920s. Mark Azadovskii's work revealing the influence of gender on tale-tellers' repertoire and performance choices (1926) and Margaret Mead's comparative study documenting extreme cultural variability in gender roles in tribal societies (1935) presaged issues still being considered today. Simone de Beauvoir's philosophical exploration of the way women have been defined as "not man" (1953) was particularly important in sparking the political feminism of the 1960s and the explosion of feminist scholarship in folklore as well as other disciplines in the 1970s and 1980s. Works by Carol Gilligan and the multiple authors of *Women's Ways of Knowing* further elaborated the groundwork of the gender perspective, arguing that women in Euroamerican cultures have been culturally conditioned to have fundamentally different (but not deficient) ways of understanding and responding intellectually and ethically to the world. The constructivist position on gender is closely tied to the deprivileging of authoritative discourses and decentering of the unitary subject central to deconstruction and poststructuralism. This perspective is also

406

entirely congruent with the movements within folklore that stressed the value of contextual interpretation, with the role folklore plays in communication between persons who identify with distinct and even hostile groups as well as within homogenous folk groups (differential identity), and with the dialogic construction of identity through aesthetic expression—that is, with the paradigms of the contextual/performance revolution in folklore theory of the 1970s and 1980s. Significantly, however, gender was not taken into account in the original formulation of these theories. Feminist critics have had to note the telling omission and argue for the essential place of gender in approaches to folklore study that rely upon a problematized notion of personal identity and group membership.

A gender-informed perspective also has shaped both topical and methodological considerations in the study of folklore. In terms of topic, perceiving gender as a cultural construct has prompted the realization that gender roles and identities are themselves traditional forms of expressive communication, that is, they are social, aesthetic accomplishments and forms of folklore in their own right. Groups defined by gender and/or sexual orientation are appreciated as significant folk groups with their own lore, practices, and types of group-internal and group-external communication. New genres and new perspectives on genre have emerged as folklorists realized that one's practice as a narrator, humorist, craftsperson, singer, or performer/creator of any type is likely to be influenced by one's gender and one's responses to gender norms in one's society. An awareness that gays and lesbians as well as heterosexual women have been defined primarily in terms of absences and deficiencies (in contrast to heterosexual male practice, silently accepted as the human norm) has prompted explorations of the positive qualities of the expressive skills practiced within these groups. Conversely, folklorists now recognize that gender must be taken into account as a source of potential difference within families and ethnic or racial groups formerly treated as homogeneous. The recognition of cross-cultural, cross-racial, cross-class, and historical variation in definitions of gender also deflects feminist folkloristics from the attractions of essentialism, counterbalancing the disposition to identify universal "women's styles" or "women's experiences."

In terms of fieldwork methodology, a gender-informed perspective has been one of the theoretical approaches most influential in overturning formerly dominant concepts of objectivity in research. Feminist folklore scholars (following the critical work of Evelyn Fox Keller and Sandra Harding in the natural and social sciences, respectively) argue that the valorization of objectivity and distance in ethnographic research has been a way of privileging a conventionally male interaction style. Current practice recognizes that the self does not have to be defined by separation from the other and that empathic and participatory ways of understanding the ethnographic subject are as valid as an objectifying, purely intellectual approach. While insisting that gender identity is variable and changeable, this perspective recognizes that the researcher's effective or perceived gender identity and sexual identity have a profound effect on fieldwork. One's own perceptions and experiences (including the lived experience of gender and sexual orientation) will necessarily influence what issues are important to the researcher and hence not only what questions one asks but also what one sees and hears in the course of complex aesthetic communicative events. Gender identity also influences access: Who the researcher is perceived to be will have an effect on how people make sense of that individual, what they think they should talk to her or him about, and hence what she or he learns about a culture or situation. Ethnographers need to learn to capitalize on the opportunities afforded by gender. Particularly for stigmatized groups—gay and lesbian communities as well as heterosexual women—many communicative activities are intentionally coded to avoid exposure. Thus, potential informants are likely to be willing to reveal themselves and share lore only with those who share their gender or sexual identity or who demonstrate that they are sympathetic. A shared gender identification may also be crucial in enabling the researcher to make sense of cues or to interpret communicative forms properly. A complete commonality between researcher and informant on the basis only of shared gender should not be assumed, however, given the variation within gender definitions.

In studying folklore through the lens of gender or studying gender by means of its expression in folklore, a constant tension exists between constructivist and essentialist tendencies. The role of ethnographic and empirical work in the social sciences (in contrast to philosophical and psychoanalytically informed theories) is to document actual cultural, racial, and class variation in gender roles, practices, and expectations. Nevertheless, given the logical explanatory connections between observed expressive forms and common gender-based activities (for example, between intentionally interruptable narrative styles employed by women and the demands of child care), it can be a tempting act of gender solidarity to generalize. Furthermore, it appears that, in practice, each person (researcher or subject) must essentialize to some extent, concluding that some ways of being or behaving are crucial to his or her identity as a gendered subject. To the extent that a gender perspective is allied with feminist theories advocating transcendence of the Cartesian mind/body split, this approach recognizes that a person's sense of self depends upon the experience of living in a particular (gendered) body with particular qualities and capabilities—although all "experience," even bodily experience, must be seen (from an Althusserian perspective) as ideologically informed and thus culturally constructed. One solution, advocated by Diana Fuss, argues that essentialism is implicated even within the most critical constructivism:

A cultural-constructivist position replaces the idea of an essential natural, biological human gender identity with the concept of gender as necessarily (essentially) created through social interaction.

Patricia E. Sawin

See also Family Folklore; Feminist Perspectives on Folklore Scholarship; Gay and Lesbian Studies and Queer Theory.

✳✳✳✳✳✳✳✳✳✳✳✳✳✳✳✳✳

References

Azadovskii, Mark. 1974. *A Siberian Tale Teller.* Trans. James R. Dow. Austin, TX: Center for Intercultural Studies in Folklore and Ethnomusicology.

Belenky, Mary Field, Blythe McVicker Clinchy, Nancy Rule Goldberger, and Jill Mattuck Tarule. 1986. *Women's Ways of Knowing: The Development of Self, Voice, and Mind.* New York: Basic Books.

Blincoe, Deborah, and John Forrest. 1993. *Prejudice and Pride: Lesbian and Gay Traditions in America.* Special issue of New York Folklore 19(1–2).

Collins, Camilla A., ed. 1990. *Folklore Fieldwork: Sex, Sexuality, and Gender.* Special issue of *Southern Folklore* 47(1).

de Beauvoir, Simone. 1953. *The Second Sex.* New York: Knopf.

Fuss, Diana. 1989. *Essentially Speaking: Feminism, Nature, and Difference.* New York: Routledge.

Gilligan, Carol. 1982. *In a Different Voice: Psychological Theory and Women's Development.* Cambridge, MA: Harvard University Press.

Goodwin, Joseph P. 1989. *More Man than You'll Ever Be: Gay Folklore and Acculturation in Middle America.* Bloomington: Indiana University Press.

Harding, Sandra, ed. 1991. *Feminism and Methodology.* Bloomington: Indiana University Press.

Herzfeld, Michael. 1985. *The Poetics of Manhood: Contest and Identity in a Cretan Mountain Village.* Princeton, NJ: Princeton University Press.

Keller, Evelyn Fox. 1985. *Reflections on Gender and Science.* New Haven, CT: Yale University Press.

Mead, Margaret. 1935. *Sex and Temperament in Three Primitive Societies.* New York: William Morrow.

Mills, Margaret. 1993. Feminist Theory and the Study of Folklore: A Twenty-Year Trajectory toward Theory. *Western Folklore* 52:173–192.

GENRE

A French word, from the Latin *genus,* used to describe a basic concept in literary theory and criticism, variably termed *form, kind,* or *type,* depending upon the period and the theory. Plato (*The Republic*) distinguishes, in the arts of the rhaphsode, between narration, imitation, and the mixture of the two, while considering the art of the actor essentially mimetic. In his *Poetics,* Aristotle differentiates narrative epic poetry from the imitative action of drama. The basic triad of generic categories—the epic, the dramatic, and the lyrical—is a Renaissance formulation that has remained viable in literary discourse up to the present. From the inception of folklore scholarship, the definitions of specific genres—the *Märchen*, the *Sage*, the legend, the ballad, the proverb, the riddle, the fable, and many others—have forged the genre as a principle concept of the discipline. Referring particularly to its literary renditions, Johann Gottfried von Herder (1744–1803) compares the *Märchen* with the *Romane* (romance, novel), considering the former to be not just a genre but also an entity that possess a spiritual quality that permeates other literary forms. Jacob (1785–1863) and Wilhelm (1786–1859) Grimm's assertion that "the fairy tale is more poetic, the legend is more historical" remains the cornerstone of many analyses of folk narrative.

Such descriptive definitions, which project the writer's own attitude, emotions, and response to the text, have failed to provide the precision in generic distinctions that is necessary for systematic research. To complicate matters, genre terms are words in ordinary languages, subject to ambiguity, vagueness, synonymy, and historical changes. The attempt to employ them with analytic precision inevitably has been burdened by their semantic history in multiple languages. Comparative analysis has addressed the problems of differing cultural perspectives, attitudes, and belief systems that have made the construction of an analytical system of genres even more difficult.

Faced with such complex systems of generic distinctions, folklorists have taken two distinct directions in their attempts to resolve the indefiniteness of folklore genres and the concept of genre in folklore. The first approach seeks ways to overcome these difficulties and to construct the concept of genre as a category of analytical classification; the second proposes to explore the difficulties and to conceive of genre as a category of cultural discourse.

GENRE AS A CATEGORY OF ANALYTICAL CLASSIFICATION

The viability of any classification system lies in its relationship to the reality of the information it stores. The system has to correspond not only to a logical order of things but also to the reality of the information in material, biological, and social life. Therefore, the formulation of a classification system of folklore genres requires a theoretical explanation that will establish its relationship to the literary-visual history, cultural use, and artistic creativity of folklore forms. Within folklore scholarship, it is possible to delineate two basic theories that answer that need, albeit from two opposing points of view. These are the theory of primary forms and the theory of ideal types.

The theory of primary forms initially was advanced by André Jolles, though it is not exclusive to his writings. The primary forms are the first verbal manifestations of human cognition that crystallize around specific semantic domains. According to Jolles, folklore forms are universal and have been known throughout history and in all cultures, though they may take different literary representations. The semantic domain of the holy manifests itself in the legend, and that of the family is manifest in the *Sage*; the nature of the creation of the universe is shown in myth; and the principle of inquiry is expressed in riddles. Proverbs represent experience, and the *Kasus* ethics. The concern with factuality crystallizes in the *Memorabile*, as naive morality does in the *Märchen*. The comic spirit finds venue in jokes. These are the elemental forms of human creativity that have the potential to evolve, multiply, and transform as society changes and moves from orality to literacy. At the basis of the generic categories, there are, hence, semantic domains that persist as elementary forms that permeate later and technically more advanced forms and means of expression. Kurt Ranke proposes to substitute psychological-spiritual needs for Jolles' semantic domains. It is the function of different genres to fulfill these needs. Accordingly, the *Märchen* function to express human aspirations for a higher order of justice, the *Sage* manifests resignation in the face of worldly tribulations, and myth expresses human needs to mediate between the known and unknown. The theory of primary forms assumes the universality of folklore genres since they are generated either by cognitive semantic domains of language or by psychological-spiritual needs that are fundamental to human beings in all societies and cultures. Therefore, as analytical categories of classification, genres have their roots in human categories of thought and language.

The theory of ideal types, which draws on a fundamental concept of Max Weber, considers genres as heuristic constructs that reflect the reality of folklore forms by approximation only. Lauri Honko, who has been the principal proponent of this theory, considers genres to be distinct configurations of contents, form, style, structure, function, frequency, distribution, age, and origin. Each genre is a construct category that involves an ideal configuration and criteria that are appropriate for each form. No single folktale, ballad, legend, or proverb, to use some common folklore forms as examples, has to meet all the standards of its ideal types; it can and need only approximate them. Genres are, hence, classificatory categories that involve not one but several distinctive features, and it is the task of researchers to determine the relations between the category and the texts that people narrate, sing, or utter in society. A failure to establish such a relation may be indicative of the formation of a new genre, the criteria of which require formulation. Honko himself has not outlined a systematic scheme of folklore genres as ideal types, but others have, even though they do not refer explicitly to Honko's theoretical formulation.

Limiting himself to the three basic forms in prose narrative—myth, legend, and folktale—and summarizing the scholarly consensus of his time, William Bascom proposes the following generic configuration:

FORM	BELIEF	TIME	PLACE	ATTITUDE	PRINCIPAL CHARACTERS
Myth	Fact	Remote past	Different world: other or earlier	Sacred	Nonhuman
Legend	Fact	Recent past	World of today	Secular or sacred	Human
Folktale	Fiction	Any time	Any place	Secular	Human or nonhuman

Scott Littleton adds *history* and *sacred history* to the genres he considers, positioning them on a grid of two polarities: the fabulous and the factual, the secular and the sacred. As the configuration between these four components changes, historically and culturally, the narration of a particular theme moves from one ideal generic pattern to another. In this scheme of analytical categories, folktale is fabulous and secular, myth is fabulous and sacred, history is factual and secular, and sacred history is sacred by definition and factual. The legend occupies a central position in relation to all four factors.

Heda Jason and Roger Abrahams, respectively, propose two of the most comprehensive schemes for the classification of folklore genres. Jason employs, first, a five-part classification system of modes: the realistic, the fabulous, the numinous, the marvelous, and the symbolic. These modes then manifest themselves in the realistic, fabulous, and symbolic genres of folklore. In her descriptions of specific genres, Jason retains theme, time, space, structure, and function as terms of analysis. Abrahams, on the other hand, extends the classificatory principles to account for the rhetoric of folklore and its social interaction. Consequently, he divides all folklore genres into three major groups: conversational genres, play genres, and fictive genres. In his scheme, it is not only the genre itself that is an analytical category. He constructs a graded scale between two polarities of interpersonal involvement and detachment (his term is *removal*). Each genre, not each text of each genre, relates to these two extreme configurations by approximation. In turn, each performance of each text may have its own position on the generic arch that Abrahams constructs.

The theories of primary forms and ideal types assume the universality of folklore genres, and in their applications to the available classificatory models, they provide for variation, modification, change, and transformation that are inherent in the social dynamics of folklore.

GENRES AS A CATEGORY OF
CULTURAL DISCOURSE

The idea of genre as a category of cultural discourse involves a different set of assumptions, problems, and research goals. First, the universals are not the genres themselves but the division of speech into different forms. In every society, speakers divide their speech into categories that they perceive and name. Apparently, there are a few recurrent principles that are universal: The idea of truth distinguishes facts from fiction, the perception of rhythm separates poetry from prose, and the ability to use tropes in language differentiates between figurative and nonfigurative language. Taking these features as given, genres of discourse become subject to specific inquiries of cultural cognition, linguistic representation, and performance. Speakers in every language name or label by other means the genres they use. These names or signs reflect the cultural taxonomy of speech, representing the features the speakers consider most distinctive in their forms of folklore. They constitute a system of local knowledge of rhetoric and speech making, a theory coded in generic names and practices.

Second, since a universal and scientific classification system becomes irrelevant to the exploration of genres as categories of cultural discourse, the identification of a particular text in terms of a preformulated system of pigeon-holes becomes methodologically irrelevant as well. The inquiry into the nature of folklore genres shifts from a deductive to an inductive method, exploring the use and performance of the genres in society through the formulation of their forms and structures, their conception within the cultural cosmology, the rules and principles for their performance, and the textual and social interrelations between the genres themselves.

Morphological-structural analysis explores generic discourse on a semantic, dramatic, or metaphoric level. The sequence of episodes in a narrative—the relationship between actions, characters, objects, or other symbols, whether in a tale, a legend, a ballad, or an epic—constitutes a dimension of the generic discourse that distinguishes one genre from another in specific societies. Morphological-structural relations serve as the generic grammar of folklore forms. Speakers, narrators, and singers—though they may not be able to formulate the grammar—have the ability to be aware of that grammar. Therefore, such an analysis becomes an essential part of the ethnography of folklore genres. Although morphological-structural analysis originally purported to advance definitions of folklore genres, assuming them to have similar patterns in all traditions, it is possible to modify this methodology in order to examine the ethnic genres of specific traditions.

In many societies, the generic system amounts to a complex set of relations between folklore forms, which their speakers relate to other domains of social life, such as religion and politics. As people establish connections

413

between their speech genres and their ideas about their world, they establish a cosmology of speech that includes ideas about the creation of speech in general and certain genres in particular. They place religious value on traditional genres of prayers, invocations, and ritual songs and consider other forms of speech as mundane, profane, or ordinary. There are narratives that account not only for the creation of speech but also for its different forms and stories about great orators and singers who excelled in delivering one genre or another. Such a "mythology of folklore genres" is an essential aspect of genres of discourse because it provides the basis for the use of such genres in society as rooted in cultural ideology.

The pragmatic exploration of ethnic genres requires an examination of their names, their cultural taxonomies, and their performances in social life. Their names reflect their cultural conception and significance, their history in tradition, and their import and function as their speakers view them. Their taxonomies underscore their relations to each other in terms of their prosodic features, the spaces and times of their performances, and their association with particular segments of society. Their performances are the basis for any analysis of the poetics of folklore genres, the use of formulas and frames, the alteration between prose and poetry, and the use of any genres of speech within or in relation to other genres of speech.

There is not a necessary and exclusive direct correspondence between genres and events as cultural categories of folklore. A single cultural event is often the occasion for the performance of several genres. The rules that dictate which genres are appropriate for which occasions are part of the cultural conventions. Similarly, a single genre may include other culturally recognized genres. Tales often include songs, epics include other tales as well as proverbs and riddles, and proverbs and riddles, when performed by themselves, may allude to tales and songs, thus semantically including themes known in different genres. Such combinations do not necessarily imply neglecting the principles of genres but rather an artistic and often playful use of these cultural categories of discourse.

Dan Ben-Amos

See also Aesthetics; Ethnoaesthetics; Ethnopoetics; Linguistic Approach; Literary Approach; Text; Texture.

❊❊❊❊❊❊❊❊❊❊❊❊❊❊❊❊❊❊❊

References

Abrahams, Roger D. 1969. The Complex Relation of Simple Forms. *Genre* 2:104–128.

Bakhtin, Mikhail M. 1986. *Speech Genres and Other Late Essays*. Trans. Vern W. McGee and eds. Caryl Emerson and Michael Holquist. Austin: University of Texas Press.

Bascom, William R. 1965. The Forms of Folklore: Prose Narratives. *Journal of American Folklore* 78:3–20.

Bauman, Richard, ed. 1977. *Verbal Art as Performance.* Rowley, MA: Newbury House.

Bausinger, Hermann. 1968. *Formen der "Volkspoesie"* (Forms of folk "poesy"). Grundlagen der Germanistik 6. Berlin: Erich Schmidt.

Ben-Amos, Dan 1969. Analytical Categories and Ethnic Genres. Genre 2:275–301.

Ben-Amos, Dan, ed. 1976. *Folklore Genres.* Publication of the American Folklore Society, Bibliographical and Special Series, vol. 26. Austin: University of Texas Press.

———. 1992. *Do We Need Ideal Types (in Folklore)?: An Address to Lauri Honko.* NIF Papers 2. Turku: Nordic Institute of Folklore.

Briggs, Charles L., and Richard Bauman 1992. Genre, Intertextuality, and Social Power. *Journal of Linguistic Anthropology* 2(2):131–172.

Gossen, Gary. 1971. Chamula Genres of Verbal Behavior. *Journal of American Folklore* 84:145–167.

Honko, Lauri. 1968. Genre Analysis in Folkloristics and Comparative Religion. *Temenos* 3:48–66.

———. 1976. Genre Theory Revisited. *Folk Narrative Research: Some Papers Presented at the Sixth Congress of the International Society for Folk-Narrative Research.* Special issue of *Studia Fennica* 20:20–26.

———. 1980. Genre Theory. ARV 36:42–45.

———. 1989. Folkloristics Theories of Genre. *Studies in Oral Narrative,* ed. Anna-Leena Siikala. Special issue of *Studia Fennica* 33:13–28.

Honko, Lauri, and Vilmos Voigt, eds. 1980. *Genre, Structure and Reproduction in Oral Literature.* Bibliotheca Uralica 5. Budapest: Akadémiai Kiadó.

Jason, Heda. 1977. *Ethnopoetry: Form, Content, Function.* Forum Theologiae Linguisticae 11. Bonn: Linguistica Biblica.

Jolles, André. 1930. *Einfache Formen* (Primary forms). 2nd edition. Tübingen, Germany: Max Niemeyer.

Littleton, Scott C. 1965. A Two-Dimensional Scheme for the Classification of Narratives. *Journal of American Folklore* 78:21–27.

Ranke, Kurt. 1967. Einfache Formen (Primary forms). *Journal of the Folklore Institute* 4:17–31.

Rosenberg, Bruce A. 1978. The Genres of Oral Narrative. In *Theories of Literary Genres,* ed. Joseph P. Strelka. Yearbook of Comparative Criticism 8. University Park: Pennsylvania State University Press.

Ryan, Marie-Laure 1979. Toward a Competence Theory of Genre. *Poetics* 8:307–337.

———. 1979. Introduction: On the Why, What and How of Generic Taxonomy. *Poetics* 10:109–126.

Sydow, Carl Wilhelm von. 1934. Kategorien der Prosa-Volksdichtung (The categories of prose tradition). In *Volkskundliche Gaben John Meier zum 70 Geburtstag dargebracht,* ed. W. Heiske. Berlin: Walter de Gruyter. (A brief synopsis in English can be found in von Sydow's Selected Papers on Folklore, ed. Laurits Bødker, Copenhagen: Rosenkilde and Bagger, 1948.)

Todorov, Tzvetan 1990. *Genres in Discourse.* Trans. Cathrine Porter. Cambridge: Cambridge University Press.

Toporov, V. N. 1974. Toward the Problem of Genres in Folklore. In *Semiotics and Structuralism: Readings from the Soviet Union,* ed. Henryk Baran. White Plains, NY: International Arts and Sciences Press.

Voigt, Vilmos 1976. Towards a Theory of Theory of Genres in Folklore. In *Folklore Today: A Festschrift for Richard M. Dorson,* eds. Linda Dégh, Henry Glassie, and Felix J. Oinas. Bloomington: Indiana University Press.

Gesture

Movement of the body, including the face, that expresses an idea or emotion. The study of such movement, called *kinesics*, has a place in several disciplines concerned with human communication, especially linguistics, psychology, anthropology, and ethnology. Folkloristic interest in gestures, though drawing from these branches of study, has focused in two particular directions: on body movements and facial expressions that contribute to the articulation of verbal and material folklore forms—that is, gestures that contribute to the paralinguistics of folklore performance—and on movements that have traditional meaning in their own right. Although recognizing that every movement means something either latently or overtly, folklorists have concentrated primarily on those gestures that are conscious and traditional.

One major category of gestures studied by folklorists are those known as *emblems*. These gestures have a direct verbal translation, generally known throughout the folk community. Performers use them with the conscious intent of sending a specific message, particularly when such factors as distance or poor acoustics have made verbal communication impractical. Emblems may stand on their own, without any verbalization. One of the simplest emblems used in various cultures is nodding one's head to signal either the affirmative or the negative. Waving upon greeting or upon leave-taking is another widely known emblem. Other familiar examples of gestures that function as emblems are "the bird," the upraised middle finger used as an insult, and a shrug of the shoulders, suggesting the gesturer's ignorance of the subject under consideration.

In some traditional contexts, especially occupations in which the noise of heavy machinery may drown out speech, systems of emblems may develop to enable workers to communicate with one another. Two gestural systems relying on emblems that have elicited folkloristic interest are the sign language used for intercultural communication among Native Americans and American Sign Language, used by the hearing- and speech-impaired. The latter, in fact, offers a method for communicating folklore forms circulated orally in other performance situations.

Illustrators are the other major category of gestures that folklorists study. Gestures that are designated as illustrators are clearly linked to another mode of communication, usually speech, and occur when spoken words need amplification or clarification. Speakers may use illustrators to indicate the size and shape of an object, to designate a direction, to emphasize a point being made, or to enumerate related elements in a discourse. A fisher, for example, may demonstrate the length of "the one that got away" by holding his or her open palms the appropriate distance apart; a pointed finger may indicate the road

416

to be taken when someone verbally gives directions; a storyteller can suggest the suddenness of the protagonist's escape from a threatening revenant with a snap of the fingers; and a homilist may differentiate the points in a sermon by ticking them off one by one on the fingers. Some performers of folklore may become associated with a particular illustrator. African-American story-teller James Douglas Suggs, whose performances were reported by Richard M. Dorson, characteristically depicted the hasty departure of a character by slapping his hands together and then sliding one quickly off the other. Ozark ballad singer Almeda Riddle became associated with the circles she made with each hand to maintain the tempo as she sang.

Folklorists also may have some interest in the category of gestures known as *regulators*, those gestures that help to guide the flow of verbal interaction by signaling beginnings and ends of discourse, topic shifts, or turns at speaking. Nodding, pointing, or changing facial expression or posture may serve such purposes.

Few studies focusing exclusively on gestures have appeared in the literature of folklore studies, though most fieldworkers recognize the necessity of recording and reporting gestures that they observe during verbal performances. The most extensive study of a single gesture, using the historic-geographic method, is Archer Taylor's examination of the "shanghai gesture" (known by other folk names), an emblem of insult in which the thumb is touched to the nose and the fingers are wagged. Other gesture studies by folklorists take a more ethnographic approach and examine gesture use in particular contexts. For example, a study of two gestures, cutting one's eyes to indicate disapproval and sucking the teeth to signal anger, suggests their African origins, but the study focuses principally upon the gestures' context-dependent meanings and usages among African-Americans in the West Indies and the United States.

Potential approaches to the study of gestures by folklorists include examining the role gestures play in affirming group identity. The signing used by urban gangs exemplifies this role of gestures, as does the use of secret handshakes by members of clubs and other organizations. Gestures may be overt signs of group identity based on religion (for example, crossing oneself), ethnicity (the Black Power salute and handshake), or voluntary association (the Boy Scout sign).

Folklorists also may concentrate on how gestures complement or replace other forms of communication. When an infielder in a baseball game raises the first and little fingers to indicate to outfielders that two players on the opposing side have made outs, he uses that particular gesture because verbal communication may be hampered by distance and crowd noise. Furthermore, raising the first and second fingers might not be as easily distinguishable as the gesture he uses.

417

Folklorists also may note the culture-specific meaning of gestures that appear to be identical but actually have different meanings. The gesture used by the infielder to mean "two outs," for example, closely resembles the gesture of the "horns," which has both insulting and prophylactic significance in Mediterranean cultures and their extensions in the Western Hemisphere. When directed at a married man, the horns emblem suggests that his wife is being unfaithful, that he is a cuckold. When directed in response to a compliment made by someone whose intentions may be suspect, the same gesture wards off the evil eye. Sports fans in the U.S. Southwest recognize the gesture as a spirit-rouser for supporters of the University of Texas athletic teams, who are known as Longhorns. Another gesture that has multiple meanings is the upraised first and middle fingers held slightly apart. This may simply mean the number two, but it also has significance because of its resemblance to the letter *v*. Associated with Winston Churchill, the British prime minister during World War II, the gesture has come to stand for "victory." During the antiwar movement of the 1960s in the United States, the gesture came to represent peace and, in fact, became an integrative device among members of the counterculture for whom its significance extended to a range of activities associated with their lifestyle.

In addition to examining how gestures are used by storytellers and other verbal artists, folklorists should look at gesture usage in such contexts as traditional ritual, where the exact way in which something is done (for example, whether the right or left hand is used) may affect the efficacy of the procedure. Moreover, gestures frequently constitute important features of games, dances, and dramatic performances.

One hindrance to the study of gestures has been the failure to develop a simple, uniform system to record them. Although some folklorists have tried to use methods based loosely upon systems such as that developed by Rudolf Laban for transferring body movement to the printed page, most have found Laban notation too cumbersome and have opted for verbal descriptions of the gestures. When the gestures are part of the performance of some other kind of folklore, transcribers may have difficulty integrating them into the text of the performance. General comments about body language in a performance note may substitute for precise indication of which gestures appeared at what precise point in the performance.

William M. Clements

See also Frame; Performance.

✳✳✳✳✳✳✳✳✳✳✳✳✳✳✳✳✳

References

Barakat, Robert A. 1973. Arabic Gestures. *Journal of Popular Culture* 6:749–793.

Birdwhistell, Ray L. 1970. *Kinesics and Context: Essays on Body Motion Communication.* Philadelphia: University of Pennsylvania Press.

de Laban, Juana. 1954. Movement Notation: Its Significance to the Folklorist. *Journal of American Folklore* 67:291–295.

Dorson, Richard M. 1956. *Negro Folktales in Michigan.* Cambridge, MA: Harvard University Press.

Fine, Elizabeth C. 1984. *The Folklore Text from Performance to Print.* Bloomington: Indiana University Press.

Graber, Robert Bates, and Gregory C. Richter. 1987. The Capon Theory of the Cuckold's Horns: Confirmation or Conjecture? *Journal of American Folklore* 100:58–63.

Mallery, Garrick. 1879–1880. Sign Language among North American Indians Compared with That among Other Peoples and Deaf Mutes. *First Annual Report of the Bureau of Ethnology.* Washington, DC: GPO.

Morris, Desmond, Peter Collett, Peter Marsh, and Marie O'Shaughnessy. 1979. *Gestures: Their Origins and Development.* New York: Stein and Day.

Rickford, John A., and Angela E. Rickford. 1976. Cut-Eye and Suck-Teeth: African Words and Gestures in New World Guise. *Journal of American Folklore* 89:294–309.

Taylor, Archer. 1956. *The Shanghai Gesture.* Helsinki: Academia Scientiarum Fennica.

GESUNKENES KULTURGUT

The idea that noteworthy cultural materials originated among the elite (or upper stratum of society) and subsequently descended to (were copied by) the lower stratum, or folk. A movement in the opposite direction is termed *gehobenes Kulturgut* (elevated culture materials). If the process involves social groups at various levels within the same presumed evolutionary stage, it may not be labeled as evolution or devolution.

The term *gesunkenes Kulturgut* was coined by the German Hans Naumann at the beginning of the twentieth century. In 1902, Eduard Hoffmann-Krayer suggested that folktales did not spring from a particular social class present in all societies, contrary to the views of romantic nationalism. He further postulated: "The folk do not produce, they re-produce." Naumann—who had espoused (in company with other folklorists such as Arnold van Gennep and Pierre Saintyves) the view that folklore originated in primitive rituals—embraced this new argument and developed it into a theory. His new postulate credited the origin of folklore to a socially superior *Oberschicht* (upper stratum, intelligentsia), whose creative responses were borrowed, copied, or imitated by the socially inferior *Unterschicht* (lower stratum, peasantry, folk). From a psychological standpoint, although the process was one of "matched dependent behavior," the behavior of the model (the *Oberschicht*) degenerated into folklore in the course of being acquired and reproduced by the *Unterschicht*. These folkloric responses of the *Unterschicht* were degenerated imitations of the original *Oberschicht* models because they were garbled and because they reflected the ignorance and misunderstanding of the unsophisticated *Unterschicht*. Naumann called the product of what was adopted from the *Oberschicht* models *gesunkenes Kulturgut*.

The arguments of Naumann, Hoffmann-Krayer, and others who viewed folklore in nationalistic terms were later incorporated into Nazi political ideology. Thus, what began as an academic, sociological, and anthropological thesis became fundamental to the development of the extreme nationalistic *Herrenvolk* (master race) ideology. The roots of this doctrine lie deep in German political theory and practice, backed by the firm beliefs that racial and folk ideals are basic to the state and that intense nationalism is an important means of survival.

In their search for the spiritual and national ancestry of the German peoples, Nazi folklorists adopted this view. Thus, the theory of the *Herrenvolk* became synonymous with the earlier concepts of the leading, higher, or formative social strata of a population—respectively, the *Führerschicht, Oberschicht,* and *Bildungsschicht*. All of these strata were thought to have served as models for the imitative behavior of lower, less gifted social groups or nations.

Thus, the first step toward a theory of imitative learning in culture was introduced by folklorists at the beginning of the twentieth century but never gained popularity because it was used by political ideologists as a scientific justification for extreme nationalism. The defeat of the ideology doomed the theory as well. With the violent downfall of the Nazi regime, Naumann's theory became debased, and the concept of imitative learning in culture was aborted.

Another form of *gesunkenes Kulturgut* is that designated in the idea of the deterioration of higher forms of cultural expressions into lesser forms. Within the realm of verse (poetry-song), this phenomenon was labeled *Zersingen* (to sing to pieces) by Friedrich von Schlegel (1772–1829)—a philologist and ideologue of German romanticism. He postulated that folksongs are formulated by a process of deterioration through transmission, whereby sophisticated poems are unwittingly rendered into songs. This hypothesis was accepted by folk narrative scholar Albert Wesselski, who was convinced that only through writing, a higher level of culture, could narrative survive. Wesselski sought to use Schlegel's postulate in order to discredit Walter Anderson's theory that attributed the stability of folktales to oral transmission and audience.

The turbulent career of Naumann's imitative-degenerative theory concerning the acquisition of folkloric responses by the *Unterschict* from the *Oberschicht* created a hostile attitude toward the mere discussion of such a learning process. Ironically, a similar theory proposed by Lord Raglan remains little known in European folklore circles because it did not acquire the political notoriety of Naumann's theory. Without referring to any specific race, nation, or social class, Raglan formulated a theory of the ritualistic origin of folklore. According to Raglan, the origins of narrative genres are to be sought in ancient, dramatic "royal ritual," developed and phrased by the royal and priestly classes. This ritual drama was imitated by the masses (lower classes), who were too unsophisticated to understand its meaning, and through an evolving process of degeneration, the ritual drama reached its present state as folklore. Thus, epic, legend, myth, and folktale were invented by an upper class and imitated by a lower class, which rendered them into their present forms.

Raglan argued that the invention of such genres could not be credited to "peasants" and "savages" (his labels for nonliterate peoples). "No popular story-teller has ever been known to invent anything," Raglan asserted, and "the peasant and the savage, though they are great hands at making up stories, are nevertheless incapable of making up the simplest story of the doings of ordinary human beings."

Raglan's theory implies that creative imagination is a sophisticated phenomenon found only among the upper classes and that the peasant and savage or illiterate possesses only "memory [which] is more or less retentive, but will add nothing to his or anyone else's ideas since it can invent nothing." Thus, the peasant and savage or illiterate merely imitates and distorts, responding negatively, and is unable to create anything himself.

In summary, Raglan's theory of the imitative learning of folkloric responses from superior classes is almost identical to Hans Naumann's. Raglan merely spoke in general terms of royalty and peasantry, whereas Naumann's theory described European *Oberschicht* and *Unterschicht*, which would later be interpreted as definite *Führerschicht* (leader stratum) (as opposed to the ignorant masses) and German *Herrenvolk* (in contrast to inferior races).

At the close of the twentieth century, the concept of or belief in the principle of sunken culture materials saw a political renaissance. The argument that culture and its institutions (economic, political) flow from the upper strata of society down to the lower strata and that the lower strata benefit from the upper's riches (possessions) became a viable theory (ideology) and social program (policy) attributed to the Republican Party in the United States. In the parlance of contemporary economic theory, it is referred to as "trickle-down economics" or "Reaganomics."

Hasan El-Shamy

See also Audience; Context; Psychological Approach.

✳✳✳✳✳✳✳✳✳✳✳✳✳✳✳✳✳✳

References

Bach, Adolf. 1960. *Deutsche Volkskunde* (German folklore). 3d. ed. Heidelberg: Quelle and Meyer.

Dundes, Alan. 1975. *Analytic Essays in Folklore*. The Hague: Mouton.

Hoffmann-Krayer, Eduard. 1902. *Die Volkskunde als Wissenschaft* (Folklore as science). Zurich: F. Amberger.

Naumann, Hans. 1921. *Primitive Gemeinschaftskultur*. Jena, Germany: Diederich.

————.1922. *Grundzüge der deutschen Volkskunde*. Leipzig, Germany: Quelle & Meyer.

Raglan, Lord. 1934. The Hero of Tradition. *Folklore* 45:212–231.

————. 1936. *The Hero: A Study of Tradition Myth and Drama*. London: Methuen.

Saintyves, Pierre. 1923. *Les contes de Perrault et les recits paralélles*. Paris: Librarie Critique.

El-Shamy, H. 1967. Folkloric Behavior. Ph.D. thesis, Indiana University, Bloomington.

van Gennep, Arnold. 1910. *La formation des legendes* (The formation of legends). Paris: E. Flammarion.

Wesselski, Albert. 1931. *Versuch einer Theorie des Märchens*. Reichenberg, Germany: F. Kraus.

Young, Kimball. 1934. *Introduction to Sociology*. New York: American Book.

GOSSIP

A form of discourse between persons discussing the behavior, character, situation, or attributes of absent others. Gossip is a speech act in which people make sense of their world by providing a charter for belief in the moral character of known social actors. Folklorist Sally Yerkovich defines gossip so as to emphasize its "morality": "a form of sociable interaction which depends upon the strategic management of information through the creation of others as 'moral characters' in talk." Unlike rumor or other forms of hearsay, most gossip is not assumed to be false; rather, its defining feature is that its target is not present while moral judgments are made.

Social scientists take three basic approaches to explain the motivation for gossip: the functional approach, the transactional approach, and the conflict approach. The functional view argues that gossip serves a function for a social system by asserting collective values. Gossip is an indirect sanction that avoids direct confrontation and strengthens group boundaries. To gossip is to be part of a community.

The transaction approach emphasizes the strategic value that gossip has for its narrator. Gossip projects individual interests through information control and is a form of impression management. Often, gossipers will become the center of attention and be viewed as people "in the know." The decision to spread gossip is closely connected to the relationship between narrator and audience and to the narrator's expectation of the receptivity of the audience.

The conflict perspective emphasizes how gossip has the potential to be utilized as a political strategy by groups for their collective purposes. The discrediting of an oppositional force through gossip, or propaganda, is a well-known technique used by those who wish to persuade others. Although gossip has not been extensively studied by Marxists, it is clear that ruling classes might encourage negative gossip against indigenous revolutionary figures to split the working class.

Many have remarked that gossip has expanded in the twentieth century through its central placement in media outlets. Gossip columnists such as Hedda Hopper, Louella Parsons, or Walter Winchell became forces to be reckoned with in the twentieth century. In the United States, gossip has seemed even more prevalent in media outlets in recent years, with the growing popularity of the *Star* and other tabloids, of *People* magazine and its imitators, and of television shows such as *Hard Copy* that center on the dissemination of personal information about celebrities. Stories about "personalities" have long had an important role in popular outlets. Sociologists Jack Levin and Arnold Arluke (1987) emphasized that media gossip has its own rules and limits, and they demonstrated that most media gossip is positive and that most gossip reporters behave in an ethical fashion.

Because oral gossip is moral discourse, concerned with the reputation of the teller and the target, its production in conversation is quite complex. In the words of Jorg Bergmann, gossip is "discreet indiscretion." The parties delicately construct the meaning of the gossip in such a way that their views of proper behavior are upheld by others. Gossip topics are proposed and accepted. Moral indignation is deployed and responded to. As Bergmann and others have demonstrated, the conversation analysis of gossip holds considerable promise for demonstrating the significance of this traditional genre.

Gary Alan Fine

See also Rumor.

✳✳✳✳✳✳✳✳✳✳✳✳✳✳✳✳

References

Abrahams, Roger D. 1970. A Performance-Centered Approach to Gossip. *Man* 5:290–301.

Bergmann, Jorg. 1993. *Discreet Indiscretions: The Social Organization of Gossip.* New York: Aldine.

Fine, Gary Alan, and Ralph Rosnow. 1978. Gossip, Gossipers, Gossiping. *Personality and Social Psychology Bulletin* 4:161–168.

Haviland, John B. 1977. *Gossip, Reputation and Knowledge in Zincantan.* Chicago: University of Chicago Press.

Levin, Jack, and Arnold Arluke. 1987. *Gossip: The Inside Scoop.* New York: Plenum.

Rosnow, Ralph, and Gary Alan Fine. 1976. *Rumor and Gossip: The Social Psychology of Hearsay.* New York: Elsevier.

Sparks, Patricia. 1985. *Gossip.* New York: Knopf.

Yerkovich, Sally. 1977. Gossiping as a Way of Speaking. *Journal of Communication* 27:192–196.

GRAFFITI

Written, anonymous, short, and frequently traditional commentaries placed on public walls, desktops, subway cars, sidewalks, and other flat surfaces. The media of choice include spray paint, pencil, and ink, or the commentaries may be scratched or etched in the surfaces. The term *graffiti* has come into English from the Italian, derived from a word meaning "to scratch." It was first used extensively by art historians to refer to the scratched or etched political slogans discovered on the walls of ancient Pompeii and to artistic designs created by scratching away the outer color layer to reveal the contrasting color beneath. A related term is *latrinalia,* or writings on public bathroom walls, which frequently tend to focus on more profane, sexual, and scatological topics. Graffiti ranges in form from doggerel to epigrams to slogans to single words, often personal names and place-names. Some graffiti is elaborate enough to be regarded as an art form, especially when stylized lettering and dramatic color schemes are utilized. Written form characterizes the genre, distinguishing graffiti from murals and other public artistic displays.

The content of graffiti usually is topical, responding to current events, political trends, and local issues. For example, "stop the bombing," "get out of Cambodia," and "make love, not war" were common graffiti during the Vietnam War. AIDS, homosexuality, and feminism became common topics during the 1990s. Whimsicality and wittiness also are distinguishing characteristics of the genre. One example is the enigmatic "Kilroy was here," which originated in World War II. Many slogans on T-shirts, bumper stickers, and coffee mugs represent a popular culture exploitation of the form. Because of its topical subject matter, most graffiti is short-lived, being either deliberately erased or replaced by another writer.

The subjects addressed in graffiti, however, are as varied as the graffiti artists themselves. Much research has been conducted regarding the differences in graffiti in various college and university buildings—the chemistry building versus the fine arts building or the men's gym versus the women's gym. Of course, the graffiti in these specialized locales generally reflects the interests and concerns of the students (and faculty) who frequent them.

Another characteristic of graffiti is its interactive quality, expressed as conversations or "runs" in which a variety of successive writers add to and comment on the original statement. For example, many sources report variations on the following run: "God is dead"—"Don't worry, Mary is pregnant again"—"God isn't dead. He just doesn't want to get involved"—"Who is god anyway?" Sometimes these runs continue until the available wall space is used up.

At the opposite end of the spectrum is urban graffiti that consists of a single person's nickname or a gang name or symbol. As a rule, the defacing of such graffiti is the catalyst for gang retaliation. A distinctive Mexican-American graffito, *con safos* (or its abbreviation, c/s), functions to prevent the defacement of any name graffiti that it accompanies because of the folk belief among Mexican-Americans that to deface such distinctively protected graffiti is to reflexively harm oneself. An oral folk rhyme expressing this same sentiment is "I'm rubber, you're glue. What you throw at me, sticks to you."

As mentioned, much urban graffiti is gang or "turf" related, and thus it functions as a boundary marker. In hotly contested areas or intersections, practically all of the walls and sidewalks may be covered with contrasting graffiti. The subway cars of New York City have provided the most dramatic example of excessive graffiti. Such gang-related graffiti utilizes a combination of gang colors, names, and symbols. In such cases, municipal authorities usually regard creating graffiti as defacing public property or vandalism punishable by fines and imprisonment. The problem with such regulations, however, is that the writers of graffiti are inherently anonymous, which usually precludes their apprehension by the authorities. In some communities, as part of negotiations to end gang violence, the authorities will work out a truce in which the various gangs come together publicly to wash off and paint over the offending graffiti of all the involved groups.

Graffiti can be classified as folklore for many reasons. Although most researchers regard graffiti as a separate and distinct genre, others make a strong case that graffiti is a specialized kind of written folk speech because of its poetic and narrative characteristics. Regardless of genre classification, graffiti is undoubtedly traditional, with a pedigree extending back historically to the ancient Romans and possibly further. It also employs traditional, doggerel verse forms that reappear generation after generation, such as latrinalia with the common introduction "Here I sit. . . ." The anonymity of the graffiti writers is another characteristic that places graffiti squarely in the purview of folklore. Finally, graffiti is associated with distinctive folk groups, ranging from the habitués of various university buildings to socially deviant groups such as gangs to various ethnic groups.

Sylvia Grider

See also Inscription.

✽✽✽✽✽✽✽✽✽✽✽✽✽✽✽✽✽✽

References

Blake, C. Fred. 1981. Graffiti and Racial Insults: The Archaeology of Ethnic Relations in Hawaii. In *Modern Material Culture: The Archaeology of Us*, eds. Richard A. Gould et al. New York: Academic.

Castleman, Craig. 1982. *Getting Up: Subway Graffiti in New York*. Cambridge, MA: MIT Press.

Dundes, Alan. 1966. Here I Sit—A Study of American Latrinalia. *Kroeber Anthropological Society Papers* 34: 91–105.

Grider, Sylvia. 1975. Con Safos: Mexican-Americans, Names, and Graffiti. *Journal of American Folklore* 88:132–142.

Grieb, Kenneth J. 1984. The Writing on the Walls: Graffiti as Government Propaganda in Mexico. *Journal of Popular Culture* 18(1):78–91.

Hentschel, Elke. 1987. Women's Graffiti. *Multilingua: Journal of Cross Cultural and Interlanguage Communication* 6(3):287–308.

Melhorn, J. Jack. 1985. Rest Room Graffiti: A Descriptive Study. *Emporia State (KS) Research Studies* 34(2–3):29–45.

Ong, Walter J. 1990. Subway Graffiti and the Design of the Self. In *The State of the Language*, eds. Christopher Ricks and Leonard Michaels. Berkeley: University of California Press.

Proctor, Lenore Feltman. 1991. Graffiti Writers: An Exploratory Personality Study. Ph.D. dissertation, Pace University, New York.

Read, Alan W. 1988–1989. Folk Criticism of Religiosity in the Graffiti of New York City. *Maledicta: The International Journal of Verbal Aggression* 10:15–30.

Smith, Moira. 1986. Walls Have Ears: A Contextual Approach to Graffiti. *International Folklore Review* 4:100–105.

Stein, Mary Beth. 1989. The Politics of Humor: The Berlin Wall in Jokes and Graffiti. *Western Folklore* 48(2):85–108.

Stewart, Susan. 1987. Ceci Tuera Cela: Graffiti as Crime and Art. In *Life after Postmodernism: Essays on Value and Culture*, ed. John Fekete. New York: St. Martin's.

Tanzer, Helen H. 1939. *The Common People of Pompeii: A Study of the Graffiti.* Baltimore, MD: Johns Hopkins University Press.

GREAT TRADITION/LITTLE TRADITION

The distinction between the higher, elite levels of a civilization (*great tradition*) and the folk or popular levels (*little tradition*). Little traditions are most often associated with the preurban stages or nonurban, nonliterate/illiterate levels of society and are products of the village or the common people. The basis of the great tradition is rooted in the little traditions of the folk level. As a society undergoes primary urbanization, the little traditions become codified, evolve into great traditions, and often fall subordinate to the aesthetics and learning of the great traditions.

In contrast to little traditions, great traditions represent the highest levels of the intellectual and aesthetic achievements of a civilization, and as such, they are transmitted and preserved in some codified, stylized "text" form. As the codified and developed cultural heritage of the society, they provide the sources for identity among members of the society by providing the rules of conduct, the primary philosophy, religion, standards, cultural norms, and aesthetic sensibilities. Great traditions are the product of the reflective, literate, philosophic few, and they are a result of urbanization. Further, they represent the mediated, codified, and intellectualized little traditions extant in a culture. The existence of a set of great and little traditions within a civilization depends upon consciousness of a common culture built on the common cultural artifacts within the little traditions.

The study of great traditions is most often associated with textual studies, such as history, the classics, or comparative religion. The focus of these disciplines is, typically, the understanding of various cultures through their great traditions. Most of these studies find their models in the traditional studies of ancient Greece and Rome and the "Oriental Renaissance" studies of classic Persian, Chinese, Japanese, and Indic texts. Little traditions, however, are most often the realm of the cultural anthropologist, the ethnographer, and the folklorist.

The useful definition and study of great and little traditions began in earnest with Robert Redfield's studies in the 1930s and with his joint projects with Milton Singer in the 1940s and 1950s. Basic to these definitions was Redfield's idea of the folk-urban continuum, which traces societies on a scale from tribal to urban as a part of human cultural development. According to this system, a society evolves from a simpler, tribal system, with its own sets of beliefs, norms, and standards (little traditions), to a more sophisticated, primary urban center, with a codified set of norms, beliefs, and aesthetic and intellectual achievements interpreted by a ruling elite (great traditions). The creation of these primary urban centers occurs in a process that Redfield defined as *orthogenetic transformation*, in which an evolving ruling group interprets and mediates between the several little traditions surrounding the developing urban center to develop and codify a great tradition.

Like little traditions, great traditions can evolve when a primary urban center comes in conflict with another culture or even with conflicting ideologies. The mediation between the cultures leads to the development of a secondary (or tertiary, quaternary, ad infinitum) urban center, with the conflicting traditions mediated by a select intelligentsia who present the new traditions to the indigenous culture and explain the existing great traditions to the interlopers. Robert Redfield defined this process as *heterogenetic transformation*, in which a conquering group destroys and replaces the great traditions of the indigenous group by way of the intelligentsia. Milton Singer offered the example of Madras in India as a heterogenetic city. There is no singular great tradition in Madras, but there are several overlapping versions of the Hindic great tradition, with a great deal of admixture among the competing versions. As a colonial city and later the primary government and commerce city for the British in southeast India, Madras was the communication point for many of the great traditions that existed there, as well as the relay point for transmitting the British ideologies to the local citizenry.

The concepts of great and little traditions are polar types; folk and urban lie at opposite ends of the spectrum, with evolving stages of little traditions turning into great traditions falling in intervals along the continuum. The traditional bias, though, has been to view the continuum in a linear fashion, with folk giving way to urban. Inherent in this bias is a view of the folk as rural and of folk groups as existing only in a rural, nonliterate or illiterate setting. For the folklorist, though, it is more useful if the term *little tradition* is defined as the traditions particular to a specific folk group and the term *great tradition* is defined as the mediated, codified, intellectualized little traditions extant within a specific culture.

Randal S. Allison

See also Folk Culture; Tradition.

****

References

Bauman, Richard, ed. 1992. *Folklore, Cultural Performances, and Popular Entertainments: A Communications-Centered Handbook*. New York: Oxford University Press.

Redfield, Margaret Park, ed. 1966. *Human Nature and the Study of Society: The Papers of Robert Redfield*, vol. 1. Chicago: University of Chicago Press.

Singer, Milton B. 1972. *When a Great Tradition Modernizes: An Anthropological Approach to Indian Civilization*. New York: Praeger Publishers.

H

Hemispheric Approach

Theory that each Western Hemisphere country's folklore should be studied in its distinctive ethnic and historical contexts. Developed by Richard M. Dorson in the 1950s, the approach sought to distinguish American folklore (specifically, that of the United States) from the traditions of Europe and other sources of immigration. The initial colonization of the Americas, the importation of slaves from Africa, and continuing waves of immigration from various cultures, especially Europe and Asia, created a set of folk traditions that lacked the holistic national identity and long-standing rootedness found in Old World societies. Western Hemisphere folklore emerged from such processes of culture contact as acculturation, retention, and revitalization. Coupled with the particular histories of Western Hemisphere nations, these processes have generated heterogeneous sets of folklore traditions.

Dorson focused primarily on the folklore of the United States. He identified several historical forces that contributed to the distinctiveness of American folklore. His list of these forces changed with the development of the approach; the final catalog of them (published posthumously) cited colonization, the revolution, the frontier, slavery, the Civil War, immigration, and industrialization. (Earlier lists had also included the presence of aboriginal Americans and the influence of the mass media.) Dorson contrasted his hemispheric approach with theories and methodologies that focused cross-culturally on themes, symbols, or patterns in folklore without regard to their cultural contexts and with approaches that examined a limited number of texts or performances of folklore only in terms of their immediate situation. A folklorist who adopted Dorson's hemispheric approach, by contrast, would place the materials of folklore within the broad currents of American cultural history. The ways in which folklore reinforced the dominant ethos of a particular society became the most important target of investigation.

Dorson positioned his approach as contrasting "American folklore" with "folklore in America." The latter perspective analyzed folklore encountered in the United States using the same methods that applied to folklore encountered elsewhere. A structural study of an Appalachian Jack tale, for instance, would utilize structural methodology that might work equally well on a *Märchen* collected in Germany. However, the hemispheric approach would consider the folktale in the context of American history and life, perhaps emphasizing the importance of regionalism in shaping its content.

The hemispheric approach's almost exclusive focus on surface content and lack of interest in structure, function, symbolism, and performance limited its appeal for folklorists concerned with those features of folklore. Moreover, folklorists who did not study Western Hemisphere folklore (or that of Australia, whose cultural history Dorson believed to be similar to that of Western Hemisphere nations) found little to interest them in the hemispheric approach. Consequently, when Dorson reviewed the approach a decade after he first published it as a formal statement, he could cite only a few studies besides his own that might be identified as using that approach. His final articulation of the approach, published two years after his death, concluded by noting that very little had been done by folklorists using the perspective.

William M. Clements

See also Historical Analysis; Worldview.

✳✳✳✳✳✳✳✳✳✳✳✳✳✳✳✳✳

References

Dorson, Richard M. 1959. *American Folklore.* Chicago: University of Chicago Press.
———. 1971. *American Folklore and the Historian.* Chicago: University of Chicago Press.
———. 1973. *America in Legend: Folklore from the Colonial Period to the Present.* New York: Pantheon.
———. 1983. A Historical Theory for American Folklore. In *Handbook of American Folklore*, ed. Richard M. Dorson. Bloomington: Indiana University Press.

Hero/Heroine, Folk

A character depicted as the center of action in real or fictitious accounts of life and living. The attributes of the hero/heroine depend on the narrator's intent (i.e., the genre through which a given cultural expression is made), as well as the psychological composition (national character, modal personality) of the social group to which the hero/heroine belongs. Also, within the same social group, demographic factors (e.g., gender, age, religion) will affect how a hero/heroine is presented and perceived. Whatever the specifics of the situation may be, a hero/heroine will evoke in the listener or reader a sense of belonging through certain psychological processes associated with vicarious instigation, such as modeling, empathy, sympathy, and positive identification. As the model, a hero/heroine's success is gratifying, and his or her failure is punitive. In certain cases in which a character's heroic attributes are not pronounced, such a narrative persona may be referred to as a protagonist. Typically, a hero/heroine is opposed to a villain—also labeled an antihero. A villain evokes a sense of alienation through negative identification; his or her failure is gratifying, and his or her success is punitive.

Certain folklore genres are more commonly associated with heroic characters and action (e.g., epics, sagas, and myths); the little-used term *hero tale* (compare *Heldensage*) was introduced to designate such narratives. Yet the hero/heroine appears across a broad spectrum of cultural expressions, being the most common and best-known figure in world folklore and mythology. The heroic character reflects the qualities needed to conquer chaos and overcome the temptations advanced by the forces of evil or darkness. Thus, in many myths and folktales, the sun, the giver of light, is identified ideally with the hero/heroine figure. The cult, lore, and mythology of the hero/heroine have thrived since prehistoric times due to the demands of war and to the traits and behaviors associated with heroism, which humanity has felt the urge to accentuate, glorify, and record in oral, graphic, and written form.

Heroic behaviors include saving individuals and nations from destructive forces or leading them from danger, discovering hidden treasure, and reuniting people with deities or the life principle. Moreover, among hero/heroine figures, there is a great variety of types—for instance, the deity-like culture

A woodcut of pioneer American folk hero Davy Crockett fighting with the Great Bear. As with most folk heroes, Crockett's attributes were determined by the social group to which he belonged.

hero, the historical figure, the trickster, the strong man, the strong woman, the ignorant hero, the ingenue, the beautiful youth, the saint, and the magician. A small sample of motifs dealing with heroes/heroines may illustrate the great diversity of this theme as it occurs in folk literature: A500–A599, "Demigods and culture-heroes"; A511.1.2, "Culture-hero speaks before birth"; A511.1.3.2, "Demigod son of king's unmarried sister by her brother"; A511.3.2, "Culture-hero reared (educated) by extraordinary (supernatural) personages"; A512.3, "Culture-hero as son of god"; A522.3.1, "Spider as culture-hero"; A522.22, "Raven as culture-hero"; L100–L199, "Unpromising hero (heroine)"; L101, "Unpromising hero (male Cinderella)"; L102, "Unpromising heroine"; L111.3, "Widow's son as hero"; L111.5, "Bastard hero"; L112.3, "Deformed child as hero"; L114.1, "Lazy hero"; L114.4, "Cheater as hero"; L160, "Success of the unpromising hero (heroine)"; M361, "Fated hero. Only certain hero will succeed in exploit"; Z292, "Death of hero"; and Z293, "Return of hero" (compare K2200–K2299, "Villains and traitors").

Joseph Campbell has shown that although hero/heroine tales and myths occur around the world and may vary in detail, close analysis reveals these stories have structural similarities that persist across cultures and historical periods. Such stories have, in other words, a universal pattern, despite arising from groups or individuals having no direct contact with each other. Repeatedly, one observes tales describing a miraculous but common birth, demonstration of superhuman strength and ability, rapid rise to prominence or power, triumphant struggle with the forces of evil, proneness to pride, and ultimate decline through betrayal or sacrifice resulting in death. Moreover, in many such stories, early weakness is offset by the emergence of a powerful mentor or guardian figure who assists in the execution of superhuman tasks that cannot be accomplished alone. For example, among Greek heroic figures, Theseus had Poseidon, god of the sea, Perseus had Athena, goddess of wisdom, and Achilles had Chiron, the centaur, as guides.

The central example of the hero/heroine motif in Western culture is the story of Jesus Christ, who is born humbly but with numerous associated miracles, reveals superhuman abilities and wonders, rises quickly to a position of high esteem among his followers, struggles with the forces of evil represented by Satan, and then suffers death through betrayal as the ultimate sacrifice for humanity. The only one of the elements listed earlier that does not appear in the Christ-as-hero story is proneness to pride. Also, the Christ story contains the added component of a miraculous return to physical life after death.

More typically, the hero/heroine sets out from a mundane home environment, is called to a quest or adventure, crosses a threshold of some kind, and is subjected to a number of trials or ordeals, culminating in an ultimate test of will and virtue—a struggle with a dragon or other creature representing the forces of darkness (in psychological terms, the unconscious). Victory over the monster is rewarded with a treasure, such as a kingdom and a beautiful princess as bride.

Cross-culturally, the hero/heroine's first goal is the conquest of self; so, besides folklorists, psychologists and students of religion are attracted to the study and analysis of heroic myth and lore. For instance, according to dream and folktale psychoanalytic interpretation, the hero/heroine embodies the triumph of the developed ego over the primitive forces of the id, or primal instincts. And from the more heterodox psychoanalytic perspective of Otto Rank, the following elements are typical of the lives of heroic figures such as Moses, Paris, Siegfried, Romulus, and Lohengrin:

1. Birth to royal or noble parents, with gestation and birth being shrouded in secrecy.
2. A tyrannical father who wishes to suppress or kill his offspring.
3. Abandonment of the offspring in a mysterious place until the child is found and raised by impoverished parents, by a poor woman, or by animals.
4. Growth to maturity, discovery of the tyrannical father, and vengeful killing of him.
5. Elevation to the father's status, along with celebration as a hero or deification.

This sequence of life events differs markedly from the one noted by Campbell as occurring in heroic myth and folklore, and it reflects early psychoanalytically inspired ideas on the universal occurrence of infantile fantasies about the father, or "the Oedipal complex," in which the father is an object of sexual envy by the son.

In contrast, from the perspective of Jungian analysis, the hero/heroine's life takes on a more spiritual cast, in which his or her typical solar attributes reflect a deepening and broadening of consciousness through the raising of unconscious images and feelings to conscious awareness, that is, illumination or enlightenment. In Jungian terms, the hero/heroine is the most widely accepted archetypal symbol of the libido, psyche, or spirit, and in the heroic life, the historical and symbolic are seen as identical, with the evolution of the hero/heroine's greater personality or self through various trials being termed *individuation*.

In interpreting heroic myth and lore at the level of culture, the hero/heroine may be seen as the restorer of healthy, positive functioning in circumstances in which a group has deviated from its pattern of collective cooperation or integration. This societal-cultural level of symbolism parallels the individual level, in which the ego or outer personality is restored to functioning in harmony with the inner self or higher nature.

Thus, across cultures, folklore and myths about the hero/heroine unfold in ways that reflect the general stages of human growth or transformation. Winnebago Indian myths, for example, show a typical development from primitive to highly sophisticated conceptions of the hero/heroine as symbolic figure representing personal evolution.

Paul Radin, in examining Winnebago hero tale cycles, reveals four discrete stages in the hero's journey through life: Trickster, Hare, Red Horn, and Twin. The Trickster cycle involves the earliest and least evolved phase of human development, when primary physical demands predominate and the hero behaves instinctually, boldly, and often childishly. This figure initially takes the form of an animal who goes through a series of mischievous adventures, being represented in American folklore by Brer Rabbit. Through the course of these exploits, Trickster changes and begins to resemble a mature individual at the end of the cycle.

The next cycle in the Winnebago tale series is that of Hare, who, like Trickster, first appears as an animal without full human attributes but nonetheless is viewed as the progenitor of human culture. This figure reflects an advance on the character of Trickster, in that Hare is becoming socialized, modifying Trickster's self-centered and childish cravings.

Red Horn, the third figure in the Winnebago hero series, reflects ambiguous qualities and meets the criteria of the typical folk hero by passing various trials, proving his courage in battle, manifesting superhuman powers, and having a powerful mentor, a thunderbird named "Storms-as-he-walks," who compensates for Red Horn's deficiencies. With the Red Horn figure, the level of humanity has been reached, albeit haltingly, and the help of supernatural powers is required to guarantee the hero's triumph over evil powers. Toward the end of the cycle, Red Horn's mentor departs, leaving him to his own devices and showing that a human being's security and well-being derive from within him- or herself.

The theme of the last cycle in the series, that of the Twins, reflects the question of how a person is to be successful in life without succumbing to his or her own pride or ego—in folk or mythic terms, the jealousy of the gods. The Twins, Flesh and Stump, although said to be sons of the Sun, are basically human and comprise a single individual, reflecting the two sides of human nature—introversion or inward directedness and extroversion or assertiveness, respectively. For a long period during the tale cycle, these figures appear to be invincible, defeating all challengers. But over time, they fall victim to pride, and their unbridled behavior brings about their downfall. Their sentence is death, but since they have become so frightened by their own reckless abuse of power, they agree to live in a constant state of rest—symbolically, the two sides of human nature thus become balanced.

The universal or archetypal quality of hero/heroine myths and folktales have given them great appeal for people of all cultures through the ages. Since they symbolize and reflect the process of both individual and societal growth and development, they resonate with the inner and outer needs and desires of all human beings and have thus attained a place of cross-cultural prominence.

Hasan El-Shamy

See also Culture Hero; Folktale; Jungian Psychology; Myth.

✳✳✳✳✳✳✳✳✳✳✳✳✳✳✳✳✳

References

Campbell, Joseph. 1949. *The Hero with a Thousand Faces*. New York: Pantheon.

Cirlot, J. E. 1962. *A Dictionary of Symbols*. New York: Philosophical Library.

Jung, C. G., ed. 1982. *Man and His Symbols*. New York: Dell.

Matthews, Boris, trans. 1986. *The Herder Symbol Dictionary*. Wilmette, IL: Chiron.

Rank, Otto. 1970. *The Myth of the Birth of the Hero: A Psychological Interpretation of Mythology*. New York: Johnson.

El-Shamy, H. 1967. Folkloric Behavior. Ph.D. thesis. Indiana University, Bloomington.

Stevens, Anthony. 1982. *Archetypes: A Natural History of the Self*. New York: Quill.

Thompson, Stith. 1955–1958. *Motif-Index of Folk-Literature*. 6 vols. Bloomington: Indiana University Press.

von Franz, Marie-Luise. 1970. *Interpretation of Fairy Tales*. Dallas, TX: Spring.

HISTORICAL ANALYSIS

Method of scholarship that examines folkloric texts over time and as a process. Since folklore is a discipline that studies traditional processes (i.e., items or performances that are rooted in the past but continue to adapt and change for current use), most folklorists have looked at historical developments to shed light on changes in a particular tradition rather than to study history as an element of folklore. Scrutinizing folklore as a process that changes over time enables us to recognize patterns and structures. This method also reveals versions and variations among and between texts and cultures, which would not be recognizable without some degree of historical depth. Thus, studies of material culture, folksong, traditional narrative, folk drama, and so on include, of necessity, a historical component. Although there are folkloric theories that do not depend upon the development and change of traditional culture to explain their perspectives, those that do look to those processes to explicate a particular outcome, provide a model to test a particular theory, or reconstruct a group's perspective of its past and rationale for the present.

The study of folklore began as the search for survivals of elite culture among European peasants. The eighteenth-century German theologian Johann Gottfried von Herder, known as the father of romantic nationalism, regarded the oral traditions of the "folk" as encompassing the wisdom of the Germanic forefathers; in the face of the French domination of Europe, such a philosophy provided a refuge in a historical past whose traditions could serve only to inspire the cultural and political unification of the Germanic states. Nineteenth-century philologists such as Jacob and Wilhelm Grimm collected and arranged *Märchen* (or folktales) in order to justify their theories about language and culture transmission, as well as to rediscover the authentic soul of "the people" during the development and consolidation of European nationalism. In nineteenth-century England, Edward Tylor, like other evolutionary anthropologists and early folklorists who were followers of social Darwinism, regarded items of traditional culture as evidence of stages in the social evolution of colonial and European cultures: Customs and beliefs among Africans or Pacific Islanders could be taken as representative of the primitive stage of humankind, and the survivals of folk customs among European peasants illustrated the barbaric stage of European peoples. Although not very good historical analysis, the perspective of Tylor and other evolutionists did depend upon a notion about historical processes that strongly influenced folklore scholarship—that the past could be reconstructed by studying contemporary "survivals" of traditional culture. Hence, the ballad studies of Francis Gummere, George Lyman Kittredge, Francis J. Child, and others constituted attempts to prove that contemporary fragments or whole texts of folksongs represented the survivals of a historical golden age, rather than functional living texts for those who performed them.

Myth-ritual scholars also were fascinated with the evolutionary question of whether ritual (action) or myth (explanation) came first. Most of the early scholars in this field did not investigate living cultures but speculated about the probable evolution and relation of myth and ritual based on classical texts. James Frazer, Max Müller, Jane Harrison, Stith Thompson, Lord Raglan, William Bascom, and others carried on years-long scholarly debates over this issue. Such analyses came to be seen as passé because of their emphasis on origins rather than function or cultural context.

Early social scientists Karl Marx, Émile Durkheim, Sigmund Freud, and Carl Jung also looked to the folklore of "primitive" peoples to illustrate their theories about political, social, and psychological developmental stages. Using historical texts derived from the Bible, creation myths, and personal narratives, they re-created their versions of human evolution. Interestingly, their scholarly antecedents tended to disregard the historical component and focus on issues of function, geographical determinism, and the structural underpinnings of cultures.

Literature scholars such as Francis J. Child also looked for and at relics, fragments, or survivals of folksong texts rather than at their performance contexts. The goal of such scholars was to speculate about the devolution of elite culture as preserved by the lower classes, as if the latter were merely vessels for past glories. Child compiled a multivolume compendium of ballads, versions, and fragments, which he arranged in a "chronological" order based on the topics of the songs. Although Child was an armchair scholar, folksong scholars Cecil Sharp and Maud Karpeles were involved with actively collecting songs from real people in England and in the United States in order to reconstruct a national folklore and teach it to schoolchildren. With the twentieth-century focus on sociology and psychology as opposed to history, the ballad and folksong scholars who persisted in debating the historical origins and transmission paths of their texts had begun to seem almost anachronistic by the time their evolutionary and devolutionary theories were summarized and laid to rest by D. K. Wilgus in 1959. By the end of the 1960s, Albert Lloyd, a member of a socialist scholars' circle in England that was consciously involved with rewriting English history to conform to a Marxist evolutionary model, had recast the story of folksong and ballad scholarship to reveal the working-class roots and thus the authenticity of Child and broadside ballads.

In the United States, a similar nationalistic impulse fueled a movement among folklorists to recover the unique American roots of traditional culture. During the early and middle years of the twentieth century, folklorists looked to American balladry to illustrate the American character and history as distinct from those of Europe. Folksong scholars employed oral history interviews and field collection methods to compile collections such as Malcolm Laws' work on Native American balladry. John Lomax and later his son Alan Lomax looked to the folksong and lore of occupational, criminal, and African-American groups to demonstrate the existence of a vibrant lower-class American culture—again as distinct from a passive European peasantry.

Twentieth-century linguists also were interested in the history of various items of folklore and particularly in traditional narratives and their component parts—motifs—in order to test theories about the spread of language over space and time. Scandinavian scholars developed what became known as the historic-geographic or Finnish method to search for the "ur" or prototypical form of a traditional narrative in order to trace the path of transmission. The American scholar Stith Thompson finished the work of Antti Aarne and published his multivolume motif index. Later scholars have tended to disregard the historical impulse that inspired the Finnish School and instead use the motif index to show how tales and fragments of tales from different cultures resemble each other.

Thompson, like American anthropologists, also looked to the folklore of indigenous peoples to demonstrate theories about the development of cultures. He focused on the transmission of narrative motifs and still employed analysis of texts as they existed over time, but others, such as Franz Boas, Melville Herskovits, Ruth Benedict, and other students of Boas, tended to take into account only "factual" history in their investigations of cultural psychology and social organization. Unlike many cultural anthropologists, however, certain folklorists who utilized a psychological or cultural approach continued to employ historical analysis to elucidate the continued relevance of traditional narratives—from blood libel legends to European *Märchen*. Alan Dundes and Jack Zipes in particular have fruitfully employed an examination of beliefs, legends, and folktales as they have developed over time to elucidate the persistence of anti-Semitism and divergent national identities.

During the middle years of the twentieth century, a new sort of historical analysis was coming into vogue, one that focused on the past and traditions of everyday people as opposed to those of the elite. During the 1930s, the Federal Writers' Project sponsored surveys by folklorists such as Benjamin Botkin, Zora Neale Hurston, Alan Lomax, Herbert Halpert, and others. Their goal was to collect and record on cylinders the lore of working people and that which exemplified regional culture. Hurston, for example, did considerable work collecting the folk history, songs, and narratives of African-Americans in her native state of Florida. Best known for her fiction, Hurston used folkloric accounts of the past to construct a feminist critique of southern life during the first half of the twentieth century.

At the same time, anthropologists were taking a renewed interest in the history of the peoples they studied. Ethnohistory, a scholarly account of a culture group's past (often before the time of contact), though recognized as a field in the early 1950s, did not come into vogue until the 1960s and 1970s among anthropologists who had come to recognize the fictive and ahistorical nature of the concept of the ethnographic present. Although such scholars as Bronislaw Malinowski and A. R. Radcliffe-Brown themselves engaged in historical researches in the 1920s and 1930s, their students tended to disregard history in the service of discovering the function of cultural practices and the structures of social institutions. Anthropologists such as E. E. Evans-Pritchard reemphasized the importance of historical research for anthropologists, but most scholars since have tended to emphasize economic, social, and psychological structures when they have looked at traditional cultural practices.

Even though such theoretical analyses did spur advances in one direction, they begged the question of change and development among individual societies—as opposed to the evolutionary stages of human society. Although scholars were slow to realize that oral tradition among both nonliterate and literate peoples actually recorded a very specific view of the past, anthropologists and folklorists eventually recognized that the native view of history was critical to understanding motives and actions in the present.

During the egalitarian 1960s, folklorists began to employ the techniques of oral history as well as library and textual sources to learn about context and function. Those who have developed the most useful theories and models have disregarded the anachronistic anthropological notion of the ethnographic present and incorporated folk and oral history from their informants into their investigations. Richard Dorson, who came out of an American civilization background at Harvard, was particularly interested in the historical development of American folklore and American and British folklorists. His book-length studies of those developments became as seminal as the work of Wilgus in explicating how folklorists came to study and theorize about their discipline. Dorson may be best known among folklorists for his use of archival data to unveil the existence of fakelore employed by lumber companies, which promulgated the legends of Paul Bunyan for commercial motives. Lynwood Montell's groundbreaking oral history of Coe Ridge demonstrated the rich possibilities available to folklorists who investigated living memories. Henry Glassie's studies of both architecture and later of Irish traditions also employed the techniques of oral and folk history to elucidate the function and context of traditional processes. Although his perspective is reminiscent of that of nineteenth-century romantic nationalists, Glassie's explicit political analysis of folk history was part of the focus on cultural empowerment and authenticity that emerged in the 1980s.

Also working in the 1960s and relying on a communications model, Dell Hymes shifted the focus of folklore research to performance studies in which context and audience as well as aesthetic criteria were the topics of study. Richard Bauman added a historical component to this approach by using records of oral performances by seventeenth-century Quakers as case studies. His use of archival texts to test an explicitly ahistorical theory reintroduced the notions of process and time. Bauman's work, combined with that of Roger Abrahams and Américo Paredes in the 1970s, resulted in a series of studies examining the historical development of perceptions about group identity. Works by Paredes, Bauman, Abrahams, and José Limón laid the groundwork for studies of authenticity and politics and the relationship of folklore to those issues.

Folklorists and anthropologists are not the only ones who have investigated the history of traditional expressive culture. Historians, particularly those of the Annales school in France and from the History Workshop and Manchester University in England, have looked specifically at folkloric items and events to construct cultural histories of European society. Emmanuel LeRoy Ladurie, Eric Hobsbawm, George Rudé, Natalie Davis, Robert Darnton, Peter Burke, Bob Bushaway, E. P. Thompson, Raphael Samuel, Peter Laslett, and Paul Thompson are just a few of the social historians who have noticed the persistence of patterned behaviors and the commentary on them by contemporary peoples in their letters, diaries, and memoirs. Unfortunately, most of these historians, because of their Marxist perspective, tend to take the view that folklore is always dead or dying, and they use that notion to prove that modernization, industrialization, urbanization, and particularly capitalism were responsible for destroying the old world of reciprocal responsibility between classes. Though none of those historians seems to have read any folklore studies, the analytic perspective is reminiscent of the folklore/fakelore debate; in the social historians' analyses, however, authenticity and invention are opposed with little comprehension of the complexities of how traditional processes grow and change.

Barbara Babcock edited the seminal work that combined historical and symbolic analysis of folklore in the 1970s, but it was not until the mid-1980s that other folklorists picked up on her direction and insight. Studies by folklorists interested in the relationship among politics, tradition, and display events and those concerned with the construction of ethnic and regional identity have engaged specifically in examinations of the historical roots and contexts of traditional enactments. Such studies both shed light on more general theoretical problems central to folklore, such as perceptions about authenticity and tradition, and provide some of the most creative elucidations of unique historical processes, which have in turn contributed to broader cultural discussions on the development of social identity in a multicultural society.

Rachelle H. Saltzman

See also Euhemerism; Evolutionary Theory; *Gesunkenes Kulturgut*; Historic-Geographic Method; History, Folk; History, Oral; Myth-Ritual Theory; Philological Approach; Romantic Nationalism; Transmission.

✻✻✻✻✻✻✻✻✻✻✻✻✻✻✻✻✻✻

References

Babcock, Barbara, ed. 1976. *The Reversible World*. Ithaca, NY: Cornell University Press.

Bauman, Richard. 1983. *Let Your Words Be Few: Symbolism and Silence among Seventeenth-Century Quakers*. Cambridge: Cambridge University Press.

Bauman, Richard, and Roger Abrahams, eds. 1981. *"And Other Neighborly Names": Social Process and Cultural Image in Texas Folklore*. Austin: University of Texas Press.

Davis, Susan. 1986. *Parades and Power*. Philadelphia: University of Pennsylvania Press.

Dorson, Richard. 1971. *American Folklore and the Historian*. Chicago: University of Chicago Press.

Dundes, Alan, ed. 1991. *The Blood Libel Legend*. Madison: University of Wisconsin Press.

Glassie, Henry. 1982. *Passing the Time in Ballymenone*. Philadelphia: University of Pennsylvania Press.

Hobsbawm, Eric, and Terence Ranger, eds. 1985. *The Invention of Tradition*. Cambridge: Cambridge University Press.

Montell, William Lynwood. [1970] 1972. *The Saga of Coe Ridge*. New York: Harper and Row.

Vansina, Jan. 1985. *Oral Tradition as History*. Madison: University of Wisconsin Press.

Historic-Geographic Method

A research method developed for the study of folklore in the 1870s, based on the comparison of variants and aimed initially at the discovery of the original form, place of creation, and age of a given item of folklore, as well as its local redactions and pathways of diffusion.

THE ROOTS AND DEVELOPMENT OF THE METHOD

The historic-geographic method—also known as the comparative method or, especially outside the United States, the historical-geographic method, the Finnish method, and the typological method—was born in Finland during the 1870s in the initial studies of Julius Krohn and their continuation by his son Kaarle Krohn. Julius observed that the greater the distance between two places, the greater the differences in their respective folklore. Further, differences and commonalities in oral tradition from one locale to the next could be studied profitably in terms of geographic distribution and spread.

The method was based on the text-critical approach of philology, aimed at determining the relations between extant manuscripts. Using this approach, for instance, the critic attempted to ascertain whether Manuscript A derived from Manuscript B or whether the two represented wholly independent developments. On the basis of such judgments, the scholar could then deduce the possible origin and authorship of a given narrative.

It should be borne in mind that the application of this method to folklore, as outlined by Julius Krohn, only could occur on the basis of a sufficiently large corpus of collected variants. Finland proved an ideal laboratory for studying the method in practice since both Finland and Estonia had amassed immense folklore archives as a product of romantic nationalism. In Krohn's time, these archives consisted primarily of folk poetry, although many *Märchen* texts had been collected there as well. Finland also was situated at the crossroads of eastern and western Europe, making it the recipient of influences from many places, and finally, the Baltic-Finnic region itself contains many distinctive cultural subregions, each with its own folklore.

Other intellectual movements of the day influenced the initial development of the Finnish method as well. Already in the first decade of the nineteenth century, German romanticist scholars had pursued the possibility of reconstructing the core of ancient mythology on the basis of extant folk beliefs. Current folklore and belief were seen as the shattered fragments of a once-coherent system. This devolutionary premise was countered in turn by the late-nineteenth-century development of evolutionary theory, which persuaded scholars that human expressions began as scattered and unrelated elements and gradually evolved into broader and more coherent entities.

Kaarle Krohn transformed his father's so-called local-historical method into the Finnish comparative method. In the process, the findings of experimental psychologists were brought to bear on the topic, especially their studies of the laws of retention and loss of memory. Krohn conceived of the development of folk poems as beginning with simple, isolated themes that subsequently underwent a long process of growth and change. Later, he proposed an entirely different theory of the development of Finnish folk poetry in his major study, *Kalevalastudien* (1924–1931). According to this later view, the heroic poems had been composed in their entirety in western Finland, undergoing transformation and devolution in the eastern tracts, where they had survived into the nineteenth and twentieth centuries. In either case, however, the pathways of development were regarded as completely predictable, demonstrable on the basis of extant evidence. The phenomena were reducible to general patterns and laws.

The historic-geographic method was formulated to study the migration of folklore and was evolutionist in the sense that it sought to apply Darwin's theory in detail to folklore itself. The discovery of mechanical laws of development became a prime goal of research in all of the humanities during the nineteenth century. Diffusionism is a broad-based research perspective that seeks to explain similar features shared by different cultures as signs of earlier contact. It engendered many similar approaches parallel to—but independent of—the Finnish method in the folklore research of other countries as well.

The historic-geographic method has become so broadly and variously adapted, however, that we can no longer speak of a single method but rather must include differing methods, researchers, and schools of thought associated with it. The so-called typological method replaced the geographic element by the 1930s. In this later development, redactions are determined on the basis of formal typology rather than geographic provenience. Because all research contains an element of comparison, it becomes difficult at times to distinguish when a study is based on the historic-geographic method itself, on a later derivative research trend of refinement, or on some entirely unrelated method.

The main purpose of the Finnish method was to use existing performances of folklore—a folk poem, *Märchen*, belief, or other item—to determine its original form, contents, idea, or core. During this early period of folklore study, researchers were less interested in what the item meant to its present performer than in where it originated and how it had spread in the past.

The historic-geographic method promoted and assumed an international orientation. In 1907, the Finn Kaarle Krohn and Dane Axel Olrik founded an organization entitled the Folklore Fellows, whose series of scientific publications—Folklore Fellows Communications—continues today. Many of the most influential folklorists of the day were students of Krohn, leading to even greater cooperation and exchange. Notable in this respect are Walter Anderson of Estonia, Bertalan Korompay of Hungary, Séamus O'Duilearga of Ireland, and Archer Taylor and Stith Thompson of the United States.

The basic concepts of the method are the *variant, normal form, hypothetical original form (Ur-form),* and *redaction.* The last term is subdivided into the categories of *subredaction* and *base redaction.* Different recordings of a given folk poem, legend, proverb, or other item are designated as *variants;* even separate performances from the same performer are distinguished from each other under this rubric. Variants that seem to resemble one another more than any of them resemble other collected variants are grouped under the term *redac-*

tion. As an aid to dealing with a large number of different forms, the folklorist constructs a "normal form" of the folklore item, bringing together the central or most salient features of the item as reflected in the corpus of texts. Sometimes, the reconstructed Ur-form of an item is identical to the normal form of a given period.

The purpose of redaction analysis is to discover the relations between different redactions and hypothesize an Ur-form or "original core." The primary or secondary nature of a given feature of a redaction or variant could be ascertained through reference to certain criteria for originality, developed by Walter Anderson. For instance, an older element could be recognized by its numerical prevalence in the collected texts, broad geographic distribution, unusualness of detail, logical fit with other old features in the reconstructed text, archaic features of language or style, and aptness as a possible source of other later developments.

A secondary feature could be recognized by its narrow geographic distribution, occurrence with other alternative features, lateness of collection, or closer fit with other genres or items of folklore. A tradition does not usually develop in the reverse direction—that is, it is unlikely that features running counter to a late, local version would prove to be original. The researcher also must take into account that the age of a feature under investigation may differ from the age of the item of folklore itself. Distinctions or connections between redactions could be observed through content or motif indexes, charts of features, or cartographic methods.

The historic-geographic method has undergone many modifications and innovations over the course of the twentieth century. It is sometimes impossible to determine the original form of an item of folklore—for example, a folksong—if the item never possessed a fixed form at the outset. Initially, folklorists assumed that the method could be applied mechanically to all genres of folklore; later, the different "life histories" of various folklore genres became recognized.

In the study of *Märchen*, the work of Antti Aarne proved very significant. Aarne's type index, *Verzeichnis der Märchentypen*, published in 1910, became the basis of international folktale research. The numbering system contained in Stith Thompson's enlarged and reedited version of the index, published in 1961, remains the internationally accepted standard for the field. In his *Motif-Index of Folk-Literature*, Thompson further sought to classify and index all narrative motifs, in other genres as well as in *Märchen*. Type indexes of *Märchen* and other narrative genres represent valuable tools for historic-geographic research, and the Folklore Fellows Communications series alone has published some 49 separate indices of this kind. The same typological method has been applied to other genres as well (e.g., Archer Taylor's systematized catalog of riddles, Matti Kuusi's index of proverbs), aiming at the elucidation of the relations of different variants over space and time.

Märchen, because of their relative length, proved an apt genre for the application of the historic-geographic method: They were international in distribution, and their types could be characterized readily. Walter Anderson's 1923 *Kaiser und Abt* (Emperor and abbot) was one of the classic applications, after which a long series of other monographs appeared devoted to specific *Märchen* or legend types. Typical examples are Jan-Ovind Swahn's *Tale of Cupid and Psyche* and Anna-Birgitta Rooth's *Cinderella Cycle*. The method has been applied to riddles, games, and legends. Of comparative studies of proverbs, Matti Kuusi's monograph on proverbs related to the co-occurrence of rain and sunshine (*Regen bei Sonnenschein*) has provided the greatest breadth. The author carefully determined the genetic relations of an international collection of variants.

In Finland, the typological method was aptly suited to the study of epic and lyric folk poetry. Matti Kuusi's major work has been to further the historic-geographic study of this genre through redaction analysis. Using this method, Kuusi discovered stylistic periods that could be differentiated from each other by formal features. He placed a large portion of the collected folk poetry in the oldest stylistic category, ascribing it to a period extending from the arrival of the Finns in Finland to the beginning of the current era.

Cartographic studies and folklore atlases, a side development of the historic-geographic method, became popular in the 1930s under the influence of German *Volkskunde*. Cartographic methods are useful for representing essential similarities and differences in redactions in all kinds of genres, oral as well as material. The map always requires some explanation, however, since diffusion not only occurs as a simple product of geographic proximity alone but also reflects historical and economic relations, religion, cultural differences, and, occasionally, temporary or nebulous factors. For example, the study of cultural similarity or difference through the quantitative comparison of proverbs is an area of historic-geographic research pioneered in the study *Proverbia Septentrionalia: 900 Balto-Finnic Proverb Types with Russian, Baltic, and German Scandinavian Parallels* (1985).

Redaction analysis can bring forth a picture of the typical singing style of a given area. With this picture as a reference point, it becomes possible to examine a singer's own improvisation or typicality of repertoire on a line-by-line basis. Groundwork of this kind also contributes to the study of collagelike techniques of composition. The personal styles of *Märchen* raconteurs also can be characterized with reference to norms of narrative performance specific to a given area and recognizable through historic-geographic analysis.

APPRAISALS

The historic-geographic method was criticized from the outset, and many critical characterizations have helped hone and strengthen the theory. It has been claimed that researchers do not pay enough attention to literary influences, although the study of a given folklore item itself generally began with the scrutiny of written and "nonauthentic" sources. Scholars have been criticized for paying too much attention to geographic aspects and too little to historical ones—for example, overlooking the possibility of vertical diffusion. The best results have been obtained when the method has been applied to folklore within a single language area; international and global connections usually prove more speculative. Although the method stresses careful attention to detail and great exactness, the conclusions of historic-geographic studies sometimes have been (somewhat maliciously) characterized as claims to scholarly clairvoyance, especially when charting diffusional pathways on a global level.

Although the historic-geographic method always has been informed by its own issues, it is nonetheless only a scholarly tool—a system of characterization that can be used as the basis for a variety of different kinds of study. It has been used too generally and for purposes for which it is ill suited. Often, the method's harshest critics have relied on the method itself as a basis for arriving at their viewpoints, rendering their criticisms more like adaptations or by-products than real challenges. Such can be said, for instance, of structuralist approaches, which represent but one of many analytical frameworks suitable for the study of folklore.

The contribution of the Finnish method to folklore research is to be found not only in the range of applications offered for redaction analysis but also in the method's insistence on consistent, scientific criteria as the basis of research. Scholars aimed at the goal of completeness in collection and analysis, preventing them from drawing conclusions based solely on a handful of selected examples. All source materials must be carefully considered and ranked according to accepted criteria. Further, the argument, once assembled, must be presented in such a way that any other scholar trained in the method could reach similar conclusions. The notion that another scholar should be able to reach the same conclusions on the basis of the material presented and principles followed remains important today.

Although the historic-geographic method is often viewed as a somewhat antiquated product of turn-of-the-century scholarship, it is evident that the significance of folklore can never be adequately described without knowledge of the cultural influences impinging from the surrounding milieu.

Leea Virtanen

See also Historical Analysis; Literary Approach; Motif; Philological Approach; Tale Type.

✳✳✳✳✳✳✳✳✳✳✳✳✳✳✳✳✳

References

Aarne, Antti. 1913. *Leitfaden der vergleichendon Märchenliteratur.* Helsinki: Suomalainen Tiedeakatemia.

Aarne, Antti, and Stith Thompson. 1961. *The Types of the Folktale*. Helsinki: Suomalainen Tiedeakatemia.

Anderson, Walter. 1930–1940. Geographisch-historische Methode (Geographic-historic method). In *Handwörterbuch des deutschen Märchens* (Handbook of German folktales), ed. Lutz Mackensen. Vol. 1, pp. 508–522. Berlin: Walter de Gruyter.

Boberg, Inger M. 1953. *Folkmindeforskningens Historie I Mellem-og Nordeuropa* (The history of folklore research in central and northern Europe). *Danmarks Folkeminder* 60. Copenhagen.

Hautala, Jouko. 1968. *Finnish Folklore Research, 1828–1918*. Helsinki: Societas Scientiarum Fennica.

Honko, Lauri. 1985. Zielsetzung und Methoden der finnischen Erzähl forschung. *Fabula* 26(3–4):318–335.

Krohn, Kaarle. 1971. *Folklore Methodology*. Trans. Roger L. Welsh. Austin and London: University of Texas Press. Originally published as Die folkloristische Arbeits methods. Oslo, 1926.

Kuusi, Matti. 1974. "The Bridge and the Church": An Antichurch Legend. In *Studia Fennica* 18:27–75. Helsinki: Suomalainen Tiedeakatemia.

Röhrich, Lutz. 1987. Geographisch-historische Methode (Geographic-historic method). In *Enzyklopädie des Märchens* (Encyclopedia of Märchens), ed. Kurt Ranke, Vol. 5, pp. 1011–1030. Berlin: Walter de Gruyter.

HISTORY, FOLK

A community's collective perceptions about past events. Every folk group has its own notion of the past, which influences the thoughts, actions, and perceptions of its members. Although often used as a synonym for *oral history, ethnohistory,* and *oral traditions,* the term *folk history* is distinct in that it involves a collective perception about what the members of a group determine to be significant about the past and about how that past affects the present. In contrast, oral history pertains to a group's or an individual's commentary and recollections about events the interviewer deems important. Folklorists are interested in a group's perceptions about its past because they contain and provide the context for all kinds of folklore, from traditional crafts to aesthetic expressions, as well as providing in-group perspectives on what has been culturally meaningful over time.

A folk history is not the same as a life history. A single individual's oral narrative, for example, does not necessarily constitute the accepted version or versions of a self-identified group. Folk history is also not merely ethnohistory, an account by scholars of a group's history before contact with outsiders. Rather, folk history encompasses a *community's* beliefs and evaluations about particular occurrences, rationales about why particular events were critical to a community, and explanations as to how particular events have affected the present. Although folk history is passed along through oral tradition, not all oral tradition is folk history, for the latter includes a range of customary expressions that have more to do with artistic meaning or passing along a skill than with a chronicle of past events. Not all folk history is found in oral tradition, and certainly, it is not found exclusively among nonliterate peoples. Diaries, letters, the media, novels, and memoirs, as well as formal historical texts, constitute sources for folk history, for all provide a specific perspective that can be found to impart a group perspective on significant historical events.

Unlike historians, folklorists do not regard folk history simply as another document to be validated or dismissed, as a document used to support or exemplify other data, or as a last resort in the absence of other sources assumed to be more reliable because they are in print. Unlike anthropologists, folklorists do not regard folk history as the sum of informal unwritten recollections or as the official narratives of the elite among non-Western cultures. Instead, folklorists rely upon a range of sources, including specific narratives about the past and the implicit evidence found in folksongs, anecdotes, legends, memorates, and personal experience narratives to examine the in-group view of circumstances and the contextual meaning of symbolic expressions.

Although folklorists, like anthropologists, seek cultural patterns in their field data, there is more of a tendency among folklorists to accept the information given at face value. Neil Rosenberg noted that historians provide their own interpretation of the past, whereas the goal of folklorists is to understand their informants' perspective. Like historians, folklorists tend to regard traditional history as a conscious expression on the part of their informants rather than considering it, as many anthropologists do, as the key to unconscious structures and thus to social, linguistic, or economic systems. Indeed, they even regard the performance of folk history as a significant text in and of itself and analyze its structural and aesthetic similarities to other forms of folklore.

For any group—national, ethnic, occupational, geographic, religious, or whatever—folk history provides a representation of the past. Such representations can justify motives and actions, explain social structures, and establish an alternative worldview. Although outsiders may view folk history as downright fabrication because it may contradict the dominant story of the past, the debate over those in-group perceptions is often couched in terms of legitimacy and authenticity or about whether the dominant or the minority view of events and motives is correct.

Although some scholars have posited that folklorists collect while historians interview informants, such a dichotomy is more theoretical than actual. Contemporary folklorists probably spend more time in the field than do oral historians, becoming familiar with community members and their culture, but they also engage in directed interviews as well as in a more general "collecting" of texts. In recording folk histories, the fieldworker encounters many versions and pieces of a story from informants. Narratives may vary according to the age, gender, occupation, or status level of the informant. After several

Johnny Appleseed is a prominent figure in traditional American folk history.

narratives have been heard, however, the elements of a coherent story emerge. No one person knows or relates the entire tale, but different informants can confirm, validate, or temper the perceptions of other group members.

Folk history, like oral history, has carried a fair amount of political baggage, which has worked over time to diminish or heighten its value. Viewed by many as the history of "the people"—oppressed, marginalized, or otherwise discounted—folk history has tended to be regarded as the province of leftist scholars. Richard Dorson, who received his training in American civilization, particularly objected to this characterization, which grew out of the leftist intellectual movement of the 1930s, and noted that "the folk" often hold conservative views about the past that differ considerably from those of the scholars who romanticize about the folk. Two of Dorson's students, Lynwood Montell and William Ivey, produced notable studies of community history that demonstrated the value of traditional, albeit nonarchival, sources. Interestingly, in commentary by anthropologists and historians on the topic, neither man is recognized as a folklorist but is instead regarded as a historian.

The particular contribution of Dorson, Montell, and Ivey, as well as Henry Glassie, was to demonstrate that the authenticity of folk history rests upon its depiction of what is significant in the past for members of a community. Hence, recent analyses by folklorists of Native American histories, occupational and community studies, studies of wars, and even analyses of performance events have made it their aim to reconstruct a past from the perspective of in-group members. Whether a particular side represents freedom fighters, patriots, rebels, or revolutionary insurgents depends upon whose folk history provides the rationale for recounting significant events. Such a perspective has been paralleled by the works of the Annales school of French historians who focus on meaningful structures in history, by British social historians who investigate how different groups construct their pasts, and by American cultural historians who seek to uncover the perspective of those viewed as not significant by the dominant culture.

Historians, anthropologists, and even folklorists have not always accepted the value of folk history as a legitimate account of the past, rather, they have regarded it as, at best, something that can fill in the blanks in the absence of more "reliable" accounts or, at worst, as a misrepresentation or downright falsification of what has occurred. Like other genres of folklore, it has been regarded as fictive filler, as an invention, or as re-creation. In fact, there are common structural elements or motifs in folk histories that are similar to those in local legends, anecdotes, and personal experience narratives. And familiarity with such motifs and/or the ability to spot probable structural patterns is necessary for a critical use of folk history. Yet rather than revealing the unreliability or inauthenticity of folk history, the very patterns and repetitious structures and motifs of community histories reveal the culturally significant data they carry and transmit. Furthermore, the collection of folk histories of a

451

community at different periods and from different sources can reveal, as do more standard historical sources, the ways in which a community's or a status group's perspectives on the past (and thus on the present) change over time. Careful attention to folk history can therefore reveal the logic for revitalization movements, riots, massacres, wars, and other apparently "irrational" and traditionally patterned behaviors.

Rachelle H. Saltzman

See also Historical Analysis; History, Oral; Invented Tradition; Legend; Life History; Memorate; Personal Experience Narrative.

✵✵✵✵✵✵✵✵✵✵✵✵✵✵✵✵✵

References

Dorson, Richard, ed. 1971. Folklore and Traditional History. Special issue of *Journal of the Folklore Institute* 8(2–3).

Glassie, Henry. 1982. *Passing the Time in Ballymenone*. Philadelphia: University of Pennsylvania Press.

Hudson, Charles. 1966. Folk History and Ethnohistory. *Ethnohistory* 13:52–70.

Mintz, Jerome. 1982. *The Anarchists of Casas Viejas*. Chicago: University of Chicago Press.

Montell, William Lynwood. [1970] 1972. *The Saga of Coe Ridge*. New York: Harper and Row.

Morton, Robin. 1973. *Come Day, Go Day, God Send Sunday*. London: Routledge & Kegan Paul.

Paredes, Américo. [1958] 1975. *With His Pistol in His Hand*. Austin: University of Texas Press.

Vansina, Jan. 1985. *Oral Tradition as History*. Madison: University of Wisconsin Press.

Whisnant, David. 1983. *All That Is Native and Fine*. Chapel Hill: University of North Carolina Press.

HISTORY, ORAL

Spoken narratives recounting and commenting upon significant past events. Folklore fieldwork inevitably involves collecting narratives about the past, but not all that is in oral tradition is oral history. Although many folklorists use the terms *oral tradition* and *oral history* synonymously, historians make the distinction between conducting formal interviews with directed questions and collecting verbal traditions that comment directly or indirectly on historically significant events. For oral historians, historical significance resides in what scholars or other recognized authorities determine to be important to the society at large. Thus, oral narratives about John Kennedy's assassination or the depression are appropriate topics, but individual or community recollections about a local murder or mining disaster are relegated to the realm of folk history. The latter, in contrast to oral history, provides commentary on what members of a socially "insignificant" group believe to have affected their lives. Although such distinctions exist, most folklorists have disregarded them in practice and used the directed methods of oral history to elicit full-fledged narratives as well as commentary about locally and nationally significant events.

It was the advent of the tape recorder in the 1940s that made documenting the words of regular people possible for those not in the broadcasting or recording industries. In 1948, Alan Nevins founded the Columbia (University) Oral History Collection to record the testimony of "great men" on their works, instead of relying on the evaluation of obituary writers. According to folklorist Neil Rosenberg, not until the 1960s, however, was oral history regarded as more than a supplement to the written record; in fact, the transcripts, not the tapes, were believed to be the important documents. The Oral History Association, founded in 1966, heralded the recognition that oral history was a special approach and not just a technological development. Oral history, which documents recent history that would otherwise go unrecorded, also gained popularity in reaction to the quantitative methods of social and labor historians in the 1960s and 1970s. Records of the lives of everyday people provide the human side of "scientifically" constructed statistics.

It could be argued, however, that the real shift in historical approach to sources occurred during the late 1930s and early 1940s, when members of the Federal Writers' Project set out to interview people from all backgrounds and occupations about their experiences during the depression and at the start of World War II. Folklorists such as Benjamin Botkin, Zora Neale Hurston, and Stetson Kennedy collected life histories of common people, of the "inarticulate" classes. Ralph Ellison, Richard Wright, Alan Lomax, Herbert Halpert, Studs Terkel, and others also were involved in the Federal Writers' Project, recording vernacular speech and lore as well as the average person's views on what was significant about the 1930s.

In 1966, in an address to the Oral History Association, folklorist Wayland Hand noted that folk legends and beliefs were particularly important sources of the history of the common man because such traditions provided oral history with a time depth. Richard Dorson, writing in 1970, expressed the need to enlarge the scope of oral history to include folk history. He emphasized, as did his students Lynwood Montell and William Ivey, the need to record a community's view of what was and is important in its past—not just commentary on elite categories.

Jan Vansina drew a further distinction between oral history and oral tradition by specifying that the latter consists of verbal messages from the past beyond the present generation; oral history consists of recollections and commentary about events within the informant's lifetime. Thus, oral history can be regarded as comparable to written documents, media reports, and so on that involve a first assessment of events. Because such narratives may be repeated or recorded at a temporal distance from the original event, however, the interviewer needs to be aware that memory, selection, elaboration, condensation, and the use of formulaic motifs as well as cultural styles of performance can all affect the historical account. Such factors become even more apparent with folk history, which may consist of reports passed along from previous generations.

Folklorists can provide a valuable perspective on oral history analysis because of their familiarity with the processes of oral traditions. Combining the methods of oral history with that of folklore collecting can serve as a corrective to culturally irrelevant questions on the part of the researcher. Ivey's study of local history in Michigan's Upper Peninsula particularly made the point that faulty methodology can skew the data. He noted that when he stopped asking the directed questions of the oral historian and began asking his informants to tell him what was significant for them, he elicited historical commentary that was far more relevant to the lives of those he was studying. That such data pointed to different or complementary interpretations of events, or when significant socioeconomic change occurred, only served to reconstruct a broader and more authentic history.

Montell's ethnographic study of Coe Ridge, which combined the sources of oral histories, local legends, anecdotes, ballads, letters and diaries, and archival research, further demonstrated the necessity of gathering data from whatever is available to reconstruct a community's folk history. He also made the critical point that oral histories are valuable historical documents in their own right and not just merely supplements to the written record.

Folklorist Henry Glassie specifically described folklore as the discipline that recorded the story of events and people that history had forgotten. In 1970, Montell noted that oral folk history consisted of a core of truth with narrative embellishments. The historical distortion that occurred could be attributed to patterning, telescoping, and legend displacement. Montell stressed that oral folk history provided a complement to written historical literature, for it added the human side and presented the individual as a person—a perspective usually absent from written documents.

Scholars from the fields of anthropology, history, and folklore suggest that what each has in common with the other is the oral interview. More than that, however, they share the philosophical perspective that oral interviews can elicit the stories of those ordinarily unheard by most of society. Dorson and Glassie particularly made the point that folklorists ought to be more aware of the historical perspective of their informants. Ivey, Glassie, and Vansina further stressed that oral history records the psychological truth about a community's past and its beliefs about the present.

Methodology as well as philosophy is critical to studying oral history. The folklore and fieldwork guides of Kenneth Goldstein, Bruce Jackson, Edward Ives, and Peter Seitel provide recommendations for approaching informants, working with tape recorders, documenting contextual data, and eliciting usable narratives. Although the techniques of folklore fieldwork overlap with those of oral historians, there are some differences in perspective and purpose; thus, such manuals should be read in conjunction with Vansina's discussion of methodology in researching oral traditions.

Rachelle H. Saltzman

See also Fieldwork; Historical Analysis; History, Folk.

✳✳✳✳✳✳✳✳✳✳✳✳✳✳✳✳✳✳

References

Allen, Barbara, and William Lynwood Montell. 1981. *From Memory to History.* Nashville, TN: AASLH.

Banks, Ann. 1981. *First Person America.* New York: Vintage Books.

Glassie, Henry. 1982. *Passing the Time in Ballymenone.* Philadelphia: University of Pennsylvania Press.

Ives, Edward D. 1980. *The Tape Recorded Interview: A Manual for Fieldworkers in Folklore and Oral History.* Knoxville: University of Tennessee Press.

Montell, William Lynwood. [1970] 1972. *The Saga of Coe Ridge.* New York: Harper and Row.

Mullen, Pat. 1992. *Listening to Old Voices.* Chicago: University of Illinois Press.

Olch, Peter D., and Forrest C. Pogue, eds. 1972. *Selections from the Fifth and Sixth National Colloquia on Oral History.* New York: Oral History Association.

Rosenberg, Neil, ed. 1978. *Folklore and Oral History.* St. John's, Newfoundland: Memorial University of Newfoundland.

Terkel, Studs. 1970. *Hard Times.* New York: Pantheon Books.

Vansina, Jan. 1985. *Oral Tradition as History.* Madison: University of Wisconsin Press.

Hymn, Folk

Most generally, a song praising God and sung in a folk group. Folk hymns may be found today in two kinds of setting: as survivals of older (often quite elaborate) practices, usually among marginal religious groups or in folk revivals, and as comparatively informal and spontaneous music for worship both within and without the religious mainstream. In the United States, folk hymns may be found among various ethnic groups and religious denominations—Jewish, Islamic, African-American, Pentecostal, Amish, Baptist, and so forth. Since the 1960s, in an attempt to attract youth, various mainstream churches have introduced innovations such as folk masses and original songs accompanied by guitars in the style of folk music revivals. Other mainstream churches have experimented with gospel music choruses characteristic of charismatic denominations. Marriage ceremonies written in part by the participants often have featured original or borrowed lyrics set to folklike melodies.

As a result of a research tradition in Europe and the United States, the term *folk hymn* has come to stand more narrowly for a particular type of Christian song whose tune exists in oral tradition. Irving Lowens defined *folk hymn* as a "secular folk-tune that happens to be sung to a religious text." Indeed, the practice of setting Christian songs to secular tunes was endorsed by Martin Luther, who asked, "Why should the devil have all the good tunes?" Lowens' definition emphasizes that though the words of a folk hymn may remain unchanged over time and place, the tune exhibits the variations that one expects from oral tradition. Scholars have further distinguished folk hymns from various other types of Christian religious folksong: *religious ballads* (folk ballads with religious texts, sung solo), *camp-meeting* and *revival spirituals* (folk hymns to which refrains and choruses were added in the nineteenth century), and *gospel music* (first-person texts that emphasize the Christian's relation to Jesus, trials and temptations in this life, and the joys of heavenly homecoming in the next). In most cases, Christian folk hymn texts are products of eighteenth-century hymn writers, such as Isaac Watts and Charles Wesley. Many emphasize God's grandeur and humankind's depravity. The majority of tunes tend to be in gapped or pentatonic modes rather than diatonic.

Lining-out is practiced in some folk hymn traditions. In this antiphonal practice, which dates back to the seventeenth century, a song leader gives out the words to a line of verse by speaking, intoning, or singing them, and then the congregation joins the leader to repeat the words, more or less in unison, to an elaborate tune different from the lining tune. Lined-out folk hymns represent one of the oldest layers of folk music tradition in the United States. They can be found among the Amish, among Old Regular Baptists (and some United Baptists) chiefly in southeastern Kentucky and southwestern Virginia, and in many African-American Baptist churches, where they are termed *meter* or *Dr. Watts* hymns. Another major folk hymn tradition in the United States is a tradition of singing conventions and gatherings using shape-note songbooks. This is a part-singing practice (the notes are written in the songbooks in various geometrical shapes to aid in identifying pitch), in contrast to the unison singing of the lined-out folk hymn tradition. Shaped-note hymnody originated in a late-eighteenth-century music literacy movement designed to supplant the lined-out "old way of singing." Many of the tunes in the shaped-note songbooks existed in oral tradition when they were written down in the nineteenth century. Today, shaped-note hymnody is undergoing a revival, and singing conventions gather in most parts of the United States.

Musicological scholarship on folk hymnody has centered on the nineteenth-century American shaped-note songbooks, chiefly in order to classify and analyze the tunes and in an attempt to trace their histories. George Pullen

Jackson pioneered in this area; Charles Seeger and Dorothy Horn employ more sophisticated musical analysis. Using a broader definition of folk hymnody and within a framework involving the study of performance and ritual, folklorists and ethnomusicologists have done historical and ethnographic research on living traditions, in which one of the chief attractions is a well-articulated body of native beliefs about the meaning of this music. Outside the United States, the School of Scottish Studies has documented a tradition of lined-out folk hymns (psalms) in Gaelic on the Isle of Lewis. Research of European folk hymn singing has been particularly strong in Finland, where F. O. Durchman notated hymn melodies from oral tradition as early as 1837 and Ilmari Krohn began a systematic collection in the 1890s. Päivikki Suojanen's *Finnish Folk Hymn Singing: A Study in Music Anthropology* shows that the tradition remains very much alive.

Jeff Todd Titon

See also Folk Music; Folksong, Lyric; Religion, Folk.

✳✳✳✳✳✳✳✳✳✳✳✳✳✳✳✳✳✳✳

References

Horn, Dorothy D. 1970. *Sing to Me of Heaven*. Gainesville: University of Florida Press.

Jackson, George Pullen. 1933. *White Spirituals in the Southern Uplands*. New York: Dover.

Patterson, Beverly Bush. 1994. *The Sound of the Dove: An Ethnography of Singing among Primitive Baptists*. Urbana: University of Illinois Press.

Patterson, Daniel. 1982. *The Shaker Spiritual*. Princeton, NJ: Princeton University Press.

Seeger, Charles. 1976. *Studies in Musicology*. Los Angeles: University of California Press.

Smith, Timothy Allen. 1981. The Southern Folk-Hymn, 1802–1860: A History and Musical Analysis, with Notes on Performance Practice. Master's thesis, California State University, Fullerton.

Suojanen, Päivikki. 1984. *Finnish Folk Hymn Singing: A Study in Music Anthropology*. Tampere, Finland: University of Tampere Institute for Folk Tradition.

Sutton, Brett, and Pete Hartman. 1982. *Primitive Baptist Hymns of the Blue Ridge*. 12" LP recording with book. Chapel Hill: University of North Carolina Press.

Temperley, Nicholas. 1981. The Old Way of Singing. *Journal of the American Musicological Society* 34:511–544.

Titon, Jeff Todd. 1988. *Powerhouse for God: Speech, Chant, and Song in an Appalachian Baptist Church*. Austin: University of Texas Press.

Wicks, Sammie Ann. 1983. Life and Meaning: Singing, Praying, and the Word among Old Regular Baptists of Eastern Kentucky. Diss. University of Texas, Austin.